JUVENILE DELINQUENCY

JUVENILE DELINQUENCY

Clemens Bartollas
University of Northern Iowa

John Wiley & Sons
New York   Chichester   Brisbane   Toronto   Singapore

COVER ART: Roy Wiemann
BOOK DESIGN: Joan Willens

Library of Congress Cataloging in Publication Data:

Bartollas, Clemens.
 Juvenile delinquency.

 Includes indexes.
 1. Juvenile delinquency—United States.
2. Juvenile justice, Administration of—United
States. 3. Juvenile delinquency—United States—
Prevention. 4. Rehabilitation of juvenile delinquents—
United States. I. Title.

HV9104.B345 1985   364.3'6'0973   84-14864
ISBN 0-471-89364-1

Printed in the United States of America

10 9 8 7 6 5 4 3 2 1

*To Phil Caldabaugh and Dick Jones
Two individuals who made a difference
in the life of a young boy*

FOREWORD

We know it from no less notable philosophers than Socrates and Aristotle that some of the youth in the ancient Greece of their time loathed work, were disobedient and disrespectful to others, engaged in crime, vandalism and deviant conduct and frustrated their parents and teachers. This litany, that the young are a major pain to a decent and sober society is almost as old as recorded history.

Through four or more millenia all sorts of explanations have been offered for this phenomenon of delinquency. In loose chronological order, disruptive, deviant and delinquent youth were thought to be evil (in a religious and moral sense), defective biologically, impaired intellectually, sick psychologically and much more recently as the products of sociocultural forces especially poverty, family breakdown and abuse and weakened community controls. There has never been a shortage of seemingly plausible reasons for that often stormy and violent period in the life cycle called adolescence. Nor, indeed, has there been any shortage of recommended panaceas. The prevailing interventions have invariably "fit" the status of children in the society. When children were disvalued and a burden economically, treatment was harsh and even cruel. When children were thought the wave of the future, as during the dreadful plagues and wars that swept over Europe over and over again, their treatment improved dramatically. Western society has never quite come to terms with its young. They hover somewhere between the products of original sin and pure innocents and closer to one pole or another depending on the social terrain. Nevertheless, it is safe to argue that all social interventions have gone beyond punishment, beyond psychological insight, beyond behavior modification and focused on three variables: work, education and discipline. Chief Justice Burger in a speech delivered in June, 1984 called for a full work week for all prisoners (including juveniles, I presume) as a necessary element in their rehabilitation. The speech was greeted with enthusiasm in all quarters and hailed as a novel idea. In fact, such pleas are recurrent. Once again, the youth population has become a burden on the economic system and, one way or another, youth must be engaged in other ways than full labor market participation. Little wonder, then, that crime in America is disproportionately youth crime. A very significant percentage of the crimes based by arrest involve juveniles; a majority or close to it, depending on year, of the property arrests are of those under 18.

In an attempt to reduce youth crime, the usual reaction has been to get tougher with juvenile predators by increasing the penalties and reducing the correctional alternatives such as probation and community care. On the other end of the delinquency spectrum, status offenders, (non-criminals by adult statutes) who are school truants, incorrigibles and runaways have been virtually eliminated from the juvenile justice system to make more room for the serious and dangerous delinquents. Pressured by the public, on the one side, and the reformers, on the other, the juvenile system is in shambles. The emergent system will most likely manage delinquent juveniles as a junior version of adult criminals emphasizing due process, harm, intent and punishment.

All of these observations and more, much more, are part of a superlative textbook, *Juvenile Delinquency*. Professor Bartollas, whose knowledge of the subject extends beyond the academic to experience as a wing director (administrator) at a maximum security juvenile facility, has written a carefully researched volume on the subject, free of jargon and of personal preferences and prejudices. It is historically accurate, insightful and, at times, profound. It leaves the reader with the uncomfortable feeling that there are no very simple techniques for dealing with an age old problem deeply embedded in history and modern cultural forms. Conversely, delinquency cannot be accepted as a *rite of passage* in the life cycle. Too many juveniles do too much harm to simply accept delinquency as an undesirable by-product of an inequitable social structure. Furthermore, far too many delinquents progress into adult criminal careers.

In this lively and readable book, Professor Bartollas has marshalled an impressive array of material which is important and current in framing social policy in combating delinquency. The standard sources and studies and ideological positions and disputes are all there. In fact, I have not seen a more comprehensive treatment of intervention techniques—personal, group and community—in any text. At least two other elements set this book apart. First, there are the insets—vignettes which offer a sense of immediacy and intimacy into the perceptions of the actors whether offender, victim or societal representative in one or another branch of juvenile justice. Second, and wholly unique, are the interviews with criminal justice scholars and practitioners—men and women who have invested their lives in processing, treating or incapacitating delinquents. Anyone who thinks that such people become inured and insensitive to the unrelieved misery of processing or even studying delinquents should read their interview statements very carefully. These interviewees, all major figures in the field, present the issues and options which daily confront them with understanding, feeling and a sense of optimism.

Professor Bartollas has done us all a service—those who teach no less than those who learn. This textbook is a job well done.

Simon Dinitz
Ohio State University

PREFACE

Juvenile delinquency—crimes committed by young people—constitutes approximately one-half of property crimes and one-fourth of crimes against persons in the United States by recent estimates. The high incidence of juvenile crime and the fact that these crimes are committed by young persons make the study of juvenile delinquency vital to any understanding of American society today.

This book examines juvenile delinquency from a sociological perspective, as most recent writings on the problem have. The book also examines the effectiveness of the way in which juvenile delinquency is controlled by the justice system, examines recent legislation and court rulings on the rights of youthful offenders, looks at the rights of adolescents in general, and assesses legal efforts to correct their antisocial behavior. Yet, this book was written primarily because the author believes that juvenile delinquency must be examined in other contexts as well.

First, instead of viewing delinquency in terms of only one context, such as that of the legal or justice system, this book examines delinquency in broader terms, the sociocultural, legal, political, economic, and historical contexts. All these contexts impinge upon present efforts to prevent and control delinquency and upon future attempts to describe the delinquent accurately. Second, because the individual delinquent sometimes is lost in the descriptions of his or her behavior, this book gives more attention to the experiences of delinquents and to the influence of these experiences in interpreting meaning, affecting interactions with others, and making decisions for or against crime. Third, this book emphasizes delinquency prevention. Although many writings have deemphasized prevention programs and strategies, perhaps because past efforts have proved so ineffective, this author believes technologies being developed today will result in more effective prevention interventions tomorrow. Fourth, the book examines treatment of juvenile delinquents more extensively than is typically done in texts on delinquency. Certainly, as anyone familiar with juvenile corrections is aware, correctional treatment today has more critics than advocates, again because past programs have proved ineffective. This text examines the technologies needed to improve correctional treatment in both community and institutional settings.

Two particular features of this volume are the sections on social policy and the interviews with authoritative spokespersons. Social policy is emphasized and each chapter ends with a section on the policy needed to improve the response of society to the delinquent in terms of the material presented in that chapter. Although much is discouraging about the handling of delinquents by society to date, the text attempts to outline strategies needed on the societal, community, and individual levels to help juveniles realize more of their potentials and, therefore, avoid involvement in crime. Finally, the interviews with spokespersons after each chapter should stimulate readers and help them integrate the materials in the chapter.

The design of this volume arose from the author's personal experiences with juvenile delinquents and the questions about American delinquency that resulted: What is the wider context in which delinquency takes place? What causes delinquency? What do we know about delinquents? How are the family, the experiences of adolescents, and the school related to delinquency? How does the delinquent see himself or herself? What can be done to control juvenile delinquency? What can be done to treat delinquency?

The outline of this book moves from statistics on juvenile crime to the causes of delinquency and then to control, prevention, and treatment of delinquency. The book is divided into six units: the measurement of delinquency, the causes of delinquency, social institutions and their impact upon delinquency, the male and female delinquent, the control of delinquency, and the prevention and treatment of delinquency. The first unit measures the nature and extent of delinquency through examining the available official and unofficial statistics. The second unit explains delinquency in five ways: (1) juveniles have free will and choose to become involved in delinquency; (2) juveniles are driven by biological and psychological factors to become delinquent; (3) juveniles are driven by social structural factors to become delinquent; (4) juveniles become delinquent through the process of interaction with others; and (5) juveniles become delinquent because they are economically exploited by powerful groups in society. The third unit examines the relationship between delinquency and problems in the family, such as child abuse, the growing pains and experiences of adolescents, and experiences in the school. The fourth unit focuses on the individual delinquent and considers such matters as the types of youthful offenders and the meaning delinquency has for these youths. The fifth unit discusses the control of delinquency. Chapters are included on an overview of the justice process, on police-juvenile relations, on the juvenile court, on community-based corrections, and on long-term institutions. The final unit considers delinquency prevention and treatment. The book closes with a summary and recommendations for policy.

A study of delinquency in American society is a blend of both theory and research, of the views of both soft-liners and hard-liners, of the concerns of victims and the justification of youths, of both treatment and punishment, of both disillusionment about past failures and increased motivation to find more effective answers. *Juvenile Delinquency* has been designed to give the student a thorough overview of juvenile delinquency by explaining what is documented about the problem and by examining delinquency in the wider context of those forces impinging on the individual adolescent and in the immediate context of the interaction of the adolescent with society.

Clemens Bartollas

ACKNOWLEDGMENTS

Several individuals have made an invaluable contribution to this text. Foremost were Jean Kennedy and Judith Sutton who edited the manuscript. They both performed countless miracles in shaping the work from rough to final copy. The interviews that Linda Bartollas conducted with youthful offenders and practitioners in the juvenile justice system, as well as the materials she wrote on the family, were extremely helpful in conceptualizing and illustrating ideas. Kurt Mielke, Gary Storm, and Ellen Millhollin also provided materials for the chapters on conflict and adolescents. I am grateful to the criminologists who consented to be interviewed; their interviews following each chapter add an essential dimension to this text. Gail Truitt and Dean Wright were reviewers whose insights were instrumental in organizing materials and resolving problems. Jerry Stockdale, Robert Claus, Gene Lutz, and Robert Kramer are colleagues whose helpful critiques have been widely followed. I am grateful to Simon Dinitz who prepared the foreword; he has been associated in one way or another with the seven books I have written. Julia Rathbone typed many drafts on the word processor that enabled me to keep the manuscript moving without interruption. I would like to thank Dean Robert Morin for his assistance in the typing and zeroxing of this book. Finally I am grateful to my daughter Kristin who prepared the index and to Butch Cooper who was my project editor at Wiley.

C.B.

CONTENTS

JUVENILE DELINQUENCY

CHAPTER 1

THE CONTEXTS OF AMERICAN DELINQUENCY

CHAPTER OUTLINE

They started walking at dusk, two teenagers casually spreading the message that the streets of West Los Angeles were no longer safe. Finally, they stopped Phillip Lerner and demanded money. Lerner had no cash; only his infant in a stroller. They let him pass and kept walking. They hailed Arkady and Rachel Muskin at a nearby intersection. The couple quickly handed over $8 and two wristwatches, and gratefully fled. Next the boys intercepted two elderly Chinese women and pulled out a pistol. When one woman tried to push the gun out of her face, ten bullets blasted out, killing both. The boys kept walking. They came upon a trio of friends out for an evening stroll. They took a watch and a few dollars and, without as much as a word, killed one of the three, a Frenchman visiting Los Angeles for the first time. The boys kept walking. At last they reached a drive-in restaurant where they found seventy-six-year-old Leo Ocon walking on the sidewalk. They argued with him for less than a minute and then shot him down. Their evening over, they climbed into an old sedan and then, much as they had started, calmly went off into the night.[1]

Juvenile delinquency, as this chilling account shows, is sometimes terrifying. The study of delinquency deals with teenage murderers, robbers, rapists, and gang members, as well as with adolescents who steal cars, commit prostitution, smoke pot and use hard drugs, skip school, and run away from home. The study of delinquency examines why juveniles break the law; considers the impact of the family, the neighborhood, and the school on delinquent behavior; examines the behaviors and social characteristics of juvenile delinquents; and discusses the measures and programs needed to prevent and control delinquent behavior.

However, the study of delinquency today is facing a major challenge. On all fronts, from the hard-liners who want to "get tough" to liberals who are searching for treatment panaceas, there is evidence of an inability to know what is the best strategy to handle youth crime in American society. The widespread belief that prevention and treatment are ineffective and that understanding the causes of delinquency is not helpful in controlling delinquency makes this challenge even more formidable.

This text proposes a contextual perspective that should help clarify the development and present dynamics of American delinquency and what can be done about the problem of delinquency. This chapter begins with an examination of that contextual perspective, which will guide the discussion of delinquency in the subsequent chapters.

THE CONTEXTUAL PERSPECTIVE AND THE STUDY OF DELINQUENCY

Delinquent behavior, as well as the means to prevent and control delinquency, are set in, and are shaped by, five contexts in America: the historical, the legal, the sociocultural, the economic, and the political.[2] The historical context defines how

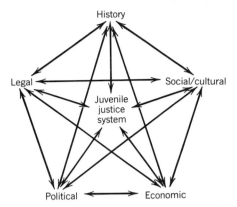

Figure 1-1 Contextual Perspectives and Their Interrelationships

juvenile delinquents have been handled in the past and influences how they are perceived and handled in the present. The legal context establishes the definition of delinquent behavior and status offense behavior and determines the legal procedures for dealing with youths in trouble. Sociocultural forces shape the norms and values of society, including its attitudes concerning youth crime. The economic context is especially important in American society because so many attitudes and behaviors are influenced by success goals and the means to achieve them. The economic context gains in importance in fiscally hard times, with high unemployment and tight budgets for all institutions in society, including those for youth. Finally, within the political context, policy decisions are made dealing with youth crime.

These five contexts do not exist in and by themselves, for they are interrelated with each other. Each context influences the others and, in turn, is influenced by the others (see Figure 1-1). Furthermore, each of the five contexts operates on three levels: the societal level; the neighborhood or community level; and the individual level.[3]

THE HISTORICAL CONTEXT

Many sociological interpretations of delinquency lack a sense of history, in that such attempts to account for the origins and emergence of typical patterns of delinquency rarely locate those origins in time and place. Such ahistorical approaches to understanding delinquency have a serious shortcoming, because these interpretations generally rest on unexamined assumptions concerning the history of particular societies or communities.[4] Thus, the history of how law-violating juveniles have been dealt with in the past is an important consideration in understanding how delinquent youths are handled today.

The Societal Level

On a societal level, the history of juvenile justice in America can be divided into five periods: colonial, houses of refuge, juvenile court, juvenile rights, and the present.

The Colonial Period (1636–1824)

The history of juvenile justice in the United States actually began in the colonial period. The colonists believed that the family was the source and primary means of social control of children. In colonial times, the law was uncomplicated and the family was the cornerstone of the community.[5] Townfathers, magistrates, sheriffs, and watchmen were the only law enforcement officials, and the only penal institutions were jails for prisoners awaiting trial or punishment.

Juvenile lawbreakers did not face a battery of police, probation, or parole officers, nor did they need to worry that members of the juvenile justice system would try to rehabilitate them. They had only to concern themselves with being sent back to their families for punishment. If still recalcitrant after harsh whippings and other deprivations, youthful offenders could be returned to community officials for further punishments, such as public whippings, dunkings, or the stocks, or, in more serious cases, expulsion from the community or even capital punishment.

The Houses of Refuge Period (1824–1899)

Later reformers became disillusioned with the family and looked for a substitute that would provide an orderly, disciplined environment similar to that of the "ideal" Puritan family.[6] Houses of refuge were proposed as the solution, juvenile institutions where discipline was to be administered firmly and harshly. These facilities, which were intended to protect wayward children from corrupting home environments, reflected a new direction in juvenile justice, for no longer were parents and family the first line of control for children. The authority of the family had been superseded by that of the state, and wayward children were placed in facilities presumably better equipped to reform them.

The houses of refuge flourished for the first half of the nineteenth century, but by the middle of the century, reformers were beginning to suspect that these juvenile institutions were not as effective as had been hoped. Some had grown unwieldy in size, and discipline, care, and order had disappeared from most. Reformers were also aware that many youths were being confined in institutions—jails and prisons—that were filthy, dangerous, degrading, and ill-equipped to manage them effectively. A change was in order, and reformers proposed the juvenile court as a way to provide for more humane care of law-violating youths.

The Juvenile Court Period (1899–1967)

First created in Cook County, this new court for children was based upon the legal concept of *parens patriae*. This medieval English doctrine sanctioned the right of the Crown to intervene into natural family relations whenever a child's welfare was threatened. The concept was explained by the committee of the Chicago Bar Association that created the new court:

> *The fundamental idea of the junvenile court law is that the state must step in and exercise guardianship over a child found under such adverse social or individual conditions as to encourage the development of crime. . . . The juvenile court law proposes a plan whereby he may be treated, not as a criminal, or legally charged with crime, but as a ward of the state, to receive*

practically the care, custody, and discipline that are accorded the neglected and dependent child, and which, as the act states, "shall approximate as nearly as may be that which should be given by its parents."[7]

Proponents of the juvenile court promised that it would be flexible enough to give individual attention to the specific problems of wayward children. These reformers believed that once the causes of deviancy were identified accurately, specific problems could be treated and cured; thus juveniles would be kept out of jails and prisons and, therefore, would not be corrupted by adult criminals.

However, the juvenile court period did not see radical changes in the philosophy of juvenile corrections since the family continued to be subservient to the state and youths still could be institutionalized. The only major new factor was the establishment of the juvenile court as another official agency to aid in controlling wayward children. But juvenile delinquents would continue under the control of the state until they were either cured or too old to remain under the jurisdiction of juvenile authorities.

Society extended its control over the young in several other ways. Police departments established juvenile bureaus. The notion of treating juveniles for their specific problems was also evidenced by the acceptance of both probation and parole agencies, which were institutionalized in the first part of the twentieth century. Incarceration in a training or industrial school, a carry-over from the nineteenth century, was reserved for those who could not be treated in their communities.

The Juvenile Rights Period (1967–1975)

In the 1960s the juvenile justice system was subjected to heavy criticism because reformers believed that youthful offenders too frequently were subjected to curbstone justice by the police, to capricious and arbitrary justice by the courts, and to punitive and repressive justice in the training schools. The pressure that the reformers placed upon the federal courts in the 1960s and 1970s led to a series of decisions by the U.S. Supreme Court (*Kent* v. *United States,* 1966; *In re Gault,* 1967; *In re Winship,* 1970; *McKeiver* v. *Pennsylvania,* 1971; and *Breed* v. *Jones,* 1975.)[8] The *In re Gault* decision, the most far-reaching of these cases, stated that juveniles have the right to due process safeguards in proceedings where a finding of delinquency could lead to confinement, and that juveniles have rights to notice of charges, to counsel, to confrontation and cross-examination, and to privilege against self-incrimination.[9] The intent of these Supreme Court decisions was to protect the fundamental constitutional rights of youthful offenders in the juvenile justice system.

Another development during this period was the expression of dissatisfaction with the traditional methods of juvenile justice. Reformers believed that inconsiderate treatment by the police, five-minute hearings in the juvenile court, and degrading and often brutal treatment in training schools fostered rather than reduced juvenile crime. Youth service bureaus, the most widely used of diversionary programs, promised to keep youthful offenders out of the formal justice system.

Community-based programs also received an enthusiastic response in the late 1960s and early 1970s, for more and more states began a process of deinstitutionalization, under which only hard-core delinquents were sent to long-term training schools. Enthusiasm for community-based corrections was so widespread in the early 1970s that many observers felt that training schools would shortly no longer be used to deal with juvenile crime.

The Present (1975–   )

Dissatisfaction with the state's role in preventing, treating, and controlling youth crime best characterizes the past decade in juvenile justice. Reformers and hard-liners alike lament the inadequate administration of juvenile justice, the failure of the rehabilitative model, and the ineffectiveness of juvenile institutions. Some critics propose massive changes in juvenile justice. Others want to get tough on youth crime. Still others want to keep the structure of juvenile corrections as it is but to concentrate on doing the job better than before. Finally, some critics contend control of juveniles would be better returned to the family because the state has obviously demonstrated its inability to provide adequately for youths in trouble.

Tradition and the Local Community

Overall societal attitudes toward handling crime, of course, have an impact upon local communities and neighborhoods within those communities. But each community also develops its own individual history of dealing with juvenile delinquency. Thus one community may have a variety of services for youth in trouble, while another has only limited services. Forest E. Eastman, a juvenile judge for more than two decades in Cedar Falls, Iowa and one of the authors of the first Iowa Juvenile Code, explained in a 1981 interview how insufficient resources affect juvenile justice:

> It is frustrating for a juvenile judge not to have the facilities or treatment programs that are obviously necessary. You may at times know or think you know what needs to be done, but you can't find anyone who provides that kind of service for this type of kid.[10]

Communities in Massachusetts, California, and Minnesota have a tradition of providing a wide and impressive network of youth services. They offer such services as substance abuse treatment, financial restitution and community service, in- and out-patient psychiatric care, in-home detention, youth service bureaus, youth shelters, runaway drop-in centers, programs for teenage prostitutes, and day treatment and residential programs.

The Youthful Offender and History

An act of crime is a product of the time and experience of the actor. This act must be viewed in terms of its emergence, transmission, perpetuation, and modifications within the historical context of the social system in which the actor lives.[11] That is, like communities, which have particular histories, each juvenile develops his or her own history of behavior in the family and larger community. Those youths who are looked upon as good boys and girls generally seek to maintain the positive image they project. Yet those youths who are looked upon as troublemakers because of their histories of law-violating behavior also have their reputations to uphold. Moreover, juveniles may be part of a family in which the parents and/or siblings have been in trouble with the law. Such families frequently are labeled as troublemaking environments, and teachers and police expect younger siblings to create the same problems as the older ones did.

THE LEGAL CONTEXT

The legal context, unlike the historical context, has received major emphasis in recent years, sometimes to the point that the other perspectives are ignored.

The Societal Level

On the societal level, the legal definitions of delinquency, the legal categories of juvenile misbehavior, and the length of jurisdiction of the juvenile court are important concerns in understanding the impact of the legal context.

Delinquency is a legal term that was initially used in 1899 when Illinois passed the first law on juvenile delinquent behavior. Juvenile delinquency is typically defined as an act committed by a minor (the age at which an individual is considered a minor varies among states, but it is sixteen or seventeen and below in most states) that violates the penal code of the government with authority over the area in which the act occurred.[12]

Juvenile court codes, which are found in every state, also specify the conditions under which the state may legitimately intervene in a juvenile's life. State juvenile codes, as part of the *parens patriae* philosophy of the juvenile court, were enacted to eliminate the arbitrary nature of juvenile justice throughout the nation, to enlarge the procedural safeguards for juveniles beyond those rights already afforded them by the U.S. Constitution, and to deal with youths more leniently because they were seen as not fully responsible for their behaviors.[13] The 1955 *In re Poff* decision aptly expresses the logic of this argument:

> *The original Juvenile Court Act enacted in the District of Columbia . . . was devised to afford the juvenile protections in addition to those he already possessed under the Federal Constitution. Before this legislative enactment, the juvenile was subject to the same punishment for an offense as an adult. It follows logically that in the absence of such legislation the juvenile would be entitled to the same constitutional guarantees and safeguards as an adult. If this is true, then the only possible reason for the Juvenile Court Act was to afford the juvenile safeguards in addition to those he already possessed. The legislative intent was to enlarge and not diminish those protections.[14]*

Juvenile court codes usually specify that the court has jurisdiction over juveniles in relation to three categories of juvenile behavior. First, the court may intervene when a youth has been accused of committing an act that would be a misdemeanor or felony if committed by an adult. Second, the court may intervene when a juvenile commits certain other acts that are not defined as criminal if committed by adults—status offenses. Incorrigibility at home, running away, and truancy at school are examples of status offenses. Third, the court may intervene in cases involving dependency and neglect. If the court determines that a child is being deprived of needed support and supervision, it may decide to remove the child from the home for his or her own protection.

The problem with these broad categories is that they lack precise criteria for determining the types of behavior that qualify as juvenile delinquency. Fortunately, some clarification has been made concerning the matter of who is and is not a delinquent. Since the passage of the 1974 Juvenile Justice and Delinquency Prevention Act, the definition of delinquency has been more and more restricted to acts committed by a juvenile that are violations of criminal law. Two recent surveys conducted by the State Legislative Leaders Foundation found that forty-seven states have agreed to deinstitutionalize status offenders and separate juveniles from adult inmates within five years. Only eleven states currently classify status offenders and juvenile delinquents in the same category, and six of these states do have some provisions for differential treatment of status offenders.[15]

Juveniles who commit minor acts that are considered illegal only because they are underage are known variously as MINS (minors in need of supervision), CHINS (children in need of supervision), JINS (juveniles in need of supervision), CHINA (children in need of assistance), PINS (persons in need of supervision), or members of FINS (families in need of supervision). They may also be termed predelinquent, incorrigible, beyond control, ungovernable, or wayward children. The legal separation between status offenders and delinquents is important because approximately half of all arrests of juveniles each year are for such acts as truancy, disobeying parents, and running away from home.

Some controversy surrounds the issue of how long juveniles should remain under the jurisdiction of the juvenile court. The National Juvenile Justice Assessment Centers, in recently surveying how states addressed the issue, found that the juvenile court has jurisdictions over youths under eighteen in thirty-nine jurisdictions, over youths under seventeen in eight jurisdictions, and over youths under sixteen in four jurisdictions.[16]

Juvenile Justice and the Local Community

Juvenile lawbreaking is dealt with in local communities by five systems: the juvenile justice system, the adult justice system, private corrections, nonjudicial agencies, and educational systems. The juvenile justice system is at the hub of the other systems, because youngsters are either referred to the juvenile court by those systems or referred to those systems by the juvenile court. The police, as well as other agencies, refer troublesome youths to the juvenile court, which makes the decision as to what will be done with them.

The juvenile court may make the decision at a transfer hearing to bind over, or certify, a youth who has committed a serious crime to the adult court. Or the juvenile court, usually at the intake proceedings, may decide to divert a minor offender or a status offender to a nonjudicial agency, such as a youth service bureau, a social welfare agency, or a mental health clinic. Or a juvenile judge may decide at the disposition stage of the court's proceedings that a particular youth needs the services of a day treatment or a residential program. Some day treatment and residential programs are operated by the county or state governments. A youth might be sent to a training school, which may be in the community and may be operated under private auspices. Finally, a juvenile judge may make the decision that a disruptive student in the public school system needs the services of an alternative school. Figure 1-2 depicts the interrelationships of the systems that deal with juvenile lawbreakers in the local community.

The Youthful Offender and the Law

Juveniles who come in contact with the juvenile justice system react to such encounters in various ways, and their behavior is affected by their response. Whether the first contact with a police officer is positive or negative may have consequences on whether a youth commits future delinquent acts. The juvenile judge, the probation officer, and the staff in a youth shelter, the youth service bureau, or the residential program also affect youthful offenders. From their contacts with actors in the system, some juvenile offenders may conclude that little payment is exacted for delinquent behavior. Others may conclude that the consequences of spending forty hours shoveling snow in a community restitution service project are bad enough to make them turn away from antisocial behavior. Some youths have positive experiences with actors in the juvenile justice process, which have short-term or long-term effects on their behavior. As one youth found, "Mr. Roberts, he turned my life around."[17]

Figure 1-2 Interrelationships of Local Systems Dealing with Youthful Offenders

THE SOCIOCULTURAL CONTEXT

A sociological perspective of delinquency assumes that a knowledge of the particular social structure and the social processes that make up the context in which delinquency occurs is important in understanding youth crime. Institutions such as the family, school, and church are part of the framework or structure of society. Culture preserves the meanings that are passed from generation to generation and is the background against which the values, symbols, and objects of a society have developed. That is, culture provides a world view with which society's members perceive reality and interpret events; it is the filter or the lens through which they see the world. Socialization is the process by which individuals internalize their culture, for from the socialization process, an individual learns the norms, sanctions, and expectations of being a member of a particular society.

The Societal Level

In terms of the larger social structure, society today is concerned about the seriousness of youth crime and with finding more effective ways to deal with youth crime. The public, alerted by the media as to the chilling realities of youth crime, is alarmed and wants something done to curb the serious problem of juvenile delinquency in American society. Official crime reports, self-report studies, and surveys of crime victims all testify to the seriousness of the problem. For example, the *Uniform Crime Reports* indicate that the police arrest nearly two million minors a year.[18] The *Uniform Crime Reports* also document that juveniles commit 34.5 percent of the property crimes and 17 percent of the violent crimes in the United States.[19] Significantly, the number of juveniles arrested has increased in the past ten years, at a time when the population of those eighteen and under has declined 10 percent.

The public also is concerned about violence and vandalism in the public schools. The 1977 report of the Subcommittee on Juvenile Delinquency of the Senate Judiciary Committee stated that violence and vandalism in the public schools "are indeed occurring with more frequency and intensity than in the past" and probably have escalated in some schools "to a degree which makes the already difficult task of education almost impossible."[20]

BOX 1-1 "Teachers—New Endangered Species"

John K., a 42-year-old Caucasian, was a high school teacher in the inner city of Los Angeles, California, from 1965 to 1977. He watched morale and discipline progressively deteriorate with a commensurate increase in school violence and vandalism. Vagrants and truants roamed the campus, disrupting classes, threatening and sometimes attacking teachers. Combat between opposing gangs was almost a daily occurrence. Participants used fists, knives, chains, lead pipes, and guns. The school's administrators seemed either powerless or indifferent to the teachers' concern for their personal safety. They were unable to keep nonstudents off campus or to control their activities.

Despite the obvious danger to his own safety, John K. was a conscientious teacher who believed it was his responsibility to intervene when gang fights occurred on campus; most other teachers had "learned to look the other way." As a consequence, John was repeatedly threatened and sometimes beaten.

Just before Christmas vacation, John entered the audiovisual control booth of the school auditorium. As he closed the door, he confronted two male students cutting power lines and smashing electrical equipment. One student fled; the other began beating John with his fists. The student who had fled returned; he held John while the other grabbed a chain and began battering the teacher's head and shoulders. John's screams and calls for help were either not heard or ignored. The battering continued, and he finally lost consciousness. After he recovered from his injuries and was released from the hospital, he resigned.

Source: Alfred M. Bloch, M.D., and Ruth Reinhardt Bloch, "Teachers—New Endangered Species," in *Violence and Crime in the Schools,* edited by Keith Baker and Robert J. Rubel (Lexington, Mass.: D.C. Heath & Company, 1980), p. 81.

A child-centered culture provides the broader social context for youth crime. This child-centered culture dictates a generally permissive approach to children and, accordingly, the least restrictive model has been widely used with status offenders and minor offenders. This approach advocates a philosophy expressed by "Don't do any more than absolutely necessary with youthful offenders. If possible, leave them alone."[21] Thus, status offenders and minor offenders are diverted from the juvenile justice system, are placed on informal probation, or are placed on probation with limited supervision placed upon them. While this soft line approach is being advocated for minor offenders, the public's mood toward juvenile delinquency is emphasizing a hard-line policy toward violent and serious juvenile criminals. Juvenile offenders who have committed serious crimes are being sent to training schools, and, if the crime is a violent one, their cases may be waived to the adult court.

The Sociocultural Context and the Local Community

Delinquency is ultimately defined in terms of the range of socially acceptable behavior of young people in a given community at a given time. But social justice is frequently different for the children of the "haves" than for children of the "have-nots." In short, it can be argued that juvenile justice from its very beginnings in America has generated class favoritism, with the result that poor children have been processed through the system, while middle- and upper-class children have been more likely to be excused. For example, the gentlemen reformers who started the houses of refuge and the child savers who founded the juvenile court both were primarily concerned about establishing institutions to control behaviors restricted at that time to lower-class youths, such as sexual licentiousness, roaming the streets, drinking, frequenting dance halls and movies, and staying out late at night.[22]

The attempt to protect wayward youths from the vices of society has particularly affected the handling of female delinquents. The community is especially sensitive to such behaviors as promiscuity and prostitution by adolescent females. The girl who is unruly or beyond control at home, the girl who runs away from home, the girl who frequents taverns or gets intoxicated, all pose a threat to the community's definition of the role of a proper young lady.

The Youthful Offender and the Sociocultural Context

Young people, like adults, are influenced by the values and norms of the larger society. The violence of youth gangs in the 1950s and the weaponry and the lethal behaviors adopted by youth gangs in the 1970s and early 1980s are not surprising in view of the infatuation with violence in American society. The victimization of the weak in juvenile training schools imitates the predatory environments of adult prisons. Property offenses committed by juveniles, from shoplifting to robbery, can be seen as an extension of the criminogenic behavior found among adults. Furthermore, the growing dependency of youths on artificial stimulants and chemicals has been learned from adults dependent on alcohol and drugs.

But the social institutions of the community can exert positive influences on adolescents' behavior. The quality of their home life, as well as the emotional support they receive, has considerable effect upon youths' world views and behavior. Similarly, their performance in school and their involvement in church groups and community activities affect their "definition of the situation" and the way they respond to the social order. Equally important, the support and reinforcement they receive from home and school influence the peer cultures they become involved with in the community or neighborhood. Adolescents are more likely to become involved in deviant teenage societies if their needs are not met by other social institutions in the community.

Yet delinquent behavior is not merely the product or consequences of societal and community forces, but is also the creation of symbol-using, self-reflexive human beings. The likelihood of a young person committing a delinquent act is largely determined by four contexts: structural, situational, interactional, and personal. The structural context pertains to the sociocultural, economic, legal, and political factors on a societal level that affect all adolescents. The situational context is defined by such matters as the racial or ethnic background, the support systems available in the neighborhood, and the family situation of each youth. The interactional context determines how youngsters develop shared symbols and derive meaning as they become involved in social interaction with others. Finally, the personal context refers to the way in which individual youngsters translate what happens to them in the other contexts through their own experiences and assumptions concerning life. Some youngsters are more influenced by external contexts than others, but all are seeking to make sense of their lives and to decide upon behavior appropriate for their perception of life. (Figure 1-3 depicts this process.)

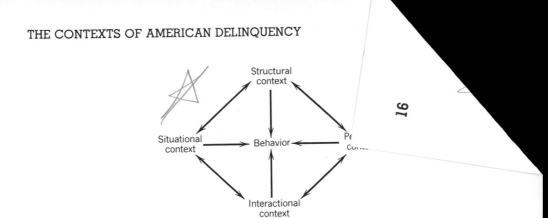

Figure 1-3 Contexts Affecting Decision Making Among Adolescents

THE ECONOMIC CONTEXT

The economic context of delinquency pertains to such factors as socioeconomic class, unemployment, and poverty. Liberals generally have seen a strong relationship between economic factors and delinquency, while conservatives have contested such a relationship.

The Societal Level

The relationship between socioeconomic class and delinquency is currently being debated widely, but little disagreement exists concerning the high cost of youth crime.

The Relationship between Socioeconomic Factors and Delinquency

Some studies have found a significant causative relationship between poverty (measured in various ways) and youth crime, while others have failed to show such a correlation.[23] Self-report studies, especially, have generally found delinquency to be spread through the social classes and, therefore, have minimized the importance of poverty of parents as a factor in delinquency causation (see Chapter 3). There is also the argument that even in the most impoverished neighborhoods, the majority of youngsters do not become involved in delinquent behavior.

But supporters of the strong relationship between poverty and delinquency (discussed in more detail in Chapter 6) argue one or more of the following positions. First, while delinquency may be spread throughout the social classes, poverty is related directly to violent and serious property offenses. Even recent self-report studies have found that lower-class youths tend to commit more frequent and more serious delinquent offenses than do middle-class youths.[24] Second, poverty is an influential intervening variable in causing delinquent behavior; that is, lower-class parents reside in neighborhoods that are more criminogenic than those of higher-class parents and their children are more likely to become delinquent simply through greater exposure to criminogenic influences. Or, the argument continues, poverty increases the likelihood of parents neglecting or abusing their children, and neglected and abused children are more likely to commit delinquent behavior. Third, young people find it difficult to react constructively to growing up in deprived environments. Economic deprivation at home, because their parents are unemployed, drives many of these youths to the streets. But, like their parents, they too face unemployment. In this regard, Allen Calvin has documented an extremely strong association between the unemployment of black youths and street crime.[25]

The Cost of Youth Crime

Juvenile delinquency is extremely expensive for American society. The economic cost of juvenile crime can be divided into direct and indirect costs, but since most juvenile crime is hidden, it is impossible to calculate accurately the real cost.

The direct costs of serious juvenile crimes are basically the out-of-pocket expenses of victims and witnesses: the loss of money or property and consequent inability to buy goods or services, and the costs of having to appear at hearings held by the police or courts. The costs of personal injury, as well as mental problems that may result from being a victim of or a witness to a violent crime, also are important. The National Juvenile Justice Assessment Centers estimated that all adult and juvenile crime cost $35 billion in 1975.[26] Of this amount, $10 million, or 28 percent, was the result of serious juvenile crimes. Property and violent juvenile crimes cost about $5 million each. The Assessment Centers also estimated that juvenile crime costs witnesses over $2 million in direct costs alone.[27]

Indirect costs are those that affect the community generally. For example, families often have to pay more for goods and services because a victimized business must raise its prices to cover its losses. Indirect losses also result when businesses must increase their insurance coverage against losses and pay for better security systems. Other indirect costs include increased taxes to pay for public and private victim compensation programs, unemployment compensation, welfare, and processing offenders through the juvenile justice system.

The Economic Context
and the Local Community

The problem of finding adequate funding for the control of delinquency in local communities is a pressing one today. Despite how important budget-line items for justice or how pressing litigation or code revision may be to some, the dollars invested are almost insignificant compared to the resources allocated to public education, to overcoming energy shortages and unemployment, or even to adult education. The low level of funding is underlined by the fact that the Law Enforcement Assistance Administration (LEAA), which had been an important source of funding for juvenile justice, was phased out in the early 1980s.

The problem of finding adequate funding for juvenile justice agencies promises to become more severe throughout the 1980s. The Office of Juvenile Justice Delinquency Prevention (OJJDP) was given $70 to $77 million for the 1982 fiscal year, a significant reduction from the $100 million level at the end of the 1970s.[28] Moreover, there is no assurance that even the current level of funding will be maintained or, indeed, that the OJJDP will continue to be authorized in the years to come. The use of local referenda to reduce property taxes, like Proposition 13 in California, appear to be gaining popularity across the nation. These referenda, as California has found, can bring severe budget cuts for such local or county juvenile justice agencies as probation, detention facilities, day treatment programs, and residential facilities.

The Youthful Offender and Economics

Juveniles are affected by the economic conditions of society in at least two ways. First, children who have been raised in poverty must accept on a daily basis the consequences of economic deprivations. It is not surprising that the children of the poor frequently turn to crime to provide what their families cannot provide. Second, adolescents in American society today must deal with economically hard times that make unemployment extremely high. Adolescents who for one reason or the other drop out of school find making it in the marketplace even more difficult. Among minority youths in urban areas, unemployment figures are sometimes as high as 40 to 50 percent. Cloward and Ohlin have pointed out that adolescents who do not have legitimate opportunities will turn to illegitimate opportunities, or crime, to survive in life.[29]

THE POLITICAL CONTEXT

Policies that affect rates of unemployment, poverty, and public assistance are made in the political arena, as are policies dealing with youth crime. This political context becomes especially important in terms of developing, implementing, and evaluating policy for the prevention and control of delinquency.

The Societal Level

Social policies and programs operate in environments in which diverse groups compete for scarce resources. Many conflicting interests are usually present, and power in these environments is generally unequally divided among them. Those seeking to achieve policy changes frequently must contend with a turbulent political and organizational environment as they attempt to demonstrate that the new policy will "work" and is somehow better than the existing policy.[30]

Recent policy changes reflect the interactions of political groups with the larger political environment. The children's rights movement emerged as a concern of interest groups in the 1970s. Considerable legislation was passed as a result, and 1979 was proclaimed the International Year of the Child. In addition, mandatory reporting laws for child abuse were passed in every state in the 1970s.

The deinstitutionalization movement of the 1970s also succeeded to the degree it did because it had the support of policymakers. The success of Jerome Miller in closing all the training schools in Massachusetts in the early 1970s was the result of Miller's ability to mobilize support in the legislature before the opposition had a chance to organize its resistance. Commissioner Miller also was able to establish and maintain good public relations, developing a good rapport with the Boston newspapers, especially the *Globe*. He took confined youths to speak to public groups throughout the state, where these youths told their audiences about the brutal and inhumane conditions of training school life. Finally, Miller had the active backing of a reform-minded governor.[31]

However, in spite of these and other policy changes, juvenile justice at present is an area of relatively marginal governmental concern. Juvenile justice currently has little general support within the states, few interest groups regularly support it, few coalitions of interest groups or governmental leaders push for change, and reports on major events relating to juvenile justice (other than incidents of crime) usually are relegated to the back pages of the newspapers.[32]

The Political Context and the Local Community

Policy decisions that affect the quality of juvenile justice services also are made in the local communities. A chief of police may make the decision to deemphasize specialized police services because of fiscal constraints, and juvenile officers trained and committed to improving juvenile/police relations are no longer available in that community. Policymakers may decide not to pick up the funding of a promising day treatment or residential program that had been dependent upon federal funding for survival. In the late 1970s and early 1980s, such events took place in countless communities across the nation, and many exemplary programs were terminated. Finally, citizens may vote down a bond issue to build a new detention facility for juveniles, and youthful offenders must continue to face the county jail.

The Youthful Offender and Politics

Political changes affect all citizens in American society, but in some ways, adolescents are affected even more than adults are. Mandatory reporting of child abuse laws has resulted in more frequent and earlier identification of youths who are being brutalized at home. The children's rights movement has influenced the courts to grant adolescents more rights in school; no longer do students leave their rights at the schoolyard gate. But the lengthening of society's definition of childhood, with its corresponding postponement of adult responsibilities, has contributed toward creating a generation of youth who feel powerless and alienated in terms of making a contribution to the larger society.

INTERRELATIONSHIPS AMONG THE CONTEXTS

The history of juvenile justice is sometimes presented as a steady march toward more humane and enlightened conceptions of childhood and democracy.[33] But in every period since the colonial one, political and economic forces have combined with sociocultural and legal forces to shape society's methods of handling troublesome youths. The concept of delinquency arose from this long process of developing new rules to govern childhood.

In the colonial period, juvenile justice was shaped principally by the cultural and religious ideas of the Puritans, but the creation of the houses of refuge in the nineteenth century emerged from more complex factors. On the one hand, the houses of refuge were a product of the Jacksonian era that saw the young American nation as having an unlimited capacity to solve its social problems. The theory behind the houses of refuge was that crime was caused by a bad environment, in which young and impressionable offenders were led astray by the breakdown of home life.[34] But, on the other hand, these institutions were also intended to care for the children of the increasing numbers of Irish immigrants arriving in America.[35]

Similarly, the juvenile court emerged from the interrelationships among the sociocultural, economic, and political contexts. Thus, how the law reached its present state, how it works on a daily basis, and how it changes in a local community all are related to each other.[36] That is, the law emerges from the mores of the people.[37] The wave of optimism that swept through American society during the Progressive era (the period from 1890 to 1920) influenced the creation of the juvenile court. Reformers believed that through the acceptance of positivism and the intervention of the state, the problems of youth in trouble could be solved.[38] The juvenile court also emerged during the wake of unprecedented industrial and urban development in America. This process was accompanied by large-scale immigration to urban centers of people of different cultural, political, and religious backgrounds from the indigenous population; the Progressives were determined to rescue the immigrant children and protect them from their families.[39] Furthermore, as Anthony Platt has forcefully argued, the creation of the juvenile court represented an expression of middle-class values and the philosophy of conservative political groups.[40]

The origins of the juvenile rights period also lie in the interrelationships among the various contexts. The spirit of the late 1960s and 1970s was conducive to reform. Traditional institutions and structures were subjected to heavy criticism, and, within this sociocultural context, reformers sought ways to reduce the autocratic rule of the juvenile court and the repressiveness of the juvenile justice system. Legal policymakers were motivated to rule on several court decisions that restricted the procedural arbitrariness of the juvenile court. Meanwhile, community-based corrections was proposed as an alternative to long-term training schools. The deinstitutionalization movement that occurred in many states resulted both from a conviction that training schools were debilitating to youths and from a desire to find more economical ways to handle youthful offenders.[41]

The sociocultural context is currently responsible for a hard-line mood toward juvenile criminals. The public, whose perceptions have been influenced by the media as well as by real changes in crime rates, has been advocating a ''get-tough'' strategy for dealing with serious juvenile delinquents. Policymakers in the political arena have been responding with tougher policies toward juveniles who commit serious offenses; yet, at the same time, policymakers have respected the public's desire to treat leniently those youths who pose little threat to the social order. The sociocultural context has also led policymakers to continue to revise juvenile court acts and to pass legislation pertaining to youth crime. For example, lawmakers in many jurisdictions now believe that the seriousness of an offense is more important a factor than the age of the offender in determining whether the adult or juvenile court should have jurisdiction. Finally, juvenile court judges are aware of the public's concern about youth crime and, therefore, are more likely to consider public safety than they have been in the past.

Today, perhaps more than ever before, economic factors appear to be influencing both the existence of and the treatment of youth crime in America. Unemployment and poverty continue to keep about one out of every seven families below the poverty level, and there is, not surprisingly, some evidence that lower-class juveniles commit a disproportionate amount of predatory crimes. The economic context also is directly related to the support given social control institutions and agencies, and federal funding and state support for juvenile justice programs has been dramatically reduced. The argument can also be made that part of the reason more youthful offenders are being kept in the community is to avoid the expense of confining juveniles in long-term institutions.

Finally, the majority of American youth violate the law at some time during their adolescent years. The explanations for such behavior are found in the various contexts that define young people's lives and their perceptions of these contexts. Yet some youths violate the law more frequently and in more serious ways than other adolescents. The explanations for their more serious delinquent behavior must be rooted in their specific reactions to the forces impinging upon them. But the choices they make sometimes are limited through the use of routine, taken-for-granted, socially recognized procedures that constitute the social world.[42]

IMPLICATIONS OF THE CONTEXTUAL PERSPECTIVE

The contextual perspective assumes that the definitions of delinquency, the social forces conducive to delinquency, and the prevention and control of delinquency emerge from the interrelationships of five contexts, each of which has societal, community, and individual levels. In studying the problem of delinquency one will find that this contextual perspective also offers five advantages.

First, the contextual perspective helps to prevent the student from getting trapped in one context and subordinating all the others to that one frame of reference. Second, the contextual perspective serves to remind one studying delinquency that youth crime is affected by a variety of forces on several levels. As delinquency is examined from the three levels, ranging from the general culture to the perspective of the individual delinquent, the student will understand why easy answers do not exist. Indeed, part of the reason why the present knowledge of delinquency barely scratches the surface is that approaches to the past have generally been so unidimensional.

Third, the contextual perspective reminds the student that theories about delinquent behavior must be understood in terms of the economic, social, political, and cultural conditions of their time. That is, this approach emphasizes the importance of why people thought as they did, how their creations reflect the time in which the theories were expressed, and what role these creations played in their particular historical setting. Did the theorists lag behind their time? Did they outdistance it? Or did they anticipate the future?[43]

Fourth, the contextual perspective helps provide a more realistic expression of the delinquent in action. One of the aims of this text is to present a picture of delinquents that accurately portrays delinquents in the real world. Frequently, the depictions of delinquency in texts do not convey the reality they purport to explain, often losing what is essential in the character of the delinquent enterprise.[44] A realistic portrait of delinquent behavior must reflect a multidimensional view rather than a unidimensional one, must report accurately how delinquents interpret the events that happen to them, and must interpret the effects of their interactions with others on their behavior.

Fifth, the contextual perspective is helpful in developing a more effective strategy for dealing with delinquency in American society. To deal effectively with the problem, we must restructure delinquency prevention and control interventions in a manner based on these interlocking perspectives. The more that the interrelationships of these perspectives are acknowledged on the societal, community, and individual levels, the more likely that our approaches to delinquency will not just be Band-Aid therapy.

SUMMARY

Each generation feels that the problem of delinquency is more serious than ever before, and this generation is no different. The public believes that delinquency is increasing, vandalism and violence in the public schools are a serious problem, and violent youth crime has made many streets in America unsafe. The history of dealing with juvenile lawbreakers has seen the state assume authority originally invested in the family. The legal context for dealing with delinquency stems from the *parens patriae* philosophy, through which the juvenile court becomes a substitute parent for wayward children. Delinquency in America takes place in a sociocultural context that has become more and more child-centered, but the least-restrictive approach to youth problems has traditionally been largely reserved for middle- and upper-class youths. Lower-class youngsters often are viewed differently and, accordingly, receive punitive sanctions from the juvenile court. Juveniles are influenced by the values and norms of society, and much of the behaviors and attitudes of delinquents are reflections of what is found in the wider society. The direct and indirect costs of delinquency today are staggering. But equally important to American society is the cost of letting vast numbers of youths grow up impoverished. As children of the poor are faced with the difficulties of daily survival, not surprisingly, many have turned to crime. The political arena is where policy on delinquency is created in this nation. Interest groups advocating reform of delinquency policy have achieved some gains, but too much of the time the prevention and control of delinquency remains a minor area of governmental concern.

The contextual perspective guides the discussion of delinquency throughout this text. Each chapter includes a social policy section representing the political context. The historical and legal contexts are discussed in nearly every chapter, and, wherever pertinent, the sociocultural and economic contexts are included. The societal, community, and individual levels, particularly in the policy sections, are emphasized. The summaries of most chapters also use the contextual perspective to integrate the material discussed. The concluding chapter reviews the entire text through the contextual perspective.

Discussion Questions

1. How has the role of the family changed throughout the history of juvenile justice in the United States?
2. Define the concept of *parens patriae*. Why is it important in juvenile delinquency?
3. What are the three categories in which the juvenile court has jurisdiction over youth?
4. Explain the contextual perspective. How is this multidimensional model helpful in understanding juvenile delinquency?
5. What are some of the reasons that make juvenile delinquency a serious problem in American society?
6. Why is juvenile delinquency a marginal area of governmental concern?

References

Krisberg, Barry, and Austin, James. *The Children of Ishmael: Critical Perspectives on Juvenile Justice*. Palo Alto, Calif.: Mayfield Publishing Company, 1978.

Phillipson, Michael. *Understanding Crime and Delinquency: A Sociological Introduction*. Chicago: Aldine Publishing Company, 1974.

Platt, Anthony M. *The Child Savers*. Chicago: University of Chicago Press, 1969.

Pound, Roscoe. "The Juvenile Court and the Law." *National Probation and Parole Association Yearbook* 1 (1964).

Rothman, David J. *The Discovery of the Asylum*. Boston: Little, Brown & Company, 1971.

Sarri, Rosemary C., and Vinter, Robert D. "Justice for Whom? Varieties of Juvenile Correctional Approaches." In *The Juvenile Justice System*, edited by Malcolm W. Klein. Beverly Hills, Calif.: Sage Publications, 1976.

Schlossman, Steven L. *Love and the American Delinquent: The Theory and Practice of "Progressive" Juvenile Justice, 1825–1920*. Chicago: University of Chicago Press, 1977.

Schur, Edwin. *Radical Non-Intervention: Rethinking the Delinquency Problem*. Englewood Cliffs, N.J.: Prentice-Hall, 1973.

Shichor, David. "Historical and Current Trends in American Juvenile Justice." *Juvenile and Family Court Journal* 34 (August 1983): 61–75.

Smith, Charles P., and Alexander, Paul S. "A National Assessment of Serious Juvenile Crime and the Juvenile Justice System: The Need for a Better Response: Summary Report." *Reports of the National Juvenile Justice Assessment Centers*. Vol. 1. Washington, D.C.: U.S. Government Printing Office, 1980.

FOOTNOTES

1. "The Plague of Violent Crime," *Newsweek* 23 March 1981, p. 1.

2. The interactionist perspective found in Michael Phillipson, *Understanding Crime and Delinquency: A Sociological Introduction* (Chicago: Aldine Publishing Company, 1974), was quite useful in developing the contextual perspective contained in this chapter.

3. Ibid., pp. 38–42.

4. Ibid., pp. 138–139.

5. David J. Rothman, *The Discovery of the Asylum* (Boston: Little, Brown & Company, 1971), pp. 46–53.

6. Ibid., pp. 225–227.

7. Roscoe Pound, "The Juvenile Court and the Law," *National Probation and Parole Association Yearbook* 1 (1944), p. 4.

8. *Kent* v. *United States,* 383 U.S. 541, 86 S.Ct. 1045, 16 L ed 2d 84 (1966); *In re Gault,* 387 U.S. 1, 18 L. Ed. 2d 527, 87 S.Ct. 1428 (1967); *In re Winship,* 397 U.S. 358, 90 S.Ct. 1968, 25 L. Ed. 368 (1970); *McKeiver* v. *Pennsylvania,* 403 U.S. 528, 535 (1971); *In re Barbara Burrus,* 275 N.C. 517, 169 S.E. 2d 879 (1969); and *Breed* v. *Jones,* 421 U.S. 519, 95 S.Ct. 1779 (1975).

9. 387 U.S. 1, 18 L. Ed. 2d 527, 87 S.Ct. 1428.

10. Interviewed in August 1981.

11. Paul C. Friday, "Interactional Review of Youth Crime and Delinquency," in *Crime and Deviance,* edited by Graeme Newman (Beverly Hills, Calif.: Sage Publications, 1980), p. 102.

12. Larry J. Siegel and Joseph J. Senna, *Juvenile Delinquency: Theory, Practice, and Law* (St. Paul, Minn.: West Publishing Company, 1981), p. 5.

13. Barry Krisberg and James Austin, *The Children of Ishmael: Critical Perspectives on Juvenile Justice* (Palo Alto, Calif.: Mayfield Publishing Company, 1978), p. 60.

14. 135 F. Supp. 224 (C.C.C. 1955).

15. David Shichor, "Historical and Current Trends in American Juvenile Justice," *Juvenile and Family Court Journal* 34 (August 1983), p 64

16. Charles P. Smith and Paul S. Alexander, "A National Assessment of Serious Juvenile Crime and the Juvenile Justice System: The Need for a Rational Response," *Reports of the National Juvenile Justice Assessment Centers,* vol. 1, *Summary* (Washington, D.C.: U.S. Government Printing Office, 1980), pp. xix–xx.

17. Interviewed in June 1972.

18. U.S. Department of Justice, Federal Bureau of Investigation, *Uniform Crime Reports, 1982* (Washington, D.C.: U.S. Government Printing Office, 1983), p. 176.

19. Ibid.

20. U.S. Senate Subcommittee on Delinquency, *Challenge for the Third Century: Education in a Safe Environment* (Washington, D.C.: U.S. Government Printing Office, 1977).

21. Edwin Schur, *Radical Non-Intervention: Rethinking the Delinquency Problem* (Englewood Cliffs, N.J.: Prentice-Hall, 1973).

22. Anthony M. Platt, *The Child Savers* (Chicago: University of Chicago Press, 1969).

23. Richard B. Freeman, "Crime and Unemployment," in *Crime and Public Policy,* edited by James Q. Wilson (San Francisco: ICS Press, 1983), p. 90.

24. Suzanne S. Ageton and Delbert S. Elliott, *The Incidence of Delinquent Behavior in a National Probability Sample of Adolescents* (Boulder, Colo.: Behavioral Research Institute, 1978).

25. Allen D. Calvin, "Unemployment among Black Youths, Demographics and Crime," *Crime and Delinquency* 27 (April 1980), pp. 234–244.

26. Smith and Alexander, "A National Assessment," pp. 59–62. Economic costs for these studies do not, of course, take recent inflationary increases into account.

27. Ibid., p. 59.

28. Information received from an administrator in the Office of Juvenile Justice Delinquency Prevention in July 1981.

29. Richard A. Cloward and Lloyd E. Ohlin, *Delinquency and Opportunity: A Theory of Delinquent Gangs* (New York: Free Press, 1960).

30. See Richard Quinney, *The Social Reality of Crime* (Boston: Little, Brown & Company, 1970) for the development of this concept of interest groups.

31. Robert Johnson et al., "Juvenile Decarceration: An Exploratory Study of Correctional Reform," in *Crossroads in Corrections: Designing Policy for the '80s,* edited by S. Zimmerman and H. Miller (Beverly Hills, Calif.: Sage Publications, 1981).

32. Rosemary C. Sarri and Robert D. Vinter, "Justice for Whom? Varieties of Juvenile Correctional Approaches," in *The Juvenile Justice System,* edited by Malcolm W. Klein (Beverly Hills, Calif.: Sage Publications, 1976), p. 169.

33. Krisberg and Austin, *Children of Ishmael,* p. 569.

34. Rothman, *Discovery of the Asylum,* p. 107.

35. Krisberg and Austin, *Children of Ishmael,* p. 24.

36. Phillipson, *Understanding Crime and Delinquency,* p. x.

37. David Matza, *Delinquency and Drift* (New York: John Wiley & Sons, 1964), p. 154.

38. David J. Rothman, *Conscience and Convenience: The Asylum and Its Alternatives in Progressive America* (Boston: Little, Brown & Company, 1980), pp. 43–60.

39. Shichor, "Historical and Current Trends," p. 61.

40. Platt, *Child Savers.*

41. A. T. Scull, *Decarceration: Community Treatment and the Deviant: A Radical View* (Englewood Cliffs, N.J.: Prentice-Hall, 1977).

42. Phillipson, *Understanding Crime and Delinquency,* p. 46.

43. Katja Vodopivec, "The Multidisciplinary Approach to Theory Evaluation," in *New Paths in Criminology,* edited by Sarnoff A. Mednick and S. Giora Shoham (Lexington, Mass.: Lexington Books, 1979), pp. 17–18.

44. Matza, *Delinquency and Drift,* p. 2.

INTERVIEW WITH MARVIN WOLFGANG

"Considering the limited resources of time, talent and money available to handle delinquents, perhaps it is that violent few, the 6 percent chronic offenders in Cohort I and the 7.5 percent chronic offenders in Cohort II, to which we should give our attention."

In this interview, Marvin Wolfgang, Director for the Center for Studies in Criminology and Criminal Law at the University of Pennsylvania, discusses some of the most important questions involved in understanding delinquency in America.

Question: What is the relationship between the past and the present in terms of how delinquency is handled in American society?

Wolfgang: Within the last decade juvenile status offenses such as truancy, incorrigibility and running away from home have been and are being eliminated from juvenile court statutes and are being treated as personal and familial problems. That elimination of status offenses is probably one of the most important changes that have occurred in recent times. Another change that has occurred within the past decade is a variety of efforts to deinstitutionalize delinquents and to divert them out of the juvenile justice system. The extent to which these efforts have been successful in reducing the business of juvenile justice or the handling of juveniles by agencies in the United States is difficult to assess. There has also developed a willingness on the part of state legislators to reduce the maximum age of the juvenile court statute

Professor Marvin Wolfgang is widely acknowledged as one of the top criminologists in the United States. The Measurement of Delinquency and Delinquency in the Birth Cohort, both of which have influenced how delinquency is perceived and handled in this nation, are among his many publications. Forthcoming publications on Cohort II also promise to have significant impact on the understanding of delinquent behavior. Interviewed in May 1984, and used with permission.

from 18 to 16, as in the case of New York State. Under inducement from the National Institute of Juvenile Justice and Delinquency Prevention, the states have been encouraged to separate the detention of juveniles from adults and, although the enabling act has indeed been working, there are still institutions housing juveniles and adults together, but there has been a considerable reduction in that phenomenon.

Question: The Philadelphia Cohort study is considered a classic in terms of understanding juvenile crime in this nation. How do you reconcile your findings in the first and second cohort studies concerning socioeconomic status with the self-report studies?

Wolfgang: In a follow-up sample of 567 males age 25 to 26 in Cohort 1, we asked a series of questions at the end of the interview that contained self-reports on 22 offenses ranging from criminal homicide to minor offenses like disorderly conduct. Dr. Paul Tracy, from our Center, has conducted special studies comparing the self-report offense frequency and type among nondelinquents, delinquents, one-time offenders, recidivists and chronic offenders. He further delineated these groups by socioeconomic status and found that there is a considerable correlation between the self-admitted commission of offenses and arrests, both by type and frequency. The chronic lower SES delinquents admitted committing many more and many more serious violent offenses for which they had never been arrested than did delinquents in any other category or nondelinquents. This finding holds across race as well. Moreover, some of the more sophisticated research literature on self-reports in comparison with arrestees among delinquents, such as the work done by the late Michael Hindelang, indicates that the previously reported disparity between self-report and arrests by SES is considerably reduced when looking at a variety of sources, including victimization surveys. The reduced disparity, or even the nonsignificant disparity, holds mostly for serious offenses and less for the trivial ones. Thus, although all of the delinquents in both Cohorts 1 and II were so designated as having an official police contact, we in general maintain that the SES differences by frequency of delinquency contact are real.

Question: The theories of delinquent behavior appear so unidimensional. What is needed to create a more multidimensional approach to understanding delinquency?

Wolfgang: I do not think that theories of delinquent behavior are very unidimensional. There are unidisciplinary perspectives but generally the authors of them do not deny the functioning of other disciplinary theoretical constructs. We at the Center for Studies in Criminology and Criminal Law at the University of Pennsylvania have generally been taking a multidisciplinary and, in some cases, an interdisciplinary perspective in our writing of proposals and in attempting to explain and interpret our observations about delinquency. We are predominantly sociological and sociopsychological because of our training, but we also are prepared to study and utilize a variety of other factors. In the efforts to integrate strain and conflict theory with control theory, there is surely a multidimensional perspective. Such efforts are not sterile eclecticism but make linkages between a variety of concepts. Learning theory, differential association, cultural conflict, subcultural theory and control theory and opportunity structures can all be brought together in an integrated fashion without denying the integrity or validity of any one specific approach.

Question: Biosociology has never been well received by American criminologists. Why is it receiving popularity at this time? What does biosociology have to contribute to our understanding of delinquent behavior?

Wolfgang: At the Center we have, for the past four and a half years, been engaging in a biosocial study of several waves of birth cohorts born between 1959 and 1964 in Philadelphia. We have obtained the files of a large-scale study originally designed as a medical survey to get baseline statistics on birth defects. This Collaborative Perinatal Study collected thousands of variables about the pre-, peri-, and postnatal histories of approximately 60,000 subjects throughout the United States. In Philadelphia we have data on approximately 10,000. These data include an enormously rich set of variables that are physiological, neurological, psychological and psychiatric as well as demographic and sociological. Our effort has been to examine the linkages between these otherwise apparently disparate factors, such as brain hemispheric laterality and neurological dysfunctions. Our report will be complete in another year but some papers have already been given, particularly by Dr. Deborah Denno, on some of these neurological factors, achievement level and IQ, minimal brain damage, as they may be relevant to deviant and delinquent behavior.

One of the reasons that we and several other groups across the country and in Europe have been studying what are commonly called biosocial factors is that historically these interests perhaps go in cycles and perhaps we may be returning to a more sensitive interest in what Talcott Parsons would call a personality system, as distinguished from the social and cultural systems. Moreover, the technological and methodological advances in physiology, neurology and biochemistry have been enormous in the last 10 to 15 years, far outpacing the innovations and scientific leaps that have been made in the social sciences. As we have learned more and more about the influence of these biological factors on human behavior and social groupings, it is not unnatural that the study of criminal and deviant behavior would be interested in exploring these relationships. Longitudinal data with biophysiological and neurological variables available, both in this country and in England and Denmark, provide excellent materials for examining these relationships.

Question: What does society need to do to more effectively control delinquency?

Wolfgang: I am favorably disposed to the policy that eliminates juvenile status offenses from juvenile court statutes. I am not unfavorable to the considerations of reducing the maximum age of delinquency from 18 to 16, primarily because I think there is compelling and convincing evidence, both historically and from scientific research, that persons age 16 and over have the cognitive awareness and capacity to understand the nature and character of their deeds, and that such cognition is not significantly different from persons age 18 and over. I am not suggesting that society's reaction to delinquency should result in harsher or more severe penalties or in more incarceration. I am only suggesting that the disparities in the dual systems we have of juvenile justice and adult criminal justice should be reduced and perhaps even eliminated. I thoroughly endorse the policy of, in general, separating juveniles from adults in any confined space such as jails or prisons. I further think that, based on our own research and that of others, the criminal career programs in jurisdictions around the United States should be taking into account a criminal career that begins much earlier than 18 in a very high proportion of cases. Our 6 percent in Cohort 1 and 7.5 percent in Cohort II who had five or more offenses before reaching age 18, many of them violent offenses, should be taken into account in any focused prosecutory program of convicting and incapacitating career criminals. A criminal justice policy or practice that permits an 18-year-old offender to start adulthood with a virgin or first offense, thereby ignoring an offense—particularly a violent offense—career as a juvenile is not adequately providing proper social protection.

In both our birth cohorts the proportion of one-time offenders was high, approaching 50 percent of all delinquents. In most cases one-time offenders committed relatively trivial offenses and, for reasons that we may not entirely appreciate, desisted, perhaps by "spontaneous remission." In any case, these one-time offenders were never arrested, at least up to age 18. Considering the limited resources of time, talent and money available to handle delinquents, perhaps it is that violent few, the 6 percent chronic offenders in Cohort 1 and the 7.5 percent chronic offenders in Cohort II, to which we should give our attention. Because Cohort II shows a higher proportion of offenders, particularly violent offenders, beginning their careers at age 13, efforts should be made, which we are seeking to do, to predict future offensive behavior at an early age at onset. Such predictions, I hasten to add, that go beyond sheer scientific inquiry should be translated into policy only for purposes of providing constructive, positive interventions and not for extending the length of time of confinement or control nor for increasing the severity of any penalties.

THE MEASUREMENT OF DELINQUENCY

CHAPTER 2

THE MEASUREMENT OF OFFICIAL DELINQUENCY

CHAPTER OUTLINE

Those who make a practice of comparing human actions are never so much at a loss as to put them together and in the same light; for they commonly contradict each other so strangely that it seems impossible that they have come from the same shop.

Montaigne

Crime is once again emerging as a major social problem in the United States. Not since the mid- to late-1960s and the early 1970s has so much fear and anxiety been generated by the unlawful elements of our society. Juveniles are responsible for a great deal of this current concern. Not only do they commit far more crime than might be expected from their numbers in the population, but their delinquency is related to such important social problems as child abuse, drug use, and violence in the schools. Yet, in spite of our certainty as to the seriousness of juvenile crime, we are not really certain how much youth crime does occur.

The purpose of this chapter is to unmask the amount, the nature, and the extent of "official" juvenile delinquency in American society. The next chapter will examine the amount, the nature, and the extent of "unofficial" delinquency. In this chapter, we identify the main tools to measure delinquency, the official statistics that report juvenile involvement in crime, the problems of official statistical approaches, and policy implications.

THE MEASUREMENT OF DELINQUENCY

Throughout history, society has developed many techniques for seeking truth. People want verifiable data to decide how best to act. Philosophy, religion, intuition, and common sense have all been called on to provide the answers to the great questions concerning the social order. The failure of these methods to provide reliable and valid information has led thinkers to search for other, better sources of truth. The contemporary answer is science, and its proponents feel science provides more accurate answers than does any other method yet used.[1]

The growth of the physical and natural sciences took place in the eighteenth and nineteenth centuries, and in the nineteenth century, a number of philosophers proposed that the methods of science could be applied equally to the study of human affairs. In the final quarter of the nineteenth century, a new school of criminology, the positive school, began to apply the methods of science to the study of criminals. In the early decades of the twentieth century, the positivists also began to examine why certain youths become delinquent and how they differ from nondelinquents. Throughout this century, empirical examination has been used to investigate countless biological, psychological, and social factors to determine the conditions that lead to delinquent behavior. Empirical investigation has also been used in recent years to measure the extent and nature of delinquency in American society.

A number of research tools have been developed to measure the extent and nature of delinquent behavior. These can be divided into official and unofficial means of measurements. The *Uniform Crime Reports, Juvenile Court Statistics,* institutional and aftercare records, and cohort studies constitute the main sources of official statistics. The sources of unofficial statistics are self-report studies and victimization surveys.

OFFICIAL STATISTICS

The *Uniform Crime Reports* and the *Juvenile Court Statistics* are based on the tabulation of data collected from the police and juvenile courts. Institutional and aftercare files consist of statistics recorded by institutional staff or aftercare officers who work with offenders. Cohort studies usually utilize raw police files along with a variety of official and unofficial data.

Uniform Crime Reports

New York, Massachusetts, and Maine were the first states to collect crime statistics, but, for the most part, record keeping by state and locality during the early years of American history was haphazard or nonexistent. In 1870, federal record keeping was authorized when Congress created the Department of Justice. Although the states and local police establishments largely ignored the task of record keeping either because of indifference or fear of federal control, this tendency began to be reversed in the early part of the twentieth century when the International Association of Chiefs of Police created a committee on Uniform Crime Reports. In 1930, the Attorney General designated the Federal Bureau of Investigation to serve as the national clearinghouse for data collected by the Uniform Crime Reports program.[2]

An examination of the *Uniform Crime Reports* indicates that juveniles are arrested for the same kinds of offenses as adults, as well as for some for which adults very seldom are arrested. For example, while both adults and juveniles are arrested for such serious offenses as murder and aggravated assault and for such less serious offenses as simle assault and carrying weapons, only juveniles can be taken into custody for running away, violating curfew, or truancy from school.[3]

The offenses for which the FBI collects information are divided into two classes of crimes, Part I and Part II offenses. Part I offenses, also known as index offenses, are subdivided further into crimes against the person, such as murder, rape, robbery and aggravated assault, and into crimes against property, such as burglary, larceny, auto theft, and arson. Juveniles arrested for the violent Part I offenses are more likely to be held for trial as adults, whereas those arrested for less serious offenses usually are processed by juvenile authorities. The exceptions to this general rule are those juveniles who have lengthy records of crime, including violent offenses, and those who are held over for trial in adult courts because they are believed to be threats to society.

Each month, police departments across the United States report to the FBI the number of offenses that come to their attention, as well as the number of offenses that the police are able to clear by arrest (clearance by arrest means that a person is arrested because he or she confesses to an offense or is implicated by witnesses or by other criminal evidence of having committed an offense). These monthly reports are summarized in year-end reports, and these yearly reports constitute our major official source of information about crime in the United States. The data are subdivided into many different statistical categories, including the backgrounds of offenders and the type of crime for which they are arrested.

Crime by Age Groups

The FBI reported that in 1982 approximately 10,000,000 arrests occurred for all offenses other than traffic violations (see Table 2-1 for the total arrests, distribution by age). The FBI data indicate that the number of arrests for Part I and Part II crimes has increased each year since 1970 with the exceptions of 1972, 1977, and 1982.[4]

Juveniles account for a disproportionate number of these arrests. Of all age categories, people over 35 are the most law-abiding and people between the ages of 19 and 35 are most heavily involved in crime. Yet in 1982 juveniles between the ages of 10 and 17, constituting about 15 percent of the population, were arrested for 17 percent of the violent crimes and 34.5 percent of the property crimes. Even youths between 13 and 15 years of age have higher arrests rates than might be expected.[5]

TABLE 2-1 Total Arrests, Distribution by Age, 1982

Offense Charged	Total All Ages	Ages under 15	Ages under 18	Ages 18 and over
Total	10,062,343	550,901	1,804,688	8,257,655
Percent distribution	100.0	5.5	17.9	82.1
Murder and nonnegligent manslaughter	18,511	183	1,579	16,932
Forcible rape	28,332	1,134	4,159	24,173
Robbery	138,118	9,114	36,480	101,638
Aggravated assault	258,899	9,463	34,145	224,754
Burglary	436,271	62,320	172,838	263,433
Larceny-theft	1,146,705	157,221	371,296	775,409
Motor vehicle theft	108,736	9,134	39,141	69,595
Arson	16,908	3,747	6,282	10,626
Violent crime	443,860	19,894	76,343	367,497
Percent distribution	100.0	4.5	17.2	82.8
Property crime	1,708,620	232,422	589,557	1,119,063
Percent distribution	100.0	13.6	34.5	65.5
Crime index total	2,152,480	252,316	665,920	1,486,560
Percent distribution	100.0	11.7	30.9	69.1

TABLE 2-1 (Continued)

Offense Charged	Total All Ages	Ages under 15	Ages under 18	Ages 18 and over
Other assaults	450,072	36,740	74,472	375,600
Forgery and counterfeiting	79,851	1,353	7,737	72,214
Fraud	265,663	7,086	18,683	246,980
Embezzlement	7,358	98	572	6,786
Stolen property: buying, receiving, possessing	114,597	8,107	28,352	86,245
Vandalism	201,463	43,814	89,274	112,189
Weapons: carrying, possessing, etc.	164,078	5,456	22,759	141,319
Prostitution and commercialized vice	11,029	253	3,014	108,015
Sex offenses (except forcible rape and prostitution)	66,320	4,138	10,783	55,537
Drug abuse violations	565,182	11,405	76,208	488,974
Gambling	36,569	155	1,270	35,299
Offenses against family and children	45,432	661	1,598	43,834
Driving under the influence	1,404,646	387	25,521	1,379,125
Liquor laws	404,797	8,597	119,157	285,640
Drunkenness	1,034,527	3,113	33,571	1,000,776
Disorderly conduct	764,324	28,902	115,993	648,331
Vagrancy	32,158	853	3,626	20,532
All other offenses (except traffic)	1,958,658	76,505	309,437	1,649,221
Suspicion	9,019	821	2,541	6,478
Curfew and loitering law violations	78,806	20,131	78,806	—
Runaways	115,214	50,010	115,214	—

Source: U.S. Department of Justice, Federal Bureau of Investigation, *Uniform Crime Reports, 1982* (Washington, D.C.: U.S. Government Printing Office, 1983), p. 176. Data derived from 9832 reporting agencies, which had a 1982 estimated population of 187,346,000.

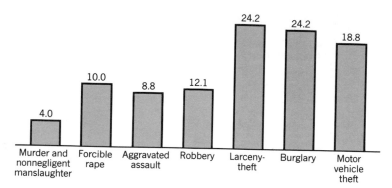

Figure 2-1 Percentage of Offenses Cleared by Arrests of Juveniles Under Eighteen in 1982

Source: Adapted from U.S. Department of Justice, Federal Bureau of Investigation, *Uniform Crime Reports, 1982* (Washington, D.C.: U.S. Government Printing Office, 1983), p. 163.

Violent crime is usually committed by older offenders, with the ages of 25 to 29 being peak years. Even so, 53 percent of all violent index offenses (not crime-cleared) involve offenders under 25 years of age and 23 percent involve offenders between the ages of 13 and 18.[6] Although crimes of violence are less numerous than property offenses, violent youth crime creates considerable fear and paranoia in American society.

Property offenses cause much of the contemporary concern over youth crime. The act of discovering a break-in, and not knowing whether or when another one will occur, has caused many citizens to change their lifestyles. Significantly, of the index property offenses, the highest rates of clearance by arrest for juveniles under 18 are for burglary and larceny theft, followed by auto theft (see Figure 2-1). Of those arrested for index property crimes, 67 percent were under the age of 25 and 36 percent were between the ages of 13 through 16.[7]

When the arrests for both violent and property index crimes are combined and examined in terms of age, another view of the distribution of youth crime emerges. Sixteen-, seventeen-, and eighteen-year-olds traditionally have been arrested more frequently than individuals of any other age category. This trend held for 1982 as well, but, in contrast to earlier years, fifteen-, sixteen-, seventeen-, and eighteen-year-olds were arrested at surprisingly uniform rates.[8]

Sex, Race, Ethnicity, and Areas of Residence

The FBI also collects information on sex, race and ethnicity, and areas of residence. These data are collected because of their relatively easy accessibility as well as for their implications for social policy in the areas of law, correctional facility construction, and crime prevention.

Juvenile delinquency is predominantly a characteristic of young males. Males were arrested at a ratio of nearly 4 to 1 over females in 1982, with males accounting for 1,431,483 arrests, and females, 373,205 arrests.[9] In the midst of the leveling off of juvenile arrests since the early 1970s, this 4 to 1 ratio has remained unchanged.

For example, in 1973, female delinquents accounted for 296,567, or 19 percent, of the total arrests of juveniles under eighteen.[10] But, as will be discussed in the next chapter, unofficial statistics report a much closer ratio between the sexes.

Criminologists have been greatly interested in race and ethnicity as correlates of delinquency. Although many argue that this approach reflects a middle-class bias in research and law enforcement against non-WASPs (White Anglo-Saxon Protestants), the statistics do focus attention on the prevalence of street crimes among some segments of the lower classes. Members of certain racial and ethnic groups are arrested and confined in numbers far out of proportion to their numbers in the general population.

In 1982, 1,291,581 whites under the age of eighteen were arrested, whereas 471,495 blacks under eighteen were arrested. Blacks made up only between 12 and 13 percent of the U.S. population, yet they accounted for 26.9 percent of all juvenile arrests and were confined at a rate equal to that of whites. American Indians and Alaskan natives accounted for 13,013 or 0.7 percent and Asian and Pacific Islanders 15,556, or 0.9 percent of all juvenile arrests. Hispanics, for whom the FBI started reporting data only in 1980, accounted for 180,613 arrests, a total of 12.1 percent of all juvenile arrests for 1982.[11]

Data on the area of residence provide researchers with a view of where crime occurs, and, although area of residence is not a perfect measure of the origins of crime because of the mobility of modern society, data on residence do help identify places where crime prevention activities should be focused. Cities, as might be expected, lead, with 1,138,289 arrests of youthful offenders from urban areas, followed by 162,620 arrests of those from suburban areas, and 61,912 of rural youth.[12]

The Rise of Youth Crime

The *Uniform Crime Reports* also provide one answer to questions on the rise and fall of youth crime. According to these official statistics, arrests of juveniles under the age of eighteen rose rather dramatically between 1960 and 1973 and then began to level off. Between 1973 and 1982, forcible rape increased 3.4 percent; aggravated assault, 23.1 percent; larceny-theft, 8.5 percent. But during this same period, murder and nonnegligent manslaughter decreased 6.9 percent; robbery, 1.6 percent; burglary, 9.6 percent; motor vehicle theft, 48.9 percent; and arson, 8.9 percent. Overall, the crime index total of juveniles under eighteen decreased 2.7 percent.[13]

But when the arrests of juveniles under eighteen between 1978 and 1982 are examined, the data become even more striking. In this five-year span, the crime index total of arrested juveniles under eighteen declined 14.5 percent. Of the index crimes, only murder and nonnegligent manslaughter increased, by .8 percent.[14] Categories of index crimes that decreased during this period, as listed by the *Uniform Crime Reports*, are:

Robbery	4.1 percent
Aggravated assault	4.5 percent
Burglary	21.6 percent
Larceny-theft	7.9 percent
Motor vehicle theft	42.9 percent
Arson	18.5 percent[15]

In short, according to the *Uniform Crime Reports,* delinquency appears to have leveled off during the mid-1970s and even to have begun to decline since then.

Controversy over *Uniform Crime Reports*

Yet experts challenge the UCRs on a number of grounds. A serious complaint is that these statistics tell us more about official police policy and practice than about the amount of crime, since the police arrest only those offenders who violate important laws and ignore most of the other offenses committed by juveniles. Also, of course, the police can make arrests only when crimes come to their attention. Since most crimes are hidden or not reported to the police, the UCRs vastly underestimate the actual amount of crime in the United States. Further, police department policies frequently change with each new administration or political party in office, as subsequent administrators either emphasize or deemphasize the "youth problems." In addition, new reporting procedures and computerization make the reporting and recording of offenses known to the police easier than ever before. The public's attitude toward reporting changes continually; recent hard-line policies encourage the reporting of more offenses. Any or all of these factors can easily be made to account for the changes in the numbers contained in the annual *Uniform Crime Reports.*

Other situations affect the statistics contained in the *Uniform Crime Reports.* Frank Zimring has pointed out that youths often are arrested in groups rather than as individuals.[16] While only one crime may have been committed, several juveniles may be arrested. Thus, if the amount of crime is estimated by the number of arrests rather than by the number of offenses, the amount of crime committed by the youth population may be overstated. Another problem of official arrest statistics is that they are based upon data from cooperating departments rather than upon reports on the total population of the United States. A closely related problem is that, as anyone who has tried to decipher *Uniform Crime Reports* knows, the data used for FBI statistics come from shifting samples. That is, different data bases or sets of jurisdictions are used for different sets of tables. These shifts in data base can account for shifts in the apparent incidence of juvenile crime.

Among other problems Zimring identified are the fact that no one audits police reports to check their accuracy; that young offenders may be easier to detect in the act of committing a crime than older offenders, with a resulting inflation of the rates for youths; that FBI statistics come from different cities and states with different trends and patterns in youth crime, thereby making generalizations risky; and that little information is available on the amount and nature of weapons used in such crimes as robbery and aggravated assault. Thus, these and other problems with the data of the *Uniform Crime Reports* mean that the amount of real information available about juvenile crime is very sketchy. For this reason, experts have turned to other statistics to supplement the UCRs.

Juvenile Court Statistics

Most information about the number of children appearing before the juvenile court each year comes from the *Juvenile Court Statistics.* In 1926, the Juvenile Court

Statistics Project was inaugurated by the Children's Bureau of the Department of Labor.[17] The basic objectives of compiling juvenile court statistics were defined as follows:

1. To furnish an index of the general nature and extent of the problems brought before the juvenile court;
2. To show the extent and nature of service given to courts in such a way that significant trends in methods of treatment and in scope and volume of juvenile work would be brought out;
3. To point out significant factors contributing to the problems coming before the courts in order to throw light on possibilities of corrections and prevention; and
4. To show the extent to which service given by courts has been effective in correcting social problems.[18]

However, the annual reports of juvenile court statistics have undergone modifications relating to reporting procedures as well as to content and project objectives. Initial reports included analyses of trends in delinquency based on factors such as sex, race, home conditions, reasons for referral, place of detention care, and disposition. Then, in 1952, the amount of information requested from jurisdictions was limited to a summary count of delinquency, dependency, neglect and traffic cases, and cases involving special proceedings. The responsibility for collecting the *Juvenile Court Statistics* was shifted from the Department of Health, Education & Welfare (HEW) to the Law Enforcement Assistance Administration (LEAA). Under a grant awarded by LEAA in 1975, the National Center for Juvenile Justice was given the responsibility for maintaining the series.

The number of children appearing before the juvenile court significantly increased from the late 1950s until the early 1970s, when it began to level off. In the late 1970s, the estimated number of delinquency cases decreased each year, as shown in Table 2-2. An estimated 1,432,000 cases were disposed of in 1976, 1,389,000 in 1977, and 1,359,000 in 1978, representing a 3 percent decrease from 1976 to 1977 and a 2.2 percent decrease from 1977 to 1978. Nevertheless, this overall 5.1 percent drop must be viewed in comparison with the child population under the jurisdiction of the courts during each of these years; that is, while the number of delinquency cases decreased yearly, the decline was merely proportional to the reduction in the child population served by the juvenile courts.[19]

Cases involving both male and female juvenile offenders declined between 1976 and 1978. The estimated numbers of cases involving males were 1,092,000 in 1976, 1,063,000 in 1977, and 1,055,000 in 1978—an overall decrease of 3.5 percent for the three-year period. For the same period, the estimated number of cases involving females decreased 10.4 percent, from 339,000 in 1976, to 326,000 in 1977, to 303,800 in 1978.[20] One explanation for the greater reduction in cases involving females may be the growing tendency to refer fewer female status offenders to the juvenile court. Significantly, the percentage of females referred to the court is still smaller than that indicated by the 4 to 1 ratio of arrested juvenile males and females reported by the *Uniform Crime Reports*.

TABLE 2-2 Estimated Number and Rate of Delinquency Case Dispositions, 1957–1981

Year	Estimated Number of Delinquency Cases[a]	Child Population 10–17 Years of Age[b]	Rate[c]
1957	440,000	22,173,000	19.8
1958	470,000	23,433,000	20.0
1959	483,000	24,607,000	19.6
1960	510,000	25,368,000	20.1
1961	503,000	26,056,000	19.3
1962	555,000	26,989,000	20.6
1963	601,000	28,056,000	21.4
1964	686,000	29,244,000	23.5
1965	697,000	29,536,000	23.6
1966	745,000	30,124,000	24.7
1967	811,000	30,837,000	26.3
1968	900,000	31,566,000	28.5
1969	988,500	32,157,000	30.7
1970	1,052,000	33,141,000	31.7
1971	1,125,000	33,643,000	33.4
1972	1,112,500	33,954,000	32.8
1973	1,143,700	34,126,000	33.5
1974	1,252,700	34,195,000	36.6
1975	1,317,000	33,960,000	38.8
1976	1,432,000	33,482,000	42.3
1977	1,389,000	32,896,000	42.2
1978	1,359,000	32,276,000	42.1
1979	1,374,500	31,643,000	43.4
1980	1,445,400	31,171,000	46.4
1981	1,350,500	30,725,000	44.0

[a]Estimates for 1957–1969 were based on data from a national sample of juvenile courts. Estimates for 1970–1981 were based on data from all units reporting consistently for two consecutive years.

[b]Based on estimates from Bureau of the Census, U.S. Department of Commerce (Current Resident Population Reports, Population Estimates and Projections, Series P-25, No. 929, Issued May 1983). Also included are population figures for Puerto Rico and the Virgin Islands.

[c]Rate was based on the number of delinquency cases per 1,000 children 10 through 17 years of age.

Source: Ellen H. Nimick, et al., *Juvenile Court Statistics: 1981* (Pittsburgh, PA: National Center for Juvenile Justice, 1983), p. 14.

Urban and semiurban courts experienced a decline in the number of delinquency case dispositions between 1976 and 1978, but, at the same time, rural areas experienced a consistent increase in the number of dispositions. Urban areas accounted for 60 percent of all delinquency case dispositions between 1976 and 1978, but there was an 8.3 percent decline in the estimated number of cases disposed of in urban areas. An estimated 931,000 cases were disposed of in 1976, 875,000 cases in 1977, and 854,000 cases in 1978. Delinquency dispositions in semiurban areas remained relatively constant between 1976 and 1977, and then declined by 5 percent in 1978; an estimated 406,000 cases were disposed of in 1976, 406,900 in 1977, and 386,000 in 1978. But an estimated 93,200 cases were disposed of in rural areas in 1976, 107,600 in 1977, and 117,400 in 1978. This increase in rural cases reflected a 27.7 percent increase in the rate of male cases over the three-year period and a 30.7 percent increase in cases involving females.[21]

The National Center for Juvenile Justice conducted a 1978 survey of juvenile courts in thirteen states and two large jurisdictions for the purpose of attaining more detailed information on the characteristics of juveniles who appeared before the court and on juvenile court transactions. This study revealed that the profile of a typical juvenile referred was that of a white male, 16 to 17 years of age, referred to the court by law enforcement agencies for a property offense. Males were typically older than females referred, and males were referred more frequently for property offenses. The majority of the females referred to court were referred for status offenses. Although the same proportion of males and females referred were detained (19 percent), cases involving females resulted more often in dismissal.[22]

This 1978 survey also revealed that a significant increase in the rate of delinquency took place with the increasing age of juveniles. The number of referrals detained also increased with age. For all age groups, property offenses were the most likely reason for referral. But older juveniles were referred more frequently for drug and alcohol offenses.[23]

Juvenile Court Statistics, like the *Uniform Crime Reports,* have some serious limitations. First, the time lag in these statistics lessens their usefulness. The most recent data available examine cases appearing before juvenile courts between 1976 and 1978, but more up-to-date statistics are needed to determine how the reduced arrests of juveniles from 1978 to 1982 affected the number of youths appearing before the court on delinquency court dispositions.

Second, the data collected by the National Institute of Juvenile Justice and Delinquency Prevention represent only an estimate of the number of juvenile crimes that come to the attention of the juvenile court. These cases make up a small percentage of the total number of juvenile crimes. Many juvenile crimes are never reported; of those that are reported, the police dismiss or informally handle a high percentage. Of those that are referred to the juvenile court, a high percentage are diverted to nonjudicial agencies.

Finally, *Juvenile Court Statistics* provide little information about juvenile court transactions or the characteristics of referred juveniles. Thus, the scope of these statistics must be expanded or supplementary studies are necessary to provide this information.

Correctional Records
and Aftercare Statistics

Institutional files typically provide data on residents' criminal history, demographic background, and physical characteristics. The results of psychological tests and information about psychiatric evaluations, IQ, and previous school performance also are usually in institutional files. Although files often constitute the only data available and must be used, the reliability of such information is, at best, dubious, for three reasons. First, ages, birthdates, IQ, and other numbers probably have been transcribed numerous times, with consequent probability of error. Second, there is some question about the adequacy of the information those compiling the files are able to find. Third, the information contained in the files is sometimes six or seven years old and may no longer be true.

Aftercare statistics are kept in some states on youths released from juvenile correctional institutions. These statistics usually indicate the type of discharge from aftercare, providing information on whether youths successfully completed aftercare or were reinstitutionalized. Some researchers have found aftercare statistics helpful in determining the recidivism rates of an institutional cohort. The basic limitation of these statistics is that the information is usually sketchy and sometimes inaccurate. That much necessary information is missing makes it difficult to draw many conclusions about the youths under examination.

Cohort Studies

Delinquency cohort studies usually include all persons born in a particular year in a city or county and follow them throughout part of or all of their lives. This procedure is extremely costly but permits researchers to determine through a year-by-year search of police files and community records, interviews, and self-report studies which persons in a cohort were arrested and which were not. Offenders can be identified early, followed throughout their lives and compared with nonoffenders, thereby giving a picture of their criminal careers and how they progressed. Findings of cohort studies conducted in Philadelphia, Columbus, Ohio, and Racine, Wisconsin have been quite useful in filling out the picture of youth crime.

Delinquency in the Philadelphia Cohort

Marvin Wolfgang and colleagues conducted two important cohort studies. The first study consisted of all males born in 1945 who resided in the city of Philadelphia at least from their tenth until their eighteenth birthdays. Official police records, data from school records, and socioeconomic data were used in the study. The principal findings of the 1945 cohort are listed below.[24] The second study consisted of all males and females born in 1958 in Philadelphia, and the chief findings of this study are discussed in Box 2-1.

1. **Delinquency in the Cohort**   Of the 9945 cohort subjects, 6470, or 65 percent, were nondelinquents, while 3475, or 35 percent, had at least one contact with the police at some time over the span of their juvenile court age.[25]

2. **Multiple Offenders**   Nearly 54 percent, or 1862 boys, committed more than one offense. Of 10,214 offenses, 8601, or 84.2 percent, were committed by the 1862 recidivists. Chronic offenders who committed five or more offenses (626, or 6.3 percent, of the total cohort) were responsible for 5305, or 51 percent, of the total number of delinquent acts.[26]

3. **Race**   Of the 7043 white youths, 2017, or 28.64 percent, had police contact, and of the 2902 nonwhite subjects, 1458, or 50.24 percent, had police contact. Nonwhites were more likely to become recidivists than were whites, and of the recidivists nonwhites were more likely to be chronic offenders.[27]

4. **Education**   Nondelinquents received more education than delinquents (11.24 years of school completed versus 9.96 years for delinquents), achieved better grades, and had higher IQs.[28]

5. **Social Class**   Boys from the lower class were more likely to be delinquents, recidivists, and chronic offenders than were boys from higher social classes.[29]

6. **Age**   The probability of whites committing an offense increased gradually to age 12, then increased rapidly to age 16, and dropped sharply by age 17; the nonwhite rates began to increase sharply by age 9, continued a steep increase through age 16, and then decreased sharply at age 17.[30]

7. **Career Chains**   The probability of becoming an adult offender increased dramatically for persons with a record of juvenile delinquency. If a youth had at least one arrest under age 19, the probability of being arrested between 19 and 26 years of age was .4357. This was three times larger than the probability of being arrested as an adult without a record as a juvenile.[31]

BOX 2-1 Interview with Marvin Wolfgang

Question: In what ways are the findings of the second cohort study similar to and different from the first cohort study?

Wolfgang: The major objective of our 1958 cohort study is a complete replication of the 1945 Philadelphia birth cohort study. The same criteria prevail with a different birth year: all subjects must have been born in the given year and must have lived in Philadelphia at least from ages 10 to 18. In general, we sought to establish the same set of estimates as were developed in the previous study in order to determine the cohort effects on delinquent behavior of growing up in the 1960s and 1970s, compared to these activities expressed by a cohort some 13 years earlier. We have intended to determine the differences, if any, which the data show between the two cohorts in such areas as: delinquent rates, correlates of delinquency, first and second offense probabilities, age at onset of delinquency and offense accumulation, relative seriousness of offenses, offender typologies, offense switching probabilities, disposition rates, incapacitation effects and prevention points.

The Cohort 1 data contain 9945 subjects, 3475 delinquents and a total of 10,214 offenses. In comparison, the Cohort II study is much larger and includes females. The 1958 data contain 28,338 subjects, 6545 delinquents and a total of 20,089 offenses.

Our data indicate that boys who were born in 1958 and reached their 18th birthday in 1976 comprised a considerably more violent cohort than their urban brothers did, who were born in 1945 and turned 18 in 1963. The 1958 cohort entered the state of delinquency in about the same proportion (32.6 percent) as the 1945 cohort (34.9 percent), so that the prevalance rate is not significantly different between the two cohorts. But the more recent group has a much higher incidence; that is, they are more delinquent in general and have engaged in much more injurious behavior. The Cohort II are more violently recidivistic and commit more index offenses before reaching age 18. They start their jury offenses earlier (age 13 as compared to age 14) and continue longer. We suspect that when we examine violent offenses according to our system of grading the seriousness of each criminal event, the present cohort will be shown to have average seriousness scores that are much higher than the earlier cohort. Once again, although just about the same proportion of males get into some kind of trouble with the law, the trouble they get into is more violent and more frequent, thus with more harm inflicted on the community. The Cohort II, depending on particular types of crimes, are three to seven times more violent than Cohort I.

The chronic offenders, those who have five or more arrests before reaching age 18, are again approximately the same proportion in Cohort II (7.5 percent of males) as in Cohort I (6 percent). The chronic offenders, however, are responsible for even more of the serious index offenses and violent offenses than were those in Cohort I. Among the males in Cohort II the data indicate that, for both races, chronic offenders continue to have the greatest share of offenses, particularly the more serious violations. For example, chronics committed 68.5 percent of the index offenses, 60.7 percent of the criminal homicides, 76.2 percent of the rapes, 73.4 percent of the robberies, 65 percent of the aggravated assaults and 66.4 percent of the injury offenses.

Interviewed in May 1984, and used with permission.

Significantly, Wolfgang et al. found that a few youths committed half or more of all juvenile offenses and an even higher percentage of the violent juvenile offenses in Philadelphia. More of these offenders were nonwhite than white. These studies also found that stricter punishments by the juvenile justice system are likely to encourage rather than to eliminate further delinquent behavior.

Delinquency in the Columbus Cohort

Donna Martin Hamparian et al. examined the records of those youths who were born in the years 1956 through 1960 and had been arrested for a violent offense in Columbus, Ohio. The researchers discovered that 1138 youths born during these five years were arrested for a violent offense or offenses in Columbus before January 1, 1976.[32] Their principal findings on the violent youthful offenders are as follows:

1. **Sex** Males outnumbered females by almost six to one in committing violent offenses; the violent cohort consisted of 84.6 percent boys and 15.7 percent girls.[33]

2. **Race** Blacks were much more likely to commit violent offenses than were whites. Indeed, in a county in which 12.5 percent of the total population was black, 54.8 percent of the violent cohort was black.[34]

3. **Social Class** The delinquents in the violent cohort came predominately from homes with incomes less than the county median. Only 14.3 percent came from homes in which the family income exceeded the median.[35]

4. **Violent Juvenile Offenders and the Overall Youth Population** Juvenile violent offenders made up a very small fraction of the total number of youths in Columbus at this time. For example, the boys arrested represented only 2.3 percent of the total number of boys in their age group.[36]

5. **Career Chains** The researchers found that juveniles do not typically progress from less serious to more serious crimes, nor do youths specialize in particular types of offenses.[37]

6. **Status Offenders** Hamparian et al. found that status offenders are not headed toward confirmed criminality. Fewer than 10 percent of the delinquents in this study began their careers with a status offense.[38]

7. **Family Background** About half the delinquent cohort came from homes in which both parents were present, and about another one-third came from homes in which only the mother was present. A considerable number of youths (12.2 percent) had siblings who were part of this violent cohort.[39]

8. **Impact of Institutional Treatment** The impact of institutional treatment was basically negative. Indeed, length of time outside an institution between arrests reduced dramatically after each commitment.[40]

The findings of the Columbus study show some agreement and some disagreement with the Philadelphia study. For example, the Columbus study also found that black and lower-class males committed the most serious offenses. But, unlike the Philadelphia study, the Columbus study did not reveal a progression of youth crime from less serious to more serious offenses.

Delinquency in the Racine Cohort

The Racine study is based on an analysis of police and court records of three birth cohorts comprising 6127 persons, male and female. Of these, 4179 had essentially continuous residence in Racine, Wisconsin from at least the age of 6 through the age of 32 for those born in 1942, through 25 for those born in 1949, and through 21 for those born in 1955.[41]

The principal findings of this study are as follows:

1. **Sex and Race** White females generally had the fewest contacts and the least serious involvements with the police, and black males had the most contacts and most serious involvements with the police.[42]

2. **Residential Distribution of Delinquency** Police contacts occurred most frequently in the inner city and its interstitial areas. However, at least half of the white males in high socioeconomic status areas had at least one nontraffic police contact during their lives.[43]

3. **Education**   Both attitude toward school and leaving school before graduation were found to be related to juvenile and adult police contact seriousness score.[44]

4. **Pattern of Delinquent Behavior**   The researchers found the most prevalent pattern of delinquent behavior to be one of declining seriousness and discontinuation after the teenage period.[45]

5. **Frequency of Delinquent Behavior**   Over 90 percent of the males in each cohort had engaged in youthful misbehavior, as had 65 to 70 percent of the females.[46]

6. **Comparison of Delinquent Behavior Among Cohorts**   Increasing involvement and seriousness of delinquent behavior was found in each cohort. The proportion of police contacts of the 1942 and 1955 cohorts more than doubled between ages 6 and 17 and more than tripled between ages 18 and 20. Delinquency among females increased even more than it did among males regardless of the measure of frequency or seriousness employed.[47]

7. **Interventions by the Justice System**   The study found that an increase in frequency and seriousness of misbehavior typically occurs in the periods following the administration of sanctions by the justice system; that is, with few exceptions, interventions by the agencies of social control do not play even a moderate role in decreasing the seriousness of delinquent or criminal behavior.[48]

8. **Adult Criminality**   Those who had police contacts as juveniles were more likely to have police contacts as adults.[49]

The conclusions of the Racine cohort study largely concur with those of the two other studies, but the Racine study demonstrated to an even greater extent that the consequence of processing juvenile offenders in the justice system was the increased likelihood that they would continue criminal careers as adults. Similarly, those juveniles who had not become so heavily involved in the justice system were less likely to evidence criminal behavior as adults.[50]

Controversy Over Cohort Studies

In spite of the strengths and insights they provide, cohort studies do have a number of problems. One major difficulty is that their findings cannot be generalized confidently beyond those persons in the cohort. Philadelphia is different from Columbus, and both urban areas are certainly different from Racine. Such studies also are very expensive and time-consuming. Keeping track of a sample of youths even up to age 35 is next to impossible because names and addresses change, some people die, and others simply drop out of sight; the same facts hold true for researchers and their assistants. Finally, to provide a true picture of the crime rate nationally would require that a sample be taken each year in every area of the country.

Still, even with these drawbacks, cohort studies remain an accepted and useful addition to other official and nonofficial statistics in illuminating the problem of delinquency and crime.

POLICY IMPLICATIONS

The analysis of official statistics measuring delinquency raises a number of questions for policymakers. To deal effectively with delinquency in American society, social researchers must provide policymakers answers to these questions.

Questions Policymakers Must Consider

The most important questions official statistics raise for policymakers are: Has youth crime leveled off after years of increase? Do lower-class youths commit more serious crimes than middle-class youths? Why are urban areas so criminogenic? Do interventions by the justice system increase rather than reduce further delinquent behavior? Does youth crime progress from less to more serious forms?

Has Youth Crime Leveled Off After Years of Increase?

The *Uniform Crime Reports* document that after years of rising arrest rates for juveniles under eighteen, delinquency apparently leveled off during the mid-1970s and has even begun to decline since then. However, hard-liners contend that because the population of those eighteen and under declined 10 percent during the past decade, the total amount of youth crime may have lessened, but the proportion of juveniles involved in crime is the same as or greater than in the past.

Do Lower-Class Youths Commit More Serious Crimes than Middle-Class Youths?

The *Uniform Crime Reports* and the cohort studies both indicate that lower-class juveniles commit more frequent and more serious delinquent acts than middle-class youths. Indeed, a small group of lower-class chronic offenders commits one delinquent act after the other. These delinquents, according to the Philadelphia cohort studies, commit half or more of the serious crimes in urban areas. But the self-report studies of delinquents themselves, discussed in the next chapter, contend that social class is not a significant variable in understanding delinquent behavior because delinquency is distributed throughout the social classes.

Why Are Urban Areas So Criminogenic?

The *Uniform Crime Reports* document the fact that youth crime is much higher in the cities than in suburban and rural areas. Some experts claim that delinquency is higher in urban areas because urban youngsters receive less supervision from parents than those in nonurban areas, because more temptations to become delinquent are present in urban areas, because urban communities provide less support than in nonurban areas, and because poverty is higher in urban areas. But other researchers argue that the greater likelihood of getting officially processed in urban areas is what creates the large differential in youth crime in urban, suburban, and rural areas.

Do Interventions by the Justice System Increase Rather Than Reduce Further Delinquent Behavior?

Both the Columbus and Racine cohort studies found that intervention by the justice system makes juveniles worse rather than better. If intervention has more of a negative than a positive impact, this presents a real quandary as to what to do with youths who commit serious and violent delinquent acts. Hard-liners contend that it is the permissiveness of the justice system that encourages delinquent behavior. When the cost of youth crime is made high enough, they argue, then juveniles will be deterred from future delinquent activities.

Does Youth Crime Progress from Less to More Serious Forms?

Conflicting evidence also exists concerning career chains for delinquent behavior. G. R. Patterson and R. Loeber both found that noncompliance with parents leads to increased statistical risks for more serious forms of antisocial behavior; that is, each step in the career chain is more criminogenic than the preceding one.[51] Marvin Wolfgang and his colleagues found that the probability of becoming an adult offender is much higher for persons with a record of juvenile delinquency than for persons without one.[52] But Donna Martin Hamparian and colleagues found that juveniles do not typically progress from less serious to more serious crimes.[53] Hardliners also contend that "get tough" interventions by the justice system will encourage the cessation of delinquent behavior before juveniles become involved in more serious offenses.

Social Research and Policymakers

The relationship between social research and the policy-making process is described in Figure 2-2. Beginning with a social problem or a negative social condition, the policy-making process can be divided into eight steps. But such constraints as political activities, availability of resources, different ideological viewpoints, and inability of social researchers to provide sound policy recommendations affect the willingness of policymakers to accept the recommendations of social researchers.

Social policy, as proposed by the contextual perspective, takes place in a political context. Citizen participation in policy decisions, such as voting for referenda, participating in hearings, and communicating directly to decision makers through letters, petitions, and demonstrations, affect the acceptance or rejection of policy proposed by social research. The availability of resources also is a factor determining the fate of social research recommendations. Furthermore, the ideology of policymakers cannot be ignored in the decision-making process. Unfortunately, policymakers frequently are reluctant to implement recommendations of social researchers unless the findings support their own position. That is, policymakers often do not pay attention to the recommendations of social researchers unless they are consistent with their own points of view.[54] However, before policymakers will become more receptive to their findings in the prevention and control of youth crime, social researchers must improve in four major areas.

First, social research must better integrate theory and research. The findings of social research are frequently presented merely as descriptive statistics. Researchers

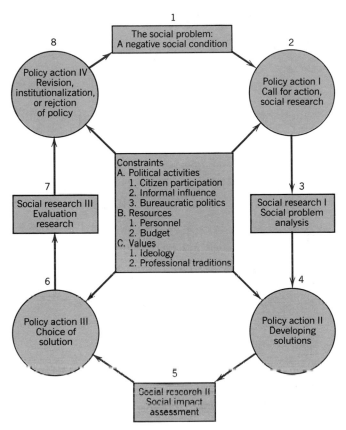

Figure 2-2 Social Research and the Decision-Making Process

Source: Kurt Finsterbusch and Annabelle Bender Motz, *Social Research for Policy Decisions* (Belmont, Calif.: Wadsworth Publishing Company, 1980), p. 33.

sometimes forget that theory and research are inextricably bound; each helps to guide and direct the other. Research finds methods to collect data, identifies variables to be studied, tests variables for their worth, analyzes related variables, and suggests new directions for theory. Theory points the way to further research, derives new variables, makes interconnections among variables, integrates new and old ideas, builds systems of thought, and leads the way to new social and theoretical conclusions. Research collects and theory analyzes; research discovers and theory explains; research disproves and theory reorders. This process never ends.[55] In short, the more that the integration of theory and research is reflected in social research findings, the more likely that these findings will be useful to policymakers.

Second, social researchers' policy recommendations must address the societal, the community, and the individual levels. The societal level of intervention mandates that adolescents be integrated more effectively into the larger society. The community level of intervention requires that more effective networks be established for youths among the family, the community, and the school. Researchers must also identify the most effective interventions for youthful offenders. For some youths, nonintervention would be the course most likely to ensure their desistance from crime.[56] For others, the second or third offense represents the optimal time for intervention. The authors of the Philadelphia cohort study found that intervention policy might most efficiently target on third offenders; beyond the third offense there was a leveling off of desistance probability.[57]

Third, social researchers must direct more of their energies into action research that will have policy implications. Such action research must be guided by the major questions facing policymakers about youth crime. Furthermore, this research must draw on multidimensional rather than unidimensional understanding of delinquent behavior. For example, the conclusions of official statistics sometimes differ in major ways from the findings of unofficial statistics. But an examination of delinquency that includes the findings of both official and unofficial statistics is more likely to capture the larger picture and to present more consistent findings.

Finally, to determine the solution to serious and violent youth crime, as well as more frequent property offenses, those concerned with the youth crime problem will need to be certain about the reliability of statistics. As any researcher knows, statistics often reflect only the responses of families, community members, and officials of the justice system to children who simply do not want to conform. They further may reflect changes in community policies and police effectiveness. Socially unacceptable behavior that was once hidden may have become known because of increased police activity. Police and community members also may pay more attention to known juvenile delinquents who have records. These youths may be brought to the attention of the juvenile court more frequently than other lawbreaking youths whom the community does not consider "bad."

SUMMARY

The measurement of juvenile delinquency is partly dependent on statistics derived from official rates of youth crime. The *Uniform Crime Reports* and cohort studies conducted in Philadelphia, Columbus, and Racine are important sources of official rates of delinquency. But juvenile court statistics, institutional files, and aftercare records also are helpful in establishing the official rates of delinquency. Cohort studies, particularly, demonstrate the use of theory and research in measuring the nature and extent of delinquency in American society. Cohort studies use sophisticated research designs to test the prevailing theory in the field and then to develop more theoretical assumptions about the nature and impact of delinquency.

Official statistics have contributed a number of important findings about youth crime in American society. First, juveniles under eighteen commit a disproportionate number of property and violent offenses. Second, lower-class youths are involved in more frequent and more serious offenses than middle-class youths; indeed, youth crime is primarily focused among lower-class youths. Third, blacks commit more frequent and more serious offenses than whites. Fourth, males commit more frequent and more serious offenses than females. Fifth, urban youths commit more frequent and more serious offenses than suburban or rural youths. Sixth, a small group of youthful offenders, primarily lower-class minority youths, commits half or more of the serious offenses in urban areas. Seventh, the interventions by the juvenile justice system frequently make youths worse rather than better. Eighth, some evidence exists that youthful offenders progress to increasingly serious forms of delinquent behavior. Finally, the evidence seems to indicate that delinquency did indeed begin to level off in the mid-1970s. But this trend does not diminish the seriousness of youth crime. The rates of juvenile delinquency are still high; violence remains a problem; and citizens are more fearful than ever before.

Discussion Questions

1. What do the *Uniform Crime Reports* generally show about official delinquency in American society?
2. What problems do the official statistics of the *Uniform Crime Reports* present researchers?
3. What do *Juvenile Court Statistics* show about juvenile delinquency in American society?
4. Identify the three cohort studies that were conducted in the United States. What are the general findings of each concerning the nature and extent of youth crime?
5. Identify several questions raised by an examination of official statistics. Why is each question important?
6. How must social researchers improve in order to make research recommendations more attractive to policymakers?

References

Hamparian, Donna Martin; Schuster, Richard; Dinitz, Simon; and Conrad, John P. *The Violent Few: A Study of Dangerous Juvenile Offenders.* Lexington, Mass.: Lexington Books, 1978.

Shannon, Lyle W. "Assessing the Relationship of Adult Criminal Careers to Juvenile Careers: A Summary." Washington, D.C.: U.S. Government Printing Office, 1982.

Shannon, Lyle W. "The Relationship of Juvenile Delinquency and Adult Crime to the Changing Ecological Structure of the City." Iowa City: Iowa Urban Community Research Center, n.d.

Smith, Daniel D.; Finnegan, Terrence; Snyder, Howard N.; Feinberg, Norma G.; and McFall, Patricia. *Delinquency 1978: United States Estimates of Cases Processed by Courts with Juvenile Jurisdiction.* Pittsburgh, Pa.: National Center for Juvenile Justice, 1981.

U.S. Department of Justice, Federal Bureau of Investigation. *Uniform Crime Reports, 1982.* Washington, D.C.: U.S. Government Printing Office, 1983.

Wolfgang, Marvin E.; Figlio, Robert M.; and Sellin, Thorsten. *Delinquency in a Birth Cohort.* Chicago: University of Chicago Press, 1972.

Zimring, Franklin E. "The Serious Juvenile Offender: Notes on an Unknown Quantity." In *The Serious Juvenile Offender: Proceedings of a National Symposium.* Washington, D.C.: U.S. Government Printing Office, 1978.

FOOTNOTES

1. Clemens Bartollas and Stuart J. Miller, *The Juvenile Offender: Control, Correction, and Treatment* (Boston: Holbrook Press, 1978), p. 384.

2. Michael D. Maltz, "Crime Statistics: A Historical Perspective," *Crime and Delinquency* 23 (January 1977), p. 33.

3. Stuart J. Miller provided an early draft of the material on the *Uniform Crime Reports*.

4. U.S. Department of Justice, Federal Bureau of Investigation, *Uniform Crime Reports, 1982* (Washington, D.C.: U.S. Government Printing Office, 1983), p. 43.

5. Ibid., pp. 176–177.

6. Ibid.

7. Ibid.

8. Ibid.

9. Ibid., pp. 178–180.

10. Ibid., p. 171.

11. Ibid., pp. 185, 188. The data for Hispanics are derived from a different survey from the ones used for the other racial groups.

12. Ibid., pp. 190, 202, 214.

13. Ibid., p. 170.

14. Ibid., p. 172.

15. Ibid.

16. The following criticisms of official statistics on youth crime come from Franklin E. Zimring, "The Serious Juvenile Offender: Notes on an Unknown Quantity," in *The Serious Juvenile Offender: Proceedings of a National Symposium* (Washington, D.C.: U.S. Government Printing Office, 1978), pp. 22–23.

17. This history of *Juvenile Court Statistics* is adapted from Linda Dahma, Howard N. Snyder, and Dennis Sullivan, *Juvenile Court Statistics, 1976–1978* (Pittsburgh, Pa.: National Center for Juvenile Justice, National Council of Juvenile and Family Court Judges, 1981), pp. 1–3.

18. I. R. Perlman, "Juvenile Court Statistics," *Juvenile Court Judges Journal* 16 (1965), p. 73.

19. Dahma et al., *Juvenile Court Statistics*, p. 22.

20. Ibid., p. 23.

21. Ibid., pp. 23–26.

22. Daniel D. Smith et al., *Delinquency 1978: United States Estimates of Cases Processed by Courts with Juvenile Jurisdiction* (Pittsburgh, Pa.: National Center for Juvenile Justice, National Council of Juvenile and Family Court Judges, 1981), pp. 36–39.

23. Ibid., pp. 45–49.

24. Marvin E. Wolfgang, Robert M. Figlio, and Thorsten Sellin, *Delinquency in a Birth Cohort* (Chicago: University of Chicago Press, 1972).

25. Ibid., p. 65.

26. Ibid., p. 88.

27. Ibid., p. 90.

28. Ibid.

29. Ibid., p. 64.

30. Ibid., p. 91.

31. Ibid., p. 131.

32. Donna Martin Hamparian et al., *The Violent Few: A Study of Dangerous Juvenile Offenders* (Lexington, Mass.: Lexington Books, 1980), p. 21.

33. Ibid., p. 39.

34. Ibid.

35. Ibid.

36. Ibid.

37. Ibid., foreword by John M. Rector, xvii.

38. Ibid.

39. Ibid., p. 40.

40. Ibid., foreword, xvii.

41. Lyle W. Shannon, *Assessing the Relationships of Adult Criminal Careers to Juvenile Careers: A Summary* (Washington, D.C.: U.S. Government Printing Office, 1982), p. v.

42. Ibid., p. 1.

43. Ibid., p. 2.

44. Ibid., p. 12.

45. Ibid., p. v.

46. Ibid., p. vi.

47. Ibid., p. 2.

48. Ibid., p. vi.

49. Ibid., p. 14.

50. Ibid., p. 15.

51. G. R. Patterson, *Coercive Family Processes* (Eugene, Ore.: Castalia Publishing Company, 1982); R. Loeber, *The Identification of Youths at Risk For Delinquency and Antisocial Lifestyles,* mimeographed (1981).

52. Wolfgang et al., *Delinquency in a Birth Cohort.*

53. Hamparian et al., *The Violent Few.*

54. See Kurt Finstenbusch and Annabelle Bender Motz, *Social Research for Policy Decisions* (Belmont, Calif.: Wadsworth Publishing Company, 1980), pp. 40–74.

55. Bartollas and Miller, *Juvenile Offender,* p. 384. See also Earl Babbie, *The Practice of Social Research,* 3d ed. (Belmont, Calif.: Wadsworth Publishing Company, 1983), pp. 27–48.

56. Edwin M. Schur, *Radical Non-Intervention: Rethinking the Delinquency Problem* (Englewood Cliffs, N.J.: Prentice-Hall, 1973).

57. Wolfgang et al., *Delinquency in a Birth Cohort.*

INTERVIEW WITH FRANKLIN E. ZIMRING

Two lessons I think have been learned from the period 1960 to 1980. One, never buy a simple explanation of a single theory unless the evidence is compelling. A lot of things are going on in the social world at once. A second lesson is that delinquency theory in particular has taken constructive steps backwards. Things have been happening which shouldn't have been happening according to the paradigmatic theories of the day.

In this interview, Franklin E. Zimring, director for Studies in Criminal Justice at the University of Chicago Law School, discusses such matters as serious youth crime, changes in trends in youth crime, the juvenile court, and the relationship between age and policy concerning youthful offenders.

Question: In an interview in *Corrections Magazine*, you say there is good news and bad news concerning youth crime. The bad news is that we don't have much of a handle on the serious youthful offender. Would you say more about that?

Zimring: If one looks over the period say since 1960s, serious violence attributed to young offenders in major metropolitan areas has been a very concentrated problem. Between 1960 and 1975, the nonwhite, 15- to 19-year-old male population of the American city increased by roughly 150 percent. But serious violent offenses, to the extent that we can measure them, went up much faster than that.

Violent offenses build through adolescence. Unlike property offenses, the probabilities of committing a violent offense at age 17 are twice as high as at age 15. Violent offenses are heavily

Professor Franklin E. Zimring, one of the most widely respected researchers on juvenile justice, has authored and coauthored many publications in juvenile and adult corrections. The Changing Legal World of Adolescents, Deterrence, with Gordon Hawkins, and Age, Crime, and Sanctions: The Transition from Juvenile to Adult Crime have been especially widely hailed for their contribution to the field. Interviewed in 1980, and used with permission.

concentrated in minority populations and concentrated in the period just around reaching 20.

When these rates increased as they did stunningly in the 60s, we have only the roughest ideas why. Nor do we know why these rates leveled off, as they have since early in the 70s. A convenient explanation is we are running out of kids. Well, when you look at the population trends with the group with the highest risk of robbery, rape, and homicide, that shouldn't explain decreases prior to the mid-1980s. Yet we have the decreases. So even though there is good news, the bad news is that we don't know why. And that's bad because you say, now what's going to happen ten years from now? With respect to runaways and vandals, I can answer the question. As a function of there being fewer kids, there's going to be less of that behavior to be absorbed. But if we cannot understand what happened last year, we're in a very poor position for projecting what's going to happen ten years from now.

Two lessons I think have been learned from the period 1960 to 1980. One, never buy a simple explanation of a single theory unless the evidence is compelling. A lot of things are going on in the social world at once. A second lesson is that delinquency theory in particular has taken constructive steps backwards. Things have been happening which shouldn't have been happening according to the paradigmatic theories of the day. If one would take Cloward and Ohlin seriously in a simpleminded way about the 60s, we would have expected reductions in crime. If we take the economic opportunity people seriously in that same simplistic way, we would have expected increases in youth violence in the 70s. Neither happened.

There's a gathering sense that we are back at square one in terms of understanding many of these fluctuations. Another thing you could expect to happen is that if this year, crime is either up or down among twelve-year-olds, then next year that trend will be reflected with thirteen-year-olds and the year after with fourteen-year-olds. The rough aggregate data that I have been looking at in the 70s, and here I've been reading arrest trends which are very difficult to obtain, suggest that when there are reductions in fourteen-year-old rates this year, there are reductions in fifteen-year-old rates not next year but this year too. This needs careful and serious study at the community level because my statements are based on very rough data.

One thing I find astonishing is that when you ask a rather simple question like this and think that somebody must have done a study—well, they haven't. This study could explain the character of that particular population of kids, or cohort. If it is true that different age cohorts fluctuate up and down together instead of with lags, and if this were established by a systematic study, then those who are looking for cultural or systemic nonindividual variations as theoretical explanations would be in relatively good shape.

Question: Do you see any changes in trends in youth crime?

Zimring: Let's start with soft stuff. You don't know where to stop by definition, because it includes everything from spitting on the sidewalk all the way to house breaking. We know that there are going to be decreases attributable to the decreases in middle adolescent population. There are just X-million fewer kids.

To the extent that we can measure, the rate for serious, violent youth crime is holding constant for changes in the population. This probably has taken place for nearly a decade in this country. When I looked at it in the late 70s, I was surprised that the flattening had occurred as early as it had. One of the reasons we didn't know it had happened was that the volume of offenses continued upward because the number of kids did. That is,

the upward trend in the serious, documented violence flattened out at the turn of the decade.

Interestingly enough, the focus on the serious youthful offender as a particular problem in sentencing policy happens now. But there was quite a time lag. The hysteria on the problem didn't start until the middle of the 70s. Law and order 1968 style was for older offenders. The crackdown legislation in criminal justice dates from 1975 to 1976. Now it's probably not the first time in human recorded history that we started slamming barn doors after the horses left. Certainly, rates are still high, but there is this interesting nonfit between the recent trend and public mood.

Question: I sense from what you have written that you are not as ready to dismiss the juvenile court as many are. Why do you continue to support the concept of the juvenile court?

Zimring: The number of theorists operating in law reform is both high and dangerous. Not only do I see value in a juvenile court administration, but I find myself even more unfashionably in support of discretion, which is the "boogie" man in American criminal justice administration. Look at the numbers of youth. I just don't know how you can run a system with the numbers which are involved without a fair amount of discretion.

Moreover, I am bothered by "just deserts" as a formula for penalty setting. Where do you get the recipe for "just deserts"? How do you begin intellectually the process of deciding what a fourteen-year-old, knife-wielding street robber on his second offense deserves? Now I don't think you can duck the question by saying: Oh, we're not asking that; we're asking whether he is a delinquent or not and, if he is a delinquent, what does he need?

I know that there are a lot of critics who say the court is too hard on soft crime and and too soft on hard crime. They say that what we need is proportionality. Proportionality relative to what and why? There isn't a balance of the agenda in any logical sense. It just sounds good, which is, of course, the prime prerequisite now for legislative action. If you get hard on hard kids, that doesn't mean we're going to get soft on soft kids. If you get soft on soft kids, that doesn't necessarily mean you're going to get hard on hard kids. If we're going to make a two by two contingency table, then there are really four different patterns. Where is reform going? It's probably going in all four directions depending on which jurisdiction you are in.

I had occasion to keynote the annual conference of the Cook County Juvenile Justice System sometime ago. A third of the probation officers in the State of Illinois are in the juvenile court of Cook County. I was trying to explain to them what those folks out there in law reform land thought they were doing. But my personal guess is that, barring technological breakthroughs, they will be dealing with the same business including the same problems ten years from now that they are dealing with now. We will be having the same discussions, and it will be essentially the same business I think it always was. The only differences are that there will hopefully be declines in detention and institutionalization.

Question: Age seems to be so important in terms of what happens to children. Would you comment on that?

Zimring: The whole issue with age today relates to punishing the serious juvenile offender. Everybody is suddenly discovering the serious juvenile offender even though he was statistically there all along. When you read something like the Juvenile Justice and Delinquency Prevention Act of 1974, you think that liberal reformers believe that all the kids who are in facilities are boy scouts and virgins. Then, when they find a serious juvenile offender, they say "goodie," now we're going to have a balanced justice system. We'll let all the status offenders go, and we'll really concentrate on the kids who ought to have the book thrown at them. I find that a trade-off that has troublesome social, political, and racial overtones.

We don't know what distributive justice or just deserts mean when it comes to kids. Similarly, I am amused by juvenile justice personnel who say,

"I know where we can find super principles for handling young offenders in juvenile court. They suggest that we turn to the jurisprudence of adult criminality, which is an intellectual and moral disaster.

The way that criminal courts are presently structured, I don't think we can have a criminal justice system extending through middle adolescence in criminal court. I find it intellectually horrifying from the standpoint of getting a balanced and fair system toward young offenders. Some of the kids who are arrested for homicide and are tried in the criminal court get life in prison. Essentially, what we do is to export the most troublesome cases from system 1 to system 2.

It makes no sense to give one sixteen-year-old kid six months in a training school while another is sent to prison when they both committed the same crime. That is injustice. That's one reason why I don't want the juvenile court abolished: this isn't the time to throw everything up for grabs.

To recapitulate, age does make a difference. So, we may have to operate on a sliding scale in choosing sentences. Presumption against loss of liberty is an effective way. But it is difficult for the justice system to admit a partial responsibility or graduation of categories. Two things must happen to achieve appropriate sliding scales for juveniles. First, we can't really have a sliding scale without discretion. Second, the lawyers need the kindness of the legal doctrine of *parens patriae*.

Right now the punishment model seems to have many adherents. Adult justice has a lot of control over juvenile justice. But I have the feeling that this will change. Frequently, we get sick of our legislation. We do this because we assume that there are large gains to be made. We need to change but not in the name of crime prevention. I will bet on the failure of any program that is labeled delinquency or crime prevention. What we need is a just sentencing system for kids.

CHAPTER 3

UNOFFICIAL ACCOUNTS OF DELINQUENT BEHAVIOR

CHAPTER OUTLINE

I started using drugs when I was eight years old. It makes you feel like you can beat anything that comes along. I thought, "Wow, this is great!" When I was nine, someone asked me if I wanted to take some acid. I figured, sure, why not? This was really great because I could sit around and watch the walls melt. My English teacher deteriorated in her chair one time at school. As the years went by, I started to peddle a lot of speed and acid. Pretty soon, I was drug dependent. I needed speed in the morning, and I had to take speed to school to make it through the day. It got to the point that I couldn't handle speed anymore. I was too juiced up. Now I regret doing so many drugs because I can't remember simple things that I should remember, like talking with someone over the phone the night before. I became spacey; in fact, people have called me spacey for two years now.

Sixteen-year-old girl[1]

The official measurement of delinquent behavior gives only part of the picture of the problem. For several reasons, official statistics must be supplemented by unofficial accounts of delinquent behavior. First, official statistics do not measure what has been called "hidden delinquency,"—unobserved or unreported delinquency. The official statistics make it appear that the number of delinquents represents only a small fraction of youths in the United States, but self-report studies show that official statistics represent only the tip of the iceberg. Second, official statistics do not tell much about the personalities, attitudes, values, and lifestyles of delinquents today. For example, the quotation from a sixteen-year-old girl that began the chapter provides insight into why teenagers take drugs and the consequences of the abuse of drugs. Insights of this nature cannot be found in official statistics. Third, official statistics are misleading about the nature of delinquency, for both the cohort studies and official files of police departments and court systems make it appear that delinquency is primarily a lower-class phenomenon. Yet self-report studies indicate that delinquent behavior is distributed throughout all social classes. Fourth, official statistics do to tell why most delinquents remain "hidden," while certain youths are swept up in the machinery of police arrest and court referral. That is, unofficial accounts of delinquent behavior and the processing of offenders through official agencies must be examined in order to understand why juveniles are handled the way they are by the juvenile justice system.

Self-report studies, victimization surveys, biographical and autobiographical sources, open-ended interviews, and participant observation are the main sources of unofficial accounts of delinquent behavior. Each of these unofficial sources are examined and evaluated in this chapter. The unofficial accounts of delinquent behavior, like official statistics, have both strengths and shortcomings, but still they furnish a much more complete picture of the extent and nature of delinquency in American society than official statistics alone offer.

SELF-REPORT STUDIES

The logic of self-report studies is based on the fundamental assumption of survey research, "If you want to know something, ask."[2] Researchers have gone to juveniles themselves and asked them to admit to any illegal acts they have committed. The self-report method has been widely used for at least two reasons: first, self-report studies enable researchers to examine the nature and extent of unreported, or hidden, delinquency; and, second, self-report studies are thought to eliminate the lower-class bias in official study produced by differential law enforcement. According to Gwynn Nettler, the various methods of self-report studies include:

1. Asking people to complete anonymous questionnaires.
2. Asking people to complete anonymous questionnaires and validating findings by later interviews or police records.
3. Asking people to confess to criminal acts on signed questionnaires validated by police records.
4. Having people complete anonymous questionnaires, identified by number, and validated by follow-up interviews and the threat of polygraph tests.
5. Interviewing respondents.
6. Interviewing respondents and validating their responses by official records.[3]

Austin Porterfield conducted the first study of hidden delinquency in the 1940s when he asked several hundred college students whether or not they had ever engaged in delinquency.[4] Although all of the students reported that they had engaged in delinquency, few of them had been brought to police or court attention. But it was James F. Short, Jr., and F. Ivan Nye in the late 1950s who pioneered the first self-report study of a delinquent population.[5] After their first study of a training school population, they conducted a self-report study with members of three Washington communities, with students in three midwestern towns, and with delinquents in training schools in Washington State.[6] In their findings from these two studies, as well as in other published papers, Short and Nye concluded that delinquency was widespread throughout the adolescent population, that the seriousness and frequency of delinquent behavior were major factors determining the actions taken against juvenile lawbreakers, and that no relationship could be found between delinquency and social class.[7]

Self-report studies, which became widely used in the 1960s, also commonly agree that practically every youth commits some form of delinquency. More specifically, the studies suggest that adolescents should not be divided into offenders and nonoffenders since the majority commit at least minor offenses and that the youth who never violates the law is a rarity.[8] But the more serious offenders who commit violent or predatory crimes or who are committed to crime as a way of life are more likely than minor offenders to be arrested and referred to the juvenile court.[9] Figure 3-1 is an example of a recent self-report study.

Figure 3-1 Example of a Self-Report Questionnaire

Please indicate how often you have done each of the following *in the last 12 months*.

| If you have not engaged in a particular activity, put ___0___ and go on to the next. | If you have, put the number of times. |

REMEMBER: YOUR ANSWERS ARE PRIVATE SO YOU CAN ANSWER HONESTLY.

During the last 12 months, how many times did you:

1. Break into a place to do something illegal? _____
2. Take something from a store on purpose without paying for it ("shoplifting")? _____
3. Steal something worth more than $100 (*not counting shoplifting*)? _____
4. Steal something worth less than $100 (*not counting shoplifting*)? _____
5. Beat up or hurt someone on purpose? _____
6. Get into any fist fights or brawls (not counting the times you beat up or hurt someone on purpose)? _____
7. Ruin, break, or damage someone else's property on purpose? _____
8. Take a car without the owner's permission? _____
9. Take money or something by threatening someone with a weapon (gun, knife, etc.)? _____
10. Take money or something by threatening someone without a weapon? _____

Source: Excerpted from a high school survey used in research by M. L. Erickson, J. P. Gibbs, and G. F. Jensen as part of a National Institute of Mental Health study entitled "Community Tolerance and Measures of Delinquency."

Two self-report studies challenge the official statistics on their assumption that youth crime is increasing. Martin Gold and David Reimer found in a national study of self-reported youth crime in 1972 that the seriousness and frequency of delinquent behavior of thirteen- to sixteen-year-old boys was lower than the delinquent behavior of that age group had been in 1967. They further concluded that youth crime began to level off in the 1960s and was less of a problem than it had been a few years earlier.[10]

In 1976, the Institute for Juvenile Research in Illinois completed a three-year study of self-reported youth crime throughout the state. Alan Berger, discussing this research, noted that the statistics on the extent of youth crime among boys closely paralleled the findings of similar studies conducted across the country over a decade previously, which would indicate that youth crime among boys had not greatly decreased. But this study did find a marked increase over the previous decade in youth crime among girls.[11]

Self-report studies also offer valuable information on the relationship between social class and delinquency; on age, sex, and race differences in delinquency; on group versus individual delinquency; and on the extent of drug and alcohol abuse among delinquents.

Social Class and Delinquency

One of the most startling findings of the self-report studies in that delinquent behavior is unrelated or only very slightly related to a juvenile's social class.[12] Jay R. Williams and Martin Gold, in their national study of thirteen- to sixteen-year-old boys and girls, forcefully make this point: "In no case is the relationship between social status and delinquent behavior strong."[13] Travis Hirschi, in his survey of 4000 junior and senior high school students in Richmond, California found that there was little association between self-reported delinquencies and income, education, and occupation, except that the sons of professionals and executives committed fewer delinquent acts.[14] Richard E. Johnson, in redefining social class as *underclass* and *earning class*, concluded: "The data provide no firm evidence that social class, no matter how it is measured, is a salient factor in generating delinquent involvement."[15] Tittle and Villemez, analyzing twenty-six self-report studies, concluded that thirteen found no significant class variation, that nine reported some relationship between social class and crime/delinquency, and that four found a relationship only for some specific subcategory of individuals in the sample.[16]

However, Elliottt and Ageton's national study in 1977 found that a different pattern emerged when juveniles were asked how many times they had violated the law during the previous year. These researchers further found that the average number of delinquent acts reported by lower-class youngsters exceeded that reported by working-class or middle-class youths. The average number of crimes against persons reported by lower-class juveniles was 1.5 times greater than that reported by the working-class group and nearly four times greater than that reported by the middle-class group. The average number of reported crimes against property was also slightly higher for lower-class than for working-class or middle-class youths.[17]

Thus, although early studies disputed the assumed relationship between social class and delinquency, Elliott and Ageton's more recent national study indicated that class membership remains important in influencing the frequency and seriousness of delinquent behavior. More research is clearly still needed on the relationship between social class and delinquency, but social class may be only one of the variables affecting delinquent behavior.

Racial Background and Delinquent Behavior

The few self-report studies that have examined specifically the factor of race and delinquency have usually been limited to comparing black and white youths. Hirschi, the first researcher who compared official statistics with self-report accounts of delinquency, found that the differences between blacks and whites were much less in self-report accounts.[18] In two national studies by Williams and Gold and by

Gold and Reimer, whites and blacks reported involvements in 17 delinquent behaviors with similar frequencies.[19] But when these two researchers tallied the seriousness of delinquency for both years, they found that the seriousness of self-reported delinquency was slightly greater for black males than for white males.[20] Furthermore, when Elliott and Ageton analyzed the ratio of black to white for the total number of offenses, they found that it was nearly two to one. They concluded that this difference was due primarily to the greater involvement of blacks in serious property offenses.[21] Nevertheless, they contended that the differences between the races are primarily related to the larger number of multiple, or chronic, black offenders.[22]

On balance, the self-report studies clearly question the finding of official sources about the relationship of race to delinquency. Yet more recent self-report national studies have shown that blacks commit more serious delinquent acts and are more likely to be chronic offenders than whites.

Gender and Delinquent Behavior

The self-report studies usually show a smaller differential between females and males engaging in delinquent acts than the official studies do. Self-report studies also indicate that girls are not specialists and that the pattern of female delinquency is much the same as that of boys.[23] Williams and Gold concluded that "American girls behave delinquently less frequently and less seriously than American boys."[24] Ageton and Elliott also found that a larger proportion of boys report having broken the law more frequently than do girls (see Table 3-1).[25] Hindelang et al. added that as the value of goods stolen increases, so does the sex ratio showing male involvement; these researchers also found that self-report items for violence show large differentials between males and females and approximate the levels indicated in official studies.[26]

Yet self-report studies disagree on whether or not delinquency among girls is rising. The Institute for Juvenile Research, as previously indicated, found an increase.[27] Gold and Reimer also reported that female delinquency rose 22 percent between 1967 and 1972, but this increase was primarily related to the use of alcohol and drugs.[28] Nevertheless, other researchers claim that the rise of female delinquency is a myth.[29]

In sum, the self-report studies indicate that girls commit more delinquent acts than official accounts of delinquency report they do, but self-report accounts do show that a larger proportion of boys break the law, break it more frequently, and commit more serious crimes than girls do.

Age and Delinquent Behavior

Official studies of delinquency have found that the incidence of arrest accelerates at age thirteen and peaks at about age seventeen, but this pattern is not so clearly evident in self-report studies. Williams and Gold did find that older juveniles are more frequently and seriously delinquent than younger ones.[30] Yet Ageton and Elliott's national survey found that the incidence of some offenses, such as assault

TABLE 3-1 Mean Number of Self-Reported Delinquent Acts by Gender

Type of Offense	Girls	Boys	Approximate Ratio
Aggravated assault	.05	.28	1:5
Sexual assault	.07	.01	1:7
Strong-armed others	.04	.18	1:4
Burglary	.03	.22	1:7
Larceny:			
$5 to $50	.24	.29	1:1
Over $50	.01	.11	1:11
Motor vehicle theft			
Stole vehicle	.00	.03	—
Joyriding	.07	.15	1:2
Damaged property	.20	1.48	1:7
Prostitution	.02	.14	1:7
Sexual intercourse	2.04	3.43	2:3
Use of drugs			
Alcohol	5.50	9.24	1:1.7
Marijuana	6.64	7.73	1:1
Hallucinogens	.12	.15	1:1
Amphetamines	.35	.63	1:1.8
Barbiturates	.39	.43	1:1
Truancy	2.61	5.43	1:2
Running away	.08	.10	1:1

Source: Suzanne S. Ageton and Delbert S. Elliott, *The Incidence of Delinquent Behavior in a National Probability Sample of Adolescents* (Boulder, Colo.: Behavioral Research Institute, 1978), Table 2.

and robbery, increases with age, while that of others peaks between ages thirteen and fifteen.[31]

In short, conflicting findings about age in self-report studies may indicate that youthful offenders are younger than official statistics indicate, but more analysis of this factor is obviously needed.

Group Delinquency

Inquiry into group delinquency also has resulted in conflicting findings. Some self-report studies have found that most delinquent behavior occurs in groups. For example, Erickson and Jensen reported that regardless of their sex or whether they are in urban settings or small towns, juveniles tend to follow herd instincts when they violate the law. They did find that drug offenses have the highest group frequency and that status offenses, other than drinking or smoking, have the lowest.[32] Moreover, the Institute for Juvenile Research found that peer group influence is the most important factor determining whether a specific youth will become delinquent.[33] Yet Erickson reported in another study that between 37 and 42 percent of delinquent acts are committed alone.[34] Hindelang further indicated that group delinquency may be overestimated.[35]

Group delinquency will be examined elsewhere, but it is evident that self-report studies show that most delinquent behavior is group-related. Not surprisingly, some kinds of delinquent behavior are more group-oriented than others.

Abuse of Drugs and Alcohol and Delinquent Behavior

More and more researchers are coming to the conclusion that drug and alcohol abuse is one of the most important correlates of delinquent behavior. The National Institute on Drug Abuse of the U.S. Department of Health and Human Services conducted a nationwide self-report survey of almost 7000 subjects. Some of the findings are as follows:

- Between 1972 and 1979 experience with marijuana and cocaine has doubled among twelve- to seventeen-year-olds.

- In the 12- to 17-year-old group, 31 percent report [in 1979] they had tried marijuana, up from 14 percent in 1972. Current use of marijuana in this age group is 17 percent—the same as in 1977. In 1972, however, they reported only 7 percent in this group were current users.

- Cocaine is second only to marijuana in its increasing popularity. Since 1972, the rate of increase for cocaine use across all age groups has been noticeably larger than the rate of increase for marijuana use.

- The number of people who have tried hallucinogens has increased significantly for all ages. Among youth, 7 percent have tried hallucinogens. . . .

- Self-reported use of PCP or angel dust in the twelve- to seventeen-year-old group decreased since 1977 from 6 percent to 4 percent.[36]

The Institute for Social Research at the University of Michigan, which gathered information from a probability sample of several thousand high school seniors from 1975 through 1979, also found that the use of marijuana and cocaine dramatically increased between 1975 and 1979. The use of alcohol, stimulants, and inhalants increased but at a lower rate; and the use of sedatives, heroin, and tranquilizers declined slightly in this population.[37]

In sum, the self-report studies have found wide use of drugs among adolescents, but the popularity of some drugs varies at different times. Alcohol and marijuana remain popular, but some evidence points to increased use of cocaine among adolescents.

Evaluation of Self-Report Studies

The desire to uncover the true rate of delinquency, as well as greater recognition that official statistics on juvenile delinquency have serious limitations, has led to a growing reliance on the use of self-report studies. The self-report studies discussed above have revealed the following conclusions:

1. There is considerable undetected delinquency, and police apprehension is low, probably less than 10 percent.

2. Both middle- and lower-class juveniles are clearly involved in considerable illegal behavior.

3. Most undetected lawbreaking would be handled informally or the cases dismissed if they were brought to the attention of the juvenile court, but not all hidden delinquency in this country involves minor offenses; a significant number of serious crimes are committed each year by juveniles who elude apprehension by the police.[38]

4. Lower-class youths appear to commit more frequent delinquent acts and are more likely to be chronic offenders than are middle-class youths.

5. Blacks are more likely than whites to commit serious criminal acts and to become chronic offenders.

6. Girls commit more delinquent acts than official statistics indicate, but boys still appear to commit more delinquent acts and to commit more serious crimes than girls do.

7. The incidence of some offenses increases with the age of juveniles, while the incidence of others peaks between thirteen and fifteen years of age.

8. Most delinquent behavior is group-related, but some kinds of delinquent acts are less likely to be performed by groups than others.

9. Alcohol and marijuana are the most widely used drugs among adolescents, but cocaine use has increased in recent years.

However, self-report studies have been criticized for three reasons: their research designs have often been deficient, resulting in the drawing of false inferences; the varied nature of social settings in which the studies have been undertaken makes it difficult to test hypotheses; and they have questionable reliability and validity.[39] Albert Reiss' survey of studies employing self-report procedures led him to this pessimistic conclusion:

> *Overall, they have contributed little either to policy programs or to a basic understanding of the phenomenon. On the contrary, these self-surveys have provided data which give an erroneous picture of the incidence of delinquency in sex, class, and race categories. Moreover, these data reinforce ideological positions which exaggerate the causal role of the enforcement process in delinquency and underestimate its role in reducing the rate.*[40]

The most serious questions concerning self-report studies rest with their reliability and validity. In terms of validity, how can researchers be certain that juveniles are telling the truth when they fill out self-report questionnaires? Juveniles may not remember their offenses and may therefore underreport delinquency, or they may remember offenses that occurred before the period in question and thus may over-report crime. Furthermore, juveniles may conceal their activities or exaggerate them, depending on the image they want to project to the researcher.[41]Short and Nye, however, noted that items (can be built into questionnaires) designed to "catch the random respondent, the over-conformist, and the individual who is out to impress the researcher with his devilishness, the truth notwithstanding."[42] Yet Michael Hindelang et al. argued that self-report studies are likely to underestimate the illegal behavior of the seriously delinquent youth, for the juvenile who has committed frequent offenses is less likely to answer the questions truthfully than is the youth who is less delinquent.[43]

Reliability is related to the consistency of a questionnaire or an interview; that is, whether repeated administration of a questionnaire or an interview will elicit the same answers from the same juveniles when they are questioned two or more times. Hindelang, examining the reliability of self-report studies, concluded that "reliability measures are impressive, and the majority of studies produce validity coefficients in the moderate to strong range."[44]

In sum, although self-report studies have some shortcomings, criminologists generally consider them to be helpful tools in measuring and understanding delinquent behavior. Throughout this book, the results of self-report studies frequently guide the discussion.

VICTIMIZATION SURVEYS

In 1972, the Census Bureau began victimization studies to determine as accurately as possible the extent of crime in the United States. These surveys involve three different procedures. The largest component of the program is the National Crime Panel, which oversees interviewing a national sample of approximately 125,000 people in 60,000 households every six months for up to three and one-half years. Data from these individuals are used to estimate the national frequency of the crimes found in the FBI's Crime Index (except for murder).[45]

The owners, managers, and clerks of 42,000 business establishments selected as a sample also have been interviewed to provide an estimate of robbery and burglary rates for businesses. However, this portion of the survey was ended in 1976.

Finally, the Census Bureau conducts victimization surveys in 26 major cities. Housing units in the central area of each city are randomly selected, and each member in the household twelve years or older is questioned about his or her experiences as a victim of crime. In addition, one-half of the respondents are asked about their perception of crimes, the extent of their fears, and other attitudes regarding criminal activities.

The National Crime Survey reports that forty-one million Americans become victims of crime each year. Table 3-2 shows that most victimizations involve theft.

The specific offenses, in order of diminishing frequency, are personal larceny without contact, household larceny, household burglary, and assault.

Victimization surveys reveal that nearly four times more Americans are victims each year than the *Uniform Crime Reports* show. The data also show declines in victimization rates from 1973 to 1976. Rape was down 11.6 percent; robbery, 4.2 percent; and motor vehicle theft, 13.7 percent. Meanwhile, larceny was up 10 percent; burglary of commercial establishments, 6.7 percent; and assault, 1.6 percent. But Table 3.3 shows that out of ten different types of victimizations examined, the rates for eight were lower in 1976 than in 1975. Thus, victimization rates appear to have stabilized or declined during the mid-1970s.

The 1976 National Crime Survey revealed that 450,000 young people under age 21 victimized others: 23,000 by rape, 1.5 million by assault, and 27,000 by robbery. Victimization surveys show the vast majority of offenders in personal crimes to be male, and blacks have higher rates of victimization for serious crimes against the person than whites. Significantly, young people are more likely to become victims than any other age group. Young males have the greatest risk of becoming victims, followed by young females, older males, and older females.[46]

Michael E. Hindelang compared the data on victimization and the official data on arrests to determine the involvement of blacks in serious personal crimes (forcible rape, robbery, aggravated assault, and simple assault). He found that both sources of data showed the percentages for robbery to be virtually the same, but the official data indicated a somewhat greater proportion of black offenders involved in the remaining three crimes than did the victimization data.[47]

Evaluation of Victimization Surveys

Victimization surveys have not been as widely used in analyzing delinquency as have the *Uniform Crime Reports, Juvenile Court Statistics,* cohort studies, and self-report studies, but they do add to what is known about crime in America. Some of the principal findings of victimization surveys are as follows:

1. Much more crime is committed than is recorded, but the discrepancy between the number of people who say they have been victimized and the number of crimes known to the police varies with the type of offense.

2. The rank order of serious offenses reported by victims, with the exception of vehicle theft, is identical to that of the *Uniform Crime Reports.*

3. The probability of being victimized varies with the kind of crime and where one lives. The centers of American cities are the more probable sites of violent crimes.

4. The most frequent crimes experienced, according to victims, are thefts of property worth less than $50 and malicious mischief.

5. Juveniles are more likely to commit crimes, especially property offenses, than any other age group, but they are themselves more likely to be victimized than any other age group.

TABLE 3-2 Estimated Number of Personal and Household Victimizations, by Type of Victimization and Reporting to Police, United States, 1980[a]

Type of Victimization	Total		Reported to Police		Not Reported to Police		Don't Know Whether Reported to Police	
	Number	Percent	Number	Percent	Number	Percent	Number	Percent
Personal victimizations:								
Rape and attempted rape	160,224	100	68,302	43	89,025	56	2,897	2
Robbery	1,138,026	100	644,944	57	471,682	41	21,400	2
Robbery and attempted robbery with injury	397,771	100	276,756	70	112,877	28	8,138	2
Serious assault	198,614	100	149,000	75	45,526	23	4,087	2
Minor assault	199,157	100	127,755	64	67,350	34	4,051	2
Robbery without injury	442,485	100	263,307	60	168,831	38	10,347	2
Attempted robbery without injury	297,770	100	104,881	35	189,974	64	2,915	1
Assault	4,371,043	100	1,984,009	45	2,244,146	51	142,888	3
Aggravated assault	1,596,780	100	869,701	54	673,037	42	54,042	3
With injury	549,279	100	330,051	60	197,709	36	21,520	4
Attempted assault with weapon	1,047,501	100	539,651	52	475,329	45	32,522	3
Simple assault	2,774,263	100	1,114,307	40	1,571,109	57	88,847	3
With injury	779,570	100	377,662	48	381,649	49	20,259	3
Attempted assault without weapon	1,994,692	100	736,645	37	1,189,459	60	68,588	3

Personal larceny with contact	517,748	100	189,827	37	321,444	62	6,476	1
Purse snatching	134,404	100	79,107	59	53,928	40	1,368	1
Attempted purse snatching	48,865	100	B	B	B	B	B	B
Pocket picking	334,479	100	102,221	31	227,150	68	5,108	2
Personal larceny without contact	13,504,961	100	3,645,660	27	9,551,430	71	307,870	2
Household victimizations:							
Burglary	6,522,461	100	3,371,648	52	3,080,957	47	69,856	1
Forcible entry	2,302,239	100	1,682,979	73	600,453	26	18,807	1
Unlawful entry without force	2,843,163	100	1,209,129	43	1,603,654	56	30,380	1
Attempted forcible entry	1,377,060	100	479,541	35	876,850	64	20,669	2
Larceny	9,787,440	100	2,731,459	28	6,974,994	71	80,987	1
Under $50	4,690,792	100	658,048	14	4,011,593	86	21,151	0
$50 or more	3,930,784	100	1,756,738	45	2,138,601	54	35,445	1
Amount not ascertained	464,440	100	127,823	28	322,941	70	13,676	3
Attempted	701,424	100	188,850	27	501,860	72	10,715	2
Vehicle theft	1,290,072	100	393,876	69	370,328	29	25,868	2
Completed	875,733	100	756,287	86	106,838	12	12,608	1
Attempted	414,339	100	137,589	33	263,489	64	13,260	3

NOTE. These estimates are based on data derived from surveys that were undertaken in connection with the Bureau of Justice Statistics' National Crime Survey program. In these surveys, conducted by the U.S. Bureau of the Census for the Bureau of Justice Statistics, representative national samples of households and businesses were drawn. In the personal and household portion of the survey, victimization data were collected for all household members who were at least 12 years of age; therefore, victimizations of those under 12 years of age were not counted in the survey. Some crimes, such as homicide, were not counted.

aSubcategories may not sum to total because of rounding.

Source: Timothy J. Flanagan and Maureen McLeod, eds., Sourcebook of Criminal Justice Statistics—1982 (Washington, D.C.: U.S. Department of Justice, Bureau of Justice Statistics, 1982), p. 292.

TABLE 3-3 Estimated Number of Personal and Household Victimizations and Percent Not Reported to Police, 1973–1980, and Estimated Number of Business Victimizations and Percent Not Reported to Police, 1973–1976, by Type of Victimization, United States[a]

Type of Victimization	1973 Estimated Number of Victimizations	1973 Percent Not Reported to Police	1974 Estimated Number of Victimizations	1974 Percent Not Reported to Police	1975 Estimated Number of Victimizations	1975 Percent Not Reported to Police	1976 Estimated Number of Victimizations	1976 Percent Not Reported to Police
Personal victimizations:								
Rape and attempted rape	152,740	51	161,160	47	151,055	44	145,193	47
Robbery	1,086,700	46	1,173,980	46	1,121,374	46	1,110,639	46
Robbery and attempted robbery with injury	376,000	35	383,470	37	353,493	34	360,700	36
Serious assault	208,800	28	215,000	32	207,114	33	175,660	32
Minor assault	167,200	42	168,460	44	146,380	37	185,041	39
Robbery without injury	396,740	43	466,400	41	467,595	41	453,867	40
Attempted robbery without injury	313,960	64	324,120	63	300,285	69	296,071	67
Assault	4,001,820	55	4,063,680	54	4,176,056	54	4,343,261	52
Aggravated assault	1,616,700	47	1,695,440	46	1,590,080	44	1,694,941	41
With injury	496,960	39	545,990	39	543,175	34	588,672	37
Attempted assault with weapon	1,197,740	51	1,149,450	49	1,046,905	49	1,106,269	43
Simple assault	2,385,120	61	2,368,240	61	2,585,976	60	2,648,320	59
With injury	603,500	51	582,190	54	687,352	51	691,534	53
Attempted assault without weapon	1,781,610	64	1,786,050	63	1,898,624	63	1,956,786	60
Personal larceny with contact	495,590	66	511,480	65	513,952	65	497,056	63
Purse snatching	103,280	51	90,230	36	119,096	36	91,595	32
Attempted purse snatching	71,260	B	62,830	B	60,912	B	55,535	B
Pocket picking	321,050	68	358,410	71	333,943	72	349,926	70
Personal larceny without contact	14,635,655	77	15,098,118	75	15,455,660	73	16,021,110	73
Household victimizations								
Burglary	6,432,350	52	6,655,070	51	6,688,964	51	6,663,422	51
Forcible entry	2,070,950	29	2,190,330	28	2,251,869	27	2,277,063	29
Unlawful entry without force	2,956,830	62	3,031,080	62	2,959,734	62	2,826,599	60
Attempted forcible entry	1,404,560	68	1,433,660	64	1,477,361	67	1,559,760	66
Larceny	7,506,490	74	8,866,060	74	9,156,711	72	9,300,854	72
Under $50	4,824,900	84	5,641,160	84	5,615,914	84	5,601,954	84
$50 or more	1,884,280	47	2,351,490	51	2,707,605	46	2,745,097	47
Amount not ascertained	263,750	77	296,000	77	277,922	81	299,350	78
Attempted	533,560	80	577,410	75	555,270	76	654,454	73
Vehicle theft	1,335,410	31	1,341,890	32	1,418,725	28	1,234,644	30
Completed	884,710	13	855,680	11	910,253	8	759,816	11
Attempted	450,710	67	486,210	68	508,472	63	474,828	61
Business victimizations:								
Robbery	264,113	14	266,624	10	261,725	9	279,516	12
Burglary	1,384,998	21	1,555,304	19	1,518,339	18	1,576,242	25

NOTE. See NOTE, Table 3-2. The business portion of the survey only counted burglaries and robberies; crimes such as shoplifting and employee theft were not counted. The business portion of the survey was not conducted after 1976. For survey methodology and definitions of terms, see Appendix 11.

[a]Subcategories may not sum to total because of rounding.

Source: Timothy J. Flanagan and Maureen McLeod, eds., *Sourcebook of Criminal Justice Statistics—1982* (Washington, D.C.: U.S. Department of Justice, Bureau of Justice Statistics, 1982), p. 293.

Type of Victimization	1977 Estimated Number of Victimizations	1977 Percent Not Reported to Police	1978 Estimated Number of Victimizations	1978 Percent Not Reported to Police	1979 Estimated Number of Victimizations	1979 Percent Not Reported to Police	1980 Estimated Number of Victimizations	1980 Percent Not Reported to Police
Personal victimizations:								
Rape and attempted rape	154,237	42	171,145	49	191,739	48	160,224	56
Robbery	1,082,936	44	1,038,074	49	1,115,870	42	1,138,026	41
Robbery and attempted robbery with injury	386,405	33	330,843	33	381,245	35	397,771	28
Serious assault	214,670	24	179,905	29	203,300	32	198,614	23
Minor assault	171,735	45	150,939	37	177,946	38	199,157	34
Robbery without injury	412,505	35	408,833	44	470,846	34	442,485	38
Attempted robbery without injury	248,026	70	298,390	72	263,778	67	297,770	64
Assault	4,663,827	55	4,730,097	56	4,845,822	54	4,371,043	51
Aggravated assault	1,737,774	47	1,707,883	46	1,768,683	44	1,596,780	42
With injury	541,411	37	576,731	36	599,136	36	549,279	36
Attempted assault with weapon	1,196,363	51	1,131,152	51	1,169,547	49	1,047,501	45
Simple assault	2,926,053	60	3,022,214	62	3,077,139	59	2,774,263	57
With injury	755,780	51	755,125	51	795,483	46	779,570	49
Attempted assault without weapon	2,170,273	63	2,267,089	66	2,281,656	64	1,994,692	60
Personal larceny with contact	461,014	62	519,967	64	510,790	64	517,748	62
Purse snatching	87,937	36	111,475	44	119,548	40	134,404	40
Attempted purse snatching	46,687	B	65,568	B	46,707	B	48,865	B
Pocket picking	326,390	66	372,924	66	344,535	70	334,479	68
Personal larceny without contact	16,469,154	74	16,492,446	74	15,861,378	74	13,504,961	71
Household victimizations								
Burglary	6,766,010	50	6,698,581	52	6,684,018	51	6,522,461	47
Forcible entry	2,300,292	27	2,199,925	29	2,154,639	27	2,302,239	26
Unlawful entry without force	2,962,705	60	2,911,696	61	3,109,280	60	2,843,163	56
Attempted forcible entry	1,503,013	67	1,586,959	67	1,420,099	67	1,377,060	64
Larceny	9,415,533	74	9,344,239	75	10,631,289	74	9,787,440	71
Under $50	5,443,697	85	5,177,916	87	5,726,441	86	4,690,792	86
$50 or more	2,851,831	52	3,125,604	54	3,666,796	55	3,930,784	54
Amount not ascertained	410,196	82	395,943	77	562,414	77	464,440	70
Attempted	709,808	73	644,776	77	675,639	75	701,424	72
Vehicle theft	1,296,759	31	1,364,549	33	1,392,837	30	1,290,072	29
Completed	797,671	11	860,016	11	920,158	13	875,733	12
Attempted	499,089	63	504,533	71	472,679	63	414,339	64
Business victimizations:								
Robbery	X	X	X	X	X	X	X	X
Burglary	X	X	X	X	X	X	X	X

6. Blacks are overrepresented in serious personal crimes, but official arrest data indicate that a somewhat greater proportion of black offenders are involved in forcible rape, aggravated assault, and simple assault than the victimization data indicate.[48]

But victimization surveys do have several limitations: information on status offenses is not included, nor on victimless crimes, such as drug abuse, prostitution, and drunkenness; information on white-collar crime is difficult to gain from victim surveys; information on age is always questionable because victims must guess at offenders' ages; and victims may give inaccurate information. Victims may forget the victimizations they have experienced, may deliberately exaggerate or fail to admit victimization, or may state that a specific crime took place within the research year when it actually occurred before or after the period.[49]

Nevertheless, victimization surveys are an important supplement to official statistics and self-report studies, adding to what is known about crime in the United States.

QUALITATIVE METHODS

Self-report studies, victimization surveys, and official accounts of delinquent behavior are helpful in understanding the nature and extent of delinquency in American society. Each of these measurements has its own shortcomings, but little knowledge of delinquency would be available without these statistical measurements. Yet a major limitation with these traditional, or quantitative methods, is that they present relatively static pictures of social life.[50] Some researchers have found that qualitative methods, such as nonstructured interviews, content analysis of written statements, and participant observation, are useful in shaping a more complete picture of delinquency in American society because they focus on processes and social dynamics. Thus, qualitative methods are widely accepted because they can be used to examine the effects of interaction between the delinquent and others in the environment and because they are able to probe in greater depth the perceptions of the delinquent. As Albert K. Cohen and James Short, Jr., have stated:

> It is our position that the meaning and function of any form of delinquent behavior can only be inferred from rich and detailed descriptive data about the behavior itself, about its position in a larger context of interaction, and about how it is perceived and reacted to by the actor itself and by other participants in their interactive context.[51]

Nonstructured Interviews

Nonstructured interviews generally permit respondents to answer the questions they are asked in whatever way they choose. This interviewing process, which is frequently combined with participant observation, requires that the interviewer establish rapport with the interviewee, especially if sensitive topics are to be discussed. BOX 3-1 presents an excerpt from an interview with a sixteen-year-old prostitute.

BOX 3-1 Interview with a Teenage Prostitute

Question: Why does a teenage girl become a prostitute?

Answer: If you're working for yourself, the money is pretty good. If you are working regular, you make $1000 or more a week if you work every night. You can either work in a massage parlor or on the streets. . . .

Question: How old are teenage prostitutes and how do they learn what to do?

Answer: They are usually fifteen and up. Older women have a lot of influence and power over younger ones. Most street prostitutes have pimps, and have a lot of control over their girls.

Question: What are the advantages of having a pimp?

Answer: Some girls feel that pimps help you as much as you can help them. They feel that their pimps care about them. When you are new to a territory, it is nice to have a man who knows the territory and will take care of you. They furnish a roof over your head, provide all the necessities that you need, and make certain you eat well. The pimp is there to bail you out when you go to jail. He makes certain that none of the other pimps hassle or rob you.

    As far as I'm concerned, there ain't no advantages in having a pimp. They would like you to believe they will take care of you, but after they get you, you might see clothes but that's about it. Some will give you a little spending money, but the majority take it all. If you need something, they will either take you out to buy it or give you money to buy it. A lot of prostitutes are into drugs, and as long as they are getting their drugs, they're happy. Coke, heroin, and weed are the drugs most widely used. . . .

Question: Do you enjoy your work?

Answer: Very few prostitutes enjoy it. They just turn their feelings off. They take it as their job and just look at the money. They go in and try to get the job done as fast as they can. It is necessary to turn your feelings back on when you are with your man [pimp].

Source: Interviewed by Linda Bartollas in June 1981 in a midwestern city.

    This excerpt provides information on the socialization process of a teenage prostitute, including her relationship with a pimp, and on her attitude toward her work. If a number of teenage prostitutes were to be interviewed from a given area, it would be possible to make some generalizations about teenage prostitutes from that area. Of course, the more the interviewer is able to examine the differences of age, race, background factors, and experiences among the prostitutes, the more valuable the interview data would be.

    Indeed, some of the most insightful studies about the nature of delinquent behavior are based on nonstructured interviews. Carl Werthman and Irving Pilivian used interviews to examine the attitudes of gang members toward the police. One youth gang member commented:

Every time something happens in this neighborhood, them motherf———g cops come looking for me! I may not be doing nothing, but if somebody gets beat or something gets stole, they'll always be coming right to my place to find out what's going on.[52]

Walter B. Miller used interviews to understand the lower-class values of gang members in the 1950s, and in the 1970s, he used interviews with professionals in the criminal justice system to understand the nature and activities of youth gangs in several major cities in the United States.[53] Howard Polsky, Rose Giallombardo, and Clemens Bartollas, Stuart J. Miller, and Simon Dinitz used interviews of both staff members and residents to understand the dynamics of life for youths in training schools.[54]

However, nonstructured interviews do have limitations. First, the process of drawing generalizations from interviews poses a problem because it typically is unclear what population would reasonably be represented by these data—usually because the data do not come from random samples. Second, the validity of the interview data is always questionable. The interviewees may not be telling the truth, or they may merely be telling the interviewer what he or she wants to hear. Interviewees also may have a distorted perspective on the topics under discussion. Third, unless youths are asked the same questions on a number of occasions, the reliability of interview material is also open to question. A youth who is asked the same questions again a month or six months later is likely not to give the same answers.

Yet the importance of nonstructured interviews in understanding delinquency cannot be minimized, because they permit an in-depth examination of the attitudes of delinquents and the measurement of the effects of interaction, both of which are difficult to obtain using quantitative methods.

Biographical Sources

Written accounts and statements by delinquents and former delinquents have been used to expand what is known about the nature of delinquency. Clifford Shaw was one of the first to bring the public the actual voice of the offender when he presented delinquents' versions of why they became delinquents, what their experiences were, and how they viewed the world. The result was a highly compelling insider's view of delinquency, which Shaw used to illuminate the processes through which individuals became delinquents and the conditions that accompanied recidivism. He collected hundreds of case studies of youthful offenders, and he encouraged others to do so as well. Shaw published two books, *The Natural History of a Delinquent Career* and *The Jack-Roller,* drawn from delinquents' autobiographical statements.[55]

Claude Brown's *Manchild in the Promised Land* describes his own adolescent years in Harlem. Brown's well-written novel describes the popularity of drugs and the pressures on youths to become involved with drugs, especially heroin; life on the streets and what it means to be "street wise"; the way that black youths are handled by the juvenile justice system; the positive and negative effects that staff in the justice system can have upon youth; and what it takes for a youth deeply involved in a delinquent career to make the decision to go straight.[56]

In addition, scores of adult offenders and inmates of adult prisons have published their stories, and some of these accounts discuss their experiences and law-violating activities as juveniles. For example, *A Criminal Addict's Story* describes the author's experiences as a member of a New York City youth gang in the 1950s.[57]

Unfortunately, biographical statements on delinquents are few in number. Shaw and Brown were especially helpful in presenting an insider's view of delinquency that was relevant for their time; biographical sources now are needed to provide an insider's view of delinquency for the 1980s.

Participant Observation

Another method used in understanding delinquency, participant observation, requires a researcher to go into a setting where delinquents are and to become involved in that culture to some degree. He or she might inform youths of an intent to do a study of a street gang, as R. Lincoln Keiser did, for which he or she needs the cooperation of the gang members.[58] The researcher then attends activities of the gang, talks with them, and may even socialize with them. The researcher immerses himself or herself in the delinquent subculture, in an attempt to understand the dynamics of that subculture, the leadership patterns, the norms and values, and the attitudes of gang members.

Some participant observers become more engaged in the culture than do others, but all are attempting to understand the culture from the perspective of its members, to perceive the interactions among members of the culture, and to identify aspects of their lives that could not otherwise be captured. For example, Bartollas, Miller, and Dinitz found participant observation helpful in perceiving the dynamics of training-school life. They used this method to identify the pecking order in each cottage, the various social roles that made up this pecking order, the factors involved in youths becoming involved in a social role, and the relationship between social roles and victimization within the cottages.[59]

In sum, participant observation is a valuable technique for understanding certain settings. But this method takes much more time than would be required to give a paper and pencil test to delinquents. The danger always exists that the researcher will be coopted by the values and outlooks of the individuals he or she is studying. Finally, unless participant observation is used along with other methods, the researcher may find it difficult to translate the impressionistic data collected into useful research findings.

COMPARISON OF OFFICIAL AND UNOFFICIAL MEASUREMENTS OF DELINQUENCY

Official and unofficial measurements of delinquency agree on many findings. First, there is widespread delinquency among juveniles. Second, youth crime appears to be leveling off and perhaps even to be declining. Third, males commit more offenses than females, with greater disparities occurring for more serious offenses. Fourth, drug and alcohol offense rates have increased significantly in recent years. Fifth, rates are higher for blacks than for whites for offenses involving violence or serious property crimes. Sixth, offense rates are higher for urban than for suburban or rural youths.

However, the various means of measurements also indicate disparate findings, although these are usually a matter of degree rather than total contradiction. First, although the *Uniform Crime Reports,* self-reports, and victimization surveys all show stable or declining offense rates for recent years, self-report data suggest this trend began earlier than do victimization or *Uniform Crime Reports* data. Second, cohort studies, as well as the *Uniform Crime Reports,* show a stronger relationship between social class and delinquency than is indicated by self-report studies. Official statistics report that the problem of juvenile crime is primarily one of lower-class youths, but self-report studies indicate that delinquent behavior is spread throughout the class structure, as the juvenile who does not break the law is a rarity. Third, unofficial statistics show a smaller ratio between male and female offenses than is found in official statistics. Fourth, the differences among racial categories in rates for serious offenses are greater in official statistics and victimization surveys than they are in self-report studies, with self-report showing little or no difference by race in the frequencies for all offenses combined.[60]

In short, both official and unofficial measurements of delinquency report that youth crime is a serious problem in the United States, but important differences are found between official and unofficial measurements of the distribution of youth crime.

POLICY IMPLICATIONS

As official statistics draw our attention to the prevalence and seriousness of lower-class youth crime, self-report studies emphasize that delinquent behavior is distributed throughout the social classes. Middle-class delinquency, as forthcoming chapters will indicate, has not received the same attention from researchers as have lower-class violent crime and gang delinquency.

Because delinquency is widespread throughout society, delinquent acts apparently are more than the economically oriented response of deprived youths to their environment. While delinquent acts by middle-class youths may not catch the public's attention as does lower-class violent crime, they do make up a significant part of the delinquency problem and pose several significant questions for policymakers: Why do so many middle-class youths become delinquent? Why is drug and alcohol abuse so prevalent among middle- and upper-class youths? Why do social institutions, including the family, provide such ineffective insulation against delinquency for many middle-class youths? What effective means of deterrence can be used to persuade middle-class youths to refrain from delinquent behavior?

Several methods have been proposed for dealing with middle-class delinquents. The most widely used approach today is to ignore the problem of middle-class offenses; if middle-class youths do come to the attention of the justice system, their cases are dismissed or they are diverted to nonjudicial agencies. This soft-line, or least-restrictive, approach is helpful in that it means these youths are not caught in the net of the justice system. An alternative approach, of course, would be to get tougher on middle-class youths who violate the law. Some jurisdictions, in fact, are doing this by assigning community service obligations to middle-class and lower-class juvenile lawbreakers. But a better way to handle middle-class delinquents would be to examine the factors in the sociocultural context that influence so many youths to become delinquent. An understanding of middle-class delinquency, then, can come only from a demonstration of how it is bound up with other aspects of social life. As emphasized throughout this book, the social institutions of society, such as the family, the school, and the community, must generate more supportive networks for all youths. The political context also appears to be important to middle-class youths, in that it is likely that the marginal role of adolescents in American society lowers their commitment to responsible and law-abiding roles until they are ready to assume adult responsibilities.

SUMMARY

This chapter has examined several nonofficial measurements of delinquent behavior. Self-report studies have revealed that most youths are involved in delinquent behavior and that upwards of 90 percent of delinquent acts are undetected or ignored. Middle-class youths, as indicated by self-report studies, are involved in a considerable amount of illegal behavior, but lower-class youths, especially minority youths, appear more likely to commit more frequent delinquent acts and to become chronic offenders. Self-report studies also indicate that girls commit more delinquency than is recorded in official accounts of delinquency, but boys still appear to commit more serious crimes than girls do. Victimization surveys reveal nearly four times as many victims each year than do the statistics in the *Uniform Crime Reports*. Juveniles may commit extensive crimes in American society, but they are more likely to become victims than are older people. Interviews, participant observation, and, to a lesser degree, biographical accounts also are helpful in understanding delinquency in American society. Together, these unofficial measurements of delinquency add to what is known officially about delinquency. Much of the material in the rest of this book draws on the official and unofficial data discussed in this chapter and the last one.

Discussion Questions

1. What can self-report studies tell us that official accounts of delinquency can not?
2. What are the main conclusions to be drawn from the self-report studies?
3. Why are youths the greatest victims in American society? Where are they victimized and how?
4. Why are interviews needed to supplement facts about delinquency?
5. Define participant observation. How is this method helpful in understanding the nature of delinquency?

References

Ageton, Suzanne S., and Elliott, Delbert S. *The Incidence of Delinquent Behavior in a National Probability Sample of Adolescents.* Boulder, Colo.: Behavioral Research Institute, 1978.

Erickson, Maynard L., and Jensen, Gary F. "Delinquency Is Still Group Behavior: Toward Revitalizing the Group Premise in the Sociology of Deviance." *Journal of Criminal Law and Criminology* 68 (1977): 388–395.

Gold, Martin, and Reimer, David J. *Changing Patterns of Delinquent Behavior among Americans 13 to 16 Years Old, 1967–1972.* Ann Arbor, Mich.: Institute for Social Research, University of Michigan, 1974.

Hindelang, Michael J. "Age, Sex, and the Versatility of Delinquency Involvements." *Social Problems* 18 (Spring 1971): 527–535.

———; Hirschi, Travis; and Weis, Joseph G. *Measuring Delinquency.* Beverly Hills, Calif.: Sage Publications, 1981.

Hirschi, Travis. *Causes of Delinquency.* Berkeley, Calif.: University of California Press, 1969.

National Criminal Justice Information and Statistics Service. *Criminal Victimization in the United States, 1980.* Washington, D.C.: U.S. Government Printing Office, 1981.

Shaw, Clifford. *The Jack-Roller: A Delinquent Boy's Own Story.* Chicago: University of Chicago Press, 1930.

Short, James F., Jr., and F. Ivan Nye. "Extent of Unrecorded Juvenile Delinquency: Tentative Conclusions." *Journal of Criminal Law, Criminology and Police Science* 49 (November-December 1958): 207–213.

Tittle, Charles R., and Villamez, Wayne J. "The Myth of Social Class and Criminality: An Empirical Assessment of the Empirical Evidence." *American Sociological Review* 43 (1978): 643–656.

FOOTNOTES

1. Interviewed in June 1981.

2. Michael J. Hindelang, Travis Hirschi, and Joseph G. Weis, *Measuring Delinquency* (Beverly Hills, Calif.: Sage Publications, 1981), p. 22.

3. Gwynn Nettler, *Explaining Crime* (New York: McGraw-Hill Book Company, 1974), pp. 73–74.

4. Austin L. Porterfield, "Delinquency and Its Outcome in Court and College," *American Journal of Sociology* 49 (November 1943), pp. 199–208.

5. James F. Short, Jr., "A Report on the Incidence of Criminal Behavior, Arrests, and Convictions in Selected Groups," *Research Studies of the State College of Washington* 22 (June 1954), pp. 110–118.

6. James F. Short, Jr., and F. Ivan Nye, "Extent of Unrecorded Juvenile Delinquency: Tentative Conclusions," *Journal of Criminal Law, Criminology and Police Science* 49 (November-December 1958), pp. 296–302.

7. James F. Short, Jr., and F. Ivan Nye, "Reported Behavior as a Criterion of Deviant Behavior," *Social Problems* 5 (Winter 1957–1958), pp. 207–213.

8. LaMar T. Empey, *Studies in Delinquency: Alternatives to Incarceration* (Washington, D.C.: U.S. Government Printing Office, 1967), pp. 27–32; Maynard L. Erickson and LaMar T.

Empey, "Court Records, Undetected Delinquency and Decision-Making," *Journal of Criminal Law, Criminology and Police Science* 54 (December 1963), pp. 456–469.

9. William T. Pink and Mervin F. White, "Delinquency Prevention: The State of the Art," in *The Juvenile Justice Process,* edited by Malcolm W. Klein (Beverly Hills, Calif.: Sage Publications, 1976), p. 9.

10. Martin Gold and David J. Reimer, *Changing Patterns of Delinquent Behavior among Americans 13 to 16 Years Old, 1967–1972* (Ann Arbor, Mich.: Institute for Social Research, University of Michigan, 1974).

11. Alan Berger made these comments at a seminar on delinquency prevention at Sangamon State University, February 1977. See Illinois Institute for Juvenile Research, *Juvenile Delinquency in Illinois* (Chicago: Illinois Department of Mental Health, 1972).

12. F. I. Nye, *Family Relationships and Delinquent Behavior* (New York: John Wiley & Sons, 1958); Short and Nye, "Extent of Unrecorded Delinquency," pp. 296–302; Robert A. Dentler and Lawrence J. Monroe, "Social Correlates of Early Adolescent Theft," *American Sociological Review* 26 (October 1961), pp. 733–743; Ronald L. Akers, "Socio-Economic Status and Delinquent Behavior: A Retest," *Journal of Research in Crime and Delinquency* (January 1964), pp. 38–46; W. L. Slocum and C. L. Stone, "Family Culture Patterns and Delinquent-Type Behavior," *Journal of Marriage and Family Living* 25 (1963), pp. 202–208; LaMar T. Empey and Maynard L. Erickson, "Hidden Delinquency and Social Status," *Social Forces* 44 (June 1966), pp. 546–554; Travis Hirschi, *Causes of Delinquency* (Berkeley, Calif.: University of California Press, 1969); J. R. Williams and Martin Gold, "From Delinquent Behavior to Official Delinquency," *Social Problems* 20 (1972), pp. 202–229; D. H. Kelly and W. T. Pink, "School Commitment, Youth Rebellion, and Delinquency," *Criminology* 10 (1973), pp. 473–485.

13. Williams and Gold, "From Delinquent Behavior to Official Delinquency," p. 217.

14. Hirschi, *Causes of Delinquency,* p. 75.

15. Richard E. Johnson, "Social Class and Delinquent Behavior: A New Test," *Criminology* 18 (May 1980), p. 91.

16. Charles R. Tittle and Wayne J. Villemez, "Social Class and Criminality," *Social Forces* 56 (December 1977), p. 475.

17. Suzanne S. Ageton and Delbert S. Elliott, *The Incidence of Delinquent Behavior in a National Probability Sample of Adolescents* (Boulder, Colo.: Behavioral Research Institute, 1978).

18. Hirschi, *Causes of Delinquency,* Table 14.

19. Williams and Gold, "From Delinquent Behavior to Official Delinquency"; Gold and Reimer, *Changing Patterns of Delinquent Behavior.*

20. Ibid.

21. Delbert S. Elliott and Suzanne S. Ageton, "Reconciling Race and Class Differences in Self-Reported and Official Estimates of Delinquency," *American Sociological Review* 45 (February 1980), p. 103.

22. Ibid., p. 104.

23. Michael J. Hindelang, "Age, Sex, and the Versatility of Delinquency Involvements," *Social Problems* 18 (April 1971), pp. 527–535; Anne Campbell, "The Role of the Peer Group in Female Delinquency," (D.Phil. thesis Oxford University); Gary Jensen and Raymond Eve, "Sex Differences in Delinquency," *Criminology* 13 (February 1976), pp. 427–448; and Nancy B. Wise, "Juvenile Delinquency among Middle Class Girls," in *Middle Class Juvenile Delinquency,* edited by Edmund W. Vaz (New York: Harper & Row, 1967).

24. Williams and Gold, "From Delinquent Behavior to Official Delinquency," p. 213.

25. Ageton and Elliott, *Incidence of Delinquent Behavior.*

26. Hindelang et al., *Measuring Delinquency*, p. 140.

27. Illinois Institute for Juvenile Research, *Juvenile Delinquency.*

28. Gold and Reimer, *Changing Patterns of Delinquent Behavior.*

29. Darrell J. Steffensmeier and Renee H. Steffensmeier, "Trends in Female Delinquency: An Examination of Arrest, Juvenile Court, Self-Report, and Field Data," *Criminology* 18 (May 1980), pp. 62–85.

30. Williams and Gold, "From Delinquent Behavior to Official Delinquency," p. 215.

31. Ageton and Elliott, *The Incidence of Delinquent Behavior.*

32. Maynard L. Erickson and Gary F. Jensen, "Delinquency Is Still Group Behavior: Toward Revitalizing the Group Premise in the Sociology of Deviance," *Journal of Criminal Law and Criminology* 68 (1977), pp. 388–395.

33. Illinois Institute for Juvenile Research, *Juvenile Delinquency.*

34. Maynard Erickson, "The Group Context of Delinquent Behavior," *Social Problems* 19 (1971), pp. 115–129.

35. M. J. Hindelang, "With a Little Help from Their Friends: Group Participation in Reported Delinquent Behavior," *British Journal of Criminology* 16 (1976), pp. 109–125.

36. U.S. Department of Health and Human Services, *A Drug Retrospective: 1961–1980* (Washington, D.C.: U.S. Government Printing Office, 1980).

37. Lloyd Johnston, Jerald G. Bachman, and Patrick M. O'Malley, *Drugs and the Nation's High Schools* (Rockville, Md.: U.S. Department of Health, Education and Welfare, 1979), pp. 23–30.

38. LaMar T. Empey, "Contemporary Programs for Adjudicated Juvenile Offenders: Problems of Theory, Practice and Research," in *Juvenile Justice Management,* edited by Gary B. Adams et al. (Springfield, Ill.: Charles C Thomas Company, 1973), pp. 425–493.

39. Nettle, *Explaining Crime,* p. 86.

40. A. Pepitone, "Commentary," in *Social Policy and Sociology,* edited by N. J. Demerath II et al. (New York: Academic Press, 1975), pp. 277–278.

41. Gary F. Jensen and Dean G. Rojek, *Delinquency: A Sociological View* (Lexington, Mass.: D.C. Heath & Company, 1980), p. 94.

42. Short and Nye, "Reported Behavior as a Criterion," p. 211.

43. Hindelang et al., *Measuring Delinquency*, p. 295.

44. Ibid., p. 126.

45. National Criminal Justice Information and Statistics Service, *Criminal Victimization in the United States, 1980* (Washington, D.C.: U.S. Government Printing Office, 1981).

46. Ibid.

47. Michael J. Hindelang, "Race and Involvement in Common Law Personal Crimes," *American Sociological Review* 43 (February 1978), p. 103.

48. Most of these findings are derived from Nettler, *Explaining Crime,* pp. 68–70.

49. L. D. Savitz, M. Lalli, and L. Rosen, *City Life and Delinquency–Victimization: Fear of Crime and Gang Membership* (Washington, D.C.: U.S. Government Printing Office, 1977), p. 11.

50. Michael Phillipson, *Understanding Crime and Delinquency: A Sociological Introduction* (Chicago, Ill.: Aldine Publishing Company, 1974), p. 60.

51. Albert K. Cohen and J. F. Short, Jr., "Research in Delinquent Sub-cultures," *Journal of Social Issues* 14 (1958), pp. 20–37.

52. Carl Werthman and Irving Piliavin, "Gang Members and the Police," in *The Police,* edited by David J. Bordua (New York: John Wiley & Sons, 1967), p. 70.

53. Walter B. Miller, "Lower Class Culture as a Generating Milieu of Gang Delinquency," *Journal of Social Issues* 14 (Summer 1958), pp. 5–19; *Violence by Youth Gangs and Youth Groups as a Crime Problem in Major American Cities* (Washington, D.C.: U.S. Government Printing Office, 1975).

54. Howard Polsky, *Cottage Six: The Social System of Delinquent Boys in Residential Treatment* (New York: Russell Sage Foundation, 1962); Rose Giallombardo, *The Social World of Imprisoned Girls* (New York: John Wiley & Sons, 1974); and Clemens Bartollas, Stuart J. Miller, and Simon Dinitz, *Juvenile Victimization: The Institutional Paradox* (New York: Halsted Press, 1976).

55. Clifford Shaw, *The Natural History of a Delinquent Career* (Chicago: University of Chicago Press, 1955); and Clifford Shaw, *The Jack-Roller: A Delinquent Boy's Own Story* (Chicago: University of Chicago Press, 1930).

56. Claude Brown, *Manchild in the Promised Land* (New York: Macmillan Publishing Company, 1965).

57. *Manny: A Criminal Addict's Story* (Boston: Houghton-Mifflin, 1978), pp. 16–17.

58. Lincoln Keiser, *The Vice Lords* (New York: Holt, Reinhart & Winston, 1969).

59. Bartollas, Miller, and Dinitz, *Juvenile Victimization.*

60. Jensen and Rojek, *Delinquency,* p. 117.

INTERVIEW WITH TRAVIS HIRSCHI

I really think that American sociologists for some reason can't come to grips with the fact that there is no longer the class society we had in the 1930s. I don't deny differences in income, occupational prestige, and education, but these differences don't seem to have the consequences for our kids they once had.

In this interview, Professor Travis Hirschi, who is the founder of social control theory and one of the most widely respected authorities on American delinquency, discusses and evaluates self-report studies, social class and its relationship to delinquency, the middle-class and female delinquent, and theoretical directions that are needed at the present time. His comments about social control theory are contained in Chapter 7 where his theory is discussed.

Question: What is your evaluation of self-report studies? What are their limitations and their strengths?

Hirschi: Self-reports seem perfectly legitimate for tests of such theories as Cohen's and Merton's. Are they legitimate and completely acceptable for other theories? Well, they are not really fully appropriate for tests of control theory. Control theory suggests that people lie, cheat, and steal. Therefore, it suggests they may also lie when they are filling out a self-report questionnaire.

The most general methodological question is whether there is a chronic offender who is qualitatively different from other offenders and who is being missed by self-report studies. As of now, I don't believe criminologists are even close to identifying an offender distinct in terms of antecedent variables from other offenders. In other words, I'm not convinced there is this kind of evidence against the self-report method. The great search for some sort of career offender that we can identify

Travis Hirschi is presently professor of sociology at the University of Arizona. He is the author of Causes of Delinquency, *which develops the theoretical underpinnings of social control theory. Professor Hirschi, who was president of the American Society of Criminology during 1984–1985, is the coauthor of* Measuring Delinquency *and such noteworthy articles as the relationship between delinquency and intelligence and between delinquency and the family.*

and lock up has so far found very little. My guess is that it will continue to find little or nothing.

Question: David Matza is one author who seems to say that there comes a cutting point where there seems to be a capturing of the will, and this person becomes different than he was before. Do you agree with this viewpoint?

Hirschi: I read a book about a detective who recovered a great deal of money, and he had to make a decision about whether to return the money or to say that he didn't get it back. He decided to return the money and remain a law-abiding person. But he knew in his heart that in that moment he could have decided the other way and gone on to a life of crime. So, I don't deny that a rational decision exists for some people. There is a moment they decide, but I don't think the ordinary criminal or delinquent deciding to buy drugs or break into a store is really making a career decision.

Question: I find your comments about social class very interesting in *Causes of Delinquency*. Social class is presently being minimized as an important factor in understanding delinquency. Do you agree?

Hirschi: The more I think about it, the more convinced I am that crime has little to do with class. Need is the ultimate base of our belief that class matters. But there's no necessity of crime following from being poor. I was just looking at some pre-test data on shoplifting. The typical shoplifter in the few cases I examined would try on a few things, put a couple in his or her pocket, and buy one in order to get out of the store. Now, is that need? These shoplifters were able to afford one of the items. Let's say you are buying a bra. That you have enough money for one bra suggests to me that you don't *have* to steal the other two. Other research indicates the same finding. For example, the more money you have, the more likely you are to use drugs. Or, the kids with the largest allowances are most likely to become delinquents.

Once you get beyond the idea that people are driven to crime out of economic necessity, then class takes on a different meaning. Now the question becomes: Are there class differences in socialization? Well, traditional stratification theory has always taught that if there is a class where people are excessively concerned about the behavior of their children, it is the lower-middle class. If that is where the crime rate should be lowest, there is little theoretical reason to be upset when one doesn't find a relation between "class" and crime.

It has always bothered me (and it has always bothered colleagues of mine, like Charles Tittle, who do the same kind of research) that we don't see a relation in the data, or if we see one that's significant, it sure doesn't look very big. If there is a correlation between class and crime, it is certainly not very large. At the same time, class is a multidimensional concept, whose meaning we have difficulty understanding. As long as the relation is small and the meaning of the concept is vague, it seems to me we're barking up the wrong tree to pursue it.

Question: Where would middle-class delinquency fit into this?

Hirschi: The middle-class kid is able to buy things. According to class theory, this kid shouldn't commit crime. The middle-class kid who hasn't been trained to defer gratification should commit criminal acts as quickly as any other kid for the same reason; that it, because he or she has little to lose. I really don't think American sociologists can come to grips with the fact that this is no longer the class society that we pictured it to be in the 1930s. I don't deny differences in income, occupational prestige, and education, but the differences don't seem to have the consequences for our kids that they once had.

Question: I've noted the recent tendency to apply mainline sociological theory to female delin-

quency. How do you see control theory being applied to female delinquency?

Hirschi: It has never crossed my mind that there would be any difference in terms of the logic of the explanation between female and male delinquency. When I see the research on female delinquency coming out today, I think I made a mistake by not including females in my analysis. I had the data, but I was afraid of interactions or differences across sexes that would unduly complicate my argument. I thought it was about as complex as I would handle at the moment anyhow. Thus, it was really a decision to simplify my argument rather than one based on the belief that there was a group that required a different theory. I never believed that we should start with the assumption that a particular group requires a particular theory. The focus on middle-class delinquency, to go back to that for a moment, in my opinion has been a serious mistake. I think that such studies should be banned from the literature. Unless you can show that there's something distinct in the middle class, then let's forget it.

Question: What directions do we need to go in terms of research and theoretical development.

Hirschi: There is nothing I dislike more than the idea that you can sit down and spell out in advance what a good theory should look like or what good research should be. When we do that, we begin to say that everybody should de longitudinal studies or some such silliness. What we have, then, are lots of longitudinal studies, but no obvious improvement over what we would have had everyone been doing the research they like to do. We also have people telling us that a theory has to have properties X, Y, and Z. I say, "You write one that has these properties because I can't. I can't think that way. I have to worry about what the phenomenon means, and I have to collect data that bear on my conceptions of what it means." Still, we are doing better. Our data are better; our ideas are better. They're far from clear and plain, but I think we are making progress. And the reason we're making progress is because we are doing what we should be doing—collecting data, thinking about what they mean, and theorizing about them.

UNIT TWO

THE CAUSES OF DELINQUENCY

CHAPTER 4

FREE WILL AND DELINQUENCY

CHAPTER OUTLINE

We have some true [juvenile] sociopaths who would not hesitate to hurt someone or kill someone if they were obstructing what the kid wanted to do. We have a kid now who is a prime example of that; he bragged on the streets that nobody could catch him. Sociopaths are a strange breed. They're almost impossible to treat. They don't feel guilty or they don't hurt [feel pain]. Just don't get in their way and you will be all right.

Juvenile probation officer[1]

This chapter, the first of five on causation, explores the concept that juveniles commit delinquent behavior simply because they have free will and choose to do so. This emphasis on free will and personal responsibility is quite different from the emphasis in the next three chapters, which deal with the positive school of criminology; that is, the philosophy that juveniles cannot help committing delinquent acts because they are controlled either by internal factors (psychological or biological deficiencies) or external factors (poverty, learning crime from others, or societal labeling). Or to put it another way, youthful offenders are objects that shift like billiard balls in response to different forces.[2]

Beginning with the basic approaches to youth crime in the juvenile justice system, this chapter examines the principles of the classical school of criminology and then applies these principles to the analysis of delinquency in America. After examining the punishment approach to delinquency, the chapter concludes with policy implications.

THREE APPROACHES TO DELINQUENCY IN AMERICAN SOCIETY

The juvenile justice system, especially the juvenile court, has always had three approaches to juvenile lawbreakers. On one end of the spectrum, the *parens patriae,* or rehabilitation model, is used as an approach with status offenders and minor offenders. These youths are presumed to need treatment rather than punishment, because they are driven to commit their unacceptable behavior; that is, their offenses are seen as caused by internal psychological or biological conditions or by sociological factors in their environment.

But on the other end of the spectrum, juveniles who commit serious crimes or continue to break the law are presumed to deserve punishment rather than treatment, because they possess free will and know what they are doing. Their delinquencies are viewed as purposeful activity resulting from rational decisions in which the pros and cons are weighed and the acts that promise the greatest potential gains are performed.[3] Chronic offenders, especially, are likely to be punished rather than treated by the juvenile court. Box 4-1 portrays a juvenile criminal who received punishment rather than treatment.

BOX 4-1 A Juvenile "Monster"

George Clancy, a fictitious name for an Indianapolis youth, was a fourteen-year-old black, 6 feet, 2 inches tall and strongly built. For at least three years, he had been a well-known problem to the community. Then, on an autumn evening in 1974, he and two associates made an armed foray into a middle-class neighborhood. They entered three retail stores, and, armed with a shotgun, they robbed each store. They emptied cash registers and forced proprietors and customers to disrobe. The tactics worked well in the first store but in the second George became aroused by the nakedness of one of his female victims and raped her. In the third store, he tried to force a male customer to rape one of the women present. Upon his refusal, George clubbed him and shoved the barrel of his shotgun into the woman's vagina. The unusually repulsive brutality of the crimes made George's case a *cause célèbre* in the Indianapolis newspapers. The disgusting nature of his crimes, as well as his unusual size, resulted in the press designating him as a "monster man." He was placed in a youth training school in another state because there were no facilities in Indiana with sufficiently secure facilities. Two years later the staff of that training school was ready to release him, but the Indiana Youth Authority opposed his release to that state. Extended negotiation finally led to his placement in still another state.

Source: John P. Conrad, *Justice and Consequences* (Lexington, Mass.: D.C. Heath & Company, 1981), pp. 15–16.

In between these two groups fall youths who see crime as a form of play and commit delinquent acts because they enjoy the thrill of getting away with illegal behavior or because they are bored and want to relieve their boredom. Although criminologists usually conclude that the crimes these juveniles commit represent purposeful activity, the youths in the middle group are not considered as bad as the serious delinquents are. They may be exercising free will, but their acts are more "mischievous acts" than delinquent behavior. Middle-class youths are especially likely to have such "mischievous" behavior excused by the justice system. Figure 4-1 illustrates the three approaches.

In summary, officials of the juvenile justice system conclude that juveniles who commit status offenses and minor offenses need treatment rather than punishment, because they are driven to commit their unacceptable behavior. A second group of youngsters also has its unacceptable behavior excused as normal adolescent activity; these juveniles' behavior may be purposeful but it is an attempt to escape boredom by seeking a little excitement or fun. However, the behavior of youths who commit one delinquent act after the other or who commit a serious property or personal offense is measured by a different yardstick. Their behavior is looked upon as being bad rather than sick and as arising from a rational decision-making process; accordingly, juvenile judges and other officials of the juvenile justice system conclude that they need punishment rather than treatment. In other words, youths in the third group are treated by the juvenile justice system more like adults than like juveniles. The theoretical underpinnings for the handling of these "bad" juveniles are found in the classical school of criminology.

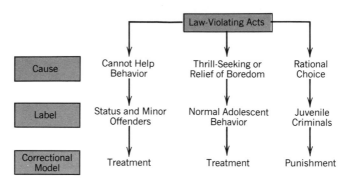

Figure 4-1 Three Approaches to Delinquency Control

THE CLASSICAL SCHOOL
OF CRIMINOLOGY

In 1764, Cesare Bonesana, Marquis of Beccaria, then only twenty-six and just out of law school, published a slim volume entitled *An Essay on Crimes and Punishment*.[4] This essay, which appeared anonymously because the young author feared reprisals if its authorship was known, was read avidly and translated into all the languages of Europe.[5] Beccaria, a child of the enlightenment and the growing force of liberalism, based the legitimacy of criminal sanctions on the social contract. The authority of making laws rested with the legislator, who should have only one view in sight, "the greatest happiness of the greatest number." Beccaria also saw punishment as a necessary evil, and suggested that "it should be public, immediate, and necessary; the least possible in the case given; proportioned to the crime; and determined by the laws."[6] Beccaria defined the purpose and consequences of punishment thus:

> *The purpose of punishment is to deter persons from the commission of crime and not to provide social revenge. Not severity, but certainty and swiftness in punishment best secure this result. Punishment must be sure and swift and penalties determined strictly in accordance with the social damage wrought by the crime. Crimes against property should be punished solely by fines, or by imprisonment when the person is unable to pay the fine. Banishment is an excellent punishment for crimes against the state. There should be no capital punishment. Life imprisonment is a better deterrent. Capital punishment is irreparable and hence makes no provision for possible mistakes and the desirability of later rectification.*[7]

In 1780, the Englishman Jeremy Bentham, another influential eighteenth-century thinker about crime, published *An Introduction to the Principles of Morals and Legislation*, which further developed the philosophy of the classical school.[8] Because Bentham believed that a rational person would do what was necessary to achieve the most pleasure and the least pain, he contended that punishment would deter criminal behavior providing it was made appropriate to the crime. He stated that punishment has four objectives: (1) to prevent all offenses, if possible; (2) if a person does decide to commit an offense, to persuade him or her to commit a less rather than a more serious one; (3) if a person has resolved upon a particular offense, "to dispose him to do not more mischief than is necessary to his purpose," and (4) to prevent the crime at as cheap a cost to society as possible.[9] Bentham derived six rules from these objectives:

1. The value of the punishment must not be less in any case than what is sufficient to outweigh that of the profit of the offense.

2. The greater the mischief of the offense, the greater is the expense which it may be worth while to . . . [exact] in the way of punishment.

3. Where two offenses come in competition, the punishment for the greater offense must be sufficient to induce a man to prefer the less.

4. The punishment should be adjusted in such a manner to each particular offense, that for every part of the mischief there may be a motive to restrain the offender from giving birth to it.

5. The punishment ought in no case to be more than what is necessary to bring it into conformity with the rules here given.

6. That the quantity actually inflicted on each individual offender may correspond to the quantity intended for similar offenders in general, the several circumstances influencing sensibility ought always to be taken into account.[10]

The basic theoretical constructs of the classical school of criminology were developed from the writings of Beccaria and Bentham: First, human beings were looked upon as rational creatures who, being free to choose their actions, could be held responsible for their behavior. This doctrine of free will was substituted for the widely accepted concept of theological determinism, which saw humans as predestined to certain actions. Second, punishment was justified because of its practical usefulness. No longer was it acceptable on the grounds of vengeful retaliation or as expiation on the basis of "superstitious" theories of guilt and repayment. The aim of punishment was the protection of society, and its dominant theme was deterrence. Third, it was presumed that the human being was a creature governed by a *felicific calculus* (pertaining to the ability to produce happiness for self) and oriented toward obtaining a favorable balance of pleasure and pain. Fourth, a rational scale of punishment was proposed that should be painful enough to deter the criminal from further offenses and to prevent others from following his or her example of crime. Fifth, sanctions should be proclaimed in advance of their use; these sanctions should be proportionate to the offense and should outweigh the rewards of crime. Sixth, equal justice should be offered everyone. Finally, proponents of the classical school urged that individuals should be judged by the law solely for their acts, not for their beliefs.[11]

Utilitarianism, as developed by the classical school, continued to gain in public acceptance and became the dominant theoretical underpinning of the development of corrections in both the United States and Europe. Criminal deterrence, social reform, and rehabilitation of offenders all were justified because of their presumed social advantage. The role of punishment was often deemphasized, especially during a period of reform, but juvenile and adult offenders were constantly reminded that they would be expected to experience punishment as part of their rehabilitation.

Utilitarian punishment philosophy was attacked on two fronts during the twentieth century, following the rise of positivism and the treatment model and the development of "just deserts" punishment philosophy. The wave of optimism that swept through America during the Progressive era (from about 1890 to 1920) led to the acceptance of positivism in the emerging juvenile court. Positivism, which is based upon deterministic underpinnings, rejected the concept of free will. Juveniles should not be punished for their offenses, reasoned the positivists, because they were driven to commit socially unacceptable behavior. The purpose of the emerging juvenile justice system came to be seen as the deterrence of delinquent behavior through rehabilitative techniques.[12]

J. D. Mabbott's seminal 1939 essay, "Punishment," represented the first step in the development of "just deserts" punishment philosophy. Mabbot argued that it is unfair to deprive a person of liberty as a consequence of that person's committing a criminal act for any reason other than that the act "deserves" to be punished and that that person committed the act.[13] This presumption that an offender deserves to be punished simply because of what he or she has done rather than for any social reasons has been sharply debated by philosophers in the decades following the publication of Mabbott's essay. One of the positive outcomes of this debate was the development of the constructs of "just deserts."

THE CLASSICAL SCHOOL REVISITED

A revival of the principles of the classical school of criminology can be found in the utilitarian punishment philosophy and in the justice model. Both positions hold that the basic purpose of the juvenile justice system should be punishment because juveniles have free will and, therefore, are responsible for their behavior.

The Utilitarian Punishment Model

In the mid-1970s, the United States returned to the philosophy of utilitarian punishment to deal with serious juvenile as well as adult crime. The utilitarian punishment philosophy is grounded on the assumption that punishment is necessary to deter youthful offenders and to protect society from crime. Thus, punishment is justified because of its presumed social advantages. Proponents of this approach, the correctional right, make the argument that if we are unable to improve youthful offenders through rehabilitative programs, we can at least assure that they are confined and that potential lawbreakers are deterred by the consequences incurred by those who do break the law.[14]

James Q. Wilson and Ernest van den Haag, leading spokespersons for utilitarian punishment philosophy, have described the main points of this hard-line approach to juvenile justice.[15] First, proponents of utilitarian punishment philosophy resent losses in the quality of American life caused by the problem of delinquency. They feel that a paramount duty of government is to provide the necessary social controls so that citizens are secure in their lives, liberties, and pursuit of happiness. Because the duty of the government is to protect the rights and liberties of its citizens, punishment is to be used against those who violate the laws of the state.[16]

Second, punishment is owed by those who violate the law, and, like debts, must be paid. However, punishment and vengeance are not the same. Vengeance is self-serving since it is arbitrarily taken by a person who feels injured and wishes to retaliate, but punishment or retribution is imposed by the courts after a guity plea or a trial in which the accused has been convicted of committing a crime.[17]

Third, punishment is an effective deterrence against delinquent behavior. Van den Haag is particularly convinced of the deterrent effects of sanctions, believing that the "first line of social defense is the cost imposed for criminal activity."[18] The higher the cost, the more likely that it will deter youth crime. He says:

> . . . if a given offender's offenses are rational in the situation in which he lives—if what he can gain exceeds the likely cost to him by more than the gain from legitimate activities he does—there is little that can be "corrected" in the offender. Reform will fail. It often fails for this reason. What has to be changed is not the personality of the offender, but the cost-benefit ratio which makes his offense rational. That ratio can be changed by improving and multiplying his opportunities for legitimate activity and the benefits they yield, or by decreasing his opportunity for illegitimate activities, or by increasing their cost to him, including punishment.[19]

Fourth, proponents of utilitarian punishment philosophy believe in free will; that is, that youthful offenders can reason and have freely chosen to violate the law. Such offenders are not controlled by any past or present forces and, therefore, they deserve punishment for the social harm they have inflicted upon society. Van den Haag expresses it this way:

> It is easy, though unfashionable, to see why justice must disregard the different needs and general disparities of temptation among persons and groups. A frustrated man rejected as repulsive by the sexual partner he craves may be more tempted to rape than another person better endowed or stimulated; an irritable person is more disposed to assault than a phlegmatic one; a poor and deprived man may be more tempted to steal than a wealthy one. But the prohibition against rape must be applied equally to repulsive (and frustrated) individuals and to attractive (and unfrustrated) ones; the prohibition against assault to the ill- and to the even-tempered; and the prohibition against stealing to rich and poor alike. Else the forbidden act would be pro-

hibited only to those not inclined or tempted to commit it. Which won't help. The purpose of the law is to forbid what some people are tempted to do, by character or by circumstance. The threat of punishment is meant to discourage those who are tempted rather than those who are not.[20]

Fifth, juvenile delinquents are deterred from crime only through the awareness that unlawful behavior will result in a period of isolation from society. Hard-liners dismiss the community-based movement, because they claim that youthful offenders do not take the justice process seriously until they "do some time." Punishment then, requires that youths be sent to long-term training schools or to adult prisons.

Sixth, punishment, rather than rehabilitation, must be the purpose of the juvenile justice system. Rehabilitation has not worked and it is an insufficient penalty for the social harm an offender has done. But Wilson explains that rehabilitation should continue to have a role in the juvenile justice system:

Now suppose we abandon entirely the rehabilitation theory of sentencing and corrections—not the effort to rehabilitate, just the theory that the governing purpose of the enterprise is to rehabilitate. We could continue experiments with new correctional and therapeutic procedures, expanding them when the evidence warrants. If existing correctional programs do not differ in their rehabilitative potential, we could support those that are least costly and more humane (while still providing reasonable security) and phase out those that are most costly and inhumane. But we would not do any of these things on the mistaken notion that we were thereby reducing recidivism.[21]

Components of the Utilitarian Punishment or Crime Control Model

An increased use of training schools, a hard-line policy toward serious juvenile delinquents, a greater use of determinate and mandatory sentences, and a get-tough policy with drug offenders are the main strategies advocated by proponents of utilitarian punishment philosophy for dealing with juvenile crime (see Chapter 14 for additional comments on this crime control model).

These advocates contend that more juvenile offenders should be placed in training schools, and they should be held there for longer periods of time. Proponents of this model also recommend that repeat offenders be incarcerated, for these offenders are the ones most likely to inflict damage upon society.[22] Moreover, incarcerating serious offenders means that they are prevented for at least a certain length of time from committing additional crimes.[23]

The *parens patriae* philosophy of the juvenile court is rejected by the hard-liners as being too permissive in dealing with serious youth crime. They believe that it is far more effective policy to transfer more serious juvenile offenders to adult court.

Advocates of the punishment model also support a wider use of determinate and mandatory sentencing. They believe that sentences fixed by the legislatures will deal with the youth crime problem better than those that depend on the discretion of juvenile judges and the aftercare process.

Proponents of utilitarian punishment philosophy are aware of the relationship today between drug abuse and juvenile delinquency, but they refuse to regard addiction as a disease and to excuse the crimes that individuals addicted to drugs commit. Van den Haag, for example, believes that if "we punish becoming addicted, fewer persons do become addicted."[24] Wilson adds that drug addicts, like other offenders, are deterred when a "get-tough" policy is enforced.[25]

In sum, supporters of utilitarian punishment philosophy want to declare war on crime. They support repressive methods in order to increase the cost of breaking the law.

The Justice Model

The justice model also holds to the belief that punishment should be the basic purpose of the juvenile justice system. Among the variants of the justice model for youth crime are those proposed by David Fogel, the Report of the Committee for the Study of Incarceration and the Report of the Twentieth Century Fund.[26]

Fogel's Justice Model

The justice-as-fairness perspective, as Fogel calls his model, is as critical of the juvenile justice system as are proponents of utilitarian punishment philosophy. To improve the justice system, Fogel emphasizes the importance of due process rights throughout the correctional process.[27] He summarizes the basic approach of the justice model with the statement: "If we cannot treat with reliability, we can at least be fair, reasonable, humane, and constitutional in practice."[28]

Fogel explains that he was influenced by a number of philosophical concepts in developing the justice model. Philosopher John Rawls had stated that the first priority of the justice system is to achieve justice.[29] From his examination of the abuses of the system in action, Fogel concluded that justice can only be achieved through fair, reasonable, humane, and constitutional practices.

Second, the concept of free will is a basic underpinning of the justice model. Fogel quotes Stephen Schafer's assertion that "although free will may not exist perfectly, the criminal law is largely based upon its presumed vitality and [free will] forms the only foundation for penal sanctions."[30]

Third, the concept of "just deserts" is the pivotal philosophical basis of the justice model. Fogel believes that youth offenders are volitional and responsible human beings and, therefore, they deserve to be punished if they violate the law. The punishment shows that the youthful offender is blameworthy for his or her conduct. The decisions concerning offenders should be based not on their needs, but upon the penalties that they deserve for their acts.[31] This nonutilitarian punishment position is not intended to achieve social benefits or advantages, such as deterrence or rehabilitation; rather, the only reason to punish an offender is because he or she deserves it. However, the punishment given the offender must be proportionate to the seriousness of the offense or the social harm inflicted upon society.[32]

Fourth, a fundamental distrust of the power of the state represents another underpinning of the justice model. Unbridled discretion, according to Fogel, is one way in which the state misuses its power over citizens. Fogel also feels that the state has misused its power with required rehabilitative programs for offenders.[33]

Fifth, a concern both for the victim and the offender underlies the justice model. Indeed, Fogel believes that officials of the juvenile justice system should place as great an emphasis on the victims of crime as they do on offenders.[34] Similarly, offenders are to be treated with respect and dignity, by permitting them to choose programs voluntarily, by providing them with all the rights dictated by law, by making certain that decisions about them are made in a just way, by creating mechanisms that permit them to bring grievance actions against unfair decisions that concern them, and by giving them an opportunity to be involved in self-government within the training school.[35]

The components of the justice model have been applied to juvenile justice in four areas: sentencing, justice-as-fairness for offenders, a victim-oriented justice system, and decriminalization of status offenders and deinstitutionalization of minor offenders.

The indeterminate sentence and the aftercare structure are to be replaced by a determinate sentencing structure.[36] Juveniles are to be treated as responsible; volitional human beings, and the governing principle of sentencing should be one of "proportionality," that is, a relation must exist between the seriousness of the offense committed and the severity of the sanctions imposed.[37]

Justice-as-fairness must characterize the processing of juveniles through the justice system. One means to ensure the due process rights of offenders is to limit the enormous discretion granted to juvenile justice practitioners.[38] Involvement in correctional treatment must be totally voluntary and should have nothing to do with the length of confinement or probation.[39] Residents of training schools must be provided an adequate formal grievance process to negotiate the decisions affecting them, thereby serving as an effective means of conflict resolution.[40] The residual or chronic offender also must be ensured of justice-as-fairness safeguards.[41]

A victim-oriented justice system means that officials of the juvenile justice system should utilize means to restore victims to their pre-crime status.[42] Financial restitution and community service sanctions are needed to restore victims.[43] Finally, status offenses are to be decriminalized and more youthful offenders diverted from the juvenile justice system to voluntary services. Training schools are to be used only as a last resort.[44]

The Report of the Committee for the Study of Incarceration

The committee's report, written by Andrew von Hirsch, begins with the statement "We take seriously Kant's view that a person should be punished because he deserves it."[45] The recommendations of this study also propose that "deserts" be used as the guiding principle of the correctional process. Offenders are to be subjected to certain deprivations, or punishments, because they deserve them—and they deserve them because they have engaged in wrongful conduct. The severity of punishment, according to von Hirsh, should be commensurate with the seriousness of the wrong. Furthermore, like Fogel, the committee recommends determinate sentencing, dismantling of rehabilitation procedures, limited use of confinement, and reduced length of sentences.[46]

The Report of the Twentieth Century Fund Task Force on Sentencing Policy toward Young Offenders

The Twentieth Century Fund Task Force, in developing a foundation for sentencing policy toward youthful offenders, was guided by four principles: culpability, diminished responsibility resulting from immaturity, providing room to reform, and proportionality. The task force decided that at age thirteen or fourteen, a youth may be considered responsible, at least to a degree, for the criminal harms he or she causes. In reaching the decision that youthful offenders should be legally responsible for intentional criminal harms, the task force concluded that these youths are capable of moral judgment and varying degrees of self-control. Yet youthful offenders should be protected from the full force of the criminal law. The task force concluded that the degree of punishment administered to youth crime should be proportional to the offense.[47]

Comparison of the Utilitarian Punishment, Justice, and Rehabilitation Models

In basic concept, the justice and utilitarian punishment, or crime control, models are based upon free will, and offenders are looked upon as individuals who are responsible for having chosen their socially unacceptable behavior. In contrast, the rehabilitation model is based upon a deterministic concept, which claims that crime is caused by some biological or psychological deficiency within the offender or by some sociological factors within society. Although the basic rationale for punishment in the justice model is the concept of "just deserts," the basic rationales for punishment in the utilitarian punishment model are the deterrence of offenders and the protection of society.

In regard to sentencing, its purpose in the utilitarian punishment model is to establish law and order in society. Doing justice, which means to minimize any harm done by the justice system and to ensure that the justice system does a good job of dispensing justice, is the basic purpose of sentencing in the justice model. But according to the rehabilitation model, the purpose of sentencing is to provide for the rehabilitation of offenders through individualized treatment.

The crime control strategy of the utilitarian punishment model is to declare war on delinquency by instituting get-tough policies. Proponents of this model hold that increasing the cost of crime will deter criminal behavior and will protect citizens from crime. The justice model holds that offenders should receive "just deserts" or "just punishments" for their socially unacceptable behavior, but that although they must be punished in proportion to the social harm they have inflicted upon society, they are to receive humane and fair treatment by the justice system. In contrast, the crime control strategy of the rehabilitation model is to eliminate the factors causing crime through a therapeutic environment or experience for offenders. (See Figure 4-2 for a comparison of the three models.)

Figure 4-2 Comparison of the Rehabilitation, Justice, and Utilitarian Punishment Models

Policy	Rehabilitation	Justice	Utilitarian Punishment
1. Approach to the offender	Deterministic or positivistic approach	Free will based upon the classical school	Free will based upon the classical school
2. Purpose of sentencing	Establish law and order	Doing justice	Doing good
3. Type of sentencing advocated	Indeterminate	Determinate	Determinate
4. Role of treatment	Basic goal of the correctional process	Voluntary but necessary in a humane system	Ineffective and dangerous because it results in coddling criminals
5. Crime control strategy	Eliminate factors causing crime through therapeutic intervention; develop improved treatment technologies	Justice-as-fairness for offenders, for practitioners in the justice system, and for victims	Declare war on crime by instituting get-tough policies

Source: Clemens Bartollas, *Correctional Treatment: Theory and Practice* (Englewood Cliffs, N.J.: Prentice-Hall, 1985).

EVALUATION AND CRITICISM OF NEOCLASSICAL THEORY

Both the utilitarian punishment and the justice models look upon delinquency as volitional activity that is the result of a rational decision in which the pros and cons are weighed and the act that promises the greatest potential gain is performed. The delinquent is seen as having free will and being responsible for his or her behavior. Of the two approaches to youth crime, the utilitarian punishment concept is more acceptable to society than "just deserts" because the former promises the presumed social benefits of deterring crime and protecting society, while the latter offers only punishment for its own sake. Or to put this another way, society would prefer to base the juvenile justice system on some utilitarian principle than on mere retribution.

In evaluating neoclassical theory, especially the utilitarian punishment approach, three questions are important: Is delinquency rational behavior? Does punishment deter crime? What are the consequences of a punishment-oriented approach to juvenile delinquency?

Is Delinquency Rational Behavior?

An analysis of delinquent behavior leads to the conclusion that some antisocial behavior appears to be purposeful and rational. For example, some observers have noted that delinquency is an enjoyable activity. Thrasher thought that a "sport motive" was more important in stealing than a desire for material gain.[48] Henry McKay, Paul Tappan, and Albert Cohen have described delinquency as a form of play.[49] J. Tobias found that middle- and upper-middle class offenders mention boredom as a major reason for engaging in delinquent acts, and that they usually discount the need for money as a contributing factor.[50]

In addition, some lower-class, as well as middle-class offenders, engage in delinquent behavior because of the low cost or risk of such behavior. This low risk has resulted from two factors: First, the *parens patriae* philosophy is based upon the presumption of innocence for the very young, as well as of reduced responsibility for those up to their mid-adolescence. Thus, in early adolescence the potential costs of all but the most serious forms of delinquent behavior are relatively slight.[51] Second, juveniles are protected from punishment by the existence of enormous caseloads in large cities, the confidentiality of juvenile court records, and the increased criticisms of long-term training schools. Youths on probation, then, can repeatedly violate the law and suffer no real consequences for their illegal behavior. Juvenile offenders, of course, understand these unwritten rules. According to a delinquent testifying before the New York State Select Committee at a hearing on assault and robbery against the elderly:

> If you're 15 and under you won't go to jail. . . . That's why when we do a "Rush and Crib"—which means you rush the victim and push him or her into their apartment, you let the youngest member do any beatings. See, we know if they arrest him, he'll be back on the street in no time.[52]

However, to conclude that the majority of delinquent behavior is the result of rational activity, in which youngsters calculate the benefits and dangers of delinquent involvements, seems questionable. This presumption also prescribes too much freedom to the delinquent. Silvan S. Tomkins expands upon this point:

> Man is neither as free as he feels nor as bound as he fears. There are some aspects of himself, as of his environment, which he may easily transform, some aspects which he may transform only with difficulty and others which he can never transform. . . . Much of the debate concerning the freedom of the will arose from a confusion between the concepts of causality and freedom and from a derivative failure to distinguish motives that are more free from motives that are less free. . . . The conventional concept of causality, which generated the pseudo problem of the freedom of the will, assumed that the relationship between events was essentially two-valued, either determinate or capricious, and that man's will was therefore either slavishly determined or capriciously free. We feel, however, that this controversy concerns man's degree of freedom rather than the determinateness of his behavior.[53]

In other words, delinquents "are neither wholly free nor completely constrained but fall somewhat between."[54] Some delinquents, of course, are less free than others. Youths who engage in obsessive-compulsive acts, such as the compulsive arsonist, kleptomaniac, or sex offender, appear to have little control over their behavior. Nor can much freedom be ascribed to those who commit acts that are characterized by irrationality, intense emotion, and "pointless" destruction of property.

Some question must be raised about the degree of freedom of the youth who is under the influence of or is addicted to drugs or alcohol. Such youths may commit delinquent acts under the influence of chemicals that they would not otherwise:

> Drugs and alcohol, that's the main reason why I'm here. All the times I broke the law I was drunk or high. I mainly just stole cars. I just liked to hot wire cars and joyride when I was wasted. I could have never have done it if I was straight; it's easy when you're drunk. I guess drugs and alcohol will be my biggest obstacle when I get out of here, that and my attitude.[55]

But even those youths who appear to have more freedom tend to drift in and out of delinquent behavior without giving a great deal of thought to the cost and consequences of their behavior.[56] Delinquency for these youths seems to arise during the course of the interactions they experience on a daily basis and to be more spontaneous occurrences than calculated or planned activities.[57]

In sum, although some youths' involvement in delinquency may be related to cost-benefit decisions and to a rational process, other explanations better explain the delinquent behavior of most youths. With the vast majority of youngsters, delinquent behavior arises without much forethought as they interact with their environment. With still other youths, compulsive behavior, the influence of alcohol or drugs, or intense emotional reaction to a situation seem to lead them to bypass any rational process.

Does Punishment Deter?

Deterrence is typically separated into general and specific deterrence. General deterrence refers to the threat and use of punishment in order to prevent illegal behavior on the part of the population in general. Specific deterrence has to do with the threat and use of punishment in order to prevent illegal behavior by specific persons who already have broken the law. In an effective justice system, law violators must be identified, apprehended, and punished swiftly and certainly, and the punishment must carry a measure of severity at least equal in magnitude to the gravity of the crime.[58]

However, the theory of using punishment to deter delinquent behavior has a number of flaws. First, the juvenile justice system has a limited ability to identify, apprehend, and punish with certainty. Indeed, a very small percentage of youthful offenders are apprehended for their illegal behavior, and of those identified and convicted by the juvenile court, very few receive any significant degree of punishment.[59]

Second, to be an effective deterrent, a perceived certainty factor must reach a certain level. Tittle and Rowe found that level to be approximately 30 percent, while Bailey places this figure closer to 50 percent.[60] Thus, unless the certainty of identification, apprehension, and punishment is regarded by the potential juvenile lawbreaker to be in the 30- to 50-percent range, the general deterrence policy probably has little value.[61]

Third, deterrence is based on the assumption of a rational humankind, yet many delinquent acts are far from rational. Some youngsters are indifferent to the consequences of their acts. The psychological makeup of a person also influences decision making. A juvenile may go along with the group because he or she does not want to risk rejection, or a youth may attempt to kill during a fit of jealousy. Furthermore, juveniles—like adults—may have perceptual distortions. They see selectively and weigh what they see with their values and ideologies.[62]

Fourth, the juvenile justice system can be seen as not even a system at all, but rather a fragmented, pluralistic, case-disposition network. Virtually unchecked discretionary power has been doled out to all the various government agencies that make up the juvenile justice system, and these agencies often go to great lengths to protect their own "turf." An effective large-scale deterrence policy would require a high level of cooperation and coordination among these many agencies, and that condition is not likely to be met in the near future.[63]

Fifth, a good argument can be made for the fact that a general deterrence policy really only "deters" those who are already law-abiding and can do little to deter those who are not internally inhibited from delinquent behavior. In other words, those who have internalized appropriate social norms from family, friends, church, and school will be deterred from delinquency, and those who have not will become involved in inappropriate behavior regardless of the threats of punishment.[64]

Finally, long ago Jeremy Bentham recognized the difficulty in establishing high levels of certainty and suggested that the problem might be overcome by increasing the severity of punishment.[65] However, considerable research has led to the conclusion that involvement with the justice system actually breeds rather than cures crime. Vito and Allen found that incarceration has an overridingly negative impact on behavior.[66] Hamparian et al. found that placing juveniles in institutions makes them more likely to commit a new offense and that the longer juveniles are in institutions, the quicker they are to commit new offenses upon release.[67] Shannon's study of three birth cohorts revealed an increase in the frequency and seriousness of misbehavior in the periods after sanctions had been administered.[68]

In sum, the theoretical and practical problems surrounding general and specific deterrence make it extremely difficult to conclude that the threat of punishment prevents the commission of a delinquent act or that increased punishment will prevent future delinquent acts by youthful offenders. In addition, a not-to-be-ignored danger is that increased punishment may cause youthful offenders to respond in anger directed at society for what the justice system has done to them.

What Are the Consequences of a Punishment-Oriented Justice System?

A punishment-oriented justice system invokes criticism on many fronts. The most widespread criticism is that a repressive response to youth crime does not work. A brutal response to youth crime has not worked in the past; nor is it likely to work in the future. The chief reason why a repressive response to youth crime will not work is that the logic underlying this approach is fundamentally flawed. This neoclassical approach assumes that youth crime takes place only when youthful offenders have calculated rationally the cost and benefits of crime, but more commonly, youth crime takes place as the result of juveniles being impoverished, addicted to drugs, emotionally distraught, or influenced by peers. That is, most youthful offenders merely respond to the needs and emotions of a particular moment.

Critics also assail the policy of increased confinement advocated by the utilitarian punishment model. Because training schools are acknowledged as being unsafe, inhumane, and criminogenic, the policy of increased confinement is charged with making the juvenile justice system more repressive. The fairness of the utilitarian punishment model is criticized as well. Critics claim that proponents of the utilitarian punishment model deny the spread of delinquency throughout American society by viewing the delinquent as an alien or as an outsider. Further, critics charge that hard-liners focus almost entirely on lower-class crime and minimize the social harm done to society by middle-class crime.

Moreover, critics charge that blaming crime solely on offenders results in ignoring the social and structural conditions in society that lead to crime. This, in turn, encourages policymakers to continue neglecting the social conditions, such as poverty and unemployment, that contribute to youth crime.

Finally, radical criminologists add that the conservative position ignores the injustice and inhumanity inherent in our society. They claim that the utilitarian punishment model works against any possible structural transformation of an exploitative capitalistic system because it solidifies the power of the ruling elites.

POLICY IMPLICATIONS

A get-tough policy on serious youth crime is currently favored by the public. The utilitarian punishment philosophy and justice models, both of which view punishment as the basic purpose of the juvenile justice system, have gained popularity because of their hard-line stances. The philosophy of these models has been incorporated in a number of states, especially New York, Washington, and California. The Omnibus Crime Bill of 1978 in New York State, commonly known as the "juvenile offender law," stripped the Family Court of jurisdiction of thirteen-year-olds accused of murder and fourteen or fifteen-year-olds accused of murder, attempted murder, and other violent offenses. In Washington a new system of determinate sentences has been adopted for juvenile offenders (Revised Criminal Code of Washington 1977). In California (Assembly Bill 3121, Chapter 1071:1–24) makes juveniles sixteen and older who are accused of a selected list of felonies more vulnerable to adult penal sanctions.

The shortcomings of the utilitarian punishment philosophy clearly outweigh its strengths. Three of these are particularly disturbing: (1) the repressiveness that is part of the utilitarian punishment model will not work; (2) this model will lead to a more inhumane and unfair justice system; and (3) this model chooses to ignore the social problems that lead to crime. Using repressive measures to declare war on youth crime may have dire consequences for American society.

The justice model, which also presumes that youthful offenders have free will and are responsible for their behavior, appears on the surface to be a viable means to deal with youth crime in the United States. Based on the "just deserts" philosophy, this model appears to be a more socially acceptable way at present of dealing with serious youth crime than is rehabilitative philosophy.

This model also has merit because its emphasis on justice-as-fairness implies a humane way of dealing with juvenile delinquents. Proponents of the justice model make the point that fair play and due process of law must be primary concerns during the correctional process. Justice-as-fairness, advocates claim, must be defined as restricting commitments to training school to those who have committed serious offenses. But for those offenders who are sent to training school, justice-as-fairness also means that they are sent there *as* and not *for* punishment and, therefore, they should be treated in a fair and humane way.

In addition, the justice model draws applause because it is the only reform strategy today encompassing a systemwide reform of juvenile justice. For example, Fogel's justice model deals with nearly every aspect of administering justice to delinquents, with the needs of victims, with the due process rights of offenders, and with the needs of the other actors in the justice process. Supporters claim that compared to Fogel's justice model, other reform strategies are either piecemeal approaches or merely projections for change in the system.

However, the justice model does appear to have two serious flaws. First, the concept of "just deserts," which states that delinquents deserve to be punished proportionately for the social harm they have inflicted upon society, is unlikely to gain acceptance in the juvenile justice system. Punishment proportionate to the seriousness of the crime, of course, may be defended as a fair and humane standard for sentencing, but admitting retribution as the ultimate aim of the juvenile correctional system will breed a policy of despair rather than of hope.[69] Indeed, the concept of "just deserts" has existed for centuries and has never totally dominated the penal policy of any advanced society, so whether this theory could ever dominate the correctional policy of this nation is questionable.[70]

Second, the justice model may be widely accepted throughout the nation, but little evidence exists that it actually is producing a more humane system. The reason for this is that the justice model, as Francis Cullen and Karen Gilbert have noted, is being used by "get-tough-with-juveniles" politicians to create more punitive sentencing structures. Unfortunately, supporters of the justice model have launched a repressive "movement that assumes the values they have opposed."[71]

The problem does not concern minor offenders and status offenders, as society and its policymakers have approved a soft-line approach with these offenders. The problem lies with serious and violent offenders; society expects a hard-line, punishment-oriented approach with them. The utilitarian punishment and justice models provide a good justification for punishment because they both presume that older juveniles have free will and, therefore, are responsible for their behavior. But both models have real flaws, the most serious of which is that ultimately they lead to a more repressive justice system.

A partial solution to the problem of serious and violent juvenile crime would be to develop a new correctional model that combined the rehabilitation, the justice, and the utilitarian punishment models. Some jurisdictions and agencies of the justice system throughout the nation are attempting this, with the logical consequences model. This model puts costs and consequences on antisocial behavior and assumes free will and responsibility on the part of offenders, but it also emphasizes treatment services with offenders (See Chapter 14 for a discussion of this model).

SUMMARY

Clearly, the punishment model of old has regained popularity in dealing with juvenile delinquents who have committed serious crimes. Policymakers are more and more coming to the conclusion that increasing its cost is the only way to reduce youth crime in the United States. To justify the punishment of juveniles, theorists have returned to the classical school of criminology, which asserts that individuals have free will and, therefore, are responsible for their behavior. Delinquent behavior, then, is viewed as purposeful behavior, as an activity resulting from a rational decision in which the pros and cons were weighed.

The contextual perspective is helpful in understanding why society has moved to a get-tough position with juvenile criminals. Youth crime has always been a serious problem, but in the early 1970s the media persuaded the public that youth crime was increasing at alarming rates and that juvenile criminals were becoming more dangerous than ever before. In the sociocultural context, the declining quality of American life was blamed on youthful offenders, especially minority offenders. The political and economic structures of American life were facing heavy criticism in the late 1960s and early 1970s, and politicians sought easy and popular solutions; the juvenile and adult criminals who had been heroes only a few years before were now villains. Conservative policymakers were attracted to the get-tough measures of the utilitarian punishment philosophy, while disillusioned liberals responded to the "just deserts" philosophy. Mandatory and determinate sentencing structures for adults were soon passed into law, and before the end of the 1970s, these same legal structures were being applied to juveniles.

Utilitarian punishment and justice models have been proposed as approaches using an explanation of delinquent behavior that will justify punishment. Unfortunately, the justice model, which recommends many promising reforms of the juvenile justice system, is actually being transformed into a policy encouraging repressive methods. Utilitarian punishment philosophy has even greater acceptance in the public sector as the answer to serious juvenile crime, but the danger is that this repressive response to crime may return juvenile corrections in America to the Dark Ages.

Discussion Questions

1. Why have the juvenile court and policymakers been so quick to apply the concept of free will to violent juvenile criminals?

2. List the philosophical underpinnings of the justice and the utilitarian models. How do these models differ from each other?

3. What are the basic flaws in using punishment to deter youth crime in America?

4. Why is the utilitarian punishment model likely to lead to a more repressive juvenile justice system? Why is this also true for the justice model?

References

Allinson, Richard. "Is New York's Tough Juvenile Law a 'Charade'?" *Corrections Magazine.* 9 (1983): 40–45.

Conrad, John P. *Justice and Consequences.* Lexington, Mass.: D.C. Heath & Company, 1981.

Cullen, Francis T., and Gilbert, Karen E. *Reaffirming Rehabilitation.* Cincinnati: Anderson Publishing Company, 1982.

Erickson, Maynard L., and Gibbs, Jack P. "Punishment, Deterrence, and Juvenile Justice." In *Critical Issues in Juvenile Delinquency,* edited by David Shichor and Delos H. Kelly. Lexington, Mass.: Lexington Books, 1980.

Fogel, David. . . . *We Are the Living Proof: The Justice Model for Corrections.* Cincinnati: Anderson Publishing Company, 1975.

Hirsh, Andrew von. *Doing Justice: The Choice of Punishments.* New York: Hill & Wang, 1976.

Rawls, John. *A Theory of Justice.* Cambridge, Mass.: Harvard University Press, 1972.

Rennie, Ysabel. *The Search for Criminal Man: A Conceptual History of the Dangerous Offender.* Lexington, Mass.: Lexington Books, 1978.

Van den Haag, Ernest. *Punishing Criminals: Concerning a Very Old and Painful Question.* New York: Basic Books, 1975.

Wilson, James Q. *Thinking about Crime.* New York: Basic Books, 1975.

FOOTNOTES

1. Interviewed in May 1981.

2. Anne Campbell, *Girl Delinquents* (New York: St. Martin's Press, 1981), p. 37.

3. Edward Cimler and Lee Roy Bearch, "Factors Involved in Juvenile Decisions about Crime," *Criminal Justice and Behavior* 8 (September 1981), pp. 275–286.

4. Cesare Bonesana Beccaria, *On Crimes and Punishments,* 1764. Trans. by H. PaoLucci (Indianapolis: Bobbs-Merrill, 1963).

5. Ysabel Rennie, *The Search for Criminal Man: A Conceptual History of the Dangerous Offender* (Lexington, Mass.: Lexington Books, 1978), p. 15.

6. Beccaria, *Essay on Crimes and Punishments,* p. 179.

7. Harry Elmer Barnes and Negley K. Teeters, *New Horizons in Criminology,* 3d ed. (Englewood Cliffs, N.J.: Prentice-Hall, 1959), p. 285.

8. Jeremy Bentham, *An Introduction to the Principles of Morals and Legislation* (1823; reprint ed., New York: Hafner Publishing Company, 1948).

9. Rennie, *Search for Criminal Man,* p. 22.

10. Bentham, *Introduction to the Principles of Morals and Legislation,* pp. 178–182.

11. Richard A. Ball, "Restricted Reprobation and the Reparation of Social Reality: A Theory of Punishment" (Paper presented at the Annual Meeting of the American Society of Criminology, Dallas, 1978), p. 6.

12. David J. Rothman, *Conscience and Convenience: The Asylum and Its Alternatives in Progressive America* (Boston: Little, Brown & Company, 1980), pp. 43–60.

13. J. D. Mabbott, "Punishment," reprinted in Frederick A. Olafson, *Justice and Social Policy* (Englewood Cliffs, N.J.: Prentice-Hall/Spectrum, 1961), p. 39.

14. John P. Conrad, *Justice and Consequences* (Lexington, Mass.: Lexington Books, 1981), p. 157.

15. Ernest van den Haag, *Punishing Criminals: Concerning a Very Old and Painful Question* (New York: Basic Books, 1975) and James Q. Wilson, *Thinking about Crime* (New York: Basic Books, 1975).

16. Van den Haag, *Punishing Criminals,* pp. 1–5.

17. Ibid., p. 11.

18. Ibid., p. 57.

19. Ibid., p. 59.

20. Ibid., pp. 44–45.

21. Wilson, *Thinking about Crime,* p. 172.

22. Ibid., p. 200.

23. Ibid.

24. Van den Haag, *Punishing Criminals,* p. 127.

25. Wilson, *Thinking about Crime,* p. 145.

26. David Fogel, . . . *We Are the Living Proof: The Justice Model for Corrections* (Cincinnati: Anderson Publishing Company, 1975; Andrew von Hirsch, *Doing Justice: The Choice of Punishments* (New York: Hill & Wang, 1976; Twentieth Century Fund Task Force on Sentencing Policy toward Young Offenders, *Confronting Youth Crime* (New York: Holmes & Meier, Inc., 1978).

27. Fogel, *"We Are the Living Proof."*

28. David Fogel and Joe Hudson, eds., *Justice as Fairness: Perspectives on the Justice Model* (Cincinnati: Anderson Publishing Company, 1981), p. viii.

29. John Rawls, *A Theory of Justice* (Cambridge, Mass.: Harvard University Press, 1972), p. 3.

30. Stephen Schafer, *The Political Criminal: The Problem of Morality and Crime* (New York: Free Press, 1974).

31. Von Hirsh, *Doing Justice,* p. 98.

32. Fogel and Hudson, *Justice as Fairness,* p. 1.

33. Fogel, *"We Are the Living Proof,"* p. 227.

34. Ibid., p. 206.

35. Fogel and Hudson, *Justice as Fairness,* p. x.

36. Fogel, *"We Are the Living Proof,* pp. 192–199.

37. Charles Shireman, "The Juvenile Justice System: Structure, Problems and Prospects," in *Justice as Fairness,* edited by Fogel and Hudson, pp. 136–141.

38. Ibid.

39. Fogel, *"We Are the Living Proof,"* p. 261.

40. Ibid., pp. 215–221.

41. Ibid., pp. 275–276.

42. Interview in Clemens Bartollas, *Correctional Treatment: Theory and Practice* (Englewood Cliffs, N.J.: Prentice-Hall, 1984), Chapter 4.

43. Joe Hudson and Burt Galaway, "Restitution and the Justice Model," in *Justice as Fairness,* edited by Fogel and Hudson, pp. 52–65.

44. Ibid.

45. Von Hirsch, *Doing Justice,* p. 6.

46. Ibid.

47. Twentieth Century Fund Task Force, *Confronting Youth Crime,* pp. 6–8.

48. F. Thrasher, *The Gang* (Chicago: University of Chicago Press, 1936).

49. H. McKay, "The Neighborhood and Child Conduct," *Annals of the American Academy of Political and Social Science* 261 (1949), pp. 32–41; P. Tappan, *Juvenile Delinquency* (New York: McGraw-Hill Book Company, 1949; and A. Cohen, "The Delinquent Subculture," in *The Sociology of Crime and Delinquency,* edited by M. Wolfgang, L. Savitz, and N. Johnston, 2d ed. (New York: John Wiley & Sons, 1970).

50. J. Tobias, "The Affluent Suburban Male Delinquent," *Crime and Delinquency* 16 (1970), pp. 273–279.

51. David F. Greenberg, "Delinquency and the Age Structure of Society," *Contemporary Crisis* 1 (1977), p. 209.

52. Ibid., p. 210.

53. Silvan S. Tomkins, *Affect, Imagery, Consciousness: The Positive Affects,* vol. 1 (New York: Springer, 1962), pp. 108–109.

54. David Matza, *Delinquency and Drift* (New York: John Wiley & Sons, 1964), p. 27.

55. Interviewed in May 1981.

56. Matza, *Delinquency and Drift.*

57. See James F. Short, Jr., and Fred L. Strodtbeck, *Group Process and Gang Delinquency* (Chicago: University of Chicago Press, 1965), pp. 248–265.

58. Chris W. Eskridge, "Flaws in the Theory and Practice of General Deterrence" (Paper presented at the Annual Meeting of the Academy of Criminal Justice Sciences, San Antonio, Texas, March 1983), p. 1.

59. Ibid., p. 3.

60. Charles Tittle and Allan Rowe, "Moral Appeal, Sanction Threat, and Deviance: An Experimental Test," *Social Problems* (1973), pp. 490–495; William Bailey, "Certainty of Arrest and Crime Rates for Major Felonies: A Research Note," *Journal of Research in Crime and Delinquency* (July 1976), pp. 145–154.

61. Eskridge, "General Deterrence," p. 3.

62. Ibid., pp. 9–10.

63. Ibid., p. 13.

64. Ibid., pp. 13–14.

65. Franklin Zimring and Gordon Hawkins, *Deterrence* (Chicago: University of Chicago Press, 1973).

66. Gennaro F. Vito and Harry E. Allen, "Shock Probation in Ohio: A Comparison of Base Expectancy Rates," *International Journal of Offender Therapy and Comparative Criminology* (January 1981), pp. 70–75.

67. Donna Hamparian et al., *The Violet Few* (Lexington, Mass.: Lexington Books, 1978).

68. Lyle W. Shannon, *Assessing the Relationship of Adult Criminal Careers to Juvenile Careers: A Summary* (Washington, D.C.: U.S. Government Printing Office, 1982).

69. William Gaylin and David J. Rothman, "Introduction" to von Hirsh, *Doing Justice,* p. xxxix.

70. Francis A. Allen, *The Decline of the Rehabilitation Ideal* (New Haven: Yale University Press, 1981), p. 69.

71. Francis T. Cullen and Karen E. Gilbert, *Reaffirming Rehabilitation* (Cincinnati: Anderson Publishing Company, 1982), p. 138.

INTERVIEW WITH
ERNEST VAN DEN HAAG

Crime pays for adults. It pays even more for juveniles. They'll [juveniles] take things seriously only when crime stops paying.

In this interview, Ernest van den Haag, who is acknowledged as one of the leading spokespersons for the utilitarian punishment model, talks about the role of punishment with juvenile lawbreakers. Professor van den Haag also indicates why he feels punishment will be a more effective deterrent than the present way juveniles are handled by the juvenile justice system.

Question: Is it possible to put enough cost on juveniles to deter delinquent behavior?

Van den Haag: Oh yes! I think that what we have done now is to make their crimes costless. We have given them an immunity from punishment, and then we are astonished that they would commit crime. I would abolish tomorrow all juvenile courts because they have been a terrible failure. I believe that anyone over thirteen should be dealt with in the adult court. A youth's attorney, of course, is free to maintain that the youth didn't have *mens rea* and could not form intention. The court in some cases may accept the argument and in some cases it may not.

Ernest van den Haag is the John M. Olin Professor of Jurisprudence and Public Policy at Fordham University. Previously he was Professor of Criminal Justice at the State University of New York at Albany and Professor of Social Philosophy at New York University. After education at Italian and French universities, he received an M.A. from the State University of Iowa and a Ph.D. from New York University. He has been a practicing psychoanalyst in New York for 25 years. Among his nine books, the two most recent are Punishing Criminals (1979) and The Death Penalty: A Debate (with John P. Conrad, 1983). He has published numerous articles in learned journals and law reviews. Interviewed in November 1983, and used with permission.

On an individual basis, I would certainly agree that juveniles quite often don't know what they are doing. But I don't think that one should say in general that a fourteen-year-old doesn't know what he is doing. That is nonsense! If you say it, the fourteen-year-old is encouraged. He or she, in effect, is told he can do what he wants with impunity.

Now I don't think that punishment is the only factor that influences the crime rate. There are many, many other factors, but they are much harder to manipulate. For instance, religion may be very desirable and better family upbringing is certainly desirable. But I don't quite know how to produce either. I do know how to impose punishment. It is simply the one thing that society can do directly, therefore, I am in favor of it.

Question: What role does rationality play in your position?

Van den Haag: My position is based more on incentives and disincentives than on the rationality of behavior. Whether a person is a juvenile or an adult, I think you can have disincentives for certain types of behavior and incentives for other types of behavior. Obviously, the purpose of the criminal law is to give disincentives strong enough to discourage criminal and delinquent behavior.

There is one complication though. You are not only trying to influence the behavior of the person being punished, but also you are trying to influence the behavior of others. General deterrence, which is what we mean by influencing the behavior of others, does require sufficient rationality to infer that when person X suffers punishment Y for doing act A, then if I do A, I may also experience punishment Y. So in this sense rationality is required, but it still plays a minor role in criminal activity.

Question: One of the problems of punishing juveniles is that we don't have much certainty of apprehension and conviction. How can we increase in certainty without increasing the severity?

Van den Haag: First of all, I would increase the severity. Many of our punishments are either trivial or ridiculous. I would greatly reduce the number of people put on probation. A first-time offender under some circumstances may merit probation, but we grant probation too freely.

As for increasing certainty, there are various ways to do that. First, increase the rate of apprehension. Second, increase the rate of conviction, which is much less costly. It seems to me that the rules we have made, such as the exclusionary rule and a variety of other rules, make conviction terribly difficult. The apprehension rate could be increased without much additional expense if the police were free to investigate a crime in a reasonable fashion. If police officers commit criminal acts during the process of an investigation, I think they should be punished. But I don't see why evidence gathered during an investigation should not be used in the case. The purpose of the court is to establish the truth, rather than to deter police officers from doing their jobs.

Of course, it is obvious that of all the crimes committed, only a very small percentage will ever lead to apprehension, but that percentage may be enough to deter those who can be deterred. There will always be a certain number who are undeterrable, even if we had 100 percent certainty of apprehension. We don't know what to do about these people. But I am quite satisfied with deterring those who are reasonably rational to use your term.

Question: If you want to dismantle the juvenile court, how about other parts of the juvenile system? Would you have a separate system for juveniles and adults?

Van den Haag: I would for punishment. I would not want to see a fourteen-year-old sent to prison with older prisoners. They should be separately dealt with. The punishment should be essentially the same but administered somewhere else. For those

under thirteen who commit offenses, I would deal with them, not through any court system, but through social agencies. I would hold the parents responsible. If the parents tell me they can't control their children, I would say that those who are *in loco parentis* would have to do something with the children rather than punishing them. Foster parents or institutions, whatever the case may be, could be used, but once offenders are over thirteen, then they should be treated as adults are. By the way, thirteen is an average age; you might get me to say twelve but not fourteen. Thirteen is a reasonable age and was the common law tradition.

Question: How should juveniles thirteen and over who have broken the law be treated by the justice system?

Van den Haag: I think the evidence is that highly controlled environments are more reformatory than uncontrolled environments. Whether their parents violently beat them or disregarded them altogether, juveniles got into trouble in the first place because they were in an unstructured environment. What youthful offenders need are strongly structured and controlled environments with firm clear rules and affection, but affection, of course, can't be provided by law.

So I would have a very strict environment and those who are school age would go to school within the compound. Those who are working age or prefer not to attend school should have an incentive to work. I have always been in favor of giving confined people normal wages with some deductions for room and perhaps restitution. But I don't believe very much in rehabilitation. I don't think it has ever worked anywhere. If anything can be helpful, it is to establish work habits. It gives the offender an alternative to the offense. He or she may not take it, but at least the offender *can* make a living without crime.

Then, if a person still wants to be a criminal, there is not much we can do about it. We should make it as unrewarding as we can, but for those who find a thrill in breaking the law, there isn't much we can do about it.

Question: How about corporal punishment during the period of institutionalization?

Van den Haag: I don't believe in corporal punishment at all. I think it is very hard to avoid being abused. I think our society finds corporal punishment repulsive, although I don't think in principle it is worse than anything else. In principle, forty lashes may be an easier burden than two years in prison. But I just don't think society will accept it. You see, this society believes that the person should in some sense be inviolable and that we don't want to interfere physically beyond confining the person. The only corporal punishment we occasionally use is the death penalty, and we try to inflict that without pain.

Question: One of the criticisms of your position is that ultimately it will create a more repressive system. What is your reaction to this criticism?

Van den Haag: Why is it more repressive to punish people than what we do now? I would just regulate it. No society has ever existed without punishing criminals. If you show me a way without punishing criminals, I could be persuaded, but I don't know how we could deter crime without punishment. I don't think crime has much to do with social justice at all. I think crime has much more to do with whether you are serious about apprehending and punishing criminals.

If you or I committed a crime, we might be irrational, because we stand a great deal to lose and relatively little to gain. But most of the people who commit crime have very little to lose and a lot to gain. They know that the chances of being punished are very small, so crime for them is perfectly rational.

Let me conclude by saying that currently crime pays. Crime pays for adults. It pays even more for juveniles. They'll [juveniles] take things seriously only when crime stops paying. Hard core offenders know that the chances of being punished are very small, so crime for them is perfectly rational. We must make crime irrational. It is not the criminal who is irrational; it is society.

CHAPTER 5

BIOLOGICAL AND PSYCHOLOGICAL EXPLANATIONS OF DELINQUENCY

CHAPTER OUTLINE

History and Development of Positivism in Criminology
Biological Positivism
    Early Theories of Biological Positivism
    Sociobiology or Contemporary Biological Positivism
Psychological Positivism
    Psychoanalytic Explanations of Delinquent Behavior
    Individual Differences and the Need for Classification
    Evaluation of Psychological Positivism
Policy Implications
Summary

to it was explained the as, in

// We had a fourteen-year-old sexual abuse case recently who had considerable emotional problems that were coming out in a lot of ways. She was a bomb that might explode any minute. She couldn't accept any kinds of authority whatsoever. She couldn't handle any kinds of rules, and she did basically what she wanted to do. She had huge temper tantrums. She couldn't deal with the other kids. She was in fights or arguments every day. When things didn't go her way, she became physically threatening. She displaced a great deal of her anger toward one staff member, which was really intended for her mother. \\

Social worker in a youth shelter[1]

Delinquents, according to the theories discussed in this chapter, cannot help committing their socially unacceptable behavior. They are controlled by either biological or psychological factors that cause them to become involved in delinquent behavior. The delinquent act, then, is determined by a preexisting and underlying biological or psychological condition. Yet this notion of partial or total determinism is in conflict with the concept of legal responsibility, for if an adolescent's delinquent act is determined or predisposed by antecedent conditions, then the adolescent, it stands to reason, cannot be held responsible for this behavior. Or to take this position to its logical conclusion, this determinist position denies the relevance of the legal and punishment process.[2]

This chapter begins with a broad discussion of positivism and then describes and evaluates a number of studies showing the relationship between delinquency and biological and psychological positivism. Finally, the chapter considers the policy implications for those youths who have biological or psychological problems that make it difficult for them to function in socially acceptable ways.

HISTORY AND DEVELOPMENT OF POSITIVISM IN CRIMINOLOGY

The basic issues in the debate over positivism concern whether human behavior is determined by external forces or whether humans exercise free will. These issues cannot be answered by either logic or research. The answers are a matter of faith and personal choice. If an individual has faith that one answer or the other is the truth, then little that anyone else can say will change that person's mind. A person tends to hear only what is compatible with existing beliefs and will tend to discount even the best argument, rationale, and logic presented in favor of the opposite views. Similar positions of belief are found even in science.[3]

Human behavior is but one more facet of a universe that is part of a natural order, but human beings can study behavior and discover how natural laws operate. Two positions diverge at this point of natural law. One view states that, since a natural order with its own laws exists, changing human behavior is impossible. Proponents of this position argue that science should be used only to discover what these laws are so that no one will attempt to interfere with them. The other view is that, just as laws operate in the medical, biological and physical sciences, laws govern human behavior, and these can be understood and used. The causes of human behavior, once discovered, can be modified to eliminate or ameliorate many of society's problems. This second position is the one accepted by most scientists. The concept, as it applies to juvenile justice, is called positivism.

Positivism became the dominant philosophical perspective of juvenile justice at the time the juvenile court was established at the beginning of the twentieth century. During the Progressive Era (the period from 1890 to 1920), the wave of optimism that swept through American society led to the acceptance of positivism. The doctrines of the emerging social sciences assured reformers that through positivism their problems could be solved. The initial step was to gather all the "facts" of the case. Equipped with these data, reformers were then expected to analyze the issues in "scientific" fashion and discover the right solution.[4]

Armed with these principles, reformers set out to deal with the problem of delinquency confident that they knew how to find the cause. Progressives looked first to environmental factors, pinpointing poverty as the major cause of delinquency. Some Progressives were attracted also to the doctrine of eugenics and believed that the biological limitations of youthful offenders drove them to delinquency. But eventually the psychological origins of delinquency came to be more widely accepted than either the environmental or biological origins.[5]

Positivism has three basic assumptions.[6] First, the character and personal backgrounds of individuals explain delinquent behavior. Positivism, relegating the law and its administration to a secondary role, looks for the cause of deviancy in the actor.

Second, the existence of scientific determinism is a critical assumption of positivism. Delinquency, like any other phenomenon, is seen as determined by prior causes; it does not just happen. Because of this hard determinism, positivism rejects the view that the individual exercises freedom, possesses reason, and is capable of choice.

Third, the delinquent is seen as fundamentally different from the nondelinquent. The task then is to identify the factors that have made the delinquent a different kind of person. In attempting to explain this difference, positivism has concluded that the wayward youth is driven into crime "by something in his physical makeup, by aberrant psychological impulses, or by the meanness and harshness of his social environment."[7]

BIOLOGICAL POSITIVISM

The attention given to biological positivism in America may be divided into two periods. The first period was characterized by the nature-nurture debate during the latter part of the nineteenth century and the early twentieth century. Sociobiology, the name usually given the second and more recent period, has stressed the interaction between the biological factors within an individual and the influence of the particular environment.

Early Theories of Biological Positivism

Lombroso's theory of physical anomalies, genealogical studies, and theories of human somatotypes, or body types, represent early approaches relating crime and delinquency to biological factors.

Lombroso and Biological Positivism

Cesare Lombroso, who is frequently regarded as the founding father of biological positivism, is best known for this theory of the atavistic criminal. According to Lombroso, the atavistic or "born" criminal was a reversion to an earlier evolutionary form or level; that is, the characteristics of primitive men periodically reappeared in certain individuals.[8] Lombroso claimed that he discovered the secret of criminal behavior when he was examining the skull of the notorious criminal Vihella:

he said—

> This was not merely an idea, but a flash of inspiration. At the sight of that skull, I seemed to see all of a sudden, lighted up as a vast plain under a flaming sky, the problem of the nature of the criminal—an atavistic being who reproduces in his person the ferocious instincts of primitive humanity and the inferior animals. Thus were explained anatomically the enormous jaws, high cheek bones, prominent superciliary arches, solitary lines in the palms, extreme size of the orbits, handle-shaped or sensile ears found in criminals, savages, and apes, insensibility to pain, extremely acute sight, tattooing, excessive idleness, love of orgies, and the irresistible craving for evil for its own sake, the desire not only to extinguish life in the victim, but to mutilate the corpse, tear its flesh, and drink its blood.[9]

Initially, Lombroso insisted that all criminals or delinquents were "born" or atavistic, but study of several thousand criminals led him to modify his theory. In 1897, by the time of the fifth edition of his book *L'Uomo Delinquente*, he had reduced his estimate of the percentage of born criminals to 40 percent. In addition to the born criminal, Lombroso also included in his classification epileptic criminals, insane criminals, and occasional criminals. This latter group was led to engage in crime by association with other criminals, by poor education, or by inspiration of patriotism, love, honor, or political ideas.[10]

Lombroso's theory of the biological inferiority of criminals lost much of its credibility when Enrico Ferri, one of Lombroso's students, found that 63 percent of Italian soldiers showed some of the same physical signs of degeneration.[11] Furthermore, Charles Goring, in a study of 3000 English convicts, along with students and sailors serving as controls, concluded that his results did not confirm Lombroso's assertions concerning the atavistic, or biologically inferior, criminal.[12]

Lombroso's theory has also been criticized on a number of other grounds. His statistical techniques, many critics have noted, were totally inadequate. Similarly, the physical signs, which Lombroso claimed identified the born criminal, have frequently been pointed out as the result of social environment and poor nutrition rather than as part of the constitutional makeup of the person. In addition, contemporary genetic theory has totally rejected the possibility of an evolutionary throwback to earlier more primitive species. Finally, critics charge that individuals with pronounced physical abnormalities are more likely to be arrested than those without such visible markings.[13]

Although Lombroso's theories of the atavistic criminal have not stood the test of scientific investigation, he did make two significant contributions to the study of juvenile delinquency. First, he provided the impetus to study the individual offender rather than the crimes committed by the person. Second, his manner of studying the criminal, which involved control groups and a desire to have his theories tested impartially, influenced the development of the scientific method.

Genealogical Studies and Delinquency

In 1877, Richard Dugdale did a detailed genealogical study of the Jukes family covering some 1200 persons and spanning nearly a century. He documented an extensive theory of "pauperism, prostitution, exhaustion, disease, fornication, and illegitimacy." This study is sometimes cited as providing evidence for the hereditary nature of crime, but only 76 of the 709 individuals traced had evidence of criminal records. Indeed, even Dugdale concluded that "environment is the ultimate controlling factor in determining [criminal] careers."[14]

In 1913, H. H. Goddard conducted another now-well-known genealogical study in a training school in New Jersey for "feebleminded" boys and girls. Upon investigating the family history of one of the wards, Deborah Kallikak, Goddard discovered that she was a descendant of a brief union between a Revolutionary War soldier and a feebleminded girl. He was able to locate 484 descendants of this union, of whom 143 were feebleminded and several were alcoholics and prostitutes. The same soldier had later married a Quaker girl and fathered a long line of upstanding citizens. Impressed by these findings, Goddard concluded that "bad stock" was the cause of feeblemindedness and that such persons should not be permitted to reproduce. Interestingly, in spite of the large number of feebleminded persons in the Kallikak family, only three of the 484 were criminals.[15]

These genealogical studies received little support, but Goddard's finding that at least half of all juvenile delinquents were mental defectives generated intense debate for over a decade.[16] William Healy and Augusta Bronner were supporters of the correlation between low intelligence and delinquent behavior. In 1926, they tested a group of delinquents in Chicago and Boston and concluded that delinquents were five to ten times more likely to be mentally deficient than were nondelinquents.[17] But the findings of John Slawson and Edwin Sutherland discouraged future investigations of the correlation between intelligence and delinquency. Slawson, studying 1543 delinquent boys in New York institutions and comparing them with a control group of New York City boys, found that delinquents were about normal in mechanical aptitude and nonverbal intelligence and lower in abstract verbal intelligence. He also found that no relationships existed among the number of arrests, the types of offenses, and IQ.[18] Edwin Sutherland, evaluating IQ studies of delinquents and criminals, concluded that the lower IQs of offenders were related more to testing methods and scoring than to the actual mental ability of offenders.[19]

Body Type Theories of Delinquency

Ernst Kretscher, a German, first developed the theory that there are two body types, the cyclothyme and the schizothyme. Schizothymes are strong and muscular, and they are more likely to be delinquent than are cyclothymes, who are soft-skinned and lack muscle.[20]

William Sheldon, author of *Varieties of Delinquent Youth*, was the first American researcher to examine the relationship between body type and delinquent behavior. Sheldon described three body types: *endomorphic* (soft, round, and fat); *mesomorphic* (bony, muscular, and athletic); and *ectomorphic* (tall, thin, and fragile). Sheldon postulated that these somatotypes had temperamental correlates. He investigated with great thoroughness 200 delinquent boys whose ages ranged from fifteen to twenty-four years. He found that the delinquents were more likely to be mesomorphic and less likely to be ectomorphic. The temperamental correlations with mesomorphy pertained to such characteristics as social assertiveness, lesser submissiveness to authority, and less-inhibited motor responses.[21] The main criticism of Sheldon's method was that using photographs was too subjective to inspire confidence in its accuracy.

Glueck and Glueck's *Physique and Delinquency* is the result of comprehensive research into persistent delinquency. They studied the causes of delinquency through a comparison of 500 persistent delinquents and 500 proven nondelinquents. Their comparison of the delinquent group with the nondelinquent group indicated marked and significant differences regarding their somatotypes (60.1 percent of the delinquents were mesomorphic as compared to 30.7 percent of the nondelinquents). "Among the delinquents, mesomorphy is far and away the most dominant component," they found, "with ectomorphic, endomorphic, and balanced types about equally represented but in relatively minor strength."[22]

Juan B. Cortes criticized the Gluecks' study for the following reasons: First, all the delinquents studied were committed to correctional institutions; in other words, the results may apply to institutionalized delinquents but not to delinquents in general. Second, the method used to estimate the somatotype was unreliable. Third, the age of the 500 delinquents ranged from nine to seventeen, with an average age of fourteen years and six months; the problem with somatotyping youths this age is the general acceleration of growth and morphological changes that take place during this period.[23]

Evaluation of Early Biological Positivism

The primitiveness of the research techniques of the early biological positivists won them few supporters. Little evidence now exists that the findings of these biological positivists have any relation to delinquent behavior. Lombroso's theory that the delinquent has distinctive physical features was quickly dismissed. The theory that criminal genes are inherited was also discredited by most biologists and social scientists. So were the body type theories, because they ignored the importance of environment in the development of the body structure of adolescents. Indeed, R. L. Means, discussing the neglect of biological influences in sociology, notes that the rule in the field appears to have been to attack biological determinism and thereby "liberate" sociology from any consideration of biological factors.[24]

Sociobiology or Contemporary Biological Positivism

Sociobiology differs from other theories of biological determinism because it links genetic and environmental factors. That is, sociobiology claims that delinquent behavior, like other behaviors, has both biological and social correlates. Recent advances in experimental behavior genetics, human population genetics, the biochemistry of the nervous system, experimental and clinical endocrinology and neurophysiology, and many related areas have led to more sophisticated knowledge of the way the environment affects the growth, development, and functioning of the human organism.[25] This recent explosion of knowledge concerning the variety of factors influencing human behavior has caused a number of criminologists to endorse enthusiastically biosocial theories.[26] Indeed, the 1978 meeting of the American Society of Criminology addressed the genetic foundations of antisocial behavior, the role of brain damage and psychopathology in delinquency, the relationship of low intelligence to delinquency, and the biochemical approaches to antisocial behavior.[27]

Sociobiologists have investigated the relationship between antisocial behavior and biological factors and environment through studies of twins and adoption, chromosomal abnormalities, electrodermal activity and psychopathy, minimal brain functioning, intelligence, physique, and orthomolecular imbalances. Researchers of the first three areas, twins and adoption, chromosomal abnormalities, and electrodermal activity, have focused more on adult criminality, while those investigating minimal brain functioning, intelligence, physique, and orthomolecular imbalances have examined primarily the relationship between sociobiology and juvenile delinquency. Minimal brain damage, or the existence of certain learning or behavioral disabilities associated with nervous system dysfunctioning, will be discussed in Chapter 11; the relationship between intelligence, physique, and orthomolecular imbalances and delinquency will be examined in the following section.

Intelligence

With the increasing popularity of sociobiology in the 1960s and 1970s, intelligence was again examined as a factor in delinquent behavior. D. J. West and D. P. Farrington conducted a longitudinal study of 411 English boys on the Raven Progressive Matrices, and this study found that those who later became criminals were characterized by lower IQs than were those who did not. The authors concluded that intelligence is a meaningful predictive factor of future delinquency.[28] Lis Kirkegaard-Sorensen and Sarnoff A. Mednick also conducted a longitudinal study on the value of adolescent intelligence test scores for the prediction of later criminality. They found that adolescents who committed criminal acts later had a lower tested intelligence score than their more law-abiding peers.[29] Robert Gordon, in comparing delinquency prevalence rates and delinquency incidence rates, concluded that nonwhite juvenile males had higher arrest rates and court appearance rates than white males or females, regardless of any specific geographical location, rural or urban. He proposed that differences in IQ may provide the greatest explanation of these persistent differences in unlawful behavior.[30]

Travis Hirschi and Michael Hindelang reexamined a number of research studies—Hirschi's 1969 data from California, Wolfgang and associates' Philadelphia data, and Weiss's data from the state of Washington, and found that "the weight of evidence is that IQ is more important than race and social class" for predicting delinquency. These researchers also rejected the contention that IQ tests are race- and class-biased in that they favor middle-class whites and are therefore invalid means of comparing lower- and middle-class youths. They concluded that low IQ affects school performance, resulting in an increased likelihood of delinquent behavior.[31]

Sociologists thought that the IQ issue was dead in the mid-1930s when the studies consistently challenged the relationship between IQ and delinquency, but recent studies have resurrected the issue. Unquestionably, whatever the correlation between IQ and delinquency, the association is strengthened by other environmental factors, such as performance in school.

Physique or Constitutional Factors and Delinquency

Some constitutional factors are more directly related to delinquent behavior than others. For example, structural disorders of the limbic system demonstrate that focal brain disease can alter the propensities of the human organism. Epilepsy-related disorders also can clearly affect the behavior of individuals. Furthermore, hormones, especially those related to sexual reproduction, have been cited as affecting the propensity of delinquent behavior in an individual.[32] Studies by Juan B. Cortes and Florence M. Gatti on body type and by Hans Eysenck on the autonomous nervous system are more indirectly related to delinquency, but they both have received wide attention.

In a 1972 study, Cortes and Gatti drew on body type theory in a biopsychosocial theory of delinquency. They examined the body types of 100 delinquent boys, 100 nondelinquent boys, and 20 criminals and found that the delinquents were decidedly more mesomorphic and somewhat less endomorphic and ectomorphic than the boys in the nondelinquent sample.[33] But Cortes and Gatti carried the discussion further than the earlier body type theorists had. They emphasized that these findings did not tell anything about the cause and effect but showed only that a greater proportion of persons with strong physiques were delinquents.[34] In developing a biopsychosocial theory of delinquency and criminality, they stated that "criminal and delinquent behaviors are the result of a negative imbalance within the individual in the interaction between (a) the expressive forces of his psychological and biological characteristics and (b) the normative forces of familial, religious, and sociocultural factors."[35]

Thus, they concluded that the answer to the problem of delinquency rests in the interaction between the particular personality and the particular environment, or even more to the point, the particular reaction of *some* persons to elements in their environment.[36] They listed some of the variables that affect either the personality or the environment, or both:

1. Mesomorphic physique—the physical component is clearly associated with delinquency.

2. Psychological deficiencies—these include defective ego and superego.

3. Excessive needs—these include addiction to narcotics or to alcohol, and other physiological needs such as hunger and sex.

4. Differential association—this involves learning crime from others.

5. Frustrations—increased frustrations enhance the likelihood of delinquent behavior.

6. Various pressures—some crimes are committed because of fear, jealousy, blackmail, or economic pressures.

7. Low intrinsic religiosity—low religiousness tends to lead to delinquency and delinquent behavior to lower religiosity.

8. Quality of family life—delinquents come from homes of conflict more so than do nondelinquents.

9. Social disorganization—the breakdown of the normative system by which behavior is regulated increases the chances of delinquency.

10. Opportunities—delinquency is related to opportunities or chances to become involved in this behavior.

11. Low social morality—cultural conflict is also related to delinquent behavior.[37]

Cortes and Gatti's interaction model is in some ways impressive. Their more advanced body type theory involves a variety of psychological and sociological variables, as well as an examination of the physique. But these researchers include so much that one wonders whether they end up with anything specific. In addition, some of the variables they identify as significant, such as religiosity, have received little support in the literature.

Hans Eysenck's theory of the autonomous nervous system, like body type theory, has its origins in the earlier attempts to understand the relationship between constitutional factors and delinquency. But his sociobiological theory goes one step further in relating the importance of both biological and environmental factors. Eysenck contends that some children are more difficult to condition than others because of the inherited sensitivity of their autonomous nervous systems. Yet the conditioning of the child or developing of a conscience in a child also depends on the quality of the conditioning the child receives within the family. Eysenck argues that types of individuals range from those in whom it is easy to excite conditioned reflexes and whose reflexes are difficult to inhibit to those whose reflexes are difficult to condition and easy to extinguish.[38]

Individuals whose consciences or autonomic nervous systems are more difficult to condition tend to be extroverts rather than introverts. The extrovert is much more likely, according to Eysenck, to become involved in delinquent behavior. Eysenck sees the extrovert as a person who craves excitement, takes chances, acts on the spur of the moment, and frequently is impulsive. He also believes that the extrovert tends to be aggressive and loses his or her temper quickly, is unable to keep his or her feelings under tight control, and is not always reliable.[39]

Eysenck's theory has come under extensive criticism. Hoghughi and Forrest point to the finding that youthful offenders are frequently more introverted than are members of control groups.[40] His research techniques also have faced strong criticism. Taylor et al. accuse him of errors of computation, biased samples that forbid any generalizations, scales with built-in biases that do not measure what they are purported to measure, unexplained inconsistencies within the data, misinterpretations and contradictions in representing the research of others, and unjustifiable manipulation of the data. They further argue that even if it were true that the physical basis of behavior lay in the reflexes of the autonomic nervous system, that fact would not explain the meaning the behavior has for the actor.[41]

Eysenck's theory does make sense on two levels. First, children are different, as any parent knows, and it is plausible that it is more difficult to help some develop moral values than others. Certainly, sufficient family histories are available to ascertain that "good" and "bad" kids sometimes exist in the same family. Second, parents do vary in their effectiveness in developing moral values in their children. But the danger of Eysenck's theory—which is the danger of all genetic theories—is the assumption that humans are malleable and conditionable and that meaning as defined by the individual is not important. The other major flaw in this theory is related to the basic concept of the autonomic nervous system itself: merely because autonomic nervous systems differ does not mean that these differences can be directly related to deviant behavior in later life.

Orthomolecular Imbalances

The term *orthomolecular* comes from two Greek words meaning "to correct the chemical imbalances in the body." Orthomolecular research has shown that some delinquent behavior can be attributed to chemical imbalances in the body or to brain toxicity. Biochemists explain such delinquent behavior through the fact that the normal functioning of the brain is affected by diet and/or genetic deficiencies, so that abnormal deficits or excesses in molecular brain concentrations lead to various mental and behavioral problems.[42] Abraham Hoffer, the father of the orthomolecular movement, adds that two symptoms result from chemical imbalances in the body: changes in perception, and hyperactivity.[43]

The connection between orthomolecular imbalances and delinquent behavior is currently receiving increased attention in the juvenile justice system.[44] Barbara Reed, a probation officer in Cuyahoga Falls County, Ohio, was one of the pioneers in investigating the association between inadequate diet and delinquent behavior. She reports that she herself suffered from dizzy spells and from serious health problems until she discovered that her inadequate diet was causing the breakdown of her physical health. She then cut out all sugar, caffeine, and refined foods, and, feeling so much better herself, began to prescribe this diet to probationers. Her results were impressive enough that judges began to assign problem probationers to her.[45]

Several studies have found that high amounts of lead in a person's system can result in increased delinquent behavior. Lead in extreme amounts can be fatal, and in smaller amounts it will cause negative behavior.[46] Other studies have found that allergies and stimulation by certain colors are directly related to negative behavior.[47]

The acceptance of the idea that chemical imbalances in the body, resulting from poor nutrition, allergies, or exposure to lead and certain colors, certainly owes p of its popularity to the health consciousness of the American society at the present time. However, the link between faulty nutrition and delinquent or criminal behavior is very weak. While a faulty diet and vitamin deficiencies may affect how a juvenile feels, it does not necessarily follow that the adolescent will become involved in delinquent behavior.

Evaluation of Sociobiology

Sociobiological theory is based upon several assumptions. First, the belief that all human beings are born with equal potential to learn and achieve is rejected, and biological differences are recognized. Second, sociobiologists place a strong emphasis on learning, but caution that the physical and social environment interact to limit or to enhance a person's capacity for learning. Third, sociobiologists emphasize the importance of the biological environment as a means of preventing crime and delinquency.[48]

The relationship between sociobiology and delinquent behavior is generating extensive debate today. C. R. Jeffrey, a criminologist and one of the proponents of sociobiology, goes so far as to propose that the biosocial interdisciplinary model should become the major theoretical framework for dealing with the prevention and control of crime and delinquency:

> [I]t must be noted that our rejection of new knowledge about human behavior, at a time when we are burning people at the stake, creates an impossible moral dilemma. Today much of the opposition to sociobiology is couched in moralistic and ethical terms. It is assumed that humanistic man cannot coexist with scientific man. The present state of world affairs suggests that perhaps we had better join the two. We have examples of an emerging bioethics, as found in The Self and Its Brain by Karl Popper, a philosopher and historian, and John Eccles, a brain scientist. Another example is The Biological Origin of Human Values by George Pugh. The ethical and social systems that appear in the Bible or in Plato's Republic, and are part of man's history, were originally a product of genetic evolution and the human brain. We cannot separate man's ethical and social systems from his brain and biological system.[49]

However, the majority of criminologists are reluctant to accept sociobiological theories for several reasons. First, the physical processes through which behavior can be inherited have not been defined and remain only speculative. Second, most criminologists are fearful that the moral and legal concepts of responsibility will be eroded further in juvenile justice if determinism by heredity forces is accepted. Third, the transformation of delinquency into a medical problem appears to represent a return to the much-maligned medical or rehabilitation model, and criminologists are concerned about the new possibilities for abuse under the guise of treatment.[50]

;ICAL POSITIVISM

Although biological factors have been given little credibility as a cause of delinquent behavior until the present, psychological factors have long been popular in the study of juvenile delinquency. Part of the reason for the early acceptance of psychological factors can be traced to the influence of the Progressive Movement and the medical model that emerged from this movement. Also, psychological positivism is accepted because of the *parens patriae* philosophy, since the very nature of that model requires treatment of wayward youth. Further, psychological positivism is popular because youths do appear to be influenced by emotional factors in their socially unacceptable behavior. That is, there are too many examples of youthful offenders who commit compulsive-obsessional acts, who become involved in irrational behavior, and who repeat endlessly the same self-destructive behaviors.

Psychoanalytic theory was first most widely used with delinquents, but, more recently, other behavior and humanistic schools of psychology have been applied to the problem of youth crime.

Psychoanalytic Explanations of Delinquent Behavior

Sigmund Freud, the founder of psychoanalysis, contributed three insights that have profoundly shaped the handling of juvenile delinquents: (1) the personality is made up of three components; (2) all normal children pass through three psychosexual stages of development; and (3) the personality traits of a person are developed in early childhood.

Freud's theory of the personality involves the id, the ego, and the superego. The id refers to the raw instincts and primitive drives of the person. The id wants immediate gratification of its needs and, therefore, tends to be primitive and savage. The ego and superego, the other two components, have the express purpose of controlling the primitive drives of the id. The ego mediates between the id and superego and is important in the socialization of the child. The superego, or the conscience, internalizes the rules of society. Thus, as a child develops, he or she learns to distinguish socially acceptable behavior from socially unacceptable behavior.[51]

Freud identified the oral, the anal, and the phallic stages as the life stages that shape personality development. The first stage, the oral one, is experienced by the newborn infant. Pleasure is experienced in this stage through eating, sucking, and chewing. In the anal stage, which takes place between one and three years of age, urinary and bowel movements replace sucking as the basic source of pleasure for the child. During the phallic stage, which takes place in normal children between the ages three to six, the child receives pleasure from the genitals. Each stage brings increased social demands on the child and affects the way in which he or she deals with basic, innate drives. The sexual and aggressive drives, in particular, create tensions that a child must learn to gratify in socially acceptable ways.[52]

Freud also argued that by the age five, all of the essential ingredients of a child's adult personality are determined. That is, the "child is father of the man"; what a child has experienced emotionally by the age of five will affect that child the rest of his or her life. This deterministic viewpoint proposes that emotional traumas experienced in childhood will cause life-long psychological problems.[53]

Freud, who believed that human nature was basically evil, devoted little attention to crime and delinquency. But his followers have identified four ways in which emotional problems developed in childhood might lead to delinquent behavior.[54]

First, delinquent behavior is related to neurotic development in the personality. Freud established a relationship between desire and behavior; that is, everything is integrated in the subconscious, and external behavior is only an expression of the subconscious drives of the organism. A youth may feel guilty over a socially unacceptable desire, such as an incestuous craving for sex with a parent, or over an act he or she committed in the past. Thus, according to Freudian theory, he or she will seek punishment to expiate the feelings of guilt. For example, an incident that lends itself to a Freudian explanation concerns a delinquent who was trying to avoid the sheriff's deputies in an automobile when one of the deputies fired at him. The deputy missed him, but the boy's younger brother who was also in the car was hit and permanently paralyzed. Subsequently, this delinquent continued to be involved in self-defeating behavior. He would immediately follow up a good event in his life by inappropriate and self-defeating behavior.[55]

Second, delinquent behavior is attributed to a defective superego. The inability to develop a normally functioning superego can result in the inability to feel guilt, to learn from experience, or to feel affection toward others.[56] Such individuals, sometimes called sociopathic or psychopathic, may constantly express aggressive and asocial behavior toward others. One youth who was labeled a sociopath had a long history of aggressive behavior toward others. In one event, he knifed a youth who got into his way in the corridor of school. Upon being questioned why he had done that, he merely said, "He got in my way." Then, the youth was asked, "Did you have any bad experiences with this youth? Were you angry with him for any reason?" The youth responded, "No, I didn't even know him, but he got in my way." The institutional social worker questioned, "Do you feel you have the right to knife anyone who gets in your way?" The youth answered, "I'll knife anyone who gets in my way."[57]

Third, violent delinquent behavior is sometimes explained by the tendency of children with an overly developed superego to repress all negative emotional feelings throughout childhood, so that these repressed feelings explode in a violent act at a later point in adolescence. For example, model adolescents occasionally become involved in violent crimes toward parents and neighbors, sometimes horribly mutilating their victims.

Fourth, delinquent involvements can be related to a search for compensatory gratification. According to Freud, children who were deprived at an early stage of development will later seek the gratification which they missed. Thus, an adolescent may become an alcoholic to satisfy an oral craving or may become sadistic because of poor toilet training received during the anal period.

In sum, several of Freud's theories have influenced the handling of delinquents throughout most of this century: failure to develop an adequate superego, or conscience, will result in antisocial behavior; moral maturity and responsibility are developed as a child moves through a series of developmental stages and avoids being fixated at infantile stages; and early childhood experiences produce deeply ingrained and enduring personality traits in the individual.

Modifications of Psychoanalytic Theory

William Healy, a psychiatrist at the turn of the twentieth century, was profoundly influenced by psychoanalytic theory. His particular adaptation of this theory was to focus upon mental conflicts that originated in unsatisfactory family relationships. Healy pioneered the establishment of psychiatric child guidance clinics in several U.S. cities under the auspices of the Commonwealth Fund Program for the Prevention of Delinquency. Although Healy specified the source of such mental conflicts to originate in the child's family relationships, he also realized the importance of the community in modifying delinquent behavior.[58]

August Aichhorn, another proponent of psychoanalytic theory, also worked extensively with youth in trouble. He emphasized the importance of transference. He thought that delinquents had considerable hatred toward their parents because of the conflictual nature of the family relationship and that they transferred this hatred toward parents to other authority figures. Aichhorn attempted to utilize transference and to permit youngsters to satisfy their impulses while under the guidance of a therapist they could rely on and trust. He believed that institutionalized delinquents, exposed to the love and acceptance of a therapeutic relationship, would learn to trust one adult figure and, in turn, would learn to respond more appropriately with other adults.[59]

Kate Friedlander provided another psychoanalytic approach to treating delinquents. She focused upon the development of antisocial characteristics in the personality, such as selfishness, impulsiveness, and irresponsibility, which she defined as the results of disturbed ego development in early childhood. Thus, delinquency becomes an alternative way of fulfilling desires the youth is unwilling to express directly.[60]

In short, a number of individuals have taken the insights of psychoanalysis and applied them to the real world situation. Although most psychotherapists today no longer hold to all the principles of psychoanalysis, this movement has deeply influenced the understanding of how delinquents in this nation should be handled.

Individual Differences and the Need for Classification

Psychological positivists throughout this century have devoted enormous energies to understanding delinquent behavior. Early classification schemes grouped delinquents into those having psychoses, psychoneuroses, and personality disorders. Psychotic persons are disorganized mentally, and they are frequently institutionalized. Psychoneuroses are disorders that develop because of anxiety and unresolved conflict within the personality. Personality disorders are usually traced to the failure to develop normal social controls in childhood. The most important group of personality disorders is that encompassing antisocial or psychopathic personalities.[61]

The psychopath (or sociopath, antisocial personality, or a host of other names) is acknowledged as the personality of the hard-core juvenile delinquent. The claim is made that these are chiefly the unwanted, rejected children, who grow up but remain as undomesticated children and never develop trust or loyalty to an adult.[62] Hervey Cleckley gave the most complete clinical description of this type of personality. He listed sixteen characteristics he had noted in his practice:

1. The psychopath is charming and of good intelligence.
2. He is not delusional or irrational.
3. There is an absence of nervousness or psychoneurotic manifestations.
4. The psychopath is unreliable.
5. He is insecure, and he is a liar who can be trusted no more in his accounts of the past than in his promises for the future.
6. He is lacking in either shame or remorse.
7. His antisocial behavior is inadequately motivated. He will commit all kinds of misdeeds for astonishingly small stakes, and sometimes for no reason at all.
8. His judgment is poor, and he never learns from experience. He will repeat over and over again patterns of self-defeating behavior
9. He is pathologically egocentric and has no real capacity for love, although he often simulates affection or parental devotion.
10. His emotions are shallow.
11. The psychopath lacks insight to a degree usually found only in the most serious mental disorders.
12. He does not respond to consideration, kindness, or trust.
13. Drunk or sober, but especially when drunk, he is guilty of fantastic and uninviting behavior.
14. Psychopaths often threaten suicide but almost never carry it out.
15. The psychopath's sex life is impersonal, trivial, and poorly integrated.
16. The psychopath shows a consistent inability to make or follow any sort of life plan.[63]

In another classification scheme, Richard J. Jenkins distinguished two broad types of delinquency: adaptive and maladaptive. Adaptive delinquency is defined as more or less planned, motivational behavior; that is, it has a purpose and is intent on pursuing that purpose. In contrast, maladaptive delinquency is defined as a stereotyped frustration response. "It is automatic rather than planful, explosive rather than considered, and stereotyped rather than flexible." The subject's emotional state interferes with his or her capacity to learn. The maladaptive delinquent repeats behavior of the past, which rather than being rewarding, tends to produce further frustration.[64]

Sheldon Glueck and Eleanor Glueck's study in *Unraveling Juvenile Delinquency* examined a sample of 500 juvenile offenders and 500 nonoffenders in an effort to discover significant distinctions in the personality traits of the two groups. The Gluecks found that the delinquents were more defiant, ambivalent about authority, extroverted, fearful of failure, resentful, hostile, suspicious, and defensive than the nondelinquents. The Rorschach test (which is used to determine personality structure through subjects' responses to ink blots) were used as the basis of the Gluecks' assessment.[65]

The Minnesota Multiphasic Personality Inventory (MMPI) has also been used to differentiate the personality traits of delinquents and nondelinquents. Hathaway and Monachesi, administering the MMPI to a sample of delinquents and nondelinquents, found that male and female delinquents tend to score high on scales indicating paranoia, psychopathic deviance, and hypomania (the subject is overproductive in both thought and action). But none of the other scales were closely associated with delinquency.[66] See Table 5-1 for a summary of biological, sociobiological, and psychological theories of delinquency.

Evaluation of Psychological Positivism

Two questions must be answered to evaluate accurately the effect of psychological positivism: First, do personality differences between delinquents and nondelinquents actually exist? Second, do psychological problems cause delinquent behavior?

Three major studies have generally concluded that there are few personality differences between delinquents and nondelinquents. First, Schuessler and Cressey reviewed studies related to personality characteristics of criminals or delinquents and noncriminals or nondelinquents and found that it is impossible to determine significant differences between criminal and noncriminal personalities.[67] Waldo and Dinitz, examining ninety-four additional studies, reported that in 81 percent of the studies, a statistical difference existed between a criminal group and noncriminal group, but they contended that the methodological weaknesses of the studies make any reliable conclusions difficult.[68] Tennenbaum also reviewed personality studies from 1966 to 1975 and presented results similar to those of Waldo and Dinitz. He found that "personality tests, per se, are no better predictors of criminal personalities now than were those of ten years ago."[69]

Second, as Richard Jenkins explained, a great deal of delinquency is committed by youths who appear as normal psychologically as nondelinquents do.[70] But psychological positivism, according to supporters, can help explain the behavior of deeply disturbed delinquents, compulsive-obsessive behavior in delinquents, and the repeated failures of some delinquents. The problem is that the popularity of psychological positivism has resulted in the forced administration of treatment to all delinquents. Some youths need treatment and do profit from it, but little positive results take place with countless others who do not want or need such interventions. Indeed, sometimes treatment does more damage than it does good.

POLICY IMPLICATIONS

An important issue for policymakers concerns the best way to deal with violent juvenile behavior. Biological and psychological positivists do not accept the punishment-oriented approach to violent behavior proposed in the last chapter. They argue

TABLE 5-1 Summary of Biological, Sociobiological, and Psychological Theories of Delinquency

The Theory	Cause of Delinquency Identified	Supporting Research
Lombroso and the born delinquent	The atavistic criminal is a reversion to an earlier evolutionary form or level	Weak
Genealogical studies	Heredity	Weak
Body type theories	Mesomorphic body type	Weak
Intelligence	IQ is a meaningful predictive factor in delinquent behavior when combined with environmental factors	Moderate
Eysenck and the autonomic nervous system	The insensitivity of the autonomic nervous system, as well as the faulty conditioning of parents, leads to delinquent behavior	Weak
Orthomolecular imbalances	Chemical imbalances in the body, resulting from poor nutrition; allergies; and exposure to lead and certain colors lead to delinquency	Weak
Psychoanalytic theory (Sigmund Freud)	Unconscious motivations resulting from early childhood experiences	Weak
Psychoanalytic theory (William Healy)	Mental conflicts originating in unsatisfactory family relationships	Weak
Psychoanalytic theory (August Aichhorn)	Hatred toward parents transferred to other authority figures	Weak
Psychotic breakdown	Disorganized mentally resulting in socially unacceptable behavior	Weak
Psychoneurotic personality	Disorders originating because of anxiety and unresolved conflict within the personality	Weak
Psychopathic personality	Unwanted, rejected children growing up without trusting or being loyal to others	Moderate

that children are sociobiologically or psychologically predisposed to violence, and thus cannot be held responsible for this behavior. But they do agree that society must be protected from predatory behavior. A possible solution suggested by some positivists is that children with a propensity to violence be identified early in life and placed in intervention programs.

The possibility of the prediction of violence is widely accepted because there is an abiding belief in our society that, while the details cannot be filled in, the general plot of people's lives can be outlined before the stories unfold. Many believe that the first few chapters of a person's life, infancy and childhood, incubate the themes that will be played out in all the rest. Almost every psychological theory, from the superego deficiencies of psychoanalysis to the modeling theory of behaviorists, supports this belief.[71] Biological explanations of behavior go back before birth, tracing the origins of behavior to the genetical makeup of the child.

Four statistical outcomes will occur in predicting any kind of future behavior. If the prediction is made that delinquency will occur and it does occur, the prediction is called a *true positive*. Similarly, if the prediction is made that delinquency will not occur and it does not, the prediction is called a *true negative*. If a prediction is made that an event will occur and it does not, the outcome is called a *false positive*. If the prediction is made that crime will not occur and it does, the outcome is called a *false negative*. Clearly, predictors of delinquency try to maximize the positive and minimize the negative outcomes.[72]

Three studies have tried to predict violent behavior among juveniles. Lefkowitz, Eron, Walder, and Huesman's 1977 study, delineated in *Growing Up to be Violent,* followed up a sample of over 400 males and females in Columbia County, New York, from ages eight to nineteen. Lefkowitz and his colleagues found that "aggression at age eight is the best predictor we have of aggression at age nineteen, irrespective of IQ, social class, or parents' aggressiveness." Other statistically significant variables included the father's upward social mobility, low identification of the child with parents, and a preference on the part of boys for watching violent television programs.[73] McCord reported on a thirty-year follow-up of 201 boys who had participated in the Cambridge-Somerville Youth Project between 1939 and 1945. She discovered that 36 percent of the incidence of later violent behavior could be accounted for by childhood predictive factors, and she concluded: "The boys who lacked supervision, whose mothers lacked self-confidence, who had been exposed to personal conflict and to aggression were subsequently more convicted for personal crimes."[74] Finally, Farrington and West, in a sophisticated longitudinal study of the development of delinquency, studied 411 males contacted in 1961 and 1962 when they were eight and nine years of age. In terms of violent behavior, they found that the more harsh the childrearing, the more violent the delinquency, and that aggression at age eight was highly predictive of aggression at age eighteen.[75]

These studies show that serious problems exist in predicting violence in children. First, little agreement is found concerning the characteristics associated with a certain probability of a child's becoming violent. Indeed, the only real agreement among the three studies is that aggression at age eight is the best predictor of later aggressive behavior. Second, these studies use individualistic variables to predict serious and violent delinquent behavior, and, as indicated by the contextual perspective, more than individualistic variables must be involved in predicting delinquent behavior. Third, because of the low level of knowledge available about predicting violent behavior, there is considerable danger in relying on such predictions to place youths in early intervention programs. The costs of these early intervention programs, as subsequent chapters explain, are those of labeling on a child's self-concept and the widening of the net of the juvenile justice system.

Thus, the pursuit of panaceas for youth violence goes on. Prediction and early intervention do not appear to be any more hopeful than repressive measures in dealing with youth crime. Violence in American society has emerged through the interrelationships of the five contexts on all three levels. Until policymakers begin to consider the historical, sociocultural, political, and economic reasons for violence and to design policy that will relieve these causes, no answers exist for youth violence.

SUMMARY

Both biological and psychological positivism are individualistic explanations of delinquency. The question of what causes delinquency is answered by pointing to biological or psychological factors within the individual. That is, all delinquent behavior, like other behavior, is seen as having an organic or psychological basis. The individual delinquent then is controlled by such factors and has no control over them. Sometimes the factors are very elusive, such as an autonomic nervous system that is difficult to condition or an inadequately developed superego, but others are more easily discerned, such as inappropriate interpersonal relationships. Both early biological and psychological positivism theories have developed into more complex explanations of delinquent behavior. Early biological positivism was replaced by sociobiology, and psychoanalysis was replaced by models less intrapsychic and more oriented to the interactions between the individual and the environment. In addition to being more interdisciplinary, research on the biological and psychological contributions to delinquency is more sophisticated than in the past. For example, control groups are more frequently used and longitudinal designs are beginning to emerge.[76]

The contextual perspective is helpful in understanding the present role of sociobiological and psychological positivism in dealing with delinquency in American society. Historically, sociology has minimized the role that biology, especially, has played in causing delinquent behavior. Even today, when more and more behavioral and social sciences are finding their roots in biology, sociologists continue to refer to sociobiologists as "new-Lombrosians." But in the legal context, juvenile judges have become much more receptive to biological and psychological positivism. They appear to be referring juveniles in larger numbers to mental health facilities, contending that more emotionally disturbed youths are appearing before them.[77] Juvenile judges also are more concerned about the role of learning disabilities than they have been in the past. In the sociocultural context, the public's search for easy answers to complex problems has led to some acceptance of these individualistic explanations of delinquent behavior. In the economic context, psychological counseling and services for children with learning problems are more likely to exist in the community than in institutions because middle-class children are retained in community programs and lower-class youngsters tend to be thrown to correctional institutions. But the reduction of federal funding is reducing the number of these programs. Finally, policymakers in some states are attracted to individualistic explanations of delinquency, but in other jurisdictions biological and psychological factors have not had the impact on policymakers that social factors have had.

Discussion Questions

1. Why have the early findings of biological positivism in the United States received so little support from criminologists?
2. How is sociobiology different from biological positivism? What do they have in common? What explains the increasing popularity of sociobiology?
3. Explain the contribution that Sigmund Freud made to psychological positivism.
4. Describe the sociopath or psychopath. Why are sociopaths so difficult to treat?

References

Aichhorn, August. *Delinquency and Child Guidance*. New York: International University Press, 1964.

Cortes, Juan B., with Gatti, Florence M. *Delinquency and Crime: A Biopsychosocial Approach: Empirical, Theoretical, and Practical Aspects of Criminal Behavior*. New York: Seminar Press, 1972.

Erikson, Erik. *Identity, Youth and Crisis*. New York: W. W. Norton, 1966.

Eysenck, H. J. *Crime and Personality*. 2nd ed. London: Routledge and Kegan Paul, 1977.

Freud, Sigmund. *A General Introduction to Psycho-Analysis*. Translated by Joan Riviere. New York: Liveright, 1935.

Glueck, S., and Glueck, E. *Unraveling Juvenile Delinquency*. Cambridge: Harvard University Press, 1950.

Hippchen, Leonard, ed. *Ecologic-Biochemical Approaches to Treatment of Delinquents and Criminals*. New York: Van Nostrand Reinhold Company, 1978.

Hirschi, Travis, and Hindelang, Michael J. "Intelligence and Delinquency: A Revisionist Review," *American Sociological Review* 42 (1977): 571–587.

Jeffery, C. R., ed. *Biology and Crime*. Beverly Hills, Calif.: Sage Publications, 1979.

Jenkins, Richard L., and Boyer, Andrew. "Type of Delinquent Behavior and Background Factors," *The International Journal of Social Psychiatry* 14 (1967): 66–76.

Mednick, Sarnoff A., and Christiansen, Karl O., eds. *Biosocial Bases of Criminal Behavior*. New York: Gardner Press, 1977.

Piaget, Jean. *The Moral Judgment of the Child*. London: Kegan Paul, 1932.

Schauss, Alexander. *Diet, Crime and Delinquency*, revised edition. Berkeley, Calif.: Parker House, 1981.

Schussler, Karl, and Cressey, Donald. "Personality Characteristics of Criminals," *American Journal of Sociology* 17 (1952): 704–729.

Shah, Saleem A., and Roth, Loren H. "Biological and Psychophysiological Factors in Criminality." In *Handbook of Criminology*, edited by Daniel Glaser. Chicago: Rand McNally Publishing Company, 1974, pp. 101–173.

Shoemaker, Donald J. *Theories of Delinquency: An Examination of Explanations of Delinquent Behavior.* New York: Oxford University Press, 1984.

FOOTNOTES

1. Interviewed in March 1981.

2. Michael Phillipson, *Understanding Crime and Delinquency* (Chicago: Aldine Publishing Company, 1974), p. 18.

3. Clemens Bartollas and Stuart J. Miller, *The Juvenile Offender: Control, Correction, and Treatment* (Boston: Holbrook Press, 1978), p. 400.

4. This section on the progressive era and the influence of positivism is largely adapted from David J. Rothman, *Conscience and Convenience: The Asylum and its Alternatives in Progressive America* (Boston: Little, Brown & Company, 1980), p. 32.

5. Ibid., pp. 43–60.

6. David Matza, *Delinquency and Drift* (New York: John Wiley & Sons, 1964), p. 5.

7. Donald C. Gibbons, "Differential Treatment of Delinquents and Interpersonal Maturity Level: A Critique," *Social Services Review* 44 (1970), p. 68.

8. Ian Taylor, Paul Walton, and Jock Young, *The New Criminology: For a Social Theory of Deviance* (New York: Harper & Row, Publishers, 1973), pp. 41–42.

9. Cesare Lombroso, introduction to Fina Lombroso Ferrara, *Criminal Man according to the Classification of Cesare Lombroso* (New York: Putnam, 1911), p. xiv.

10. Taylor, Walton, and Young, *New Criminology*, p. 42.

11. M. F. A. Montagu, "The Biologist Looks at Crime," *Annals of the American Academy of Political and Social Science* 217 (1941), pp. 46–57.

12. Charles Goring, *The English Convict: A Statistical Study, 1913* (Montclair, N.J.: Patterson Smith, 1972).

13. Taylor, Walton, and Young, *New Criminology*, pp. 42–43.

14. Saleem A. Shah and Loren H. Roth, "Biological and Psychophysiological Factors in Criminality," *Handbook of Criminology*, edited by Daniel Glaser (Chicago: Rand McNally Publishing Company, 1974), p. 107.

15. Ibid., p. 108.

16. Henry Goddard, *Efficiency and Levels of Intelligence* (Princeton, N.J.: Princeton University Press, 1920).

17. William Healy and Augusta Bronner, *Delinquency and Criminals: Their Making and Unmaking* (New York: Macmillan Publishing Company, 1926).

18. John Slawson, *The Delinquent Boys* (Boston: Budget Press, 1926).

19. Edwin Sutherland, "Mental Deficiency and Crime," in *Social Attitudes*, edited by Kimball Young (New York: Henry Holt, 1973).

20. William Sheldon, *Varieties of Delinquent Youth* (New York: Harper & Row, Publishers, 1949).

21. Ibid.

22. S. Glueck and E. Glueck, *Physique and Delinquency* (New York: Harper & Row, Publishers, 1956), p. 9.

23. Juan B. Cortes with Florence M. Gatti, *Delinquency and Crime: A Biopsychosocial Approach: Empirical, Theoretical, and Practice Aspects of Criminal Behavior* (New York: Seminar Press, 1972), pp. 18–19.

24. R. L. Means, "Sociology, Biology, and the Analysis of Social Problems," *Social Problems* 15 (1967), pp. 200–212.

25. Shah and Roth, "Biological and Psychophysiological Factors," p. 101.

26. Saleem A. Shah, Sarnoff A. Mednick, and C. R. Jeffery are some of the main proponents of sociobiology.

27. C. R. Jeffery, *Biology and Crime* (Beverly Hills, Calif.: Sage Publications, 1970), p. 14.

28. D. J. West and D. P. Farrington, *Who Becomes Delinquent?* (London: Heinemann, 1973).

29. Lis Kirkegaard-Sorensen and Sarnoff A. Mednick, "A Prospective Study of Predictors of Criminality: Intelligence." In *Biosocial Basis of Criminal Behavior,* edited by Sarnoff A. Mednick and Karl O. Christiansen (New York: Gardner Press, 1977).

30. Robert A. Gordon, "Prevalence: The Rare Datum in Delinquency Measurement and Its Implications for the Theory of Delinquency," in *The Juvenile Justice System,* edited by Malcolm Klein (Beverly Hills Calif.: Sage Publications, 1976), pp. 201–284.

31. Travis Hirschi and Michael Hindelang, "Intelligence and Delinquency: A Revisionist Review," *American Sociological Review* 42 (1977), pp. 471–486.

32. Shah and Roth, "Biological and Psychophysiological Factors," pp. 115–126.

33. Cortes and Gatti, *Delinquency and Crime,* p. 21.

34. Ibid., pp. 36–37.

35. Ibid., p. 189.

36. Ibid., p. 191.

37. Ibid., pp. 191–194.

38. Hans Eysenck, "The Technology of Consent," *New Scientist* 26 (June 1969), p. 689.

39. Hans Eysenck, *Fact and Fiction in Psychology* (Harmondsworth, England: Penguin, 1965), pp. 260–261.

40. M. Hoghughi and A. Forrest, "Eysenck's Theory of Criminality," *British Journal of Criminology* 10 (1970), pp. 240–254.

41. Taylor, Walton, and Young, *New Criminology,* p. 50.

42. William E. Thornton, Jr., Jennifer James, and William G. Doerner, *Delinquency and Justice* (Glenview, Ill.: Scott, Foresman & Company, 1982), p. 81.

43. A. Hoffer, "The Relation of Crime to Nutrition," *Humanist in Canada* 8 (1975), pp. 3–9.

44. See Alexander Schauss, *Diet, Crime, and Delinquency* (Berkeley, Calif.: Parker House, 1981).

45. U.S. Congress, Senate, Hearing before the Select Committee on Nutrition and Human Needs, June 22, 1977.

46. O. David, J. Clart, and K. Voeller, "Lead and Hyperactivity," *The Lancet* 2 (1972), pp. 900–903.

47. J. A. Wacker, *The Reduction of Crime through the Prevention and Treatment of Learning Disabilities* (Dallas: J. A. Wacker, 1974); and A. Borcal and L. Y. Rabkin, "A Precursor of Delinquency: The Hyperkinetic Disorder of Childhood," *Psychiatric Quarterly* 48 (1974), p. 384.

48. Larry J. Siegel and Joseph J. Senna, *Juvenile Delinquency: Theory, Practice, and Law* (St. Paul, Minn.: West Publishing Company, 1981), p. 77.

49. Jeffery, *Biology and Crime*, pp. 16–17.

50. Thornton, James, and Doerner, *Delinquency and Justice*, p. 83.

51. Sigmund Freud, *An Outline of Psychoanalysis* (New York: reprint ed., W. W. Norton, 1963).

52. Ibid.

53. Ibid.

54. LaMar T. Empey, *American Delinquency: Its Meaning and Construction* (Homewood, Ill.: Dorsey Press, 1982), pp. 172–173.

55. The author worked with this youth from 1970 to 1972.

56. Hervey Cleckley, *The Mask of Sanity* (St. Louis: Mosby, 1955), pp. 382–417.

57. The author worked with this youth from 1971 to 1972.

58. William Healy, *Twenty-Five Years of Child Guidance*, Studies from the Institute for Juvenile Research, Series C, no. 256 (Illinois Department of Public Welfare, 1934), pp. 14–15.

59. August Aichhorn, *Wayward Youth* (New York: Viking Press, 1963).

60. Kate Friedlander, *The Psychoanalytic Approach to Juvenile Delinquency* (London: Routledge & Kegan Paul, 1947).

61. Richard L. Jenkins, "Delinquency and a Treatment Philosophy," in *Crime, Law and Corrections*, edited by Ralph Slovenko (Springfield, Ill.: Charles C Thomas, 1966), pp. 135–136.

62. Ibid., p. 136.

63. Cleckley, *Mask of Sanity*, pp. 382–417.

64. Jenkins, "Delinquency and a Treatment Philosophy," p. 137–138.

65. S. Glueck and E. Glueck, *Unraveling Juvenile Delinquency* (Cambridge: Harvard University Press for the Commonwealth Fund, 1950).

66. S. Hathaway and E. Monachesi, "The MMPI in the Study of Juvenile Delinquents," *American Sociological Review* 17 (1952), pp. 704–709.

67. Karl Schussler and Donald Cressey, "Personality Characteristics of Criminals," *American Journal of Sociology* 55 (1955), pp. 476–484.

68. Gordon Waldo and Simon Dinitz, "Personality Attributes of the Criminal: An Analysis of Research Studies 1950–1965," *Journal of Research in Crime and Delinquency* 4 (1967), pp. 185–201.

69. D. J. Tennenbaum, "Personality and Criminality: A Summary and Implications of the Literature," *Journal of Criminal Justice* 5 (1977), pp. 225–235.

70. Jenkins, "Delinquency and a Treatment Philosophy."

71. John Monohan, "Childhood Predictors of Adult Criminal Behavior," in *Early Intervention and Juvenile Delinquency*, edited by Fernand N. Dutile, Cleon H. Foust, and D. Robert Webster (Lexington, Mass.: Lexington Books, 1982), p. 11.

72. Ibid., pp. 12–13.

73. M. Lefkowitz et al., *Growing Up to Be Violent* (New York: Pergamon Press, 1977).

74. J. McCord, "Some Child Rearing Antecedents to Criminal Behavior in Adult Men," *Journal of Personality and Social Psychology* 37 (1979), pp. 1477–1486.

75. D. P. Farrington and D. J. West, "The Cambridge Study in Delinquency Development," mimeographed (1980).

76. Donald J. Shoemaker, *Theories of Delinquency: An Examination of Explanations of Delinquent Behavior* (New York: Oxford University Press, Inc., 1984), p. 35.

77. Statement that interviewed judges consistently made to the author.

INTERVIEW WITH
RICHARD L. JENKINS, M.D.

It's always destructive to reject a child or to punish him without offering anything else through which he can redeem himself. . . . The delinquent child comes in and looks upon you as the enemy. You've got to handle him in such a way that (1) he respects your power; (2) he respects your fairness; and (3) he knows that you're interested in his life.

In this interview, Dr. Richard L. Jenkins, professor emeritus of child psychiatry and former chief of the child psychiatry service of the University of Iowa, discusses such important matters as the reasons for the youth crime problem, the relationship between emotional deprivation and delinquency, between neurosis and delinquency, and between status offenders and other delinquents. He also expresses his opinion on the treatment of status offenders and hard-core offenders, as well as the policy implications that are needed to deal more effectively with delinquents in the United States.

Question: Why do we have such a serious problem with youth crime in this nation?

Jenkins: I would like to reverse that question: I don't think it is as useful to ask why some kids become delinquent as to ask why all kids don't become delinquent. In one sense, practically all kids, at one time or the other, do something that legally is delinquent.

The matter of teaching people to respect the rights of others and to live within a given framework is a matter which is a bit more difficult

Richard L. Jenkins is Professor of Child Psychiatry Emeritus at the University of Iowa College of Medicine. He was for ten years Chief of the Child Psychiatry Service. Dr. Jenkins has a particular interest in the problems of juvenile delinquency and has worked with the juvenile courts in Chicago and Detroit, at the New York State Training School for Boys at Warwick, and at the Eldora Training School in Iowa. He is the author of Breaking Patterns of Defeat, *J. B. Lippincott Co., Philadelphia, 1954,* Behavior Disorders of Childhood and Adolescence, *Charles C Thomas, Springfield, Illinois, 1973, and over 150 scientific and professional articles. Interviewed in June 1983, and used with permission.*

in these times for several reasons. First, the changes in society are reflected in the instability of our homes, institutions, and economic system. During the Great Depression, the rates of delinquency dropped. Delinquency generally rises with prosperity and goes down with depression. My own explanation of this is that the kids are pretty much unsupervised when both parents are working. When dad and mom are at home, they may be unhappy and there may be economic hardships, but there is some form of control and supervision. I also think that the uncertainties of the nuclear age add something. Today, nobody can count comfortably on the future. The breakdown of traditional sexual mores has certainly contributed to misbehavior. Finally, the growth in the use of drugs and alcohol by the young has had a very pronounced effect and has contributed both directly and indirectly to the rise of youth crime.

Question: Beginning with Freud, the psychological model of causation suggests that there is a relationship between emotional deprivation and delinquent behavior. What is your reaction to this psychological model of causation?

Jenkins: Well, I don't dispute the importance of Freud in the development of child psychiatry. But I wouldn't ascribe the statement you made to Freud. He focused on the overguilty and the role of guilt in the production of neurosis. Now I believe emotional deprivation in children results in a cry for parental affection and a cry for parental support. Parental impatience or lack of parental support results in behavior the child interprets as parental rejection. I think that showing affection is something that has to be learned. An individual who has never had a relation with a parent which was mutually giving and nourishing on the part of the adult doesn't become a socialized person and doesn't develop a sensitivity to others. There is a great deal of support in the literature that the unsocialized aggressive and unfeeling kinds of behavior go with the lack of parental acceptance and parental nurture. They go with parental rejection.

Question: What do you see as the relationship between the neurotic and the delinquent?

Jenkins: In the first place, there is a slight but definite negative correlation between neurosis and delinquency. Delinquents are less neurotic than nondelinquents. When someone asks me, "What conflict leads to this kid's delinquency," I usually respond, "It is the conflict he *does not have.*" This is true for the unsocialized kid, who is uninhibited and unconflicted about acting on his feelings.

There are two basic groups of delinquents; one is likely to have neurotic conflict, and the other is not. The undersocialized delinquent does not tend to have neurotic conflict. The undersocialized delinquent is divided into the undersocialized aggressive (my original term for this delinquent was the unsocialized aggressive) and the undersocialized nonaggressive, who is prone to such behaviors as running away. The socialized delinquent, being a socialized person, is capable of a neurotic conflict and can often get into it in terms of conflict between such conscience as he has and his behavior. The socialized delinquent—and I'm making things clearer than they are—is a youth who was accepted by his mother and made into a responsive socialized human being, but grew up with an absent, perhaps an alcoholic or criminal father, who failed to give the guidance, control, and direction which an adolescent boy wants and needs. This youth then picked out as a male model some older delinquent on the street. But this group offers a far better prognosis than the undersocialized.

Question: What is the relationship between the status offender and the delinquent? Are their behaviors that different?

Jenkins: I think that no one has been able to distinguish two separate groups. The status offenders, such as the runaways and those beyond the control of their parents, are basically more unsocialized than the group delinquents and offer, in my judgment, a worse prognosis. People do not consider what the social meaning of status offenses is or the risks of status offenses. They insist on applying adult thinking to children. It's not illegal for adults to desert the home, so a child shouldn't be penalized for doing so. An adult doesn't have to go to school or, in this country, to obey his parents, so children shouldn't be declared delinquent for not doing so.

The American Psychiatric Association favors the juvenile court having control over status offenders. The National Council of Juvenile and Family Court Judges also favors that. But the children's rights people, with whom I can't see eye-to-eye, say it is unjust and discriminatory. I don't have any quarrel if they want to say they're not delinquent, but I do have a quarrel with saying they should not be under the jurisdiction of the juvenile court. A single runaway may not mean much. Running away can be a sign of health, if the home is bad. Repeated runaways indicate something wrong in the home or the individual, usually the home, and it is necessary for the court to intervene.

Question: What is the best way to treat the status offender?

Jenkins: I think the best way is to prevent their behavior from happening. Early family therapy can adjust some of their problems. A study in San Francisco a few years ago examined twenty runaway girls. Some of them were running from problems in the home, and they were able, with one exception, to get the problems resolved through family therapy. Others were running from the drug scene, their boyfriends, the gay life, or the sex life. They had very poor success in holding them outside of an institution.

Question: What can be done with that group of chronic offenders who commit the more frequent and serious youth crimes?

Jenkins: Well, I'm in favor of residential treatment. For example, this institution [Eldora Training School] is a good one. The living units are a little larger than would be ideal, but we have responsible—and I do mean responsible—people in charge.

As long as a kid experiences being able to push through the barriers, he doesn't hear you. When a kid finds that he can get away with negative behavior, then he will continue that behavior. But if you can make a favorable and understanding contact at that time, he will begin to compromise on his negative behavior. The matter of treating a severely delinquent child is a matter of teaching compromise and getting him motivated in the right direction of doing what you want because he finds that it is to his welfare or best interest.

Question: Where does punishment fit in your scheme of treating children?

Jenkins: I know that punishment is increasingly used in juvenile justice. Determinate sentencing has been advocated under the Juvenile Justice Standards developed by the Institute of Judicial Administration and the American Bar Association. Under these standards no one could reduce the judges sentence by more than 5 percent. So any effort to motivate the kid to earn his way out is thrown away. The State of Washington has a determinate sentencing law.

I believe punishment is necessary, but I don't like to see it used stupidly. And that set of national standards and the Washington law are simply stupid. They try to motivate the delinquent to do better by punishment, but the delinquent will see this as mistreatment or vindictiveness. The delinquent, then, will keep this feeling a long, long time after he is punished.

It's always destructive to reject a child or to punish him without offering anything else through which he can redeem himself. He needs to find something to do that you can reward him for. The delinquent child comes in and looks upon you as the enemy. You've got to handle him in such a way that (1) he respects your power; (2) he respects your fairness; and (3) he knows that you're interested in his life.

Question: What policy recommendations do you think are needed to deal more effectively with delinquents in this nation?

Jenkins: I think we need to do what we can do to strengthen the family, and there are many cases where public policy does the opposite. We need to adopt the school experience to the exceptional child, and that is increasingly being done with those kids who do not fit the usual pattern, the mentally retarded, the physically handicapped, and the hyperkinetic. We need very much more in the way of rewards offered to teenagers for work. I think the CCC was one of the most constructive means that Roosevelt developed, in terms of rewards for work. Finally, I think the emphasis on children's rights has been unwisely overdone. The first thing that is wrong with children's rights is that children are not adults.

CHAPTER 6

SOCIAL STRUCTURE THEORIES

CHAPTER OUTLINE

The life histories of the five brothers make it possible to give a preliminary answer to the crucial question: To what extent is a criminal career a result of personality traits and to what extent is it a product of the situation in which the person is born and reared?

With each of the five brothers social factors are more important than personality traits in influencing their behavior. The entrance and progress of each brother in a delinquent career appears to be almost a direct outcome of the residence of a poverty-stricken immigrant family in a neighborhood of boys' gangs and criminal traditions. . . .

Clifford R. Shaw, Henry D. McKay, and J. F. McDonald[1]

This chapter and the next examine sociological explanations of delinquent behavior. The basic flaw of explanations based on the individual, according to social structure theorists, is that such interpretations fail to come to grips with the underlying social and cultural conditions giving rise to delinquent behavior. These theorists add that the overall crime picture reflects conditions requiring collective social solutions and that, therefore, social reform, not individual counseling, must be given the highest priority in efforts to reduce crime problems.[2]

The setting for delinquency, as suggested by social structure theories, is the social and cultural environment in which adolescents grow up or the subcultural groups in which they choose to become involved. Social structure theorists, using official statistics as their guide, claim that such forces as cultural deviance, social disorganization, status frustration, and social mobility are so powerful that they induce lower-class youths to become involved in delinquent behavior.

This chapter examines cultural deviance and strain theories. Both cultural deviance and strain theory attempt to explain why official delinquency rates are higher in lower-class areas. These theories also have been modified to answer why middle-class youngsters commit delinquent acts.

CULTURAL DEVIANCE THEORIES

Clifford R. Shaw and Henry D. McKay, members of the Chicago School of urban criminology, and Walter B. Miller, an anthropologist, developed theoretical perspectives viewing delinquent behavior as an expression of conformity to cultural values and norms that are in opposition to those of the larger American society.

Clifford R. Shaw and Henry D. McKay

The pioneering investigations of Shaw and McKay established that delinquency varies in inverse proportion to the distance from the center of the city; that it varies inversely with socioeconomic status; and that delinquency rates in a residential area persist regardless of changes in racial and ethnic composition of the area.[3]

Social Disorganization and Delinquency

Shaw and McKay viewed juvenile delinquency as resulting from the breakdown of social control among the traditional primary groups, such as the family and the neighborhood, because of the social disorganization of the community. Rapid industrialization, urbanization, and immigration processes also contributed to the disorganization of the community. Delinquent behavior became an alternative mode of socialization through which youths who were part of disorganized communities were attracted to deviant lifestyles.[4] These delinquent values and traditions, which replaced traditional ones, were passed on from one generation to the next.

Shaw and McKay turned to ecology to show this relationship between social disorganization and delinquency. In 1929, Shaw reported that marked variations in rates of school truancy, juvenile delinquency, and adult criminality existed among different areas in Chicago. These rates varied inversely with the distance from the center of the city; that is, the nearer a given locality was to the center of the city, the higher its rates of delinquency and crime. Shaw also found that areas of concentrated crime maintained their high rates over a long period, even when the composition of the population changed markedly.[5] In a study Shaw and McKay performed for the National Commission on Law Observance and Enforcement (1931), they reported this basic ecological finding was true for a number of other cities also.[6]

In 1942, Shaw and McKay published their classic work, *Juvenile Delinquency in Urban Areas,* which developed these ecological insights in greater scope and depth.[7] What Shaw and McKay had done was to study males brought into the Cook County Juvenile Court on delinquency charges in 1900–1906, 1917–1923, and 1927–1933. They discovered that over this thirty-three year period, the vast majority of the delinquent boys came from either an area adjacent to the central business and industrial areas or along two forks of the Chicago River. Then, applying Burgess's concentric zone hypothesis of urban growth—that urban areas grow in concentric circles—they constructed a series of concentric circles, like the circles on a target, with the bullseye in the central city. Measuring delinquency rates by zone and by areas within the zones, they found that in all three periods the highest rates of delinquency was in Zone I (the central city), the next highest in Zone II (next to the central city), and so forth, in progressive steps outward to the lowest in Zone V. Significantly, although the delinquency rates changed from one period to the next, the relationship among the different zones remained constant, even though in some neighborhoods the ethnic compositions of the population had changed totally. During the first decade of the century, the largest portion of the population was German or Irish, but thirty years later, it was Polish and Italian.[8]

Shaw and McKay, in analyzing the official data, found that a number of factors were related to high rates of delinquency. First, buildings were allowed to deteriorate in anticipation of the expansion of industry. Second, as a result of the anticipated displacement of residence by industry, the residential population began to decrease. Third, the percentage of families in the area that received financial aid from the

United Charities and the Jewish Charities increased. Fourth, lower-class blacks and foreign born individuals were attracted to these inner-city areas.[9]

Opportunity Structure and Deliquency

Shaw and McKay eventually moved the focus of their analysis from the influence of social disorganization of the community to the importance of economics on high rates of delinquency. They found that the economic and occupational structure of the larger society was more influential in the rise of delinquent behavior than was the social life of the local community. They concluded that the reason members of lower-class groups remained in the inner-city community was less a reflection of their newness of arrival and their lack of acculturation to American institutions than it was a function of their class position in society.[10]

The consequence of this differential opportunity structure led to a conflict of values in local communities, as some residents embraced illegitimate values while others maintained allegiance to conventional ones. Delinquent groups were characterized by their own distinctive standards, and Shaw and McKay became increasingly involved in examining the process through which delinquents came to learn and to pass on these standards.[11]

Shaw and McKay summarized this relationship between ecology and social disorganization and cultural transmission theories thusly:

1. Delinquency rates vary widely throughout the city. The probability of adolescents becoming delinquent and getting arrested and later incarcerated depends on their living in one of these high-rate areas.

2. Delinquency is a product of the socialization mechanisms existing within a neighborhood. Unstable neighborhoods have the greatest chance of producing delinquents.

3. High delinquency rates indicate the breakdown of social institutions and of the ability of society to care for and control its citizens.

4. Delinquency is not the property of any one ethnic or racial group. Members of any racial or ethnic group will be delinquent if they live in the high-rate areas. Their crime rate will be reduced once they leave these areas.

5. Delinquency rates correlate highly with economic and social conditions such as poverty, poor health, and deteriorated housing.

6. Areas disrupted and in transition are the most likely to produce delinquency. After the transition has ended, a drop in the delinquency rate occurs.

7. Since the community is the major source of delinquency, it is evident that control of delinquency should be community-based.[12]

Evaluation of Shaw and McKay's Cultural Deviance Theory

Few studies in the area of delinquency have been as influential in the development of research, theory, and social action as those of Shaw and McKay. Indeed, although their basic findings were published over forty years ago, controversy over the validity of their findings continues; even the most recent theoretical statements draw upon them for support or in criticism.[13]

Shaw and McKay also provide a theoretical framework bridging both sociological and social psychological explanations. Images of the delinquent held at each stage of development of the Shaw and McKay tradition permit such bridging; they viewed the delinquent as "disaffiliated" in the social disorganization stage, as a "frustrated social climber" in the functionalist stage, and as an "aggrieved citizen" in the interactionist stage. These images of the delinquent offer the promise of synthesis between sociological and social psychological explanations of delinquency. These cultural and structural aspects of social differentiation are combined with the systematic study of individual and collective aspects of delinquency.[14]

Shaw and McKay founded the Chicago Area Projects, one of the most significant attempts to develop community organization within local communities. Shaw, especially, was concerned that slum dwellers learn to deal with their own problems and to do a better job of running their own lives. The Chicago Area Projects, described further in Chapter 20, have also been among the most effective juvenile delinquency prevention programs.

Furthermore, Shaw and McKay contributed important insights on gang formation. They looked upon the delinquent gang as responding normally to the slum conditions and the social deprivations of the local environments. In this regard, Shaw and McKay regarded delinquent behavior as an understandable choice given the lack of legitimate opportunity for lower-class families in the inner city. In developing the Chicago Area Projects, Shaw and McKay were able to persuade former delinquents to become involved as leaders of neighborhood groups working with youth, primarily because they viewed these former delinquents not as different from nondelinquents but as individuals who had made normal choices to deal with life in a deprived social environment.

However, critics have dismissed Shaw and McKay's contention that youngsters growing up in slum neighborhoods are bound to become delinquents on two counts. First, even in the neighborhoods of highest rates of delinquency, a good percentage of young people do not turn to a delinquent career.[15] Second, Shaw and McKay's theory assumes that higher economic class protects youngsters from delinquency, and the self-report studies have clearly shown that delinquent behavior is spread throughout the social classes. In addition, Shaw and McKay's analysis of delinquent behavior was based upon official statistics, and, as previous chapters have indicated, official rates of delinquency distort the picture of juvenile delinquency.

Finally, Shaw and McKay's theoretical analysis was flawed because they did not succeed in relating successfully the interaction between the processes of the local community and the forces of social disorganization. For example, if social disorganization always leads to some degree of personal disorganization, how could personally disorganized individuals be capable of forming gangs with a high degree of organization?[16]

Nevertheless, regardless of the theoretical and empirical shortcomings of Shaw and McKay's contributions, their work has had an enduring impact on the study of delinquency in America.

Lower-Class Culture and Delinquent Values

Walter B. Miller, in another variation of cultural deviance theory, argues that the motivation to become involved in delinquent behavior is endemic to lower-class culture:

> . . . the cultural system which exerts the most direct influence on [delinquent] behavior is that of the lower-class community itself—a long-established, distinctively patterned tradition with an integrity of its own—rather than a so-called "delinquent subculture" which has arisen through conflict with middle-class culture and is oriented to the deliberate violation of middle-class norms.[17]

Membership in One-Sex Peer Groups

The one-sex peer group, according to Miller, is a significant structural form in the lower-class community. This group is a reaction to female-dominated homes, where the male parent is absent from the household, present only occasionally, or, when present, only minimally involved in the support and rearing of children. The male-oriented peer group, then, represents the first real opportunity for lower-class boys to learn the essential aspects of the male role in the context of peers facing similar problems of sex-role identification. The desire to prove their masculinity, reasons Miller, is what attracts lower-class boys to these one-sex peer groups. Delinquent behavior is seen as the lower-class boy's attempt to prove that he is grown up and no longer tied to his mother's apron strings. Delinquent offenses are motivated primarily by the desire to achieve ends, status, or qualities valued within the youth's most significant cultural milieu.[18]

Focal Concerns of Lower-Class Culture

Miller argues that the lower-class culture is characterized by a set of focal concerns—that is, areas or issues that command widespread attention and a high degree of emotional involvement. They are: trouble, toughness, smartness, excitement, fate, and autonomy.[19]

Miller contends that staying out of trouble represents a major challenge for lower-class citizens, and that, therefore, personal status is often determined in terms of this law-abiding/non–law-abiding dimension. But which of the two qualities is valued depends largely upon the individual and his or her circumstances. An overt commitment may be made to abiding by the law, while a covert commitment is given to breaking the law. Miller adds that membership in adolescent gangs may be contingent on a commitment to the law-violating alternative.

Physical prowess, as demonstrated by strength and endurance, is valued in lower-class culture; the tough guy who is hard, fearless, undemonstrative, and a good fighter is the ideal person in the eyes of lower-class boys. Miller contends that the intense concern over toughness is directly related to the fact that a significant proportion of lower-class males are reared in matriarchal households and, therefore, a nearly obsessive concern with masculinity is found in these youths. The homophobia evident in this culture is another indication of this obsession with masculinity.

The capacity to outsmart, outfox, outwit, con, dupe, and "take" others is valued in lower-class culture; one must also be able to avoid being outwitted, "taken," or duped himself. Smartness also is necessary to achieve material goods and personal status without physical effort.

The search for excitement or a thrill is another of the focal concerns of lower-class life. The widespread use of alcohol by both sexes and gambling of all kinds spring from this quest for excitement. Going out on the town is the most vivid expression of the searching for a thrill, but, of course, pursuits of this nature frequently lead to trouble. In between periods of excitement, lower-class life is characterized by long periods of inaction or passivity.

Lower-class individuals often feel that their lives are subject to a set of forces over which they have little control; they may accept the concept of destiny, meaning that their lives are guided by strong spiritual forces. Getting lucky or being in luck might rescue the individual from lower-class life; this belief in fate encourages the lower-class person to gamble.

The desire for personal independence is an important concern, partly because the lower-class individual feels controlled so much of the time. A consequence of this desire for autonomy is the inability to deal with controlled environments such as schools or correctional facilities. Table 6-1 provides a comparison of these focal concerns.

TABLE 6-1 Focal Concerns of Lower-Class Culture

Area	Perceived Alternatives (state, quality, condition)	
1. Trouble	law-abiding behavior	law-violating behavior
2. Toughness	physical prowess, skill; "masculinity"; fearlessness, bravery, daring	weakness, ineptitude; effeminacy; timidity, cowardice, caution
3. Smartness	ability to outsmart, dupe, "con"; gaining money by "wits"; shrewdness, adroitness in repartee	gullibility, "con-ability"; slowness, dull-wittedness, gaining money by hard work; verbal maladroitness
4. Excitement	thrill; risk, danger; change, activity	boredom; "deadness," safeness; sameness, passivity
5. Fate	favored by fortune	being ill-omened, being "unlucky"
6. Autonomy	freedom from external constraint; freedom from superordinate authority; independence	presence of external constraint; presence of strong authority; dependency, being "cared for"

Source: Walter B. Miller, "Lower-Class Culture as a Generating Milieu of Gang Delinquency," *Journal of Social Issues* 14 (1958), p. 12. Reprinted by permission.

In sum, Miller contends that the lower class has a distinctive culture of its own. Its focal concerns, or values, make lower-class boys more likely to become involved in delinquent behavior. They want to demonstrate that they are tough guys, able to outwit the cops. The pursuit of crime is looked upon as a thrill. Yet lower-class boys are protected by the fatalistic belief that if an individual is going to get caught, there is nothing he or she can do about it. Crime, then, permits one to show personal independence from the controls placed upon him or her; crime also provides an avenue through which one can gain material goods and personal status with a minimum of physical effort.

Evaluation of Miller's Thesis of Lower-Class Culture

Miller's theory appears most plausible when applied to the behavior of lower-class gang delinquents. These gang cultures do appear to establish their own values and norms, distinct from the values and norms of the larger culture. In addition, Marvin Wolfgang and Franco Ferracuti argue that there is a subculture of violence among young males in the lower social classes that legitimates the use of violence in various social situations.[20]

However, Miller's contention that the lower classes have distinctive values has been widely criticized. Some critics argue that the evidence shows that lower-class youths hold to the same values as those of the larger culture. For example, Travis Hirschi has found that little disagreement exists among youngsters from different classes concerning their attachment to the social bond.[21] As discussed later in this chapter, Albert K. Cohen and Richard A. Cloward and Lloyd E. Ohlin claim that lower-class youths have internalized middle-class values and that their delinquent acts are a reflection of these middle-class values.[22]

STRAIN THEORY

Strain theorists look upon delinquency as a consequence of the frustration individuals feel when they are unable to achieve the goals they desire. Robert K. Merton, Albert K. Cohen, and Richard Cloward and Lloyd Ohlin all have contributed variations of strain theory.

Robert K. Merton and the Theory of Anomie

Merton has made an important contribution to understanding how deviant behavior is produced by different social structures. According to Merton, "Socially deviant behavior is just as much a product of social structure as conformist behavior. . . . Our primary aim is to discover how some social structure exerts a definite pressure upon certain persons in the society to engage in nonconforming rather than conforming behavior."[23]

In *Social Theory and Social Structure,* Merton considers two elements of the social and cultural systems. The first is the set of "culturally defined goals, purposes, and interests held out as legitimate objectives for all or for diversely located members of the society." These are the goals that people feel are worth striving for; they may be considered cultural goals. A second important aspect "defines, regulates, and controls the acceptable means of reaching out for these goals." Although a specific goal may be attained by a variety of means, not all of these means are sanctioned by the culture. The acceptable method is referred to as the institutionalized means. Merton contends that the two elements must be reasonably well integrated if a culture is to be stable and smooth running. If individuals feel that a particular goal is important, they should have a legitimate means of attaining it. When such integration is lacking in a culture, then a state of normlessness, or anomie, occurs. Merton further asserts that contemporary American culture seems to "approximate the polar type in which great emphasis upon certain success-goals occurs without equivalent emphasis upon institutional means."[24] The lower classes are asked to orient their behavior toward the prospect of accumulating wealth, while they are largely denied the means of doing so legitimately. It is this opposition of the cultural emphasis and the social structure that creates intense pressure for deviation.

Merton developed a typology of the modes of adaptation that can be used when an individual is confronted with anomie. In Table 6-2, five types of individual adaptation are listed: a plus (+) signifies acceptance, a minus (−) signifies rejection, and a plus-or-minus (±) signifies a rejection of the prevailing values and a substitution of new ones. These modes of adaptation are used to explain how deviant behavior in general is produced by the social structure, but they can also be applied specifically to juvenile lawbreaking.

Conformity

If a society is well integrated and, thus, anomie is absent, conformity both to cultural goals and to institutionalized means will be the most common and most widely found adaptation. The conforming juvenile accepts the cultural goal of society as well as the institutional means of attaining it; he works hard in legitimate ways to become a success.

Innovation

When adolescents accept the cultural goal but reject the institutional means of attaining it, they may pursue other paths that frequently will not be legitimate in terms of cultural values. Merton expresses the opinion that innovation resulting in deviant behavior is especially likely to occur in a society that offers success as a goal for all, but at the same time withholds from a segment of the population the legitimate means of attaining that goal. For example, lower-class youths who have accepted the cultural goal of success are likely to steal if they are denied legitimate opportunities to achieve the goal they have internalized.[25] Unable to "make it" in socially acceptable ways, they tend to pursue the success goal in law-violating ways.

Ritualism

Although they may have abandoned the cultural goals, some juveniles will continue to abide by the acceptable means for attaining them. Ritualism consists of "individually seeking a private escape from the dangers and frustrations . . . inherent in the competition for major cultural goals by abandoning these goals and clinging all the

TABLE 6-2 Merton's Theory of Anomie

Modes of Adaptation	Cultural Goal	Institutional Means
1. Conformity	+	+
2. Innovation	+	−
3. Ritualism	−	−
4. Retreatism	−	−
5. Rebellion	±	±

Source: Robert K. Merton, "Social Structure and Anomie," *American Sociological Review* 3 (1938): 676. Reprinted by permission.

more closely to the safe routines and institutional norms."[26] Some of these young-sters, for example, while keeping their behavior within the confines of the law, stop trying to achieve in school. They go through the motions of attending classes and studying, but have abandoned the goal of being a success in life.

Whereas innovation is a mode of adaptation typical of the lower class, ritualism is encountered more frequently in the lower middle class because parents of lower-middle-class children exert continuous pressure upon them to abide by the moral mandates of society.

Retreatism

When individuals have rejected both the goals of the culture and the institutionalized means of attaining them, they have, in effect, retreated from their society. The juvenile drug addict exemplifies this mode of adaptation. Drug addicts have di-vorced themselves from the cultural goal of success and must break the law to obtain and use their drugs. Yet even though they have none of the rewards held out by society, these socially disinherited persons face few of the frustrations involved in continuing to seek those rewards.

Rebellion

Rebellion consists of rejecting one's culture's values and institutions and substituting in their place a new set of values and institutions. The rebellious juvenile, for example, may commit himself to a political ideology, such as Marxism, that is intent on establishing a new social order that has a "closer correspondence between merit, effort, and reward."[27]

Merton used monetary success to exemplify the major cultural goal of our society, but mentioned some other alternative acceptable values. Intellectual or artistic achievement, for example, offer alternative career patterns that are not necessarily financially rewarding.

Evaluation of Merton's Theory of Anomie

Merton's theory has received much criticism. It is argued that his theory is not logically adequate. In retreatism, Merton rejects both cultural goals and institutional means. In rebellion, however, he establishes new goals and new means. According to logical development, intervening steps belong between retreatism and rebellion. A new set of cultural goals should be established and the institutional means rejected; then the cultural goals should be rejected and a new set of institutional means substituted.

The theory also appears to fall short of pragmatic adequacy—which relates to the ability of a theory to offer a solution for the particular problems that initiated the research inquiry—for it merely describes the effect of anomie on a success-oriented culture without explaining why and how such behavior occurs. As a result, Merton does not provide solutions to the problem of deviant behavior. Nor does his typology contain practical suggestions for controlling deviant behavior.

Furthermore, his theory lacks operational adequacy (which relates to whether or not it can be tested). Even though his typology describes behaviors typical of the real world, it has not been developed to the level of a working hypothesis that can be tested. Nor does Merton's theory explain why some of those who have attained success become involved in crime. Neither does it deal with the importance of interaction with peers, a crucial variable in juvenile crime. Nor is adequate consideration given to the psychological characteristics of offenders.

But Merton appears to be on more solid ground in terms of empirical adequacy— which relates to the degree of agreement between theoretical claims and empirical evidence—because his typology of deviant behavior is exemplified by the lives of youngsters who walk the streets of nearly every city in this nation. Conformists, innovators, and retreatists may be more plentiful, but rebels and ritualists also can easily be located.

Cohen and the Theory of Delinquent Subculture

Albert K. Cohen's thesis in his *Delinquent Boys: The Culture of the Gang* is that lower-class youths are actually protesting against the values of middle-class culture.[28] Because boys in the delinquent subculture are unable to attain the goals of middle-class culture, they experience status frustration, or strain. This strain explains their membership in delinquent gangs and their nonutilitarian, malicious, and negativistic behavior.[29]

The Delinquent Subculture

The delinquent subculture is nonutilitarian because delinquents commit crimes "for the hell of it," without intending to gain or profit from their crimes. For example, most steal, Cohen proposes, because they want the items to eat, to wear, or to sell. But the delinquent subculture steals things that are often discarded, destroyed, or casually given away.[30] Also, Cohen claims that malice is evident in the crimes of the delinquent subculture, displaying an enjoyment in the discomfort of others and a delight in the defiance of taboos.[31] Further, the delinquent subculture takes norms from the larger culture but turns them upside down. The delinquent's conduct is right by the standards of the subculture precisely because it is wrong by the norms of the larger culture.[32]

In terms of its spirit, the delinquent demonstrates versatility in its delinquent acts. Although a gang may be involved in stealing more than other offenses, members' delinquent acts tend to run the gamut; that is, they do not specialize as do many adult criminal gangs and "solitary" delinquents.[33]

The delinquent subculture also is characterized by "short-run hedonism." It has little interest in planning activities, setting long-term goals, budgeting time, or gaining knowledge and skills that require practice, deliberation, and study. Instead, gang members hang around the corner waiting for something to turn up. They respond impulsively to a suggestion, without considering the gains and costs of the activity.[34]

A further characteristic of this subculture is its emphasis on group autonomy—that is, it is intolerant of any restraint except the informal pressures of the gang itself. Gang members are generally resistant to attempts to regulate their behavior at home, at school, or in community activities. But in terms of their involvements in the gang, they develop intense loyalty and solidarity.[35]

From the behavior of the delinquent subculture, Cohen turns to an analysis of the social structure of American society. He sees the social structure as the most important frame of reference motivating and justifying individuals' conduct. The social structure in American society, claims Cohen, has an immense hold on citizens; even twelve- or thirteen-year old children know about the class system.[36] This class system defines the middle-class values and norms children are expected to aspire to and to achieve:

> These norms are, in effect, a tempered version of the Protestant ethic which has played such an important part in the shaping of American character and American society. In brief summary, this middle-class ethic prescribes an obligation to strive, by dint of rational, ascetic, self-disciplined, and independent activity, to achieve in worldly affairs. A not irrebuttable but common corollary is the presumption that "success" is itself a sign of the exercise of these moral qualities.[37]

Status at school especially is measured by these middle-class standards. First, the teacher is hired to foster the development of middle-class personalities. Second, the teacher is likely to be a middle-class person, who values ambition and achievement and quickly recognizes and rewards these virtues in others. Third, Cohen points out, the educational system itself favors "quiet, cooperative, 'well-behaved' pupils" who make the teacher's job easier; it greets with disapproval the "lusty, irrepressible, boisterous youngsters who are destructive of order, routine, and predictability in the classroom."[38]

A pivotal assumption in Cohen's theory is that lower-class boys internalize these middle-class norms and values but then are unable to attain these middle-class goals. Status frustration takes place, and the mechanism of reaction-formation is used to handle it. On one hand, according to Cohen, the delinquent claims that the middle-class standards do not matter, but, on the other hand, he directs irrational, malicious, unaccountable hostility toward the norms of the respectable middle-class society.[39]

In turn, the delinquent subculture offers the lower-class youth the status he does

not receive from the larger culture. But, of course, the status offered by the delinquent subculture is status only in the eyes of his fellow delinquents. Thus, according
to this theory, the same middle-class value system in America is instrumental in
generating both respectability and delinquency.[40]

Evaluation of Cohen's Theory of Delinquent Subculture

Cohen's theory views the subculture as the product of a single problem of adjustment
to a single social system and its social stratification. He claims that delinquent
activities frequently appear to represent a direct denial of the middle-class values of
getting ahead by hard work and material acquisition. But because lower-class boys
are ill-prepared by their home and social environments to perform effectively in
terms of the middle-class measuring stick, they must create their own criteria for
status and reward.[41]

Cohen's theory has done much to spark the development of delinquency theory.
Short and Strodtbeck used it to develop their research design to study youth gangs.[42]
Cloward and Ohlin's later subcultural theory profited from Cohen's earlier discussion.[43] Furthermore, the issues and controversies raised by Cohen's theory have
done much to enhance the development of delinquency theory.

In contrast to Merton's theory, which views deviance as an abrupt and sudden
product of strain or anomie, Cohen identifies the sequential or developmental nature
of delinquent behavior. His concept of the interaction between the youth and others
contends that delinquency arises during a continuous interaction process whereby
changes in the self result in changes in the activities of others:

> *The history of a deviant act is a history of an interaction process. The an-
> tecedents of the act are an unfolding sequence of acts contributed by a set
> of actors. A makes a move, possibly in a deviant direction; B responds; A
> responds to B's response, etc. In the course of the interaction, movement in
> a deviant direction may become more explicit, elaborated, definitive—or it
> may not. Although the act may be socially ascribed to only one of them,
> both ego and alter ego help to shape it.*[44]

However, a number of criticisms have been leveled at Cohen's theory. Travis
Hirschi questioned the feasibility of using status frustration as the motivational energy to account for delinquency, because most delinquent boys eventually become
law-abiding, even though their lower-class status does not change. Thus, since the
lower-class boy's position in the economic structure is relatively fixed, his eventual
reform cannot be attributed to changes in the conditions that originally drove him
into delinquency.[45]

David Matza challenged Cohen's radical distinction between the delinquent and
the conventional actor. Matza, who sees the values of the delinquent as largely in
harmony with those of the larger culture, rejected the oppositional viewpoint between delinquent and conventional values.[46] David Greenberg argued that the
choice of target may be more rational than Cohen allows because, rather than
engaging only in nonutilitarian, malicious, and negativistic activities, some delinquent youths can be seen as rational and committing crime for profit or gain.[47]

Furthermore, while Cohen's theory may apply to a small population of delinquent boys who commit destructive acts, it fails to explain the delinquent behavior of many American adolescents who drift in and out of delinquency during their teenage years.[48] In addition, it ignores those youths who commit delinquent acts on their own. Finally, Cohen does not offer any empirical evidence to support his theory. Indeed, the vagueness of such concepts as reaction formation and lower class internalization of middle-class values make it difficult to test his theory.

Cohen, along with James Short, Jr., has developed a more complex model of delinquency to answer these criticisms. These two have expanded the original theory into five delinquent orientations: parent male subculture, conflict-oriented subculture, drug addict subculture, semiprofessional theft, and middle-class subculture.[49] In the interview at the end of this chapter, Cohen further updates and modifies his theory.

Cloward and Ohlin's Opportunity Theory

Cloward and Ohlin also have had a major impact on delinquency research and action programs. They argue that Merton only discussed the availability of legitimate means for achieving material success and ignored illegitimate means. All youths, according to Cloward and Ohlin, internalize middle-class success goals at an early age, but in most lower-class neighborhoods legitimate avenues for mobility and success are largely closed.[50] Thus, those youths seek out illegitimate means to achieve success, and they usually do it through one of three specialized gang contexts: "criminal," "conflict," and "retreatist."[51]

The Criminal Subculture

The criminal subculture is based principally upon criminal values. Participants in this subculture are organized primarily for the pursuit of material gain by such illegal means as extortion, fraud, and theft. In the value orientation of young people in this subculture, delinquent and criminal behavior is accepted as a means of achieving success goals:

> The dominant criteria of in-group evaluation stress achievement, the use of skill and knowledge to get results. In this culture, prestige is allocated to those who achieve material gain and power through avenues defined as illegitimate by the larger society. From the very young to the very old, the successful "haul"—which quickly transforms the penniless into a man of means—is an ever-present vision of the possible and desirable. Although one may also achieve material success through the routine practice of theft or fraud, the "big score" remains the symbolic image of quick success.[52]

The criminal subculture provides the socialization by which a member learns to admire and respect older criminals and to adopt their lifestyles and behavior. He masters the techniques and orientations of the criminal world through delinquent episodes. Hostility and distrust are exhibited toward representatives of the larger society, who are regarded as suckers to be exploited whenever possible. Successful people in the conventional world are viewed as also having a "racket," and with this attitude the delinquent is able to neutralize successfully the controlling effect of conventional norms. But in dealing with the in-group, he remains loyal, honest, and trustworthy because he must prove himself reliable and dependable in his contacts with criminal associates.[53]

The Conflict Subculture

Violence is the keynote in the conflict subculture, whose members pursue status, or "rep," through the manipulation of force or threat of force. The warrior youth gangs that attract so much attention in the press exemplify this subculture. The "bopper," who is the basic role model, fights with weapons to win respect from other gangs and to compel a fearful deference from the conventional adult world. The bopper is expected to have great courage in the face of personal danger, demonstrating a willingness to defend his personal integrity and the honor of the gang.[54]

The immediate aim of fighting gangs is to acquire a reputation for toughness. A "rep" both ensures respect from peers and poses a threat to adults and assures a way of gaining access to the scarce resources for pleasure and opportunity in underprivileged areas. Relationships between gang members and the adult world are weak, for gang members are unable to find appropriate adult role models who would designate a structure of opportunities leading to adult success. Thus, faced by the apparent indifference of the adult world, the gang member seeks to win by coercion the attention and opportunities he could not otherwise achieve.[55]

The Retreatist Subculture

The subculture emphasizes the consumption of drugs. Members of this subculture have become alienated from conventional roles in the family or occupational world. They have withdrawn into an arena where the ultimate value consists of the "kick." Participants in this subculture look upon themselves as culturally and socially detached from the lifestyle and everyday preoccupations of members of the conventional world. The "kick" may mean alcohol, marijuana, hard drugs, unusual sexual experiences, hot jazz, or any combination of these, but whatever he chooses, the retreatist is seeking an intense awareness of living and a sense of pleasure that is "out of this world."[56]

The retreatist group generates a new order of goals and criteria of achievement. But instead of seeking to impose its system of values on the world of the "straights," the adolescent in retreat is content to strive for status and deference only within his own subculture. The retreatist subculture, then, provides substitutes for success goals, which members feel are beyond their reach.[57]

Cloward and Ohlin admit that while these three subcultures exhibit essentially different orientations, in reality subcultures frequently appear in somewhat mixed form. A subculture predominantly involved with conflict may on occasion become involved in systematic theft; members of a criminal subculture may sometimes engage in combat in the streets with a rival gang.[58]

Evaluation of Cloward and Ohlin's Opportunity Theory

Cloward and Ohlin's basic thesis is that "pressure toward the formation of delinquent subcultures originates in marked discrepancies between culturally induced aspirations among lower-class youth and the possibility of achieving them by legitimate means."[59] Lower-class youths are faced with competitive disadvantages in pursuing the legitimate channels of success. But because a young person rejects or is denied access to legitimate means does not mean that he or she will become delinquent, for first he or she needs an opportunity to learn how to become delinquent. Young persons, according to Cloward and Ohlin, are granted access to illegitimate opportunity through subcultural membership.

Irving Spergel, examining Cloward and Ohlin's contention that different patterns of delinquency are found in neighborhoods with varying opportunity structures, identified three subcultural neighborhoods in New York City, each of which had an opportunity structure consistent with the socioeconomic status of the neighborhood. His study was accepted as support for Cloward and Ohlin's theory.[60] Palmore and Hammond's study of children in the Aid to Dependent Children welfare program also found that delinquency was more common in sections of the city where family and neighborhood disorganization were present; in turn, delinquency rates were lower in areas exhibiting stable family patterns and low disorganization.[61]

The research of James F. Short, Jr., and associates offered mixed support for Cloward and Ohlin's opportunity theory. On one hand, they did find discrepancies between juveniles' aspirations and their expectations for fulfillment by legitimate means. But Short also found that while blacks experienced the greatest discrepancy between aspirations and achievement expectations, they were the least delinquent.[62]

The findings of several other studies show even sharper disagreement with Cloward and Ohlin's opportunity theory. Walter B. Miller's previously discussed research found that lower-class youths do not aspire to middle-class values, because they have focal concerns of their own.[63] Travis Hirschi, conducting a self-report study in the San Francisco Bay Area, found that delinquent youth lack the loyalty and cohesiveness to the group suggested in Cloward and Ohlin's theory.[64] Furthermore, studies of gang delinquency have found that more than one type of gang exists in a particular area.[65]

Nevertheless, Cloward and Ohlin's opportunity thesis is important because of the impact it has had on the development of delinquency theory. For example, Delbert S. Elliott and Harwin L. Voss used variables implicit in Cloward and Ohlin's theory to design their influential study on dropouts from school.[66] Cloward and Ohlin's theory is also notable for the impact it has had on public policy. Such delinquency prevention programs as Mobilization for Youth in New York City were established on the basis of the theoretical notion that youths who do not have legitimate avenues for success will pursue illegitimate ones. Indeed, a basic rationale of the 1960s War on Poverty welfare programs was to provide legitimate opportunities for lower-class youths so that they would not need to pursue illegitimate ones.

A further contribution of Cloward and Ohlin's theory is the importance it focuses on the relationship between economic factors and delinquency. While that emphasis has been challenged, as will be discussed later in this chapter, it does help to explain why delinquency rates are so high in ghetto areas.

The chief criticism of Cloward and Ohlin's opportunity theory pertains to its unidimensional approach to delinquency causation. More than economic factors are involved in delinquent behavior and, likewise, young people become involved in adolescent peer groups for reasons other than being denied access to legitimate means. In addition, their theory does not explain middle-class delinquency or delinquent acts committed by youths who are not part of a subcultural group.

MIDDLE-CLASS DELINQUENCY

Average citizens, if faced with the question of the degree of antisocial behavior among middle-class youths, probably would take one of two extreme positions. Most would either say that middle-class youths are relatively free of unlawful behavior and that the delinquent problem rests solely in lower-class neighborhoods, or they would contend that middle-class juvenile offenders are involved in extensive antisocial behavior, including sexual promiscuity, heavy drinking, drug use, and serious vandalism.

Prior to the 1960s, the answer was thought to be clear. The deprivations and circumstances of lower-class living were believed to drive youths to unlawful behavior, and the studies of delinquency concentrated almost entirely on lower-class youths. But since the late 1960s, researchers have been examining the middle class very carefully to see whether or not its members, too, are heavily engaged in crime. The truth appears to lie somewhere between two extreme beliefs. Few researchers question that crime among suburban youth has increased; in fact, the nearly three-to-one ratio of arrests of city to suburban arrests of juveniles under the age of eighteen would undoubtedly be even smaller if police patrolled middle-class neighborhoods as much as they do lower-class ones and used the same criteria for arresting middle-class youths as for lower-class ones. However, most studies find middle-class offenses to be relatively petty in nature.

Theories of Middle-Class Delinquency

Theories of middle-class delinquency are generally an extension of the perspectives developed to explain lower-class delinquency. Subculture, strain, and socialization theories all have been modified to deal with why middle-class youths commit crime.[67]

Subculture Theories

Youth culture theories are the most popular subculture explanations applied to middle-class delinquency. Affluence is viewed as the catalyst for the growth of youth culture. Because middle-class life requires little personal sacrifice, it is reasoned, the lifestyle encourages an essentially purposeless consumerism. Adolescents, sensing the futility behind the moral bankruptcy of the middle-class, may respond in several ways. They may join countercultures or become politically active. Or they may respond to the meaningless of life by constructing a peer alternative, a youth culture that focuses on conspicuous consumption and is characterized by the pursuit of artificial excitement.[68]

Fred J. Shanley notes that middle-class delinquency has resulted from broad changes in American social structure, involving weakening of the deferred gratification pattern. This shift has led to the emergence of a youth culture set off from the world of adults.[69] Albert K. Cohen, in an essay on middle-class delinquency, also agrees that alterations in the social structure have weakened the deferred gratification pattern. Middle-class youngsters in increasing numbers no longer accept the belief that attainment of future goals rests upon ascetic, scholarly behavior while one is young. Instead, the values of youth culture focus around hedonistic pursuits in the company of one's peers. Although most of the behavior of the youth culture is nondelinquent in form, pleasure seeking does have the potential to develop into delinquency.[70] Ralph England further observes that American youth have been removed from functional roles and been placed in an in-between period of neither childhood nor adulthood. England also contends that the youth culture with its irresponsible hedonism results in the transformation of adult values into delinquent behavior, such as drinking, drug use, premarital sex, and petty theft.[71]

These theories of middle-class delinquency stress the importance of peer groups in developing alternative values. In contrast to lower-class delinquent subcultures, which are presumed to be an inversion of middle-class morality, middle-class youth cultures are seen as determined by boredom rather than rage. Adolescents turn to peers in order to relieve restlessness and anxiety. The pursuit of pleasure is their basic concern, and clothing, cars, and precocious sexuality are used to give meaning to an otherwise empty existence. Delinquency provides a kick that is missing from the easy consumerism of daily life. The more that middle-class youngsters adopt these hedonistic values, the more they resemble lower-class youngsters and the more they increase their chances of delinquent behavior.[72]

Socialization Theories

Middle-class delinquency is sometimes seen as the work of lower-class juveniles who have only recently entered middle class. Such youngsters were socialized in lower-class attitudes and values, and even when the families moved up to middle-class status, the children retained the values and outlook of the lower class.[73] Another popular socialization theory is that the changes in middle-class socialization patterns in the years since World War II have resulted in increased permissiveness. Parents no longer instill in their children traditional middle-class values such as self-control and deferred gratification that can serve as barriers to delinquent behavior. Instead, an emphasis on individual development and indulgence has produced a generation that lives for the here and now and that demands immediate gratification of its needs. These new values are likened to those of the lower-class and, therefore, are thought to lead to delinquency for many of the same reasons.[74]

Strain Theories

Strain theories of middle-class delinquency focus on the similarities between middle-class and lower-class youths in dealing with the anxieties and frustrations of growing up in contemporary society. Misbehavior of middle-class boys thus may be traced to anxieties felt over masculinity. Many middle-class boys, like lower-class ones, grow up in female-dominated homes, and, therefore, they experience the need to prove their "manliness," which may lead them to socially unacceptable behavior.[75]

Another theory is that middle-class youngsters experience strain because of the difficulty of achieving meaningful increases in status over that of their parents. These youths realize that significant changes in status are unlikely regardless of how much effort they invest; yet middle-class culture still stresses the achievement ideology. This very middle-class status anxiety generates feelings of injustice that, in turn, can lead either to passive acquiescence or to angry retaliation in the form of delinquency.[76]

Middle-class youths further experience strain in dealing with the transition from childhood to adolescence. During this period, they are largely excluded from the labor market, yet the peer group culture places pressure on them to engage in a hedonistic social life. This pressure may lead to thefts and burglary to finance their increasingly expensive pursuits of pleasure.

In short, common to these theories about middle-class delinquency is a view of this delinquency as a result of a relationship between affluence and deviance. Middle-class delinquents are seen as caught in an affluent but largely meaningless lifestyle; they appear as basically passive individuals who respond to the social forces operating upon them in ways that they do not understand. This purposeless image of the middle-class delinquent has led theorists to search for causes of delinquency in internal individual motivations. Researchers have been preoccupied with the individual pathology of the middle-class delinquent and more attention has been given to the individuals involved in the activity than in the actual delinquent behavior. Thus, middle-class delinquency theories have focused on individual coping strategies and neglected factors of social structure that could be related to delinquency.[77] See Table 6-3 for a comparison of the structural theories of delinquent causation.

EVALUATION OF SOCIAL STRUCTURE EXPLANATIONS OF DELINQUENCY

Social structure explanations of delinquency relate delinquent behavior to the structural and cultural characteristics of American society. A youth may become delinquent because he or she lives in a disorganized community, because he or she is unable to achieve middle-class standards, because he or she becomes part of a delinquent subculture due to status frustration, or because of the lower-class values of the subculture to which he or she belongs.

These theories ultimately rest on the importance of class as a significant variable in the explanation of delinquent behavior. But, as previously indicated, recently the relationship between social class and delinquency has been deemphasized in delinquency research. Self-report studies show that delinquent behavior is widespread through all social classes.[78] Charles Tittle and his associates, for example, flatly declare that the relationship between social class and delinquency is a myth.[79]

However, Delbert S. Elliott and David Huizinga's national sample found that class differences among males are found in the prevalence and incidence of all serious offenses and in the incidence of nonserious and total offenses. Among females, the only significant and persistent class differences involved felony assault and public disorder offenses.[80] A survey by John Braithwaite also found that research does tend

TABLE 6-3 Summary of Social Process Theories of Delinquency

The Theory	Cause of Delinquency Identified in the Theory	Supporting Research
Cultural deviance		
Shaw and McKay	Delinquent behavior becomes an alternative mode of socialization through which youths who are part of disorganized communities are attracted to delinquent values and traditions	Moderate
Miller	Lower-class culture has a distinctive culture of its own and its focal concerns, or values, make lower-class boys more likely to become involved in delinquent behavior	Weak
Strain		
Merton	Social structure exerts pressure upon those youths who cannot attain the cultural goal of success to engage in nonconforming behavior	Weak
Cohen	Lower-class boys are unable to attain the goals of middle-class culture and, therefore, they become involved in nonutilitarian, malicious, and negativistic behavior	Weak
Cloward and Ohlin	Lower-class boys seek out illegitimate means to attain middle-class success goals if they are unable to attain them through legitimate means, usually through one of three specialized gang contexts	Moderate
Middle-class subculture	Adolescents become involved in a youth culture, and delinquency provides a kick that is missing from the easy consumerism of daily life	Moderate
Socialization	Lower-class juveniles who have only recently moved up to the middle class while retaining the values and behavior of the lower-class	Weak
Strain	Middle-class youths, like lower-class ones, become involved in delinquent behavior because of the anxieties and frustrations of growing up	Weak

to support higher offense rates among lower-class juveniles. He adds that studies not reporting these higher rates are particularly susceptible to methodological criticism. Braithwaite concludes: "The sociological study of crime does not need to 'shift away from class-based theories' as Tittle et al. [advocate]. What we require are class-based theories which explain why certain types of crime are perpetuated disproportionately by the powerless, while other forms of crime are almost exclusively the prerogative of the powerful."[81] Robert Gillespie's survey of 57 studies shows considerable support for a relationship between unemployment and property crime. He found that the relationship is most evident in studies using such variables as class, crime, and delinquency in a methodologically sophisticated manner.[82] Similarly, Donald Clelland and Timothy Carter insist that arguments and research contradicting the relationship between class and delinquency are neither theoretically nor methodologically sophisticated and that methodologically sophisticated studies would tend to find a relationship between social class and delinquency.[83]

Thus, recent evidence would support a relationship between class, the economic structures of society, and delinquency. But the flaw with the theories presented in this chapter lies in the one-sided presentation they give as to why delinquent behavior occurs. They disclose how structural and cultural values are imposed on individuals in American society, without much concern for how individuals choose to respond to the influence of the sociocultural context and to the economic factors in their immediate environment. These theories leave two basic questions unanswered: what explains the fact that many youths in the same cultural setting do not become delinquent; and why is it that many culturally deprived youths who do become delinquent desist from delinquent behavior at the end of their teenage years, even when their social and economic situations remain the same?

POLICY IMPLICATIONS

Social structural theories examine areas that are vitally important in allowing young people to realize their potential. First, they deal with the basic survival needs of the child. Economic deprivation is first felt at home, and the squalor of their home experiences is what drives many youths to the streets. Mothers and fathers cannot make do on a day-to-day basis when they live on the edge of economic survival. Not surprisingly, the father frequently leaves, children are neglected and abused, and the mother is gone much of the time simply trying to make ends meet. The harsh realities of a lack of food, of clothing, and of a warm environment may lead a youth to conclude that "life is a bitch" and "you have to learn to hustle at an early age if you want to make it."[84]

Second, social structural theories discuss the impact of disorganized communities on adolescents. Learning to adapt to a disorganized community may easily lead adolescents to an acceptance of cultural patterns that are conducive to delinquent behavior. For youths who experience economic deprivations at home—and probably the majority of youngsters in disorganized communities are in this category—the streets offer the promise of attaining goods and services that their parents could never afford. In these disorganized communities, youth gangs typically are well-established; in many communities youngsters may feel required to join a gang for safety. Disorganized communities also offer drugs of every type, everyday contact with adult criminals, and an on-going exposure to violence.

Third, social structural theories describe the difficulty of coping in constructive ways when one is not able to meet the success goals of society. This inability to meet the success goals usually becomes evident at school. Both lower- and middle-class youths may respond to lack of success with disruptive behavior, truancy, and crime.

Inability to find a job or to compete in the marketplace further encourages a youth to pursue illegitimate means.

Consequently, because the structural conditions of society lead to delinquency for some youth, changes in these conditions are needed so that more youths will have the opportunity to realize their potentials. The task of policymakers, then, is to design policy that will more adequately enable lower-class youths to succeed.

In terms of the community level, every family must be guaranteed an adequate standard of living. Granted that not all poor youths become delinquent, the likelihood of delinquent behavior increases in relation to cultural and economic deprivation. In the local community, groups that take on the task of community problems and develop the leadership and organization to deal with these problems can do much to resolve the criminogenic conditions of lower-class communities. Policymakers must ensure that these neighborhood groups receive adequate funding support and that bureaucratic obstacles do not impede their progress.

In terms of the individual youths, it is imperative that they be provided with as many success experiences as possible. They need success experiences at school, in which they receive positive reinforcement. They need to become involved with prosocial individuals in the community who offer them constructive activities in which to become involved. They also need proper training and guidance so that they can find suitable jobs.

SUMMARY

This chapter has described some of the best-known theories in sociology. Shaw and McKay, members of the Chicago School, showed the ecological importance of where a young person lives. The closer youths live to the inner city, the more likely they are to become involved in delinquency. But the explanation for the delinquency in these areas goes beyond that of social disorganization, for a cultural tradition passes these criminogenic norms from one generation to the next. Robert K. Merton's social structure and anomie theory states that the social structure of a society influences the behavior that occurs in that society. Youths who are caught in anomie or normlessness are more likely to become deviant or delinquent than those who are not. Albert K. Cohen's theory of lower-class gang cultures, which derives from the work of Merton as well as others, contends that lower-class youths aspire to middle-class values but, because they are unable to attain them, they invert these values and become involved in negativistic, malicious, and nonutilitarian behavior. Cloward and Ohlin argue that lower-class gang youth do aspire to middle-class values but become involved in illegitimate pursuits because they are unable to attain these pursuits legitimately. Yet Walter B. Miller contends that lower-class youths do not aspire to middle-class values because they have their own focal concerns, and it is these focal concerns that encourage involvement in delinquent behavior. Finally, theories of middle-class delinquency state that middle-class youths are also caught by the structural conditions of American society and that some of these youths respond with delinquent behavior.

Social structure theories provide one important part of the equation of delinquent behavior; namely, that the larger social structure influences the behavior of juveniles within that society. The youths from impoverished families are more likely than others to become involved in delinquent behavior on an on-going basis. But middle-class youths also experience status frustration because of the success orientation of American culture, and some of them too become involved in delinquent behavior. Yet this side of the equation requires the other; namely, a discussion of the social processes involved in a juvenile becoming a delinquent. The next chapter will discuss the process of becoming a delinquent.

Discussion Questions

1. According to Shaw and McKay, what is the relationship between ecology, social disorganization, and transmission of a deviant culture?
2. Which of the theories in this chapter impressed you as being most logical? Why?
3. Should poverty exclude a youngster from responsibility for delinquent behavior? Why or why not?
4. Do you believe that lower-class youngsters aspire to middle-class values? Or do they have their own values?
5. Reflecting for a moment on your own period of adolescence, why did you—or others you know—become involved in delinquent acts?

References

Braithwaite, John. "The Myth of Social Class and Criminality Reconsidered," *American Sociological Review* 46 (February 1981): 36–57.

Clelland, Donald, and Huizinga, David. "Social Class and Delinquent Behavior in a National Youth Panel," *Criminology* 21 (1980): 318–336.

Cloward, Richard A., and Ohlin, Lloyd E. *Delinquency and Opportunity: A Theory of Delinquent Gangs.* New York: Free Press, 1960.

Cohen, Albert K. *Delinquent Boys: The Culture of the Gang.* New York: Free Press, 1955.

———. "Middle-Class Delinquency and the Social Structure." In *Middle-Class Juvenile Delinquency,* edited by Edmund W. Vaz. New York: Harper and Row, 1967.

Elliott, Delbert S., and Huizinga, David. "Social Class and Delinquent Behavior in a National Youth Panel," *Criminology* 21 (May 1983): 149–177.

England, Ralph W. "A Theory of Middle-Class Juvenile Delinquency," *The Journal of Criminal Law, Criminology and Police Science* 50 (April 1960): 535–540.

Miller, Walter B. "Lower-Class Culture as a Generating Milieu of Gang Delinquency," *Journal of Social Issues* 14 (Summer 1958): 5–19.

Richards, Pamela, Berk, Richard A., and Forster, Brenda. *Crime as Play: Delinquency in a Middle Class Suburb.* Cambridge, Mass.: Ballinger Publishing Company, 1979.

Shaw, Clifford R., and McKay, Henry D. *Social Factors in Juvenile Delinquency: Report on the Causes of Crime, Vol. II.* Washington, D.C.: National Commission on Law Observance and Enforcement; U.S. Government Printing Office, 1931.

———. *Juvenile Delinquency and Urban Areas.* Chicago: University of Chicago Press, 1942.

Short, James F., Jr., ed. *Delinquency, Crime, and Sociology.* Chicago: University of Chicago Press, 1976.

FOOTNOTES

1. Clifford R. Shaw, Henry D. McKay, and James F. McDonald, *Brothers in Crime* (Chicago: University of Chicago Press, 1938), pp. 326–328.

2. Edwin Schur, *Our Criminal Society* (Englewood Cliffs, N.J.: Prentice-Hall, 1969), p. 15.

3. Albert J. Reiss, Jr., "Settling the Frontiers of a Pioneer in American Criminology: Henry McKay," in *Delinquency, Crime and Society,* edited by James F. Short, Jr. (Chicago: University of Chicago Press, 1976), p. 79.

4. Harold Finestone, *Victims of Change: Juvenile Delinquents in American Society* (Westport, Conn.: Greenwood Press, 1976), p. 90.

5. Clifford R. Shaw, *Delinquency Areas* (Chicago: University of Chicago Press, 1929), pp. 198–203.

6. Clifford R. Shaw and Henry D. McKay, *Social Factors in Juvenile Delinquency; Report on the Causes of Crime,* vol. II (Washington, D.C.: National Commission on Law Observance and Enforcement, 1931), p. 60.

7. Clifford R. Shaw and Henry D. McKay, *Juvenile Delinquency and Urban Areas* (Chicago: University of Chicago Press, 1942).

8. Ysabel Rennie, *The Search for Criminal Man* (Lexington, Mass.: Lexington Books; 1978), p. 129.

9. Finestone, *Victims of Change,* pp. 83–84.

10. Ibid., p. 92.

11. Ibid., p. 99.

12. Shaw and McKay, *Juvenile Delinquency and Urban Areas,* pp. 38–39.

13. James F. Short, Jr., "Introduction" to *Delinquency, Crime and Society,* p. 1.

14. Ibid., p. 3.

15. S. Kobrin, J. Puntil, and E. Peluso, "Criteria of Status among Street Gangs," *Journal of Research in Crime and Delinquency* 4 (January 1967), pp. 98–118.

16. Finestone, *Victims of Change,* p. 112.

17. Walter B. Miller, "Lower-Class Culture as a Generating Milieu of Gang Delinquency," *Journal of Social Issues* 14 (1958), pp. 9–10.

18. Ibid., pp. 14–16.

19. Ibid., pp. 11–14.

20. Marvin E. Wolfgang and Franco Ferracutti, *The Subculture of Violence* (London: Tavistock, 1957).

21. Travis Hirschi, *Causes of Delinquency* (Berkeley, Calif.: University of California Press, 1969).

22. Richard A. Cloward and Lloyd E. Ohlin, *Delinquency and Opportunity: A Theory of Delinquent Gangs* (New York: Free Press, 1960) and Albert K. Cohen, *Delinquent Boys: The Culture of the Gang* (Glencoe, Ill.: Free Press, 1955).

23. The following analysis of social structure and anomie is adapted from Robert K. Merton, *Social Theory and Social Structure,* 2d ed. (New York: Free Press, 1957).

24. Morton Deutsch and Robert M. Krauss, *Theories in Social Psychology* (New York: Basic Books, 1965), p. 198.

25. Cloward and Ohlin, *Delinquency and Opportunity.*

26. Merton, *Social Theory and Social Structure,* p. 151.

27. Ibid., p. 155.

28. Cohen, *Delinquent Boys,* p. 9.

29. Ibid., p. 25.

30. Ibid., p. 26.

31. Ibid., p. 27.

32. Ibid., p. 28.

33. Ibid., p. 29.

34. Ibid., p. 30.

35. Ibid., p. 31.

36. Ibid., p. 82.

37. Ibid., p. 87.

38. Ibid., pp. 113–114.

39. Ibid., p. 133.

40. Ibid., p. 137.

41. Michael Phillipson, *Understanding Crime and Delinquency: A Sociological Introduction* (Chicago: Aldine Publishing Company, 1974), pp. 153–154.

42. James F. Short, Jr., and Fred L. Strodtbeck, *Group Process and Gang Delinquency* (Chicago: University of Chicago Press, 1965).

43. Cloward and Ohlin, *Delinquency and Opportunity.*

44. Albert K. Cohen, "The Sociology of the Deviant Act: Anomie Theory and Beyond," *American Sociological Review* 30 (1965), p. 9.

45. Hirschi, *Causes of Delinquency.*

46. Matza, *Delinquency and Drift.*

47. David F. Greenberg, "Delinquency and the Age Structure of Society," *Contemporary Crisis* 1 (1977), p. 199.

48. However, Cohen does deal with middle-class delinquency in the article "Middle-Class Delinquency and the Social Structure," in *Middle-Class Delinquency,* edited by E. W. Vaz (New York: Harper & Row, 1967), pp. 207–221.

49. Albert K. Cohen and James Short, Jr., "Research on Delinquent Subcultures," *Journal of Social Issues* 14 (1958), pp. 25–31.

50. Cloward and Ohlin, *Delinquency and Opportunity.*

51. Ibid., p. 20.

52. Ibid., p. 22.

53. Ibid., p. 23.

54. Ibid., p. 24.

55. Ibid., p. 25.

56. Ibid., pp. 25–26.

57. Ibid., p. 27.

58. Ibid., p. 21.

59. Ibid., p. 40.

60. Irving Spergel, *Racketville, Slumtown, Haulberg* (Chicago: University of Chicago Press, 1964).

61. Erdman B. Palmore and Phillip E. Hammond, "Interacting Factors in Juvenile Delinquency," *American Sociological Review* 29 (December 1964), pp. 848–854.

62. James F. Short, Jr., Ramon Rivera, and Ray Tennyson, "Perceived Opportunities, Gang Membership and Delinquency," *American Sociological Review* 30 (1965), pp. 56–57.

63. Miller, "Lower-Class Culture."

64. Hirschi, *Causes of Delinquency.*

65. Short, Jr., and Strodtbeck, *Group Process and Gang Delinquency.*

66. Delbert S. Elliott and Harwin L. Voss, *Delinquency and Dropout* (Lexington, Mass.: Lexington Books; 1974), p. 9.

67. Pamela Richards, Richard A. Berk, and Brenda Forster, *Crime as Play: Delinquency in a Middle-Class Suburb* (Cambridge: Ballinger Publishing Company, 1979), pp. 10–15.

68. Ibid., p. 11.

69. Fred J. Shanley, "Middle-Class Delinquency as a Social Problem," *Sociology and Social Research,* vol. 51 (January 1967), pp. 185–198.

70. Cohen, "Middle-Class Delinquency."

71. Ralph England, "A Theory of Middle-Class Juvenile Delinquency," *Journal of Criminal Law, Criminology, and Police Science* 50 (1960), pp. 535–540.

72. Richards et al., *Crime as Play,* p. 11.

73. Ibid., p. 13.

74. Ibid.

75. Cohen, *Delinquent Boys,* p. 164.

76. Richards et al., *Crime as Play,* p. 14.

77. Ibid., p. 16.

78. See Chapter 3 for the findings of these self-report studies.

79. Charles R. Tittle, Wayne J. Villemez, and Douglas A. Smith, "The Myth of Social Class and Criminality: An Empirical Assessment of the Empirical Evidence," *American Sociological Review* 43 (October 1978), pp. 643–656.

80. Delbert S. Elliott and David Huizinga, "Social Class and Delinquent Behavior in a National Youth Panel," *Criminology* 21 (May 1983), p. 169.

81. John Braithwaite, "The Myth of Social Class and Criminality Reconsidered," *American Sociological Review* 46 (February 1981), p. 49.

82. Robert Gillespie, "Economic Factors in Crime and Delinquency: A Critical Review of the Empirical Evidence," *Hearings, Subcommittee on Crime of the Committee of the Judiciary, House of Representatives 95th Congress,* serial 47 (Washington, D.C.: U.S. Government Printing Office, 1978), pp. 601–625.

83. Donald Clelland and Timothy Carter, "The New Myth of Class and Crime," *Criminology* 18 (1980), pp. 319–336.

84. Interviewed in July 1977.

INTERVIEW WITH ALBERT K. COHEN

I think it is a safe generalization that, in the past fifteen years or so, the literature is coming to focus more and more on the nature, the character, and the individual circumstances of persons. Thus, rather than seeing the delinquent act as something that occurs in an interactive situation and is the product of an interaction, the delinquent's actions are interpreted through that person's personality and background.

In this interview, Albert K. Cohen emphasizes the importance of a sociological understanding of delinquency. He also discusses a number of important issues relating to his classic work, *Delinquent Boys: The Culture of a Gang,* including some notions of what would be involved in reformulating his thesis. Furthermore, Professor Cohen discusses middle-class delinquency and his reactions to such theorists as Travis Hirschi and David Matza.

Question: Let's begin with the thesis that you expressed in *Delinquent Boys* thirty years ago. Would you express it any differently today?

Cohen: I don't know what form it would take, except that it would be different. It has been subject to a lot of criticisms, and I have developed some of my own reservations about it which have not necessarily been embodied in the public criticism in the literature. It obviously would have to be rethought.

But I think in certain respects my own thinking has not altered—the notion that most delinquent activity, like most human activity, consists of actions that people do more or less together, or that are at least oriented to other people, is still true. The motivation to engage in those activities always is to some extent the function of a person's relationships to other people and one's participation in those activities is in some sense instrumental to the promotion of satisfying relationships with others.

Albert K. Cohen, professor of sociology at the University of Connecticut, is the author of the classic study, Delinquent Boys: The Culture of the Gang. *He has also authored* Deviance and Control *and edited the* Sutherland Papers *and* Prison Violence. *Interviewed in November 1983, and used with permission.*

This, I think, is the fundamental premise of the whole book; it's a basic premise, I think, to the whole idea of sociology.

What has bothered me most in the years since the publication of that book is not so much the declining influence or acceptance of some of the ideas specific to that particular interpretation of delinquency, but rather the decline of this general perspective on human conduct as applied to delinquency. I think it is a safe generalization that, in the past fifteen years or so, the literature is coming to focus more and more on the nature, the character, and the individual circumstances of persons. Thus, rather than seeing the delinquent act as something that occurs in an interactive situation and is the product of an interaction, the delinquent's actions are interpreted through that person's personality and background.

Delinquency needs to be perceived and treated as events performed in company of others or oriented to others guided somehow by the norms, expectations, and beliefs that are derived from and are sustained by one's communication with other people. The delinquent act is an event in a matrix of interaction and in that matrix there are a number of people. One of the persons will be the person to whom the act will be accredited. Amongst all the people there is one person whom we point the finger at and we say, "That's the person who did it!" But if you are trying to explain the action or the event, you don't explain it by saying, "This person did it," and then look at that person and try to find out what's special about that person, because the event was a product of the whole context in which it was embedded. What was going on at the time will include all the contributions by all the participants.

Question: Your book talks about the importance of social class on the behavior of boys. There is a tendency today to dismiss class as a significant variable in understanding delinquency. Do you still see the importance of social class as much as you did when you wrote *Delinquent Boys*?

Cohen: I'm much less clear in my own mind than I was at the time. I recognize that delinquency is much more widely distributed within the class structure than I assumed it was at the time that I wrote that book. I was well aware, of course, of middle class delinquency, but I had the feeling that it was dwarfed by working class delinquency. I have the feeling today that, notwithstanding the results of so much research utilizing self-report delinquency, the delinquency that constitutes a social problem is still more heavily concentrated in these same classes, the working class.

I think that there are some real problems with the interpretation of the self-report delinquency methods, and a large literature has reported these problems. It's a very interesting example of where the progress of theory itself is tied up with questions of methodology. Whether you perceive a phenomenon to be out there and to be explained depends upon whether the methods you use give credence to the existence of the phenomenon. If it's not there, there is nothing to explain. The position that many people have taken is that a class differential in delinquency is not a problem to explain because it's not there. Well, I question that. I rather think that one of the things that has not been considered is that the controversy may be in part confused by the fact that historically the class distribution of delinquency has itself changed. I was writing out of my own experience growing up in a society in which this class difference was very marked. I was writing at a time when that class differential was diminishing. I suspect we may be moving into a time when that class differential may be reestablished.

Question: Where does middle class delinquency fit into this?

Cohen: This is very speculative, of course, but I've gotten extremely interested in the phenomenon of middle class delinquency. The preoccupation and concern with and the visibility of middle class delinquency may be largely a product since World War II. I suppose what it really boils down to is this: that during the 50s and 60s and to a large extent the 70s, the kind of self-discipline, the kind of preoccupation with long-run goals, and the deferral of gratification tended to break down as a consequence of what was happening in the society.

I think that throughout American history the values of the middle class were shaped by the Protestant Ethic, but the structural basis of the Protestant Ethic practically disintegrated in the 50s and 60s. Through the eyes of a child the world was a vast cornucopia. Come Christmas, and the gifts were heaped so high! I remember sitting with families around the Christmas tree for hours unpacking gifts. After unwrapping the 50th, 80th, and 100th gift, the kids would be trying to simulate enthusiasm and excitement. I remember asking myself: What does the world look like to these kids? What will it look like when they grow up? An era of sustained affluence created a generation for whom the satisfaction of desire did not depend on deferral of gratification.

In contrast, I remember most vividly that growing up in a middle-class household was no ticket to success during the Depression Era. It meant that you had the support of a family that was ambitious and whose members would pull together and sacrifice for one another in order to advance the social standing of the family and to encourage the progress of the children through the school system. Part of growing up was the knowledge that everybody was tightening their belts and deferring to one another's needs. You would see people struggle. They don't have to lecture you. You know it's a hard row to hoe. You know anything that counts comes at some cost.

In terms of middle class delinquency, let me add that in *Delinquent Boys* the emphasis was on positive motivation, that is, what you might call the pay-off of crime and delinquency. The rewards can be material or relational rewards. Delinquency, like play in general, can be fun. It's doing things together with other kids that sound exciting and some of these activities yield material rewards. Or it can be ways of demonstrating to other people certain of your qualities, like your manhood, which bring gratification when recognized by others. But then the question arises, and it was not addressed to that extent in *Delinquent Boys*: Why do people refrain?

I've been influenced by Travis Hirschi in this regard, although I did deal with this in an article I wrote before I read Hirschi. I suspect that the increase of middle class delinquency also occurred during the 1950s and 1960s because of the weakening of the control systems of society. The controls that stem from the school system, the family systems, and other social systems were not as strong as in the past. If I were to write *Delinquent Boys* over again, it would confront the question of delinquency in other social levels much more squarely, and it would treat it in a more serious manner. A large part of the answer or investigation would be couched in very Hirschi-type language. That is to say, what has happened to the controls conceptualized in terms of the social bond that entails commitments, involvements, and attachments?

Question: How do delinquent and nondelinquent youths differ?

Cohen: Now you can look at those kids who do things and ask: Why are they different from kids who don't commit delinquent acts? What is it about their respective personalities and their relationships to those around them that explains the differences between them? I would call this the psychological level. Hirschi's concern is focused on the individual level or the psychological level as I am inclined to call it. He is interested in explaining why some kids are more delinquent than other kids. This is reflected in the nature of his research. He looks at the delinquent kids and those who are not delinquent. He looks at their individual attributes, relationships to their families, and schools, and so on. No two kids have the same constellation.

I use Hirschi's language now with some facility because I think that it's very helpful to think of kids as linked to their respective environments in terms of commitments, attachments, and so on. But the question that I go on to say is: If you take the environments or attachments as the givens—this kid is different from that kid because he has more attachments to his family, to peers, to

schools than this kid over here. But again, we must inquire why delinquency fluctuates. Why do delinquency rates vary from one society to another? From one city to another? From one community to another? What is it *about the society* that produces this? If delinquency is a function of social control conceived of as attachments, then the distribution of delinquency obviously has to correspond to a distribution of attachments. You can map the attachments in a society. Then you have to ask: What is it about the society that produces the distribution or mapping of attachments?

I think the psychological paths are very important. I think there is a very fundamental kind of linkage between the sociological and the psychological level. But having answered the psychological question, you are still left with the sociological question. I think *Delinquent Boys* was in a way quintessentially sociological. That doesn't make it superior to Hirschi or other studies of delinquency. The sociological question is not any more legitimate than the psychological question. But this book was addressed to the sociological question. By this I mean, it looked at certain kinds of events, in this case delinquency. It located these events in a certain space and that space was within the social system. It raised such questions as: What's going on in this society? Where does it happen? On what scale? And why?

Question: Do you see as much status frustration as there was when you wrote *Delinquent Boys*?

Cohen: I hesitate to answer that question because if the world looks different to middle class kids, as I have suggested, I suspect that being working class changes with time too. When I wrote *Delinquent Boys*, I read everything that had been written on the subject. When I say everything, I mean everything that was descriptive of working class life, and especially of being a working class child. But that wasn't such a great feat because there wasn't that much. Now there's a vastly greater literature, and I don't pretend to have any command of it. I suspect that the change was greater, that the world changed more for middle class kids than it did for working class kids. For the working class kid, life still remained problematic in many of the same ways.

But in terms of status frustration, I suspect that the working class youth has as much status frustration as when I wrote *Delinquent Boys*. Conceivably, for many of them, this status frustration may be aggravated. The reason for this is that in the era of affluence, those who don't have very much, whether that consists of material goods, esteem, or recognition, will experience rather intense frustration. They must deal with the frustration that comes from not having when most people whom you know do have these kinds of things. It's a matter of relative deprivation.

Now I will tell you something else about a way in which my thinking has been shaken. Not so much as a result of criticism but as a result of trying to reconcile my own theory with some facts. Some that I think are rather plain. One of the key ideas in *Delinquent Boys* is the notion of counter-suggestibility; this is the reaction formation notion that the delinquent subculture takes its form in large part from the fact that it is a denial of and rejection of the middle class culture or the standard American culture. It stands the conventional culture on its head. In doing that, it legitimizes a whole world of activity and it disvalues respectable activity. It is actually hostile toward and rejects the conventional world. This is a notion that goes along with practically all of the subcultural formulations: the idea that delinquents are comfortable doing what they are doing because they just don't put any stock in conventional morality. They reject and don't believe in it.

I'm afraid, however, that that's not true. It should have been apparent to me then and I guess in some corner of my mind I was aware of it. Suppose you were to ask most delinquents or most criminals and put it to them this way, "Look, you do all these terrible things. You do them frequently and, as far as I can tell, you don't lose any sleep over them. You don't seem to be obsessed by guilt." You can talk to professional criminals, and they feel good if they have had a good day's work. They feel bad if they have had a bad day, but they don't go home and pitch and toss all night because of having deprived this widow of her mite. And they have been doing this for years. So you would say to these people, "Obviously, all of this middle class morality of stealing and this and that,

you don't put any stock in it. If you had the opportunity to rewrite the laws yourself, you would probably throw out all that garbage about theft and whatever it is that you yourself engage in. Stealing would be OK." I am quite convinced that a professional thief would look at you and say, "You are crazy." If you give him the opportunity to rewrite the laws, he would rewrite them pretty much the way they are. You ask them, "But why?" And he would say, "Its got to be that way."

As a matter of fact, Matza does make that point. The whole idea of techniques of neutralization is oriented to the assumption that delinquents do not reject the conventional systems. I am sure that I must have been to some degree influenced by reading that. Matza's position is that these kids are perfectly capable of respecting and admiring people who live exemplary lives. Their mental constitution is such that it does make it possible to subscribe to conventional morality, while at the same time to engage systematically in acts that violate that morality. He says the answer is techniques of neutralization.

I have been coming around to something that formulates it somewhat differently. It is a question of the possible ways in which people can relate to normative systems. One way is simply to reject them literally. Another is to accept them. But then again you get different possibilities and one of them is what I call the gamester attitude, which in effect translates the moral rules into a kind of game rules. This is not in the sense of what you should or shouldn't do, but in terms of a set of rules that define the game. There are people whose job it is to observe the players, and if they catch the players violating the rules, they penalize them. If you think of basketball, hockey, or football, the job of the player is to make points and to lose as few points as possible while violating the so-called rules. But you need to do this unobtrusively so you won't be penalized for it. You win some, and you lose some. You are not mad at the umpire if he calls you offside. He's doing his job. You're doing yours.

That's the way it goes. Obviously, you don't reject the rules. You think they ought to be what they are. This is something that, if I were rewriting *Delinquent Boys*, I would want to think through and come to terms with and see where that fits in. Also, how it, the gamester attitude, relates to the cultures in which the boys participate. In other words, the ways of relating to the normative system, to conventional morality, and to rules in general are more complex than what we have thought them to be.

I think there is some evidence of the malice that I talked about. It becomes very visible in a great deal of vandalism. The classic example is the student defecating on the teacher's desk. You may wonder what he is trying to say but it's hard to impute more than one meaning to that message. Catholic kids will go around and break the school windows, but they won't break the church windows. What does this mean? There is a sense of resentment, a sense of being humiliated, a sense of being put down by people in institutions. They have been made to feel small or of no consequence. People don't see you when they're looking around at people. You don't count. This engenders a certain amount of bruising of the ego, and this resentment expresses itself in hostile actions. But I would be very careful about generalizing as freely as I did about the pervasiveness of this.

Again, I think you have to go back and look much more closely at the phenomenon you're trying to explain. You can only go so far speculating in a vacuum. I think that it's still true today. There really is not enough careful ethnographic study of the object that we're trying to explain. Most research tends to look at a sample of delinquents and a sample of nondelinquents and to compare their personalities and biographies. You can research from now to doomsday, and you won't have the answers. Go out and look at what they're *doing*. They're sitting on the stoop or sidewalk, and a half an hour later, they're robbing something. They're breaking into something. How do they get from here to there? We need, in effect, a minute by minute, blow by blow description of how they got from here to there, who said what, the emotion that was expressed in this situation, what it is that engenders excitement, how the act was conceived, how it grew, how it culminated. We need to know information from which we can make some inferences about the states of mind that are influencing their conduct. There's very little, even today, of the kind of research that is calculated to give the answers to these kinds of questions.

CHAPTER 7

SOCIAL PROCESS THEORY

CHAPTER OUTLINE

I'm here because my older brothers have all been in trouble. Some were here and are now in prison, and I didn't really have anything to follow but just their footsteps. I just wanted to fit into the crowd. The only time I feel happy with myself is when I'm high on drugs. Drugs make you feel like you are worth something. . . . I heard the principal and a teacher talk about me one day. They were comparing me to my older brother who was a terror in school. So I thought why should I try?

Seventeen-year-old male in a training school[1]

Social process theories, the focus of this chapter, examine the interactions between individuals and their environments that influence them to become involved in delinquent behavior. These sociopsychological theories became popular in the 1960s because they provided a theoretical mechanism for the translation of environmental factors into individual motivations. One of these theories examines how delinquents learn crime from others. A second proposes that any examination of the process of becoming a delinquent must take seriously both the internal components of the individual and the influences of the external environment. Another theory discusses how the creation and enforcement of the rules of society play an important role in determining the nature and extent of delinquency. Still another social process theory provides an explanation both of why youths do not become delinquent as well as of why they do become delinquent. Finally, several of these theories involve such important concepts as deviant identity, delinquent career, and commitment to delinquency.

Differential association, drift, control, and labeling are the social process explanations of delinquency described and evaluated in this chapter.

DIFFERENTIAL ASSOCIATION THEORY

Edwin H. Sutherland's formulation of differential association proposes that delinquents learn crime from others. His basic premise was that delinquency, like any other form of behavior, is a product of social interaction. In developing the theory of differential association, Sutherland was influenced by symbolic interactionism, which holds that individuals are constantly being changed as they take on the expectations and points of view of the people with whom they interact in intimate small groups.[2] Sutherland began with the notion that criminal behavior is to be expected of those individuals who have internalized a preponderance of definitions favorable to law violations.[3] In 1939, the theory of differential association was first developed in his text *Principles of Criminology*, and he continued to revise it until its final form appeared in 1947.

Propositions of Differential Association

Sutherland's theory of differential association is outlined in the following nine propositions:

1. Criminal Behavior Is Learned   Delinquent behavior, like other behavior, is learned from others. That is, delinquent behavior is not an inherited trait, but an acquired one.

2. Criminal Behavior Is Learned in Interaction with Other Persons in a Process of Communication   Delinquent behavior, according to Sutherland, is learned through a youth's active involvement with others in a process of communication. This process includes both verbal and nonverbal communication.

3. The Principal Part of the Learning of Criminal Behavior Occurs within Intimate Personal Groups   Adolescents, Sutherland says, learn delinquent behavior from their most intimate social groups. The meanings derived from these intimate relationships are far more influential for adolescents than any other form of communication, such as movies and newspapers.

4. When Criminal Behavior Is Learned, the Learning Includes: Techniques of Committing the Crime, Which Are Sometimes Very Simple; the Specific Direction of Motives, Drives, Rationalizations, and Attitudes   Sutherland suggests that youths learn the techniques of committing delinquent offenses from others. For example, a youth may learn how to "hot wire" a car from a delinquent companion with whom he is involved; he also acquires from others the attitudes or "mind set" that will enable him to set aside the moral bounds of the law.

5. The Specific Direction of Motives and Drives Is Learned from Definitions of Legal Codes as Favorable and Unfavorable   Adolescents come into contact both with persons who define the legal codes as rules to be observed and with those whose definitions of reality favor the violation of the legal codes. This creates culture conflict; the next proposition explains how this conflict is resolved.

6. A Person Becomes Delinquent Because of an Excess of Definitions Favorable to Violation of Law over Definitions Unfavorable to Violation of Law   This proposition expresses the basic principle of differential association. A person becomes delinquent, according to Sutherland, because he or she has more involvement with delinquent peers, groups, or events than with nondelinquent peers, groups, or events. Both an excess of contacts with delinquent definitions and isolation from antidelinquent patterns are important.

7. Differential Associations May Vary in Frequency, Duration, Priority, and Intensity   The impact that delinquent peers or groups have upon a young person depends upon the frequency of the social contacts, over how long a period of time the contacts take place, the age at which a person experiences these contacts, and the intensity of these social interactions.

8. The Process of Learning Criminal Behavior by Association with Criminal and Anticriminal Patterns Involves All of the Mechanisms That Are

Involved in Any Other Learning   The learning of delinquent behavior is like other learning experiences and is not restricted to mere imitation of others' behavior.

9. Though Criminal Behavior Is an Expression of General Needs and Values, It Is Not Explained by Those General Needs and Values Since Non-criminal Behavior Is an Expression of the Same Needs and Values   Sutherland concludes by suggesting that the motives for delinquent behavior are different from those for conventional behavior. What differentiates delinquent from nondelinquent behavior is that it is based on an excess of delinquent definitions learned from others.[4]

Sutherland assumes that delinquents must be taught antisocial behavior. Those who do not engage in socially unacceptable behavior have been socialized or acculturated to conventional values, but those who become involved in delinquent behavior do so because they have been taught other values. Sutherland develops a quantitative metaphor, in which conventional and criminal value systems are composed to elementary units called "definitions." Each unit can be weighted by the modalities of frequency, priority, duration, and intensity of contact. Thus, delinquency or criminality is determined by the algebraic sum of these weighted units.[5] Donald R. Cressey, who has been the spokesperson for differential association theory since Sutherland's death, further explains this theory in Box 7-1.

BOX 7-1 Interview with Donald R. Cressey

Question: What do you feel are the best features of differential association theory and do you see any areas which need to be reformulated?

Cressey: The strongest characteristic of differential association theory is its orientation to the scientific method and, thus, to empiricism. This means that its users do not assume that human behavior is prompted by deeply hidden "pushers," whether they be biological, psychological, or social. On the contrary, the theory is based on an assumption that every social scientist used to make, namely that human events are as "natural" as physical and biological events. Put more specifically, down deep under differential association theory is an assumption that humans come into the world as complex but unprogrammed computers. Then, during the course of their lives, they get programmed to behave in certain ways. The programming is not systematic or consistent, as it is when a technician programs a real computer. Still, various rules for behavior are fed into us, and we behave accordingly. No behavior that has not been programmed into a person will ever show up in that person's actions. Nowadays a lot of people object to that scientific assumption. They want the human to be more dignified and majestic than other animals so they give us a soul, a psyche, a mind, or a "will." But because such "pushers" are not observable or measurable, differential association theory assumes that we must look elsewhere for explanations of why people behave as they do.

So, starting with that assumption, all the differential association theory says is that if people are programmed to behave in a certain way, they will act that way. If you are programmed to know only that "honesty" is the best policy," then you will be honest. If you are programmed to know only that it is all right to steal, then you will steal. But the matter is not so simple because, starting when we are at our mothers' knees, we are programmed in both ways. What the theory says, then, is that whether you will steal or not depends on the *ratio* of these two kinds of behavior patterns that have been put into the computer which is you.

Now that's a great oversimplification of what differential association theory says about human learning. If you start to explore the process seriously and in detail, it gets very complicated in a hurry. The biggest problem I see with the theory is the idea that the effects of behavior patterns—whether favorable to crime or unfavorable to it—are cumulative. It isn't that behavior patterns are not observable. At least hypothetically, one can measure the ratio of the two kinds of behavior patterns a person has learned. But no one has shown how behavior patterns presented at one time in a person's life link up with behavior patterns presented at a later time, if indeed they do.

The strength of differential association is that it makes good sense of the so-called "factors" that are correlated with high crime and delinquency rates. Indeed, the theory makes better sense of the sex ratio, the age ratio, and the social class ratio in crime and delinquency than does any other theory. Consider poverty. Street crimes are clearly associated with poverty, and a popular theory is that poverty causes crime and delinquency. But if you think about the relationship for a moment, it will dawn on you that poverty doesn't grab people by the shoulders, kick them in the butt, and make them commit crime. Girls living in ghetto areas are in equal poverty with boys, but their delinquency rates are much lower than the rates for boys. So something else is at work. The "something else" that accounts for the differences in the rates is association differentially with the behavior patterns unfavorable or favorable to delinquent behavior.

Differential association theory is often misinterpreted. Some think it refers to association with delinquents or criminals, but it doesn't. It refers to association with criminal *behavior patterns*, which often are presented by mothers, fathers, and others who are not criminals. The idea that differential association is a theory about criminality in general also is in error. The error stems from the way the theory is presented, but if you think about it for a while, it's clear that differential association is really a theory about specific kinds of crime. For example, if you have an excess of associations favorable to shoplifing sweaters from local department stores, as teenaged girls are likely to do, that doesn't mean you have an excess of associations favorable to burglary, robbery, or stealing hubcaps. People don't become criminals in general. They are programmed to believe that committing only some kinds of crime is "really" bad, indecent, immoral, or otherwise unacceptable.

Interviewed in November 1983, and used with permission.

Evaluation of Differential Association Theory

Some support for the differential association theory can be found in the literature. James S. Short, Jr., tested an institutional sample of 126 boys and 50 girls and found that a consistent relationship existed between delinquent behavior and delinquent associations and that such associations were significant for both boys and girls.[6] Albert Reiss and A. Lewis Rhodes, using a sample of 378 white males, also found a youth's chance of committing a delinquent act depended on whether other members of his friendship group committed the same act.[7] Brenda S. Griffin and Charles T. Griffin, testing differential association theory in two studies of drug use among adolescents, found that the findings generally supported Sutherland's theory.[8]

The differential association theory still retains such an important place in the study of delinquent behavior because it is difficult to reject the argument that juveniles learn crime from others. Because juveniles learn their basic values, norms, skills, and perception of self from others, it seems irrefutable that they also learn crime from "significant others." Learning crime from those who have a greater number of definitions favorable to law violations appears to be particularly true for juveniles because of their extreme vulnerability to the influence of the group.

The positive nature of the differential association theory also has appeal, as this theory does not reduce delinquency to psychological and biological models, which postulate that personal inadequacies cannot be penetrated by outside influence. Instead Sutherland sees individuals as changeable and as subject to the opinions and values of others. Thus, the chief task in delinquency prevention becomes one of affecting change on small groups in which adolescents are involved, rather than attempting to change an entire society.[9]

The enduring impact of the differential association theory on the study of juvenile delinquency is apparent in the attempts to revise this theory. Melvin DeFleur and Richard Quinney, in reformulating the nine propositions of differential association theory, argue that the theory could be formally tightened if it were based on the concepts of symbolic interaction and attitude formation.[10] Daniel Glaser's modification of differential association theory is called "differential identification." The theory of differential identification is stated as follows: "A person pursues criminal behavior to the extent that he identifies himself with real or imaginary persons from whose perspective his criminal behavior seems acceptable."[11] Glaser's revision allows for human choice and stresses the importance of motives existing in the wider culture independent of direct intimate association. Robert Burgess and Ronald Akers' differential reinforcement theory propose a step-by-step restatement of differential association according to such ideas as reinforcement and punishment. Thus, they are contending that criminal or delinquent behavior is primarily learned "in those groups which comprise the individual's major source of reinforcements."[12]

The criticisms of the differential association theory can be grouped into three areas. First, critics point out that differential association theory has no room for human purpose and meaning, because it ultimately reduces the individual to an object that merely reacts to the bombardment of external forces and cannot reject the material being presented.[13] That is, the delinquent is viewed as a passive recipient into which various definitions are poured, and the resultant mixture is something over which he or she has no control.[14]

Second, differential association theory has been accused of proposing a view that does not deal with several critical questions relating to the process of learning crime from others. For example, why does one youth succumb to delinquent definitions and another does not? Why do youths who are exposed to delinquent definitions still perform conforming behavior most of the time? How did the first "teacher" learn delinquent techniques and definitions to pass on? Why do most youths desist from delinquent behavior at the age of seventeen or eighteen? Why do youths frequently continue delinquent behavior even after the removal of the aversive stimuli (delinquent peers)? Finally, what is the effect of punishment on delinquents?

Third, the terms of the differential association theory are so vague that it is nearly impossible to test the theory empirically. For example, how can "excess of definitions toward criminality" be measured statistically? How can "frequency, duration, priority, and intensity" be studied? What defines an intimate personal group? What exact techniques, motives, and rationalizations are learned from others?

However, although differential association theory has been under sharp attack in recent years, it remains one of the best known and most enduring theories of delinquent behavior.

DELINQUENCY AND DRIFT

David Matza's *Delinquency and Drift* discusses the process of becoming a delinquent.[15] Matza's concept of drift and differential association shares many assumptions in common, but Matza's drift theory does place far greater importance than differential association theory on the exercise of juveniles' choices and on the sense of injustice that juveniles feel about the discriminatory treatment they have received.

The process of becoming a delinquent, Matza says, begins when a juvenile neutralizes himself or herself from the moral bounds of the law and drifts into delinquency. Drift, according to Matza, means that "the delinquent *transiently* exists in limbo between convention and crime, responding in turn to the demands of each, flirting now with one, now the other, but postponing commitment, evading decision. Thus, he drifts between criminal and conventional action."[16]

Matza, having established that the delinquent is one who drifts back and forth between convention and deviancy, then examines the process by which legal norms are neutralized. But fundamental to his analysis is the contention that delinquent youths remain integrated into the wider society and that a violation of legal norms does not mean surrendering allegiance to them.[17]

There are millions of occasions during which a delinquency may be committed. Except for occasions covered by surveillance, virtually every moment experienced offers an opportunity for offense. Yet delinquency fails to occur during all but a tiny proportion of these moments. During most of the subcultural delinquent's life he is distracted and restrained by convention from the commission of offenses. Episodically, he is released from the moral bind of conventional order. This temporary though recurrent release from the bind of convention has been taken for compulsion or commitment. It is, instead, almost the opposite. During release the delinquent is not constrained to commit offense; rather, he is free to drift into delinquency. Under the condition of widely available extenuating circumstances, the subcultural delinquent may choose to commit delinquencies.[18]

Delinquency becomes permissible when responsibility is neutralized. The sense of responsibility, then, is the immediate condition of drift. But other conditions of drift include the sense of injustice, the primacy of custom, and the assertion of tort.

The delinquent, as part of a subculture, is filled with a sense of injustice. Matza claims that the subculture of delinquency depends on a memory file that collects examples of inconsistency; incompetence of officials of the juvenile justice system, especially the juvenile court judge; and favoritism. When the delinquent feels pushed around, or controlled by external forces, he may experience the mood of fatalism. This, in turn, results in the drift into delinquent behavior and provides a justification for such behavior.[19]

The primacy of custom relates to the delinquent's observation of the virtues of his subculture; these virtues stress the "traditional precepts of manliness, celebrating as they do the heroic themes of honor, valor, and loyalty."[20] In the group setting, the delinquent must demonstrate valor and loyalty when faced with dare, challenge, and insult. Although the acts emerging from the behavior of subcultural delinquents are in the nature of boyish antics, the delinquent knows they are wrong—but they are less wrong because they are motivated and inspired by noble sentiments.[21]

The assertion of tort occurs when the subcultural delinquent considers a harmful wrong as a tort instead of a crime. A tort has to do with a private transaction between the accused and the victim, and subcultural delinquents frequently believe that the justice process cannot be invoked unless the victim is willing to make a complaint or to press the charge.[22]

Other means of neutralization include the denial of responsibility, the denial of injury, the denial of the victim, the condemnation of the condemners, and the appeal to higher loyalties. These means permit the delinquent to insulate himself or herself from blame for deviant behavior.[23]

However, Matza concludes that "the breaking of the moral bind to law arising from neutralization and resulting in drift does not assure the commission of a delinquent act."[24] The missing element that provides "the thrust or impetus by which the delinquent act is realized is *will*."[25] The will is activated both on mundane occasions and in extraordinary situations.[26] But the subcultural delinquent is not likely to have the will to repeat an old offense if he or she has failed in the past: "Few persons—clowns and fools are among them—like to engage in activities they do badly."[27] Desperation, reasons Matza, also can activate one's will to commit infractions. Matza sees desperation intertwined with the mood of fatalism; that is, because the delinquent feels pushed around, he or she needs to make something happen to restore the mood of humanism.[28] Crime then enables the subcultural delinquent to see himself or herself as cause rather than as effect.[29]

David Matza's *Becoming Deviant* develops even further the steps in this process of becoming a delinquent. This process occurs in three stages: affinity, affiliation, and signification.[30] Affinity means that "persons, either individually or in aggregates, develop predispositions to certain phenomena."[31] Affiliation is the process by which the individual is "*converted* to conduct novel for him but already established for others." Affiliation provides the context and process by which the neophyte may be "turned on" or "out."[32] Affiliation begins with contagion, but the juvenile must be converted; that is, the individual decides to become committed to delinquent behavior.[33] Signification means that the juvenile is willing to stand up for, in the sense of representing or exemplifying, delinquent behavior.[34] That is, the juvenile has become committed to delinquency during affiliation and now is willing to exemplify or demonstrate delinquent behavior and values.

Matza developed the drift theory to account for the majority of adolescents who, from time to time, engage in delinquent behavior. But those youths who develop ongoing involvements with delinquent behavior he defines as being committed to delinquency and being willing to stand up for their commitment. This latter group, of course, consists of the chronic offenders, who constitute one of the most serious problems in dealing with youth crime in America.

Evaluation of Drift Theory

Drift, or neutralization, theory has several strengths. First, drift theory builds on the assumption that delinquent behavior is a learning process that takes place in interactions with others. It examines the influence of the group in encouraging youths to take a vacation from the moral binds of the law.

Second, drift theory can be used to account for the fact that the majority of adolescents commit occasional delinquent acts but then go on to accept roles as law-abiding adults. That is, drift theory accounts for the fact that delinquency will decline as adolescents approach adulthood. Matza's plausible explanation is that such individuals were not committed to delinquent norms in the first place. Matza does not categorize delinquent norms as either conventional or delinquent, but instead sees delinquent behavior as arising in a certain situational context among those who basically comply with societal norms.

Third, drift theory is extremely helpful in analyzing the situational aspect of delinquent behavior. Matza, in trying to explain how the situation affects the delinquent, provides an internal perspective that focuses on the delinquent as an author of action who is pressured by a situational context and by the norms of that context to engage in delinquent behavior. This critique of sociological positivism or determinism uses appreciation rather than condemnation to understand how the delinquent youth tries to make sense of his or her social reality.

Fifth, Matza's concept of the youth who becomes committed to delinquency and is willing to stand up for that commitment offers a step in developing a greater theoretical understanding of the career, or chronic offender. Unfortunately, such concepts as that of the will are extremely difficult, if not impossible, to examine empirically, but these exploratory concepts do offer promising theoretical considerations for understanding delinquent behavior.

Support for drift, or neutralization, theory has been mixed, but it would appear that many of these conflicting results can be resolved by more careful specification of the environmental context, the nature of the particular delinquency involved, and a search for intervening variables.[35] Richard Ball developed and used a neutralization attitude scale with a sample of youth at the Fairfield School for Boys in Lancaster, Ohio, and with a sample of core-city high school boys. He found that delinquents tended to give more excuses for various offenses than do nondelinquents. These differences were used for both personal and property offenses. Thus, Ball concluded that delinquents will accept the influence of neutralization more readily than non-delinquents.[36] Walter C. Reckless and Shlomo Shoham developed another theory of neutralization, which they called norm erosion. As the opposite of norm retention, norm erosion is a process of "give" in moral and ethical resistance; norm erosion can be applied to behavior that is embraced even when contrary to or in violation of the moral norms the delinquent or criminal originally internalized.[37] But Michael Hindelang questioned whether delinquents in fact subscribe to the same moral code as to nondelinquents and, therefore, whether neutralization actually takes place.[38] In support, Robert Regoli and Eric Poole, upgrading Hindelang's study, concluded that delinquents possibly do drift in and out of delinquent behavior because the attitudes of delinquents and nondelinquents are very similar.[39]

Several major criticisms can be raised about drift theory. Hirschi accuses drift theory of a logical deficiency; that is, "the strain that prompts the effort at neutralization also provides the motive force that results in the subsequent deviant act."[40] He adds that Matza overstates the conformity of delinquent youth: "Many persons do not have an attitude of respect toward the rules of society; many persons feel no moral obligation to conform regardless of personal advantage."[41] Taylor et al. accuse Matza of having a unidimensional view of the poor. In spite of the introduction of will into the explanation of subcultural recruitment, they claim, the deviant has no choice but to move toward the two poles of desperation and humanism; that is, between a despairing and a less despairing handling of his or her situation.[42]

Nevertheless, David Matza, in grounding his theory in the theoretical distributions of those who preceded him, such as Sutherland's differential association theory, has provided one of the most useful expressions of the dynamics of why individuals become involved in delinquent behavior. A recent restatement of his theory is found in the interview following this chapter.

CONTROL THEORY

The core ideas of control theory have a long history and go back to at least the nineteenth century. Control theorists agree on one fundamental point: that human beings must be held in check, or somehow controlled, if delinquent tendencies are to be repressed. Control theorists also generally agree that delinquency is the result of a deficiency in something; that is, juveniles commit delinquency because some controlling force is absent or defective.[43] Walter C. Reckless' containment theory and Travis Hirschi's social control theory are the two best known control theories.

Containment Theory

Walter C. Reckless developed containment theory in the 1950s and 1960s in order to explain crime and delinquency. Containment theory, which can explain both conforming behavior and deviancy, has two reinforcing elements: an inner control system and an outer control system. The assumption is that strong inner and reinforcing external containment provide insulation against deviant behavior. However, Reckless notes that containment theory does not explain the entire spectrum of delinquent behavior, for it does not account for delinquency that emerges from strong inner pushes, such as compulsions, anxieties, and personality disorders, or from organic impairments, such as brain damage.[44]

Elements of Containment Theory

Reckless defines the ingredients of inner containment as self-components, such as self-control, positive self-concept, ego strength, well-developed superego, high frustration tolerance, high resistance to diversions, high sense of responsibility, ability to find substitute satisfactions, goal orientations, and tension-reducing rationalizations. Outer containment, or external regulators, represent the structural buffers in the person's immediate social world or environment that are able to hold him or her within bounds. External controls consist of such items as the presentation of a consistent moral front to the person; institutional reinforcement of his or her norms, goals, and expectations; effective supervision and discipline; provision for a reasonable scope of activity, including limits and responsibilities; and opportunity for acceptance, identity, and belongingness.

Internal pushes consist of the drives, motives, frustrations, restlessness, disappointments, rebellion, hostility, and feelings of inferiority that encourage a person to become involved in socially unacceptable behavior. Environmental pressures are conditions associated with poverty or deprivation, conflict and discord, external restraint, minority group status, and limited access to success in an opportunity structure. Finally, the pulls of the environment consist of distractions, attractions, temptations, patterns of deviancy, carriers of delinquent patterns, and criminogenic advertising and propaganda in the society.

Relationship of Internal and External Containment and Delinquency

If a youth has a weak outer containment, the external pressures and pulls will need to be handled by the inner control system. If the youth's outer buffer is relatively strong and effective, his or her inner defense does not have to play such a critical role. Similarly, if the youth's inner controls are not equal to the ordinary pushes, an effective outer defense may help hold him or her within socially acceptable behavior. But if the inner defenses are in good working order, the outer structure does not have to come to the rescue. Juveniles who have both strong external and internal containment, then, are much less likely to become delinquent than those who have only either strong external or strong internal containment. Youths who have both weak external and internal controls are the most prone to delinquent behavior, although weak internal controls appear to result in delinquent behavior more often than weak internal controls.

The Self-Concept as an Insulation Against Delinquency

Containment theory, which has its origins in symbolic interactionism, involves both outer and inner containment, but inner containment, or self-concept, has received far more attention than has outer containment. Walter C. Reckless, Simon Dinitz, and their students spent over a decade investigating the effects of self-concept on delinquent behavior. The subjects for this study were sixth-grade boys living in the area of Columbus, Ohio, that had the highest white delinquency rate. Teachers were asked to nominate those boys who, in their point of view, were insulated against delinquency, and in the second phase of the study, teachers in the same area schools were asked to nominate sixth-grade boys who appeared to be heading toward delinquency. Both the "good boy" group and the "bad boy" group were given the same battery of psychological tests; the mothers of both groups too were interviewed.[45]

Reckless and Dinitz concluded from these studies that one of the preconditions of law-abiding or delinquent conduct is a good self-concept. This "insulation" against delinquency may be viewed as an ongoing process reflecting an internalization of nondelinquent values and conformity to the expectations of significant others—parents, teachers, and peers. Thus, a good self-concept, the product of favorable socialization, steers youths away from delinquency by acting as an inner buffer or "containment" against delinquency.

Reckless and Dinitz then undertook a four-year intervention project in the 1960s, which involved seventh-grade boys in all of the Columbus junior high schools and was designed to improve the self-concept of potential delinquents. But the follow-up data indicated that the special classes had no appreciable impact.[46]

A number of other studies have examined the efficacy of a positive self-concept in insulating adolescents from delinquent behavior. E. D. Lively and colleagues, who investigated self-concept in teenage children of various ethnic groups in Akron, Ohio, found that self-concept appears to improve as one moves away from the inner city.[47] H. B. Kaplan and A. D. Pokorny investigated the relationship of a broken home and self-derogation (negative self-concept) and found that a broken home in itself does not lead to a poor self-concept. Such factors as race, sex, and socioeconomic class, along with instability within the home, join together to create a negative self-concept.[48] In another study in Hawaii, Gary F. Jensen examined specific variables of self-concept and their relationship to "inner containment." He found that the greater the self-esteem, the less likely the youth is to become involved in delinquent behavior.[49] The result of a study of delinquency by Ferracuti and colleagues in San Juan, Puerto Rico, also supported the relationship of poor self-concept to delinquent behavior.[50] Furthermore, a recent study by H. B. Kaplan examined delinquent behavior as a coping strategy to defend against negative self-evaluation. He found that some students did become involved in particular activities with new membership groups in order to enhance self-esteem with those groups and, if they had negative experience with nondeviant groups, they would turn to delinquent-oriented groups to achieve a positive self-experience.[51]

The major flaw of inner containment, or self-concept theory, is the difficulty of defining self-concept in such a way that researchers can be certain they are accurately measuring the key variables of this concept. Simon Dinitz and Betty A. Pfau-Vicent, in updating the self-concept studies, have summarized why measurement of the self-concept is difficult:

> In short, we do not know what the crucial variables are in defining self-concept, nor how to use what we do know to adequately predict and control delinquent behavior. What is needed now is careful and thorough research aimed at accurate operationalization of self-concept. Only when we have identified these crucial variables will improved prevention efforts find fallow ground in which to take root in our efforts to enhance a young person's self-concept in the service of the prevention and control of serious juvenile delinquency.[52]

M. Schwartz and S. S. Tangri also questioned whether knowledge of others' perceptions was incorporated into a boy's self-concept. They suggested that poor self-concept might have other outcomes besides vulnerability to delinquency. They also disputed the adequacy of Reckless and Dinitz's measures of self-concept, saw the definitions of terms as confusing, and questioned the effects of labeling on the subsequent behavior of both the "good" and "bad" boys.[53]

Social Control Theory

Social control theory was developed by Travis Hirschi in *The Causes of Delinquency*. Hirschi, linking delinquent behavior to the bond an individual maintains with society, states that "delinquent acts result when an individual's bond to society is weak or broken."[54]

Two theoretical underpinnings undergird this sociological explanation of delinquent behavior. First, Hirschi is indebted to Emile Durkheim, who throughout his writings expressed the importance of the social bond in society:

> The more weakened the groups to which [the individual] belongs, the less he depends on them, the more he consequently depends only on himself and recognizes no other rules of conduct than what are founded on his private interests.[55]

Second, Hirschi accepts the view propounded by Thomas Hobbes, Puritan theologians, and Sigmund Freud that humans are basically antisocial and sinful. While this view may not be fashionable in sociological circles, Hirschi argues that their basic impulses motivate humans to become involved in crime and delinquency unless there is reason for them to refrain from antisocial behavior. Thus, instead of the standard question, "Why do they do it?," Hirschi says the more important question is, "Why don't they do it?"[56]

Elements of the Bond

Hirschi theorizes that the social bond is made up of four main elements: attachment, commitment, involvement, and belief.

The first element of control theory is an individual's attachment to conventional others. The sensitivity toward others, argues Hirschi, relates to the ability to internalize norms and to develop a conscience.[57] Attachment to others also refers to the ties of affection and respect children have to parents, teachers, and friends. The stronger the attachment to others, the more likely that an individual will take this into consideration when and if he or she is tempted to commit a delinquent act.[58] The attachment to parents is the most important variable insulating a child against delinquent behavior. Even if a family is broken by divorce or desertion, the child needs to maintain attachment to one or both parents. Indeed, "If the child is alienated from the parent," Hirschi asserts, "he will not develop an adequate conscience or superego."[59]

The second element of the bond is commitment to conventional activities and values. An individual is committed to the degree that he or she is willing to invest time, energy, and himself or herself in conventional activities, such as educational goals, property, or reputation. When a committed individual considers the cost of delinquent behavior, he or she uses common sense and thinks of the risk of losing the investment already made in conventional behavior.[60] Hirschi contends that if juveniles are committed to these conventional values and activities, they develop a stake in conformity and will refrain from delinquent behavior.

Involvement also protects an individual from delinquent behavior. Because time and energy are limited, involvement in conventional activities leaves no time for delinquent behavior. "The person involved in conventional activities is tied to appointments, deadlines, working hours, plans, and the like," reasons Hirschi, "so the opportunity to commit deviant acts rarely arises. To the extent that he is engrossed in conventional activities, he cannot even think about deviant acts, let alone act out his inclinations."[61]

The fourth element is belief. Delinquency results from the absence of effective beliefs that forbid socially unacceptable behavior.[62] Respect for the law and for the social norms of society are important components of belief. This respect for the values of the law and legal system is derived from intimate relations with other persons, especially parents. Hirschi develops a causal chain "from attachment to parents, through concern for the approval of persons in positions of authority, to belief that the rules of society are binding on one's conduct."[63]

Evaluation of Social Control Theory

Travis Hirschi tested his theory by administering a self-report survey to 4077 junior and high school students in Contra Costa County, California. He also used school records and police records to analyze the data he received on the questionnaires. His analysis of the data yielded data on the basic elements of the social bond.

Hirschi analyzed attachment of respondents in the sample to parents, to the school, and to peers. The greater the attachment to parents, he found, the less likely is the child to become involved in delinquent behavior. But more so than the fact of communication with the parents, the quality or the intimacy of the communication is the critical factor. The more love and respect that is found in the relationship with parents, the more likely that the child will recall the parents when and if a situation of potential delinquency arises.[64]

Hirschi also found that in terms of attachment to the school, students with little academic competence and those who perform poorly are more likely to become involved in delinquent behavior. Significantly, Hirschi found that students with weak affectional ties to parents tend to have little concern for the opinions of teachers and to dislike school.[65]

The attachment to peers, Hirschi found, does not imply lack of attachment to parents. Those respondents who were most closely attached to and respectful of their friends were least likely to have committed delinquent acts. Somewhat surprisingly, delinquents were less dependent on peers than nondelinquents. Hirschi theorizes from his data "that the boy's stake in conformity affects his choice of friends rather than the other way around."[66]

In terms of commitment, Hirschi found that if a boy claims the *right* to smoke, drink, date, and drive a car, he is more likely to become involved in delinquency. The automobile, like the cigarette and bottle of beer, indicates that the boy has put away childish things. Also, the more a boy is committed to academic achievement, the less likely he is to become involved in delinquent acts. Finally, Hirschi found that the higher the occupational expectations of boys, the less likely that they would become involved in delinquent behavior.[67]

The more that a boy is involved in school and leisure activities, the less likely he was to become involved in delinquency. That is, the more that boys in the sample felt that they had nothing to do, the more likely they were to become involved in delinquent acts. Hirschi theorizes that lack of involvement and commitment to school releases a young person from a primary source of time-structuring.[68]

In another confirmation of his control theory, Hirschi found that the less boys believed they should obey the law, the less likely they were to obey it. Significantly, he added that delinquents were relatively free of concern for the morality of their actions; delinquents, therefore, were relatively amoral and differed significantly in values from nondelinquents. Also, the data in this study failed to show much difference between lower- and middle-class young people in terms of values.[69] Travis Hirschi expresses some recent thoughts about social control theory in a 1983 interview:

BOX 7-2 Interview with Travis Hirschi

Question: If you were to rewrite *Causes of Delinquency*, would you reformulate control theory in any way?

Hirschi: Control theory as I stated it can't really be understood unless one takes into account the fact that it was attached to a particular method of research. When I was working on the theory, I knew that my data were going to be survey data; therefore, I knew I was going to have mainly the perceptions, attitudes, and values of individuals as reported by them. So I knew the theory had to be stated from the perspective of individuals committing or not committing delinquent acts. Had I data on other people, or on the structure of the community, I would have had to state the theory in a quite different way. There are lots of control theories, but the major differences among them stem from differences in the vantage point of the theorists, not from differences in their understanding of the theory.

For example, I was aware at the time I wrote my theory that it was well within the social disorganization tradition. I knew that, but you have to remember the status of social disorganization as a concept in the middle 1960s when I was writing. I felt I was swimming against the current in stating a social control theory at the individual level. Had I tried to sell social disorganization at the same time, I would have been in deep trouble. So I shied away from that tradition. As a result, I did not give social disorganization its due. I went back to Durkheim and Hobbes and ignored an entire American tradition that was directly relevant to what I was saying. But I was aware of it and took comfort in it. I said the same things the social disorganization people had said, but since they had fallen into disfavor I had to disassociate myself from them. Further, as Ruth Kornhauser so acutely points out, social disorganization theories had been associated with the cultural tradition. That was the tradition I was working hardest against; so in that sense, I would have compromised my own position or I would have introduced a lot of debate I didn't want to get into had I dealt explicitly with social disorganization theory. Now, with people like Kornhauser on my side, and social disorganization back in vogue, I would emphasize my roots in this illustrious tradition.

Question: Can control theory be expanded? What would be its main propositions and underpinnings of this expanded control theory?

Hirschi: Jack Gibbs mentioned the other day that traditionally the problem with social control as a concept is that it tends to expand until it becomes synonymous with sociology, and then it dies. It dies because then there is nothing unique or distinct about it. This danger is present even when the concept is limited initially to delinquency. I enjoy papers that apply my theory to areas other than delinquency, such as Watergate and white collar crime, but I recognize the risk. Because of it, generality is not something I would move toward. Instead, I would try to focus on the theory's image of criminality and ask how far that might take us. I think I've generally worked with a too restrictive image of delinquency. I did this because I thought the field had made a mistake by bringing things into delinquency that were not delinquency. If, for example, smoking and drinking are part of delinquency, they cannot be causes of delinquency. I thought that was a mistake because I wanted to use those kinds of behaviors as independent variables. I now believe that smoking and drinking are delinquency.

Source: Interviewed in November 1983 and used with permission.

Other researchers have found support for control theory. Wiatrowski, Griswold, and Roberts explored the degree to which the four dimensions of the social bond are mutually independent, as well as the direct and indirect effect of socioeconomic class. Using self-reports of 2213 tenth-grade boys, they concluded that items considered as indicators of attachment to school, parents and peers, future occupational commitment, and school involvement are mutually independent predictors of moderate delinquent behaviors.[70] Krohn and Massey also found a moderate relationship between a wide range of delinquent behaviors and social bond measures.[71] But both of these studies concluded that the social bond factors tell only a partial story, for other factors also are needed to understand delinquent behavior.[72] Michael Hindelang, using subjects in the sixth through twelfth grades in a New York State school system, essentially supported Hirschi's social control findings. The attachment to peers was the major difference between his study and Hirschi's, for Hindelang found, as have many other researchers, that identification with peers was directly related to delinquent involvements.[73]

Control theory has several strengths. First, it is amenable to empirical examination. In contrast to other theorists discussed in this unit, Hirschi was able to test his theory with a population of adolescents. The basic theoretical constructs of control theory are clearly defined—such terms as attachment to parents, involvement in school, and commitment to conventional activities.

Second, integrated theories that have recently emerged have used the social control perspective to weave together the socialization settings of control theory into a unified conceptualization of socialization processes.[74] Both Elliott and colleagues and Johnson have used the concept of social bond to synthesize other theories into a single explanatory paradigm.[75]

Third, social control theory has provided valuable insights concerning delinquent behavior. For example, the importance of the intrafamily relationship has been substantiated. The relationship between the school and delinquency is another important area addressed by social control theory. Hirschi explored such areas as aspirations, achievement, affection toward teachers, time spent on homework, and the influence of class on school performance. Furthermore, he examined peer relationships perhaps in greater depth than any other researcher, and, while his findings concerning peers and delinquency may be questioned, the issues he raised are extremely helpful in understanding these relationships. In addition, Hirschi discussed the importance of work, occupational aspiration, use of the automobile, and leisure-time activities, among other factors, all of which have significantly increased our knowledge of delinquent behavior.

But Hirschi's theory does have limitations. First, he uses a limited array of items in evaluating the dimensions of the social bond, and the questionnaire items he used to measure delinquency list only a few relatively minor behavior problems.[76] Second, there are some theoretical problems with social control theory. It fails to describe the chain of events that weaken the social bond, and it divides delinquents into either socialized or unsocialized youths. That division is criticized both because it ignores the political and economic contexts of crime and because it ignores the findings among self-report studies of the widespread nature of youthful law-breaking activities. Third, the importance of other factors in the explanation of delinquency is indicated by the amount of delinquent behavior not explained by social control variables. Few estimates exceed 50 percent; this figure is impressive compared to other explanations of delinquency but far from allowing one to conclude that social control variables determine delinquency.[77]

In summary, social control theory has more empirical support today than any other explanation of delinquency. Although control theory does have methodological and theoretical limitations, researchers are increasingly using this theory to develop integrated explanations of delinquent behavior.

LABELING THEORY

The labeling perspective claims that society creates the deviant by labeling those who are apprehended as "different" from other youth when in reality they are different only because they have been "tagged" with a deviant label. The view that formal and informal societal reactions to delinquent behavior can influence the subsequent attitudes and behavior of delinquents has been recognized for most of this century.[78] Frank Tannenbaum, Edwin Lemert, and Howard Becker are the chief proponents of the labeling perspective.

Frank Tannenbaum: The Dramatization of Evil

In 1938, Frank Tannenbaum developed the earliest formulation of labeling theory in his book *Crime and the Community*. Tannenbaum examined the process whereby a juvenile came to the attention of the authorities and was "tagged" or labeled as different from other juveniles. Tannenbaum theorized that this process produced a change in both how those individuals were then handled by the justice system and how they came to view themselves:

> The process of making the criminal, therefore, is a process of tagging, defining, identifying, segregating, describing, emphasizing, making conscious and self-conscious; it becomes a way of stimulating, suggesting, emphasizing, and evoking the very traits that are complained of.[79]

Tannenbaum called this process "the dramatization of evil." He wrote that the process of tagging a juvenile resulted in the youth becoming involved with other delinquents and that these associations represented an attempt to escape the society that was responsible for negative labeling. The delinquent, then, became involved in a deviant career and, regardless of the efforts of individuals in the community and justice system to stamp out his or her "evil" behavior, the negative behavior became "hardened" and resistant to positive values. Tannenbaum proposed that the less the evil is dramatized, the less likely youths are to become involved in deviant careers.[80]

Edwin Lemert: Primary and Secondary Deviation

Lemert's concept of primary and secondary deviation is regarded as one of the most important theoretical constructs of the labeling perspective. According to Lemert, primary deviation consists of the behavior of the individual, and secondary deviation is society's response to that behavior. The social reaction to the deviant, Lemert charged, could be interpreted as forcing a change in status or role; that is, society's reaction to the deviant resulted in a transformation in the individual's identity.[81] The social reaction to the deviant, whether a disapproving glance or a full-blown stigmatization, is critical in understanding the progressive commitment of a person to a deviant mode of life. For example, Lemert claims that the label given to female prostitutes creates a need to resolve conflicts between their roles and identities and, . thereby, results in closer relationships with pimps.[82]

Lemert saw this process of becoming deviant as having the following stages:

The sequence of interaction leading to secondary deviation is roughly as follows: (1) primary deviation; (2) social penalties; (3) further primary deviation; (4) stronger penalties and rejection; (5) further deviation, perhaps with hostilities and resentment beginning to focus upon those doing the penalizing; (6) crisis reached in the tolerance quotient, expressed in formal action by the community stigmatizing of the deviant; (7) strengthening of the deviant conduct as a reaction to the stigmatizing and penalties; (8) ultimate acceptance of deviant social status and efforts at adjustment on the basis of the associated role.[83]

The social reaction to deviance is expressed in this process of interaction. *Social reaction* is a general term summarizing both the reactions of others in terms of moral indignation toward deviance and the action directed to its control.[84] This concept encompasses both social organizational and social psychological perspectives. As an organizational response, the concept of social reaction refers to the capacity of control agents to impose such constraints upon the behavior of the deviant as are reflected in terms like "treat," "correct," or "punish."[85]

Howard Becker and the Deviant Career

Howard Becker, another major labeling theorist, conceptualized the relationship between the rules of society and the process of being labeled as an outsider:

Social groups create deviance by making the rules whose infraction constitutes deviance, and by applying those rules to particular people and labeling them as outsiders. From this point of view, deviance is not a quality of the act the person commits, but rather a consequence of the application by others of rules and sanctions to an "offender." The deviant is one to whom that label has successfully been applied; deviant behavior is behavior that people so label.[86]

Once a person is caught and labeled, that person becomes an outsider and gains a new social status, with consequences for both self-image and one's public identity. The individual is now regarded as a different kind of person.[87] Although the sequence of events that leads to the imposition of the label of deviant is presented from the perspective of social interaction, the analytical framework shifts to that of social structure once the label is imposed. In other words, before a person is labeled, he or she participates in a process of social interaction, but once labeling has occurred the individual is assigned a status within a social structure.[88]

The conception of the deviant career supports this shift from a process orientation to a structural orientation. The imagery implied by the concept of career involves the movement from status to status within some encompassing social structure:

> A useful conception in developing sequential models of various kinds of deviant behavior is that of career. Originally developed in studies of occupations, the concept refers to the sequence of movement from one position to another in an occupational system made by any individual who works in that system. Furthermore, it includes the notion of "career contingency," those factors on which mobility from one position to another depends. Career contingencies include both objective facts of social structure and changes in the perspectives, motivations, and desires of the individual.[89]

The concept of deviant career is apparent throughout an offender's contact with the juvenile justice system. A particular youthful offender may become involved in delinquent acts from time to time, but then one night he and two companions are arrested during the break-in of a liquor store. He is a lower-class youth whose two brothers have been involved in delinquent acts throughout their adolescent years; the younger brother has been sent to training school. This youth is referred to the juvenile court and during the adjudication stage of the court's proceedings, he is judged a delinquent and placed on probation. Once labeled, this youth begins the process of interaction that leads him to pursue behaviors consistent with his new social identity. Before long, he has internalized a deviant label and is engulfed in a delinquent career. Because he has accepted the role and status of his new career, he continues to commit delinquent acts.

Evaluation of the Labeling Perspective

The labeling perspective has consistently received mixed responses. Gary Jensen found that official labels are strongly related to the self-definition of a delinquent and that white youths are more affected by official labels than are black youths.[90] Susan Ageton and Delbert Elliott also found from a longitudinal study that the self-concepts of white youths declined after they had police contact.[91] But Jack Foster, Walter Reckless, and Simon Dinitz found that labeling by the juvenile justice system during an early stage of processing did not produce either changes in self-concept or increased delinquent behavior.[92] Stuart J. Miller examined the effect of labeling during the institutional process and also concluded that such labels as emotionally disturbed or aggressive behavior had very little predictive power in the future behavior of hard-core delinquents.[93]

However, labeling theory has several strengths. First, it provides an explanation for why youths who become involved in the juvenile justice process typically continue delinquent acts until the end of their adolescent years. The official labeling process has identified them as different from other adolescents, and they continue to live up to their reputations.

Second, labeling theory emphasizes the importance of rule making and power in the creation of deviance. Considering the broader contexts of the labeling process lifts the focus of delinquency from the behavior of an individual actor to the interactions of an actor and his or her immediate and broader influences. Because society is emphasized as contributing to the process of becoming deviant, the rules made and the enforcement of those rules are critical in understanding the phenomenon of delinquency.

Third, such concepts as career and identity become meaningful when the delinquent behaviors of chronic offenders are examined. Those youths involved in one delinquent act after the other do see their lives largely in terms of delinquency. It is, in fact, a career to them, and they have internalized a deviant identity. This statement becomes evident in working with hard-core offenders who talk about "walking away from crime" and "starting a new life in the community." Their words and thought patterns obviously relate to concepts like career and identity.

Fourth, as part of a larger symbolic interactionist perspective, labeling theory points out that individuals do take on the roles and self-concepts expected of them; that is, they are indeed victims of self-fulfilling prophecies. A student who is reinforced typically attempts to seek more reinforcement; likewise, the student who is "put down" by a teacher often is discouraged and continues to engage in negative or self-defeating behaviors.

However, the theoretical basis of the labeling approach has been widely criticized. Jack Gibbs charges that the labeling approach lacks clear-cut definitions, fails to produce a coherent set of interrelated propositions and testable hypotheses, and, therefore, ought not to be considered a theory in any sense.[94] Gibbs adds that the labeling approach raises major questions:

> But the new conception has left at least four crucial questions unanswered. First, what elements in the scheme are intended to be definitions rather than substantive theory? Second, is the ultimate goal to explain deviant behavior or to explain reactions to deviation? Third, is deviant behavior to be identified exclusively in terms of reaction to it? Fourth, exactly what kind of reaction identifies behavior as deviant?[95]

The labeling perspective also is criticized for ignoring the importance of delinquent behavior. Society is made the culprit, and the behavior of the delinquent is excused. In addition, this approach fails to take seriously the motivation of the delinquent for such behavior; this particularly becomes important when dealing with actors who are aware of the high probability of apprehension for their behavior.[96]

Finally, David Bordua suggests that the labeling perspective lacks empirical verification.[97] Other social researchers add that this perspective has not clarified its basic assumptions to the point that they can be tested.[98]

EVALUATION OF SOCIAL PROCESS THEORIES

Social process theories can be fitted into the deterministic framework of the past three chapters because they conceive of the delinquent as being acted upon. But some of these theories are more deterministic than others. Differential association, for example, views the delinquent as a passive being who merely responds to the definitions of crime to which he or she is exposed. Likewise, labeling theory expresses the deterministic view that society creates the delinquent through official processing. Containment theory portrays an individual who becomes what others make him or her; the youth whose experiences have resulted in a good self-concept will be insulated from delinquency, while the youth with a poor self-concept is likely to become involved in delinquent behavior. Social control and drift theory do regard the delinquent as a decision-maker, but with the freedom to make choices for or against crime limited by the established social bond and subcultural group. Matza expresses this state in terms of the concept of soft determinism; the juvenile has freedom and choice to a point, but ultimately is responsive to the wishes of the group.

The strength of social process theories rests in their analyses of the individual level of the delinquent. The stages of becoming deviant, the careers, the identities and the self-concept are key concepts in these theories. Similarly, the commitment to the social bond or to delinquent behavior is addressed by two of these theories. The picture offered of the delinquent, particularly the drift and social control theories, seems to fit more accurately delinquents in the real world than do those of the theories discussed in the past three chapters. In addition, theories in this chapter go a step further as they attempt to describe the process or stages of becoming delinquent. Finally, the continued development of integrated theory promises to clarify even more the socialization processes that lead to or away from delinquent behavior.

However, as the strength of these theories is found in their microanalysis of the meaning, behavior, and interactions of the individual delinquent, their major flaw lies in terms of macroanalysis. These theories fail to consider seriously the impact of the larger political and economic systems upon the delinquent. Even in labeling theory, the sociocultural context and the use of power in the creation and enforcement of rules in this context appear to be divorced largely from the influence of economics and politics.

In short, as the major weakness in the social structure explanations of delinquency lies in their ignoring of the level of the individual delinquent, the major limitation of social process theories is their preoccupation with that level of analysis. But together these two types of sociological analysis can provide a much stronger explanation for why delinquency occurs and persists in American society, summarized in Table 7-1.

TABLE 7-1 Summary of Structural Theories of Delinquency

The Theory	Cause of Delinquency Identified in the Theory	Supporting Research
Differential association	Delinquent behavior is expected of those individuals who have internalized a preponderance of definitions favorable to law violations	Moderate
Drift	Juvenile neutralizes himself or herself from the moral bounds of the law and drifts into delinquent behavior	Moderate
Containment	Strong inner and reinforcing external containment provide an insulation against delinquent behavior	Strong
Social control	Delinquent acts result when a juvenile's bond to society is weak or broken	Strong
Labeling	Society creates the deviant by labeling those who are apprehended as "different" from other juveniles when in reality they are different only because they have been given a deviant label	Moderate

POLICY IMPLICATIONS

Each of the social process theories in this chapter has a contribution to make to policymakers. Differential association theory suggests that delinquents learn from their association with small groups and, therefore, the more that they are exposed to prosocial groups, the more likely it is that they will be deterred from delinquent behavior. Such treatment technologies as positive peer culture and guided group interaction show that certain delinquent youths are influenced by positive group norms. Thus, the task is to generate opportunities for delinquency-prone youths to be exposed to more positive definitions of the social order.

Social control theory suggests that the more attached youths are to the social bond, the more likely it is that they will refrain from delinquent behavior. Thus, attachment to the family, positive experiences in school, and exposure to prosocial groups in the community become important components in the design of delinquent prevention and control programs. Containment theory also proposes that positive experiences in the home, in the school, and in the community will lead to good self-concepts, thereby insulating youths from delinquent behavior.

Both drift theory and labeling theory suggest that a key element in the process of becoming delinquent is the reaction of society to socially unacceptable behavior. Delinquency in America is widespread throughout the social order, and the danger is that identifying and tagging individuals who have come to the attention of the justice system will increase their chances of continuing delinquent behavior. Or even worse, their official contacts with the system may encourage them toward a delinquent career. Thus, policymakers would be wise to discourage the labeling of youths, both in the school system and in the justice system.

SUMMARY

The social process theories discussed in this chapter provide additional pieces of the puzzle of why youngsters become involved in delinquent behavior. Their findings can be summarized as follows:

- The more that youths are exposed to antisocial definitions by peer groups, the more likely they are to become involved in delinquent behavior.
- The more that youths internalize negative feelings toward themselves, the more likely they are to become involved in delinquent behavior.
- The more that youths lack an attachment for the family, a desire to do well in the school, and an involvement in community activities, the more likely they are to become involved in delinquent behavior.
- The more that youths experience unfairness in the way they are handled by the juvenile justice system, the more likely they are to become involved in delinquent behavior.
- The more negative labels youths receive, the more likely they are to become involved in delinquent behavior.

These findings, along with the ones discussed in previous chapters, contribute to our understanding of the causes of delinquent behavior. But because the association between cause and effect for any behavior, delinquent or nondelinquent, is generally multidimensional, it is unlikely that any one theory can explain why a particular adolescent became involved in delinquent behavior. Some theories, of course, explain the behavior of particular youths better than others, but generally the reasons a youth becomes involved in delinquent behavior include psychological, social structural, social process, and sometimes even biosociological levels of explanations.

Discussion Questions

1. Why is differential association theory called a learning theory?
2. The self-concept, according to containment theory, is vitally important in affecting one's behavior. Do you agree?
3. David Matza and Travis Hirschi present two different understandings of commitment. Define how each uses it and explain which one you prefer.
4. Matza and Hirschi also propose different interpretations of the degree to which delinquents are identified with the norms and values of society. Define the position of each and explain which one you prefer.
5. What is the labeling perspective's definition of why adolescents become delinquent? Do you agree with this interpretation?

References

Burgess, Robert L., and Akers, Ronald L. "Differential Association Theory of Criminal Behavior," *Social Problems* 14 (Fall 1966): 128–147.

Glaser, Daniel. "Criminality Theories and Behavioral Images," *American Journal of Sociology* 61 (March 1956): 433–444.

Hirschi, Travis. *Causes of Delinquency*. Berkeley: University of California Press, 1969.

Johnson, Richard E. *Juvenile Delinquency and Its Origins*. Cambridge: Cambridge University Press, 1979.

Matza, David. *Delinquency and Drift*. New York: Wiley, 1964.

Matza, David. *Becoming Deviant*. Englewood Cliffs, N.J.: Prentice-Hall, 1969.

Reckless, Walter C. "A New Theory of Delinquency and Crime," *Federal Probation* 25 (December 1961): 42–46.

Shoemaker, Donald J. *Theories of Delinquency: An Examination of Explanations of Delinquent Behavior*. New York: Oxford University Press, 1984.

Sutherland, Edwin H. "Development of a Theory," in *The Sutherland Papers*, edited by Albert K. Cohen, Alfred Lindesmith, and Karl Schuessler. Bloomington: Indiana University Press, 1956.

Sutherland, Edwin H., and Cressey, Donald R. *Principles of Criminology*. 5th ed. Philadelphia: J. B. Lippincott, 1955.

Sykes, Gresham M., and Matza, David. "Techniques of Neutralization: A Theory of Delinquency," *American Sociological Review* 22 (September 1957): 129–142.

FOOTNOTES

1. Interviewed in April 1983.

2. Charles H. Cooley, *Human Nature and the Social Order* (1902; reprinted. New York: Schocken Books, 1964); George H. Mead, *Mind, Self and Society* (Chicago: University of Chicago Press, 1934.)

3. Edwin H. Sutherland, "A Statement of the Theory," in *The Sutherland Papers*, edited by Albert Cohen, Alfred Lindesmith, and Karl Schuessler (Bloomington: Indiana University Press, 1956), p. 9.

4. Edwin H. Sutherland, *Principles of Criminology* (Philadelphia: J. B. Lippincott, 1947).

5. Harold Finestone, *Victims of Change: Juvenile Delinquents in American Society* (Westport, Conn.: Greenwood Press, 1976), p. 157.

6. James S. Short, Jr., "Differential Association as a Hypothesis: Problems of Empirical Testing," *Social Problems* 8 (1960), pp. 14–25.

7. Albert Reiss and A. Lewis Rhodes, "The Distribution of Delinquency in the Social Class Structure," *American Sociological Review* 26 (1961), p. 732.

8. Brenda S. Griffin and Charles T. Griffin, "Marijuana Use among Students and Peers," *Drug Forum* 7 (1978), pp. 155–165.

9. LaMar T. Empey, *American Delinquency: Its Meaning and Construction* (Homewood, Ill.: Dorsey Press, 1982), p. 218.

10. Melvin DeFleur and Richard Quinney, "A Reformulation of Sutherland's Differential Association Theory and a Strategy for Empirical Verification," *Journal of Research in Crime and Delinquency* 3 (January 1966), pp. 1–11.

11. Daniel Glaser, "Criminality Theory and Behavioral Images," *American Journal of Sociology* 61 (1956), pp. 433–444.

12. R. Burgess and R. Akers, "A Differential Association-Reinforcement Theory of Criminal Behavior," *Social Problems* 14 (1966), pp. 128–147.

13. Steven Box, *Deviance, Reality and Society* (New York: Holt, Rinehart and Winston, 1971), p. 21.

14. C. R. Jeffery, "An Integrated Theory of Crime and Criminal Behavior," *Journal of Criminal Law, Criminology and Police Science* 49 (1959), pp. 533–552.

15. David Matza, *Delinquency and Drift* (New York: John Wiley & Sons, 1964).

16. Matza, *Delinquency and Drift*, p. 28.

17. Ibid., p. 49.

18. Ibid., p. 52.

19. Ibid., p. 69.

20. Ibid., p. 101.

21. Ibid., p. 88.

22. Ibid., p. 156.

23. Gresham M. Sykes and David Matza, "Techniques of Neutralization: A Theory of Delinquency," *American Sociological Review* 22 (December 1957), pp. 664–666.

24. Matza, *Delinquency and Drift*, p. 181.

25. Ibid.

26. Ibid., p. 184.

27. Ibid., p. 185.

28. Ibid., p. 188.

29. Ibid., p. 189.

30. David Matza, *Becoming Deviant* (Englewood Cliffs, N.J.: Prentice-Hall, 1969).

31. Ibid., p. 90.

32. Ibid., pp. 101–102.

33. Ibid., p. 102.

34. Ibid., p. 156.

35. Richard A. Ball, "Development of Basic Norm Violation: Neutralization and Self-Concept Within a Male Cohort," *Criminology* 21 (February 1983), p. 78.

36. Richard A. Ball, "An Empirical Exploration of Neutralization Theory," *Criminologia* 4 (1966), pp. 22–32. See also Richard Allen Ball, "A Report to the Ohio Youth Commission and Columbus Public Schools" based on Ph.D. dissertation, Ohio State University, 1965.

37. Walter C. Reckless and Shlomo Shoham, "Norm Containment Theory as Applied to Delinquency and Crime," *Excerpta Criminologica* 3 (November-December 1963), pp. 637–644.

38. Michael Hindelang, "The Commitment of Delinquents to Their Misdeeds: Do Delinquents Drift?" *Social Problems* 17 (1970), pp. 50–59.

39. Robert Regoli and Eric Poole, "The Commitment of Delinquents to Their Misdeeds: A Reexamination," *Journal of Criminal Justice* 6 (1978), pp. 261–269.

40. Traius Hirschi, *Causes of Delinquency* (Berkeley: University of California Press, 1969), p. 24.

41. Ibid., p. 25.

42. Ian Taylor, Paul Walton, and Jack Young, *The New Criminology* (New York: Harper & Row, 1973), p. 186.

43. Donald J. Shoemaker, *Theories of Delinquency: An Examination of Explanations of Delinquent Behavior* (New York: Oxford University Press, 1984), p. 153.

44. The principles of containment theory are adapted from Walter C. Reckless, "A New Theory of Delinquency and Crime," *Federal Probation* 24 (December 1961), pp. 42–46.

45. Simon Dinitz and Betty A. Pfau-Vicent, "Self-Concept and Juvenile Delinquency: An Update," *Youth and Society* 14 (December 1982), pp. 133–158.

46. Walter C. Reckless and Simon Dinitz, *The Prevention of Juvenile Delinquency: An Experiment* (Columbus: The Ohio State University Press, 1972).

47. E. D. Lively, Simon Dinitz, and Walter C. Reckless, "Self-Concept as a Prediction of Juvenile Delinquency," *American Journal of Orthopsychiatry* 32 (1962), pp. 159–168.

48. H. B. Kaplan and A. D. Pokorny, "Self-Derogation and Childhood Broken Home," *Journal of Marriage and the Family* 33 (1971), pp. 328–337.

49. G. F. Jensen, "Inner Containment and Delinquency," *Criminology*, 64 (1973), pp. 464–470.

50. F. Ferracuti, Simon Dinitz, and E. Acosta de Brenes, *Delinquents and Nondelinquents in the Puerto Rican Slum Culture* (Columbus: Ohio State University Press, 1975).

51. H. B. Kaplan, *Deviant Behavior in Defense of Self* (New York: Academic Press, 1980).

52. Dinitz and Pfau-Vicent, "Self-Concept and Juvenile Delinquency," p. 155.

53. M. Schwartz and S. S. Tangri, "A Note on 'Self-Concept as an Insulator against Delinquency'," *American Sociological Review* 30 (1965), pp. 922–926.

54. Hirschi, *The Causes of Delinquency*, p. 16.

55. Emile Durkheim, quoted in Hirschi, *Causes of Delinquency*, p. 16.

56. Ibid., p. 34.

57. Ibid., p. 18.

58. Ibid., p. 83.

59. Ibid., p. 86.

60. Ibid., p. 20.

61. Ibid., p. 22.

62. Ibid., p. 198.

63. Ibid., p. 200.

64. Ibid., p. 108.

65. Ibid., pp. 110–134.

66. Ibid., pp. 135–161.

67. Ibid., pp. 162–185.

68. Ibid., pp. 187–196.

69. Ibid., pp. 197–224.

70. Jerald Bachman, *Youth in Transition* (Ann Arbor, Mich.: Inter-University Consortium for Political and Social Research, University of Michigan, 1975).

71. Marvin D. Krohn and James L. Massey, "Social Control and Delinquent Behavior: An Examination of the Elements of the Social Bond" (unpublished paper, 1980).

72. Richard Salem, "Commitment and Delinquency: Social Attachments and Behavioral Change in Group Homes" (paper presented at the Annual Meeting of the Wisconsin Sociological Association, October 22, 1982), p. 5.

73. Michael J. Hindelang, "Causes of Delinquency: A Partial Replication and Extension," *Social Problems* 20 (Spring 1973), pp. 471–487.

74. Mark Colvin and John Pauly, "A Critique of Criminology: Toward an Integrated Structural-Marxist Theory of Delinquency Production," *American Journal of Sociology* (November 1983), p. 523.

75. Richard E. Johnson, *Juvenile Delinquency and its Origins* (Cambridge: Cambridge University Press, 1979) and Delbert S. Elliott, Suzanne S. Ageton, and Rachelle J. Canter, "An Integrated Theoretical Perspective on Delinquent Behavior," *Journal of Research in Crime and Delinquency* 16 (1979), pp. 3–27.

76. Salem, "Commitment and Delinquency," p. 3.

77. Shoemaker, *Theories of Delinquency,* p. 175.

78. Ibid., p. 180.

79. Frank Tannenbaum, *Crime and the Community* (New York: Columbia University Press, 1938), pp. 19–20.

80. Ibid.

81. Harold Finestone, *Victims of Change: Juvenile Delinquents in American Society* (Westport, Conn.: Greenwood Press, 1976), p. 198.

82. Edwin M. Lemert, *Social Pathology* (New York: McGraw-Hill Book Company, 1951), p. 16.

83. Ibid., pp. 16–17.

84. Finestone, *Victims of Change,* p. 192.

85. Ibid., p. 198.

86. Howard S. Becker, *Outsiders* (New York: The Free Press, 1963), pp. 8–9.

87. Ibid., pp. 31–32.

88. Finestone, *Victims of Change,* p. 208.

89. Becker, *Outsiders,* p. 24.

90. Gary Jensen, "Labeling and Identity," *Criminology* 18 (1980), pp. 121–129.

91. Susan Ageton and Delbert Elliott, "The Effect of Legal Processing on Self-Concept" (Boulder, Colorado: Institute of Behavioral Sciences; University of Colorado, 1973).

92. Jack Foster, Simon Dinitz, and Walter C. Reckless, "Perceptions of Stigma Following Public Intervention for Delinquent Behavior," *Social Problems* 18 (1970), p. 202.

93. Stuart J. Miller, "Post-Institutional Adjustment of 443 Consecutive TICO Releases," Ph.D. dissertation, The Ohio State University, 1971.

94. Edwin M. Schur, *Labeling Deviant Behavior: Its Sociological Implications* (New York: Harper & Row, 1971), p. 35.

95. Jack P. Gibbs, "Conceptions of Deviant Behavior: The Old and the New," *Pacific Sociological Review* 9 (Spring 1966), pp. 9–14.

96. Schur, *Labeling Deviant Behavior,* p. 14.

97. David Bordua, "On Deviance," *Annals* 312 (1969), p. 121.

98. Gibbs, "Conceptions of Deviant Behavior," pp. 9–14.

INTERVIEW WITH DAVID MATZA

I still do not think that very many youngsters are committed to delinquency. I am not sure how fruitful the debate is since "commitment" is a very slippery term. Commitment to an institution is a much firmer basis for subsequent juvenile delinquency than anything so intangible as an attitudinal commitment.

In this interview, David Matza updates some of the assumptions he made about delinquency in *Delinquency and Drift*. Professor Matza also emphasizes the importance of racial and economic oppressiveness upon youth in terms of delinquent behavior.

Question: Has your thinking changed concerning the process of becoming a delinquent since you wrote *Delinquency and Drift?*

Matza: Not too much but some. I would now place more emphasis on racial oppression and the class correlates of racial oppression. The underlying social and political basis for the sense of injustice is left too implicit in *Delinquency and Drift*. Partly that was because the usual theories in the early sixties were based on class injustice and such theories were not very firmly based in fact as I tried to point out in sections of the book and in *Becoming Deviant*. In my opinion, the thesis of racial injustice is based much more securely in the known facts of American history and social structure and very accurately reflected in the composition of prison and juvenile correctional populations.

Question: Are you as convinced that most subcultural delinquents adhere to societal norms as you were when you wrote *Delinquency and Drift?*

Matza: I am not as convinced, yet I still believe that even in rebellion against a morality whose application is unjust, a belief in the truth of an uncorrupted morality is asserted. When Frederick Douglass asserted that to be free, the slave was compelled to break most, if not all of the rules of the oppressor, he was not by that statement breaking with the idea of society or with the belief in morality. Increasingly, I have come to think that what we call juvenile delinquency is, in part, the behavior of the youthful section of what traditionally has been termed the dangerous classes. The nineteenth century ideas of the dangerous classes are today lodged in the writings of Edward Banfield. Without understanding the oppressive context of social life among oppressed populations, the dangerous behavior of youth is likely to be misconceived as deriving from biological factors, a tendency which is once again rampant in criminology and sociology thanks to ideologues like Banfield and his followers.

Question: Commitment to delinquency is one concept in your publications which has been widely debated. What is your reaction to this concept today?

Matza: I still do not think that very many youngsters are committed to delinquency. I am not sure how fruitful the debate is since "commitment" is a very slippery term. Commitment to an institution is a much firmer basis for subsequent juvenile delinquency than anything so intangible as an attudinal commitment.

Question: In a 1971 interview, you indicated that *Delinquency and Drift* is a "confused jumbling of conservative, liberal, and radical views" and that "*Becoming Deviant* is sort of liberal and radical, maybe a little conservative too." What did you mean by these comments?

David Matza is professor of sociology at the University of California, Berkeley. He is the author of Delinquency and Drift and Becoming Deviant and coauthor of "Techniques of Neutralization." More recently, Professor Matza is the coauthor of "Poverty and Disrepute," which appeared in Merton and Nisbet, Contemporary Social Problems, and of the "Ordeal of Consciousness" which appeared in Theory and Society. Interviewed in April, 1984, and used with permission.

Matza: I meant to imply that I was quite disappointed if not angry at the way criminal justice systems were already beginning to twist much of the writings of the sixties toward their punitive and correctional ends. I guess I thought and still think that if my writing was unclear enough to appeal to conservatives I must have been pretty confused. I was being critical of myself and perhaps others of similar perspective for having presented material so easily absorbed by an establishment which between 1970 and 1984 abandoned and then turned against improving or at least reforming the penal system. I also meant that I was not very happy about my work, that a deeper formulation of the phenomenon would eliminate some of the philosophical ambiguity.

Question: Interest and research in the attributes, motivations, and socialization of youthful offenders have largely waned today. Instead, theorists are discussing the neoclassical revival, biosociological focus, radical, or critical, criminology, and the labeling perspective. What is your reaction to this current emphasis? Does this take us further away from the real delinquent?

Matza: I think the emphasis is intellectually and scientifically repressive, taking us very far from the actual person caught breaking the rules. My reaction is to continue being critical of such tendencies in my classroom teaching and perhaps awaiting the opportunity to propose more realistic theories of practice when the population finally realizes its conservative binge has led absolutely nowhere with regard to the problems of poverty, injustice and crime. Even talking about crime to students over the past fifteen years has been difficult. Under the conservative mentality the study of crime is not really possible, not in any deep scientific or intellectual sense.

Question: Structural explanations of delinquency have also been deemphasized today. What do you feel is the relationship between class and delinquency or delinquency and poverty?

Matza: I think I covered this matter at least briefly in an earlier question. Class and poverty are important in enabling a freedom from the regulation of thus discredited moral norms and facilitating a "drift" into delinquency. Racial oppression is I think even more important. The three operate in a similar manner.

Question: What other thoughts about the prevention and control of delinquency in American society would you like to add?

Matza: Delinquency cannot be controlled when government is hostile to poor and working people. Delinquency can only be prevented by a just and peaceful social order.

CHAPTER 8

CONFLICT THEORY AND DELINQUENCY

At the present time the capitalist system is under attack from many quarters. Victims of inequality, alienation, racism, sexism, irrationality, and imperialism are engaged in simultaneous struggles to overcome their oppression, and they are finding that capitalism is one of their principal enemies. The very existence of such challenges suggest that capitalism is neither a smoothly operating system in which little protest is heard nor a system unsusceptible to any change. On the contrary, the entire history of the capitalist era has been marked by resistance from those whom capitalism has sought to subordinate. Often this resistance has been overcome only through the use of violent force and coercion by the state.[1]

Conflict theorists argue that Watergate, political assassinations, criminal activities engaged in by the FBI and CIA, and other corporate and governmental scandals are reasons to question the traditional values system in America. In addition, these theorists point to the civil rights and the women's rights movements, the protests against the Vietnam War, and the cross-cultural struggles against colonialism as evidence that conventional values and existing social arrangements are being questioned.[2]

Conflict theorists further contend that a new approach to juvenile justice is needed because traditional perspectives have been inadequate. In contrast to the theories discussed in the previous three chapters, which explain delinquency through the perspectives of biological, psychological, and sociological positivism, conflict theory sees delinquency as a product of the conflict that results when groups or classes with differing power and interests interact with each other. Radical conflict theory, based on a Marxist orientation, argues that crime and delinquency in capitalist society emerge because of the efforts of the powerful to maintain their power at all costs, with the result that the working class is exploited. Radical theorists go on to say that true economic, social, and political equality for all cannot be achieved under the present capitalist system.[3]

This chapter begins with a discussion of the two basic approaches to analyzing the nature of society, continues by examining the three dimensions of conflict theory and the radical, or new, criminology's explanation of delinquent behavior, and concludes with an evaluation of the radical perspective and the policy implications that the conflict perspective suggests.

THE NATURE OF SOCIETY

The concept of order is usually included in the discussion of conflict in a society. Consensus and coercion are likewise frequently mentioned. In fact, the polar dichotomies of order/conflict and consensus/coercion have provided the basis for the emergence of two schools of sociology—functionalist and conflict—with each tak-

The assistance of Kurt Mielke was invaluable in the research and development of this chapter.

ing a different approach to the study of crime. These two schools of thought are frequently presented as polar opposites, with functionalists cast as "conservative defenders of the status quo" and "lackeys of the bourgeoisie" and with conflict theorists being viewed as equally one-sided. This sort of oversimplified presentation certainly does not do justice to two great bodies of work, within both of which there is as much variation as there is between the two. Nevertheless, certain distinctions can be drawn between the functionalist and conflict paradigms.

Structural-Functional Theory

The functionalist model of Talcott Parsons and his contemporaries is greatly indebted to a vast number of scholars from diverse disciplines. But the systematic aspect of the functionalist model grew from the works of Auguste Comte, Herbert Spencer, and Emile Durkheim, who in turn were influenced by the biological discoveries of their day.[4] Taking their cue from biology, these theorists contended that society is best understood when it is viewed as an organic body composed of interrelated parts, all functioning for the maintenance of the system. That is, society is a persistent stable structure that is well integrated and that is based on a consensus of values.[5]

The social order and the criminal laws of a society are the products of that consensus. Crime involves the breaking of consensus-based norms and values and is "functional" in that it "illustrates the boundaries between acceptable and unacceptable behavior."[6] C. Ronald Huff, in this regard, observes:

> Criminal behavior, as a challenge to dominant social values, helps to reinforce these values among the citizens. Likewise, the state's punishment of criminal behavior serves to dramatize the importance of boundary maintenance and provides a method for symbolically expressing the group's moral indignation against the transgressor.[7]

From this point of view, the delinquent is viewed as a person who is for some reason out of step with the values of the larger society, and emphasis is placed on determining the reasons why the delinquent has deviated from society's prescribed course of action. In other words, the institutions and the laws of society are unquestionably correct, and the delinquent is psychologically maladjusted or the product of a disturbed environment.

Thus, the functionalist is mainly concerned with the behavior of delinquents. This focus, in turn, leads to a preoccupation with the rehabilitation of delinquents and with "finding answers to the practical problems of crime control."[8]

Conflict Theory

The development of the conflict model is indebted to the concept of "dialectics." This concept, like order, can be traced back to the philosophers of ancient Greece. In antiquity, the term *dialectics* referred to the art of conducting a dispute or of bringing out the truth by disclosing and resolving contradictions in the arguments of opponents.[9]

Georg F. Hegel used this concept of dialectical thinking to explain human progress and social change. A prevailing idea, or "thesis," according to Hegel, would eventually be challenged by an opposing idea, or "antithesis." The resultant conflict usually would result in the merging of the two, or "synthesis." The synthesis gradually would be accepted as the thesis, but then would be challenged by a new antithesis and so forth throughout history.[10] Karl Marx, rather than applying the method to ideas as Hegel did, applied the concept to the material world. Marx's theory became one of dialectical materialism, as he contended that the conflict was one of competing economic systems, in which the weak must ward off exploitation by the strong or powerful in society.[11]

Georg Simmel, a twentieth-century conflict theorist, argued that unity and discord are inextricably intertwined and together act as an integrative force in society. Simmel added that "there probably exists no social unit in which convergent and divergent currents among its members are not inseparably interwoven."[12] Thus, Simmel's notion of dialectics acknowledged the existence of tendencies for order and disorder.

More recently, Lewis A. Coser and Rolf Dahrendorf contend that functionalists misrepresented reality by being overly concerned with order and consensus. Dahrendorf argues that the functionalists present a description of a utopian society—a society that never has existed and probably never will. Dahrendorf proposes that social researchers would be wise to opt for the conflict model because of its more realistic view that society is held together by constraint rather than consensus, and not by universal agreement but by the coercion of some by others.[13]

The conflict perspective views social control as an outcome of the differential distribution of economic and political power in society; laws then are seen as created by the powerful for their own benefit.[14] Richard Quinney argues, for example, that criminal law is a social control instrument of the state "organized to serve the interests of the dominant economic class, the capitalist ruling class."[15] William Bonger earlier made this same point: "in every society which is divided into a ruling class and a class ruled, penal law has been principally constituted according to the will of the former."[16]

The conflict approach sees delinquency as rooted in alienation and powerlessness. Until society deals with the root causes of crime, the economic and racial discrimination against the lower classes, delinquency will continue to be a serious problem. Class, status, and race, according to conflict theorists, are of primary importance in explaining the selective enforcement of juvenile law statutes.[17]

DIMENSIONS OF CONFLICT THEORY

Because a great deal of variation exists among the ideas of conflict theorists, no single conflict theory can be identified. Some theories emphasize the importance of socioeconomic class, some focus primarily on power and authority relationships, and others emphasize group and cultural conflict.

Socioeconomic Class and
Radical Criminology

Even though Karl Marx actually wrote very little on the subject of crime as the term is used today, he inspired a new school of criminology that emerged in the early 1970s. This school is variously described as "radical," "Marxist," "critical," "socialist," "left-wing," or "new." Marx was concerned both with deriving a theory of how societies change over time and with discovering how to go about changing society. This joining of theory and practice is called "praxis."[18]

Marx saw the history of all societies as the history of class struggles, with crime a result of these class struggles.[19] He wrote in the *Communist Manifesto:*

Freeman and slave, patrician and plebian, lord and serf, guildmaster and journeyman, in a word, oppressor and oppressed, stood in constant opposition to one another, carried on an uninterrupted, now hidden, now open fight, a reconstruction of society at large, or in the common ruin of the contending classes.[20]

Emerging with each historical period, according to Marx's theory, is a new class-based system of ranking. Marx contended that with capitalism, "society as a whole is more and more splitting up into two great classes directly facing each other—bourgeoisie [capitalist class] and proletariat [working class]."[21] The relations between the bourgeoisie and the proletariat become increasingly strained as the ruling class or bourgeoisie comes to control more and more of the society's wealth and the proletariat is increasingly pauperized. In this relationship between the oppressive bourgeoisie and the pauperized proletariat lie the seeds of the demise of capitalism.[22]

In the Marxist perspective, the state and the law itself are ultimately tools of the ownership class, which reflect mainly the economic interests of that class. Capitalism, rather than human nature, produces egocentric, greedy, and predatory human behavior. The ownership class is guilty of the worst crime—the brutal exploitation of the working class; revolution is a means to counter this violence and is generally both necessary and morally justifiable. Conventional crime is caused by extreme poverty and economic disenfranchisement, products of the dehumanizing and demoralizing capitalist system.[23]

In the early 1970s, such writers as Richard Quinney, William Chambliss, Tony Platt, Paul Takagi, Harold Pepinsky, Herman Schwendinger and Julie Schwendinger, Raymond Michalowski, and Barry Krisberg applied the Marxist perspective to the study of criminal law and criminology. Richard Quinney, a leading proponent of Marx's notion of socioeconomic class conflict, summarizes radical theory or the new criminology in these propositions:

1. American society is based on an advanced capitalist economy.

2. The state is organized to serve the interests of the dominant economic class, the capitalist ruling class.

3. Criminal law is an instrument of the state and ruling class to maintain and perpetuate the existing social and economic order.

4. Crime control in capitalist society is accomplished through a variety of institutions and agencies established and administered by a governmental elite, representing ruling-class interests, for the purpose of establishing domestic order.

5. The contradictions of advanced capitalism—the disjunction between existence and essence—require that the subordinate classes remain oppressed by whatever means necessary, especially through the coercion and violence of the legal system.

6. Only with the collapse of capitalist society and the creation of a new society, based on socialist principles, will there be a solution to the crime problem.[24]

Quinney thus implies that an understanding of crime in a capitalist society necessitates an understanding of the natural products and contradictions inherent in capitalism: alienation, inequality, poverty, unemployment, spiritual malaise, and economic crisis.

Quinney sees class as also affecting the broad categories of crime—crimes of domination and repression as well as crimes of accommodation and resistance. Crimes of domination and repression are committed by the elite class in capitalist society as well as by their agents (e.g., law enforcement agents). Crimes of accommodation and resistance are committed by the *lumpenproletariat* (a term used by Marx to indicate those cast out of the productive work force) and by the working class respectively.

Power and Authority Relationships

A second important dimension of conflict theory is the focus on power and authority relationships. Max Weber, Rolf Dahrendorf, and Austin Turk all have been major contributors to this body of scholarship.[25]

Max Weber's theory, like the Marxist perspective, contains a theory of social stratification that has been applied to the study of crime. Although Weber recognized the importance of the economic context in the analysis of social stratification, he did not believe that such a unidimensional approach could explain satisfactorily the phenomenon of social stratification. He added power and prestige to the Marxist emphasis on property and held these three variables responsible for the development of hierarchies in society. Weber also proposed that property differences led to the development of classes, power differences to the creation of political parties, and prestige differences to the development of status groups.[26] Further, Weber discussed the concept of ''life chances'' and argued that life chances were differentially related to social class. From this perspective, criminality exists in all societies and is the result of the political struggle among different groups attempting to promote or enhance their own life chances.[27]

Both Dahrendorf and Turk have extended the Weberian tradition in the field of criminology by emphasizing the relationships between authorities and their subjects. Dahrendorf contends that power is the critical variable explaining crime. He argues that although Marx built his theory on only one form of power, property ownership, a more useful perspective could be constructed by incorporating broader conceptions of power.[28] Turk, constructing his analysis on the work of both Weber and Dahrendorf, postulates that every society is characterized by norms of deference and norms of domination within the authority structure.[29] The distribution of power and prestige among individuals and groups in a society has been an important variable in Turk's conflict theory, for which he lists the following ten "informal working premises":

1. *Individuals diverge in their understanding and commitments.*

2. *Divergence leads, under specific conditions, to conflict.*

3. *Each conflicting party tries to promote his or her own understanding and commitments.*

4. *The result is a more or less conscious struggle over the available resources, and therefore of life chances.*

5. *People with similar understanding and commitments tend to join forces, and people who stay together tend to develop similar understandings and commitments.*

6. *Continuing conflicts tend to become routinized in the form of stratification systems.*

7. *Such systems (at least at the intergroup level) are characterized by economic exploitation sustained by political domination in all forms, from the most clearly violent to the most subtly ideological.*

8. *The relative power of conflicting parties determines their hierarchical position; changes in position reflect only changes in the distribution of power.*

9. *Convergence in understanding and commitment is generated by the (not necessarily voluntary) "outsiders," and the natural environment.*

10. *The relationship between divergence and convergence in human understanding and commitments is a dialectical one, ergo the basic social process or dynamic is one of conflict.*[30]

This perspective of conflict theory, focusing on power and authority relationships, examines the relationships between the legal *authorities* who create, interpret, and enforce right/wrong standards for individuals in the political collectivity and those who accept or resist but do not make such legal decisions.[31]

Group and Cultural Conflict

Another dimension of the conflict perspective focuses on group and cultural conflict. Thorsten Sellin and George Vold advocate this approach to the study of crime. Sellin argues that to understand the cause of crime, it is necessary to understand the concept of "conduct norms." This concept refers to the rules of a group concerning the ways its members should act under particular conditions. The violation of these rules guiding behavior arouses a group reaction.[32] Individuals are members of many groups (family group, work group, play group, political group, and religious group), and each group has its own particular conduct norms.[33] Sellin explains:

> The more complex a culture becomes, the more likely it is that the number of normative groups which affect a person will be large, the greater is the chance that the norms of these groups will fail to agree, no matter how much they may overlap as a result of a common acceptance of certain norms.[34]

Sellin also notes that an individual experiences a conflict of norms "when more or less divergent rules of conduct govern the specific life situation in which a person may find himself."[35] The act of violating conduct norms is "abnormal behavior," and crime represents a particular kind of abnormal behavior distinguished by the fact that crime is a violation of the conduct norms defined by criminal law.[36] Regarding criminal law, Sellin writes:

> The criminal law may be regarded as in part a body of rules, which prohibit specific forms of conduct and indicate punishments for violations. The character of these rules . . . depends upon the character and interests of those groups in the population which influence legislation. In some states these groups may comprise the majority, in others a minority, but the social values which receive the protection of criminal law are ultimately those which are treasured by the dominant interest groups.[37]

Sellin also has developed a theory of "primary and secondary culture conflict." Primary culture conflict occurs when an individual or group comes into contact with an individual or group from another culture and the conduct norms of the two cultures are not compatible. Secondary culture conflict refers to the conflict arising whenever society has diverging subcultures with conduct norms.[38]

George B. Vold, like Sellin and in the tradition of Simmel, also analyze the dimension of group conflict. He views society "as a congeries [an aggregation] of groups held together in a shifting, but dynamic equilibrium of opposing group interests and efforts."[39] Vold formulates a theory of group conflict and applies it to particular types of crimes, but he did not attempt to explain all types of criminal behavior. He contends that group members are constantly engaged in defending and promoting their group's status. As groups move into each other's territory or sphere of influence and begin to compete in those areas, intergroup conflict is inevitable. The outcome of a group conflict results in a winner and a loser, unless a compromise is reached—but compromises never take place when one group is decidedly weaker

Figure 8-1 Comparison of Conflict Perspectives	Legal Definitions	Legal Order	Purpose of Conflict	Capitalism
Socioeconomic class (Radical)	Rejection	Rejection	Revolution	Rejection
Power and authority relationships	Acceptance	Acceptance	Reform	Acceptance
Group and cultural conflict	Acceptance	Acceptance	Reform	Acceptance

than the other. Like Simmel, Vold believes that group loyalty develops and intensifies during group conflict.[40]

Vold further posites that "the whole political process of law making, law breaking, and law enforcement directly reflects deep-seated and fundamental conflicts between interest groups and their more general struggles for the control of the police power of the state."[41] Vold addresses both "crime as minority group behavior" and the "political nature of much criminal behavior."[42] Crime as minority group behavior is exhibited by individuals who band together because they "are in some way at odds with organized society and with the police forces maintained by that society."[43] Vold also contends that "many kinds of criminal acts must be recognized as presenting primarily behavior in the front-line fringes of direct contact between groups struggling for the control of power in the political and cultural organization of society."[44] Crimes of a political nature are, for example, those resulting from a political protest movement, from conflict between company management and labor unions, and from attempts to overcome the caste system or racial segregation.[45]

In sum, conflict criminologists can be divided into three basic groups—those emphasizing socioeconomic class, those emphasizing power and authority relationships, and those emphasizing group and cultural conflict. However, those who emphasize socioeconomic class call themselves radical, critical, or new criminologists and do not identify with the other two groups. Indeed, some rather significant differences do exist between the radicals and the other two groups. The others emphasize a plurality of interests and power and do not put the single emphasis on capitalism as do the radicals. Nor do the nonradical conflict criminologists reject the legal order as such or the use of legal definitions of crime. Furthermore, they favor reform as opposed to revolution. See Figure 8-1 for a comparison of the three groups.[46]

CONFLICT THEORY AND EXPLANATIONS OF DELINQUENT BEHAVIOR

Conflict theory about juvenile delinquency is still in the early stages of development. However, in the 1970s, radical criminologists in America began to examine delinquency according to a Marxist framework. They see little to be gained by trying to understand the causes of delinquent behavior, believing that what needs to be examined are how the political economy and social structure create conditions conducive to feelings among youth of powerlessness and alienation. They further contend that the dominant classes create definitions of crime to oppress the subordinate classes, that the economic system exploits lower-class youth, and that social justice is lacking for lower-class youth.

Alienation and Powerlessness among Youth

Radical theorists argue that the problem of delinquency must be seen as part of the larger problem of alienation and powerlessness among American youth. In Krisberg and Austin's *The Children of Ishmael,* they note that youth in a capitalist society generally are seen as a group of people who are in a sense expected to remain in a holding pattern until they can take their places in the work force.[47] They add that "young people form a subservient class, alienated, powerless, and prone to economic manipulation."[48]

Young people, according to Krisberg and Austin, also are excluded from full participation in society's political institutions. Young people lack organized lobbies, have limited voting power, and hold few positions of authority. Moreover, youths are subjected to controlling forces by the state, and, just like any other subordinate group in society, they have their rights, privileges, and identities defined by the "powers that be."[49]

Theorist David F. Greenberg states that "the exclusion of young people from adult work and leisure activities forces adolescents into virtually exclusive association with one another, cutting them off from alternative sources of validation for the self."[50] Greenberg claims that the long-term consequences of increased age segregation created by changing patterns of work and education have increased the vulnerability of youths to the expectations and evaluations of their peers.[51]

In short, radical theorists conclude that lengthening the time before youths assume adult roles and are given adult responsibilities has contributed to powerlessness and alienation among youth, which, in turn, has contributed to delinquent behavior.

Definitions of Delinquency

Radical criminologists argue that certain acts are termed *delinquent* because it is in the interest of the ruling class to so define them.[52] Thus, the law is seen by radical criminologists as an oppressive force that is used to promote and stabilize existing socioeconomic relations. The law maintains order, but it is an order imposed upon the powerless by the powerful.[53] Anthony Platt's *The Child Savers,* which describes the role played by wealthy "child-saving" reformers in the nineteenth century, explains how dominant classes create definitions of crime to control the subordinate classes:

> *The juvenile court system was part of a general movement directed towards developing a specialized labor market and industrial discipline under corporate capitalism by creating new programs of adjudication and control for "delinquent," "dependent," and "neglected" youth. This in turn was related to augmenting the family and enforcing compulsory education in order to guarantee the proper reproduction of the labor force.[54]*

In other words, because delinquents are unsocialized children, who are in danger of producing not only more crime but more children like themselves, it has been necessary to find legal means to discipline them. Otherwise, they would be unprepared to supply labor for the alienating work of capitalism.[55] Definitions of delinquency, then, are enforced upon the children of the "dangerous classes" as a means of forcing them to conform to alienating work roles.

Economic Exploitation of Youth

Radical criminologists charge that the "haves" exploit the "have-nots," with the result that the children of the have-nots become a marginal class. Barry Krisberg, studying twenty-two gang members in Philadelphia, found that the harsh realities of ghetto existence fostered a psychology of survival as a functional adaptation to an uncompromising social situation or environment.[56] Significantly, the gang members perceived "survival" in Spencerian terms; one gang leader put it this way: "Survival, man, is survival of the fittest. You do unto others before they do unto you, only do it to them first."[57]

But Krisberg noted a contradiction in the gang leaders' view of hustling as a means of survival. Many claimed that the hustle is a fantastic means of meeting one's needs. But others, as the following account reveals, felt that "hustling was the mode of a desperate man, and that the rewards were small"[58]:

> *Like, your stomach gets to griping at one end, your ribs get to meeting your backbone, and . . . you get to saying I got to get me some money to get me something to eat. When you try to get this money, you try to get enough to hold you over, to keep you from doing this for a while. But it just don't happen that way, man, like, you take off something or somebody and you only wind up getting $20 out of the thing, and you got a half-assed room, the rent $20—you got to give the scratch right up. And you keep doing it. That's how these things go down.[59]*

Herman Schwendinger and Julia Schwendinger also contend that capitalism produces a marginal class of people who are superfluous from an economic standpoint.[60] They further argue that socialization agents within the social system, such as the school, tend to reinvent within each new generation the same class system: "The children of families that *have* more *get* more, because the public educational system converts human beings into potential commodities."[61] That is, the schools tend to be geared toward rewarding and assisting those youths who exhibit early indications of achieving the greatest potential success in institutions of higher learning and later in the job market. Yet, this selection is made at the expense of those who do not exhibit such potential in their early encounters with the educational system.[62]

David L. Greenberg discusses juvenile theft in terms of structural obstacles to legitimate sources of funds. He points out that the persistent decline in teenage employment, especially among black teenagers, has left adolescents less and less capable of financing an increasingly costly social life, the importance of which is enhanced as the age segregation of society grows. Thus, adolescent theft occurs as a response to the disjunction between the desire to participate in social activities with peers and the absence of legitimate means to finance this participation.[63] Greenwood illustrates this point by quoting from Carl Werthman's study of San Francisco delinquents:

> *Shoplifting . . . was viewed as a more instrumental activity, as was the practice of stealing coin changers from temporarily evacuated buses parked in a nearby public depot. In the case of shoplifting, most of the boys wanted and wore the various items of clothing they stole; and when buses were robbed, either the money was divided among the boys, or it was used to buy supplies for a party being given by the club.*[64]

Mark Colvin and John Pauly, in one of the most significant articles relating the radical perspective to juvenile delinquency, claim that delinquency is a latent outcome of the reproduction process of capitalism. They develop an integrated theory of delinquency, grounded in Marxian insights on the role of productive relations in shaping other relations. Supporting their model from empirical evidence from the research of others, Colvin and Pauly predict that parents' experience of coerciveness in workplace control structures is associated with their developing alienated bonds. This, in turn, contributes to the development of more coercive family control structures, which leads to more alienated initial bonds in juveniles. Juveniles with alienated initial bonds, according to these theorists, are more likely to be placed in more coercive school control situations, which reinforce their alienated bonds. Juveniles' alienated bonds, then, lead them to greater association with alienated peers, who form peer group control structures. These peer group control structures, along with interaction with class-related, community, and neighborhood distributions of opportunities, create two different paths of delinquent involvement. In the first path, the experience of coerciveness in peer group control relations mutually interacts with their alienated bonds to propel them into serious, patterned, violent delinquent behavior. In the second path, the experience of remuneration from illegitimate sources creates an alternative utilitarian control structure which interacts with newly formed calculative bonds to propel these juveniles into serious, patterned, instrumental delinquent behavior.[65]

In sum, according to these studies, the structural conditions of capitalistic society lead to the exploitation of lower-class youths. This exploitation, in turn, creates a marginal role for these lower-class juveniles and influences their pursuing illegitimate means to satisfy their desires.

Social Injustice in the Justice System

Radical criminologists argue that social justice is lacking in American society for three reasons. First, poor and disadvantaged youth tend to be disproportionately represented in the juvenile justice system despite research indicating that actual acts of delinquent behavior are uniformly distributed throughout the social spectrum.[66] Second, female status offenders are subjected to sexist treatment in the juvenile system.[67] Third, racism is present and blacks are dealt with more harshly than whites.[68]

William J. Chambliss analyzes this issue of social justice in his study entitled "The Saints and the Roughnecks." He studied two groups of boys, one consisting of eight upper-middle-class boys (the Saints) and the second consisting of six lower-class boys (the Roughnecks). He found the Saints to be continually occupied with truancy, drinking, wild driving, petty theft, and vandalism. The parents of the Saints, as well as the community at large, tended to see the Saints as being essentially "good" boys who only occasionally engaged in "sowing a few wild oats." In contrast, the Roughnecks were "constantly in trouble with the police and community even though their rate of delinquency was about equal with that of the Saints."[69]

Radical criminologists also have begun to question the handling of female delinquents by the juvenile justice system, focusing especially on the double standard that is applied to female status offenders. The evidence shows that girls charged with status offenses receive harsher treatment than girls suspected of delinquent behavior at the level of referral to the court, pretrial detention, and confinement. Girls are also much more likely than boys to be brought into the court system as status offenders; indeed, the court sometimes punishes the noncriminal behavior of female adolescents as harshly as it does the criminal behavior of male adolescents.[70] Such extralegal paternalism is cited as further evidence of sexism.

Radicals also contend that the juvenile justice system is racist, since blacks are treated more punitively than whites. At the time of arrest, nonwhite youths are more likely to be referred to the juvenile court than are whites. Once referred to the court, they are less likely than whites to be diverted to nonjudicial agencies. Furthermore, minority youths are more likely than whites to be found delinquent during the adjudication stage of the juvenile court proceedings; and during the disposition stage, they are more likely to be sent to training school than are whites.[71]

In short, radical criminologists believe that the formal juvenile justice system, as well as the informal justice system, administers different sorts of justice to the children of the "haves" and to the children of the "have-nots," to boys who commit delinquent offenses and to girls who commit "moral" offenses, and to white youths and to nonwhite youths.

EVALUATION OF RADICAL PERSPECTIVES ON THE CAUSES OF DELINQUENCY

The theoretical contributions of contemporary criminologists working within the radical perspective diverge from mainstream liberal assumptions, ideology, and practice. Their theoretical position is radical in the sense that the implied policy would dramatically alter the way crime is defined, criminals are treated, theories are formulated and tested and, quite possibly, even dramatically alter the sociopolitical-economic structure of the United States.

That a theoretical position is labeled radical should never be reason for automatic condemnation or for automatic acceptance. Too often theories are either attacked because they are viewed as threatening to the status quo, or automatically elevated to the top of a sacred pedestal, thereby destroying any hope of ever attaining a higher level of understanding. Following either of these paths will undoubtedly lead away from the ultimate goal—a more humane society and a more effective juvenile justice system.

The strengths of the radical pespective lie in the several criticisms it makes of present-day society and the social control measures used with juveniles. First, the radical perspective is correct in its accusation that social justice is frequently unequal for adolescents in American society. The cases of middle- and upper-class youths who commit delinquent offenses are more likely to be handled nonjudicially than are those of lower-class youths who commit the same offenses. Nonwhite youths, especially at the disposition stage of juvenile court proceedings, tend to receive more punitive dispositions than do white youths.[72] In addition, although adolescent females who commit noncriminal offenses may be treated more fairly now than in the past, their gender still too frequently influences how they are handled by the justice system.[72]

Second, the radical perspective is important because of its desire to use societal or more "macro" strategies to eliminate alienation, inequality, poverty, unemployment, and other such problems. Although the overriding concern of the past four chapters has been with the offender and with whether or not he or she is responsible for delinquent behavior, that preoccupation tends to excuse society from dealing with these social problems. Moreover, the radical pespective is a reminder that no easy solutions exist for the complex problems of American society.[74]

Third, radical theorists have provided valuable insights for understanding crime and delinquency through their efforts to demystify the law and legal practices. They have discussed how the meaning of delinquency, as defined by juvenile court law, is influenced by sociocultural, political, and economic factors. They also have helped clarify the importance of extralegal factors in juvenile court decision making.

Fourth, the radical perspective correctly advocates more power for young people. The subservient status of American adolescents does result in some young people feeling alienated, powerless, and economically manipulated or used. The poorer a young person is, the more likely he or she is to face this subservient position in American society. The theorists of the radical perspective, as well as other interest groups, are advocating more rights for children in all areas of their lives.

Finally, radical theory has questioned the ability of the state to deliver beneficial and fair programs for delinquent youth. For example, radical theorists have surmised correctly that rehabilitative programs sometimes are used more as punishment than as treatment; not surprisingly, some youths get worse rather than better with "treatment."[75] In addition, the tendency of positivism to separate youths into delinquents and nondelinquents ignores the fact that lawbreaking is widespread among adolescents and rationalizes punitive handling of those who are processed in the system, frequently lower-class and minority youth.

However, a number of criticisms can be made about the radical theory explanation as well. First, radical theory tends to be "enslaved by its own emancipation."[76] That is, just as positivism is typically ensnared in behavioral considerations, radical theory tends to overemphasize the political nature of delinquency and the influence of economic factors upon delinquency.[76] Although this criticism does not deny the importance of the radical position, it is a reminder that crime or delinquency arises from a number of forces (as indicated by the contextual perspective of this book), and it cannot be explained solely by political or economic factors any more than by legal or cultural factors alone.

Second, self-report studies reveal that a great deal of youth crime is neither politically nor economically motivated. The existence of middle- and upper-class youth crime particularly calls into question the Marxist thesis that economic exploitation is what generates delinquency in American society. Also, some recent research shows that delinquency rates may rise during times of prosperity, rather than during times of recession.[78] Lamar Empey has noted, "The loosened controls that are associated with increasing affluence and opportunity may be somewhat more important than poverty per se."[79]

Third, radical theory has romanticized the delinquent, leading to a deterministic viewpoint that, like labeling, minimizes the delinquent act. Radical theory's fascination with the victimized offender ends by regarding the lawbreaker as a political criminal, seen as no more responsible for his or her antisocial behavior than positivism would have it.

Fourth, some radical theorists have little interest in what it considers to be piecemeal reform of the juvenile justice system. Radical criminologist David Greenberg explains why this is so:

> Some radicals have feared that successful campaigns to achieve short-run goals might make a socialist revolution hard to achieve. . . . If some concessions are won, this argument goes, militant opposition to the state will dry up. Behind this concern lies an implicit "big bang" model of how revolutions are made: conditions get worse and worse until the oppressed can't stand it anymore and one day explode. In the industrialized capitalist world such a model seems farfetched. In fact, it is a pernicious model, since it encourages socialists to sit back and do nothing while social conditions deteriorate. . . .[80]

The position that true justice must await the arrival of a wider socioeconomic revolution weakens the possibility of reform and change in the justice system.[81] The danger, of course, is that a system that is not undergoing reform and change will become only more repressive.

Fifth, the radical perspective has some serious theoretical and empirical deficiencies. Its orientation to the future has discouraged an empirical orientation among radical theorists.[82] Radical thought has emphasized the sketching of institutions which do not exist, and this speculative aspect has not encouraged programs of research.[83]

Furthermore, logical deficiencies are apparent in radical thought—e.g., in the claim that the rules that define crime and delinquency lead to the injuries or social harm caused by crime. All societies, whether capitalist or socialist, experience the injuries of crime and have seen fit to condemn the lawbreaker.[84]

Finally, a number of questionable assumptions are made in radical theory. Radical theorists frequently speak of radical criminology as a unique paradigm in American criminology, but this emerging theoretical position certainly has been shaped by other theories such as social pathology, structural-functionalism, and labeling.[85] Radical theory also overstates the evilness of the state and the goodness of human nature. That is, as John Hagen and Jeffrey Leon showed in their study of the development of the juvenile court in Canada, the notion that the criminal law is purely a reflection of the interests and ideologies of the governing class is overstated.[86] In addition, radical thinkers exaggerate the oppressiveness of social science research; the contention that social researchers are merely "lackeys of the state" working to maintain the status quo, may be true of some, but is hardly true of all.

POLICY IMPLICATIONS

The three conflict perspectives have several contributions to make to handling youth crime in America. The emphasis on improving human rights is a reminder to policymakers, as well as to all interest groups for children, that the potential of youths to achieve their maximum potential in American society is very much affected by the larger issue of human rights. Whether or not racial justice and the ability to earn an adequate standard of living are guaranteed affect whether minority children and those from impoverished families face discrimination and poverty as they grow up. Similarly, women's rights affect the thousands of children across the nation reared in one-parent homes. Finally, children's rights promise that youths will be granted or guaranteed more of the basic rights that adults enjoy.

Conflict theory also has much to teach children's advocacy groups about how power and domination affect the creation of policy. For example, conflict theory contends that in our society control is gained by those groups who wield the most power and resources; that once a group achieves dominance over others, it seeks to use the available societal mechanisms to its advantage to maintain that dominance; that laws are formulated in the interests of the dominant group, with the result that those behaviors common to the less-powerful groups may be restricted; and that the law enforcement and control systems operate to process disproportionately the less powerful members of society.[87]

Finally, the conflict perspective points out that the opportunity structure and economic exploitation of a society become key variables in understanding lower-class youth crime. Societies in which economic exploitation is extreme and in which opportunity is limited can be expected to have high rates of delinquency. Thus, an adequate standard of living for all Americans and increased employment possibilities for teenagers become critical issues in deterring youth crime.

SUMMARY

Although sociology as a discipline is a relatively recent phenomenon, many concepts used by sociologists today date back to antiquity. *Conflict* is one such example. Heraclitus of Ephesus, Herodotus, Aristotle, and Polybius are but a few of the classical thinkers who incorporated this concept into their discussions of the state. Today, the notion of conflict continues to be widely discussed in the analysis of society.

Radical theorists are critical of the capitalist system. They claim that true economic, social, and political equality cannot be achieved under the present capitalist system in the United States. They also say that crime in capitalist society is caused by the efforts of the elite to maintain their power at all costs, with exploitation of the working class. Radical theory about juvenile delinquency is still fragmented and in its early stages of development. But most radical theorists generally relate delinquency to alienation and powerlessness among youth, especially lower-class youth; to the dominant classes' creation of definitions of crime to control subordinate classes; to the economic exploitation of the lower class; and to the lack of social justice in American society.

Examining the past five chapters readily leads to the conclusion that no one theory can be used to explain all delinquency. Each of the main theories about the causes of delinquency provides a small piece of the puzzle, but combined they are even more helpful in understanding youth crime in America. The task is to increase the explanatory power of these theories by building on the strengths of each. The past chapters do provide some directions, or building blocks, which should be useful in providing a greater synthesis of the various explanations of delinquent behavior. First, as discussed in Chapter 6, to understand delinquent behavior a multilevel theoretical approach is needed, with its offer of the promise of synthesis between sociobiological, psychological, and macro and micro sociological explanations. Second, as discussed in the past two chapters, integrated theory is helpful in weaving together the disconnected socialization settings of control theory into a unified conceptualization of socialization processes. That is, retaining the conception of the bonding processes, integrated theory follows the juvenile through life-cycle encounters with various socializing agencies.[88]

Discussion Questions

1. What are the two basic models of society? Explain the differences between them.
2. What are the various dimensions of conflict theory? How do they differ?
3. What are the explanations of delinquency according to radical theory? Evaluate each of these explanations.

4. What is your reaction to the conflict perspective? What must policymakers learn from this perspective?

References

Afanasyer, V. *Marxist Philosophy*. Moscow: Foreign Language Publishing House, n.d.

Colvin, Mark, and Pauly, John. "A Critique of Criminology: Toward an Integrated Structural-Marxist Theory of Delinquency Production," *American Journal of Sociology* 89 (November 1983): 513–551.

Dahrendorf, Rolf. "Out of Utopia: Toward a Reorientation of Sociological Analysis." In *Sociological Theory: A Book of Readings,* edited by Lewis Coser and Bernard Rosenberg. New York: Macmillan Publishing Company, 1976.

Huff, C. Ronald. "Conflict Theory in Criminology." In *Radical Criminology,* edited by James Inciardi. Beverly Hills, Calif.: Sage Publications, 1980.

Krisberg, Barry, and Austin, James, eds. *The Children of Ishmael: Critical Perspectives on Juvenile Justice*. Palo Alto, Calif.: Mayfield Publishing Company, 1978.

Marx, Karl, and Engels, Frederick. *The Communist Manifesto*. Reprint. New York: International Publishers, 1979.

———. *Collected Works: Marx and Engels 1851–1853*. Vol. II. New York: International Publishers, 1979.

Platt, Anthony. *The Child Savers*. 2d ed. Chicago: University of Chicago Press, 1981.

Quinney, Richard. *Class, State, and Crime*. 2d ed. New York: Longman, 1980.

Sellin, Thorsten. *Culture, Conflict, and Crime*. New York: Social Science Research Council, 1938.

Taylor, Ian, Walton, Paul, and Young, Jock. *The New Criminology: For a Social Theory of Deviance*. London: Routledge & Kegan Paul, 1973.

Vold, George B. *Theoretical Criminology*. 2d ed. Prepared by Thomas J. Bernard. New York: Oxford University Press, 1979.

FOOTNOTES

1. Richard C. Edwards, Michael Reich, and Thomas E. Weisskopf, *The Capitalist System: A Radical Analysis of American Society* (Englewood Cliffs, N.J.: Prentice-Hall, 1972), p. 462.

2. Barry Krisberg and James Austin, eds., *The Children of Ishmael: Critical Perspectives on Juvenile Justice* (Palo Alto, Calif.: Mayfield Publishing Company, 1978), p. 4.

3. Richard Quinney, *Class, State, and Crime,* 2d ed. (New York: Longman, 1980), pp. 57–66.

4. Jonathan H. Turner, *The Structure of Sociological Theory* (Homewood, Ill.: Dorsey Press, 1978), pp. 20–26.

5. Rolf Dahrendorf, *Class and Class Conflict in Industrial Society* (Palo Alto: Stanford University Press, 1959), pp. 161–163.

6. Turner, *Structure of Sociological Theory,* pp. 25–26.

7. C. Ronald Huff, "Conflict Theory in Criminology," in *Radical Criminology,* edited by James Inciardi (Beverly Hills, Calif.: Sage Publications, 1980), p. 62.

8. John F. Galliher, "The Life and Death of Liberal Criminology," *Contemporary Crisis,* 2 (1978), p. 248.

9. V. Afanasyer, *Marxist Philosophy* (Moscow: Foreign Language Publishing House, n.d.), p. 14.

10. Ron E. Roberts and Robert Marsh Kloss, *Social Movements: Between the Balcony and the Barricade,* 2d ed. (St. Louis: C. V. Mosby Company, 1979), p. 18. This interpretation of Hegel's "thesis—antithesis—synthesis" is frequently questioned. See Roberts and Kloss, *Social Movements,* p. 16.

11. Stephen Spitzer, "Toward a Marxian Theory of Deviance," *Social Problems* 22 (1975), p. 638.

12. Georg Simmel, *Conflict,* trans. Kurt H. Wolf (Glencoe, Ill.: Free Press, 1955), pp. 15–30.

13. Rolf Dahrendorf, "Out of Utopia: Toward a Reorientation of Sociological Analysis," in *Sociological Theory: A Book of Readings,* edited by Lewis A. Coser and Bernard Rosenberg (New York: Macmillan Publishing Company, 1976), p. 198.

14. David Schichor, "The New Criminology: Some Critical Issues," *The British Journal of Criminology* 20 (1980), p. 3.

15. Richard Quinney, *Critique of Legal Order: Crime Control in Capitalist Society* (Boston: Little, Brown & Company, 1973), p. 16.

16. William Bonger, *Criminality and Economic Conditions,* abridged ed. (Bloomington: Indiana University Press, 1969), p. 24.

17. Krisberg and Austin, *Children of Ishmael,* p. 87.

18. Turner, *Structure of Sociological Theory,* p. 124.

19. Karl Marx and Frederick Engels, *The Communist Manifesto* (reprinted, New York: International Publishers, 1979), p. 9.

20. Ibid.

21. Ibid.

22. Ibid., pp. 9–21.

23. David O. Friedrichs, "Radical Criminology in the United States: An Interpretative Understanding," in *Radical Criminology,* p. 38.

24. Richard Quinney, *Criminal Justice in America: A Critical Understanding* (Boston: Little, Brown & Company, 1974), p. 24

25. This section on power and authority relationships is largely derived from Huff, "Conflict Theory in Criminology," pp. 72–74.

26. Max Weber, "Class, Status, Party," in *Class, Status and Power,* edited by R. Bendix and S. M. Lipset (New York: Macmillan Publishing Company, 1953), pp. 63–75.

27. Ibid.

28. Dahrendorf, *Class and Class Conflict.*

29. A. T. Turk, "Class, Conflict, and Criminalization," *Sociological Focus* 10 (August 1977), pp. 209–220.

30. Austin T. Turk, "Analyzing Official Deviance: For Nonpartisan Conflict Analysis in Criminology," in *Radical Criminology,* pp. 82–83.

31. Ian Taylor, Paul Walton, and Jock Young, *The New Criminology: For a Social Theory of Deviance* (Boston: Routledge & Kegan Paul, 1973), p. 241.

32. Thorsten Sellin, *Culture, Conflict, and Crime* (New York: Social Science Research Council, 1938), p. 28.

33. Ibid., p. 29.

34. Ibid.

35. Ibid.

36. Ibid., pp. 32, 57.

37. Ibid., p. 21.

38. Ibid., pp. 104–105.

39. George B. Vold, *Theoretical Criminology*, 2d ed., prepared by Thomas J. Bernard (New York: Oxford University Press, 1979), p. 283.

40. Ibid.

41. Ibid., p. 288.

42. Ibid., pp. 288–296.

43. Ibid., p. 289.

44. Ibid., p. 292.

45. Ibid., pp. 293–295.

46. Friedrichs, "Radical Criminology in the United States," p. 39.

47. Krisberg and Austin, *Children of Ishmael,* p. 219.

48. Ibid., p. 1.

49. Ibid., pp. 1–2.

50. David F. Greenberg, "Delinquency and the Age Structure of Society," *Contemporary Crisis* 1 (1977), p. 196.

51. Ibid.

52. W. J. Chambliss, "Toward a Political Economy of Crime," *Theory and Society* 2 (Summer 1975), p. 152.

53. J. R. Hepburn, "Social Control and the Legal Order: Legitimate Repression in a Capitalist State," *Contemporary Crisis* 1 (1977), p. 77.

54. Anthony M. Platt, "The Triumph of Benevolence: The Origins of the Juvenile Justice System in the United States," in *Criminal Justice in America,* edited by Richard Quinney (Boston: Little, Brown & Company, 1974), p. 377.

55. Lamar T. Empey, *American Delinquency: Its Meaning and Construction* (Homewood, Ill.: Dorsey Press, 1982), p. 430.

56. Barry Krisberg, "Gang Youth and Hustling: The Psychology of Survival," in Krisberg and Austin, *Children of Ishmael,* p. 244.

57. Ibid.

58. Ibid., p. 245.

59. Ibid.

60. Herman Schwendinger and Julia R. Schwendinger, "Marginal Youth and Social Policy," *Social Problems* 24 (December 1976), pp. 84–91.

61. Ibid., p. 188.

62. Ibid.

63. Greenwood, "Delinquency," pp. 196–197.

64. Carl Werthman, "The Function of Social Definitions in the Development of Delinquent

Careers," in *Task Force Report: Juvenile Delinquency* (Washington, D.C.: U.S. Government Printing Office, 1967), p. 157.

65. Mark Colvin and John Pauly, "A Critique of Criminology: Toward an Integrated Structural-Marxist Theory of Delinquency Production," *American Journal of Sociology*, 89 (November 1983), p. 543.

66. Krisberg and Austin, *Children of Ishmael*, p. 53.

67. See Chapter 12 for a discussion of sexism in the juvenile justice system.

68. See Chapters 15 and 16 for discussion of racism in the justice system.

69. Willam J. Chambliss, "The Saints and the Roughnecks," *Society* 11 (1973), pp. 341–355.

70. Media Chesney-Lind, "Judicial Paternalism and the Female Status Offender: Training Women to Know Their Place," in Krisberg and Austin, *Children of Ishmael*, p. 385.

71. Terence P. Thornberry, "Race, Socioeconomic Status, and Sentencing in the Juvenile Justice System," *Journal of Criminal Law and Criminology* 64 (1973), pp. 90–98; Charles W. Thomas and Anthony W. Fitch, *An Inquiry into the Association between Respondents' Personal Characteristics and Juvenile Court Dispositions* (Williamsburg, Va.: Metropolitan Criminal Justice Center, College of William and Mary, 1975); and Rosemary C. Sarri and Robert D. Vinter, "Justice for Whom? Varieties of Juvenile Correctional Approaches," in *The Juvenile Justice System*, edited by M. W. Klein (Beverly Hills, Calif.: Sage Publications, 1976).

72. Thornberry, "Race, Socioeconomic Status, and Sentencing"; Thomas and Fitch, "Respondents' Personal Characteristics and Juvenile Court Dispositions."

73. Since the 1974 Juvenile Justice and Delinquency Prevention Act, fewer status offenders, female and male, have been sent to juvenile correctional institutions. Also, this author's participant observation in juvenile court failed to support the criticism that female status offenders at present are being treated very differently from male status offenders.

74. Harold F. Pepinsky, "A Radical Alternative to 'Radical' Criminology," in *Radical Criminology*, p. 308.

75. H. E. Pepinsky, *Crime Control Strategies: An Introduction to the Study of Crime* (New York: Oxford University Press, 1980).

76. Francis A. Allen, *The Crimes of Politics* (Cambridge: Harvard University Press, 1974).

77. David Shichor, "New Criminology," p. 7.

78. William E. Thornton, Jr., Jennifer James, and William G. Doerner, *Delinquency and Justice* (Glenview, Ill.: Scott, Foresman & Company, 1982), p. 180.

79. Empey, *American Delinquency*, p. 389.

80. David F. Greenberg, *Crime and Capitalism: Readings in Marxist Criminology* (Palo Alto, Calif.: Mayfield Publishing Company, 1981), p. 489.

81. Francis T. Cullen and Karen E. Gilbert, *Reaffirming Rehabilitation* (Cincinnati: Anderson Publishing Company, 1982), p. 21.

82. Shichor, "New Criminology," p. 13.

83. T. B. Bottomore, *Varieties of Political Expression in Sociology* (Chicago: University of Chicago Press, 1972), p. 4.

84. Empey, *American Delinquency*, p. 436.

85. Robert F. Meier, "The New Criminology: Continuity in Criminological Theory," *Journal of Criminal Law and Criminology* 67 (1977), pp. 461–469.

86. John Hagan and Jeffrey Leon, "Rediscovering Delinquency: Social History, Political Ideology, and the Sociology of Law," *American Sociological Review* 42 (August 1977), pp. 587–598.

87. Franklin P. Williams III, "Conflict Theory and Differential Processing: An Analysis of the Research Literature," in *Radical Criminology,* p. 215.

88. Colvin and Pauly, "A Critique of Criminology," p. 523.

INTERVIEW WITH RICHARD QUINNEY

Justice in a capitalist society is limited to the overall needs of a continuing capitalist system. Justice is largely limited to "criminal justice," a punitive model that does not deal with the inadequacies of the system.

In this interview, Professor Richard Quinney, who has published numerous books and articles advancing a Marxist analysis of crime, discusses such topics as the lack of social justice in American society, the contradictions of capitalism, the need for a religious socialist culture, and the reasons why the capitalist state is oppressive and coercive.

Question: In your book *Class, State, and Crime*, you write about a "religious socialist culture." What do you mean by this phrase and why is it needed?

Quinney: The theologian Paul Tillich, in the 1930s, advanced a critique of developing capitalist society that combined a Marxist understanding of capitalism with the Judeo-Christian perspective on prophetic religion. Today the movement continues in the form of "liberation theology" in Latin America. A religious socialist culture— as an ideal that is realized in popular struggle—is a culture that: (1) supports a society based on equal distribution of goods and services, with the material means of production owned and controlled by workers; and (2) attends to the spiritual (as well as material) needs of people. It is a culture that allows human beings to live in a world filled with sacred as well as secular meaning. Everyday life is thereby filled with ultimate concern. In a socialist culture we would be able to live our lives deliberately, with care for each other, and live a life that has mean-

Richard Quinney received his Ph.D. from the University of Wisconsin, and he is presently professor of sociology at Northern Illinois University. The Social Reality of Crime, Criminology, Class, State, and Crime, Providence: The Reconstruction of Social and Moral Order, and Social Existence are some of the books that have brought Dr. Quinney's analysis of crime and social problems to the attention of readers throughout the world. Interview conducted in February 1984, and used with permission.

ing both within the moment and in the larger transcendent universe.

Question: Why is social justice lacking in American society?

Quinney: Justice in a capitalist society is limited to the overall needs of a continuing capitalist system. Justice is largely limited to "criminal justice," a punitive model that does not deal with the inadequacies of the system. Social justice, on the other hand, would serve the needs of all people, including their economic well-being. The goal of social justice can be attempted in our capitalist society, but true social justice can be achieved only in a socialist society. The struggle for social justice is a struggle for the transformation of our present society in the United States.

Question: What are the chief contradictions of capitalism and how do they contribute to the extent and nature of crime in American society?

Quinney: There are many contradictions in capitalism. The basic contradiction is between the goal of progress and a better society, on the one hand, and the reality of the inability of capitalism to ever attain this goal because of the inherent class structure of capitalism. The capitalist class owns and controls the means of production and distribution and, as such, assures that a subordinate class of workers and consumers will be dominated politically and economically—to assure the continuation of the capitalist system. Classes outside of the capitalist class commit crimes out of need, frustration, and brutalization. Members of the capitalist class commit crimes out of greed and power. The rates of crime under capitalism can never be substantially reduced. Capitalism generates its own crime and rates of crime.

Question: Why is the capitalist state oppressive and coercive?

Quinney: The capitalist state exists to perpetuate capitalist economics and the social relations of capitalism. It is the policy and enforcement arm of capitalist society. Thus, the actions carried out by the branches of the state are of a control nature, including the activities associated with dispensing education, welfare, and criminal justice. The state must also provide benefits for those who suffer and fail under capitalist economics, but even these services have a control function, attempting to assure the continuation of the capitalist system.

Question: How does the early Quinney differ from the Quinney of today? Or how has your approach to the crime problem changed?

Quinney: I have moved through the various epistemologies and ontologies in the social sciences. After applying one, I have found that another is necessary for incorporating what was excluded from the former, and so on. Also, I have tried to keep my work informed by the latest developments in the philosophy of science. In addition, I have always been a part of the progressive movements of the time. My work is thus an integral part of the social and intellectual changes that are taking place in the larger society, outside of criminology and sociology. One other fact has affected my work in recent years: the search for meaning in my life and in the world.

Question: What directions do you anticipate the new criminology or critical criminology will take in the 1980s?

Quinney: This is the time to substantiate the critical Marxist perspective through studies of specific aspects of crime. We know generally the causes of crime. Further work is in large part a political matter—showing others through the accepted means of research. In the long run, however, our interests must go beyond the narrow confines of criminology and sociology. The theoretical, empirical, political, and spiritual issues are larger than the issue of crime.

Question: Critical or new criminology theorists have written much less about delinquency than criminality in American society. What more needs to be contributed by Marxists in this area?

Quinney: Our society emphasizes youth and the youth culture while at the same time increasingly excluding youth from gainful and meaningful employment. Youth are being relegated to the consumption sector—without the economic means for consumption. Education—including college—has traditionally provided a place for youth that are not essential to a capitalist society. But with the widening of the economic gap between classes, will education be an outlet and opportunity for the majority of adolescents and young adults? We are approaching a structural crisis (and personal crises) that will require a solution beyond what is possible in a capitalist society. Our challenge is to understand the changes that are taking place around us and the courage to be a part of the struggle that is necessary.

UNIT THREE

ENVIRONMENTAL INFLUENCES ON DELINQUENCY IN AMERICA

CHAPTER 9

THE FAMILY AND DELINQUENCY

CHAPTER OUTLINE

My mom and I can't stay in the same house without jumping down each other's throat. My dad has had to pull my mom off of me a couple of times. She really scared me one time. I can't remember what we were arguing about, but I started to take off out the back door. She caught me, knocked me against the cupboard, and grabbed hold of my neck. She began to hit my head against the cupboard. Dad pulled her off. You get used to it after a while and learn how far you can push her. There isn't a whole lot I can do about it. She is my mom, and I've got to do what she says."

Fifteen-year-old girl[1]

The family represents the primary agent for the socialization of children. The family is the first social group a child encounters and is the group with which most children have their most enduring relationships. The family gives a child his or her principal identity and of course even his or her name.[2] The family teaches social roles, moral standards, and society's laws, and it disciplines children who fail to comply with those norms and values. The family either provides for or neglects children's emotional, intellectual, and social needs; the neglect of these basic needs can have a profound effect upon the shaping of a child's values and attitudes.

This chapter discusses the general problems of the American family, the relationship between the family and delinquency, and the types and impact of child abuse and neglect.

GENERAL PROBLEMS OF THE AMERICAN FAMILY

The American family is racked with problems. Some observers of social life even argue that the family as a social unit no longer functions in a useful way. Divorce, isolation, role problems, unemployment, alcohol and drug abuse, and violence are some of the problems affecting the family today.

The United States has the highest divorce rate of Western countries; in 1979, nearly nine million Americans reported themselves as divorced.[3] The number of children under eighteen affected by parents' divorces increased from 361,000 in 1956 to 1.12 million in 1974.[4] The rise of divorce means that single-parent families have been increasing; in 1979, there were ten million such families. In a five-year study of one-parent families in Baltimore, Freudenthal identified five major problems: (1) financial hardship; (2) a sense of incompleteness and frustration; (3) a sense of failure; (4) feelings of guilt; and (5) some degree of ambivalent feelings between the parent and child or children.[5]

Isolation also is a major problem of many American families. Isolation is the result of urbanization, increased mobilization, dehumanizing jobs, and the disintegration

The assistance of Linda Dippold Bartollas was invaluable in shaping the contents of this chapter.

of communities, neighborhoods, and support networks. The decline of the extended family, which traditionally offered numerous advantages to children because it relieved some of the pressures of parenting, has further contributed to the problem of isolation.

The American family is experiencing more role problems than in the past. The increased numbers of working mothers, as well as the impact of the women's liberation movement, have made it necessary for both males and females to redefine their roles within the household. Disagreement about the role obligations of husband and wife can be an important factor in the breakup of the family structure.

Unemployment is a critical problem for many families. In the late 1970s, 6 to 7.8 million Americans were unemployed in any particular year. This rate nearly doubled in the early 1980s; indeed, in some areas of the country, 15 to 20 percent of the work force was unemployed or laid off work, and in urban neighborhoods, 40 to 50 percent of the work force was unemployed. Unemployment rates are typically higher for women than for men, higher for blacks and other minority groups than for whites, and higher for the young workers.[6]

Alcohol and drug abuse, as well as mental illness, cause problems for more and more American families. In a 1978 Gallup poll, nearly one-fourth of the respondents said liquor had been a cause of trouble in their families. By 1979, an estimated 11 million Americans had drinking problems; a smaller percentage of adults also had problems with drugs.[7] The number of Americans suffering from some degree of mental disorder is difficult to ascertain, but it has been estimated that 30 to 55 million suffer from mental disorder and perhaps 80 percent of the population has at least mild psychiatric symptoms.[8]

Violence has been a major characteristic of the family in past times, and it is no stranger to family life today. Aggravated assaults between husbands and wives make up a significant percentage of all such reported assaults. For example, in 1971, 52 percent of the reported aggravated assaults in Detroit involved husbands and wives.[9] A study in Delaware found that 12 percent of those surveyed reported hitting a spouse with a hard object, while 22 percent had used a hand. Furthermore, more than 60 percent of the couples reported at least one violent act in their marriage.[10] With this general acceptance of violence within the family, it is not surprising then that some parents also act out their aggressions on their children.

THE FAMILY AND DELINQUENCY

The importance given the family as a contributing factor to delinquency has varied through the years. Karen Wilkinson has classified the attention given to the family into three periods: 1900–1932, 1933–1950, and 1950–1972. In the first period the role of the family as a contributing factor to delinquent behavior was emphasized. A broken home was considered a major cause of delinquency, and a great deal of research was done to measure its influence. In the second period the family was minimized in comparison to the school, social class standing, and learning of delinquent behavior from peers. In the third period, there was revived interest in the family. Wilkinson attributes this to the fact that oth~~~~~bles studied as causes of delinquency did not yield conclusive find~~~~~ ~~~~~in this post–1950 period also broadened their inquiry to en~~~~~ ~~~~~ ~~~~~ ~~~~~e relationship between parents and children, parental disc~~~~~ ~~~~~ ~~~~~nd family integration.[11]

Delinquency research on the fan~~~~~ ~~~~~ ~~~~~ on the following factors: broken homes, the child's birth order in the family, family size, delinquency among siblings, family rejection and conflict, and discipline in the home.

The Broken Home

Considerable empirical evidence supports the commonly accepted notion that delinquency results from a broken home.[12] In 1924, Mangold declared, "The broken home is probably the single most important cause of delinquency."[13] Hodgkiss's 1933 study in Cook County (Chicago) also revealed a strong difference in the incidence of broken homes among delinquents compared to nondelinquents: the delinquents had 66.9 percent and the nondelinquents 44.8 percent.[14] Sheldon and Eleanor T. Glueck's classic study, which compared five hundred delinquents and five hundred nondelinquents, reported stronger evidence of the importance of broken homes: 60.4 percent of delinquents compared to 34.2 percent of nondelinquents came from broken homes.[15] However, several studies have questioned the relationship between broken homes and delinquency. Nye's highly respected study of the family and research by Dentler and Monroe found no significant direct relationship between delinquency and family composition.[16] L. Rosen recalculated statistical relationships for eleven different studies of broken homes and male delinquency conducted between 1932 and 1968 and discovered that virtually all the studies yielded only very weak positive relationships between broken homes and delinquency.[17]

Other researchers have shed further light on this debate. Sterne, Toby, and Monahan reported that the factor of broken homes affects girls more than boys.[18] Datesman and Scarpitti found that the relationship for girls between broken homes and delinquency depends on the type of offense involved.[19] Both Hirschi and Gold found the greatest rate of delinquency in families with stepfathers.[20] Chilton and Markle initially found that children living in broken homes are more frequently involved in status and delinquent offenses, but upon reclassifying the families on the basis of income, they found that economics appeared to have more to do with the rate of referral to the juvenile court than family composition.[21] Furthermore, several studies have reported that poor quality of home life, measured by marital adjustment and harmony within the home, affects the rate of delinquent behavior among children more than whether or not the family is intact. Nye found the happiness of the marriage to be the key to whether or not children become involved in delinquent behavior.[22] The Gluecks reported good marital relationships and strong family cohesiveness in homes of more nondelinquents than delinquents.[23] McCord, McCord, and Zola, and Audry, further concluded that well-integrated and cohesive families produce fewer delinquents than do less well-adjusted families.[24]

The Child's Birth Order in the Family

Some evidence supports the notion that delinquent behavior is more likely to be exhibited by middle children than first or last children. The first child, according to this view, receives the undivided attention and affection of parents, while the last child benefits from the parents' experience in raising children, as well as from the presence of other siblings, who serve as role models. The Gluecks, Nye, and McCord, McCord, and Zola all reported that intermediate children were more likely to be delinquents.[25]

Family Size

Hirschi explained the higher rate of delinquency with middle children as the result of family size rather than ordinal position.[26] Joachim, in further analyzing Hirschi's data, found that larger family size seems to be a negative indicator for different delinquent offenses, among blacks and whites, and among youths whose fathers fall in the same education category.[27] The theory that family size is more important than ordinal position is based on the assumption that large families lack the economic resources, discipline, and ability to provide socialization needed to prevent delinquency among children. In other words, parental controls and economic resources are spread too thin in large families and, accordingly, children from large families are more likely to be involved in delinquent behavior.

Delinquency among Siblings

Some evidence indicates that siblings learn delinquency from others in the family. Healy and Bronner found that 78 percent of delinquent children in two child families had delinquent siblings, but in six-child families, the figure was 43 percent.[28] The Gluecks also reported that a much higher proportion of delinquents than nondelinquents had delinquent sibling or criminal mothers or fathers.[29] But William C. Kvaraceus's study revealed that most brothers and sisters of delinquent children are not delinquent; of the 761 delinquents in his study who were members of 687 families and had an average of four brothers and sisters, nine out of ten were the only juveniles in their families with delinquent records.[30]

Family Rejection

Several studies have found a relationship between parental rejection and delinquent behavior. Kirson Weinberg found that parents of delinquents had rejected their children.[31] McCord, McCord, and Howard reported that some rejecting parents often exhibited aggressive behavior as well.[32] Nye found that the father's rejection is more often significantly related to delinquency than the mother's rejection.[33] But a number of other studies concluded that rejection from mothers is more related to involvement with delinquency.[34] McCord, McCord, and Zola reported that only a small percentage of delinquents had affectionate relationships with parents.[35] The

Gluecks and Audry also found that parental affection is less apparent in the homes of delinquents than in those of nondelinquents.[36] Slocum and Stone further discovered that children from affectionate homes tend to be more conforming in behavior.[37]

Discipline in the Home

Inadequate supervision and discipline in the home have been commonly cited to explain delinquent behavior. Hirschi found that the rate of delinquency increased with the incidence of mothers employed outside the home. He attributed this finding to the fact that unemployed mothers spent more time supervising their children's activities and behavior.[38] Nye found a slight causal relationship between the employment of the mother and delinquent behavior.[39] But the Gluecks' study failed to reveal a strong association between working mothers and delinquent behavior.[40] Jensen and Eve further found that the degree of supervision within the home was not a significant factor in the amount of delinquent activity of children.[41]

Nye reported that the type of discipline employed in the home had an effect upon delinquent behavior, for both strict and lax discipline and unfair discipline were associated with high rates of delinquent behavior. Nye also added that the disciplinary role of the father was more closely related to delinquent behavior than was the disciplinary role of the mother.[42] McCord, McCord, and Zola and McCord and McCord further found a relationship between inconsistent discipline and delinquent behavior.[43]

Summary

Conflicting findings make drawing conclusions about delinquency and the family difficult, but the following observations have received wide support:

1. Family conflict and poor marital adjustment are more likely to lead to delinquency than is the structural breakup of the family.

2. Children who are intermediate in birth order and who are part of large families appear to be involved more frequently in delinquent behavior, but this is probably related more to parents' inability to provide for the emotional and financial needs of their children than to ordinal position or family size.

3. Children who have delinquent siblings or criminal parents may be more prone to delinquent behavior than those who do not.

4. Rejected children are more prone to delinquent behavior than those who have not been rejected. Children who have experienced severe rejection are probably more likely to become involved in delinquent behavior than those who have experienced rejection to a lesser degree.

5. Consistency of discipline within the family seems to be important in deterring delinquent behavior.

7. The rate of delinquency appears to increase with the number of unfavorable factors in the home.

8. Nearly all of the studies on family and delinquency examine lower-class youths; the impact of the above factors may be quite different on middle- and upper-class youths.

CHILD ABUSE AND NEGLECT

Child abuse and neglect, as do the other family problems noted in this chapter, has a profound influence on shaping the behavior and attitudes of adolescents and children. Child abuse and neglect is usually divided into three areas: neglect, physical and emotional abuse, and sexual abuse.

Extent and Nature of Child Abuse and Neglect

Child abuse has a long history. Indeed, the unsparing use of the rod and the cruelty to children in nineteenth-century America makes contemporary treatment of children seem benevolent. But several events in the past several decades have focused public attention on child abuse and resulted in the documentation of its extent and nature. C. Henry Kempe first exposed child abuse as a major social problem with his groundbreaking essay on the battered child syndrome.[44] Kempe's research led to an avalanche of writing on neglect, physical abuse, and sexual abuse during the late 1960s and 1970s. The passage of legislation in all fifty states in the late 1960s requiring mandatory reporting of child abuse and neglect cases also focused attention on these problems. In addition, the passage by Congress of the Child Abuse and Prevention Act and the establishment of the National Center on Child Abuse in 1974 focused further attention on these problems.

Neglect
Neglect generally refers to disregarding the physical, emotional, or moral needs of children or adolescents. The Children's Division of the American Humane Association established a comprehensive definition of neglect, stating that physical, emotional, and intellectual growth and welfare are jeopardized when a child can be described in the following terms:

1. *Malnourished, ill-clad, dirty, without proper shelter or sleeping arrangements.*

2. *Without supervision, unattended.*

3. *Ill and lacking essential medical care.*

4. *Denial of normal experiences that produce feelings of being loved, wanted, secure and worthy (emotional neglect).*

5. *Failure to attend school regularly.*

6. *Exploited, overworked.*

7. Emotionally disturbed due to constant friction in the home, marital discord, mentally ill parents.

8. Exposed to unwholesome, demoralizing circumstances.[45]

The national figures on child neglect are twice as large as those for child abuse.[46] Douglas J. Desharov, director of the National Center on Child Abuse and Neglect, estimates that approximately one million children are mistreated by their parents each year; of these 100,000 to 200,000 are physically abused, 60,000 to 100,000 are sexually abused, and the rest are neglected.[47] Moreover, neglect is from one-and-a-half to two times more likely to result in a need for medical attention or hospitalization than is abuse. Neglect also appears to be more strongly related to poverty than is abuse.[48]

In studying the case records of 180 families that had come to the attention of authorized agencies, Young separated them into cases of severe and moderate neglect and severe and moderate abuse. She defined severe neglect as inadequate feeding. Such parents failed to provide the most necessary and elementary of all human needs. They also failed to keep the children clean, to furnish adequate clothing, and to provide proper medical care. Parents involved in moderate neglect usually fed their children, but the children were not kept clean, nor did they have adequate clothing or proper medical care.[49]

Norman A. Polansky et al., who studied neglect in Georgia and North Carolina, identified five types of mothers who are frequently guilty of child neglect. The apathetic-futile mother is emotionally numb to her children and neglects both their physical and emotional needs. The impulse-ridden mother is restless and craves excitement, movement, and change. She is unable to tolerate stress or frustration and is aggressive and defiant. Typically, she neglects her children by simply taking off on an escapade, either with a husband or a boyfriend, and letting the children fend for themselves. The mentally retarded mother has difficulty providing adequate care for her children, especially if her I.Q. is below 60. If emotional problems are combined with mental deficiency, then severe neglect is even more likely. The mother in a reaction depression is preoccupied with a loss of a loved one or some other traumatic event. Her persistent feelings of despair and sadness can lead to bodily illness so that she is unable to cope with her own reality, much less provide for her children. Finally, the borderline or psychotic mother may forget to feed the children since she is lost in her fantasies, or she may even kill the children and herself in a psychotic outburst.[50]

Polansky and colleagues replicated their Appalachian study with an examination of neglect in Philadelphia. This study concluded that a general immaturity or high degree of infantalism was the strongest predictor of maternal neglect. The neglectful mother was likely to have been abused as a child, was isolated from informal helping networks, had a low rate of participation in formal organizations, had a lower I.Q. than the mothers used as controls, had more emotional pathology than the controls, and was "dirt" poor. The researchers also found that apathy-futility and impulse-ridden mothers were far more common in the Philadelphia study than in the Appalachian study.[51]

Physical and Emotional Abuse

Physical abuse refers to intentional behavior directed toward a child by the parents or caretaker to cause pain, injury, or death. Estimates of the extent of abuse in the United States vary. Richard Nagi estimates that 167,000 cases of abuse are reported annually, while another 91,000 cases go unreported.[52] However, Vincent Fontana contends that as many as 1.5 million cases of child abuse take place each year.[53] Richard Gelles and Murray Straus, from their national survey, also estimate that between 1.4 and 1.9 million children are abused annually by their parents.[54]

The American Humane Association, analyzing 662 cases of child abuse reported in newspapers in 1962, found that children were beaten with bare fists, electric cords, straps, TV aerials, rubber hoses, ropes, sticks, fan belts, pool cues, wooden spoons, broom handles, bottles, chair legs, and baseball bats. Some children had their hands, arms, and feet burned by gas burners, cigarette lighters, electric irons, or hot pokers. Other children were strangled or suffocated by pillows held over their mouths or plastic bags thrown over their heads. Several were drowned in bathtubs, and one was buried alive. Children were also stabbed, shot, bitten, thrown violently to the floor or against a wall, subjected to electric shock, or stamped on.[55] Douglas J. Besharov, director of the National Center on Child Abuse and Neglect, estimates that more than 2000 children die each year in circumstances that suggest abuse or neglect.[56]

Emotional abuse is more difficult to define than physical abuse since it involves a disregard of the psychological needs of a child or adolescent. Emotional abuse encompasses a lack of expressed love and affection, as well as deliberate withholding of contact and approval. Emotional abuse may include a steady diet of putdowns, humiliation, labeling, name calling, scapegoating, lying, demanding excessive responsibility, seductive behavior, ignoring, fear-inducing techniques, unrealistic expectations, and extreme inconsistency.[57] Randy, a sixteen-year old boy, tells of emotional abuse he suffered:

> My father bought me a baby raccoon. I was really close to it, and it was really close to me. I could sleep with it, and it would snug up beside me. The raccoon wouldn't leave or nothing. A friend of mine got shots for it. My father got mad one night because I didn't vacuum the rug, and there were seven or eight dishes in the sink. He said "Go get me your raccoon." I said, "Dad, if you hurt my raccoon I'll hate you forever." He made me go get my raccoon, and he took a hammer and killed it. He hit it twice on the head and crushed its brains. I took it out and buried it.[58]

David G. Gil, in developing a classification of families, found that seven situations accounted for 97.3 percent of the reported abuse cases:

1. *Psychological rejection leading to repeated abuse and battering.*

2. *Disciplinary measures taken in uncontrolled anger.*

3. *Male babysitter acting out sadistic and sexual impulses in the mother's temporary absence, at times under the influence of alcohol.*

4. Mentally or emotionally disturbed caretaker causing mounting environmental stress.

5. Misconduct and persistent negative behavior of a child leading to his own abuse.

6. Female babysitter abusing child during the mother's temporary absence.

7. Quarrel between caretakers, at times when under the influence of alcohol.[59]

Research findings conflict concerning at what age a child is most vulnerable to abuse by parents. According to some researchers, from three months to three years of age is the most dangerous period in a child's life.[60] Other researchers have discovered considerable abuse among older children. Urie Bronfenbrenner contends that the highest rate of abuse occurs among teenagers.[61] David Gil found that half of the confirmed cases of abuse were children over six years of age and that nearly one-fifth were teenagers.[62] In a study of college students at an eastern university, 8 percent of the 250 students stated that they had been physically abused by parents during the last year they lived at home.[63] On balance, it seems clear that child abuse takes place at ages from birth through adolescence, but the more serious cases are still more likely to occur with infants and young children who are more susceptible to injury. Teenagers are more physically durable, able to protect themselves better, and can leave the home when parents become too abusive.

Child abuse occurs throughout the United States. Although there is little variation among regions, Southerners appear to have the lowest rates and Midwesterners have the highest rates of child abuse.[64] Child abuse also seems to be more prevalent in urban areas than suburban or rural settings. The fact that urban areas have better resources to detect child abuse does not entirely explain why so many more cases are reported to urban police. Obviously, the congested populations and poverty of the city, which lead to other social problems, largely account for the fact that abuse is predominantly an urban problem.

Official statistics on child abuse typically show that blacks and other minorities make up a greater proportion of child abusers. Increased rates of abuse among minorities may be the result of lower incomes, greater stress, or different cultural values, or the rates may be explained by the fact that minorities are more likely to be singled out by those who compile official statistics. Thus, two studies found that blacks were not as violent toward their children as whites.[65] Variations among racial groups is one of the many aspects of child abuse that needs more research, and as more data are gathered on the dynamics of the family lives of both whites and minorities, a clearer picture should emerge concerning the variations of child abuse among racial groups.

In the abusive situation, there is often one parent who is aggressive and one who is passive. Commonly, the passive parent defends the aggressive one, denies the realities of the family situation, and clings to the intact family and to the abusive partner. The passive parent behaves as if he or she is prisoner in the marriage relationship, condemned to a life sentence. This parent usually does not consider the option of separating from the aggressive partner because he or she is committed to the marriage, no matter how miserable the home situation may be.[66]

Sexual Abuse

Sexual abuse, or incest, refers to any sexual activity that involves physical contact or sexual arousal between nonmarried members of a family. Oral-genital relations, fondling erogenous areas of the body, mutual masturbation, and intercourse are the main expressions of incest within a family setting.[67] The National Center on Child Abuse and Neglect defines incest as "intrafamily sexual abuse which is perpetrated on a child by a member of that child's family group and includes not only sexual intercourse, but also any act designed to stimulate a child sexually, or to use a child sexually, or to use a child for sexual stimulation, either of the perpetrator or of another person."[68]

The seriousness of the problem of incest is becoming more apparent as states pass more effective legislation on reporting of incest cases. According to Blair and Rita Justice, 50 to 500 percent increases in confirmed cases of incest are being reported both in urban areas and at the state level. For example, the number of confimed incest cases that came to the attention of child welfare departments in Texas in 1974 was 214; in 1976, 630; and in 1977, 1,153. The well-known Child Sexual Abuse Treatment Program in Santa Clara County, California received 36 referrals in 1971, 180 in 1974, and 600 in 1977.[69]

Incest, or sexual abuse, reportedly occurs most frequently between a natural father or stepfather and a daughter, but it also may involve brother and sister, mother and son, and father and son. A father's sexual abuse of a daughter usually is a devastating experience to the girl that sometimes has lifelong consequences. Stepfathers also sexually victimize stepdaughters, but natural fathers appear to be involved in more cases of sexual abuse than are stepfathers. The average incestuous relationship lasts about three-and-a-half years.[70] The completed act of intercourse is more likely to take place with adolescents than with younger children.

Helen, a sixteen-year-old, was sexually victimized by her father for three years. She had great difficulty getting anyone to believe that her father was committing incest. When the father was finally prosecuted, she made the statement:

> When I was thirteen, my father started coming into my room at night. He usually did it when he was drinking. He would force me to have sex with him. I told my mother. I told my teachers at school. But nobody would believe me.[71]

Some evidence exists that brother-sister incest takes place more frequently than father-daughter incest, but its long-term consequences are usually less damaging because it does not cross generational boundaries and often occurs as an extension of sex play.[72] But brother-sister incest can have damaging consequences for the girl if the act is discovered and she is blamed for being sexually involved with her brother. If the girl feels she has been seduced or exploited, then the damage may be even greater.

Mother-son incest is less common and only rarely reported, largely because of the strong stigmas and taboos attached to the idea of sex between boys and their mothers.[73] Mother-son incest usually begins with excessive physical contact, which eventually becomes sexually stimulating. "Don't leave me" or "don't grow up" messages are communicated to the son as the mother seeks ways to prolong physical contact with him, sleeping with him, bathing him, or dressing him.[74]

Father-son incest also is rarely reported, largely because it violates both the moral code against incest and the one against homosexuality. The stress of an incestuous relationship, as well as the threat to masculinity, often results in serious consequences for the boy when father-son incest does occur. Sons involved in father-son incest usually experience acute anxiety because they feel damaged, dirty, and worthless; they may cope by retreating into their own world and losing contact with reality.[75]

The National Center on Child Abuse and Neglect has identified five factors that are usually present when incest takes place: (1) the daughter's voluntary or forced assumption of the mother's role; (2) some sexual incompatibility between the parents; (3) the father's reluctance to seek a partner outside the family unit; (4) the family's fear of disintegration; and (5) unconscious sanctions by the mother.[76]

Blair and Rita Justice have developed a classification of fathers who commit incest which is extremely helpful in understanding their behavior.[77] They divide incestuous fathers into four groups: symbiotic personalities, psychopathic personalities, pedophilic personalities, and a small group of "others." According to these researchers, the first group makes up 70 to 80 percent of the incestuous fathers.

Symbiotic personalities have strong unmet needs for warmth and for someone to whom to be close. They hunger for a sense of belonging and intimacy. These fathers are out of touch with their needs and do not know how to meet them in healthy ways. This type, more than the others, looks to the family to satisfy all their emotional needs. As relationships with their wives deteriorate, they turn to their daughters to satisfy their emotional and physical needs. They use a variety of rationalizations to justify their sexual abuse—e.g., that physical intimacy is the highest form of love a father can show his daughter, or that a father has exclusive property rights over the daughter and, therefore, can do whatever he wants. Alcohol is often used to loosen restraints on these fathers' behavior; after the sexual activity, they often blame the alcohol rather than themselves.

Psychopathic personalities seek stimulation and excitement through incestuous relationships. Sex is simply a vehicle to express the hostility they feel and to provide the excitement they have felt deprived of in the past. The psychopath feels no guilt and has little capacity to love; he simply wants immediate gratification of his needs. Fortunately, this type of incestuous father is rare.

Pedophilic personalities are attracted to young girls who show no signs of physical and sexual development. These extremely immature fathers have erotic cravings for children. They want sexual activity with someone who will not reject or belittle them. Only a small amount of incest is committed by these immature and inadequate personalities.

The Justices' "other types" include psychotic fathers and those who come from a subculture that permits incest. Psychotic fathers experience hallucinations and delusions, and they are most often responsible for using force in incest. About 3 percent of incestuous fathers are psychotic. In some cultural groups, it is normal for the oldest daughter to assume her mother's role, both in the kitchen and in bed. The youngest daughter also is often introduced to sex by her father or brothers. Because little culturally sanctioned incest exists in the United States, this group of fathers accounts only for a small fraction of the cases of incest.

Relationship of Child Abuse and Neglect to Delinquency and Status Offenses

For several reasons, an abused or neglected child is more likely to become involved in delinquency or status offenses. Neglect or abuse has a negative impact on the emotional development of the child; it leads to truancy and disruptive behavior in school, encourages running away from home, and generates so much pain that alcohol and drugs are sometimes viewed as a needed escape. Neglect or abuse causes so much self-rejection, especially for victims of incest, that these youths may vent their self-destructiveness through prostitution and may even commit suicide; and neglect or abuse also creates so much anger that abused youngsters sometimes commit aggressive acts against others.

Emotional Trauma of Child Abuse and Neglect

Victimized children have never received the love and nurturing necessary for healthy growth and development. They often feel abandoned and lack the security of being a part of a "real" family. They struggle, sometimes all their lives, to get the nurturing and the feeling of being cared for that they have never experienced.

Victims of child abuse and neglect often have low self-esteem, considerable guilt, high anxiety, mild to serious depression, and high internal conflict.[78] Physically, they may experience disturbances in sleeping patterns, weight loss or gain, or continual illnesses. They also tend to have poor social relationships.[79] Psychotherapists report a large number of child sexual abuse victims among their clients.[80] They also note that women who were sexually abused as children often suffer from depression.[81]

Sometimes, the emotional problems of abused children are so serious that they have difficulty functioning in family, social, or institutional settings. A social worker in a Midwestern youth shelter describes one such youth:

Some parents are really, really sick, but they don't see it. You can't get them to treatment. You get into some really messy situations. Their kids receive so little support that they feel so rejected and so mishandled that their only hope for survival into adulthood is to find someone in some institution or in some foster family that will make a commitment to them and will help them survive on their own. These kids need someone that will help them realize that what happened to them in their lives was not their fault and that they need to develop their own strengths so that they can feel good about themselves.[82]

Runaways

Teenagers who have been abused frequently run away from home. One sexually abused girl explained: "I never thought about where I was running to—only what I was running from."[83] Running away becomes a way of coping with the pain of neglect, physical abuse, and sexual abuse. The youth often sees running away as the only way to manage an unmanageable problem. Parents sometimes tell a child to get out, for they want to rid themselves of the problems that the abusive situation has created.

When abused adolescents are placed in foster homes, typically their running does not stop. They often choose to reject their new family rather than risk the possibility that they might be rejected again. Unfortunately, sometimes children are removed from an abusive home only to experience abuse all over again in a foster home.

Disruptive and Truant Behavior in School

Several studies have found that abused and neglected children have greater difficulty in school than children who are not abused.[84] According to Kempe and Kempe, "many of these children become academic and social failures almost immediately upon entering school."[85] Abused and neglected school-age children tend to perform gross motor tasks poorly,[86] have deficiencies in language development,[87] are more frequently placed in special education classes,[88] are more likely to be assigned to EMH (educable mentally handicapped) classes,[89] have more learning problems,[90] are more disobedient and have a greater problem accepting authority,[91] and have more conflict with peers.[92]

Teachers who have worked with abused and neglected children add that they have difficulty in concentrating, are aloof, have little or no confidence, frequently have emotional outbursts, have not internalized rules, and are often destructive of property.[93] In other words, abused and neglected children are often labeled disruptive in the public school, are assigned to special learning classes, and are set up for failure.

Drug and Alcohol Abuse

In an effort to blot out their pain and isolation, many abused children turn to drug and alcohol abuse.[94] A girl from an abusive home said, "Drugs became my great escape; there wasn't nothing I wouldn't try to get high."[95] Abused children often feel they have nothing to lose by taking drugs, for they are concerned only with forgetting their insecurity, anxiety, and lack of confidence. A type of love/trust relationship that they have never had with people before sometimes develops through drugs. They can finally belong, experiencing closeness and security with peers who also take drugs.

Barbara L. Myers, former director of Christopher Street, Inc., and a victim of sexual abuse as a girl, tells why she turned to drugs:

I was eleven years old when I first discovered that drugs could make the terrible world around me disappear. . . . When I was on drugs, I felt high, happy, and in control of my life. When I was high, I had peers; I finally belonged somewhere—in a group with other kids who took drugs. Whatever

*the others were taking, I took twice as much or more. I wasn't aware like
the rest of them; I got high without worrying about how much I could handle or what it would do to me. It made me feel big and powerful because I
didn't care what happened to me.*   .

*People said that taking too many drugs would burn out your brains. I used
to think that I could become a vegetable if only I could succeed in burning
out my brains. I wanted to be a vegetable. I used to picture myself as a head
of lettuce. I used to look at mentally retarded people and think that they
were so happy and didn't care about anything. I envied them because you
could spit at them, and they would smile; they didn't seem to understand
what hurt was.*[96]

Deviant Sexual Behavior

Some evidence exists that sexual abuse victims themselves often become involved in
deviant sexual behavior. Promiscuity appears to be high among female sexual abuse
victims.[97] Many female sexual abuse victims also become involved in prostitution,[98]
and sexual abuse is frequently a part of the background of male prostitutes.[99]

It is not surprising that female sexual abuse victims are attracted to prostitution,
because they have come to see themselves as shamed, marked, and good only for
delivering sex. The self-destructive aspect of prostitution serves as another way of
expressing rage for never having been loved and for having been sexually and/or
physically abused. In prostitution, sexual abuse victims take control by making
strangers pay for sex. Detachment has already been learned in childhood; therefore,
it is relatively easy for them to disassociate themselves from brief sexual encounters.[100]

Homicide and Abuse

While female victims of mistreatment are more likely to become self-destructive,
male abuse victims tend to express their anger in ways that hurt others. A strong link
appears to exist between abuse and homicide. Researchers found in one study that
85 percent of a group of teenagers who had committed murder unrelated to another
crime had received severe corporal punishment as children.[101] Another investigation
of crimes showed that in one-third of all homicides committed by adolescents in the
State of New York, the delinquent had been either neglected or abused at home.[102]
Child abuse appears in the backgrounds of many famous murderers; for example,
Charles Manson was severely abused as a child. In 1979, this link between homicide
and abuse was legally recognized when a jury acquitted a youth who had murdered
five young women as being "innocent by virtue of insanity," because he had multiple personalities created by the severe abuse he had received at home.[103]

CHILD ABUSE AND
THE JUSTICE SYSTEM

All states have statutes requiring that suspected abuse and neglect cases be reported.
Procedures vary from state to state, but typically a child abuse unit of the social

services or welfare department receives the child abuse or neglect report. The unit usually has twenty-four hours to investigate the report, unless the child is deemed to be in immediate danger, in which case the unit is expected to make a call at the home within an hour. A police officer accompanies the social worker on the child abuse or neglect investigation for four reasons: the social worker is protected in case the parents become assaultive; the peace officer has the authority to take the child out of an abusive home if necessary; the police officer may gather evidence and take pictures if court evidence is present; and the presence of the police officer permits the social worker to focus on the family rather than to be preoccupied with the legal investigation.

If the decision is made to take the child out of the home, the juvenile court judge must be called for approval as soon as the social worker and police officer leave the house. A temporary removal hearing is held in the juvenile court within three to five days if the child has been taken out of the home. At the temporary removal hearing, the juvenile judge can decide to leave the child in the temporary placement, whether a foster home, youth shelter, or group home, or the judge can return the child to the parents.

An adjudication, or fact-finding, hearing is held if a petition of abuse or neglect has been filed by the department of social services. Juvenile courts hear about 150,000 child abuse and neglect cases a year. Present at the adjudication hearing are the assistant district, state, or county attorney; the youth and his or her attorney; the parents and their attorney; the social worker assigned to the case; and the police officer who made the investigation. After the evidence has been presented, the juvenile court judge decides whether the petition charging neglect or abuse has been substantiated. If it has, a disposition hearing is set for about four weeks later.

The concept of the supremacy of parental rights continues to receive widespread support among juvenile court judges and departments of social services or welfare. This concept can be defined as "a strong presumption for parental autonomy in child rearing and the philosophy that coercive intervention is appropriate only in the face of serious specifically defined harm to the child."[104] The concept of the supremacy of parental rights also has received strong support from national standards groups. The National Advisory Commission on Criminal Justice Standards and Goals and the joint Juvenile Justice Standards Project of the American Bar Association and the Institute of Judicial Administration have both proposed that coercive intervention by the state should be only a last resort.[105]

The prosecution of the parents in criminal court depends largely upon the seriousness of the injury to the child and upon the attitude of the district, state, or county attorney's office toward child abuse. The cases most likely to be prosecuted are those in which a child has been seriously injured or killed and those in which a father or stepfather has sexually abused a daughter or stepdaughter. The most common charges in prosecutions are simple assault, assault with intent to commit serious injury, and manslaughter or murder.

In terms of present procedures, it must be remembered that reported cases represent only the tip of the iceberg. Abuse and neglect cases among lower-class families are more likely to be reported than those among middle-class families. The procedures and effectiveness of dealing with abusive homes also vary from one state to the next. Moreover, much remains to be learned about dealing more effectively with abusive families, about creating the type of placements that will serve the best interests of the child, and about creating the kind of public policy necessary to reduce the amount of abuse and neglect in this nation.

POLICY IMPLICATIONS

Ideally, children are entitled to a home life in which they can fully realize their potential. Although structural breakup of the family, conflict in the home, and rejection and inconsistent discipline interfere with that process, neglect and abuse appear to have even more long-range debilitating consequences. David G. Gil offered a comprehensive and exemplary definition of proper child care and of child abuse at a hearing on the Child Abuse Prevention Act before the Subcommittee on Children and Youth of the U.S. Senate:

> *Every child, despite his individual differences and uniqueness, is to be considered of equal intrinsic worth, and hence should be entitled to equal social, economic, civil, and political rights, so that he may fully realize his inherent potential and share equally in life, liberty, and happiness. Obviously, these value premises are rooted in the humanistic philosophy of our Declaration of Independence.*
>
> *In accordance with these value premises then, any act of commission or omission by individuals, institutions, or society as a whole, and any conditions resulting from such acts or inaction, which deprive children of equal rights and liberties and/or interfere with their optimal development, constitute, by definition, abuse or neglected acts or conditions.*[106]

To provide for this "optimal development" of children would be a staggering undertaking requiring major societal changes. But even preventing abuse and neglect in the family would be no easy task and would require certain societal changes. First, the norms that legitimize and glorify violence in this society must be eliminated. Second, the stresses leading to family conflict and violence, such as unemployment, substandard housing, and health and dental problems, must be reduced. Third, families must again be integrated into a network of kin and community in order to diminish the problem of social isolation. Finally, a national program for screening potential abusers must be instituted, and voluntary programs must be made available for high-risk parents.[107] Given the unlikeliness of such large-scale changes taking place in the near future, the treatment of abusers and victims becomes an even more important issue for the present.

Treatment

A number of programs are available for abusers and victims who request help. Hot lines and self-help groups, such as Parents Anonymous and Youth Self-Help Groups, are the most widely used programs. Parents Anonymous, which has over 150 chapters and 1500 members, is able to meet the needs of abusive parents because such parents feel more comfortable telling their problems to those who are or have been in the same predicament.[108] Crisis nurseries and day-care centers also are operated in some areas of the United States.

The most innovative program at present is the Comprehensive Child Sexual Abuse Program in Santa Clara County, California. This program, established by Henry Giarretto, is made up of three interdependent components: a professional staff, volunteers, and self-help groups. Parents United and its adjunct, Daughters and Sons United, provide the self-help components of this program.[109]

The Santa Clara County chapter of Parents United has over 200 members at present, and attendance at its weekly meetings averages 125. A new member had this to say about Parents United:

> Well, I came to Parents United's Wednesday night meeting. I don't have to tell you what I expected to find. However, what I found was a room full of normal, everyday-looking people—hugging and kissing, smiling, and greeting each other as if they were all family and hadn't seen each other for years.
>
> What I discovered that first night was that they were a family, a very special family held together by a common bond of unconditional love and understanding, of honest truth and caring. I began to feel warm inside. I felt alive again. I began to feel that "I, too" might be a worthwhile person.[110]

The counselor's first step, in dealing with the incestuous family, is to design a treatment program that usually takes the following sequence: (1) individual counseling for the child, mother, and other family members; (2) mother-daughter counseling; (3) marital counseling to help the family become reunited; (4) father-daughter counseling; (5) family counseling; and (6) group counseling. The father is usually facing court charges, but, because of the credibility of the CSATP program, he is usually given a suspended sentence or is sentenced to the local rehabilitation center for a few months.[111]

In 1977, CSATP was evaluated by the California state director of health. Dr. Jerome A. Kroth, who led the evaluation team, concluded: "The evaluator's overall conclusion is that the impact of CSATP family therapy in the treatment of intrafamilial child sexual abuse is positive, conclusive and unmistakable."[112]

In sum, because of the unlikelihood of major social change at this time, the treatment of child abuse and neglect becomes an even more critical concern. Although the programs discussed in this section are a start, many more are needed throughout the nation to deal with the problem of child abuse and neglect.

SUMMARY

The American family has serious problems today. Studies on the relationship between the family and delinquency have generally concluded that the quality of life within the home is more important than whether or not the home is intact, that parental rejection is associated with delinquent behavior, and that inconsistent, lax, or severe discipline is associated with increased delinquency. This research also leads to the conclusion that delinquent behavior among the children increases proportionately with the accumulation of unfavorable factors within the family.

The contextual perspective is helpful in understanding the problem of child abuse and neglect in American society. Treating children violently has been a sordid legacy throughout our history. Legally, the concept of the supremacy of parental rights has perpetuated the mistreatment of children by their parents; indeed, the state is reluctant to interfere unless severe physical injury, gross neglect, or sexual abuse has taken place. Within the sociocultural context, the acceptability of violence within American society and the social isolation, especially of lower-class families, have contributed to the mistreatment of children. Both neglect and abuse are influenced by poverty—poor people are more likely to neglect and abuse their children than are middle- and upper-class families. In terms of the political context, mandatory reporting and federal funding for treatment programs for abusers and victims are calling the public's attention to the extent and nature of the abuse problem.

Research findings have consistently linked child abuse and neglect to delinquent behavior and status offenses. Children who have been neglected and abused are likely to experience psychological problems, to run away from home, to become involved in truancy and disruptive behavior in school, and to turn to drug and alcohol abuse. Some neglected and abused youngsters also become involved in deviant sexual behavior and in aggressive acts toward others.

The contextual perspective also serves as a reminder that the mode of intervention chosen should fit the situational needs of the family. Intervention directed toward social control, either at the family system level or at the community organization level, becomes feasible only if basic survival needs are being met. Thus, intervention focused on basic survival, through family assistance, supersedes any other intervention, but control of the social environment comes next. Intervention with the family system itself should usually occur only when problems at the other levels are being dealt with. However, in those homes in which child abuse and neglect are taking place, the intervention must occur while the other situational needs of the family are being provided for.[113] A sound social policy regarding the family's role in delinquency control, then, must take all three levels into consideration.

Discussion Questions

1. What are the most serious problems of the family? What impact do these family problems have upon children?

2. What conditions within the family are more likely to result in delinquent behavior by the children?

3. What is neglect? What are some examples of neglect within the home?

4. Define emotional and physical abuse. What are some examples of physical and emotional abuse within the home?

5. Define and discuss incest. What type of father is most likely to become involved in incest?

6. How are child abuse and neglect related to status offenses and delinquent behavior?

7. What is the general procedure when child abuse or neglect is reported to the department of social services or welfare?

References

Finkelhor, David. *Sexually Victimized Children.* New York: Free Press, 1979.

Freeman, Michael D. *Violence in the Home: A Socio-Legal Study.* Westmead, England: Gower, 1980.

Garbarino, James, and Gilliam, Gwen. *Understanding Abusive Families.* Lexington, Mass.: D.C. Heath & Company, 1980.

Giaretto, Henry. "A Comprehensive Child Sexual Abuse Treatment Program." In *Sexually Abused Children and Their Families,* edited by Patricia B. Mrazek and C. Henry Kempe. Oxford, England: Pergamon Press, in press.

Gil, David G. *Child Abuse and Violence.* New York: AMS Press, 1979.

Glueck, Sheldon, and Glueck, Eleanor T. *Unraveling Juvenile Delinquency.* Cambridge: Harvard University Press for the Commonwealth Fund, 1950.

Hirschi, Travis. *Causes of Delinquency.* Berkeley: University of California Press, 1969.

Johnstone, John W. C. "Delinquency and the Changing American Family." In *Critical Issues in Juvenile Delinquency,* edited by David Shichor and Delos H. Kelly. Lexington, Mass.: D.C. Heath & Company, 1980.

Justice, Blair, and Justice, Rita. *The Broken Taboo: Sex in the Family.* New York: Human Sciences Press, 1979.

Kempe, R. S., and Kempe, C. H. *Child Abuse.* Cambridge: Harvard University Press, 1978.

Nye, F. I. *Family Relationships and Delinquent Behavior.* New York: John Wiley & Sons, 1958.

Pelton, Leroy H. "Child Abuse and Neglect: The Myth of Classlessness." In *The Social Context of Child Abuse and Neglect,* edited by Leroy H. Pelton. New York: Human Sciences Press, 1981.

Polansky, Norman A.; Chalmers, Mary Ann; Buttenwieser, Elizabeth; and Williams, David P. *Damaged Parents: An Anatomy of Child Neglect.* Chicago: University of Chicago Press, 1981.

Smith, Charles P.; Berkman, David J.; and Fraser, Warren M. *A Preliminary National Assessment of Child Abuse and Neglect and the Juvenile Justice System: The Shadows of Distress.* Reports of National Juvenile Justice Assessment Centers. Washington, D.C.: U.S. Government Printing Office, April, 1980.

Straus, Murray A.; Gelles, Richard J.; and Steinmetz, Suzanne K. *Behind Closed Doors.* New York: Doubleday, 1980.

Young, Leontine. *Wednesday's Children: A Study of Child Neglect and Abuse.* New York: McGraw-Hill Book Company, 1964.

FOOTNOTES

1. Interviewed in September 1980.
2. Robert Bierstedt, *The Social Order* (New York: McGraw-Hill Book Company, 1957).

3. P. C. Glick, "A Demographer Looks at American Families," *Journal of Marriage and the Family* 37 (February 1975), pp. 15–26.

4. U.S. Bureau of the Census, *Divorce, Child Custody, and Child Support* (Washington, D.C.: U.S. Government Printing Office, 1979), p. 9.

5. K. Freudenthal, "Problems of the One-Parent Family," *Social Work* 4 (January 1959), pp. 44–48.

6. U.S. Department of Labor, *Employment and Training Report of the President* (Washington, D.C.: U.S. Government Printing Office, 1980), p. 249.

7. U.S. Bureau of the Census, *Statistical Abstract of the United Staes, 1980* (Washington, D.C.: U.S. Government Printing Office, 1981), p. 129.

8. Robert H. Lauer, *Social Problems and the Quality of Life,* 2d ed. (Dubuque, Iowa: Wm. C. Brown Company Publishers, 1982), p. 502.

9. J. Boudouris, "Homicide and the Family," *Journal of Marriage and the Family* 33 (November 1971), pp. 666–667.

10. S. K. Steinmetz, "Occupational Environment in Relation to Physical Punishment and Dogmatism," in *Violence and the Family,* edited by S. Steinmetz and M. Straus (New York: Harper & Row, 1974), pp. 167–172.

11. Karen Wilkinson, "The Broken Family and Juvenile Delinquency: Scientific Explanation or Ideology," *Social Problems* 21 (June 1974), pp. 726–739.

12. W. D. Morrison, *Juvenile Offenders* (London: T. Fisher Unwin, 1896), pp. 146–147; Sophonisba P. Breckenridge and Edith Abbott, *The Delinquent Child and the Home* (New York: Russell Sage Foundation, 1912), pp. 90–91; William Healy, *The Individual Delinquent* (Boston: Little, Brown & Company, 1915), pp. 290–291; William Healy and Augusta Bronner, *Delinquents and Criminals: Their Making and Unmaking* (New York: Macmillan Publishing Company, 1926), p. 123; and Ernest H. Shideler, "Family Disintegration and the Delinquent Boy in the United States," *Journal of Criminal Law and Criminology* 8 (January 1918), pp. 709–732.

13. George B. Mangold, *Problems of Child Welfare,* rev. ed. (New York: Macmillan Publishing Company, 1924), p. 406.

14. Margaret Hodgkiss, "The Influence of Broken Homes and Working Mothers," *Smith College Studies in Social Work* 3 (March 1933), pp. 259–274.

15. Sheldon and Eleanor T. Glueck, *Unraveling Juvenile Delinquency* (Cambridge: Harvard University Press for the Commonwealth Fund, 1950), p. 123.

16. F. I. Nye, *Family Relationships and Delinquent Behavior* (New York: John Wiley & Sons, 1958); and R. A. Dentler and L. J. Monroe, "Social Correlates of Early Adolescent Theft," *American Sociological Review* 28 (1961), pp. 733–743.

17. L. Rosen, "The Broken Home and Delinquency," in *The Sociology of Crime and Delinquency,* edited by M. E. Wolfgang et al. (New York: John Wiley & Sons, 1970), pp. 489–495.

18. Richard S. Sterne, *Delinquent Conduct and Broken Homes* (New Haven, Conn.: College & University Press, 1964), p. 65; J. Toby, "The Differential Impact of Family Disorganization," *American Sociological Review* 22 (1957), pp. 505–512; T. P. Monahan, "Family Status and the Delinquent Child: A Reappraisal and Some New Findings," *Social Forces* 35 (1957), pp. 250–258; and T. P. Monahan, "Broken Homes by Age of Delinquent Children," *Journal of Social Psychology* 51 (1960), pp. 387–397.

19. Susan K. Datesman and Frank R. Scarpitti, "Female Delinquency and Broken Homes: A Re-Assessment," *Criminology* 13 (May 1975), p. 51.

20. Travis Hirschi, *Causes of Delinquency* (Berkeley: University of California Press, 1969); and M. Gold, *Delinquent Behavior in an American City* (Monterey, Calif.: Brooks-Cole, 1970).

21. R. J. Chilton and G. E. Markle, "Family Disruption, Delinquent Conduct and the Effect of Subclassification," *American Sociological Review* 37 (February 1972), pp. 93–99.

22. Nye, *Family Relationships and Delinquent Behavior,* pp. 47, 51.

23. Glueck and Glueck, *Unraveling Juvenile Delinquency.*

24. William McCord, Joan McCord, and Irving Zola, *Origins of Crime* (New York: Columbia University Press, 1959); and R. C. Audry, *Delinquency and Parental Pathology* (London: Methuen, 1960).

25. Glueck and Glueck, *Unraveling Juvenile Delinquency*; Nye, *Family Relationships and Delinquent Behavior*; and McCord, McCord, and Zola, *Origins of Crime.*

26. T. Hirschi, *Causes of Delinquency.*

27. T. Joachim, "Family Size, Social Class, and Delinquency," unpublished manuscript (1978).

28. Healy and Bronner, *Delinquents and Criminals.*

29. Glueck and Glueck, *Unraveling Juvenile Delinquency.*

30. William C. Kvaraceus, *Juvenile Delinquency and the School* (Yonkers, N.Y.: World Book Company, 1945), pp. 78–79.

31. S. Kirson Weinberg, "Sociological Processes and Factors in Juvenile Delinquency," in *Juvenile Delinquency,* edited by Joseph S. Roucek (New York: Philosophical Library, 1958), p. 108.

32. J. McCord, W. McCord, and A. Howard, "Family Interaction as Antecedent to the Direction of Male Aggressiveness," *Journal of Abnormal Social Psychology* 66 (1963), pp. 239–242.

33. Nye, *Family Relationships and Delinquent Behavior,* p. 75.

34. J. Bowlby, *Maternal Care and Mental Health* (Geneva: World Health Organization, 1951); Hirschi, *Causes of Delinquency*; M. J. Hindelang, "Causes of Delinquency: A Partial Replication," *Social Problems* 21 (Spring 1973), pp. 471–487; R. L. Austin, "Race, Father-Absence, and Female Delinquency," *Criminology* 15 (February 1978), pp. 484–504.

35. McCord, McCord, and Zola, *Origins of Crime.*

36. S. Glueck and E. Glueck, *Unraveling Juvenile Delinquency*; and R. G. Audry, "Faulty Parental and Maternal Child Relationships, Affection, and Delinquency," *British Journal of Delinquency* 8 (1958), pp. 34–38.

37. W. L. Slocum and C. L. Stone, "Family Culture Patterns and Delinquent-Type Behavior," *Marriage and Family Living* 25 (1963), pp. 202–208.

38. Hirschi, *Causes of Delinquency.*

39. Nye, *Family Relationships and Delinquent Behavior,* p. 59.

40. Glueck and Glueck, *Unraveling Juvenile Delinquency.*

41. G. F. Jensen and R. Eve, "Sex Differences in Delinquency: An Examination of Popular Sociological Explanations," *Criminology* 12 (1976), pp. 427–448.

42. Nye, *Family Relationships and Delinquent Behavior.*

43. McCord, McCord, and Zola, *Origins of Crime*; and W. McCord and J. McCord, *Psychopathy and Delinquency* (New York: Grune & Stratton, 1956).

44. C. Kempe et al., "The Battered-Child Syndrome," *Journal of the American Medical Association* 181 (July 1962), pp. 17–24.

45. *In the Interest of Children: A Century of Progress* (Denver: American Humane Association, Children's Division, 1966), p. 25.

46. Leroy H. Pelton, "Child Abuse and Neglect: The Myth of Classlessness," in Leroy H. Pelton, ed., *The Social Context of Child Abuse and Neglect* (New York: Human Sciences Press, 1981), p. 34.

47. Douglas J. Besharov, "The Legal Aspects of Reporting Known and Suspected Child Abuse and Neglect," *Villanova Law Review* 23 (1978), p. 458.

48. Pelton, "Child Abuse and Neglect," p. 34.

49. Leontine Young, *Wednesday's Children: A Study of Child Neglect and Abuse* (New York: McGraw-Hill Book Company, 1964).

50. Norman A. Polansky, Christine Deaix, and Shlomo A. Sharlin, *Child Neglect: Understanding and Reaching the Parent* (New York: Welfare League of America, Inc., 1972), pp. 21–52.

51. Norman A. Polansky et al., *Damaged Parents: An Anatomy of Child Neglect* (Chicago: University of Chicago Press, 1981), pp. 113–114.

52. R. Nagi, "Child Abuse and Neglect Programs: A National Overview," *Children Today* 4 (May-June 1975), pp. 13–17.

53. V. Fontana, *The Maltreated Child: The Maltreatment Syndrome in Children* (Springfield, Ill.: Charles C Thomas, 1971).

54. Richard Gelles and Murray Straus, "Violence in the American Family," *Journal of Social Issues* 35 (1979), pp. 15–39.

55. *Protecting the Battered Child* (Denver: American Humane Association Children's Division, 1962).

56. Besharov, "Legal Aspects of Reporting Child Abuse," pp. 515–539.

57. Garbarino and Gilliam, *Understanding Abusive Families,* p. 68.

58. Interviewed in May 1981.

59. David G. Gil, *Violence against Children: Physical Abuse in the United States* (Cambridge: Harvard University Press, 1970), pp. 130–132.

60. Kempe et al., "Battered Child Syndrome," pp. 17–24; V. Fontana, *Somewhere a Child Is Crying: Maltreatment—Causes and Prevention* (New York: Macmillan Publishing Company, 1973); R. Galdston, "Observations of Children Who Have Been Physically Abused by Their Parents," *American Journal of Psychiatry* 122 (1965), pp. 440–443.

61. Urie Bronfenbrenner, "The Origins of Alienation," *Scientific American* 231 (1974), p. 53.

62. Gil, *Violence against Children.*

63. M. A. Mulligan, *"An Investigation of Factors Associated with Violent Modes of Conflict Resolution in the Family"* (M.A. thesis, University of Rhode Island, 1977).

64. Murray A. Straus, Richard J. Gelles, and Suzanne K. Steinmetz, *Behind Closed Doors: Violence in the American Family* (Garden City, N.Y.: Anchor Books, 1980), p. 127.

65. Ibid., pp. 134–136; and Andrew Billingsley, "Family Functioning in the Low-Income Black Community," *Social Casework* 50 (1969), pp. 563–572.

66. Young, *Wednesday's Children,* p. 48.

67. Blair Justice and Rita Justice, *The Broken Taboo: Sex in the Family* (New York: Human Sciences Press, 1979), p. 25.

68. Ibid., p. 27.

69. Ibid., p. 16.

70. K. C. Meiselman, *Incest: A Psychological Study of Causes and Effects with Treatment Recommendations* (San Francisco: Jossey-Bass, 1978).

71. Interviewed as part of a court case with which the author was involved.

72. Justice and Justice, *The Broken Taboo*, p. 192.

73. A. Nicholas Groth, "Patterns of Sexual Assault against Children and Adolescents," in *Sexual Assault of Children and Adolescents* (Lexington, Mass.: D.C. Heath and Company, 1978), p. 17.

74. Justice and Justice, *The Broken Taboo*, p. 194.

75. Ibid., p. 196.

76. National Center on Child Abuse and Neglect, *Child Sexual Abuse*.

77. Ibid., pp. 59–91.

78. E. Newberger and R. Bourne, "The Medicalization and Legalization of Child Abuse," *American Journal of Orthopsychiatry* 48 (October 1977), pp. 593–607; and Straus, Gelles, and Steinmetz, *Behind Closed Doors*, pp. 181–182.

79. Garbarino and Gilliam, *Understanding Abusive Families*, pp. 173–176.

80. J. Herman and L. Hirschman, "Father-Daughter Incest," *Signs* 2 (1977), pp. 1–22; and C. Swift, "Sexual Victimization of Children: An Urban Mental Health Center Survey," *Victimology* 2 (1977), pp. 322–327.

81. J. Henderson, "Incest—A Synthesis of Data," *Canadian Psychiatric Association Journal* 17 (1972), pp. 299–313; B. Molnar and P. Cameron, "Incest Syndromes: Observations in a General Hospital Psychiatric Unit," *Canadian Psychiatric Association Journal* 20 (1975), pp. 1–24; and P. Sloane and F. Karpinsky, "Effects of Incest on Participants," *American Journal of Orthopsychiatry* 12 (1942), pp. 666–673.

82. Interviewed in May 1981.

83. "Incest: If You Think the Word Is Ugly, Take a Look at Its Effects" (Minneapolis: Christopher Street, Inc., 1979), p. 10.

84. For a review of these studies, see Diane D. Broadhurst, "The Effect of Child Abuse and Neglect in the School-Aged Child," in *The Maltreatment of the School-Aged Child,* edited by Richard Volpe, Margot Breton, and Judith Mitton (Lexington, Mass.: D.C. Heath & Company, 1980), pp. 19–41.

85. R. S. Kempe and C. H. Kempe, *Child Abuse* (Cambridge: Harvard University Press, 1978), p. 125.

86. H. P. Martin, "Neurological Status of Abused Children," in *The Abused Child: A Multidisciplinary Approach to Developmental Issues and Treatment,* edited by H. P. Martin (Cambridge: Ballinger Publishing Company, 1976), p. 78.

87. F. Blager and H. P. Martin, "Speech and Language of Abused Children," in *Abused Child,* p. 85.

88. D. F. Kline and J. Christiansen, *Educational and Psychological Problems of Abused Children* (Logan: Utah State University Department of Special Education, 1975), p. 107.

89. Martin, "Neurological Status of Abused Children," p. 77.

90. Ibid.

91. M. Halperin, *Helping Maltreated Children* (St. Louis: C. V. Mosby Company, 1979), p. 77.

92. Kline and Christiansen, *Educational and Psychological Problems*, p. 107.

93. Comments made by teachers interviewed in 1981.

94. T. Houten and M. Golembiewski, *A Study of Runaway Youth and Their Families* (Washington, D.C.: Youth Alternatives Project, 1976); and J. Streit, "A Test and Procedure to Identify Secondary School Children Who Have a High Probability of Drug Abuse," *Dissertation Abstracts International* 34 (1974), pp. 10–13.

95. "Incest: If You Think the Word Is Ugly," p. 11.

96. Ibid., pp. 11–12.

97. David Finkelhor, *Sexually Victimized Children* (New York: Free Press, 1979), p. 214.

98. J. James and J. Meyerding, "Easy Sexual Experiences as a Factor in Prostitution," *Archives in Sexual Behavior* 7 (1977), pp. 31–42.

99. Justice and Justice, *Broken Taboo,* p. 197.

100. See "Incest: If You Think the Word Is Ugly," p. 13.

101. E. Tanay, "Psychiatric Study of Homicide," *American Journal of Psychiatry* 120(1963), pp. 386–387.

102. J. Alfaro, *Summary Report on the Relationship between Child Abuse and Neglect and Later Socially Deviant Behavior* (New York: Select Committee on Child Abuse, 1978).

103. Michael S. Wald, "State Intervention on Behalf of Neglected Children: A Search for Standards for Placement of Children in Foster Care, and Termination of Parental Rights," *Stanford Law Review* 26 (1976), pp. 626–627.

104. National Advisory Commission on Criminal Justice Standards and Goals, *Juvenile Justice and Delinquency Prevention* (Washington, D.C.: U.S. Government Printing Office, 1976), p. 335.

105. Ibid.; and Institute of Judicial Administration/American Bar Association Juvenile Justice Standards Project, *Standards Relating to Abuse and Neglect* (Cambridge: Ballinger Publishing Company, 1977), p. 3.

106. David G. Gil, *Violence against Children: Physical Abuse in the United States* (Cambridge: Harvard University Press, 1970), pp. 130–132.

107. Freeman, *Violence in the Home,* pp. 109–111.

108. Ibid., p. 114.

109. Henry Giarretto, "A Comprehensive Child Sexual Abuse Treatment Program," in *Sexually Abused Children and Their Families,* edited by Patricia B. Mrazek and C. Henry Kempe (Oxford, England: Pergamon Press, in press).

110. Ibid.

111. Ibid.

112. Jerome A. Kroth, *Child Sexual Abuse: Analysis of a Family Therapy Approach* (Springfield, Ill.: Charles C Thomas, 1979), p. 137.

113. John W. C. Johnstone, "Delinquency and the Changing American Family," in *Critical Issues in Juvenile Delinquency,* edited by David Shichor and Delos H. Kelly (Lexington, Mass.: D.C. Heath & Company, 1980), p. 94.

INTERVIEW WITH RICHARD J. GELLES

People do not lose social status for being violent toward family members. You don't see people intervening when children are spanked at supermarkets. So there is a general lack of cost to family members today for being violent toward family members.

In this interview, Richard Gelles, an acknowledged authority on violence in the family, discusses such matters as the factors related to family violence, the relationship between family violence and child abuse, the relationship between the structural breakup of the family and violence, and the policy changes that are needed to improve the quality of family life.

Question: What are the most important factors contributing to family violence?

Gelles: That is a complicated question because of the emotions that child abuse and wife abuse

Richard J. Gelles is a Professor of Sociology and Anthropology at the University of Rhode Island. His book, The Violent Home, *was the first systematic empirical investigation of family violence and continues to be highly influential. He is also the author of* Family Violence *and coauthor of* Behind Closed Doors: Violence in the American Family, *the first national survey of family violence in the United States. He coedited* The Dark Side of the Family: Current Family Violence Research *and* International Perspectives on Family Violence. *He is also the coauthor of* Social Problems *with Michael Bassis and Ann Levine. Gelles received his B.A. from Bates College (1968), an M.A. in sociology from the University of Rochester (1971), and a Ph.D. in sociology from the University of New Hampshire (1973). He edited* Teaching Sociology *from 1973 until 1981 and received the American Sociological Association, Section on Undergraduate Education "Outstanding Contribution to Teaching Award" in 1979. Gelles has authored numerous articles and chapters on family violence and has presented innumerable lectures to policy making groups, practitioners, and media groups (including the Today Show, Good Morning America, The Merv Griffin Show), on family violence research. In addition to his position at the University of Rhode Island, he is a lecturer on Pediatrics at Harvard Medical School and a Research Director for Louis Harris and Associates, the national survey research firm.*

arouse in people; people seem to want to search for simple answers. In the 1960s, the simple answer was only somebody who was mentally disturbed would abuse a child or abuse a wife. In the 1970s, the popular theory was that family violence (wife abuse or child abuse) was confined to poor people or black people in the community. The other popular notion was the deterministic statement that people who were abused as children grow up to be child abusers and wife abusers. There is a consistent trend toward oversimplification in the field. With that preface, I am now going to oversimplify.

I think that child abuse and wife abuse have multidimensional causes—psychological causes, social-psychological causes, socio-structural causes, and socio-cultural causes. If I were pressed to break those multitude of causes down into simple categories, I would say that one was the cultural attitude toward violence in the United States, which accepts violence as both an instrumental act—a way of solving a problem—and as an acceptable way of expressing oneself. From our television, to corporal punishment being allowed in schools, to our lack of gun control, to our acceptance of capital punishment, to the acceptance of spanking of children in the home, to the acceptance of hitting wives under certain conditions, there is a learning environment and a moral correctness ascribed to certain forms of family violence.

The second factor would be (drawing from Merton's paradigm of goals and means) the cultural goal of being a father, mother, husband, and wife is consistent across the country and the distribution of means to reach or approach that goal. Everyone has essentially the same goal, but few people can reach it. You have to be a perfect father, a perfect mother, a loving husband, a loving wife, and those people who are deprived of the resources to reach those goals of family sanctity and sacredness tend to be more likely to adopt the violent way of dealing with family members. If I, for instance, were under considerable stress, I might say to my wife, "Let's get a babysitter for the children and go away for the weekend." I have the economic resources to do that. Should I not have those economic resources, I think it might be different.

Theoretically, I approach family violence with an exchange/social control theory. I borrow the exchange theory from family sociology and the social control approach from Hirschi's social control perspective on juvenile delinquency. The oversimplified version of this theoretical approach is that people abuse family members because they can. If you were a student reading this textbook and you felt you had been treated unfairly by your professor and you were really angry, the chances are you would not take a swing at your professor because (1) your professor could have you thrown out of school, (2) the professor might hit you back and hurt you, and (3) the professor might call the police and they would come and arrest you. If you have the same anger toward a family member, none of these costs are going to be inflicted upon you. You don't get fired from a family. The police very rarely come quickly and when they do come, they are much more interested in restoring order than in making an arrest. People don't lose social status for being violent toward family members. You do not see people intervening when children are spanked at supermarkets. So there is a general lack of cost to family members today for being violent toward family members. The attitudes of the police and the criminal justice system also reduce the costs of being violent. Thus, I think that we are violent as families because there is a structural and a moral situation that allows us to hit family members which would then prohibit us from hitting people at work or citizens on the street.

Question: What relationship do you feel exists between family violence, especially child abuse and juvenile delinquency?

Gelles: The accumulated evidence suggests that abused children are more likely to engage in violent juvenile crimes than nonabused children. However, one has also to keep in mind the warning that once a child is identified as abused in the official reporting system, that may well enhance the chances that the child will later be defined as deviant as well. What we haven't done yet is follow abused children and see what their behavior looks like as juveniles and compare them to a reasonable scientific comparison group.

Question: Is child abuse on the increase today?

Gelles: If you go by the official statistics, you would say yes. The largest collector of official statistics is the American Humane Association in Denver. They note the consistent increase in child abuse and neglect reporting. In the last eight years, perhaps a 20 to 30 percent increase is what they report. However, I believe that the increase is much more a reflection of social recognition of child abuse and neglect than actual changes in true behavior. Although I don't have data, because I haven't done longitudinal research, my theory is that as official reporting and detection go up, abusive and neglectful behavior toward children decreases slightly because people become concerned that they are going to get caught up in the system. They also see that child abuse is not just those horrible cases in the *National Enquirer,* and they begin to question their own behavior toward children. If we had true scientific evidence, my guess is we would see a slight decline in child abuse over the last thirty to fifty years.

Question: Has the structured breakup of the family contributed significantly to family violence?

Gelles: I think the increase in single parents has influenced the extent of family violence. We still have to remember that part of that structural breakup of the family is caused by people feeling that they can divorce violent partners, which means that structured family breakup is in fact one of the solutions to family violence. But structured family breakups do create single parents households. Ninety percent of single parents are women who frequently do not get proper financial support. Child support payments are not enforced regularly, which then creates a class of poor among the single parents. So if you are a single parent and you are poor, you probably do have a slightly greater risk of abusing your children.

Question: The perpetuation of family violence from one generation to the next appears to be present in many homes. What can be done to stop this vicious cycle?

Gelles: First of all, you have to understand it's not present in *all* homes. We have an unfortunate and a very sad tendency to oversimplify and turn probabilistic statements into deterministic ones. If you were abused as a child, you really only have a 50/50 chance of growing up to be an abuser yourself. This means that readers of this book who were themselves abused should not think that they have been "prewired" or predetermined to be violent. But one way of reducing the perpetuation in the household in terms of the generational cycle is to take a multifaceted approach to family violence. To change the structural system that allows it to happen in so many stressed families, especially poor families without coping abilities, is a major challenge today. Other challenges are to change the cultural attitudes toward violence, to get the deadly weapons out of family households, and to prohibit people from spanking their children. I tend to find that it's wife abuse rather than child abuse that is more common around the world. Wife abuse is particularly common in societies where women are dominated. To break this cycle of child abuse, we need gender equity, economic and political justice, and banning on spanking of children. In terms of the latter, we need to say to parents, "No, you're going to have to find another way to raise your children. You can't spank them."

Question: What policy changes are needed to improve the quality of family life in the United States?

Gelles: David Gil and a lot of others favor reducing poverty. I would be in favor of reducing poverty, even if it didn't have an effect on family violence. I think again you have to go back and remember that this is a multidimensional problem, and it is going to take multidimensional resources.

To list them off, I would greatly increase the number of shelters for battered women. I think that any community that has shelters for animals must have shelters for battered women. I would greatly increase the daycare opportunities for the family. I think that one of the unfortunate consequences of industrialization is that you move work from the home, and we have left to women the twenty-four-hour a day responsibility for rearing children. Even those who work come home and have to rear their children, and I think that we don't provide safe, careful, useful daycare for those people who need it whether they work or don't work. I think we need drastically improved child welfare services. They must be able to respond to emergency situations within twenty-four-hours and to provide compassion and support for families, and control where needed. We don't do that today.

Today, the social worker who deals with child abuse is the poorest trained, poorest paid, and most overworked professional in the child welfare system. The police and courts must stop viewing this as a family matter and stop thinking that their only responsibility is to restore temporary order. Larry Sherman and Richard Berk's recent research in Minneapolis, which was just published in the *American Sociological Review,* indicates clearly (although it hasn't been replicated yet) that arrests of a violent husband reduce the chances that he will be violent again. Walking a husband around the block or trying to calm things down or bringing a social worker with you is much less effective than simple arrest. Women's legal rights must be enforced. In terms of prevention, I have a number of steps that I consider absolutely necessary.

First would be to eliminate the cultural norms which legitimize and glorify violence in society and in the family; TV violence, guns, capital punishment, and spanking of children all have to be eliminated. The second step would be to take policy steps to reduce the violence-provoking stress created by society (unemployment, poverty, and stress of work). The third step would be to make a major effort to integrate families into a network of kin and community. The more isolated families are, the higher the rates of family violence. Community resources provide families with help and support under stress and also provide for more control so that small conflicts don't escalate into larger conflicts and violence. The fourth step would be to change the sexist character of society and family. Again, I think that much of family violence is power related and that, if we empowered women, we would probably reduce the level of child abuse and wife abuse. The last step would be to break the cycle of violence in families by eliminating spanking and violence toward children as an acceptable way of raising America's kids.

CHAPTER 10

DELINQUENCY AND ADOLESCENCE

CHAPTER OUTLINE

In 1963, *Look* magazine referred to youth as the "Tense Generation"; in 1966 as the "Open Generation"; in 1968 as the "Abandoned Generation." A survey of other contemporary magazines during the last decade or so indicates that youth have been characterized as the "Quiet Generation" (youth of the 1950s), the "Committed Generation" (Peace Core and Civil Rights volunteers), the "Uncommitted Generation" (flower children and hippies), the "Alienated Generation" (drug users and social dropouts), the "Militant Generation" (S.D.S., Black Panthers, antisocial protesters), and more recently, the "Generation of Futility and Hopelessness.

Robert D. Barr[1]

Adolescence is a term defining the life interval between childhood and adulthood. The term has been used only in the last few decades to mark a new stage of human growth and development, but there really is no way to pinpoint this period chronologically or to restrict it within biological boundaries. For the purposes of discussion in this chapter, adolescence will be considered to mean the years from ages twelve to eighteen. Within this transitional period, youngsters experience many biological changes; develop new attitudes, values, and skills to guide them through their young adult years; and become involved in a variety of experiences—some of which may lead to delinquent behavior.

Delinquent behavior is on the upswing during the adolescent years for several reasons. First, these years bring increasing freedom from parental scrutiny, and with this freedom come more opportunities to be involved in socially unacceptable behavior. Second, new tastes (often expensive ones) are acquired, for such things as stereos, clothing, automobiles, drugs, and alcohol; yet, legitimate means for satisfying these tastes are often not available. Third, the lengthening of adolescence in American culture has increased the crises and struggles of this life period, thereby increasing the chance of antisocial reactions to the authority of the law, the school, and the home. Fourth, in some cases the unmet needs and frustrations of childhood begin to fester into socially unacceptable behavior. One adolescent's experience that led to delinquent behavior is described in Box 10-1.

BOX 10-1 Becoming a Dope Addict

"When I was fourteen-years-old, my uncle used to put me on a streetcar in Chicago to deliver packages. But I didn't know what was in those packages. A woman got wind of it, and she offered to turn on five of us on my birthday with sex and heroin. I went last to see if anything was going to happen to them. They were all high and sick. I was really reluctant to go on with it. I was sitting there wanting to do it and yet not wanting to do it. She

The assistance of Kurt Mielke and Gary Storm was invaluable in shaping the contents of this chapter.

coaxed me into it by saying, "If you do it, I'll give you some ass." She gave me the dope, and I was too sick to have sex with her.

I didn't shoot any more dope for three months until I saw her again. I told her, "Don't you owe me something?" She said, "No, I paid you. When you go on another trip for your uncle, let me know and I will really make it worth your while." She conned me through sex into bringing the dope to her. I still didn't know what was in the packages. Later, I found out that she was taking half an ounce from the package and filling it with whatever kind of mix she had. Then she would send me on my way. She did that three times, but I finally figured out what was in the package. That one shot of dope made my mind more aware of street life. That first high, even though you are sick, makes a dope addict go back. And before I knew it, I was shooting dope with her all the time.

Source: Interview conducted in November 1980.

This chapter discusses the history of childhood, the adolescent years as a period of crisis, the environmental influences that affect adolescents, the degree to which adolescents are in conflict with the larger culture, the values and behaviors of adolescents that encourage involvement in delinquent behavior, and the social policy needed to enable adolescents to realize more of their potential.

DEVELOPMENT OF MODERN CHILDHOOD

Adolescence, as a new stage of human growth and development, evolved out of the modern notion of childhood. The concept of childhood, as reflected in today's child-centered culture, is a relatively recent phenomenon.[2] Much of recorded history reveals abuse and indifference to be the fate of many children. Lloyd de Mause depicts the past history of childhood as a time when children were "killed, abandoned, beaten, terrorized, and sexually abused"; he prefaces this statement by saying that "the history of childhood is a nightmare from which we have only recently begun to awaken."[4]

Throughout history, infanticide has been part of this sordid legacy, a product not only of Eastern societies but Western as well. In ancient Greece, unwanted babies were abandoned; to encourage adoption, charms and other valuables were left near them. Often mutilated and disfigured unwanted children were turned out as beggars, their grotesque shapes drawing both laughter and pity.[4] During the Middle Ages, failure or refusal to nourish the young may have constituted the most common form of infanticide.[6] Girls were deemed of little value and were often either killed outright or left to starve to death. The abandonment or killing of unwanted or illegitimate babies occurred regularly in ancient times, lessened somewhat during the Middle Ages, but, nonetheless, continued into the nineteenth century. Anthropologist Marvin Harris says of modern times, "Only an incredible degree of self-righteous pigheadedness prevents us from admitting that infanticide is still being practiced on a cosmic scale in the underdeveloped societies."[6]

However, indifference, more so than infanticide, has constituted the treatment toward children throughout history. The concept of "institutional abandonment" served to legitimize this active indifference.[7] The most prevalent form of institutionalized abandonment, recorded from Biblical times to the twentieth century, has been the wet-nurse.[8] Other forms included the sale of children and the use of children as political hostages or servants.

High infant mortality rates appear to have contributed more to this indifference than any inhumane motivations. The rapid transition from the cradle to the grave of many infants encouraged parents to remain emotionally detached from their children simply to preserve their sanity. The French essayist Montaigne noted, "I have lost two or three at nurse, not without regret but without grief."[9] Childhood illnesses were often fatal, and, according to Barbara Greenleaf, "society saw no point in making any emotional or educational investment in a youngster until he had survived them."[10]

Throughout history, children have worked, but until the Industrial Revolution, their work was usually done within or around the house, often out of doors. As work moved from the home to the factory, children were looked upon as a source of cheap labor. It was not unusual for them to work in the worst of conditions for sixteen hours a day, six days a week.[11] Until the child labor laws were actually enforced, children as young as four or five years of age were to be found working in the mines, mills, and factories.

During the seventeenth and eighteenth centuries in America, children had begun to be viewed as less threatening, and parents began to try to understand their children. Raising children became less a process of conquering their spirits, and more a process of training and socializing them. Since the mid-twentieth century, parents in the United States have emphasized a helping relationship, attempting to meet the expanding needs of their children in a democratic and supportive environment.[12]

Adolescence as a Social Invention

Although the notion of adolescence has its roots in the writings of Aristotle and Jean Jacques Rousseau, the concept per se did not exist until the late nineteenth century. As the concept of adolescence evolved out of changing conceptions of childhood, the idea of adolescence as a stage of life began with the recognition that it is a period of instability and passion yet with awakening intellectual capabilities.[13] John Kett concludes his major treatise on the evolution of adoelscence with this statement:

> [T]o speak of the "invention of the adolescent" rather than of the discovery of adolescence underscores [that] . . . adolescence was essentially a conception of behavior imposed on youth, rather than an empirical assessment of the way in which young people actually behaved.[14]

Several major social movements influenced the acknowledgment by American society of adolescence as a social reality. First, with advancing technology and mechanization, children and adolescents were no longer needed in the labor market and by 1914 every state but one had passed laws prohibiting the employment in industry of children under a certain age, generally fourteen. Second, compulsory education laws evolving out of social and religious views of adolescents as needing guidance and control kept them in school, thereby further removing them from the employment world and the mainstream of society. Finally, special legal protections for juveniles again highlighted the perception of adolescents as needing special attention, guidance, and support.[15]

Thus, because adolescents had lost their economic utility and because they were viewed as vulnerable to a wide range of corrupting influences, new goals and new roles were established for them. A variety of adult-sponsored youth organizations, such as the YMCA and YWCA, were formed. The number of years of compulsory education also was increased, thereby instituting the separation of adolescents from the adult world and the workplace.[16]

ADOLESCENCE: CRISIS OR STABILITY?

The adolescent years have traditionally been regarded as a period of crisis and stress. *Crisis* may be defined as "a serious interruption in the normal way of life of an individual or group . . . [that] requires the development of new modes of thought and action"; whereas, *stress* may be defined as "any disturbing emotional experience due to frustration (expressed then in anger, anxiety, or confusion)."[17] The notion that the period of adolescence is a time of crisis and stress goes back to Plato and other Greek philosophers. This view was also strongly championed by German philosopher/psychologists of the nineteenth century, as well as by the psychoanalysts of the twentieth century.[18]

However, the view of adolescence as a period of "stress and storm" is currently being challenged by research findings that are finding the adolescent years to be relatively stable and peaceful. In 1957, Kestley and Elkin found that, contrary to previous opinions, the adolescent years are relatively peaceful and tension-free.[19] The findings of their study were supported by research by Douvan and Adelson, Offer, and Bandura.[20] John C. Coleman, examining this contradiction in adolescent theory, concludes that adolescence can be a time of disturbance, but that this stress affects the few and not the many.[21]

Although recent empirical investigations have shown that adolescence may not necessarily be a time of storm and crisis, the potential for crisis is there, and these disruptions do affect some youths during these years. Many of these potential areas of crisis have been examined in the literature.

First, adolescence is a period of extensive physical and psychological growth. Irene Josselyn mentions these physical and psychological changes:

> [The] onset [of adolescence] can be determined by observation of physical changes—changes usually begin at about the age of ten in girls and the age of twelve in boys. Clinical evidence shows that modification of the psycho-

logical structure takes place at approximately the same time as the physical change occurs.[22]

Second, adolescence may represent a period of insecurity and high anxiety. These feelings may arise as adolescents deal with shifting concepts of self, causing fluctuation of moral standards, instability and irregularity of impulse control, and often turbulent interpersonal relationships. Thus, adolescents may have rapidly changing moods and behaviors, which make them sensitive, easily hurt, and quarrelsome.[23]

Third, the potential for crisis during this period is present because the adolescent is in limbo between childhood and adulthood. The adolescent must remain in the home while he or she is "processed" and equipped to take his or her place as an adult in society.[24] Garabarino and Gilliam aptly express this waiting period:

American teenagers are in the awkward position of being simultaneously indulged and oppressed, by and large constrained from contributing anything meaningful, and shielded legally from the consequences of their own acts. The contrived position of youth in the society may act either as a direct irritant or as an unconscious source of frustration. In other words, adolescents may not see it as such, but their arbitrary roles limit the contributions they can make, and the effects of that limitation are the real sources of irritation they feel. We do not know how much of their frustration teenagers carry from the outside world into their own homes.[25]

Fourth, adolescents may feel they are denied some basic needs. Garabarino and Gilliam note that adolescents need certain essentials to grow into competent adults:

They need to feel powerful, that they can affect the world around them. They need identity, to know who they are and with whom they belong. They need acceptance from their parents, an unconditional regard that allows them to experiment and make mistakes. They need consistency in order to believe that the world is predictable. They need to feel worthwhile. They need affection.[26]

THE SOCIAL AND CULTURAL ENVIRONMENTS INFLUENCING ADOLESCENTS

Human beings acquire their values and the means to realize them (knowledge, skills, practical dispositions, and behaviors) through interactions with their many and varied environments. At a broad level of abstraction, it is possible to distinguish between "natural," "cultural," and "social" environments. Since our attention will be focused almost entirely on the social and cultural environments that influence the lives of adolescents, a more refined scheme for classifying these environments is necessary.[27]

Many social scientists divide cultural environments into material and nonmaterial elements. The nonmaterial dimension of culture includes the beliefs, values, traditions, customs, mores, laws, and institutions that have been developed and passed along through history. The material culture includes all the physical artifacts created by human beings—tools of all kinds, vehicles for communication and transportation, art and architecture, and, very importantly, records (books, tapes, films, songs, television) describing and evaluating the nonmaterial culture. The social environment of an individual or group is made up of the people with whom the individual interacts.

Figure 10-1 illustrates the several important levels of the sociocultural environments, each of which is the locus for interactions between adolescents and the social groups and institutions on which their lives and well-being depend.

The Home or Family

During the early stages of life, the home environment of the child, and the persons who inhabit and regularly frequent this environment, shape the child's experiences. The dominant element of socialization at this stage is the family, nuclear or extended, or, in some cases, a social unit that has guardianship responsibilities for the child—a foster or adoptive family, an orphanage, or a child-care institution. In some instances, children are raised in collective or communal "families." Even though the family is still considered the primary socializing element, currently day-care centers provide daily care for many young children.

As indicated in the previous chapter, the influence of the home varies from one adolescent to the next. Travis Hirschi found that the more a child is attached to and identifies with his or her parents, the less likely the child is to become involved in delinquent behavior. That is, the more a child is attached to his or her parents, the more likely it is that he or she is bound to the parents' expectations and, therefore, the probability is increased that the child will conform with the legal norms of the larger social order.[28]

The Neighborhood

As children reach an age that allows them to spend time outside the home and away from direct supervision of parents or guardians, the neighborhood becomes an important locus of their expectations. The neighborhood, for our purposes, will simply be defined as that geographical area within ready physical access to children and adolescents, without the use of motorized transportation. Great differences exist, of course, between neighborhoods in urban and rural contexts. For an urban child, exploration of the neighborhood brings contact with a variety of social groups and institutions. The rural child is more likely to become familiar with nature and with the work done by his or her parents. The boundaries of a child's neighborhood expand as he or she matures physically and can walk or bicycle further from home. This expansion is also influenced by restrictions on mobility imposed by parents or other adults responsible for the child's care and supervision.

Until recently, educational and child-care institutions (nursery schools and

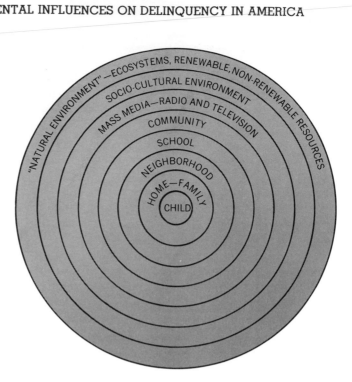

Figure 10-1 The Social and Cultural Environments Influencing the Development of Adolescents

Source: Contributed to this volume by Gary Storm.

elementary and secondary schools) were the dominant neighborhood institutions, organized on either a religious or a secular basis. With the advent of integration and busing, on the one hand, and the increase of working mothers, on the other, these institutions began to lose their neighborhood character. Now, schools are less likely to be neighborhood centers serving the educational, recreational, and cultural needs of children in the neighborhood.

The advent of the automobile and improved systems of public transportation also have reduced the influence of the neighborhood on adolescence. Travis Hirschi found that car ownership, driving, and the importance of a car are all related to delinquent activity; that is, the more important an automobile is to the adolescent, the more likely he or she is to commit delinquent acts.[29]

It can be argued that insufficient attention has been given to the role the neighborhood plays in shaping the experiences and the values of adolescents. Some evidence exists that the reduced impact of the neighborhood has contributed to the increased feeling among adolescents that they have nothing to do; this is especially important because adolescents are more likely to commit delinquent behavior when they feel they have nothing to do.[30] In addition, the sociological literature on youth gangs highlights many of the negative influences of the urban neighborhood. When adolescents become members of a street gang, the gang becomes their point of reference.

The gang affiliation not only provides them protection and security in their urban neighborhood but also supplies a source of identity. A youth is able to say, "I'm a Vice Lord, mighty, mighty Vice Lord." He knows what clothes to wear and how to dress. He knows how to greet other Vice Lords. He knows what norms are acceptable and the consequences of violating those norms.[31]

The Community

Except in the best urban neighborhoods, most of the educational, recreational, and cultural opportunities available to adolescents are located outside their immediate residential neighborhood, as are health and social services designed for children who experience problems of one sort or another. The various institutions of the juvenile justice system (police, courts, and correctional services) are also usually housed outside the neighborhood.

With the exception of neighborhood youth gangs, it is in the larger community rather than the local neighborhood that adolescents develop relationships with teenage societies. These microsocial systems are sometimes highly structured, and their members often develop their own norms of behavior, language, and dress. The concept of *reference groups* is probably more useful than that of *peer groups,* a term which has become vague and ambiguous. Muzafer Sherif and Carolyn W. Sherif define a reference group as "the group with which the individual identifies or [to which he or she] aspires to belong."[32] The Sherifs also elaborate on the function of reference groups:

> Once formed, informally organized groups, with their bounded demarcation, role patterns defining mutual expectations, and internally binding code cherished by members, become the source of the sense of belongingness, of amounting to something, the sense of mutual obligation and support. Henceforth, the approval or disapproval, blame or praise, the bounds of propriety and impropriety which are to be heeded, are intimately tied to the extent of the importance of the group in the scheme of the individual's life at the given time. In conceptual terms, the attitudes the individual upholds and cherishes, the rules that he/she considers binding for regulating his/her behavior, are those defined by such reference groups.[33]

One of the key theoretical problems in the delinquency literature concerns the relationship between personal characteristics and associational patterns.[34] Most studies have found a positive relationship between attachment to peers and delinquent behavior; that is, the greater the attachment, the greater the delinquency.[35] But one study reported that attachment to peers is a barrier to involvement in delinquency, even among adolescents with several delinquent friends.[36] More recently, Jensen and Erickson found attachment to peers to be unrelated to delinquent behavior.[37] Clearly, as Hirschi found in his study, the relationship between peers and delinquency is a complex one and depends upon both the delinquent-proneness of adolescents and the delinquent-proneness of the groups to which they belong.[38]

The Mass Media

The popular media, especially radio and television, have probably contributed more to the development of a widespread, relatively homogeneous mass culture than any other cultural influence in American society. No matter what socioeconomic and ethnic background an adolescent is from, he or she is likely to be familiar with the acceptable language, dress, music, and folk heroes of the moment. The influence of radio and television has so permeated our society that the "tube" is often seen as a member of the family. And as Henry Malcolm points out:

> Every adult over the age of thirty-five has seen the entrance of the television set into the house, not as another piece of furniture but as an ultimate source of information about the world beyond the home.

> The vast majority of children, on the other hand, see the television set as part of the home environment—like beds, chairs, and record players. In this sense the world is as much inside the home as outside.[39]

The generally mixed findings on the effects of the media on delinquent behavior make any clear conclusions difficult.[40] Several studies have found that the effect of violent, erotic, or crime-oriented media lead to an increase in delinquent behavior. S. H. Lovibond, in a study of 374 sixth through eighth grade male students, argued that the more a boy watched television, read comic books, or attended movies, the more likely he was "to endorse an ideology which makes the use of force in the interest of egocentric needs the essential context of human relationships."[41] L. D. Eron and his colleagues claim to have "demonstrated that there is a probable causative influence of watching violent television programs in early formative years on later aggression."[42] The three-year, $1-million research project by the Surgeon General's Scientific Advisory Committee on Television and Social Behavior concluded that violence on television can induce mimicking behavior in children shortly after exposure and that under *certain circumstances* viewing television violence can lead to an increase in the number of aggressive acts.[43]

In answer to these and other studies, however, it can be argued that showing an association does not necessarily demonstrate a causal relationship. In other words, delinquent children may be media-oriented or choose certain programs because of preexisting behavior patterns and attitudes. Their delinquent behavior, then, leads them to the media presentations; the media does not affect their behaviors and attitudes. Critics also have claimed that the research has focused largely on either the immediate impact or the differences among individuals, so that its findings cannot be applied to the impact of the media in the long run or on society as a whole.[44]

The Sociocultural Environment

In 1965, Glock and Stark observed that, "Looking at American society as a whole [one sees that] organized religion at present is neither a prominent witness to its own value system nor a major focal point around which ultimate commitments to norms, values, and beliefs are formed."[45] Most of the research on religious belief and church membership have found that this also holds true for adolescents.[46] Jensen and Rojek, in analyzing the research on religion and delinquency, developed the following generalizations:

1. Church participation is more likely to be related to illegal drug use than to other delinquent offenses.

2. Church participation is most relevant to drug use in denominations that prohibit such activity and is more relevant to delinquent offenses in general among ascetic or fundamentalistic denominations than among liberal denominations.

3. When religious groups are characterized by norms of abstinence, peripheral or fringe members appear to violate those norms to a greater degree than fringe members of other religious groups.[47]

Ethnocultural background appears to be a greater influence on the attitudes and behaviors of adolescents than is religious belief or church participation. A Mexican-American youth in an impoverished barrio sees the world much differently from a white youth in an upper-class neighborhood. The Mexican-American adolescent has far different daily experiences and learns to cope with life in ways that are totally foreign to the upper-class adolescent. A fifteen-year-old Brooklyn youth discusses the world view and values of his culture:

In Brooklyn you fall into one of two categories when you start growing up. The names for the categories may be different in other cities, but the categories are the same. First, there's the minority of the minority, the "ducks," or "suckers." These are the kids who go to school every day. They even want to go to college. Imagine that! . . . they're wasting their lives waiting for a dream that won't come true.

The ducks are usually the ones getting beat up by the majority group—the "hard rocks." If you're a real hard rock you have no worries, no cares. Getting high is as easy as breathing. You just rip off some duck. You don't bother going to school; it's not necessary. You just live with your mom until you get a job—that should be any time a job comes looking for you. Why should I bother to go look for it? Even your parents can't find work.

I guess the barrier between the ducks and the hard rocks is the barrier of despair. The ducks still have hope, while the hard rocks are frustrated. They're caught in the deadly, dead-end environment and can't see a way out. Life becomes the fast life—or incredibly boring—and death becomes the death that you see and get used to every day. They don't want to hear any more promises. They believe that's just the white man's way of keeping them under control.[48]

The Natural Environment

The natural environment has less influence on adolescents now than in the past. As more and more of this nation's population moves to cities, fewer adolescents are involved in farming and in agricultural pursuits. Yet there are still numerous adolescents who thrive on activities in the "great outdoors," such as downhill and cross-country skiing, hiking, mountain climbing, fishing, and hunting. But little evidence exists that sports, recreation, or hobbies serve as a deterrent to delinquent behavior.[49]

Effect of Environments

As illustrated in Figure 10-1, adolescents develop both the values and the personal means required to pursue them through interaction with concentric social and cultural environments. If adolescents develop realizable values that are at least minimally consistent with one another and with the values of the social groups and institutions to which they look for their livelihoods and well-being, they will enjoy the process of growth and will be less likely to become involved in delinquent behavior.

CONFLICT OF VALUES
WITH THE LARGER CULTURE

Considerable disagreement exists whether adolescents and adults are in conflict over values—whether a "generation gap" exists between adults and adults. James S. Coleman's study of adolescent culture two decades ago found that adolescents were turning to teenage reference groups for values and norms and away from the authority and approval of parents and teachers:

> Our adolescents today are cut off, probably more than ever before, from the adult society. They are still oriented toward fulfilling their parents' desires, but they look very much to their peers for approval as well. Consequently, our society has within its midst a set of small teenage societies which focus teenage interests and attitudes on things far removed from adult responsibilities, and which may develop standards that lead away from these goals established by the larger society.[50]

Ernest Smith also argued that a "youth culture" existed that was in conflict with the adult culture.[51] Talcott Parsons contended that youth culture was a center for rebellion.[52] Ralph England attributed much of the increase in delinquency to the rise in "youth culture."[53] During the 1960s and early 1970s, the media also frequently commented on the "generation gap" between adolescents and parents.

However, recent studies provide little support for this supposed conflict in values.[54] Guy R. Lefranciois perhaps best summarizes the consensus of these studies:

> If there is a youth culture in general, it is clearly not a counterculture as many have been led to believe. On the other hand, it is appropriate to consider various minorities among adolescents as representative of specific countercultures. Among these could be included some activist groups, drug-centered groups, delinquent groups, and various quasi-criminal gangs.[55]

In other words, the values of adolescents in general do not appear to be in conflict with those of their parents, but some adolescent reference groups do adhere to values that are in conflict with those of the larger culture and that often lead members of these groups into delinquent behavior. There appear to be five groups of adolescents present in American society.

The first group accepts the value systems of its parents and no real generation gap exists between these youths and their parents. These adolescents are achievement-oriented in school, are committed to the values of the society, are involved in conventional activities, have little, if any, contact with the law, and have nondelinquent friends.

A second group of adolescents largely accepts the value systems of parents, but its members also turn to reference groups, or teenage societies, to fulfill some basic needs. Although the reference groups they turn to have largely internalized the values and attitudes of the larger society, participants in this group may drift in and out of socially unacceptable behavior. But if these youths do come in contact with the juvenile justice system, their cases are likely to be dismissed or to be diverted to nonjudicial agencies.

A third group finds the teenage years turbulent ones, and the stresses and conflict these youths experience affect their relationships with parents and their performance at school. Their relationships with the opposite sex may also be affected by the "storm of adolescence," and they are not as likely to develop attachments to peers as are those in the first two groups. If they have conflict with their parents, they are more likely to become involved in status offenses, such as running away from home, than they are to commit delinquent offenses.

Those in a fourth group feel alienated from parents and sometimes from the school and other social institutions as well. These youngsters are attracted to teenage reference groups, or teenage societies, through which they find their identity, acceptance, consistency, and feelings of achievement. Although the degree of commitment these adolescents have to conformity or delinquency is dependent on a number of factors, they tend to seek out teenage reference groups who will reinforce their values and behaviors.

Finally, a fifth group feels alienated from both the values of parents and those of the larger society. This group is likely to be highly involved in delinquent behavior and to be labeled as disruptive in the public school. The use of drugs is also more frequent among this group than the others. Chronic juvenile offenders, as well as members of street gangs, are in this fifth group.

THE PATH FROM CONFORMITY
TO DELINQUENCY

How do delinquents differ from nondelinquents in terms of their attitudes and behaviors? What makes this question so difficult to answer is that self-report studies reveal that most adolescents commit delinquent acts at one time or the other. Frequently, the major difference between a delinquent and nondelinquent is that the delinquent was unfortunate enough to get caught. But for the purpose of discussion here, let us assume that the major difference between a delinquent and a nondelinquent is that the delinquent commits more frequent and more serious antisocial acts. Two questions, then, merit consideration in our examination of adolescence: Are there behaviors that contribute to the process of becoming delinquent? What attitudes characterize those adolescents who commit more frequent and more serious delinquent acts?

Behaviors Leading to Delinquency

Three behaviors appear to contribute to the process of becoming a delinquent: running away from home, the use of drugs and alcohol, and disruptive behavior in school. The first two are discussed here, and the third will be examined in the next chapter.

Running Away

A runaway is defined as a youth between the ages of ten and seventeen who is absent from the home overnight without permission of a parent or guardian.[56] A national study of runaways conducted by the Department of Health, Education, and Welfare found that the Northeast and the South had significantly lower proportions of runaway youth than the north central states and the West. In addition, runaways occurred more frequently in heavily populated cities and small towns and less frequently in rural and suburban areas. Rates for white and black families were similar, but Hispanic households had rates higher than the national average. Furthermore, the rate of runaways was higher for families with incomes under $7000 a year.[57]

About 50 percent of the more than 500,000 runaway youth in the study by Brennan et al. became involved in delinquent behavior. As the time away from home increased, survival became more difficult through legal means. Runaways became involved in such delinquent acts as petty theft (30 percent), grand theft (15 percent), and selling marijuana (20 percent) or hard drugs (11 percent). Those who had run away several times (multiple runaways) became more involved in delinquent acts than those who had run away once (single runaways). Of course, some of the delinquent acts, such as the use of drugs, are a continuation of past behavior, but others arise from the runaway's need to survive on a day-to-day basis.[58] See Table 10-1 for the differences in delinquent behavior for runaways, nonrunaways, and single and multiple runaways.

Brennan et al., in defining seven types of runaways, found that the first three types are not highly delinquent, while the last four are delinquent and alienated runaways.

**TABLE 10-1 Delinquent Behavior for Runaways,
Nonrunaways, and Single and Multiple Runaways (%)**

Specific Behaviors Committed During Last 12 Months	Single	Multiple	All Runners	All Non-runners
Fake excuse for school absence	50.7	56.1	54.0	29.0
Taken things worth $5 or less	39.7	40.7	40.5	15.1
Broken into place without permission	9.6	16.5	13.3	2.3
Taken car for drive without owner's permission	15.0	16.5	15.7	3.4
Taken something from locker without asking	11.0	15.4	13.9	11.8
Damaged property for fun	20.5	31.9	26.6	9.8
Beat up kids or adults for heck of it	12.3	19.8	16.3	6.3
Participated in gang fights	24.6	30.8	27.9	8.1
Taken something worth $50 or more	8.2	12.1	10.3	1.6
Used force to get money	5.5	8.8	7.9	2.0
Used marijuana	61.6	75.9	69.7	20.9
Sold marijuana	23.2	41.9	34.0	4.0
Skipped school without legitimate excuse	63.1	66.0	64.8	30.6
Sniffed glue or toxic fumes	2.8	6.6	4.8	4.0
Used hard drugs	17.8	36.3	28.5	5.3
Sold hard drugs	2.8	16.5	10.3	1.3
Bought or drank beer, wine, or liquor	83.6	85.8	84.9	52.9

Source: Reprinted by permission of the publisher, from *The Social Psychology of Runaways* by Tim Brennan, David Huizinga, and Delbert S. Elliott (Lexington, Mass.: Lexington Books, D.C. Heath and Company, copyright 1978, D.C. Heath and Company).

Those last four subtypes have these features in common:

High conflict with parents
Rejecting parents
Highly delinquent peers
High commitment to delinquent peers
High levels of personal delinquent behavior
High school alienation
Serious problems at school
Low self-esteem[59]

In summary, running away is a status offense, but about half of all runaways commit delinquent acts. The delinquent runaway, as opposed to the nondelinquent runaway, has conflicts with parents, feels alienated from the school, and is involved with delinquent peers. The longer runaways are away from home, and the more frequently they run, the more likely they are to become involved in delinquent behavior.

The Use of Alcohol and Drugs

The use of alcohol and drugs is at present normative behavior for American adolescents. The U.S. government Report on Alcohol and Health found that by the senior year of high school, 89.9 percent of boys and 83.2 percent of girls have taken a drink at least once.[60] A survey of seniors in 1977 showed that half the seniors had used marijuana, and most recent surveys suggest an increase in marijuana use among adolescents.[61] Among a sample of 1978 and 1979 high school seniors, daily use had nearly doubled when compared with a 1975 class.[62] A counselor in a youth service bureau in a midwestern city of 100,000 commented on adolescents' use of drugs:

> They'll take anything anybody gives them just to be "street." It's not just the poor folk, middle-class folk, or rich folk; it's everybody. They are also trying drugs at a younger age. Grass is like cigarettes. And they're taking more pills, heroin, and cocaine. Coke is a big thing now. Where they're coming up with enough money in junior high school for coke is another question.[63]

Alcohol is the most frequently used drug, followed by marijuana. Stimulants, including amphetamines, cocaine, and Ritalin, also are frequently used. The use of amphetamines, or "speed," and cocaine appears to be rapidly increasing among adolescents. The use of sedatives, such as barbiturates and tranquilizers, and hallucinogens, including LSD and PCP, seems to be decreasing among adolescents. Finally, narcotics, including heroin, opium, and morphine, are of less popularity with adolescents.[64] Table 10-2 summarizes the characteristics of these drugs.

Adolescents vary, of course, in terms of how frequently they use drugs and the types of drugs they use. The variables of age, sex, urban or rural setting, social class, and availability strongly affect the types of drugs used and have some effect on the frequency of drug use. Some adolescents use drugs only at parties and on special occasions; some reserve them for weekends; and some use drugs every day. Typical adolescent rationales for the use of drugs include "everybody does it," "it makes me feel good," "it helps me relax," and "I need it to get through the day." The adolescents quoted in Box 10-2 express some of these justifications.

BOX 10-2 "The High Is Where It's At"

The first and second graders in a school I work with smoke pot they get from the 5th and 6th graders. They think, "Wow, this is great! Think the high is where it's at and they can beat anything with drugs.

Counselor in a youth service bureau

I went to bed at night high, and, as soon as I woke in the morning, I got high. I would get in my mother's medicine cabinet and get me some pills to give me a buzz until I could get some pot or something stronger.

Sixteen-year-old boy in a youth service bureau

Coke gives you a real euphoria. You feel wonderful, but about thirty minutes later, you want another hit. If you do coke, you want more and more. It is called the "rich man's high."

Eighteen-year-old girl who formerly was on probation

The high makes you feel good. If I weren't high, I would be out fighting.

Fifteen-year-old boy in a training school

I did drugs to get high. I wanted to feel good. If I got a headache, I smoked a joint to get rid of it. Other people take an aspirin to get rid of their headache, but I would smoke a joint.

Sixteen-year-old boy in a training school

Source: Interviews conducted in two Midwestern states in 1981 and 1982.

The use of alcohol is a status offense, and the use of other drugs is a criminal offense. But most adolescents using alcohol and drugs do not enter the juvenile justice system. What generalizations can be made to distinguish those who come to the attention of the system and those who do not?

- The more that an adolescent uses drugs, the more likely he or she will come to the attention of the juvenile justice system.
- The more that an adolescent uses drugs other than alcohol and marijuana, the more likely he or she will become physically and/or psychologically dependent on drugs.
- The more that an adolescent is physically and/or psychologically dependent on drugs, the more likely he or she will commit delinquent acts to support the drug habit.
- The more that an adolescent is physically and/or psychologically dependent on drugs, the more likely he or she will become involved in a highly delinquent teenage society or subculture.
- The more that an adolescent commits delinquent acts and is involved in a highly delinquent subculture, the more likely he or she will be adjudicated delinquent and be placed under the supervision of the juvenile court.[65]

The Spirit of Delinquency

Once an adolescent has become a delinquent, whether in terms of commitment to delinquency or of lack of commitment to the social bond, three attitudes seem to capture his or her spirit of delinquency: the restless search for excitement, a disdain

TABLE 10-2 Controlled Substances: Uses and Effects

	Drugs	Often Prescribed Brand Names	Medical Uses	Physical Dependence	Psychological Dependence
Narcotics	Opium	Dover's Powder, Paregoric	Analgesic, antidiarrheal	High	High
	Morphine	Morphine	Analgesic	High	High
	Codeine	Codeine	Analgesic, antitussive	Moderate	Moderate
	Heroin	None	None	High	High
	Meperidine (Pethidine)	Demerol, Pethadol	Analgesic	High	High
	Methadone	Dolophine, Methadone, Methadose	Analgesic, heroin substitute	High	High
	Other narcotics	Dilaudid, Leritine, Numorphan, Percodan	Analgesic, antidiarrheal antitussive	High	High
Depressants	Chloral hydrate	Noctec, Somnos	Hypnotic	Moderate	Moderate
	Barbiturates	Amytal, Butisol, Nembutal, Phenobarbital, Seconal, Tuinal	Anesthetic, anticonvulsant, sedation, sleep	High	High
	Glutethimide	Doriden	Sedation, sleep	High	High
	Methaqualone	Optimil, Parest, Quaalude, Somnafac, Sopor	Sedation, sleep	High	High
	Tranquilizers	Equanil, Librium, Miltown, Serax, Tranxene, Valium	Antianxiety, muscle relaxant, sedation	Moderate	Moderate
	Other depressants	Clonopin, Dalmane, Dormate, Noludar, Placydil, Valmid	Antianxiety, sedation, sleep	Possible	Possible

TABLE 10-2 (Continued)

Tolerance	Duration of Effects (in hours)	Usual Methods of Administration	Possible Effects	Effects of Overdose	Withdrawal Syndrome
Yes	3 to 6	Oral, smoked	Euphoria, drowsiness, respiratory depression, constricted pupils, nausea	Slow and shallow breathing, clammy skin, convulsions, coma, possible death	Watery eyes, runny nose, yawning, loss of appetite, irritability, tremors, panic, chills and sweating, cramps, nausea
Yes	3 to 6	Injected, smoked			
Yes	3 to 6	Oral, injected			
Yes	3 to 6	Injected, sniffed			
Yes	3 to 6	Oral, injected			
Yes	12 to 24	Oral, injected			
Yes	3 to 6	Oral, injected			
Probable	5 to 8	Oral	Slurred speech, disorientation, drunken behavior without odor of alcohol	Shallow respiration, cold and clammy skin, dilated pupils, weak and rapid pulse, coma, possible death	Anxiety, insomnia, tremors, delirium, convulsions, possible death
Yes	1 to 16	Oral, injected			
Yes	4 to 8	Oral			
Yes	4 to 8	Oral			
Yes	4 to 8	Oral			
Yes	4 to 8	Oral			

TABLE 10-2 (Continued)

	Drugs	Often Prescribed Brand Names	Medical Uses	Physical Dependence	Psychological Dependence
Stimulants	Cocaine[a]	Cocaine	Local anesthetic	Possible	High
	Amphetamines	Benzedrine, Biphetamine, Desoxyn, Dexedrine	Hyperkinesis, narcolepsy, weight control	Possible	High
	Phenmetrazine	Preludin	Weight control	Possible	High
	Methylphenidate	Ritalin	Hyperkinesis	Possible	High
	Other stimulants	Bacarate, Cylert, Didrex, Iona-min, Plegine, Pondimin, Pre-Sate, Sanorex, Voranil	Weight control	Possible	Possible
Hallucinogens	LSD	None	None	None	Degree unknown
	Mescaline	None	None	None	Degree unknown
	Psilocybin-Psilocyn	None	None	None	Degree unknown
	MDA	None	None	None	Degree unknown
	PCP[b]	Sernylan	Veterinary anesthetic	None	Degree unknown
	Other hallucinogens	None	None	None	Degree unknown
Cannabis	Marihuana Hashish Hashish oil	None	None	Degree unknown	Moderate

[a]Designated a narcotic under the Controlled Substances Act.

[b]Designated a depressant under the Controlled Substances Act.

Source: U.S. Department of Justice, Drug Enforcement Administration, *Drugs of Abuse* (Washington, D.C.: U.S. Government Printing Office, n.d.).

TABLE 10-2 (Continued)

Tolerance	Duration of Effects (in hours)	Usual Methods of Administration	Possible Effects	Effects of Overdose	Withdrawal Syndrome
Yes	2	Injected, sniffed	Increased alertness, excitation, euphoria, dilated pupils, increased pulse rate and blood pressure, insomnia, loss of appetite	Agitation, increase in body temperature, convulsions, possible death	Apathy, long periods of sleep, irritability, depression, disorientation
Yes	2 to 4	Oral, injected			
Yes	2 to 4	Oral			
Yes	2 to 4	Oral			
Yes	2 to 4	Oral			
Yes	Variable	Oral	Illusions and hallucinations (with exception of MDA); poor perception of time and distance	Longer, more intense "trip" episodes, psychosis, possible death	Withdrawal syndrome not reported
Yes	Variable	Oral, injected			
Yes	Variable	Oral			
Yes	Variable	Oral, injected, sniffed			
Yes	Variable	Oral, injected, smoked			
Yes	Variable	Oral, injected, sniffed			
Yes	2 to 4	Oral, smoked	Euphoria, relaxed inhibitions, increased appetite, disoriented behavior	Fatigue, paranoia, possible psychosis	Insomnia, hyperactivity, and decreased appetite reported in a limited number of individuals

for work and the desire for a "big score," and the acceptance of aggressive behavior.[66]

The Restless Search for Excitement

The delinquent's life is frequently characterized by adventurous exploits that are valued for the stimulation they provide:

> First, . . . delinquents are deeply immersed in a restless search for excitement, "thrills," or "kicks." The approved style of life, for many delinquents, is an adventurous one. Activities pervaded by displays of daring and charged with danger are highly valued in comparison with mundane and routine patterns of behaviors.[67]

Indeed, the delinquent sometimes courts physical danger, experiments with the forbidden, and provokes the authorities in a deliberate attempt to manufacture excitement.[68] Many adolescents, of course, are looking for excitement and thrills, but the adolescent who commits delinquent acts on an ongoing basis pursues excitement to a greater degree than the casual delinquent or the nondelinquent; the delinquent also is more likely to seek excitement or kicks regardless of the social norms this behavior may violate.

Part of the reason why the delinquent seeks excitement so much of the time is his or her disengagement from conventional attitudes. For example, the delinquent is typically alienated from school; that is, he or she is generally unmotivated to be involved at school, to do homework at night, or to participate in school activities in the evenings and on weekends. The delinquent also tends to seek immediate rather than delayed gratification of his or her desires. Living only in the here-and-now, not surprisingly, increases the importance of excitement and thrills in the present.

A Disdain for Work and Desire for the "Big Score"

A second aspect of the "spirit of delinquency" concerns the delinquent's attempt to attain "the material rewards of society while avoiding, in the manner of a leisure class, the canons of school and work with their commitments to methodism, security, and routine."[69] The delinquent, as Robert K. Merton indicated, wants to attain the cultural goal of success, but does not want to pursue acceptable societal means to achieve success.[70] Or the delinquent may feel that only through illegitimate means can he or she attain the material rewards of society.[71]

Delinquents are not naïve. They are aware, especially if they have dropped out of school, that menial and low-paying jobs are probably the only ones available. With the high rates of unemployment in recent years, even these menial jobs may not be available. Although the delinquent can deal with the employment situation by showing a disdain for work, the problem still remains that he or she usually needs large amounts of money. The "big score" becomes important because it can satisfy the need for money without involving work. Dealing drugs has become a popular means for delinquents to attain the big score. A sixteen-year-old girl who was drug dependent talks about how she was able to raise money from drugs so she could "take care of business":

> When you are drug dependent, you need to raise the money somehow. With me it was either selling my body or dealing drugs. But when I was dealing drugs, I was so popular. You feel so important. I got into dealing through older people. You need to raise over $100 to start. You need someone to front for you. I would sell three ounces and have one for myself.[72]

The Acceptance of Aggressive Behavior

The third aspect of the "spirit of delinquency" concerns aggression. According to Matza and Sykes:

> This theme is most likely to be selected as pointing to the delinquent's alienation from the larger society. Verbal and physical assaults are a commonplace, and frequent reference is made to the delinquent's basic hostility, his hatred, and his urge to injure and destroy.[73]

A persuasive argument can be made that one major difference between delinquents and occasional offenders or nondelinquents is that the delinquent tends to be more aggressive toward others. The delinquent's use of aggression may occur as part of the process of maintaining his or her "rep" or in the course of committing a crime. Yet chronic property offenders and drug offenders commit one delinquent act after the other but may not be any more likely to assault others than are nondelinquents.

In short, certain behaviors and attitudes arising in adolescence are likely to lead to ongoing involvements in delinquent behavior. The chronic runaway, the habitual user of drugs and alcohol, and the disruptive student in school tend to become involved more deeply in the delinquent enterprise. Further, such attitudes as a restless search for excitement, a disdain for work, and the acceptance of aggressive behavior typically discriminate delinquents from occasional or nondelinquents.

POLICY IMPLICATIONS

Psychologist Eric Erickson has observed, "Childhood . . . is the model of all oppression and enslavement, a kind of inner colonization, which forces grown-ups to accept inner repression and self-restriction."[74] A chief reason for the repression of childhood is the lack of rights given to young persons. The area of children's rights, which shows the interrelationships among the sociocultural, the legal, and the political contexts, has generated intense debate in recent years.

In 1959, the United Nations General Assembly unanimously passed a Declaration of the Rights of the Child. Nutrition, housing, recreation, medical service, education, and protection from neglect and exploitation were identified as rights of children. In the 1960s, interest groups began to examine the special needs of children, and in the 1970s, the use of the term *rights* increased in popularity.

Four influences contributed to the children's rights movement. First, as women fought against the stereotypes of traditional sex roles in the 1960s and 1970s, concern arose over the welfare of children as well and the nature of their upbringing. Second, the public school came under fire during the 1960s and 1970s for failing to serve the needs of children. Third, evidence of the failure of the juvenile court to provide constitutional guarantees of due process led to widespread concern. Finally, the civil rights movement and the protests against the war in Vietnam paved the way for a human rights movement that represented a group of citizens discriminated against because of their age.[75]

Richard Farson has suggested a far-reaching bill of rights centering on self-determination for all individuals regardless of sex, ethnic group, or age. Individuals, according to this bill, should have the right to a relevant education, to a meaningful job and to a guaranteed wage, to a supportive home, to personal property, to sexual relationships of their choice, to all available information without censorship, to expression of political opinions, and to suffrage.[76] The Children's Defense Fund, a strong advocate of children's rights, has emphasized four basic issues: rehabilitation of the juvenile justice system, use of the least restrictive (as opposed to the best) placement, access to a good education, and provisions of independent legal counsel for minors.[77]

The children's rights movement presently encompasses a spectrum of approaches. Despite its supporters' deep commitment to children, writing an effective national policy with accompanying legislation has been difficult because each of the numerous interest groups involved defines one specific need as the most important. But while unable at present to form coalitions because no single goal or strategy can be identified for the movement, individuals and groups have made significant progress on specific issues in the legal context. For example, progress has been made in questions of custody in divorce cases, guardianship for foster children, due process in the justice system, protection of the rights of privacy, independent access to medical care, and child abuse legislation.[78]

But further progress in the children's rights movement faces serious problems. With unemployment rates reaching new highs, it is inconceivable that the government, powerful labor unions, or the large masses of unskilled workers would favor a radical increase in the labor pool by adolescents. Nor is the school likely to grant rights of self-determination to children that would jeopardize the authority of teachers and administrators. Furthermore, making school attendance noncompulsory would drastically undermine the financial basis of the public school system.[79] Thus, it is unlikely that the moral reformers in the children's rights movement will be able to do away with childhood as we now know it.

SUMMARY

Adolescence represents a rite of passage from childhood to adulthood. The "discovery" of adolescence, in terms of the contextual perspective, occurred largely in response to the social changes that took place in America in the late nineteenth and early twentieth centuries. The principal reason for prolonging the years of childhood was to fulfill the aims of the new urban-industrial society that developed so rapidly following the Civil War. That is, adolescence was "invented" because public concern over social conditions led to the development of three major social movements: compulsory (and characteristically public) education, child labor legislation, and special legal protection for juveniles. Although these movements were strongly motivated by humanitarian considerations, the influences of the major economic, social, and political forces in society also affected their development.

Adolescence represents a period of extensive physical and psychological growth. These teenage years become a period of crisis and storm for some adolescents, while others adjust well to the changes taking place in their lives. The likelihood of becoming involved in delinquent behavior is affected by the environmental influences at home, in the neighborhood or the community, and in the sociocultural context. Although the values of adolescents have not been found to be generally in conflict with those of their parents, some adolescent reference groups do adhere to values that are in conflict with the larger culture, leading them into involvement in delinquent behavior. Running away from home, the habitual use of drugs and alcohol, and disruptive behavior in school all are related to the process of becoming a delinquent. Furthermore, the delinquent spirit appears to be characterized by a restless search for excitement, a disdain for work and the desire for a big score, and the acceptance of aggressive behavior toward others.

Discussion Questions

1. Do you see adolescence as a period of crisis or of stability?
2. What are the main social and cultural environments influencing adolescents? How does each environment influence the behavior of an adolescent?
3. Are adolescents usually in conflict with the values of their parents?
4. What behaviors appear to increase the likelihood of delinquent behavior? Why?
5. What are the three attitudes that describe the spirit of the delinquent enterprise? Why is each important?

References

Adams, Gerard R., and Gullotta, Thomas. *Adolescent Life Experiences.* Monterey, Calif.: Brooks/Cole Publishing Company, 1983.

Aries, P. *Centuries of Childhood.* New York: Knopf, 1962.

Bakan, David. "Adolescence in America: From Idea to Social Fact." *Daedalus* 100 (1971): 979–995.

Beschner, George M., and Friedman, Alfred S. *Youth Drug Abuse: Problems, Issues, and Treatment.* Lexington, Mass.: D.C. Heath & Company, 1979.

Coleman, James S. *The Adolescent Society.* New York: Free Press, 1961.

De Mause, Lloyd, editor. *The History of Childhood.* New York: Psycho-history Press, 1974.

Farson, Richard. *Birthrights.* New York: Macmillan Publishing Company, 1974.

Greenleaf, Barbara Kaye. *Children through the Ages: A History of Childhood*. New York: McGraw-Hill Book Company, 1978.

Josselyn, Irene M. *The Adolescent and His World*. New York: Family Service Association of America, 1952.

LeFranciois, Guy R. *Adolescents*. 2d ed. Belmont, Calif.: Wadsworth Publishing Company, 1981.

Leger, Robert G. "Where Have All the Flowers Gone? A Sociological Analysis of the Origins and Content of Youth Values of the Seventies." *Adolescence* 15 (Summer 1980).

Matza, David, and Sykes, Gresham M. "Subterranean Traditions of Youth." *American Sociological Review* 26 (October 1961): 712–719.

FOOTNOTES

1. Robert D. Barr, "Today's Youth: Cluttered Values and Troubled Dreams," *Values and Youth,* edited by Barr (Washington, D.C.: National Council for Social Sciences, 1971), p. 13.

2. Ellen Millhollin's research and assistance was invaluable in the development of this modern childhood section.

3. Lloyd de Mause, ed., *The History of Childhood* (New York: Psycho-history Press, 1974), p. 1.

4. Barbara Kaye Greenleaf, *Children through the Ages: A History of Childhood* (New York: McGraw-Hill Book Company, 1978), p. 19.

5. de Mause, *History of Childhood,* p. 150.

6. Marvin Harris, *Cows, Pigs, Wars, and Witches* (New York: Random House, 1978), pp. 68–69.

7. de Mause, *History of Childhood,* p. 32.

8. Ibid., pp. 34–35.

9. Ibid., p. 311.

10. Greenleaf, *Children through the Ages,* p. 32.

11. George Henry Payne, *The Child in Human Progress* (New York: G. P. Putnam, 1969), p. 324.

12. Gerald R. Adams and Thomas Gullotta, *Adolescent Life Experiences* (Monterey, Calif.: Brooks/Cole Publishing Company, 1983), p. 6.

13. Ibid., p. 7.

14. J. F. Kett, *Rites of Passage: Adolescence in America, 1790 to the Present* (New York: Basic Books, 1977), p. 243.

15. Adams and Gullotta, *Adolescent Life Experiences,* pp. 7–8.

16. Ibid., p. 8.

17. George A. Theodorson and Achilles G. Theodorson, *A Modern Dictionary of Sociology* (New York: Thomas Y. Crowell, 1969), pp. 88, 422.

18. John C. Coleman, "Current Contradictions in Adolescent Theory," *Journal of Youth and Adolescence* 7 (1978), p. 2.

19. Ibid., p. 3.

20. Ibid.

21. Ibid., p. 7.

22. Irene M. Josselyn, *The Adolescent and His World* (New York: Family Service Association of America, 1952), p. 5.

23. Nathan W. Ackerman, *The Psychodynamics of Family Life* (New York: Basic Books, 1958), p. 231.

24. James S. Coleman, *The Adolescent Society* (New York: Free Press, 1961), p. 3.

25. James Garabarino and Glen Gilliam, *Understanding Abusive Families* (Lexington, Mass.: Lexington Books, 1980), p. 145.

26. Ibid., p. 146.

27. Gary Storm contributed the material on social and cultural environments.

28. Travis Hirschi, *Causes of Delinquency* (Berkeley: University of California Press, 1969), p. 94.

29. Ibid., p. 169.

30. Ibid., p. 193.

31. See David Dawley, *A Nation of Lords: The Autobiography of the Vice Lords* (Garden City, N.Y.: Anchor Books, 1973).

32. Muzafer Sherif and Carolyn W. Sherif, *Reference Groups* (New York: Harper & Row, 1964), p. 55.

33. Ibid., p. 54.

34. David J. Bordua, "Some Comments on Theories of Group Delinquency," *Sociological Inquiry* 22 (1962), p. 258.

35. M. J. Hindelang, "Causes of Delinquency: A Partial Replication," *Social Problems* 21 (Spring 1973), pp. 471–487; Lamar T. Empey and S. G. Lubeck, *Explaining Delinquency* (Lexington, Mass.: Lexington Books, 1971); M. L. Erickson and Lamar T. Empey, "Class Position, Peers and Delinquency," *Sociology and Social Research* 49 (April 1965), pp. 268–282; D. S. Elliott and H. L. Voss, *Delinquency and Dropout* (Lexington, Mass.: Lexington Books, 1974).

36. Hirschi, *Causes of Delinquency*, pp. 145–161.

37. G. F. Jensen and M. L. Erickson, "Peer Commitment and Delinquent Conduct," mimeographed (1978).

38. Hirschi, *Causes of Delinquency*, pp. 145–161.

39. Henry Malcolm, *Generation of Narcissus* (Boston: Little, Brown & Company, 1971), p. 4.

40. The materials on the media and delinquency are largely derived from Gary F. Jensen and Dean G. Rojeck, *Delinquents: A Sociological View* (Lexington, Mass.: D.C. Heath & Company, 1980), pp. 234–241.

41. S. H. Lovibond, "The Effects of Media Stressing Crime and Violence upon Children's Attitudes," *Social Problems* 15 (Summer 1967), pp. 91–100.

42. L. D. Eron et al., "Does Television Violence Cause Aggression?" *American Psychologist* 27 (1972), pp. 253–262.

43. U.S. Surgeon General's Scientific Advisory Committee on Television and Social Behavior, *Television and Growing Up: The Impact of Television Violence* (Washington, D.C.: U.S. Government Printing Office, 1971).

44. Jensen and Rojeck, *Delinquency*, p. 239.

45. C. Y. Glock and R. Stark, *Religion and Society in Tension* (Chicago: Rand McNally, 1965), p. 184.

46. Travis Hirschi and Rodney Stark, "Hellfire and Delinquency," *Social Problems* 17 (Fall 1969), pp. 202–213; S. R. Burkett and M. White, "Hellfire and Delinquency: Another Look," *Journal for the Scientific Study of Religion* 13 (December 1974), pp. 455–462; G. F. Jensen and M. L. Erickson, "The Religious Factor and Delinquency: Another Look at the Hellfire Hypothesis," in *The Religious Dimension*, edited by R. Wuthnow (New York: Academic Press, 1979).

47. Jensen and Rojeck, *Delinquency*, p. 246.

48. Deairich Hunter, "Ducks vs. Hard Rocks," *Newsweek* 18 (August 1980), pp. 14–15.

49. Hirschi, *Causes of Delinquency*, pp. 189–191.

50. Coleman, *Adolescent Society*, p. 9.

51. E. A. Smith, *American Youth Culture: Group Life in Teenage Society* (New York: Free Press, 1962).

52. Talcott Parsons, "Youth in the Context of American Society," in *Social Structure and Personality*, edited by Parsons (New York: Free Press, 1964).

53. Ralph England, "A Theory of Middle-Class Juvenile Delinquency," in *Middle Class Juvenile Delinquency*, edited by E. W. Vaz (New York: Harper and Row, 1967), pp. 242–244.

54. Coleman, "Current Contradictions in Adolescent Theory," p. 2.

55. Guy R. Lefranciois, *Adolescents*, 2d ed. (Belmont, Calif.: Wadsworth Publishing Company, 1981), p. 246.

56. Tom Brennan, David Huizinga, and Delbert S. Elliott, *The Social Psychology of Runaways* (Lexington, Mass.: D.C. Heath & Company, 1978), p. 4.

57. Ibid., pp. 131–132.

58. Ibid., pp. 234–235.

59. Ibid., p. 281.

60. U.S. Department of Health, Education and Welfare, *The Special Report to the U.S. Congress on Alcohol and Health* (Washington, D.C.: U.S. Government Printing Office, 1978).

61. U.S. Department of Health, Education and Welfare, *Marijuana and Health: Sixth Annual Report to the U.S. Congress* (Washington, D.C.: U.S. Government Printing Office, 1977).

62. U.S. Department of Health, Education and Welfare, *Marijuana and Health: Eighth Annual Report to the U.S. Congress* (Washington, D.C.: U.S. Government Printing Office, 1980).

63. Interviewed in October 1980.

64. U.S. Department of Health and Human Services, *A Drug Retrospective: 1961–1980* (Washington, D.C.: U.S. Government Printing Office, 1980).

65. These generalizations are derived from the interviews conducted with over one hundred adolescent drug users in two Midwestern states in 1981 and 1982.

66. David Matza and Gresham M. Sykes, "Subterranean Traditions of Youth," *American Sociological Review* 26 (October 1961); pp. 712–719.

67. Ibid, p. 713.

68. Ibid, p. 713.

69. Ibid, p. 714.

70. Robert K. Merton, *Social Theory and Social Structure,* rev. and enlarged ed. (New York: Free Press, 1957).

71. Richard A. Cloward and Lloyd E. Ohlin, *Delinquency and Opportunity: A Theory of Delinquent Gangs* (New York: Free Press, 1960).

72. Interviewed in January 1982.

73. Matza and Sykes, "Subterranean Traditions of Youth," p. 714.

74. Erik H. Erikson and Huey P. Newton, *In Search of Common Ground* (New York: W. W. Norton, 1973), p. 52.

75. C. R. Margolin, "Salvation Versus Liberation: The Movement for Children's Rights in a Historical Context," *Social Problems* 25 (April 1978), pp. 441–452.

76. Richard Farson, *Birthrights* (New York: Macmillan, 1974).

77. Rochelle Beck and John Butler, "An Interview with Marian Wright Edelman," *Harvard Educational Review* 44 (1974), pp. 53–73.

78. Margolin, "Salvation versus Liberation," p. 446.

79. Ibid., p. 447.

80. David Bakan, "Adolescence in America: From Idea to Social Fact," *Daedalus* 100 (1971), pp. 979–995.

INTERVIEW WITH JAMES S. COLEMAN

So the fact of being superfluous in some sense and of being part of a holding pattern, . . . means that many young people have no reason to have all the virtues that adults would want them to have. They are being held in waiting and there is not the immediacy of a goal that a person who is needed has.

In this interview, James S. Coleman, professor of sociology at the University of Chicago and an acknowledged authority on both adolescence and public education, discusses how the adolescent culture differs today from the one he studied more than twenty years ago, the quality of public education, the rights of adolescents, and policy implications for adolescents in American society.

Question: How have adolescents changed since *The Adolescent Society* was published twenty years ago?

Coleman: That's a question I could better answer if I were still studying adolescents as intensely as I was then. So I must give an answer based on fairly good knowledge at that time and on a general impression at this time. Adolescents are in many respects more worldly wise than they were when I wrote the book. I think that's largely due to changes in the structure of communication, especially television. Even though television was around at that time, children hadn't grown up with it then to the extent that they do now.

I think that one thing that has changed is that adolescents now look even more to other young people for their social rewards than they did then. That is, I think that adolescent society which was

James S. Coleman has been author or coauthor of seventeen books and monographs. His publications in the general areas of adolescence and education include The Adolescent Society, Adolescents and the Schools, Equality of Educational Opportunity, Youth: Transition to Adulthood, *and* High School Achievement: Public, Catholic, and Private Schools Compared. *He is also the author of nearly two hundred scientific and professional articles.*

existent to some degree then is much more extensive now. But I think that it has changed from being a localized adolescent society to one in which aspects of it cut across local communities of adolescents. It's not as much contained within a single school. There is much more communication across schools than before. I think the period of the youth movement in the late 1960s and early 1970s had something to do with bringing that about. I think also the existence of rock music is partly an indicator of that and also partly a determinant of that.

Let me make one more point on this subject. When I studied adolescents in 1957, only a very small fraction of kids in each high school were Elvis Presley fans. This somewhat deviant subculture was seen as quite outside the central dominant group of adolescents within a given school. This is still true in some schools; that is, the leading crowd in most schools is not a crowd which is principally concerned with rock music. But this kind of youth culture has come to be far more widespread among young people.

Question: In your book on adolescent society, I am not certain you talked about drugs at all. Why have drugs been so widely used by adolescents in the past fifteen years? What trends in American society are reflected in this widespread drug use by adolescents?

Coleman: No, I didn't write about drugs in that book because drugs were simply not a factor. I asked young people about drinking beer and whiskey. This was something that differentiated young people from one another quite sharply. Drugs, for all intents and purposes, didn't exist.

To answer the other part of your question, part of the answer has to come from the question— Why was there such a big youth revolt in the 1960s anyway? Where did this youth revolt come from? This question is fairly easy to answer, because I think it's a purely demographic phenomenon. I think it occurred largely because there was a very large cohort of young people. The institutions in society were not equipped to cope with this large cohort. The voluntary institutions, like the scouts and church groups, were simply not prepared for such a cohort, nor were the schools, and the youth began to look much more to one another because they were a much larger fraction of the society than they had been before. I don't know the mechanism through which it came about, but once that pattern of inward-looking among youth increased to that extent, this was to some degree responsible for the widespread drug use among youth.

Question: What do you feel are the most important findings of the Coleman report?

Coleman: Well, there were two findings which have been most widely used. One was used in the civil rights movement, and this finding stated that black students performed better academically in schools that were predominantly middle class than in schools that were predominantly lower class. This had direct implications for affirmative integration; namely, that one way to improve black achievement would be to increase school integration. So the report was used fairly widely in court cases and in school board deliberations for school desegregation.

A second finding that had a great deal of impact was the finding that differences in family background were far more important than differences in school characteristics for achievement. This led some people to say that schools don't make a difference at all, but this was not really what the report said. But that did lead to a number of questions about the kinds of effect school resources had upon students and about how you went about improving the school; whether you improved the school through simply putting more books in the library and hiring teachers with more advanced training or whether there was something else that was more important in improving the school.

Question: What are the basic findings of your recent study of private versus public school, and what are the implications of these findings in terms of American education?

Coleman: There were also two basic findings of this study. One was that students in private schools seemed to be performing better, even when family background of students and their orientation to college are controlled. So one finding was that students are achieving more highly in the private sector than in the public sector. The other finding was that the overall impact on the private sector of racial integration in the schools was very little. This was especially true when you looked at the country as a whole. There were two compensating factors here: there are fewer blacks in the private sector than in the public schools, but then given the proportion of blacks in the private sector, they were more integrated in the private sector than in the public sector. So the two effects balanced each other out, and the overall effect on segregation was minimal.

I think one of the implications of the achievement findings is the potential impact for American schools. What are the private schools doing that the public schools can be or should be doing? And the answer to that is making stronger academic and disciplinary demands. But how can the public sector begin to make those kinds of demands? Alternatively, how is it possible to introduce some kind of choice processes within the public sector? Public school principals and teachers are the first to point out that private school principals and teachers are in a much different situation than public schools because they do have greater levers. However, what many people fail to recognize is that many of these levers could exist in the public sector if the idea of children being assigned to a specific school rather than having some choice between schools was not taken as fixed.

Question: What policy changes do you think are needed for the adolescent to function better in our society? What changes are needed to reduce delinquency, suicide, alcoholism, and drug addiction?

Coleman: That's a fundamental and very serious

question. One of the major changes that has occurred in society over a long period of time is that young people are no longer needed in society in the way that they were before. So the fact of being superfluous in some sense and of being part of a holding pattern, even if you are in college, has an impact on American youth. In the mid-1960s there was major growth in the number of students going to college. This is when the small teachers colleges turned into branches of state universities and expanded enormously.

This fact in itself means that many young people have no reason to have all the virtues that adults would want them to have. They are being held in waiting and there is not the immediacy of a goal that a person who is needed has. I think one of the most damaging things to a person in society is to be without function or not to be needed. I believe this is one of the psychological problems housewives faced before a large proportion of them came into the labor market. No longer was keeping the house an occupation that could make them content, unless they had a large number of children.

I think that somehow we need to find a function for young people. I don't know how we do that, but if we could bring ourselves to require a year of national service for young people, that would be a solution that would have enormous benefits of all sorts. But I don't think we can reach that degree of consensus.

Question: What rights do adolescents need in our society?

Coleman: Well, to go back to your earlier question, I think that the problems of young people, such as delinquency, drugs, and suicide, arise much less from lack of rights than from lack of functionality and lack of being needed. I feel this very strongly. I know that the problem is often put in terms of a lack of rights, but I think that one of the major things that has occurred for young people in the past twenty years is that there has been a reduction of attention to young people on the part of adults.

As a country we are not as interested in children as many countries are. Some people say that we just don't like kids, but I don't think it's quite that bad. I spent a year in West Berlin a couple of years ago, and in West Berlin there are not many young children there. The character of the population is very peculiar because there are a lot of young people going to the two universities in Berlin and then there are a lot of older persons who are really left over from prewar Berlin. There are far fewer people in between [the two groups], and there are many fewer families in formation. These older persons in the Berlin population really don't like children.

I wouldn't say that is true for us, but I just think that we are not interested in children. It's not that we positively dislike them but that we don't have a natural interest in them because there are many fewer of them around. Even though we have child-centered families, etc., we don't take children seriously in considering how to organize our society. I remember being at a party at which there was a small child about a year and a half old. The people at this party were mostly young, white middle-class Americans, but there were some young black middle-class Americans, two older black women, and one young Lebanese man. The three people who showed the most interest in the child were the two older black women and the young Lebanese man. The young black and the young white middle-class Americans seemed to be leery of the child. They didn't know how to pick a child up, how to fondle it, or how to play with it. More importantly, they were not especially interested, and I see that as a really sad commentary on our society. I think we need to find ways of changing that.

Question: How well are we serving the minority student in our schools?

Coleman: One unfortunate thing about the way American education has developed is that our increased affluence has meant much more possibility of people moving into areas such that the schools are reasonably homogeneous in social class and outlook, much more than was true in the past. As a consequence, too often lower-class children, especially if they are black or of another minority, will tend to be segregated in a school. That is a serious disadvantage, not only for them, but also a serious disadvantage for whites and middle-class children who also don't have this cross-section of experience. That's one reason that National Service can be a great virtue because it mixes a population up in a way that it doesn't get mixed up in the schools because people segregate themselves residentially.

Question: Say more about this National Service. You've mentioned this a couple of times.

Coleman: Well, a number of people have worked hard and thought a lot about how to create a situation which addresses several problems. One is the problem of extended education for young people which keeps them out of any kind of functional role for a long period of time. Another is the problem of not having some kind of commitment or a means by which a young person can carry out some kind of social service in a way that is a commitment to others. One of the bad characteristics of school is that it focuses wholly on selfish aims. It doesn't focus on any kind of aims that benefit other persons at all. One of the attractions of something like the Peace Corps or the other services of that sort was that it provided a way that persons could engage in some kind of service rather than focusing wholly on themselves. But unless something like that is imposed or required, only a small fraction of young people do it. Although there are a lot of disadvantages and defects to military drafts and to military service, which are exemplified by some veterans and servicemen of the Vietnam era being deeply involved in drugs, yet military service does have, as anyone who served in World War II knows, a lot of virtues, such as bringing people from different parts of this society closer together and developing a sense of camaraderie in working for a common goal. This enables people to develop identification with other people that doesn't occur in our ordinary ways of socialization.

CHAPTER 11

PLAYGROUND CLOSES AT DUSK

VANDALS WERE HERE REPAIRS WILL BE MADE AS SOON AS POSSIBLE. PRCA VANDALISM CONTROL SQUAD

CH
A
D
PRO

THE SCHOOL AND DELINQUENCY

CHAPTER OUTLINE

I had a dynamic counselor in high school. She and a few teachers were the only ones who saved me from getting my ass thrown into reform school. They really did a wonderful, wonderful job with me.

Youth service bureau counselor who was labeled
as a delinquent during her adolescence[1]

On the first day the principal told new teachers that you don't have to worry about violence here. It didn't take me long to realize that whenever the three administrators walked on campus, they always walked in twos and had a walkie-talkie in their hands. They would never go out alone.

Coach in a Los Angeles high school[2]

I kicked in the guidance counselor's desk. I threatened teachers and the principal. I got caught smoking on purpose. I was suspended quite a few times. It was just a joy trip.

Sixteen-year-old girl in a training school[3]

Throughout history, in nearly every society, the education of youth has been a major concern. Today, the educational system in the United States is wracked with criticism. For example, Jonathan Kozol's *Death at an Early Age* documents the harm done to children by repressive educational systems.[4] John Holt contends that schools are ruining children by teaching them the wrong values, denying their innate potential for expression, and overemphasizing trivia.[5] Herbert Kohl's *Thirty-Six Children* adds that the educational needs of minority children are being ignored today.[6] Thus, because the current state of the educational process may lead to alienation of students and to delinquent behavior, the subject of public education is an important consideration in a delinquency textbook.

This chapter begins with a brief review of public education in the United States, followed by a discussion of the most significant problems faced by public education. It then examines the relationship between schools and delinquency, the emerging emphasis on the rights of students, and the policy implications for the school.

HISTORY OF EDUCATION IN AMERICA

The U.S. Constitution says nothing about public schools, but by 1850 nearly all the northern states had enacted free education laws. By 1918, education was both free and compulsory in nearly every state of the union. The commitment to public education arose largely from the growing need for a uniform approach to socialization of the diverse groups immigrating to this country.[7] Joel Spring, a historian, writes of this movement:

Education during the nineteenth century has been increasingly viewed as an instrument of social control to be used to solve the social problems of crime, poverty, and Americanization of the immigrant. The activities of public schools tended to replace the social training of other institutions, such as the family and church. One reason for the extension of school activities was the concern for the education of the great numbers of immigrants arriving from eastern and southern Europe. It was feared that without some form of Americanization immigrants would cause a rapid decay of American institutions.[8]

During most of the nineteenth century, American schools were chaotic and violent places where teachers unsuccessfully attempted to maintain control over unmotivated, unruly, and unmanageable children through novel and sometimes brutal disciplinary methods.[9] For example, Horace Mann reported in the 1840s that in one school with 250 pupils he saw 328 separate floggings in one week of five school days, an average of over 65 floggings a day.[10]

Because of widespread dissatisfaction with the schools at the turn of the twentieth century, the Progressive education movement arose. Its founder, John Dewey, advocated reform in classroom methods and curriculum so students would become more questioning, creative, and involved in the process of their own education. In short, Dewey was more concerned about individualism and personal growth than rigid socialization.[11]

The 1954 U.S. Supreme Court decision that ruled racial segregation in public schools unconstitutional was a pivotal event in the history of American education, for it obligated the federal government to make certain integration in schools was achieved "within a reasonable time limit."[12] The busing of children to distant schools, which arose out of the Supreme Court decision and which has resulted in the shift from neighborhood schools, remains a hotly debated issue.

During the 1960s, open classrooms, in which the teacher served as a "resource person" who offered students many activities from which to choose, were instituted as an alternative to the earlier teacher-oriented classrooms. As was the case with the Progressive education movement, the open-classroom concept was accepted more widely in private schools than in public ones.

The baby boom of the 1950s resulted in larger enrollments and more formalized student-teacher contacts in public schools in the 1960s and early 1970s. Public education also became more expensive in the 1970s because the increasing numbers of children in the classroom meant that more equipment had to be purchased (including expensive items such as computers, scientific equipment, and audiovisual aids). At the same time, teachers' unions took a firmer stance during contract talks, and many larger cities saw teachers' strikes during this decade.

PROBLEMS FACING THE PUBLIC SCHOOLS

Repressive methods of education, a task too large for available resources, and crime in the schools are problems presently facing public education that are important aspects of a discussion of delinquent behavior in junior and senior high schools across the nation.

Repressive Methods of Education

Public schools can be characterized as repressive because of their authoritarian atmosphere and because of the likelihood of failure by many students, especially those with limited learning abilities. The repressive methods of education, as Martin Gold has noted, make school one of the most difficult experiences for adolescents in American society.[13]

Charles Silberman, author of the widely hailed *Crisis in the Classroom*, offered an analysis of the atmosphere in public schools in 1970 that is for the most part true of today's schools:

> *Because adolescents are harder to "control" than younger children, second-ary schools tend to be even more authoritarian and repressive than elementary schools; the values they transmit are the values of docility, passivity, conformity, and lack of trust.*[14]

A number of other characteristics contribute to this authoritarian atmosphere. First, the doctrine of adolescent inferiority, as well as downward communication flow, discourage student participation in school decisions. Second, batch processing of students, routinization of activity, dependence on rules and regulations, and future-reward orientations result in bored and frustrated students. Third, large physical structures and the tracking of students into vertical groups lead to alienation and rebellion on the part of students.[15]

Haney and Zimbardo have even drawn a comparison between high schools and prisons. High schools, like prisons, have stark, impersonal architecture and drab interiors, give arbitrary power to teachers to punish and humiliate the pupil whose behavior is unacceptable, have regimentation and many regulations, including movement in lines and at signals from bells, restrict movement within the building, and regulate personal appearance through dress codes. The impersonality of large classes also has taught students, like inmates, to lose themselves in the crowd.[16]

The high probability of failure, especially for students with limited ability or learning problems, also makes American education repressive. Several studies have addressed the painful experience of failure in school.[17] Vinter and Sarri point out that the school frequently uses grades for a variety of negative sanctions designed to curb student malperformance. They found that students performing "below a certain standard received adverse grades and might (as a consequence of poor grades) be denied . . . a wider variety of privileges and opportunities within the school."[18] For example, they might no longer be eligible for "minor but prestigeful classroom or school assignments (or) [might be] excluded from participation in certain extracurricular activities."[19] Albert K. Cohen is skeptical as to whether many youths can tolerate the censure and disparagement they receive at school:

> *The contempt or indifference of others, particularly of those like school-mates and teachers with whom we are constrained to associate for long hours every day, is difficult, we suggest, to shrug off. It poses a problem with which one may conceivably attempt to cope in a variety of ways. One*

may make an active effort to change himself with the expectations of others; one may attempt to justify or explain his inferiority. . . . One may tell himself he really doesn't care what these people think; one may react with anger and aggression. But the most probable response is simple, uncomplicated, honest indifference.[20]

Failure in school, of course, would have no effect on students who lacked a desire to achieve in the first place. But overwhelming evidence leads to the conclusion that the vast majority of students do want to achieve in school. Vinter and Sarri found that almost all the students they studied were interested in at least passing their courses.[21] Turner further found that all the boys he studied wanted to finish high school and that 85 percent of them desired at least some postsecondary education.[22]

Thus, the repressiveness of public education has resulted in creating bored, frustrated, dissatisfied, and alienated students. In one study, students consistently rated themselves as more bored in school than in any other setting.[23] Urie Bronfenbrenner adds that "the schools have become one of the most potent breeding grounds of alienation in American society."[24]

Too Large a Task

The school has long been regarded as one of the main socializing institutions of society. Often the first institution entrusted with the care of a child away from the protective cloak of his or her family, the school has been charged with producing good citizens, with helping the individual better himself or herself, and with preparing the individual to maximize his or her own development.[25] Schafer and Polk enumerate the socially expressed responsibilities of the school:

We assume that all children and youth must be given the skills, attitudes, and values that will enable them to perform adult activities and meet adult obligations. Public education must ensure the maximum development of general knowledge, intellectual competence, psychological stability, social skills, and social awareness so that each new generation will be enlightened, individually strong, yet socially and civically responsible.[26]

However, the school has been unable to fulfill these immense responsibilities because it cannot take the place of parents in teaching values and social skills, because it cannot negate the influence of the peer group, and because it cannot handle effectively the increasing number of disruptive students.

First, the supposition that the school can teach values and skills that children have not learned at home is certainly questionable. Indeed, a more realistic supposition would be that children are influenced by the family climate in their adjustment in school. Thurston, Feldhusen, and Benning in fact found that the family climate is the most critical factor on misconduct in school.[27] Rudolf Dreikurs also attributed much of the problem of student misbehavior to poor family climate.[28] The Berkeley Center for the Study of Higher Education concluded that a positive family climate is directly related to a student's academic motivation.[29] Furthermore, child abuse and neglect appear to generate learning problems.[30]

Second, the ability of the school to fulfill its role as a socializing institution is restricted by the influence of the peer group. The adolescent peer culture, as indicated in Chapter 10, has varying effects upon juveniles, but with some adolescents the peer culture is critical in determining their attitudes and behaviors. A direct relationship appears to be present between performance in school and commitment to the values and norms of an adolescent peer culture; that is, the more problems adolescents have in school, the more likely they will turn to peers for support and acceptance. Conversely, the more adolescents have become affiliated with a delinquent subculture, the less receptive they tend to be to the process of academic education.

Third, disruptive behavior is currently an especially serious problem in many of this nation's classrooms. Such behavior takes many forms: defiance of authority, manipulation of teachers, inability or unwillingness to follow rules, lack of motivation to learn, fights with peers, destruction of property, use of dope in school, and physical or verbal altercations with teachers. Disruptive students require a great deal of time from teachers and counselors in order to make them accountable for their behavior and to teach them acceptable behavior. The unstructured periods of the school day, between classes, during lunch hours, and immediately after school hours give disruptive students ample time to participate in a variety of unacceptable behaviors.

Vandalism and Violence

Violence and vandalism are serious problems in the public schools. These problems came to public attention in the early to mid-1970s when the Senate Subcommittee to Investigate Juvenile Delinquency began an extensive examination of that phenomenon. Much of the material collected by the subcommittee appeared to show dramatic increases in overt acts of criminal violence and vandalism on the part of students. The public became alarmed, and demands were made for Congress and the executive branch of government to "do something." Congress responded to the public's concern by mandating that the Department of Health, Education and Welfare prepare a definitive report on the status of crime, violence, and vandalism in the nation's schools. That report, which was published in 1978 as *Violent Schools—Safe Schools: The Safe School Study Report to Congress,* took three years to complete and cost $2.4 million.[31] Box 11-1 presents a few of the findings of the Safe School Study.

BOX 11-1 Violent Schools—Safe Schools

1. *Attacks:* 1.3 percent of all secondary-school pupils are attacked each month; 42 percent of those have some injury, while only 4 percent of the 1.3 percent require medical attention (0.052 percent of the total population). These attacks are 42 percent interracial and are reported to police about 30 percent of the time; and in 75 percent of the cases, offenders are known by name to the victims.

2. *Age and attacks:* although only 1.3 percent of all secondary-school pupils are attacked in one month, 36 percent of all assaults on twelve- to nineteen year-olds occur in school, while fully 50 percent of all assaulted twelve- to fifteen-year-olds are attacked in schools.
3. *Thefts:* 2 percent of all secondary-school pupils report theft of items valued over $10 in one month. About 54 percent of this theft occurs in classrooms.
4. *Robberies:* 0.05 percent of all secondary-school students are robbed by force or threat in one month; 47 percent of those robbed know their offenders by name; 9 percent of those robbed receive minor injury; 2 percent of those robbed (0.01 percent of all secondary-school students in one month) require medical attention. In most robberies the victims are the same age, sex, and race as the perpetrators.
5. *Crime costs:* 57 percent of all crime occurs in suburban schools—which comprise only 38 percent of all schools. Total crime costs equal about $200 million per year—66 percent ($132 million) for replacement and repair of the physical plant; 24 percent ($48 million) for replacement of lost equipment; and 10 percent ($20 million) for replacement of supplies and books.
6. *Location of violence:* 13 percent of all violent acts occur in the classroom; 16 percent occur in restrooms; 43 percent in hallways and [on] stairs; and 9 percent in the cafeteria.
7. *Status of offenders:* between 74–98 percent of all offenders (except trespassers and burglars) are currently students.
8. *Vandalism:* 28 percent of all schools experience vandalism in one month, with the average loss being $81 per incident.

Source: Robert J. Rubel, "Extent, Perspectives and Consequences of Violence and Vandalism in Public Schools," in *Violence and Crime in the Schools*, edited by Keith Baker and Robert J. Rubel (Lexington, Mass.: Lexington Books, 1980), p. 19.

Another dimension of violence and vandalism in the public school is the threat of assault, murder, or rape of teachers. According to the National Education Association, 70,000 teachers were assaulted in 1978.[32] If all assaults on teachers were actually reported, the number, of course, would be much higher.

In a study of 575 inner-city teachers in Los Angeles, each teacher reported that his or her environment was extremely stressful and that violence and vandalism were out of control. They reported that violence directed toward them included threats of murder, rape, actual physical assault, and injury by students with and without weapons, as well as theft, arson, and other forms of vandalism of their personal property. Open-locker searches in their schools had revealed drugs, dynamite, knives, stilettos, ammunition, rifles, and handguns. Gang warfare caused a particularly volatile situation. Not surprisingly, most of these teachers had repeatedly petitioned their principals to transfer them to less violent schools.[33]

Violence and vandalism have had a number of consequences in public schools. First, personal freedom has been lost with the rise of fear among both students and teachers. The *Safe School Study* reported that 8 percent of all large-city junior high school students had reported actually staying home at least one day in the previous month out of fear. Second, teachers become less open and outgoing; staff members do not want to stay after school to work with pupils; and staff demand greater assurances of physical safety. Third, violence and vandalism have encouraged many schools to overlook minor rule infractions, such as extorting small amounts of money or smoking marijuana. Fourth, the final link in this "chain of consequences" is that violence and vandalism contribute to the loss of respect for authority. It is apparent, then, that unsafe schools cannot be tolerated and the problem must be corrected.[34]

DELINQUENCY AND THE SCHOOL

Achievement in school, social class, learning disabilities, and absenteeism are factors in the school setting most frequently cited as related to delinquency in schools.

Achievement in School

A number of researchers have found a direct relationship between delinquent behavior and poor academic achievement.[35] The 1967 report by the Task Force on Juvenile Delinquency concluded that boys who failed in school were seven times more likely to become delinquent than those who did not fail.[36] Studies by Palmore, Short, and Strodtbeck and by West found that delinquents tend to have lower general aptitude for achievement in school or lower intelligence.[37] Studies by Glueck and Glueck, by Liddle, and by Silberberg and Silberberg blame delinquents' poor performance in school on deficient reading skills.[38] Travis Hirschi claims that the following causal chain may eventually lead to delinquent behavior:[39]

Academic incompetence	→	Poor school performance	→	Dislike of school	→	Rejection of school's authority	→	Commission of delinquent acts

However, a number of researchers have pointed out that delinquents' lack of achievement in school is related to other factors besides academic skills. Several studies have found that delinquents are more rejecting of the student role than are nondelinquents.[40] For example, Schafer and Polk assert, "There is considerable evidence that students who violate school standards pertaining to such things as smoking, truancy, tardiness, dress, classroom demeanor, relations with peers, and respect for authority are more likely to become delinquent than those who conform to such standards."[41] Ferracutti and Dinitz, Glueck and Glueck, and West also found that delinquents tend to be more careless, lazy, inattentive, and "irresponsible" in school than nondelinquents.[42]

Delinquents' performance in school may be further affected by their relationships with classmates and teachers. A number of studies have found that delinquent or delinquency-prone youngsters tend to be less popular and have poorer relations with classmates and peers in school than nondelinquents.[43] In addition, several researchers relate delinquent behavior to the absence of warm, supportive relations between teachers and students.[44] In this regard, Cardinelli found that schools tended to have more problems when teachers lacked genuine interest in students, and Goldman further observed that good relationships among administrators, teachers, students, and even school custodians were associated with low levels of school vandalism.[45]

In short, the evidence points clearly to the conclusion that poor achievement in school is directly related to delinquent behavior, but the explanations for poor academic achievement are more complex than lack of general aptitude or intelligence.

Social Status and Delinquency in the School

Albert K. Cohen's influential study of delinquent boys was one of the most comprehensive analyses ever undertaken of the role of the school in the development of delinquent subcultures. Working class boys, as was discussed in Chapter 6, feel status deprivation when they become aware that they are unable to compete with middle-class youths in the school. Although avoiding contact with middle-class youths might solve the problem, working class boys cannot do this because they are forced to attend middle-class schools established upon middle-class values. Consequently, they reject middle-class values and attitudes and form delinquent subcultures, which provide them the status denied in school and elsewhere in society.[46] Jackson Toby, in a study based on a variation of Cohen's thesis, contends that a lower-class background makes school success difficult because lower-class youths lack verbal skills and encouragement from home.[47] John C. Phillips proposes the steps by which low status in school can lead to deviant behavior:[48]

| School status | → | [Negative] affect toward school | → | Involvement in an anti-school subgroup | → | Deviant behavior |

However, the relationship between social class and delinquency in the school has been challenged. Cohen's argument that middle-class rewards, such as high grades, are of great importance to working-class boys has been particularly disputed. Polk, Frease, and Richmond also found that any boy who does poorly in school, regardless of class background, is more likely to become involved in delinquent behavior than one who performs well in school.[49] Arthur Stinchcombe concluded that rebellious behavior is largely "a reaction to the school itself and to its promises, not a failure of the family or community."[50]

On balance, although the existence of a relationship between social class and delinquency in the school has mixed support, a relationship between school achievement and delinquency is much clearer.

Learning Disabilities (LD)

The link between juvenile delinquency and learning disabilities is at present one of the most popular subjects for research in juvenile corrections. LD research, which is still in its infancy, has its origin in 1948, when scientists labeled an organic disorder in children a "hyperkinetic impulse."[51] The most widely used definition of learning disabilities is the one adopted by the National Advisory Committee on Handicapped Children:

> *Children with special learning disabilities exhibit a disorder in one or more of the basic psychological processes involved in understanding or using spoken or written language. They may be manifested in disorders of listening, thinking, talking, reading, writing, or arithmetic. They include conditions which have been referred to as perceptual handicaps, brain injury, minimal brain dysfunction, dyslexia, developmental aphasia, etc. They do not include learning problems which are due to visual, hearing, or motor handicaps, to mental retardation, emotional disturbance, or to environmental disadvantages.*[52]

States' definitions of learning disorders vary. Some state legislatures refer to children with "minimal brain dysfunction"[53] or "specific learning disabilities,"[54] or to those "who deviate from the so-called normal person in physical, mental, social or emotional characteristics or abilities to such an extent that specialized training techniques and equipment are required."[55]

Terms used to designate the problems of learning disabilities include:[56]

aphasia	dysphasia
alexia	dyslexia
acululia	dyscalculia
apraxia	dyspraxia
apraphia	dysgraphia

Causes of LD include birth injury or anything contributing to premature birth; infant or childhood disease; environmental trauma, such as a head injury; or lack of proper health care or nutrition.[57]

The existence of a link between learning disabilities and juvenile delinquency has received considerable debate. In 1977, a LEAA study developed two hypotheses for the link: a susceptibility rationale and a school failure rationale.[58] The susceptibility rationale is based on the fact that a variety of socially troublesome personality characteristics accompany certain types of LD, such as impulsiveness and an inability to learn from experience. Children with these characteristics, according to this hypothesis, develop poor self-concepts as LD leads to uncontrollable antisocial behavior. Accordingly, they are placed with adolescents who are accepting of delinquent norms. The second rationale rests on the labeling of the child: LD children acquire a negative self-concept because they are labeled as failures both by peers and by adults. Thus, no matter how hard LD children try, they are bound to fail in the normal classroom setting. They may choose to withdraw, or they may attempt to gain recognition by acting out.

Those who acknowledge the LD/JD link generally postulate some variation of the following pattern in a youth moving from learning disabilities to delinquent behavior: because of their learning disabilities, some children experience early school failure, which leads to frustration and acting-out behavior. These children begin to involve themselves in truancy, but are apprehended and returned to school, where they experience further frustration. Accordingly, they develop a poor self-image, experience alienation, and finally are pushed out or drop out of school as a response to an overwhelming sense of defeat.[59]

Among the research supporting the existence of this link is Berman's sample of forty-five institutionalized male delinquents, 56 percent of whom were found to be learning disabled.[60] Compton's study of 444 institutionalized male delinquents found 90.4 percent to be learning disabled.[61] In a study in Washington County, Minnesota, 66 percent of the 187 clients were found to have severe learning disabilities.[62]

However, other research findings do not show a clear link between LD/JD. A four-year study for the National Center for State Courts in conjunction with the Association for Children with Learning Disabilities, designed as a comprehensive examination of the LD/JD link, failed to support a causal link between learning disabilities and delinquency. The self-report data gathered indicate that children with learning disabilities did not engage in more delinquent acts and showed these children are only slightly more likely to be caught committing delinquent acts, although apparently learning disabled children are more likely to be processed through the juvenile justice system.[63] Also, most of the studies establishing a link between LD/JD can be criticized for flaws in their methodology. For example, Compton's study must be questioned because his broad definition of LD included anything that prevented a youth from achieving success in a normal classroom setting.

On balance, although the link between LD/JD is questionable, youngsters with learning disabilities do frequently fail in school and officials of the justice system seem to be influenced by this school failure to process them through the juvenile justice system.

Absenteeism

The rates of absenteeism, including truancy and dropping out, are reaching epidemic proportions in many junior high and high schools in the United States.[64] Several studies show that school administrators rate this as their most critical disciplinary problem.[65] Absence from school is a cause of great concern even in suburban high schools.[66]

From the perspective of administrators, absenteeism creates not only problems but also solutions to some of the woes of the schools. On one hand, high absenteeism rates may jeopardize funding, since the size of the school's budget is often based on calculations of average daily attendance. Also, high absenteeism rates threaten the school's legitimacy as an institution legally required to educate all young people. But, on the other hand, high absenteeism rates both ease overcrowding and cut down on behavior problems, because many of those who are truant would cause trouble if they were in school. Of course, school administrators often suspend or expel pupils who cause trouble in the school.[67] In this regard, a West Coast teacher noted: "I don't think the school is dangerous through the day. Part of the reason is that they expelled 200 kids the first five or six months of the school year.

Some of these students were really bad. Some of these kids were sent to an alternative school as soon as they enrolled."[68]

From the societal perspective, high school absenteeism presents more serious problems. The short-term problems come from the delinquency which occurs when large numbers of adolescents are out of school with nothing constructive to occupy their time. Long-term difficulties arise from the failure of students with high absenteeism rates to acquire the credentials or basic competencies necessary to function successfully as adults in work environments.[69]

Explanations for high school absenteeism focus on society, school, and student levels. Several are related to problems in society. The correspondence argument contends that differential rates of absenteeism and high school completion reflect inequalities in the social order and are beyond the control of school administrators. The citizenship argument attributes high absenteeism rates to the school's failure to provide activities suited to all students' roles as citizens. The articulation argument views high absenteeism as a reflection of the loose linkages among social institutions in society, meaning that students no longer perceive school as useful for meeting their future needs. Explanations for absenteeism that focus on the school are related to the influence of peer groups with negative attitudes toward school, the alienation that students feel because of their lack of participation in school governance, and the fear of violence in the school. Explanations that focus on students place the blame on those who have inadequate socialization in childhood, who lack parental support, and who find other activities more interesting.[70]

An ESEA Title II project in St. Paul, Minnesota describes the student likely to become a dropout as:

> . . . one who is unable to function properly within the traditional classroom setting; who is generally recognized as an underachiever . . . ; who fails to establish goals regarding his future occupation; who has a record of tardiness as well as absenteeism; who lacks motivation, direction, and drive; who comes from a stressful family situation which appears to have a detrimental effect; who is hostile toward adults and authority figures; who has difficulty with community agencies and the law; who generally is not involved in any school activities; and, finally, who has had serious economic problems which threaten the completion of school.[71]

The relation of delinquency to absenteeism is a complex one. Delbert Elliott and Harwin Voss carried out the authoritative study of the school dropout. They studied 2721 youths who entered the ninth grade in seven junior high schools in 1963, following them through their normal graduation year of 1967. Elliott and Voss discovered that the dropouts had much higher rates of police contact, officially recorded delinquent behavior, and self-reported delinquent behavior while in school than did those who graduated. However, the dropouts' delinquent behavior declined dramatically in the period immediately after they left school and then continued to decline. In contrast, the official delinquency and self-reported delinquency of the youths who remained in school gradually increased during these years.[72]

Elliott and Voss postulated a chain of behavior in which delinquency increased the probability of dropping out, but in which dropping out decreased the incidence of subsequent delinquent behavior. Marriage and employment, which helped the dropouts make the transition from adolescent to adult roles, were suggested as the factors accounting for the lowered delinquency after leaving school.[73]

RIGHTS OF STUDENTS

The school's authority over students comes from two principal sources: the concept of *in loco parentis* and state enabling statutes.[74] Reutter summarized *in loco parentis* as follows:

> *The common law measure of the rights and duties of school authorities relative to pupils attending school is the* in loco parentis *concept. This doctrine holds that school authorities stand in the place of the parent while the child is at school. Thus, school personnel may establish rules for the educational welfare of the child and may inflict punishments for disobedience. The legal test is whether a reasonably knowledgeable and careful parent might so act. The doctrine is used not only to support rights of school authorities, . . . but to establish their responsibilities concerning such matters as injuries that may befall students.*[75]

State enabling statutes authorize local school boards to establish reasonable rules and regulations for operating and keeping order in schools, which do not necessarily have to be in written form.[76] A classic statement on this type of authority was made in the 1966 case of *Burnside v. Byars:*

> *The establishment of an educational program requires the formulation of rules and regulations necessary for the maintenance of an orderly program of classroom learning. In formulating regulations, including those pertaining to the discipline of schoolchildren, school officials have a wide latitude of discretion. But the school is always bound by the requirement that the rules and regulations must be reasonable. It is not for us to consider whether such rules are wise or expedient but merely whether they are a reasonable exercise of the power and discretion of the school authorities.*[77]

The courts have become involved in the schools through a number of important areas: procedural due process, freedom of expression, hair and dress codes, and safety.[78]

Procedural Due Process

Dixon v. Alabama State Board of Education (1961) was a major breakthrough for students' rights because the appeals court held for the first time that due process requires a student to receive notice and some opportunity for hearing before being expelled for misconduct.[79] In 1969, the U.S. Supreme Court issued its far-reaching decision in *Tinker* v. *Des Moines Independent School District,* declaring that students do not shed their constitutional rights of freedom of speech at the schoolhouse gate.[80] In January 1975, the U.S. Supreme Court took up the problem of due process in the schools, stating in *Goss* v. *Lopez* that students may not be summarily suspended, even for one day, without following fundamentally fair and fact-finding procedures.[81] In suspensions of ten days or less, a student is entitled to oral or written notice of the charges, an explanation of the evidence, and an opportunity to be heard. *Wood* v. *Strickland,* issued a month after the *Goss* decision, found that school officials may be subject to suit and held financially liable for damages if they deprive a student deliberately of his or her clearly established constitutional rights.[82]

The issue of corporal punishment came before the U.S. Supreme Court in *Baker* v. *Owen* and *Ingraham* v. *Wright.*[83] Although *Baker* v. *Owen* merely affirmed a lower court ruling (423 U.S. 907, affirming 395 F. Supp. 294 [1975]), *Ingraham* v. *Wright* held that reasonable corporal punishment is not cruel and unusual punishment under the Eighth Amendment to the U.S. Constitution.

Freedom of Expression

A number of court cases have defined students' rights to freedom of religion and expression in schools. In *West Virginia State Board of Education* v. *Barnette,* the Supreme Court held that students could not be compelled to salute the flag if that action violated their religious rights.[84] In *Tinker,* the wearing of black arm bands was declared symbolic speech and, therefore, within the protection of the First Amendment.[85]

Hair and Dress Codes

Court cases testing the power of school administrators to suspend students for violations of hair and dress codes were widespread in the late 1960s and early 1970s. In *Yoo* v. *Moynihan,* a student's right to style his hair was held to be under the definition of his or her constitutional right to privacy.[86] Then, in *Richards* v. *Thurston,* the Court ruled that a student's right to wear long hair derived from his interest in personal liberty.[87] In *Crossen* v. *Fatsi,* a dress code prohibiting "extreme style and fashion" was ruled unconstitutionally vague, unenforceable, and an invasion of the student's right to privacy.[88] Other decisions have held that schools cannot prohibit the wearing of slacks,[89] dungarees,[90] or hair "falling loosely about the shoulders."[91]

Safety

As a result of limitations on the school concerning the rules under which youth could be disciplined (*Tinker*) and because of the requirements for procedural due process imposed upon school administrators taking disciplinary action (*Goss, Ingraham,* and others), local school authorities have become increasingly wary of using tough methods to discipline students. Principals became reluctant, for example, to suspend youths for acts such as acting insubordinate, wearing outlandish clothing, loitering in halls, and creating classroom disturbances, which would have drawn a quick notice of suspension only a few decades earlier. Thus, increased judicial intervention in the academic area has contributed to (but has not caused) an increase in unruly behavior, and thereby has reduced the safety of students in the public schools.[92]

In sum, judicial intervention in the school has had both positive and negative impacts. Because the courts have made it clear students do not shed their constitutional rights at the schoolgates, students' rights are less likely to be abused than in the past. However, because school administrators often perceive themselves as handcuffed by recent court decisions, they have become reluctant to take firm and forceful action against disruptive students, with the result that violence and delinquency in the schools has increased.

POLICY IMPLICATIONS

The school experience cannot be overlooked in an examination of delinquency in American society. Feldhusen, Thurston, and Benning's longitudinal study of a decade ago found school relationships and experiences to be the third most predictive factor in delinquency, exceeded only by family and peer group relationships.[93] Hirschi, in assessing the independent effect of each variable in his study, found that liking school proved more closely associated with nondelinquency than did either communication with father or liking teachers, and that it was almost as closely associated with nondelinquency as was delinquent friends.[94] Elliott and Voss found that for males, limited academic achievement, school normlessness, association with delinquent classmates, and commitment to peers are the most powerful predictors of delinquency. But for females, they found, parental rejection, school normlessness, association with delinquent classmates, and commitment to peers are the best predictors of delinquency.[95] Stinchcombe found that failure in school leads to rebelliousness—which leads to more failure.[96]

These and other studies support the belief that the school is one of the critical social contexts for the generation of delinquent behavior. To reduce delinquency in the schools, the quality of the school experience must be improved so that youngsters will be motivated to achieve their maximum potential, and the creation of overlapping relationships between the school, the family, and the community must be encouraged.

These two goals cannot be separated. That is, delinquency and the quality of the public school experience must be analyzed within the larger context of school-community relationships. This chapter has again emphasized the belief that delinquent behavior can be best understood as the product of complex socialization processes operating at many different levels within the social system. The reduction of delinquency in the schools, then, requires a comprehensive approach that includes home, school, church, youth groups, and other institutions and persons who participate in the social processes affecting the lives of students (Figure 11-1 compares integrated versus unintegrated sets of role patterns involving the school, family, and community).[97]

A number of steps must be taken to achieve these two goals. First, education must

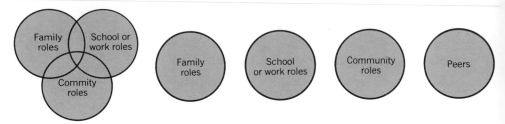

Figure 11-1 Integrated and Nonintegrated Role Patterns

Source: Paul C. Friday and John Halsey, "Patterns of Social Relationships and Youth Crime: Social Integration and Prevention," in *Youth Crime and Juvenile Justice,* edited by Friday and V. Lorne Stewart (New York: Praeger Publishers, 1977), p. 149.

be made more individually oriented. Achievement should be defined in terms of a student's individual progress, not that of others in the class. This is particularly important for low achievers, who need the best facilities and the most effective teachers to allow them to realize their potentials.[98]

Second, tracking systems, which classify students according to their abilities, should be abolished. Tracking systems tend to establish class systems within the school.[99] In schools that use tracking systems, lower-track students typically receive lower grades than other students, develop a value system that rewards misbehavior rather than the academic success they feel they can never achieve, and lose self-esteem from being stigmatized.[100]

Third, alternative schools must be expanded throughout the nation. Alternative schools, the most widely used means of delinquency prevention in the educational system, often are able to succeed with pupils who have been failures in the public school system. These schools have smaller classes and teachers trained to work with this type of population who are usually able to deal more appropriately with negative behavior in the classroom. Alternative schools will be examined more extensively in Chapter 19, but here a student in an alternative school explains why she prefers that setting to the public school:

> *The teachers here are fantastic. They're not just a teacher but here to be your friend, too. If you have a problem, you can tell them that you want to talk and they will always talk with you. In the public school, all the teachers are concerned about is your stupid work. They give you work that you don't understand and then they pass you [on to the next grade] just to get rid of you. It is one less student they have to worry about. Here, the classes are smaller, the teachers are younger, and there is not a whole lot of generation gap between us. They know what is going on, and a whole lot of them have experienced their own problems on the streets. They have worked with students like us before, and they are qualified in what they do. They take time to make sure you understand what they teach.*[101]

Fourth, students must be guaranteed three rights: the opportunity to attend a safe and lawful school, the opportunity to be taught by qualified and dedicated teachers, and the opportunity to be involved in the operation of the school. Safety is one of the most important prerequisites of involvement in the educational process; that is, unless students feel safe, they are unlikely to involve themselves very deeply in the school experience. To ensure safety, a critical problem in large urban schools, administrators must take firm action to reduce the violence and delinquency in these settings.

Good teaching is still the first line of defense against misbehavior.[102] Good teaching can also make students feel wanted and accepted and can encourage students to have more positive and successful experiences in the classroom. Gertrude Moskowitz and John L. Hayman, in a research project at three inner-city junior high schools in Philadelphia, found significant differences between effective and ineffective teachers. The best teachers expressed their feelings and enabled the students to express their emotions. They combated student boredom and restlessness with timely topics, discussions, and open-ended questions. They smiled more than ineffective teachers did and when they disciplined students, they did not raise their voices.[103]

Students also have the right to be involved in the operation of the school. Youths too frequently see themselves as immersed in an educational system that is beyond their control and unresponsive to their needs. This perception, of course, does little to increase an adolescent's desire to maintain or create positive relationships with teachers, counselors, or administrators.[104]

Fifth, schools should adopt more flexible hours and schedules so that students can become oriented to the world of work. Because modern society has extended the period of adolescence, thereby isolating the individual from the working world, schools should incorporate work into education, particularly for those between the ages of 13 and 15. The value of such experiences is that they may foster the establishment of positive work role relationships at the peak age of delinquency involvement, thus reducing the negative effects of strong peer role relationships or lack of intimate role relationships.[105]

Finally, the community at large must become involved in the school to a greater extent. One way to achieve this goal would be to include community studies in the secondary educational process, allowing representatives from various parts of the community to interact with students and explain their roles in society. Another way would be for the school to open its facilities for community events as well as to sponsor a wide range of activities designed to integrate the family, community, and students. Or families and other community members could be used more in the actual education of youth. For example, parents and elderly people could become teacher aides, on a volunteer or paid basis. Finally, joint classes for parents and children could be conducted. Such classes, which could focus on family relations, community services, or politics, might also have an effect on parents' attitudes toward education and school.[106]

In sum, to reduce the amount of delinquency generated by the school, policymakers are challenged to improve the quality of the school experience and to develop social networks linking the school with community institutions and agencies.

SUMMARY

Historically, the school has been acknowledged as an important agent in the socialization of children, but today public education is under extensive criticism. Public schools are widely accused of being repressive and of failing in their task of educating and socializing American youth. In addition, in the 1970s, vandalism and violence became serious problems in many schools. These general problems lead to lower academic achievements and to unsafe conditions on school grounds for both students and school officials. Level of achievement in school appears to be directly related to delinquent behavior, while learning disabilities and absenteeism from school are more indirectly related. The legal context, in terms of court decisions, has provided the mechanism for students to regain their rights to free speech and due process when they enter the school gate. Interest groups in the political arena have encouraged the courts to become involved in the school. To improve public schools today, public policy must be directed to two additional goals: the quality of the school experience must be improved so that youngsters will be motivated to achieve their maximum potential, and school-community networks must be reestablished.

Discussion Questions

1. What is the relationship between repressive education and delinquency?
2. What are the consequences of violence and vandalism in the public school?
3. What factors are most frequently cited as contributing to the link between schools and delinquency? Rank them in importance.
4. Discuss the rights of students in the public school. What are the positive and negative aspects of the movement to ensure due process rights to students?
5. What kind of policy is needed to reduce the amount of delinquency in the public school?

References

Baker, Keith, and Rubel, Robert J. *Violence and Crime in the Schools*. Lexington, Mass.: Lexington Books, 1980.

Cusick, Philip A. *Inside High School*. New York: Holt, Rinehart, & Winston, 1967.

Elliott, Delbert S., and Voss, Harwin L. *Delinquency and Dropout*. Lexington, Mass.: Lexington Books, 1974.

Holt, John. *Why Children Fail*. New York: Pitman, 1967.

Kvaraceus, W. C. *Juvenile Delinquency and the School*. New York: World Book Company, 1945.

Kozol, Jonathan. *Death at an Early Age*. Boston: Little, Brown & Company, 1968.

Polk, Kenneth, and Schafer, Walter E., eds. *Schools and Delinquency*. Englewood Cliffs, N.J.: Prentice-Hall, 1972.

Silberman, Charles. *Crisis in the Classroom*. New York: Random House, 1970.

Stinchcombe, Arthur L. *Rebellion in a High School*. Chicago: Quadrangle Press, 1964.

Wall, John S.; Hawkins, J. David; Lishner, Denise; and Mark Fraser. *Report of the National Juvenile Assessment Centers Juvenile Delinquency Prevention: A Compendium of 36 Program Models*. Washington, D.C.: U.S. Government Printing Office, 1981.

U.S. Department of Health, Education and Welfare. *Violent Schools—Safe Schools: The Safe School Study Report to Congress*. Washington, D.C.: U.S. Government Printing Office, 1977.

FOOTNOTES

1. Interviewed in October 1980.

2. Interviewed in July 1982.

3. Interviewed in March 1981.

4. Jonathan Kozol, *Death at an Early Age* (Boston: Little, Brown & Company, 1968).

5. John Holt, *Why Children Fail* (New York: Pitman, 1967).

6. Herbert Kohl, *Thirty-Six Children* (New York: Random House, 1968).

7. Frank R. Scarpitti, *Social Problems* (New York: Holt, Rinehart, & Winston, 1974), p. 219.

8. Joel H. Spring, *Education and the Rise of the Corporate State* (Boston: Beacon Press, 1972), p. 62.

9. Joan Newman and Graeme Newman, "Crime and Punishment in the Schooling Process: A Historical Analysis," in *Violence and Crime in the Schools*, edited by Keith Baker and Robert J. Rubel (Lexington, Mass.: Lexington Books, 1980), p. 11.

10. Horace Mann and the Reverend M. H. Smith, *Sequel to the So-Called Correspondence between the Rev. M. H. Smith and Horace Mann* (Boston: W. B. Fowle, 1847).

11. John Dewey, "My Pedagogic Creed" (1897), reprinted in *Teaching in American Culture*, edited by K. Gezi and J. Meyers (New York: Holt, Rinehart, & Winston, 1968).

12. *Brown v. Board of Education of Topeka, Kansas* (1954).

13. Martin Gold, "School Experiences, Self-Esteem, and Delinquent Behavior: A Theory for Alternative Schools," *Crime and Delinquency* 24 (1978), pp. 294–295.

14. Charles Silberman, *Crisis in the Classroom* (New York: Random House, 1970), p. 234.

15. Philip A. Cusick, *Inside High School* (New York: Holt, Rinehart, & Winston, 1967), p. 217.

16. Craig Haney and Philip G. Zimbardo, "The Blackboard Penitentiary—It's Tough to Tell a High School from a Prison," *Psychology Today* 9 (June 1975), p. 106.

17. D. H. Hargreaves, *Social Relations in a Secondary School* (London: Routledge & Kegan Paul, 1967); W. C. Kvaraceus, *Juvenile Delinquency and the School* (New York: World Book Company, 1945); K. Polk and F. L. Richmond, "Those Who Fail," in *Schools and Delinquency*, edited by Polk and W. E. Schafer (Englewood Cliffs, N.J.: Prentice-Hall, 1972); W. M. Ahlstrom and R. J. Havighurst, *400 Losers* (San Francisco: Jossey-Bass, 1971).

18. R. D. Vinter and R. C. Sarri, "Malperformance in the Public School: A Group-Work Approach," *Social Work* 10 (1965), p. 9.

19. Ibid.

20. Albert K. Cohen, *Delinquent Boys: The Culture of the Gang* (New York: Free Press, 1955), pp. 123–124.

21. Vinter and Sarri, "Malperformance."

22. R. Turner, *The Social Context of Ambition* (San Francisco: Chandler, 1964), p. 43.

23. M. Csikszentimihalyi, R. Larson, and S. Prescott, "The Ecology of Adolescent Activities and Experience," *Journal of Youth and Adolescence* 6 (1977), pp. 281–294.

24. U. Bronfenbrenner, "The Origins of Alienation," *Scientific American* 231 (1973), pp. 41–53.

25. Robert H. Lauer, *Social Problems and the Quality of Life,* 2d ed. (Dubuque, Iowa: Wm. C. Brown Company Publishers, 1982), p. 446.

26. William E. Schafer and Kenneth Polk, "Delinquency and the Schools," in *Task Force Report: Juvenile Delinquency and Youth Crime* (Washington, D.C.: U.S. Government Printing Office, 1967), p. 224.

27. J. Feldhusen, T. Thurston, and J. Benning, "A Longitudinal Study of Delinquency and Other Aspects of Children's Behavior," *International Journal of Criminology and Penology* 1 (1973), pp. 341–351.

28. Referred to in Jeane Westin, "Let's End Family Warfare," *PTA Magazine* 68 (November 1973), p. 14.

29. J. W. Trent et al., "Technology, Education, and Human Development," *Educational Record* 67 (Spring 1965), p. 97.

30. Refer to Chapter 9 for these studies.

31. U.S. Department of Health, Education and Welfare, *Violent Schools—Safe Schools: The Safe School Study Report to Congress* (Washington, D.C.: U.S. Government Printing Office, 1977), p. 177.

32. Alfred M. Bloch, M.D., and Ruther Reinhardt Bloch, "Teachers—A New Endangered Species?," in *Violence and Crime in the Schools,* p. 82.

33. Ibid., p. 84.

34. Robert J. Rubel, "Extent, Perspectives, and Consequences of Violence and Vandalism in Public Schools," in *Violence and Crime in the Schools,* pp. 24–27.

35. L. Empey and S. G. Lubeck, *Explaining Delinquency* (Lexington, Mass.: Lexington Books, 1971); M. Gold, *Status Forces in Delinquent Boys* (Ann Arbor, Mich.: Institute for Social Research, University of Michigan, 1963); M. Gold and D. W. Mann, "Delinquency as Defense," *American Journal of Orthopsychiatry* 42 (1972), pp. 463–479; T. Hirschi, *Causes of Delinquency* (Berkeley: University of California Press, 1969); H. B. Kaplan, "Sequelae of Self-Derogation: Predicting from a General Theory of Deviant Behavior," *Youth and Society* 7 (1975), pp. 171–197; and A. L. Rhodes and J. J. Reiss, Jr., "Apathy, Truancy, and Delinquency as Adaptations to School Failure," *Social Forces* 48 (1969), pp. 12–22.

36. Task Force on Juvenile Delinquency, *Juvenile Delinquency and Youth Crime* (Washington, D.C.: U.S. Government Printing Office, 1967), p. 51.

37. E. B. Palmore, "Factors Associated with School Dropouts and Juvenile Delinquency among Lower-Class Children," in *Society and Education,* edited by R. J. Havighurst, B. L. Neugarten, and J. M. Falls (Boston: Allyn & Bacon, 1967); J. F. Short and F. L. Strodtbeck, *Group Process and Gang Delinquency* (Chicago: University of Chicago Press, 1965); and D. J. West, *Present Conduct and Future Delinquency* (New York: International Universities Press, 1969).

38. S. Glueck and E. Glueck, *Unraveling Juvenile Delinquency* (Cambridge: Harvard University Press, 1950); G. P. Liddle, "Existing and Projected Research on Reading in Relationship to

Delinquency," in *Role of the School in Prevention of Juvenile Delinquency,* edited by W. R. Carriker (Washington, D.C.: U.S. Government Printing Office, 1963); and N. E. Silberberg and M. C. Silberberg, "School Achievement and Delinquency," *Review of Educational Research* 41 (1971), pp. 17–31.

39. Hirschi, *Causes of Delinquency.*

40. M. L. Erickson, M. L. Scott, and L. T. Empey, *School Experience and Delinquency* (Provo, Utah: Brigham Young University, 1964); R. J. Havighurst et al., *Growing Up in River City* (New York: John Wiley & Sons, 1962); W. Healy and A. F. Bronner, *New Light on Delinquency and Its Treatment* (New Haven: Yale University Press, 1963), W. C. Kvaraceus, *Juvenile Delinquency and the School* (New York: World Book Company, 1945).

41. Schafer and Polk, "Delinquency and the Schools," p. 233.

42. F. Ferracutti and S. Dinitz, "Cross-Cultural Aspects of Delinquent and Criminal Behavior," in *Aggression,* edited by S. H. Frazier (Baltimore: Williams & Williams, 1974); Glueck and Glueck, *Unraveling Juvenile Delinquency;* and West, *Present Conduct and Future Delinquency.*

43. Glueck and Glueck, *Unraveling Juvenile Delinquency;* Ferracutti and Dinitz, "Delinquent and Criminal Behavior"; Havighurst et al., *Growing Up in River City;* West, *Present Conduct and Future Delinquency.*

44. C. F. Cardinelli, "Relationship of Interaction of Selected Personality Characteristics of School Principal and Custodian with Sociological Variables to School Vandalism." (Ph.D. diss., Michigan State University, 1969); Ferracutti and Dinitz, "Delinquent and Criminal Behavior"; Gold, *Status Forces in Delinquent Boys;* N. Goldman, "A Socio-Psychological Study of School Vandalism," *Crime and Delinquency* 7 (1961), pp. 221–230; M. J. Hindelang, "Causes of Delinquency: A Partial Replication and Extension," *Social Problems* 20 (1973), pp. 471–487; Hirschi, *Causes of Delinquency;* C. W. Thomas, G. A. Kreps, and R. J. Cage, "An Application of Compliance Theory to the Study of Juvenile Delinquency," *Sociology and Social Research* 61 (1977), pp. 156–175; and S. Vandenberg, "Student Alienation: Orientation toward and Perceptions of Aspects of Educational Social Structure," *Urban Education* 10 (1975), pp. 262–278.

45. Cardinelli, "Interaction of Selected Personality Characteristics"; and Goldman, "School Vandalism."

46. Cohen, *Delinquent Boys.*

47. Jackson Toby, "Orientation to Education as a Factor in the School Maladjustment of Lower-Class Children," *Social Forces* 35 (1957), pp. 259–266.

48. John C. Phillips, "The Creation of Deviant Behavior in American High Schools," in *Violence and Crime in the Schools,* p. 124.

49. Kenneth Polk and F. Lynn Richmond, "Those Who Fail," in *Schools and Delinquency,* p. 67.

50. Arthur L. Stinchcombe, *Rebellion in a High School* (Chicago: Quadrangle Press, 1964), p. 179.

51. Karen V. Unger, "Learning Disabilities and Juvenile Delinquency," *Journal of Juvenile and Family Courts* 29 (1978), pp. 25–30.

52. *Issues in the Classification of Children,* edited by N. Hobbs, vol. 1 (San Francisco: Jossey-Bass, 1975), quoted in J. Podboy and W. Mallory, "The Diagnostic of Specific Learning Disabilities in a Juvenile Delinquent Population," *Federal Probation* 42 (1978).

53. Arizona Revised Statutes, §15–1011(3)(g) 1975; but the term "learning disabled" was used after July 1, 1980.

54. Florida Statutes Annotated §228:041(19) (West Supp. 1965).

55. Hawaii Revised Statutes §301–21(1)(1968).

56. Wilma Jo Bush and Kenneth W. Waugh, *Diagnosing Learning Disabilities,* 2d ed. (Columbus, Ohio: Charles E. Merrill Publishing Company, 1971), pp. 8–9.

57. Unger, "Learning Disabilities and Juvenile Delinquency"; and Mulligan, "Dyslexia, Specific Learning Disability and Delinquency," *Juvenile Justice* 23 (1976), pp. 20, 22.

58. C. A. Murray, quoted in B. McCullough, B. Zaremba, and W. Rich, "The Role of the Juvenile Justice System in the Link between Learning Disabilities and Delinquency," *State Court Journal* 3 (Spring 1979), p. 24.

59. Charles H. Post, "The Link between Learning Disabilities and Juvenile Delinquency: Cause, Effect and 'Present Solutions'" *Juvenile Family Court Journal* 32 (March 1981), p. 61.

60. A. Berman, "Delinquents are Disabled: An Innovative Approach to the Prevention and Treatment of Juvenile Delinquency," Final report of the Neuropsychology Diagnostic Laboratory at the Rhode Island Training Schools, December, 1974.

61. R. C. Compton, in *Youth in Trouble,* edited by B. L. Kratoville (San Rafael, Calif.: Academic Therapy Publications, 1974), pp. 44–56.

62. Podboy and Mallory, "Diagnostic of Specific Learning Disabilities."

63. McCullough, Zaremba, and Rich, "Role of the Juvenile Justice System," p. 45.

64. *Newsweek* (27 August 1979), p. 44.

65. J. S. Wright, "Student Attendance: What Relates Where?" *NASSP Bulletin* 62 (February 1978), pp. 115–117; D. Duke, "How Administrators View the Crisis in School Discipline," *Phi Delta Kappa* 59 (January 1978), pp. 325–330; J. Meyer, C. Chase-Dunn, and J. Inverarity, *The Expansion of Autonomy of Youth: Responses of the Secondary School to the Problems of Order in the 1960s* (Stanford: Laboratory for Social Research, Stanford University, 1971).

66. "The 2.4 Million Children Who Aren't in School," *U.S. News and World Report,* March 15, 1976, pp. 43–44.

67. Beatrice F. Birman and Gary Natriello, "Perspectives on Absenteeism in High Schools: Multiple Explanations for an Epidemic," in *Violence and Crime in the Schools,* p. 170.

68. Interviewed in June 1982.

69. Birman and Natriello, "Absenteeism in High Schools," p. 170.

70. Ibid., pp. 171–175.

71. National Advisory Council on Supplementary Centers and Services, *Dropout Prevention* (Washington, D.C.: U.S. Government Printing Office, 1975), p. 2.

72. Delbert S. Elliott and Harwin L. Voss, *Delinquency and Dropout* (Lexington, Mass.: Lexington Books, 1974), pp. 127–128.

73. Ibid.

74. S. Goldstein, "The Scope and Sources of School Board Authority to Regulate Student Conduct and Status: A Nonconstitutional Analysis," 117 *U. Pa. L. Rev.* 373, 1969.

75. E. Edmund Reutter, Jr., *Legal Aspects of Control of Student Activities by Public School Authorities* (Topeka, Kans.: National Organization on Legal Problems of Education, 1970).

76. *Hanson* v. *Broothby,* 318 F.Supp. 1183 [D.Mass., 1970].

77. 363 F.2d 744 (5th Cir. 1966).

78. This section on the rights of students is derived from Robert J. Rubel and Arthur H. Goldsmith, "Reflections on the Rights of Students and the Rise of School Violence," in *Violence and Crime in the Schools,* pp. 73–77.

79. 294 F.2d 150, 158 (5th Gr., 1961, cert. den., 368 U.S. 930).

80. 393 U.S. 503.

81. 419 U.S. 565.

82. 420 U.S. 308.

83. *Baker* v. *Owen* (423 U.S. 907, affirming 395 F.Supp. 294 [1975]); and *Ingraham* v. *Wright* (430 U.S. 651 [1977]).

84. 319 U.S. 624.

85. 393 U.S. 503.

86. 20 Conn. Supp. 375 [1969].

87. 424 F. 2d 1281 [1st Cir. 1970].

88. 309 F. Supp. 114 [1970].

89. *Scott* v. *Board of Education, U.F. School District #17, Hicksville,* 61 Misc. 2d 333, 305 N.Y.S. 2d 601 [1969].

90. *Bannister* v. *Paradis,* 316 F. Supp. 185 [1970].

91. *Richards* v. *Thurston,* 424 F. 2d 1281 [1970].

92. Rubel and Goldsmith, "Reflections on the Rights of Students," pp. 98–99.

93. J. Feldhusen, J. Thurston, and J. Benning, "A Longitudinal Study of Delinquency and Other Aspects of Children's Behavior," *International Journal of Criminology and Penology* 1 (1973), pp. 341–351.

94. Hirsch, *Causes of Delinquency,* pp. 131–132, 156.

95. Elliott and Voss, *Delinquency and Dropout,* p. 204.

96. Stinchcombe, *Rebellion in a High School,* p. 158.

97. Jacqueline R. Scherer, "School-Community Relations Network Strategies," in *Violence and Crime in the Schools,* p. 61.

98. Paul C. Friday and John Halsey, "Patterns of Social Relationships and Youth Crime: Social Integration and Prevention," in *Youth Crime and Juvenile Justice,* edited by P. C. Friday and V. L. Stewart (New York: Praeger, 1976), p. 149.

99. Ibid., p. 150.

100. Schafer and Polk, "Delinquency and the Schools," pp. 196–200.

101. Interviewed in May 1981.

102. M. Powell and J. Bergem, "An Investigation of the Differences Between Tenth-, Eleventh-, and Twelfth-grade 'Conforming' and 'Nonconforming' Boys," *The Journal of Educational Research* 56 (December 1962), pp. 184–190; K. H. Mueller, "Programs for Deviant Girls," in *Social Deviancy among Youth,* edited by William W. Wattenburg (Chicago: University of Chicago Press, 1966).

103. Gertrude Moskowitz and John L. Hayman, *Human Behavior* (September 1974).

104. Friday and Halsey, "Social Relationships and Youth Crime," p. 152.

105. Ibid.

106. Ibid., pp. 150–151.

INTERVIEW WITH KENNETH POLK

There is a well established conservative tradition in this country whereby we try to solve contemporary problems by restoring things back to what they were. But schools which try to go back to old time standards and old time solutions don't work.

In this interview, Kenneth Polk, professor of sociology at Oregon State University and one of the acknowledged authorities on the American school, discusses several pertinent issues concerned with the quality and effectiveness of the public schools.

Question: The American school is under extensive criticism today. Do you think this criticism is justified?

Polk: Some criticisms of the American schools are certainly justified. However, there are at least three criticisms that are not justified. First, in recent months there have been charges, especially by the United States Government, that discipline has deteriorated in schools and that violence and vandalism are increasing. The data would not seem to bear these claims out. The cost of vandalism is down, and delinquency itself seems to be on a downward trend. In talking with different school people and different teachers all around the country, I see no particular reason why there would be an increase in violence or an increase in vandalism today. Nor do I see any basis for these claims.

Second, schools are often blamed for unemployment. Many western countries, such as Australia, are creating what they call transition-education programs on the assumption that school-based programs solve the problems of unemployment. Unemployment, unfortunately, results from eco-nomic changes and the rapid discontinuation of jobs, particularly teenage jobs. If there are not jobs for young people, no amount of education by itself can function to find people jobs. Thus, it simply is not appropriate to blame schools for the economic problems of the larger society.

Third, there is a well established conservative tradition in this country whereby we try to solve contemporary problems by restoring things back to what they were. But schools which try to go back to old time standards and old time solutions don't work. Schools of 1890 and schools of 1950 are no solution to the problems of today. Schools of today want quality education and no one can fairly call them bad schools. The conservative solution of focusing on standards of discipline deflects attention away from major crises of today that are urgent in education.

But there are some criticisms of the American school that are justified and that should be corrected. Schools can be criticized for not responding quickly enough to changes of contemporary times. The curricula we have are outdated for an advanced technological society. Furthermore, we cannot ignore the devastating consequences of those who are denied credentials by the schools.

Question: How do public schools today contribute to delinquent behavior?

Polk: The schools continue to be a major force in shaping the life of the contemporary adolescent. There still is a very strong relationship between how a person stands in the school stratification system based on academic success and deviant behavior. I think this results because the successful students today have two kinds of rewards. It is the successful young person who reaps the rewards of the school in terms of activities in government, special favors, and so forth. The successful stu-

Kenneth Polk is the editor of Schools and Delinquency, one of the most widely cited volumes on schools and delinquency, coauthor of Measuring Delinquency and Delinquency Prevention Through Youth Development, and author or coauthor of many articles in professional and scientific journals on schools and delinquency. Interviewed in May 1984 and used with permission.

dents are the ones who have a sense of the future. They look forward to going to college and to the possibilities of a high status job after that. The sense of the future then also works backwards into the present because the successful student has both a rational sense of why school work is important and a rational constraint if publicly labeled as a juvenile delinquent. But the unsuccessful young person becomes marginal for two reasons. First, the routine of the school, as well as the daily life of the unsuccessful student, is unpleasant and degrading. They are told that they are incompetent, and they are pushed to the social margins.

It is at this point that my views have changed a bit on the power of the school over the life of young people. In earlier years, those of us studying marginality focused primarily on the immediate consequences of failure with students. But equally devastating consequences, which will become even more important tomorrow, is that young people are coming to understand that, as a result of their failure, they have almost no economic future as well. Increasingly, they are coming to see that rather than having a future limited to a working class job, which has been true, they now know that they may never be able to work. This is a new marginality; one with enormous potential for education.

Question: What is the relationship between economics and politics in public education?

Polk: Well, the relationship between economics and politics is one that we have to deal with on two levels. One, we can descriptively account for how education and the economy are connected. Including analysis of how economic changes are altering the life future of young people. For example, the work world has devastating changes for young people. There is now an enormous decline not only in teenage jobs, but in teenage jobs in particular sectors of the economy. Young people are losing access especially to white collar work (the sector expanding most rapidly for adults). The particular kinds of jobs that young people used to do are increasingly being closed off. This knowledge must be fed back into the educational system.

Policy is another level that we must deal with the relationship between economy and education. A conservative trend is influencing policy today. This trend has to do with enforcing standards, improving discipline, and bringing control in the classroom. It certainly has to do with each crisis in crime control and delinquency control in the United States. There is no evidence that these policies are of benefit. I'm absolutely amazed that so little is known by politicians of the future changes that are occurring in employment for young people and the importance of those changes.

Question: What policy recommendations are needed to make the schools a more effective force in the prevention of juvenile delinquency?

Polk: The most important thing is to recognize the large numbers of people who are being defined as marginal by our schools. If we are going to have our future education become vital by reaching out to all young people, we must provide a wider range of success experiences and a future for all youth. Vital education must experiment with different aspects of the world of young people. Vital education must be more work oriented and must prepare young people more for their careers. It must also open up access to the work world through a combination of work and job training experience.

UNIT FOUR

THE FEMALE AND MALE DELINQUENT

CHAPTER 12

FEMALE DELINQUENCY

CHAPTER OUTLINE

What are little boys made of?
Snips and snails, and puppy dog tails,
That's what little boys are made of.
What are little girls made of?
Sugar and spice, and everything nice,
That's what little girls are made of.

Anonymous

Females . . . are now being found not only robbing banks singlehandedly, but also committing assorted armed robberies, muggings, loan-sharking operations, extortions, murders, and a wide variety of other aggressive, violence-oriented crimes which previously involved only men.

Freda Adler[1]

In the mid-1970s, several factors converged to convince the public that changes were taking place in the rate and nature of crime among women. First, the *Uniform Crime Reports* documented a dramatic increase in crime committed by women. Second, the activities of the Symbionese Liberation Army brought into the public eye Patty Hearst, Emily Harris, and other women offenders. Two women, Sara Jane Moore and Lynette Fromme, were charged with separate attempts to assassinate President Gerald Ford. Third, Freda Adler's *Sisters in Crime* appeared and offered a plausible explanation of the new woman criminal; she described a violent, aggressive female criminal who was influenced by the women's liberation movement to commit crimes traditionally committed only by male criminals.[1]

The juvenile female offender also began to receive more attention during the 1970s. The vast amount of recent writing on female delinquency has appeared in part because of a desire to offset the preponderance of theories and studies centered on males, in part as a response to the perceived "dramatic increases" in the amount and versatility of involvement in delinquency by juvenile girls, and in part because of the unsubstantiated belief that the women's liberation movement has had a significant impact on female involvement in crime.[2] The recent research on female delinquency has examined the following assumptions:

- Females are showing increased frequency and versatility of involvement in delinquent acts.
- Sexual offenses, incorrigibility, and "running away" make up the delinquent repertoire of girls.[3]
- Female delinquents are far more abnormal and pathological than are male delinquents.[4]
- Females are less involved in delinquency than men because they are less masculine.[5]
- Social factors, such as class, societal reaction, and subcultures, are largely irrelevant to an understanding of female delinquency.[6]

- The women's liberation movement has influenced the extent and nature of female delinquency.
- Female delinquents are treated more leniently by the juvenile justice system than are male delinquents.

The biological, psychological, and sociological explanations of why females become involved in delinquent acts are examined in this chapter, and then assumptions about female delinquency, the offenses of juvenile girls, and the implications for policy are discussed.

EXPLANATIONS OF FEMALE DELINQUENCY

Earlier explanations of female delinquency focused on biological and psychological factors, but more recent explanations have examined sociological factors.

Biological Explanations

In *The Female Offender*, published in 1903, Cesare Lombroso deals with crime as atavism, or the survival of "primitive" traits in individuals.[7] First, he argues that women are more primitive, or lower on the evolutionary scale, because they are less intelligent and have fewer variations in their mental capacities than men: "even the female criminal is monotonous and uniform compared with her male companion, just as in general women are inferior to man."[8] Second, Lombroso contends that women are unable to feel pain and, therefore, are insensitive to the pain of others and lack moral refinement.[9] He states:

> Women have many traits in common with children; that their moral sense is deficient; that they are revengeful, jealous. . . . In ordinary cases these defects are neutralized by piety, maternity, want of passion, sexual coldness, weakness, and an undeveloped intelligence.[10]

Third, he argues, women are characterized by a passive and conservative approach to life. Although he admits that women's traditional sex roles in the family bind them to a more home-centered life, he insists that women's passivity can be directly traced to the "immobility of the ovule compared with the zoosperm."[11]

Lombroso contends that because most women are born with "feminine" characteristics, their innate physiological limitations protect them from crime and predispose them to live unimaginative, dull, and conforming lives. But women criminals, he argues, have inherited male characteristics, such as excessive body hair, moles, wrinkles, crow's feet, and abnormal craniums.[12] He adds that the female criminal, being doubly exceptional as a woman and as a criminal, is likely to be more vicious than the male criminal.[13]

Recently, with the biosocial revival in criminology, biological or physiological explanations for delinquency have regained some popularity. In a 1968 study,

Cowie et al. presented data on an English approved school [training school] sample which emphasize genetic factors as the major cause of delinquency.[14] These researchers even proposed that these genetic factors might be specific enough to determine the types of crimes the sexes will commit.[15] T. C. N. Gibbens also has reported a high rate of sex chromosomal abnormalities in delinquent girls.[16] Furthermore, Cowie et al. noted the above-average weight of their institutional sample and suggested that physical overdevelopment tends to draw a girl's attention to sex earlier in life, resulting in sexual promiscuity.[17] In addition, they claimed that menstruation is a distressing reminder to females that they can never be males, and that this distress makes them increasingly prone to delinquent acts.[18]

The viewpoints of Lombroso and other supporters of biological explanations for female delinquency can be regarded as merely a testimony to the historical chauvinism of males. Unfortunately, the study of female criminality has not yet fully recovered from the idea "that the cause of a socially generated phenomenon might be reduced to a genetically transmitted biological unit."[19]

Psychological Explanations

The "innate nature" of women is the basis of much of the writings on female delinquency.[20] W. I. Thomas, Sigmund Freud, Otto Pollak, and Gisela Konopka have addressed this "innate" female nature and its relationship to deviant behavior.

W. I. Thomas's works mark a transition from physiological explanations to more sophisticated theories embracing physiological, psychological, and social-structural factors. In *Sex and Society,* he suggests there are basic biological differences between the sexes. Maleness, according to Thomas, is "katabolic," from the animal force that involves a destructive release of energy and allows the possibility of creative work through this outward flow, but femaleness is "anabolic," motionless, lethargic, and conservative.[21] Thomas's underlying assumptions are physiological ones, for he credits men with higher amounts of sexual energy that lead them to pursue women for sexual pleasure. In contrast, he attributes to women maternal feelings devoid of sexuality, so that they exchange sex for domesticity.[22]

In his 1923 work *The Unadjusted Girl,* Thomas deals with female delinquency as a "normal" response under certain social conditions.[23] He argues that a girl is driven by four wishes or ambitions: the desire for new experience, for security, for response, and for recognition. He assumes that the delinquent girl's problem is not criminality but immorality, and he confines himself almost exclusively to a discussion of prostitution. The major cause of prostitution lies in the girl's need for love, and a secondary factor is her wish for recognition or ambition. Thomas maintains that it is not sexual desire that motivates delinquent girls, because they are no more passionate than nondelinquent girls, but that they are using male desire for sex to achieve their own ultimate needs.[24]

> The beginning of delinquency in girls is usually an impulse to get amusement, adventure, pretty clothes, favorable notice, distinction, freedom in the larger world. . . . The girls have usually become "wild" before the development of sexual desire, and their casual sex relations do to usually awaken

sex feeling. Their sex is used as a condition of the realization of other wishes. It is their capital.[25]

Freud's work begins with the assumption that women's sex organs make them anatomically inferior to men. Freud contends that a little girl assumes she has lost her penis as punishment and, therefore, she feels traumatized and grows up envious and revengeful. A woman becomes a mother in order to replace the "lost penis" with a baby. Freud also argues that women are inferior because they are concerned with personal matters and have little social sense.[26] Women, according to Freud, have weaker social interests than men and less capacity for the sublimation of their interests.[27]

The delinquent girl, in the Freudian perspective, is one who is attempting to be a man. Because she is aggressively rebellious, her drive to accomplishment is the expression of her longing for a penis. Obviously, this deviant girl needs to be treated so that she can adjust to her sex role.

Otto Pollak's *The Criminality of Women* (1950) advances the theory that women are more criminal than is usually believed, but that their crimes largely go unreported or are hidden. Pollak credits the nature of women themselves for the traditionally low official rates of female crime, because women are inherently deceitful and, therefore, act as instigators rather than perpetrators of criminal activity. The roles played by women are a factor in hidden crimes as well because such roles as domestics, nurses, teachers, and housewives enable them to commit undetectable crimes. The "chivalry" factor is further advanced as a root cause of hidden crime; that is, the police and the court forgive a girl for the same act for which they would convict a boy.[28]

Pollack also suggests two factors that influence girls to become juvenile delinquents. First, he says, early physical development and sexual maturity allow a girl more opportunities to engage in immoral or delinquent behavior. Second, a girl's home life, especially one who has criminal parents or grows up in a broken home, may cause her to seek outside substitutes for her poor home life. She is likely to seek the company of other maladjusted girls, and they will eventually become involved in a life of petty crimes.[29]

Gisela Konopka's study of delinquent girls links a poor home life with a deep sense of loneliness and low self-esteem. Konopka's conception of delinquency relies heavily on the notion of individual pathology, as she concludes that only a girl who is "sick" can become delinquent.[30] Konopka identifies four key factors contributing to female delinquency: (1) a uniquely dramatic biological onset of puberty; (2) a complex identification process because of a girl's competitiveness with her mother; (3) the changing cultural position of females and the resultant uncertainty and loneliness, and (4) the hostile picture that the world presents to some young girls.[31]

The psychological impairment of delinquent girls has been supported by a number of other writers. Clyde Vedder and Dora Somerville's *The Delinquent Girl* suggests that the delinquent behavior of girls usually indicates a problem of adjustment to family and social pressure.[32] R. Morris, in a study conducted in Flint, Michigan, adds that delinquent girls experience relational problems more frequently than nondelinquents.[33] Mary Riege asserts that delinquent girls evidence excessive loneliness, low self-esteem, estrangement from adults, and low capacity for friendship.[34] Werner and Smith further found in their longitudinal study that "emotional instability" and the "need for long-term mental health services in the early elementary grades" were the best prediction of delinquency in girls.[35] Finally, Wattenberg and Saunders' Detroit study found a pattern of broken or disrupted homes connected with female delinquency.[36]

The relationship between psychological impairment and delinquency in girls is also widely accepted by practitioners in the juvenile justice system. A social worker in a youth shelter put it this way:

> *A lot of these girls feel they've done something wrong and that it was their fault. They don't feel they are good for anything else. Some of their anger toward self is expressed in drug and alcohol abuse, multilating self, running away, and getting themselves into situations where they will be abused again. These girls tend to be very hard toward women because their anger is toward their mother, and very soft and flirtatious with men.*[37]

In sum, considerable research support perpetuates the notion that personal maladjustment characterizes the female delinquent. She either has a psychological problem, is unable to perform her proper sex role adequately, or suffers from the ill effects of a bad home life.[38]

Sociological Explanations

In the late 1970s and early 1980s, a number of studies proceeded from the assumption that sociological processes traditionally related to males could also affect the delinquent involvement of females. Thus, in addition to the effects of the women's liberation movement, researchers focused on such sociological factors as blocked opportunity, social control, masculinity, and the influence of peers.

The Women's Liberation Movement and Female Delinquency

Freda Adler's *Sisters in Crime* suggests that the rise in official rates of female crime reflects the changes brought about by the liberation of women. Adler says:

> *Women are no longer behaving like subhuman primates with only one option. Medical, educational, economic, political, and technological advances have freed women from unwanted pregnancies, provided them with male occupational skills, and equalized their strength with weapons. Is it any wonder that, once women were armed with male opportunities, they should strive for status, criminal as well as civic, through established male hierarchical channels?*[39]

Adler thus argues that the rise in crime among women is directly related to the fact that females are becoming more competitive with males, more aggressive, and more "masculine" in general.

Three criticisms have been leveled against the assumption that the increase in female crime figures can be traced to the women's liberation movement. First, Laura Crites points out that female offenders most often come from minority groups. They are frequently unemployed and usually are responsible for their own support and often for that of their children. In addition, their employment potential is limited in that over half have not graduated from high school and their work experience has generally been in the low-wage, low-status occupations. Crites reasons that the psychological independence and expanded economic opportunities of the women's rights movement are almost meaningless for this group; instead of being concerned with the ideological constructs of the women's liberation movement, the typical female offender is caught up in a struggle for economic, emotional, and physical survival.[40]

Second, Darrell J. Steffensmeier asserts that the women's liberation movement and changing sex roles have had no impact on levels of female crime, because "the changes we observed began prior to the late 1960s when the movement could be expected to have its greatest impact on levels of property crime."[41] That is, the movement can be shown to have had little impact because official female crime rates have gradually increased rather than rising dramatically at the time when interest in the movement sharply increased.

Third, Joseph G. Weis claims that the national arrest data and self-reports of delinquent behavior show that the new female criminal is more a social invention than an empirical reality, so that the women's liberation movement cannot be held responsible for changes in female criminal and delinquent behavior that data indicate simply have not happened.[42]

Peggy C. Giordano and Stephen A. Cernkovich add that Steffensmeier and Adler both tend to see liberation in terms of an individually held set of attitudes and behaviors.[43] However, Giordano and Cernkovich found that the concept of sex roles must be understood as multidimensional, partly because important differences exist between an offender's attitudes about women in general and herself in particular. These researchers further challenge the causal influence of the sex role attitudes of the women's liberation movement because of the fact that no systematic differences in attitudes between more and less delinquent girls are present.[44]

In sum, Freda Adler's view that there is a direct relationship between the women's liberation movement and the rise of female criminality attributes to women criminals and delinquents a set of motivations and attitudes that are quite remote from their everyday lives.[45] Giordano and Cernkovich are correct in their appraisal that female sex roles are multidimensional and require a more sophisticated analysis than one based on an individual's attitudes and behaviors.

Blocked Opportunity

The role of blocked or limited opportunity has received considerable attention in the sociological analysis of male delinquency. Strain theory explains that juveniles are "pushed" into delinquency as a result of lack of access to opportunities that are legitimate avenues for the realization of a set of success goals. Thus, those who are denied legitimate achievement of their success goals often turn to delinquency as a means of reaching desired goals or of striking back at an unfair system.[46]

The usefulness of such variables in studying female delinquency has been largely ignored because males are seen as concerned with achieving short- and long-term status and economic success, while juvenile girls are likely to be viewed as possessing no such aspirations but instead being satisfied to occupy a role dependent on males.[47] However, Datesman et al., in a 1975 study based on data collected in 1968 and 1969, found that perception of limited opportunity was more strongly related to female delinquency than it was to male delinquency. Both black and white female delinquents regarded their opportunities less positively than did the nondelinquents in their sample. Status offenders also perceived their opportunities as being less favorable than did nondelinquents.[48]

Cernkovich and Giordano, in a study of self-report data gathered from 1355 male and female high school students, showed that in general blocked opportunity was more predictive of delinquency than any other variable. But the effect of perception of blocked opportunity differed according to the racial background of the juvenile. For both male and female nonwhites, blocked opportunity had no effect whatever on subsequent delinquency involvement. Yet for white males and females, perception of limited opportunity was a strong predictor of delinquency.[49]

Overall, although strain theory has been applied solely to male delinquents, both the Datesman and the Cernkovich and Giordano studies show that the perception of blocked opportunity may be even more strongly related to female involvement in delinquency than to male involvement. Cernkovich and Giordano also suggest that the racial background of the juvenile may be more important in determining the importance of this factor on delinquency than the gender of the juvenile. The relationship between perception of blocked opportunity and female delinquency clearly needs more examination.

Social Control Theory

Travis Hirschi's social control theory states that delinquency results when a juvenile's bond to the existing social order is weakened or broken.[50] Proponents of social control theory contend that females are less involved in delinquency than males because sex role socializations result in a greater tie to the social bond for females than for males. That is, girls may have less opportunity to engage in delinquent behavior because they are more closely supervised by parents. Girls are also more dependent on others, while boys are encouraged to be more independent and achievement-oriented. Thus, differences in sex role socialization supposedly promote a greater allegiance to the social bond among girls, which insulates them from delinquency more than it does boys.[51]

Furthermore, sex role socialization results in greater belief in the legitimacy of social rules by girls than by boys, claim social control theorists. Austin Turk, analyzing the greater involvement of boys than girls in officially recorded crime, concluded that females are more likely to abide by legal norms than are males because their patterns of activity are more restricted than those of males.[52] Jensen and Eve, using the same data that Hirschi used in the development of control theory, found that it did provide Hirschi's social control perspective with some empirical support but that significant differences still remained between male and female delinquency.[53]

In sum, lack of commitment to the social bond appears to influence the development of delinquency in both boys and girls. There is some evidence that socialization practices cause adolescent girls to have stronger commitments to the social bond than do boys, with the result that girls require a greater "push" before becoming involved in delinquent acts. However, much more research is needed on the relationship between social control and female delinquency.

Masculinity Hypothesis

Several studies of female delinquents have proposed a masculinity hypothesis. Freda Adler contends that as girls become more boy-like and acquire more "masculine" traits, they become more delinquent.[54] Cullen, Golden, and Cullen found that the more adolescents (male and female) possessed "male" personality traits, the more likely they were to become involved in delinquency, but the relationship between masculinity and delinquency was stronger for males than for females.[55] Thornton and James found a moderate degree of association between masculine self-expectations and delinquency, but concluded that males were still more likely to be delinquent than females, regardless of their degree of masculinity.[56]

However, Norland et al., examining gender roles and delinquency, found that "when sex . . . and degree of social support for delinquency were held constant, males and females who hold more traditionally masculine expectations for themselves were no more likely to be highly delinquent than were their counterparts who hold less traditionally masculine expectations."[57] Giordano and Cernkovich also found no strong correlations between nontraditional sex role attitudes and female delinquency.[58]

In sum, any indicator of female delinquency appears to be more complex than the notion that as females become more male-like, they become more delinquent. Perhaps if it is applied in conjunction with another sociological explanation, the masculinity hypothesis will offer a better explanation of the relationship between sex differences and delinquency.[59]

Influence of Peer Groups

The importance of peer group influence on male delinquency has been widely documented, but friendship networks generally have been presumed to be not as important in the lives of adolescent girls.[60]

Giordano and Cernkovich, pioneering the investigation of the importance of the peer group for delinquent girls, argue that peer associations must be given a central role in understanding changing patterns of delinquency involvement with girls. In terms of the social context in which female delinquency took place, these researchers found that a girl was most likely to commit a delinquent act when she was in a mixed-sex group. The second highest number of delinquent acts were committed by a girl who was alone, then with a group of girls, with one other girl, with a group of boys, and finally with one boy. Significantly, the majority of delinquent acts occurred in a mixed-sex context with boys who were regarded simply as friends.[61] Girls, Giordano and Cernkovich reason, appear to learn delinquent modes of behavior from boys, but this does not mean that a boyfriend simply uses a girl as an "accomplice" or in some other passive role while he commits the crime. These researchers also note that other girls are the most important reference group of delinquent girls and that black females are more likely to commit delinquent acts with a group of girls than alone.[62]

Thus, some evidence exists that delinquent girls learn delinquent modes of behavior from others. But much more research is clearly needed. For example, what are the particular ways association with males exerts a delinquent influence? What other interacting variables along with friendship increase the degree of delinquency involvement among girls?

Evaluating the Explanations of Female Delinquency

The discussion of female delinquency thus leads to the conclusion that biological explanations are the least predictive factors. Assumptions of sexual inferiority appear to be tied more to the historical context of male chauvinism than to the reality of female delinquency. Personal maladjustment hypotheses may have some predictive ability in determining the frequency of delinquency in girls, but these variables, too, have been overemphasized in the past. Sociological explanations appear to be far more predictive of female delinquency. Strain theory, social control theory, and differential association theory all have received some support. Labeling, containment, and conflict theories may also be promising areas of inquiry concerning the relationship between sex differences and delinquency.[63]

EXTENT AND NATURE OF FEMALE DELINQUENCY

Three important questions have been raised about the extent and nature of female delinquency.[64] First, is female delinquency increasing? Second, are juvenile girls becoming more violent in their delinquent acts? Third, are juvenile girls' choices of delinquent acts becoming more varied?

Is Female Delinquency Increasing?

Two views have been expressed on the issue of changing patterns of female delinquency: (1) the perspective, usually based on the official statistics, that female participation in delinquency has increased significantly, particularly in areas that traditionally have been considered "masculine" crimes; and (2) the argument that not much has changed.

Official Statistics

According to the *Uniform Crime Reports,* juvenile crime among girls under eighteen more than tripled between 1960 and 1982. Arrests increased from 70,925 in 1960 to 299,061 in 1982, a rise of 321.6 percent. Violent crime (murder, robbery, and aggravated assault) among girls increased more than 509.4 percent, and property crime (burglary, larceny-theft, and motor vehicle theft) rose 487.6 percent.[65] The most rapidly increasing crimes are shown in Table 12-1.

TABLE 12-1 Increases in Crime Among Female Delinquents, 1960 and 1982

Crime	1960	1982	Percent Change
Larceny-theft	13,661	83,186	508.9
Aggravated assault	676	4,591	579.1
Robbery	355	1,752	393.5
Stolen property (buying, receiving, possessing)	189	2,197	1062.4
Driving under the influence	63	2,494	3858.7
Narcotics violations	195	10,529	5299.9

Source: U.S. Department of Justice, Federal Bureau of Investigation, *Uniform Crime Reports 1982* (Washington, D.C.: U.S. Government Printing Office, 1983), p. 173. Data reported by 7559 agencies representing an estimated 1982 population of 158,051,000.

Rita Simon, analyzing UCR statistics between 1953 and 1972, concludes that the major increases for females have been in the area of property crimes.[66] Darrell J. Steffensmeier has examined trends in female crime in rural America and has analyzed female involvement in property and violent crimes.[67] He, like Simon, concludes that the increases are largely in the area of property offenses, but he provides a different interpretation of the meaning of such changes.[68] Simon builds an opportunity theory to account for these changes as she emphasizes the greater labor force participation of women, but Steffensmeier counters with the argument that the changes are largely the result of increases in shoplifting, a relatively nonserious and traditionally female crime.[69]

Self-Report Studies

Self-report studies generally show that female involvement in delinquency has increased and that females are involved in more delinquent acts than are reflected in official statistics. The Gold and Reimer study, designed to make comparisons over a period of years, reported that female delinquency rose 22 percent between 1967 and 1972, but that the change was primarily related to the use of alcohol and drugs.[70] The Institute for Juvenile Research also found that delinquency among girls is increasing.[71] Patricia Y. Miller found that while the rate of male delinquency involvement remained relatively stable throughout the 1960s and early 1970s, female participation increased significantly.[72]

But Steffensmeier and Steffensmeier, in an attempt to compare the male/female differences in delinquency involvement over time, used a number of self-report studies conducted from 1955 through 1977 and concluded that male/female differences in self-reported delinquency have remained fairly stable over the past ten to fifteen years. Slight female gains are observed for property damage and petty theft, but no discernible changes exist in the rates for truancy, joyriding, fistfighting, gang fighting, carrying weapons, strong-arm theft, and major theft.[73]

Suzanne S. Ageton, however, using a national probability sample of adolescents to analyze the extent and nature of female delinquency from 1976 to 1980, found that the incidence of female delinquency generally declines or remains stable as girls move through adolescence, while the proportion of girls involved declines significantly over the same period. Furthermore, she concludes that delinquent behavior is not attracting the same number of females today as it did in the past. That is, fifteen–seventeen-year-old females in 1980 were significantly less involved in delinquency than were their same-age peers in 1976.[74]

In sum, official and many self-report studies show that delinquent behavior among girls has increased in the past two decades; the self-report studies also reveal that more girls are involved in delinquent behavior than is suggested in official statistics. But some evidence exists that delinquency among girls leveled off or even decreased during the late 1970s.

Are Adolescent Girls Committing More Violent Delinquent Acts?

In *Sisters in Crime,* Freda Adler argues that crime among adolescent girls is increasing because girls are abandoning the traditional three offenses, incorrigibility, running away, and promiscuity, and are becoming involved instead in more aggressive and violent acts.[75] As she reported:

> *"I know it's happening but I'll be damned if it still doesn't shock me when I see it,"* explained one exasperated sergeant who was slumped in the chair of a district precinct house in Washington, D.C. He was talking about the new problems which girls have created for police. "Last week, for instance, we got a call of a disturbance at the high school. A fight . . . after school. So we get down there and pull up and here is a hell of a crowd yelling and screaming at the kids in the center, who are fighting. I push my way through the crowd—they're going crazy like it is really a mean fight and when I get to the middle . . . I liked to fell over. Here are two husky broads, and they are fighting . . . now I don't mean any hair-pulling face-scratching kind of thing; I mean two broads squared off and duking it out. Throwing jabs and hooking in at each other and handling themselves like a couple of goddamned pro sparring partners. I mean, I got to ask myself, what the hell is going on? What in the name of God is happening to these girls anymore?"[76]

Adler's thesis has not received much corroboration in the United States. But Anne Campbell's study of aggression among adolescent girls in Great Britain found that every one of the 251 sixteen-year-old schoolgirls from a workingclass area of London had seen a fight and 89 percent had been in at least one themselves. The majority of these fights took place when the girls felt their personal integrity had been challenged. The rules governing fighting proscribed the use of either bottles or knives, although it was considered acceptable to punch and slap. When Campbell extended her study to girls from Borstal, a training school, she found that they were more likely to use weapons during a fight and that police involvement was far more likely.[77]

Self-report studies clearly have rejected the notion of the increasingly violent adolescent girl. Cernkovich and Giordano argue that "the acts least frequently engaged in by both males and females are the more serious personal and property offenses, although males tend to engage in these more often than females do."[78] However, they, as well as Ageton, did find that nonwhite females have higher involvement rates in the more serious personal offenses, such as fistfighting, using a weapon to attack someone, gang fighting, extortion, and carrying weapons, than do white females.[79]

In sum, while Adler's profile of the increasingly violent juvenile and adult female offender has received much attention, the evidence does not lead to the conclusion that, overall, adolescent girls are becoming more violent. Yet nonwhite adolescent girls may be more likely to become involved in violent acts, especially during a fistfight, extortion or robbery, or gang activity.

Are Adolescent Girls Committing More Varied Delinquent Acts?

In the early studies, female delinquency was limited to incorrigibility,[80] various sex offenses,[81] running away from home,[82] truancy,[83] and shoplifting.[84] However, researchers recently are finding that female delinquents seem to commit more varied delinquent acts than the official records and earlier self-report studies indicated.

Michael Hindelang, for example, found that males may commit more delinquent acts but that the types of delinquent involvements were virtually identical for males and females.[85] Kratcoski and Kratcoski also found that there were few sex differences regarding involvement in hedonistic types of offenses such as running away. Thus, they agreed that "the delinquencies of boys and girls, particularly for less serious offenses, are becoming quite similar."[86] Cernkovich and Giordano found that racial differences affected patterns: i.e., white females were more similar in their delinquency involvements to white males than they were to nonwhite females, while nonwhite females were more like nonwhite males than they were like white females.[87]

But while the types of delinquent involvements may be nearly identical for males and females, males still commit more delinquent acts.[88] For example, Ageton and Elliott found that more boys reported having broken the law more frequently than did girls who reported delinquent acts.[89] Williams and Gold also concluded that girls committed less frequent and serious delinquent acts than boys.[90]

In sum, females appear to commit more varied delinquent acts than the early studies suggested, but males are still more frequently involved in delinquent acts. Some evidence exists that the behavior of males and females may be converging, at least in terms of the types of delinquency involvements.

TYPES OF FEMALE
JUVENILE OFFENDERS

The literature is filled with methods for classifying male delinquents, but because of traditional acceptance of the erroneous assumption that female delinquents are primarily involved in status offenses and minor offenses, little work has been done to date in developing a typology of female delinquents.

However, a classification scheme based upon the offenses of female delinquents seems possible. Although this scheme has not been empirically tested, it is based upon this author's years of working in corrections with both male and female delinquents, upon questionnaires administered to female institutionalized delinquents in a southern state, and upon extensive interviews conducted recently with female delinquents in three midwestern states. The chief types of female offenders, according to this scheme, are noncriminal offenders, emotionally disturbed offenders, situational offenders, and chronic offenders. Noncriminal youths are further classified into status offenders and dependent and neglected children. Situational offenders include property, violent, and drug offenders, and chronic offenders are further divided into prostitutes and gang members:

> Noncriminal youths
>   dependent and neglected children
>   status offenders
> Emotionally disturbed offenders
> Situational offenders
>   property offenders
>   violent offenders
>   drug offenders
> Chronic offenders
>   prostitutes
>   gang members

Noncriminal Youths

Girls classified as noncriminal offenders either have committed offenses that would not be crimes if they were adults, or are dependent and neglected children. These two groups both come to the attention of the juvenile justice system primarily because of problems in the home.

Dependent and Neglected Children

Neglect cases generally involve children abandoned by parents or those whose parents fail to care for them properly. Dependency cases usually are related to parents' physical, emotional, and financial inability to provide for their children. These youths are referred to the juvenile court because of the problems with their homes; they often also have been victims of child abuse.

Status Offenders

Incorrigibility at home, sexual acting-out behavior, truancy, and running away are the most frequent status offenses committed by girls. Female status offenders tend to place the blame for their problems on their parents. They often feel that their need for a warm, accepting, and meaningful relationship with parental figures is not being fulfilled, so they see themselves as rejected and neglected. Female status offenders frequently reject the limits placed on their behavior both in and outside the home. A juvenile probation officer describes the difficulty of dealing with female status offenders:

> Status offenders are basically out of control and may have some emotional problems. I think they're tougher to work with than delinquents. It's easier to define what you can do with a delinquent. If you do this, you tell the delinquent, then this is what's going to happen. But with the status offender, you have no control over them; no one really does. They have been out of control for a long time, and you're not going to get them back into control unless you take some strict measures. And the code is not very helpful at all.[91]

The line between status offenses and delinquent behavior is often very thin. For example, female runaways from home frequently become involved in delinquent acts, such as using drugs, shoplifting or burglary, or prostitution. Kobrin et al., in this regard, did find that female status offenders are less likely to commit delinquent acts than are male status offenders.[92]

Emotionally Disturbed Offenders

Youths whose emotional problems interfere with their everyday functioning and whose behaviors bring them into the juvenile justice system are included in the broad category of emotionally disturbed offenders. These youths may be labeled emotionally disturbed, prepsychotic, psychotic, or schizophrenic by psychiatrists and clinical psychologists. Psychological evaluations frequently record that they have poor self-concepts, anxiety symptoms, neurotic guilt, little self-awareness, restricted ego capacities, and a high degree of rejection; are unable to control their impulses; resist authority; have pathological relationships with family members; have a tendency to act out inadequacies; and have many internal conflicts.[93]

There appear to be two types of emotionally disturbed female offenders: those who exhibit persistent behavioral problems, and those who commit violent crimes. The first type is found much more frequently than the second type; these adolescents exhibit acting-out behavior in all areas of their lives. They often are self-destructive or strike out toward others. The second type is less infrequently seen, but these girls sometimes involve themselves in crimes that receive wide media coverage—e.g., the adolescent girl who killed two of the children for whom she was babysitting.[94]

Situational Offenders

Property, drug, and violent offenders are the three main types of situational offenders. Situational offenders, as described by David Matza, drift in and out of crime because of boredom, group pressure, or financial need. Other than their occasional excursions into the deviant world, these youths remain basically law-abiding. Matza states that the "bind of law" must be neutralized before a juvenile drifts away from it. But before giving herself the "moral holiday" implicit in drift, the female situational offender must learn from others that the crime is fairly easy to do. Thus, Matza believes that the situational offender is in limbo between convention and crime; influenced by the group, she evades decision and commitment.[95]

Situational offenders generally are dependent on the peer group. Whether they are middle-class girls shoplifting for thrills or using drugs, or lower-class girls marginally involved in a youth gang, the peer group very much influences their behavior. This emotional hold enables them to neutralize the "bind of law," to develop the feeling necessary to commit a new infraction and to activate the will to repeat a crime.[96]

Situational offenders usually continue to drift in and out of lawbreaking until they either outgrow the desire to commit crime or they are apprehended by the police and processed by the juvenile justice system. Their contact with the system may deter them from future delinquent behavior, or it may be the start of their being labeled as delinquent or bad kids. Youths who live up to these labels have passed the threshold from the situational into the chronic offender category.

Property Offenders

Property offenders are those girls who break into a building or vehicle, steal or buy stolen goods, joyride, or steal a motor vehicle. Shoplifters and girls who commit burglaries to provide themselves with goods that can be sold to buy drugs constitute the two basic categories of property offenders.

Girls appear to be involved in shoplifting more than in any other offense for several reasons. The first explanation is the simple opportunity thesis; that is, the more exposure adolescent females have to goods and shops, the more likely they are to shoplift.[97] Anne Campbell, in her study of shoplifting among adolescent girls in Great Britain, drew this conclusion:

> With so many demands on incomes that are often quite low, it is hardly surprising that girls are heavily involved in shoplifting. The pressures—material, psychological, social, romantic—assault from every side. The shops invite them to touch, smell, feel, and wear everything that they need for instant success in all these spheres. When the temptations are all weighed up and the chances of detection calculated, it is remarkable that so few girls do it.[98]

Second, appearance is important to many girls.[99] Third, peer relationships encourage adolescent females to negate the moral binds of the law; a fourteen-year-old girl asserted, "I've ripped off stuff from stores, but I have never gotten caught. I did it because my friends dared me."[100] Fourth, some adolescent girls become involved in shoplifting because they see it as a challenge; an eighteen-year-old girl explained, "I did a lot of shoplifting when I was younger. It was a challenge. I wanted to see if I could beat the system."[101]

Empirical investigation has not yet established the number of girls who commit burglaries in order to buy drugs. However, interviews with female adolescents, including a sample of fifty who were physically and/or emotionally addicted to drugs, revealed that stealing to buy drugs takes place frequently with this population. Peer pressure appears to be a determining factor in adolescent female drug abusers' decisions to commit burglaries or robberies. A fifteen-year-old girl who was drug-dependent said, "When you break into a house, everybody thinks you are cool. Most of the kids I run around with feel it's a lot better way to get drugs than selling your body anyhow."[102]

Drug and Alcohol Abusers

Drug and alcohol abusers are widely represented among female adolescents. These girls differ from those who occasionally use drugs, because they use drugs on an ongoing basis. Alcohol and marijuana are the most widely used drugs, but female adolescents appear to use fewer narcotics, such as heroin and cocaine, and more chemicals than do adolescent males (see Table 10-2 for the various types of chemicals used).

Peer pressure among adolescents is one of the factors that make it difficult for adolescent girls "to walk away from drugs." A seventeen-year-old girl explained:

The hardest thing I've had to do in my life was to quit drugs. In jail, I knew I had three choices: spend time in and out of jail; eventually take an overdose; or stay clean. To quit drugs was like asking me not to breathe. I asked myself, "What am I going to do?" All my friends get high. Any social event I went to had drugs. To walk away from drugs, you literally had to isolate yourself.[103]

Increasing numbers of adolescent girls are dealing in drugs, usually because they need the money to provide for their own drug habits. A sixteen-year-old girl who was drug dependent describes the period when she was selling drugs to other adolescents:

It is really easy to make money off of drugs. It has got to be the easiest job anyone could do. All you have to do is to sit on your butt and wait for people to call. My boyfriend was dealing in drugs, and he was making nearly $200 a day. The money is nice, but when you get caught, it is another story. But I have never been caught. I've broken into houses too, but I have never been caught doing that either. They had a good idea it was me, but they didn't have any positive proof.[104]

Violent Offenders

Female adolescents are involved in such crimes against the person as assault against parents, teachers, and peers, as well as gang fighting.

Fistfighting at school and hitting parents are the most common violent offenses committed by adolescent girls. The girl who becomes involved in an altercation at school tends to be an urban nonwhite who feels that her personal integrity is being attacked or that another girl is "leaning on her." The girl who becomes involved in a fight with her parents tends to be white, and the altercation is usually with her mother: "My mother just kept hitting me, so I started to hit her back."[105]

Chronic Delinquents

Known by many labels—serious delinquent, violent offender, dangerous offender, hard-core delinquent, career delinquent, and chronic offender—the predominant characteristic of the chronic delinquent is his or her commitment to crime and involvement in one crime after another, often very serious crimes against persons and property. The prostitute and gang delinquent appear to be the most common female chronic offenders.

Prostitutes

The area of adolescent female prostitution has received little empirical examination, but interviews with a number of teenage girls involved in prostitution as well as with juvenile justice practitioners who work with female adolescent prostitutes produced the following observations:

Teenage girls involved in prostitution usually have a pimp.
Teenage girls who run away from home and end up in urban areas frequently become involved in prostitution.
Teenage girls involved in prostitution are likely to be drug dependent.
Teenage girls involved in prostitution often have a background of sexual abuse.
Teenage girls involved in prostitution typically continue their careers into their adult years.

A staff member who worked with adolescent female prostitutes made this observation:

A lot more girls are selling their bodies. There are more younger hookers, thirteen- and fourteen-year-olds. They just don't care. It's a way they can have all the clothes they want, all the blue jeans and shoes they want. The mentality of society is "money is great"; you can have anything you want if you have money. So, kids will do anything they can to get money. Girls sell their bodies to get money. If it was legal and had a tax on it, they would find something else.[106]

Gang Members

More attention has recently been given to adolescent girls who join gangs. In *Sisters in Crime*, Adler discusses female gangs in Philadelphia and in New York.[107] Walter B. Miller studied the Molls, a group of gang girls in an inner-city district of an Eastern seaport.[108] Giordano, in a recent examination of institutionalized girls in Ohio, reported that 53.7 percent of the 108 institutionalized girls indicated that they had been part of a group of girls that could be called a gang, and 51.9 percent of these said that their gang had a name.[109]

W. K. Brown carried out a more comprehensive study of female participation in youth gangs in Philadelphia.[110] She suggests that female gang participation is usually limited to sexually integrated gangs. Among the functions performed by girls involved in integrated gangs in Philadelphia are to serve as participants in gang wars or in individual and small group combats fights, and to act as spies to gain information about activities being planned by other gangs. Brown notes that most girls join Philadelphia gangs to be popular and to be "where the action is." But she did find one all-female black gang. The "Holly Whores" are heavily involved in the subculture of violence. These girls have been accused of knifing and kicking pregnant females and of badly scarring and mutilating "cute" girls. "Getting a body" (knifing) is said to be an important part of their "rep."[111]

POLICY IMPLICATIONS

The assumption that the adult female offender is protected by the old norms of chivalry and receives more lenient treatment by the justice system is frequently accepted in adult corrections. But if this is true for adult female offenders, strong evidence exists that it is not so for adolescent females.

Even though many of the writers on female delinquency in the twentieth century have claimed that girls are protected more than boys because they receive the benefits of chivalrous treatment, Steven Schlossman and Stephanie Wallach show that girls have been treated more harshly than boys from the time of the founding of the juvenile court at the turn of the century. These researchers, using old court records and secondary sources, assert that female juvenile delinquents often have received more severe punishments than males, although boys usually have been charged with more serious crimes. They conclude that the harsh discriminatory treatment of female delinquents during the Progressive era resulted from racial prejudice, new theories of adolescence, and Progressive-era movements to purify society.[112]

Etta A. Anderson, as well as Chesney-Lind and Rogers, provides evidence that the fear of sexual activity on the part of girls has resulted in their discriminatory treatment by the juvenile justice system.[113] This perspective sometimes sees adolescent females as turning to delinquency for purely sexual reasons regardless of whether the crime itself is a sex offense.[114] Society, then, must protect her against these sexual desires, and the juvenile justice system becomes a moral chastity belt for wayward adolescent females.

Jean Strauss notes that juvenile court judges commonly place adolescent girls in confinement for even minor offenses because they assume these girls have engaged in sexual activity and believe they deserve punishment.[115] Yona Cohn, in her study of the disposition recommendations of probation officers, found that girls constituted only one-sixth of her sample of youths in a metropolitan court, but yet they constituted nearly one-fifth of the youths sentenced to institutional care. She attributes this uneven distribution to the fact that female adolescents frequently violate the sexual norms of the middle-class probation officer.[116] Chesney-Lind further found that police in Honolulu, Hawaii were likely to arrest girls for sexual activity and to ignore the same behavior among boys.[117] Furthermore, in her study of a training school for girls in Connecticut, Kristine Olson Rogers found the treatment staff greatly concerned with the girls' sexual history and habits.[118] Both Rogers and Chesney-Lind also comment on the practices of juvenile courts and detention homes whereby females are forced to undergo pelvic examinations and submit to extensive questioning about their sexual activities, regardless of the offenses with which they are charged.[119]

Robert Terry, in a study of 9000 youths apprehended by police in a midwestern city, found that girls were more likely to be referred to the juvenile court than boys, and if referred, were more likely to receive an institutional sentence.[120] Rogers found that girls' average period of confinement in Connecticut was longer than that of boys.[121] Bartollas and Sieverdes, in a study of institutionalized youths in North Carolina, found that 80 percent of the confined girls had committed status offenses and that they had longer institutional stays than the boys.[122]

Rosemary C. Sarri concludes that juvenile law has long penalized females. She claims that the law may not be discriminatory on its face, but that the attitudes and ideologies of juvenile justice practitioners administering it may result in violations of the Fourteenth Amendment under the equal protection clause by leading them to award females longer sentences than males under the guise of "protecting" the female juvenile.[123] She adds:

> Data compiled by the National Assessment of Juvenile Corrections as well as by federal agencies and many other students of juvenile justice clearly indicate that females are overrepresented in critical areas of the justice system. One of the most critical areas pertains to placement in adult jails, lockups, and detention facilities. Females have a greater probability of being detained and held for longer periods than males, even though the overwhelming majority of females are charged with status offenses. Moreover, in the juvenile jurisdiction reporting a ratio of one female to four male arrests, the ratio for placement in detention is typically one to three.[124]

Some evidence exists that the discriminatory treatment of female delinquents has been declining since the passing of the Juvenile Justice and Delinquency Prevention Act. No longer do many states send status offenders to training school with delinquents. But the long tradition of sexism in juvenile justice will be difficult to change. Due process safeguards for female delinquents must be established to assure them of greater social justice in the juvenile justice system. The intrusion of the sociocultural context into the decision-making process in the legal context has led to discrimination toward the adolescent female that must become a relic of the past.

SUMMARY

This chapter began by raising several commonly accepted assumptions regarding female delinquency. The evidence shows that six of these seven assumptions can be rejected. Sexual offenses, incorrigibility, and running away do not make up the delinquent repertoire of girls; indeed, the offenses of male and female delinquents appear to be converging and to reflect a similar pattern. Social factors are not irrelevant to an understanding of female delinquency, but instead appear to be more influential than psychological or biological factors. The women's liberation movement has not influenced the extent and nature of female delinquency, although more research is necessary to determine what concurrent social changes may be having an impact. Female delinquents are not treated more leniently by the juvenile justice system than are male delinquents; indeed, they actually receive harsher treatment from the system. The assumption that females become involved in delinquency as they become more male-like is questionable, and there is little evidence to show that female delinquents are more abnormal and pathological than male delinquents. Finally, the frequency and variety of female delinquent acts do appear to have increased, but adolescent males still commit more delinquent acts, commit them more frequently, and commit more serious delinquent acts.

In terms of the contextual perspective, the sociocultural context dominates the others when it comes to the female adolescent delinquent. In the legal context, extralegal or social factors influence the decision-making process in the juvenile court. For example, there is some evidence that adolescent girls are treated punitively for status-type offenses, especially when sex is involved, but that they receive the benefits of chivalry when they commit delinquent offenses. Similarly, the usual effect of the economic context is sometimes reversed when it comes to female delinquency; that is, middle-class girls are treated more punitively than lower-class girls when they commit status offenses, although they normally receive less punitive treatment when they commit delinquent offenses. The political context also frequently perpetuates the sociocultural context and the discriminatory treatment of the female delinquent.

The progress recently made in understanding female delinquency promises that this area of inquiry may be a fruitful one in the future. For example, much more research is needed into sociological explanations, such as blocked opportunity, influence of peers, and the impact of labeling. Second, although adult women and adolescent girl offenders appear to have much in common, the significant differences between them need further examination. Third, cross-cultural comparisons that show similar patterns in female delinquency in the United States and in other cultures should be utilized more fully. Fourth, little has been discovered about female delinquents' perception of their treatment by the juvenile justice system or the impact of the justice system upon these youths.

Discussion Questions

1. Why has the study of female delinquency lagged behind the study of male delinquency?
2. Why has society been so sensitive to the sexual behaviors of adolescent girls? What have been the consequences of this concern?
3. How do the delinquencies of males and females compare?
4. Explain the classification scheme of female offenders. How should each group be treated by the juvenile justice system?

5. How has the social context affected the legal context in terms of female delinquency?

References

Adler, Freda. *Sisters in Crime: The Rise of the New Female Criminal.* New York: McGraw-Hill Book Company, 1975.

Ageton, Suzanne S. "The Dynamics of Female Delinquency, 1976–1980." *Criminology* 21 (November 1983): 555–584.

Cernkovich, Stephen A., and Giordano, Peggy C. "Delinquency, Opportunity, and Gender." *Journal of Criminal Law and Criminology* 70 (1979): 145–151.

———. "A Comparative Analysis of Male and Female Delinquency." *Sociological Quarterly* (Winter 1979): 131–145.

Datesman, S. K., and Scarpitti, F. R. "Female Delinquency: An Application of Self and Opportunity Theories." *Journal of Research in Crime and Delinquency* 12 (1975): 107–123.

Giordano, Peggy C., and Cernkovich, Stephen A. "On Complicating the Relationship Between Liberation and Delinquency." *Social Problems* 26 (April 1979): 468–281.

Jensen, Gary J., and Eve, Raymond. "Sex Differences in Delinquency: An Examination of Popular Sociological Explanations." *Criminology* 13 (February 1976): 427–448.

Steffensmeier, Darrell J., and Steffensmeier, Renee Hoffman. "Trends in Female Delinquency: An Examination of Arrest, Juvenile Court, Self-Report, and Field Data." *Criminology* 18 (May 1980): 62–82.

Thornton, William E., and James, Jennifer. "Masculinity and Delinquency Revisited." *British Journal of Criminology* 19 (1977): 87–104.

Weis, Joseph. "Liberation and Crime: The Invention of the New Female Criminal." *Crime and Social Justice* 6 (Fall–Winter 1976): 17–27.

Williams, J. R., and Gold, Martin. "From Delinquent Behavior to Official Delinquency." *Social Problems* 20 (Fall 1972): 209–229.

FOOTNOTES

1. Freda Adler, *Sisters in Crime: The Rise of the New Female Criminal* (New York: McGraw-Hill Book Company, 1975).

2. Peggy C. Giordano and Stephen A. Cernkovich, "On Complicating the Relationship between Liberation and Delinquency," *Social Problems* 26 (April 1979), p. 467.

3. Peggy C. Giordano, "Girls, Guys, and Gangs: The Changing Social Context of Female Delinquency," *Journal of Criminal Law and Criminology* 69 (1978), p. 126.

4. Lesley Shacklady Smith, "Sexist Assumptions and Female Delinquency: An Empirical Investigation," in *Women, Sexuality and Social Control,* edited by Carol Smart and Barry Smart (London: Routledge & Kegan Paul, 1978), p. 76.

5. William E. Thornton and Jennifer James, "Masculinity and Delinquency Revisited," *British Journal of Criminology* 19 (July 1979), p. 226.

6. Smith, "Sexist Assumptions and Female Delinquency," p. 76.

7. Cesare Lombroso, *The Female Offender* (New York: Appleton, 1920).

8. Ibid., p. 122.

9. Ibid., p. 151.

10. Ibid.

11. Ibid., p. 109.

12. Dorie Klein, "The Etiology of Female Crime: A Review of the Literature," *Issues in Criminology* 8 (Fall 1973), p. 9.

13. Lombroso, *Female Offender,* pp. 150–152.

14. J. Cowie, B. Cowie, and E. Slater, *Delinquency in Girls* (London: Heinemann, 1968).

15. Ibid., p. 17.

16. T. C. N. Gibbens, "Female Offenders," *British Journal of Hospital Medicine* 6 (1971), pp. 279–286.

17. Cowie, Cowie, and Slater, *Delinquency in Girls.*

18. Ibid.

19. Anne Campbell, *Girl Delinquents* (New York: St. Martin's Press, 1981), p. 46.

20. Ibid., p. 48.

21. W. I. Thomas, *Sex and Society* (Boston: Little, Brown & Company, 1907).

22. Ibid.

23. W. I. Thomas, *The Unadjusted Girl* (New York: Harper & Row, 1923).

24. Campbell, *Girl Delinquents,* p. 52.

25. Thomas, *Unadjusted Girl,* p. 109.

26. Sigmund Freud, *An Outline of Psychoanalysis,* trans. James Strachey (New York: W. W. Norton, 1949), p. 278.

27. Sigmund Freud, *New Introductory Lectures on Psychoanalysis* (New York: W. W. Norton, 1933), p. 183.

28. Otto Pollak, *The Criminality of Women* (Philadelphia: University of Pennsylvania Press, 1950), p. 8.

29. Ibid., pp. 125–139.

30. Gisela Konopka, *The Adolescent Girl in Conflict* (Englewood Cliffs, N.J.: Prentice-Hall, 1966).

31. These key factors from Konopka's *Adolescent Girl* are listed in Peter C. Kratcoski and John E. Kratcoski, "Changing Patterns in the Delinquent Activities of Boys and Girls: A Self-Reported Delinquency Analysis," *Adolescence* 18 (Spring 1975), pp. 83–91.

32. Clyde Vedder and Dora Somerville, *The Delinquent Girl* (Springfield, Ill.: Charles C Thomas, 1970).

33. R. Morris, "Attitudes towards Delinquency by Delinquents, Nondelinquents, and Their Friends," *British Journal of Criminology* 5 (1966), pp. 249–265.

34. Mary Gray Riege, "Parental Affection and Juvenile Delinquency in Girls," *British Journal of Criminology* (January 1972), pp. 55–73.

35. Emmy E. Werner and Ruth S. Smith, *Kauai's Children Come of Age* (Honolulu: University Press of Hawaii, 1977).

36. William Wattenberg and Frank Saunders, "Sex Differences among Juvenile Offenders," *Sociology and Social Research* 39 (1954), pp. 24–31.

37. Interviewed in May 1982.

38. Peggy C. Giordano and Stephen A. Cernkovich, "Changing Patterns of Female Delinquency" (A research proposal submitted to the National Institute of Mental Health, February 28, 1979), p. 24.

39. Adler, *Sisters in Crime*, pp. 10–11.

40. Laura Crites, "Women Offenders: Myth vs. Reality," in *The Female Offender*, edited by Crites (Lexington, Mass.: Lexington Books, 1976), pp. 36–39.

41. Darrell J. Steffensmeier, "Crime and the Contemporary Women: An Analysis of Changing Levels of Property Crime," *Social Forces* 57 (1978), pp. 566–584.

42. Joseph G. Weis, "Liberation and Crime: The Invention of the New Female Criminal," *Crime and Social Justice* 6 (1976), pp. 17–27.

43. Giordano and Cernkovich, "Relationship between Liberation and Delinquency," p. 468.

44. Giordano and Cernkovich, "Female Delinquency," p. 25.

45. Giordano, "Girls, Guys and Gangs," p. 127.

46. Robert K. Merton, "Social Structure and Anomie," *American Sociological Review* 3 (October 1938), pp. 672–682; Albert K. Cohen, *Delinquent Boys: The Culture of the Gang* (New York: Free Press, 1955); and Richard A. Cloward and Lloyd E. Ohlin, *Delinquency and Opportunity: A Theory of Delinquent Gangs* (New York: Free Press, 1960).

47. Talcott Parsons, "Age and Sex in the Social Structure of the United States," *American Sociological Review* 7 (October 1942); James S. Coleman, *The Adolescent Society* (New York: Free Press, 1961); and Ruth Rittenhouse, "A Theory and Comparison of Male and Female Delinquency" (Ph.D. diss., University of Michigan, Ann Arbor, 1963).

48. Susan K. Datesman, Frank R. Scarpitti, and Richard M. Stephenson, "Female Delinquency: An Application of Self and Opportunity Theories," *Journal of Research in Crime and Delinquency* 12 (1975), p. 120.

49. Stephen A. Cernkovich and Peggy C. Giordano, "Delinquency, Opportunity, and Gender," *Journal of Criminal Law and Criminology* 70 (1979), p. 150.

50. Travis Hirschi, *Causes of Delinquency* (Berkeley: University of California Press, 1969).

51. William E. Thornton, Jr., Jennifer James, and William G. Doerner, *Delinquency and Justice* (Glenview, Ill.: Scott, Foresman, & Company, 1982), p. 268.

52. Austin Turk, *Criminality and the Legal Order* (Chicago: Rand McNally, 1969), pp. 164–165.

53. Gary J. Jensen and Raymond Eve, "Sex Differences in Delinquency: An Examination of Popular Sociological Explanations," *Criminology* 13 (February 1976), pp. 427–448.

54. Adler, *Sisters in Crime*.

55. F. T. Cullen, K. M. Golden, and J. B. Cullen, "Sex and Delinquency: A Partial Test of the Masculinity Hypothesis," *Criminology* 17 (1979), pp. 301–310.

56. William E. Thornton and Jennifer James, "Masculinity and Delinquency Revisited," *British Journal of Criminology* 19 (July 1979), pp. 225–241.

57. S. Norland and N. Shover, "Gender Roles and Female Criminality: Some Critical Comments," *Criminology* 15 (1977), pp. 87–104.

58. Giordano and Cernkovich, "Relationship between Liberation and Delinquency," pp. 467–481.

59. Thornton and James, in "Masculinity and Delinquency Revisited," found limited support

for the merger of social control theory and the masculinity hypothesis in explaining delinquency in girls, but perhaps other combinations would be more fruitful.

60. Giordano and Cernkovich, "Female Delinquency," p. 26.

61. Ibid., p. 62.

62. Giordano, "Girls, Guys and Gangs," p. 132.

63. Giordano, and Cernkovich, "Female Delinquency," pp.24–28.

64. This section on increasing female delinquency is adapted from Giordano and Cernkovich, "Female Delinquency," pp. 16–22.

65. U.S. Department of Justice, Federal Bureau of Investigation, *Uniform Crime Reports 1982* (Washington, D.C.: U.S. Government Printing Office, 1983), p. 173.

66. Rita James Simon, *Women and Crime* (Lexington, Mass.: D.C. Heath & Company, 1975).

67. Darrell J. Steffensmeier, "Crime and the Contemporary Women: An Analysis of Changing Levels of Female Property Crime, 1960–1975," *Social Forces* 57 (1978), pp. 566–584.

68. Darrell J. Steffensmeier and Renee Hoffman Steffensmeier, "Trends in Female Delinquency: An Examination of Arrest, Juvenile Court, Self-Report, and Field Data," *Criminology* 18 (May 1980), pp. 62–82.

69. Simon, *Women and Crime*, pp. 36–42.

70. Martin Gold and David J. Reimer, *Changing Patterns of Delinquent Behavior among Americans 13 to 16 Years Old, 1967–1972* (Ann Arbor, Mich.: Institute for Social Research, University of Michigan, 1974).

71. Illinois Institute for Juvenile Research, *Juvenile Delinquency in Illinois* (Chicago: Illinois Department of Mental Health, 1972).

72. Patricia Y. Miller, "Gender, Delinquency and Social Control," mimeographed.

73. Steffensmeier and Steffensmeier, "Trends in Female Delinquency," pp. 22–23.

74. Suzanne S. Ageton, "The Dynamics of Female Delinquency, 1976–1980," *Criminology* 21 (November 1983), pp. 555–584.

75. Adler, *Sisters in Crime*, p. 106.

76. Ibid., pp. 96–97.

77. Campbell, *Girl Delinquents*, p. 150.

78. Stephen A. Cernkovich and Peggy Giordano, "A Comparative Analysis of Male and Female Delinquency," *Sociological Quarterly* (Winter 1979), p. 139.

79. Ibid., p. 142; and Ageton, "Dynamics of Female Delinquency," pp. 577–578.

80. Gordon H. Barker and William T. Adams, "Comparison of the Delinquencies of Boys and Girls," *Journal of Criminal Law, Criminology and Police Science* 53 (1962), pp. 470–475; Vedder and Somerville, *Delinquent Girl*.

81. Clyde D. Vedder, *The Juvenile Offender* (New York: Doubleday, 1954); Barker and Adams, "Delinquencies of Boys and Girls"; Vedder and Somerville, *Delinquent Girl*; Media Chesney-Lind, "Judicial Enforcement of the Female Sex Role: The Family Court and the Female Delinquent," *Issues in Criminology* 8 (1973), pp. 51–69; Datesman, Scarpitti, and Stephenson, "Female Delinquency."

82. Lois G. Forer, *No One Will Listen: How Our System Brutalizes the Poor* (New York: John Day, 1970); Chesney-Lind, "Judicial Enforcement of the Female Sex Role"; Vedder and Somerville, *Delinquent Girl*.

83. Forer, *No One Will Listen*; Vedder and Somerville, *Delinquent Girl*; Walter B. Miller, "Race, Sex, and Gangs: The Molls," *Society* 11 (November-December 1973), pp. 32–35.

84. Adler, *Sisters in Crime*.

85. Hindelang, "Age, Sex, and the Versatility of Delinquency Involvements," *Social Problems* 18 (1971), p. 533.

86. Kratcoski and Kratcoski, "Delinquent Activities of Boys and Girls," p. 88.

87. Cernkovich and Giordano, "Male and Female Delinquency," pp. 142–143.

88. Hindelang, "Age, Sex, and the Versatility of Delinquent Involvement," p. 533.

89. Suzanne S. Ageton and Delbert S. Elliott, *The Incidence of Delinquent Behavior in a National Probability Sample of Adolescents* (Boulder, Colo.: Behavioral Research Institute, 1978).

90. J. R. Williams and Martin Gold, "From Delinquent Behavior to Official Delinquency," *Social Problems* 20 (Fall 1972), p. 213.

91. Interviewed in May 1982.

92. Solomon Kobrin, Frank R. Hellum, and John W. Peterson, "Offense Patterns of Status Offenders," in *Critical Issues in Juvenile Delinquency*, edited by David Shichor and Delos H. Kelly (Lexington, Mass.: D.C. Heath & Company, 1980), p. 215.

93. Clemens Bartollas, Stuart J. Miller, and Simon Dinitz, *Juvenile Victimization: The Institutional Paradox* (New York: Halsted Press, A Sage Publication, 1976), p. 152.

94. A probation officer interviewed in May 1982 worked with this case.

95. David Matza, *Delinquency and Drift* (New York: John Wiley & Sons, 1964), pp. 184–190.

96. Ibid.

97. D. Hoffman-Bustamante, "The Nature of Female Criminality," *Issues in Criminology* 8 (1973), pp. 117–136.

98. Campbell, *Girl Delinquents*, p. 131.

99. Ibid., p. 127.

100. Interviewed in May 1982.

101. Interviewed in November 1981.

102. Interviewed in July 1982.

103. Interviewed in July 1982.

104. Interviewed in May 1982.

105. Interviewed in August 1982.

106. Interviewed in October 1981.

107. Adler, *Sisters in Crime*.

108. Miller, "Molls," pp. 32–55.

109. Giordano, "Girls, Guys and Gangs," p. 130.

110. Waln K. Brown, "Black Female Gangs in Philadelphia," *International Journal of Offender Therapy and Comparative Criminology* 21 (1970), pp. 221–229.

111. Ibid., pp. 223–227.

112. Steven Schlossman and Stephanie Wallach, "The Crime of Precocious Sexuality: Female Juvenile Delinquency in the Progressive Era," *Harvard Educational Review* 48 (February 1978), p. 65.

113. Etta A. Anderson, "The 'Chivalrous' Treatment of the Female Offender in the Arms of the Criminal Justice System: A Review of the Literature," *Social Problems* 23 (1976), pp. 350–357; Chesney-Lind, "Judicial Enforcement of the Female Sex Role"; and Kristine Olson Rogers, "For Her Own Protection . . . Conditions of Incarceration for Female Juvenile Offenders in the State of Connecticut," *Law and Society Review* 7 (1973), pp. 223–246.

114. Anderson, " 'Chivalrous' Treatment of the Female Offender," p. 153.

115. Jean Strauss, "To Be Minor and Female: The Legal Rights of Women under Twenty-One," *Ms.* 1 (1972), p. 84.

116. Yona Cohn, "Criteria for Probation Officer's Recommendations to Juvenile Court," *Crime and Delinquency* 1 (1963), pp. 272–275.

117. Chesney-Lind, "Judicial Enforcement of the Female Sex Role."

118. Rogers, "For Her Own Protection."

119. Chesney-Lind, "Judicial Enforcement of the Female Sex Role"; and Rogers, "For Her Own Protection."

120. Robert Terry, "Discrimination in the Police Handling of Juvenile Offenders by Social Control Agencies," *Journal of Research in Crime and Delinquency* 14 (1967), p. 218.

121. Rogers, "For Her Own Protection."

122. Clemens Bartollas and Christopher M. Sieverdes, "Games Juveniles Play: How They Get Their Way," mimeographed.

123. Rosemary C. Sarri, "Juvenile Law: How It Penalizes Females," in *The Female Offender,* pp. 68–69.

124. Ibid., p. 76.

INTERVIEW WITH PEGGY G. GIORDANO

I talked with a sixteen-year-old girl who said that she liked to work alone. When she was twelve or thirteen, she used to go out on jobs with boys, but she picked up a little knowledge and learned a few things. She proceeded to tell me about the house burglaries she had been involved in. She stole such items as money, guns, and stereos. To her, that was normal behavior.

In this interview, Peggy G. Giordano, professor of sociology at Bowling Green State University and one of the most widely respected researchers on female delinquency, discusses the most important insights she has learned about female delinquency, the relationship between peer groups and female delinquency, the behavior of chronic female delinquents, the effects of drugs on female delinquency, and the relationship between female delinquency and sociological theory.

Question: What are the most important insights you have learned about female delinquency from your research?

Giordano: In our research we have been looking at the extent to which everyday social processes lead to delinquency. The image of the female delinquent was always that she was a disturbed and sexually provocative loner who was guided into delinquency through her attachment to boys. Our data demonstrate that girls tend to get involved in delinquency in much the same fashion as do boys. We found that even our most delinquent girls have important peer ties, and so we have increasingly focused on the relationship between friendship

Dr. Giordano, with her colleague Steven Cernkovich, has published articles on female delinquency in Social Problems, The Journal of Criminal Law and Criminology, Sociology Quarterly, *and other journals. Their work on friendship groups, female delinquency and women's liberation, chronic offenders, and the relationship between mainline sociology and female delinquency is widely cited in the literature.*

patterns and delinquency. Second, I think there has been a lack of understanding about who these females are, how they go about doing their crimes, and what kinds of crimes they do. These data basically indicate that while females are involved in less crime than males, the patterning of delinquency for females is much the same as it is for males. If you rank order the kinds of things females do, they don't murder people very often; males don't murder very often either. The most frequent offenses for males are drinking, vandalism, and so on, and those are also the high frequency crimes for females. We have also found that the way in which they commit crimes is quite similar, in terms of their degree of planning, how far they will travel, their stated reasons for committing the acts, etc. Another finding from our research is that girls seem to take other girls as their most important reference group. Girls seem to need the support of other females in much the same way that males need the support of their same sex group.

Question: In terms of your work on friendship groups, why do females have more influence on females?

Giordano: Well, first of all, some females are still influenced by males. We found in our latest study that almost 35 percent of the institutionalized girls we interviewed were with their boyfriends when they committed delinquent acts. So the traditional pattern of males influencing them in a delinquent direction may be there for some girls. But that leaves about 65 percent who don't fit this traditional pattern. These girls need some kind of legitimization from *other girls* to give them a sense that what they are doing is appropriate, "cool" or acceptable. If they have strong negative reinforcement from other girls, I just don't think they will get involved.

Question: There seems to be some debate whether delinquent kids seek out other groups to reinforce their values or whether they become involved in groups and then are influenced by these groups to become involved in delinquency. Do you see the female adolescents you have studied as being influenced by groups to become delinquent or do they seek out groups to reinforce their delinquent values?

Giordano: I think that is probably one of the most important questions in delinquency research: The extent to which selection into the group or socialization once they are involved in the group is more important in fostering delinquent behavior. It is very difficult to nail this down without longitudinal data, but it would appear from our data and the data of other people (especially Kandel) that both processes operate about equally. It is simply not true that these kids are total angels who are suddenly "sucked in" and influenced by a delinquent group; there are areas of similarity in attitudes and behavior even before the friendships are formed. But the group does have a more profound influence than is suggested by control theory. Proponents of this theory would depict these groups as a kind of loose affiliation of losers, whose relationships are cold and brittle and who really don't have a strong influence on each other. Our recent research found that this "cold and brittle" assumption is inaccurate. This position assumes social disability—that is, that these kids are incapable of developing important and close friendships with each other and that they are just held together by the common quality of being losers. They are doing "bad" things and, therefore, they must be unable to develop "good" and close primary relationships.

We have examined this very carefully because of its importance to delinquency theory. We have over 125 questions in our interviews about what respondents' groups are like, what effect they have on each other, how much they fight with each other, how much they disclose of themselves with one another, and what are the rewards they get from these friendships. We have been focusing on this so much that my colleague, Stephen Cernkovich, is always asking: Is this a friendship study or a delinquency study? What we have found is that there are no major differences in levels of intimacy across groups who do vary considerably in their degree of involvement in delinquent behavior. On a few dimensions the nonoffender (the adolescent involved in almost *no* delinquency) does differ from other adolescents—but in the opposite direction from what might be predicted from a control theory framework—these kids appear *less* attached and less intimate with friends than their more delinquent counterparts. In looking at sex differences, we found that even the girls we classified as major offenders had friendships which were much more intimate than the friendships of comparable males. In other words, girls simply have closer relationships with their friends, regardless of involvement in delinquency. Girls talk more, and more intimately with friends than boys do. They have a greater sense of caring and trust, and so on.

We also found race differences in these friendship patterns which may have important implications for delinquency theory. At the risk of oversimplification, the friendship styles of the blacks in our sample appeared somewhat less intense. While their friendships had greater stability, they were less likely to say that they exerted pressure on each other, and scored somewhat lower on overall intimacy. This leads us to hypothesize that peer influence may have a more direct link to delinquency for white in comparison to black adolescents.

Question: How about the chronic female delinquent? How is she different from other female delinquents?

Giordano: We are concerned about the typical way delinquency is measured (using self-report surveys) and the extent to which this fails to capture serious offenders, male or female. Surveys using school samples have largely excluded such "hard core" youth. Now, some recent national studies using home interviews represent an improvement over the use of school samples. But we have found that the behavior of those kids who represent the most delinquent group in these neighborhood surveys does not hold a candle to the level of involvement of the average institutionalized youth. This is an unpopular viewpoint because we like to think that the only difference between those kids who are institutionalized and those on the streets are that they were, as labeling theory suggests, unlucky enough to get caught. Labeling does occur—there are few affluent kids in the institutions. There is certainly repression in the system. But the institutionalized offenders do admit to more serious, more frequent, and more persistent involvements in almost every type of delinquency than do their neighborhood counterparts.

It has become somewhat unfashionable to go into the institutions anymore because they represent a biased sample, but there are things we can learn from this group which would be difficult to find out using the neighborhood technique alone.

I talked with a sixteen-year-old girl in the institution who said that she liked to work alone. When she was twelve or thirteen, she used to go out on jobs with boys, but she picked up a little knowledge and learned a few things. She said that she doesn't need them anymore. She proceeded to tell me about the house burglaries she has been involved in. She stole such items as money, guns, and stereos. To her, that was normal behavior. That was her way of surviving. Because there are not that *many* serious property or violent female offenders in the general population, we would probably not encounter someone like her in the average neighborhood survey. If we aren't going into the institutions, we need to develop other kinds of strategies to find these more experienced offenders.

Question: How about the effects of drugs?

Giordano: I am not personally interested in drug use as a research topic, but I do think it is an area (like alcohol use) where there is relative equality between males and females. We can see the greatest convergence in these areas, which do not involve a great deal of technical skill (as in auto theft). To become involved in drugs, all that is necessary is to be placed into social contexts where they are used and defined as acceptable. But girls do become involved in other law violations stemming from these experiences. I don't mean in the sense that drug use necessarily forces them to go out to steal money to support their habit, but just that it introduces them to another set of contacts and opportunities where other kinds of crimes are more commonplace.

Question: I like the statement that you have made in your published work that we need to move into more main-line sociological theory to understand female delinquency. I would like you to couch your empirical findings into a theoretical framework.

Giordano: We have emphasized the influence of friendships to a great extent, which seems to be most compatible with differential association and subcultural theories. The field appears to be moving toward a so-called integrated model and this is also reflected in our data. This model suggests that combining elements of control, strain and subcultural theory can better account for delinquency than can any pure model alone. Elliott and colleagues, as well as Richard Johnson both find empirical support for this kind of integrated model.

What I think we need to do now is to move toward greater specificity and a more subtle understanding about each of these aspects of the causal model. We have known for some time that peers are important. We need to examine more comprehensively the multiple ways in which peers exert influence on each other. What causes the initial attraction to more delinquent groups? What are adolescents getting out of these friendships that results in their continuing them? What causes conflict and change to different friendships? In the same way, we need to draw upon the more general literature in sociology of the family to learn more about the role of particular family dynamics in fostering or deterring delinquency (e.g., what specific aspects of parental control and socialization differ by sex, and are these differences becoming less dramatic over time?). There is more to be learned from the literature which does not deal directly with delinquency than from most of the literature which does.

CHAPTER 13

THE MALE DELINQUENT

CHAPTER OUTLINE

Two brothers broke into a house and beat an elderly man to death. The older one had been in and out of training school three times. He was waived to the adult court and was found guilty of first degree murder.

A first-time offender gets into a fight, and with one punch he kills another kid. He is charged with involuntary manslaughter. He's a kid who just likes to fight.

I had a fifteen-year-old boy who killed his father on my caseload. He had been terribly abused all his life.

Statements from probation officers[1]

In the 1970s, the media described criminals as showing a wanton disregard for life and property and depicted crime as being out of control in American society. By spotlighting crime in the 1970s, the media intensified fear of the adult male criminal and effected a change in how the public viewed the male criminal offender. No longer was the criminal a hero; no longer was crime romanticized as it sometimes had been in the past.

Changed attitudes toward the adult male criminal also affected perceptions of the juvenile male criminal. As the 1970s progressed, male delinquency was viewed with greater and greater intolerance by the public. "Get tough with youth crime" became a cry sounded by a variety of groups across the nation. In the early 1980s, as previously noted, "hard" and "soft" approaches emerged in juvenile corrections; i.e., a "hard line" approach has been taken with delinquents who commit serious crimes and a "soft line" approach with those involved in status offenses and minor crimes.

This chapter briefly discusses the extent and nature of male delinquency; the types of male offenders, with an emphasis on violent and gang delinquents; and policy implications for dealing with chronic or hard-core delinquents.

THE EXTENT AND NATURE OF MALE DELINQUENCY

Official statistics make it appear that the number of delinquents constitute only a small fraction of American youths, yet self-report studies show that the official statistics represent only the tip of the iceberg. Indeed, self-report studies consistently show that the majority of males break the law in minor ways but are not apprehended by the police for their socially unacceptable behavior.[2] However, only a small percentage of adolescent males commits serious and sometimes violent offenses, and, not surprisingly, these offenders are the ones most likely to be apprehended by the police and to be found delinquent by the juvenile court.[3]

A number of variables must be considered to obtain a clearer understanding of male delinquents in American society: sex, race, social class, area of residence, and group behavior.

Male and Female Delinquency

Official statistics show a wider differential between male and female delinquency than do self-report studies. According to the official statistics, males were arrested at a ratio of nearly four to one over females in 1982, with males accounting for 1,431,483 arrests and females, 373,205 arrests.[4] Yet self-report studies show that although a larger proportion of boys do report breaking the law more frequently and more seriously than girls, the pattern of delinquent behavior is much the same for boys and girls. Self-report studies also typically show that the ratio or differential between the sexes increases as the offense becomes more serious.[5]

Race and Male Delinquency

A number of studies dealing with race and delinquency have found that black males are disproportionately represented in the juvenile justice system. In 1982, the *Uniform Crime Reports* documented that whites under the age of eighteen accounted for 1,291,581 arrests, whereas blacks accounted for 471,495 arrests. Blacks represented only 12 to 13 percent of the population, but they accounted for 26.9 percent of all juvenile arrests and were confined at rates equal to those of whites. Hispanics, who had the second largest number of arrests among minority groups, had 180,613 arrests in 1982.[6] Frank R. Scarpitti and Richard M. Stephenson, in a study of sixteen- and seventeen-year-old delinquents, found that "blacks are overrepresented in institutions, [have] higher delinquency history scores (DHS), and [are] more likely to be recidivists."[7] Donald J. Black and Albert J. Reiss also reported that black juveniles have higher arrest rates than whites.[8] The Philadelphia cohort study further reported that chronic offenders are more likely to be nonwhite than white and that nonwhites are more likely than whites to become recidivists.[9] In addition, Frank Zimring, in a report for the Twentieth Century Fund, observes: "Most young offenders who commit acts of extreme violence and pursue criminal careers come from minority, ghetto, and poverty backgrounds; so do their victims."[10]

Social Class and Male Delinquency

The self-report studies have generally concluded that delinquency is unrelated or only slightly related to a boy's social class.[11] For example, of the twenty-six self-report investigations of social class and delinquency, only nine found the expected relationship of lower class to delinquency.[12] Yet Elliott and Ageton's 1977 national self-report study found that lower-class juveniles reported a greater number of offenses than workingclass or middle-class youths. The average number of crimes against persons reported by lower-class juveniles also was 1.5 times greater than that reported by the middle-class groups.[13] Moreover, Wolfgang et al., in the Philadelphia cohort study, found that a small number of lower-class males were committing the majority of personal and property crimes in urban areas.[14]

Much of the remainder of this chapter focuses on lower-class male delinquents, but first four basic types of middle-class offenders will be identified. The first category is made up of boys who have family problems. These youths tend to be loners and their offenses typically involve running away, truancy, and incorrigibility. When these status offenders do become involved in such delinquent offenses as shoplifting or alcohol or drug offenses, it is usually because they are seeking attention from their parents or are attempting to embarrass them.

A second group also includes boys in conflict with their parents, but these youths are seeking approval and acceptance from a peer culture. Their offenses, which are group-related, may include alcohol or drug offenses, senseless destruction of property, shoplifting or other forms of larceny, joyriding in "borrowed" cars, and disturbing the peace.[15]

A third group of middle-class offenders is influenced primarily by the desire for hedonistic gratification.[16] These affluent youths are bored with their lives and are seeking new thrills. While they generally have no serious problems with their parents, they are very concerned with generating excitement in their lives. They become involved in such delinquent activities as destroying or damaging public or private property, joyriding, larceny, drug or alcohol abuse, and disturbing the peace.

The fourth group of middle-class delinquents is made up of juveniles whose families have only recently moved up to middle-class status. Their fathers, who formerly held lower-class jobs, have been promoted to middle-class positions, such as lower management, plant foremen, and skilled workers. Robert H. Bohlke explains the behavior of this group through status inconsistency, for the children of the "nouvelle bourgeoisie" still carry lower-class values with them.[17] These adolescents sometimes cluster in gangs and, if the gang has an antisocial leader, the group may become involved in serious delinquent behavior, such as assault, robbery, auto theft, and sexual offenses.

Residence and Male Delinquency

Official statistics show that nearly five out of every six arrests of juveniles under eighteen are urban arrests. In 1982, 1,138,289 of the juveniles arrested were from urban areas, followed by 162,620 from suburban areas and 61,912 from rural areas.[18] The ecological approach to delinquency, which was discussed in Chapter 6, suggests that youth crime is more heavily concentrated in urban areas because of the disorganization and lack of services of such communities.[19]

However, some evidence exists that there has been a recent increase of delinquency in nonmetropolitan areas. Between the years 1971 and 1976, the average yearly increase in offenses reported to the police was greatest in rural areas and cities under 10,000. The lowest yearly mean increase was in the largest cities.[20] Yet both the early and more recent studies support the contention that rural youth seem to be involved in less serious offenses than their urban counterparts, although the differences are not large.[21]

Group Behavior and Male Delinquency

Group behavior, as previously noted, is an important correlate of male delinquency. Erickson and Jensen reported that whether male or female or whether in urban settings or small towns, juveniles tend to follow herd instincts when they violate the law.[22] Although recent studies have begun to show increasing involvements of females in group delinquency, male adolescents are still more likely to commit delinquent acts, especially serious offenses, in groups than are female adolescents. Walter B. Miller, in his analysis of youth gangs in fifteen major cities, has identified eighteen types and subtypes of law-violating youth groups (see Table 13-1).[23] Significantly, only three of these eighteen types and subtypes are designated as gangs. The others are designated as groups, cliques, rings, bands, networks, and crowds.[24]

Summing Up

Although official and self-report data sometimes disagree and wide gaps are present in our understanding of the variables relating adolescent males to delinquency, the available data seem to lead to the conclusions that: (1) males continue to commit more offenses than females, especially serious ones; (2) white males commit more offenses than nonwhites, but recidivists and chronic offenders are more likely to be nonwhite; (3) social class is related to male delinquency only in regard to serious and violent offenses; (4) the vast majority of male arrests still take place in urban areas, and (5) groups, especially for male delinquents, continue to be the setting for serious antisocial acts.

TYPES OF MALE OFFENDERS

The status offender, the emotionally disturbed offender, the property offender, the violent offender, and the gang delinquent are described in this section.

Status Offenders

Kobrin et al., evaluating data from a national study of status offenders, identified three groups of such offenders: the "heavies," who were predominantly serious delinquent offenders; the "lightweights," who committed misdemeanors as well as status offenses; and the conforming youths, who occasionally became involved in status offenses. The meaning of status offenses, according to this study, differed for each group. For heavies, a status offense was likely to be an incidental event. For lightweights, the pattern was one of minor and intermittent delinquent acts as well as status offenses. Conforming youth were likely to restrict themselves to multiple status offenses perhaps as an outburst of rebellion against adult authority.[25]

Further analysis indicated that most of those receiving a citation for a status offense were juveniles for whom no official record existed of a prior offense of any kind. These youths principally were between the ages of thirteen and sixteen, equally distributed between males and females, and more likely to be whites than nonwhites. Significantly, of those with no prior status or delinquent offenses, 83.1 percent remained free of subsequent offenses of any kind.[26]

Of those youths with offense records prior to a status offense arrest, the majority of whom were male, about one in ten had committed only status offenses. About one-quarter continued to confine their infractions to status offenses, another quarter

TABLE 13-1 Types and Subtypes of Law-Violating Youth Groups

Number	Designation
1	Turf gangs
2	Regularly-associated disruptive local groups/crowds
3	Solidary disruptive local cliques
4	Casual disruptive local cliques
5	Gain-oriented gangs/extended networks
6	Looting groups/crowds
7	Established gain-oriented cliques/limited networks
7.1	Burglary rings
7.2	Robbery bands
7.3	Larceny cliques and networks
7.4	Extortion cliques
7.5	Drug-dealing cliques and networks
7.6	Fraudulent gain cliques
8	Casual gain-oriented cliques
9	Fighting gangs
10	Assaultive cliques and crowds
10.1	Assaultive affiliation cliques
10.2	Assaultive public-gathering crowds
11	Recurrently-active assaultive cliques
12	Casual assaultive cliques

Source: Adapted from Walter B. Miller, *Crime by Youth Groups and Gangs in American Cities* (Washington, D.C.: Government Printing Office), chap. 25, chart 2, 1979.

showed a subsequent record of delinquent offenses, and approximately half remained free of recorded offenses.[27] But among those youths who had committed two or more prior status offenses, also more widely represented by males, there was an equal chance that their subsequent offenses would be of the delinquent or the status variety. In other words, those for whom status offense behavior had become chronic appeared to be as likely to commit misdemeanor and criminal offenses subsequently as to confine themselves to status offenses.[28]

Thus, this study challenges the findings of Charles Thomas's examination of status offenders, which found that status offenders differed very little in offense behavior from delinquent offenders and tended to progress from status to delinquent offenses.[29] But yet, because one-third of the Kobrin study consisted of status offenders who had committed delinquent offenses, some of whom continued to commit delinquent offenses, some male status offenders do differ very little in offense behavior from delinquent offenders.

Emotionally Disturbed Offenders

There appear to be three groups of emotionally disturbed offenders among male offenders: (1) youths who are given the label because of persistent behavior problems; (2) youths who are labeled because of a psychotic breakdown, and (3) conforming youths who are given the label because of a single violent act.

Youngsters with persistent behavior problems often are referred to mental health agencies because they are unable to function in everyday life. They seem to react more negatively than the typical incorrigible child to rejection and neglect at home. They also have difficulties in relating to their peers. Sonny, a sixteen-year-old boy with persistent behavior problems, had this to say about himself:

> To get out of St. Francis [psychiatric hospital], I had to sign a paper agreeing to rules. I was willing to do anything to get out of there. I was supposed to help around the home, be in at eleven, not swear, not have problems at school, and not threaten my mother, but I broke every one of these rules when I got home.[30]

A second group of youths who are labeled emotionally disturbed are those who have psychological breakdowns prior to or following the commitment of delinquent offenses. One youth experienced a psychotic break because of a sexual assault he received during his second day of confinement in a training school. He became extremely withdrawn and delusional and was subsequently diagnosed as a paranoid schizophrenic.[31]

A third group is made up of conforming youths who commit violent crimes that seem totally out of character. For example, one middle-class youth was considered an ideal young man. He was a good student in school, active in the Boy Scouts, attended Sunday School, appeared to have a happy home life, and had no prior status or delinquent offenses. Yet one night, he took a shotgun, shot his parents repeatedly, and then quartered them. The community was shocked and could not understand how such a quiet, well-mannered youth from a good middle-class home could commit such an act. But in working with this youngster, it became clear that he had exploded in such a violent way because he had been full of unexpressed rage against his parents.[32]

Property Offenders

Situational offenders, as previously indicated, drift in and out of delinquent behavior. But the unacceptable behavior of those situational offenders who commit property offenses can be divided into two groups: (1) those who commit only minor property offenses; and (2) those who commit more frequent and more serious property offenses.

Offenders in the first group are influenced by their peer group, tend to have some involvement with alcohol and drug use, and are not specialists in their offenses. This first group also generally is more committed to conforming values than to delinquent values. These youths occasionally become involved in serious property offenses, such as burglary, breaking and entering, auto theft, and arson, but they typically commit minor offenses: for example, destruction of private and school property, vandalism, and "joyriding." Middle-class offenders are more heavily represented in the first group of property offenders than in the second group, and generally either their offenses do not come to the attention of the authorities or they are diverted to nonjudicial agencies. In addition, the offenses of the first group tend to be less goal-oriented than those of the second group. A seventeen-year-old, in a fairly representative statement, noted:

> We used to do a lot of shit a few years ago. We would break into houses for the hell of it. I remember one time we burned a barn down. On Halloween, we really used to do a lot of stuff, like doing a lot of damage to the houses of people we didn't like. But we never got caught. My parents had no idea what we were doing. I don't do that kind of thing anymore. I plan to go to college next year.[33]

The second group of property offenders seems to have more commitment to delinquency than the first group; that is, these youths appear to be more involved in the spirit of delinquency discussed in Chapter 10 and to be more alienated from social norms. They also are more deeply involved in drug and alcohol use than those in the first group. Furthermore, although their offenses include both minor and serious property offenses, they are more frequently involved in serious property crimes. In addition, their delinquent behavior tends to be more purposeful than that of those in the first group; that is, they may break into a house because they intend to steal items in order to buy drugs or they may break into a store because they need spending money. Lower-class offenders tend to be overrepresented in the second group, and, not surprisingly, their more serious offenses are more likely to result in arrest by the police and a punitive disposition by the court. A male who appears to fall in the second group asserted:

> We robbed one place and got $140 cash, and they didn't know about that. We stole $3000 worth of postage stamps and sold them for $1000. We ripped off the truck when we stole the stamps. I used the parts on my car. They think I'm a small punk who goes around and takes rinky dink stuff, but the big jobs, I plan them out.[34]

Violent Delinquents

Violent youth crime inspires concern and fear among the public because of the personal threat it poses. A person is just as dead when shot by a fourteen-year-old as when gunned down by a thirty-year-old. But just how real is the problem of dangerous and violent juveniles?

Paul A. Strasburg summarizes the research on violent delinquents with these observations:

1. *Violent acts appear, for the most part, to be occasional occurrences within a random pattern of delinquent behavior, rather than a "specialty" of juveniles.*
2. *When committing a violent act, a delinquent is more likely to do so in company with at least one other juvenile than alone.*
3. *Older juveniles tend to be more seriously violent than younger juveniles, but there is growing evidence, including data in the Vera study, that the younger age groups (thirteen to fifteen) are catching up.*
4. *Minority youths (and especially black youths) tend to be both more delinquent and more violent than white youths.*
5. *The great majority of violent delinquents are not psychotic or otherwise seriously disturbed emotionally, although many are neurotic and characterized by poor impulse control.*
6. *Many if not most delinquents have learning problems, but the cause of those problems and their relationship to delinquency and violence are not easy to establish.*
7. *A two-parent family seems to offer some protection against delinquent behavior, but the presence of both parents has little to do with whether a delinquent becomes violent.*
8. *Within community boundaries, differences in socioeconomic status appear to be weakly correlated with juvenile violence, although children from poor communities (particularly from ghettos in large metropolitan centers) are more likely to become delinquent and violent than children living in more affluent communities.*[35]

The *Uniform Crime Reports* also document the fact that the juvenile crime problem is only minimally a problem of violence. Violence, which is defined as murder, forcible rape, robbery, and aggravated assault by the *Uniform Crime Reports,* occurs about one-ninth as frequently as such property crimes as burglary, larceny-theft, and motor vehicle theft. An examination of violent youthful offenders reveals two basic types: the first-time offender and the career offender.

First-Time Violent Offenders

These youths commit crimes of passion, generally directed against family members. E. I. Megargee refers to this type of offender as "the overcontrolled." These juveniles usually have a history of being overly compliant and have experienced considerable rejection.[36] They have learned to displace their aggression or to substitute a less drastic behavior. Meanwhile, their aggression builds up until their controls can no longer override it, and when they finally explode, they release all of their pent-up anger. The model youth becomes a murderer, perhaps shooting or knifing the victim repeatedly or dismembering the victim. Typically, following the release of their repressed anger, these youths immediately revert to their passive state.[37]

Career Violent Offenders

The second type of juvenile violent offender is the career offender. This type of violent offender is not restricted to violent offenses. Megargee describes this youth as "undercontrolled," with weak controls against aggression. Whenever he is frustrated or provoked, he strikes out against others.[38] He is often diagnosed as a psychopath or sociopath because of the chronic pattern of violence against persons. Some evidence exists that career violent offenders often are physically abused as children.[39] The career offender may commit murder unintentionally. He habitually carries a weapon, usually a gun; the weapon is readily available in any situation where he feels he must defend himself, such as in a robbery or a fight, and the weapon may be used suddenly and impulsively.[40] This youth frequently comes from a subculture of violence, and he sees violence as a necessary part of the struggle for survival. Finally, according to all of the cohort studies, these career or violent offenders are primarily male, black, poor, and young; and they are involved in violent acts for a number of reasons, most frequent among them material gain.[41]

Career violent offenders appear to be more likely to continue into adult crime than other male and female offenders. James Collins, Jr., used a 10 percent sample (or 971 individuals) of the Wolfgang et al. study and followed this smaller cohort to age thirty. He found that the follow-up sample contained 14.8 percent, or 144, chronic offenders who committed 74 percent of all offenses in Philadelphia and an even higher percentage of the serious ones. Data also revealed that youths who became chronic offenders early committed 82 percent more offenses than those who became chronic offenders only later.[42]

The following statements were made by typical career violent offenders:

That old man thought he was tough or something. Wouldn't give me his wallet, so I had to cut him up. He shouldn't be around when I need money if he doesn't want to give it to me.[43]

I'll hurt anyone who messes with me.[44]

We went into this liquor store to rob it. This old man behind the counter reached for something, and I thought it was a gun. I filled his stomach with lead.[45]

Gang Delinquents

Gang delinquency is an acknowledged problem in large urban areas. But even though "gang" has been the major concept used to guide the examination of collective youth crime in urban areas the past fifty years, little or no consensus exists as to what a gang actually is. Frederick Thrasher was one of the first to attempt to define the juvenile gang:

A gang is an interstitial group originally formed spontaneously and then integrated through conflict. It is characterized by the following types of behavior: meeting face to face, milling, movement through space as a unit, conflict, and planning. The result of this collective behavior is the development of tradition, unreflective internal structure, esprit de corps, solidarity, morale, group awareness, and attachment to local territory.[46]

More recently, Walter B. Miller, as part of his nationwide examination of urban gangs, asked his respondents for a definition of a gang. In an analysis of 1400 definitional elements provided by respondents, six major elements were found to be cited most frequently—being organized, having identifiable leadership, identifying with a territory, associating continuously, having a specific purpose, and engaging in illegal activity.[47] Miller combined these elements to create the following definition:

A youth gang is a self-formed association of peers, bound together by mutual interests, with identifiable leadership, well-developed lines of author- ity, and other organizational features, who act in concert to achieve a specific purpose or purposes which generally include the conduct of illegal activity and control over a particular territory, facility, or type of enterprise.[48]

Theories of Gang Formation

The most well-developed theories for the origins of juvenile gangs and gang delin- quency have come from Herbert A. Bloch and Arthur Niederhoffer, Richard A. Cloward and Lloyd E. Ohlin, Albert K. Cohen, Walter B. Miller, and Lewis Yablon- sky.

Bloch and Niederhoffer's theory is based on the idea that joining a gang is part of the experience male adolescents need to grow up to adulthood. The basic function of the gang thus is to provide a substitute for the formalized puberty rites found in other societies. Beliefs of the gang include such symbolically manly behavior as fighting, being loyal, developing a reputation for toughness, and dealing with the struggles of life. Also encouraging involvement in a gang are the beliefs that there is a greater chance of success in the gang, that hard work does not guarantee success, that conformity to the gang is the only acceptable kind, and that life is hard and individuals are worth little.[49]

Cloward and Ohlin's theory, as previously discussed, is based on the notion that lower-class boys interact with and gain support from other alienated individuals. These youngsters pursue illegitimate means to achieve the success they were unable to gain through legitimate means. In other words, lower-class adolescents would be able to meet the formal criteria for success were they not deprived of opportunities to do so. Cloward and Ohlin specify three subcultural orientations: criminal subcul- tures, conflict subcultures, and retreatist subcultures. Criminal subcultures are con- cerned with theft and other gain-producing delinquencies; conflict subcultures are concerned with violence, fighting, and inter-gang conflict; and retreatist subcultures are basically drug-oriented.[50]

Cohen's theory, also discussed in Chapter 6, is that gang delinquency represents a subcultural and collective solution to the problem of acquiring status that faces lower-class boys when they find themselves evaluated according to middle-class values in the schools. Cohen maintains that the delinquent subculture provides an organization within which lower-class youths can meet their status needs that remain unsatisfied in their interactions with middle-class social institutions. Cohen has identified a number of characteristics of the gang: it is nonutilitarian, malicious, negativistic, versatile; it engages in short-run hedonism; and it emphasizes group autonomy.[51]

Miller holds that there is a definite lower-class culture and that gang behavior is an expression of that culture. This lower-class culture, according to Miller, is conducive to law-violating behavior. The focal concerns of the culture in approximate order of importance are trouble, toughness, smartness, excitement, fate, and autonomy. Miller postulates that the concern of lower-class adolescents with becoming adults leads to the expression of these lower-class concerns with little regard for the legitimacy of the means of expression. Miller sees gang leadership as based mainly on smartness and on toughness. He views the gang as very cohesive and with high conformity to gang norms.[52]

Finally, Yablonsky is concerned with only one type of delinquent gang, the violent or conflict-oriented gang, and he proposes that conflict-oriented delinquent gangs arise out of certain conditions found in urban slum areas. Those conditions encourage the development of the sociopathic personality in adolescents, and such sociopathic individuals become the core leadership of a near-group or violent gang. The basic function of the near-group or violent gang is to offer a way to act out aggression or hostility in a more acceptable way than the other means available in the community.[53]

Each of the five theories of gang formation has received both support and criticism. But because these theories were based primarily on 1950s gangs, considerable research is needed into current expressions of gang activity in the United States.[54]

Changing Nature of Gang Activity

From the late 1940s through the early 1960s, teenage gangs in nearly every major urban area struck fear into the hearts of citizens. But when gangs began to reduce their activities or even to disappear from some urban areas in the mid- and late 1960s, some observers thought that the problem was coming to an end. New York City is one of the urban areas in which gang activity decreased significantly in the 1960s. The major reason offered for this apparent reduction of activity has been the use of hard-core drugs, while lesser reasons include the civil rights movement, urban riots, growth of militant organizations, Vietnam, and an exodus from the ghettos.[55]

A leader of a large Bronx gang in New York City reflected on the lack of gangs in the 1960s: "You can't keep a brother interested in clicking [gang activities] if he's high or nodding."[56] A college student who was a heroin addict for several years in Spanish Harlem in New York City during the 1960s also blamed drugs for the lack of gang activity:

> My brother was a big gang member. But we did not go for that kind of thing. Man, we were on drugs. That was cool. We were too busy trying to score to buy our drugs to fool around with gang activity. It was everybody for himself.[57]

However, as one city after another reported serious problems with youth gangs in the early 1970s, it became apparent that the gangs had returned. The youth gangs of the 1970s and early 1980s, which are as violent as the gangs of the 1950s, seem more intent on making money from crime. They are more systematic in their efforts to extort local merchants, engage in robberies, shake down students for money, intimidate local residents, and sell stolen goods. The security manager of a large grocery store in Brooklyn remarked:

> These gangs know exactly what they're doing. They send guys in here to watch the cash registers. They note who's getting a lot of change. Out in the parking lot, other kids try to rip them off.

> They'll send two guys in here. One guy deliberately acts very suspicious, to draw our attention; meanwhile, his confederate is boosting [stealing] stuff. We lose about $800 a week in meat they steal from us.

> You know what happens with it? They have a regular "meat route" nearby, a list of people they sell the meat to. They'll even take orders before going out to grab the stuff.[58]

Some gangs have become so sophisticated that the police regard their activities as organized crime. Those gangs keep attorneys on retainer. Indeed, some even print up business cards to further their careers in extortion, and they sell the cards to businesses for "protection" and to warn away rivals.[59]

Walter B. Miller, investigating the problem of youth gangs in the 1970s, conducted a national survey of gangs in major urban cities. Through interviews, questionnaires, and visits to those cities, he came to the conclusion that gang members were committing as much as one-third of all violent juvenile crimes, terrorizing whole communities and keeping many urban schools in a state of siege.[60]

Professionals in the justice system agreed that youth gangs are a problem of the utmost seriousness, for in Miller's study they reported problems with gangs in ten of the fifteen largest metropolitan areas. Respondents in six cities—New York, Philadelphia, Los Angeles, Chicago, Detroit, and San Francisco—considered gang problems to be especially serious. Miller estimates that during the 1970s the number of gangs in these six cities ranged from 760 to 2700 and included from 28,500 to 81,500 gang members.

Of these six cities, Miller found that New York appeared to experience a lull in gang violence between 1965 and 1971, followed by a dramatic rise in the number of gangs and gang crimes up to 1973. The number of gang-related killings declined markedly after 1973, but the number of reported gangs, gang members, and gang-member arrests remained at a high level. Chicago experienced the rise and fall of a number of supergangs between 1965 and 1973, with gang killings peaking in 1969. Rising gang-member arrest rates, as well as the growth of smaller and more traditional gangs, characterized gang activity in Chicago between 1973 and 1975. In Los Angeles, Spanish American gangs created problems between 1965 and 1971, primarily in established Spanish-American communities. Black gangs began to increase around 1972, and they contributed the bulk of the record number of killings there in the mid-1970s. In Philadelphia, problems with black gangs were intense throughout the 1960s and police reported an average of about forty gang-related killings per year. Although the number of gang-related killings decreased in the

1970s, the number of gangs and gang members in Philadelphia continued to remain at a high level. Detroit reported a decline in the gang problem during the first part of the 1960s, but larger gangs experienced growth between 1968 and 1973 and smaller gangs also increased in number between 1973 and 1975. Finally, San Francisco saw a decline in black gangs early in the 1960s, with the proliferation of a small number of highly criminal Chinese gangs during this period. The number of relatively small Asian gangs, especially Filipino, increased between 1971 and 1975, and a resurgence of black gangs also seemed to occur during this time.

Miller found that gang members have a number of assault techniques. Significantly, in the mid-1970s, the rate of murder by firearms or other weapons was higher than ever before; the five cities that had the most serious gang problems averaged at least 175 gang-related killings a year between 1972 and 1974. Forays by small bands, armed and often motorized, seemed to have replaced the class "rumble." But gang members, whether they were involved in assaults on others or in the destruction of community property, appeared primarily to be motivated by desire for material gain and for control over public facilities (in defense of their turf).

Social characteristics of gang members in the 1970s resembled those reported for past periods. They were primarily male, ranged in age from about ten to twenty-one, came from low-income communities, and were largely black and Hispanic, although gangs with a variety of Asian origins seemed to be on the increase (see Table 13-2).

In 1975, Miller predicted that in the late 1970s and early 1980s youth gang problems would worsen in Los Angeles, Detroit, and San Francisco, improve in Philadelphia, and remain stable in New York and Chicago. Failing to see any immediate relief from gang violence and predatory activity in this country, he concluded his landmark study with these words:

> The basic question—"How serious are problems posed by youth gangs and youth groups today, and what priority should be granted gang problems among a multitude of current crime problems?"—must be approached with considerable caution, owing to a persistent tendency to exaggerate the seriousness of gang activity and to represent the "gang of today" as more

TABLE 13-2 Major Ethnic Categories of Gang Members in Six Cities

	Number	Percent
Black	29,000	47.6
Hispanic	22,000	36.1
Non-Hispanic white	5,400	8.8
Asian	4,600	7.5

Source: Walter B. Miller, *Violence by Youth Gangs and Youth Groups as a Crime Problem in Major American Cities* (Washington, D.C.: U.S. Government Printing Office, 1975), p. 66.

violent than at any time in the past. Exercising such caution, the materials presented in this report appear amply to support the conclusion that youth gang violence is more lethal today than ever before, that the security of a wider sector of the citizenry is threatened by gangs to a greater degree than ever before, and that violence and other illegal activities by members of youth gangs and groups in the United States of the mid-1970s represents a crime problem of the first magnitude which shows little prospect of early abatement.[61]

THE JUVENILE JUSTICE SYSTEM
AND THE URBAN DELINQUENT

What is it like to be an urban delinquent who commits violent crimes? Obviously, this question can be answered literally only by a juvenile who grows up in an urban environment, but this section will attempt to capture a glimpse of what experiences these youths have.

Luis, a fifteen-year-old Latin youth, had had to struggle to survive for as long as he could remember. He believed that life was basically survival of the fittest: You do unto others before they do unto you.[62] Life for him was a continued hustle and a struggle. Stealing was the only kind of work he had ever done. Luis never worried about the terror he inflicted on his victims or about their physical loss. His only concern was that he might attack someone armed with a gun or that he might get caught. He sometimes attacked his victims with his bare hands, sometimes with a knife with a six-inch blade, and sometimes with the assistance of others:

Sometimes you run up in the back and yoke him with an arm around the neck, and the other boys take the money out of his pocket.[63]

Luis, who fought with his parents, spent little time at home and as much time as possible with a gang in which he was involved. He looked upon school as a total waste of time, and, not surprisingly, was continually involved in disruptive and truant behavior.

Social workers and psychiatrists were called in to evaluate Luis, and the decision was made to refer him to the juvenile court for a foster care placement. The juvenile court adjudicated him as a MINS [minor in need of supervision], and he was placed in the care of the department of social service, which sent him to a foster care placement. But Luis did not care for that placement and ran away on the second day. He returned home, was picked up by the police, returned to the foster home, and ran away again on the second day. This process continued for some time, until the juvenile court made the decision to adjudicate Luis to a private training school several hours away from his home. There, he received the "benefit" of guided group interaction and was taught the basic principles of transactional analysis. Luis looked upon such therapy as a "bunch of bull shit," but he did decide to improve his behavior to earn the privilege of a home furlough. The home furlough was given, and he assured his "keepers" that he would return. But he had no intention of returning.

This youth, as many others, got lost in the system, and no attempt was made to pick him up.

Once he was back on the streets, his task became one of avoiding apprehension by the police while he and other members of the gang survived through robbing whomever they could. He looked upon the police as the enemy, but this did not come so much from bad experiences with police officers as it did from the "cop-and-robber" game that Luis and his companions played with the police. Their job was to avoid arrest, and the job of the police was to catch them.

Soon Luis found himself referred to the juvenile court and was adjudicated a delinquent. The juvenile judge decided to give him a chance and place him on probation. Luis resented the routine of reporting to the probation officer and he missed his weekly appointments whenever he could. He did not object to his probation officer, but he did mind the court interfering with his life.[64]

Probation, like all the other treatment approaches used with Luis, did not work. He was returned to court on three occasions, on the first two of which he was reassigned to probation with a lecture from the judge. But all he was concerned with was the bottom line, whether he could return home and go back to the streets or would be sent to a state institution.

Finally, the judge lost his patience, and Luis was adjudicated to the custody of the state department of corrections. The staff at the diagnostic center made the decision, given Luis' long-term involvement in juvenile crime, to send him to an end-of-the-line institution.

Luis, as a fifteen-year-old, was younger than most of the other residents of the institution. On the second day, a black resident tried to extort cigarettes from Luis, provoking a fight. Both boys were placed on restriction. Ten days later, upon being released to the general population, Luis was approached about sex. He grabbed a chair and hit the other youth. While being restrained by a cottage supervisor, he yelled to the other residents that he would kill "any f————er who tried to mess with him."

From that point on, Luis had his reputation. Nobody "messed with him," and he eventually became the leader of the peer subculture in his cottage. But Luis was in constant trouble with the staff: he instigated a riot on one occasion, attempted to escape twice, and developed an exploitation ring of weaker students. At each review, he was turned down for release, and eventually the decision was made not to release Luis until he turned eighteen.

Luis finally got back on the streets, after spending over two years in that "damn training school." But nearly all of his old gang was gone. One member had been killed in a gang fight, several were in adult prison, and others were in training school. In terms of his struggle for survival, Luis had to decide whether he would continue his criminal activity as an adult or would settle down and find a legitimate job.

POLICY IMPLICATIONS

Violent youth crime is unarguably a serious matter today. Simon Dinitz and John Conrad proposed five principles of system intervention for the violent offender:

1. *There must be an adverse consequence for every delinquent act. It should follow that intervention must never be nominal; the message should be clear at every stage of a delinquent career that his situation will get worse with every new delinquency.*
2. *At every stage, decision makers must be governed by the principle of minimum penetration of the system. Once a consequence has been set in convincing manner, a limit must also be set. The juvenile and his family must be likewise convinced that there is a way out of the mess he is in.*
3. *At all points, the disposition of the juvenile offender should be the least severe possible, consistent with public safety. If possible, the child should remain at home. If he must be removed, he should not have to go any farther away than necessary from the community in which he lives. If he must be committed to a state facility, it should be for as brief a period of time as is consistent with his safe restoration to the community.*
4. *At all points, there is a responsibility on the part of all agents of the system and contractors for service to identify strengths in the child on which building toward citizenship can be grounded, and unsatisfactory conditions of health, education, and socialization which can be remedied.*
5. *There must be a recognition that for certain chronic offenders, especially those who have exceeded a level of seriousness in the nature of their delinquencies, extended restraint will ordinarily be necessary. This restraint may be in a correctional facility; it may also be a heavily programmed community-based control.*[65]

In the short-range or systematic context of the justice system's handling of violent offenders, Dinitz and Conrad's recommendations provide positive guidelines. But, Weis and Hawkins' social development model offers an interlocking of the sociocultural, economic, and political perspectives that could have long-range consequences for dealing with youth crime in American society.[66]

The social development model is based upon the integration of social control theory and cultural learning theory. According to social control theory, the weakening, absence, or breakdown of social controls leads to delinquency.[67] Cultural learning, or cultural deviance, theory emphasizes the role of peers and the community in the rise of delinquency. In disorganized communities, then, youths are at greater risk of delinquency.[68]

Social control theory focuses on the individual characteristics that lead to delinquent behavior and the impact of the major socializing institutions on delinquency, while cultural learning theory examines the role of the community context in the process of learning criminal and delinquent attitudes and behaviors. Social control theory proposes that youths become delinquent because of inadequate social controls, and cultural learning theory adds that juveniles become socialized to delinquency in disorganized communities. Thus, the social development model integrates these two perspectives, and it may well offer the most promise for explaining and preventing juvenile delinquency.[69] Figure 13-1 provides a schematic expression of the social development model.

The social development model proposes that the development of attachments to

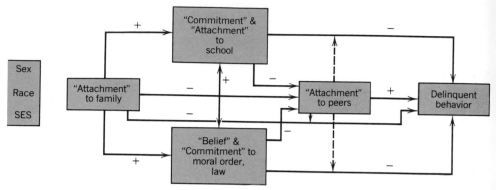

Figure 13-1 The Social Development Model of Delinquency

Source: U.S. Department of Justice, *Prevention of Violent Juvenile Crime Research and Development Program* (Washington, D.C.: U.S. Government Printing Office, 1982), p. 63.

parents will lead to attachments to school and a commitment to education, as well as a belief in and commitment to conventional behavior and the law. Learning theory describes the process by which these bonds develop. If juveniles are given adequate opportunities for involvement in legitimate activities and are able to acquire the necessary skills within a consistent reward structure, they will develop the bonds of attachment, commitment, and belief. However, a disorganized community with high rates of delinquency and crime reduces the potential of social control because the socializing institutions are weakened by higher rates of family disorganization, inadequate educational facilities, few material and social resources, and less respect for the law. Consequently, those youths who are not receiving adequate support and direction from their families and who are not experiencing success in school are most vulnerable to delinquency.[70] The social development model implies the following principles for prevention and control of delinquency in those neighborhoods characterized by high rates of serious and violent delinquency:

1. *A key to delinquency prevention is community organization against delinquent behavior.*
2. *Community control of prevention efforts and of other services for youth should be encouraged.*
3. *The participation of youth, as well as adults, should be encouraged.*
4. *Delinquent groups and gangs should be coopted into constructive activities or disbanded.*
5. *Access to illegitimate opportunities should be restricted, and legitimate educational, employment, and social activities should be accessible to all youth.*
6. *Efforts to improve the control effectiveness of the family should be directed at enhancing its direct control function and its ability to develop self-control among children.[71]*

The implementation of the social development model into policy appears to offer the most effective long-term means to reduce violent crime in American society. But, again, implementing these strategies would require major societal changes.

SUMMARY

The likelihood of an adolescent's becoming a delinquent is largely determined by four contexts: structural, situational, interactional, and personal. The structural factors pertain to the sociocultural, economic, legal, and political contexts on a societal level that affect all adolescents. The doctrine of adolescent inferiority is a major thread that ties these societal contexts together.

The situational factors include the racial background, residential location, environmental influences in the neighborhood, and family situations of a particular youngster. Thus, white males commit more offenses than nonwhites, but chronic offenders are more likely to be nonwhite. Social class appears to be related to male delinquency only in terms of serious and violent offenses. The vast majority of arrests still take place in urban areas, but nonmetropolitan delinquent crimes appear to be increasing.

In the interactional context, a youngster derives meaning and has his (or her) needs met or ignored in his (or her) social contacts with family members, peers in the community, teachers and fellow students at school, and leaders and participants in churches, community organizations, and school activities. With some youngsters, their needs are met in the various interactional contexts, and they find little reason to become involved in law-violating activities. But with others, their needs are not met at home or at school and, therefore, they become attracted to drug subcultures or to delinquent gangs. Significantly, group behavior continues to be the setting for male serious antisocial acts, and drug and alcohol abuse is one of the most important correlates of male delinquency.

Finally, the personal context is probably the most important of all because each youngster translates what happens to him in the other individual contexts through his (or her) experiences and assumptions concerning life. While one youngster may make the decision to become involved in a drug culture, another may decide to work hard in school and to make something of himself. Thus, beyond the cases discussed in this chapter are real male adolescents who are seeking to make sense of their lives.

Although the view of the media and many citizens that male delinquency is becoming increasingly violent and out of control is overstated, male delinquency is a serious social problem and requires attention from policymakers at all levels. The social development model of delinquency, combined with short-term intervention strategies, appears to be the most effective means of reducing serious male delinquency in American society. Our degree of success in dealing with these offenders in the 1980s will largely determine the degree of safeness of our streets in the 1990s.

Discussion Questions

1. How does the classification scheme used in this chapter differ from the one in the chapter on the female delinquent? What do these differences have to say about the patterns of male and female delinquency?

2. Discuss the most important variables affecting the nature and extent of male delinquency.

3. What attitudes would the middle-class delinquent have toward the juvenile justice system? Why would these attitudes be different than those of Luis and other lower-class delinquents?

4. What should society do about chronic offenders? Can they be rehabilitated?

5. What could an urban school dominated by predatory gangs do to make the environment safer for both pupils and teachers?

References

Ageton, Suzanne S., and Elliott, Delbert S. *The Incidence of Delinquent Behavior in a National Probability Sample of Adolescents.* Boulder, Colo.: Behavioral Research Institute, 1978.

Bloch, H. A., and Niederhoffer, A. *The Gang: A Study in Adolescent Behavior.* New York: Philosophical Library, 1958.

Cloward, Richard A., and Ohlin, Lloyd E. *Delinquency and Opportunity: A Theory of Delinquent Gangs.* Glencoe, Ill.: Free Press, 1960.

Cohen, Albert K. *Delinquent Boys: The Culture of the Gang.* Glencoe, Ill.: Free Press, 1955.

Megargee, E. I. "Uncontrolled and Overcontrolled Personality Types in Extreme Antisocial Aggression." *Psychological Monographs* 80 (1980).

Miller, Walter B. "Lower-Class Culture as a Generating Milieu of Gang Delinquency." *Journal of Social Issues* 14 (1958): 5–19.

———. *Violence by Youth Gangs and Youth Groups as a Crime Problem in Major American Cities.* Washington, D.C.: U.S. Government Printing Office, 1975.

Shichor, David, and Kelly, Delos H., eds. *Critical Issues in Juvenile Delinquency.* Lexington, Mass.: D.C. Heath & Company, 1980.

Weis, Joseph G., and Sederstrom, John. *The Prevention of Serious Delinquency: What to Do?* National Institute for Juvenile Justice and Delinquency Prevention, Office of Juvenile Justice and Delinquency Prevention, Washington, D.C.: U.S. Government Printing Office, 1981.

Yablonsky, Lewis. *The Violent Gang.* New York: Macmillan Publishing Company, 1962.

FOOTNOTES

1. Interviewed in May through August 1982.

2. Donald G. Gibbons, *Delinquent Behavior,* 3d ed. (Englewood Cliffs, N.J.: Prentice-Hall, 1981), p. 53.

3. Refer to Marvin E. Wolfgang et al., *Delinquency and the Birth Cohort* (Chicago: University of Chicago Press, 1973), which was discussed in Chapter 2.

4. Data are derived from the *Uniform Crime Reports, 1983* (Washington, D.C.: U.S. Government Printing Office, 1983), p. 173.

5. See Chapter 12 for the specific findings of these self-report studies.

6. *Uniform Crime Reports, 1983,* p. 185.

7. Frank R. Scarpitti and Richard M. Stephenson, "A Study of Probation Effectiveness," *Journal of Criminal Law, Criminology and Police Science* 59 (September 1968), pp. 361–369.

8. Donald J. Black and Albert J. Reiss, "Police Control of Juveniles," *American Sociological Review* 35 (1970), pp. 63–77.

9. Wolfgang et al., *Delinquency and the Birth Cohort,* p. 90.

10. Franklin E. Zimring, "Confronting Youth Crime," in *Twentieth Century Fund Task Force Report on Sentencing Policy toward Young Offenders* (New York: Holmes & Meier, 1978), p. 4.

11. F. I. Nye, *Family Relationships and Delinquent Behavior* (New York: John Wiley & Sons, 1958).

12. Charles R. Tittle and Wayne J. Villemez, "Social Class and Criminality," *Social Forces* 56 (December 1977), p. 475.

13. Suzanne S. Ageton and Delbert S. Elliott, *The Incidence of Delinquent Behavior in a National Probability Sample of Adolescents* (Boulder, Colo.: Behavioral Research Institute, 1978).

14. Wolfgang et al., *Delinquency and the Birth Cohort.*

15. See William Kvaraceus and Walter B. Miller, "Norm-Violating Behavior in Middle-Class Culture," in *Middle-Class Juvenile Delinquency,* edited by Edmund W. Vaz (New York: John Wiley & Sons, 1967), pp. 233–241, for an explanation of the behavior of this group that focuses on the upward diffusion of workingclass values and behavior patterns into the middle class.

16. See Joseph W. Scott and Edmund W. Vaz, "A Perspective on Middle-Class Delinquency," in *Middle-Class Juvenile Delinquency,* pp. 207–222, for a discussion of the hedonistic gratification of the youth culture in America.

17. Robert H. Bohlke, "Social Mobility, Stratification Inconsistency and Middle-Class Delinquency," in *Middle-Class Juvenile Delinquency,* pp. 222–233.

18. *Uniform Crime Reports, 1983,* pp. 191, 203, 215.

19. See Clifford Shaw and Henry D. McKay, *Juvenile Delinquency and Urban Areas* (Chicago: University of Chicago Press, 1942); Harold Finestone, *Victims of Change* (Westport, Conn.: Greenwood Press, 1976), pp. 116–150.

20. *Uniform Crime Reports* from 1971 to 1976, cited in Christine Alder, Gordon Bazemore, and Kenneth Polk, "Delinquency in Nonmetropolitan Areas," in *Critical Issues in Juvenile Delinquency,* edited by David Shichor and Delos H. Kelly (Lexington, Mass.: Lexington Books, 1980), p. 48.

21. Ibid., p. 50.

22. Maynard L. Erickson and Gary F. Jensen, "Delinquency Is Still Group Behavior: Toward Revitalizing the Group Premise in the Sociology of Deviance," *Journal of Criminal Law and Criminology* 68 (1977), pp. 388–395.

23. Walter B. Miller, "Gangs, Groups, and Serious Youth Crime," in *Critical Issues of Juvenile Delinquency,* pp. 115–118.

24. Ibid., p. 130.

25. Solomon Kobrin, Frank R. Hellum, and John W. Peterson, "Offense Patterns of Status Offenders," in *Critical Issues in Juvenile Delinquency,* p. 211.

26. Ibid., p. 230–231.

27. Ibid., p. 231.

28. Ibid., p. 232.

29. Charles W. Thomas, "Are Status Offenders Really So Different?" *Crime and Delinquency* 22 (1976), pp. 438–455.

30. Interviewed in May 1982.

31. The author worked with this youth in an institution in Ohio.

32. The author worked with this youth in an institution in Ohio.

33. Interviewed in October 1982.

34. Interviewed in June 1982.

35. Paul A. Strasburg, *Violent Delinquents: A Report to the Ford Foundation from the Vera Institute of Justice* (New York: Simon & Schuster, 1978), pp. 78–79.

36. E. I. Megargee, "Uncontrolled and Overcontrolled Personality Types in Extreme Antisocial Aggression," *Psychological Monographs* 80 (New York: Tavistock, 1969).

37. Vicki L. Agree, *Treatment of the Violent Incorrigible Adolescent* (Lexington, Mass.: Lexington Books, 1979), p. 90.

38. Megargee, "Uncontrolled and Overcontrolled Personality Types."

39. See Chapter 9 for a discussion of these studies.

40. Agree, *Treatment of the Violent Incorrigible Adolescent,* p. 91.

41. Muriel Gardiner, *The Deadly Innocents: Portraits of Children Who Kill* (New York: Basic Books, 1976), p. xx.

42. James Collins, "Chronic Offender Careers" (Paper presented to the American Society of Criminology, Tucson, Arizona, November 4–7, 1976), p. 5.

43. James Garabarino and Glen Gilliam, *Understanding Abusive Families* (Lexington, Mass.: Lexington Books, 1980), p. 175.

44. Interviewed in January 1972.

45. Interviewed in May 1973.

46. Frederick Thrasher, *The Gang* (Chicago: University of Chicago Press, 1927), p. 57.

47. Walter B. Miller, "Gangs, Groups, and Serious Youth Crime," in *Critical Issues in Juvenile Delinquency,* pp. 120–121.

48. Ibid., p. 121.

49. H. A. Bloch and A. Niederhoffer, *The Gang: A Study in Adolescent Behavior* (New York: Philosophical Library, 1958).

50. Richard A. Cloward and Lloyd E. Ohlin, *Delinquency and Opportunity: A Theory of Delinquent Gangs* (Glencoe, Ill: Free Press, 1960).

51. Albert K. Cohen, *Delinquent Boys: The Culture of the Gang* (Glencoe, Ill.: Free Press, 1955).

52. Walter B. Miller, "Lower-Class Culture as a Generating Milieu of Gang Delinquency," *Journal of Social Issues* 14 (1958), pp. 5–19.

53. Lewis Yablonsky, *The Violent Gang* (New York: Macmillan Publishing Company, 1962).

54. Nicholas A. Reuterman, "Formal Theories of Gangs," in *Gang Delinquency,* edited by Desmond S. Cartwright, Barbara Tomson, and Hershey Schwartz (Monterey, Calif.: Brooks/Cole Publishing Company, 1975), p. 43.

55. Craig Collins, "Youth Gangs of the 70s," *Police Chief* 42 (September 1975), p. 50.

56. Ibid.

57. Interviewed in March 1974.

58. Collins, "Youth Gangs of the 70s," p. 52.

59. Paul Weingarten, "Mean Streets," *Chicago Tribune Magazine,* 19 September 1982, p. 12.

60. Walter B. Miller, *Violence by Youth Gangs and Youth Groups as a Crime Problem in Major American Cities* (Washington, D.C.: U.S. Government Printing Office, 1975). Much of the following materials is derived from Chapter 15 of Miller's study.

61. Ibid., p. 205.

62. See Barry Krisberg, "Gang Youth and Hustling: The Psychology of Survival," *Issues in Criminology* 9 (Spring 1974), pp. 115–129.

63. Joseph B. Treaster, "Crime at an Early Age: On the Violent Streets of Luis Guzman," *New York Times,* 9 November 1981, p. 17.

64. See Peggy C. Giordano, "The Sense of Injustice: An Anaylsis of Juveniles' Reactions to the Justice System," *Criminology* 14 (May 1976), for reactions of youthful offenders to the probation process.

65. Simon Dinitz and John Conrad, "The Dangerous Two Percent," in *Critical Issues in Juvenile Delinquency,* p. 152.

66. Joseph G. Weis and J. David Hawkins, *Background Paper for Delinquency Prevention Research and Development Program* (Washington, D.C.: National Institute for Juvenile Justice and Delinquency Prevention, Office of Juvenile Justice and Delinquency Prevention, Washington, D.C.: U.S. Government Printing Office, 1979).

67. Travis Hirschi, *Causes of Delinquency* (Berkeley: University of California Press, 1969).

68. Clifford R. Shaw, *Delinquency Areas* (Chicago: University of Chicago Press, 1929); Clifford Shaw and Henry D. McKay, *Juvenile Delinquency in Urban Areas* (Chicago: University of Chicago Press, 1942).

69. U.S. Department of Justice, *Violent Juvenile Offender Program: Part II: Prevention of Violent Juvenile Crime Research and Development Program* (Washington, D.C.: U.S. Government Printing Office, 1982), p. 63.

70. Joseph G. Weis and John Sederstrom, *The Prevention of Serious Delinquency: What to Do?* (National Institute for Juvenile Justice and Delinquency Prevention, Office of Juvenile Justice and Delinquency Prevention, Washington, D.C.: U.S. Government Printing Office, 1981).

71. Ibid.

INTERVIEW WITH JAMES F. SHORT, JR.

Knowledge of general processes and forces in the production and control of delinquency can be derived only from crosscultural research. The other side of this coin, of course, is that knowledge of the particular cultural context is indispensable as well.

In this interview, Professor James F. Short, Jr., talks about delinquent gangs, the Chicago Area Projects, the insights of the Shaw and McKay tradition, the importance of multidimensional models in understanding delinquency, and the continuities and discontinuities that exist in delinquency theory. Professor Short has written widely on these topics and is one of the most highly respected researchers on delinquency in the United States.

Question: What do you feel are the central insights that the Shaw and McKay tradition have contributed to understanding delinquency in America?

Short: This question can only be answered properly in light of the state of knowledge of sociology and the "situation" of the discipline during the 1920s and 30s. Clifford Shaw and Henry McKay were very much a product of the intellectual excitement of the Chicago School of urban sociology. They drew heavily on the work of Park and of Burgess, and Burgess in particular remained one of their most ardent supporters for the remainder of his life. Burgess' "Study of the Delinquent as a Person" was published in 1923, six years before *De-*

James F. Short, Jr., is professor of sociology and director of the Social Research Center at Washington State University, where he was also dean of the graduate school from 1964 to 1968. He received the M.A. and Ph.D. degrees from the University of Chicago. Dr. Short has authored or edited ten books, including Suicide and Homicide *(with A. F. Henry, 1954);* Group Process and Gang Delinquency *(with F. L. Strodtbeck, 1965); and* Delinquency, Crime, and Society *(1974). His current research activities include study of the social impacts of crime, juvenile delinquency, and other hazards and the sociology of risk assessment. Interviewed in February 1984, and used with permission.*

linquency Areas. Shaw and McKay were part of the "second generation" of Chicago sociologists to study the city as a laboratory. In this they were building on the foundation established, not only by Park and Burgess, but by Small, Thomas, Henderson, and others, some of whom, such as Charles E. Merriam, were from other disciplines.

Much has been made of the importance of their small town and rural backgrounds for the work that Shaw and McKay did. Having known both of them reasonably well, I think the Chicago School influences were much greater than any such personally idiosyncratic factors on what they did and how they went about it. I suppose I knew Henry much the better of the two, because Shaw died so early. Henry was a thoroughgoing urbanite. He lived in an apartment on the South Side, and enjoyed urban life immensely.

Having said this, the answer to your question goes directly back to what the Chicago School was doing and how they went about it. The human ecology perspective was a natural, of course, and Shaw and McKay pursued it very well. But the Cooley-Dewey-Mead influence was equally strong, as was that of W. I. Thomas, and Thomas provided an excellent role model for how to study personalities and communities. Shaw and McKay found a way to combine these influences, by studying the distribution in space of court cases, relating this distribution to community characteristics, to the empirical finding that most offenses were committed in the company of others, and to case studies of individual delinquent boys. For me, this combination of methods and theoretical perspectives has always been the greatest contribution of the Shaw and McKay collaboration. Ironically, this is perhaps the greatest need today in the study of delinquency.

Question: In your introduction to *Delinquency, Crime, and Society*, you suggest that a multidimensional approach is needed to explain delinquency in American society. Would you develop more what this multidimensional approach would look like?

Short: It would involve combinations of theoretical and methodological approaches. It would not be culture-bound, though surely studies of delinquency and of delinquents within particular cultures are important. But it would seek generalization beyond particular cultures, as well as generalization within particular cultural contexts. Shaw and McKay did not do this, though they sought to extend their generalizations beyond the particular context of Chicago. But they did do something else which a multidimensional approach must do, namely they related their findings and the interpretations to the mainstream of the discipline. Regrettably, disciplinary specialization has led often to insularity of subdisciplines from the mainstream. Shaw and McKay's references were mainly to work other sociologists, social psychologists, and psychologists were doing, rather than to other delinquency studies.

A multidimensional approach would recognize and relate different levels of explanation to one another: the individual, and the macro- and microsociological levels (or micro- and macroeconomic, political, etc., levels). Al Cohen and I have written about this problem, in Merton and Nisbet's social problems book, as Bob Meier and I have in *The State of Sociology*. It is a problem that I am even now working on, for a book Bob Meier is editing.

Question: What are the most important continuities and discontinuities in delinquency research?

Short: In a way, I have discussed this question above. The continuities lie in the empirical and theoretical traditions that have survived the past half-a-century of delinquency studies, and, more importantly, sociology as a discipline. They include socialization theory (of which differential association may be considered a special case), social control theory, cultural deviance or subcultural

theory, and strain theory—though I dislike these labels and fervently believe they do a disservice both to social reality and to those who are most prominently identified with each. The empirical continuities, of course, are identified in the main with particular theories, though there is considerable overlap: subcultural theory with ecological methods and with field observation, socialization theory with case studies and clinical observation, survey research with each of the theoretical traditions to some extent, etc. Discontinuities relate to our failure to combine these levels of explanation effectively, or even to replicate studies so as at least to learn the limits of generalization.

Among our greatest failures, in my opinion, is to formalize theory. In part this is due to the failure to relate delinquency studies to the mainstream, though the mainstream has not advanced very far in this respect, either.

Let me return to the first question briefly. One would have to say that the Shaw and McKay tradition sensitized us forever to the importance of economic and ecological forces in shaping the particular behaviors represented in court statistics (youngsters and police, courts, etc.), and they demonstrated quite clearly that the community milieu was important in how boys related to institutions and to each other. These insights were more important than were specific empirical findings or theoretical statements. Neither Shaw nor McKay was a great theorist. Henry was a meticulous statistician, a skeptic who helped to keep all with whom he associated on their toes intellectually. And Shaw's action orientation was more important in general orientation than in specifics, e.g., as to the role and the possibility of indigenous leadership.

Question: Does the Chicago Area Project still present a viable model for dealing with delinquency in urban areas?

Short: I think the answer to this question depends largely on what you mean by a "model." If you mean a process by which indigenous leaders are identified and encouraged to involve themselves and their communities in activities aimed at keeping young people out of trouble, helping them to identify with community institutions, and in some measure to gain control over their lives, I think the answer is yes. If you mean a program of specific activities designed to appeal to young people, keep them busy, even involving their parents in doing so, the answer is no. There are recent examples of the former: some of the programs now being supported by the Eisenhower Foundation, for example, in Philadelphia, in San Juan, and a few other places. The Chicago Area Project also provides some examples, though in some cases community committees appear to function more like the second description above. I am no longer close enough to the program to be certain or to generalize. A few years ago I gave a talk to a conference sponsored by the Illinois Delinquency Prevention Commission, in Springfield. I think you may have been there. If so, you may recall that my theme was that Shaw's was an experimental approach, and that the Area Projects should remain true to his vision in that respect. I warned, perhaps gratuitously, against the ossification of ideas and programs which often accompanies institutionalization of even the best of approaches.

Question: What is the state of the art of gang delinquency research today? Have we really moved beyond the 1960s? What new directions does gang research need to go?

Short: What research? I know of no ongoing systematic research on gangs, though I am told that Mac Klein may be doing such research. Here is another great discontinuity. Cities all over the country complain about gangs, or "loose groups," yet the best research on youth gangs is nearly twenty years old and I have heard no great outcry for research—only for "doing something" about the problem. To answer your questions specifically, I do not think we have moved much beyond the 1960s in gang research. Most of what has happened since that time has been journalistic or impressionistic on the part of youth workers, law enforcement officials, and others, including sociologists. It really is quite disgraceful. The relationship between gangs and politics appears in some cities to have changed, principally as a result of the aftermath of the 1960s Great Society and War on Poverty programs, and law enforcement, all of which were largely uninformed about the nature of youth groups and politically naïve. In Chicago, the release from prison of some gang leaders has apparently led to more sophisticated underworld activities on the part of some youth groups and others not so young. But we really know very little about these matters, and this is both tragic and shortsighted.

Question: What can the crosscultural context teach us about delinquency in American society?

Short: I have already alluded to the question of the necessity of crosscultural research if theories are not to be culture-bound. Knowledge of general processes and forces in the production and control of delinquency can be derived only from crosscultural research. The other side of this coin, of course, is that knowledge of the particular cultural context is indispensable, as well. But we need to know what it is about age and sex, and the nature of particular social systems, for example, that produces delinquency.

JUVENILE CORRECTIONS

CHAPTER 14

AN OVERVIEW OF THE JUVENILE JUSTICE PROCESS

CHAPTER OUTLINE

It used to be crime out of boredom, just having fun. Now, it's crime for profit. We've some fifteen-, sixteen-, and seventeen-year-old youthful offenders who are functioning on adult levels. Traditional treatment does not know how to deal with these kids. The only thing that seems to have an impact is when you take them off the streets and put them in jail or training school.

Juvenile probation officer[1]

The juvenile justice system has the difficult task of correcting and controlling youth crime. Three challenges make this task even more difficult: the hard-line mood of society, the limitations of the juvenile justice system, and the conflicting philosophies and strategies involved in correcting juveniles. In an effort to meet these challenges, reformers developed various strategies in the 1970s. Among the results of these strategies were the rise of a movement for deinstitutionalization, a national trend to improve juvenile justice standards, and a growing commitment to entry level and preservice training.

This chapter first examines the systematic nature of the juvenile justice process and then describes the challenges and responses of the system to these challenges. The chapter concludes with a section on the policy needed to improve the juvenile justice process.

THE SYSTEMATIC NATURE OF THE JUVENILE COURT PROCESS

Like most systems, whether private or public, the juvenile justice system is concerned first with maintaining its equilibrium and surviving. The system is able to survive by maintaining internal harmony while simultaneously managing environmental inputs. The police and the juvenile court, juvenile probation, residential and day treatment programs, detention facilities, long-term juvenile institutions, and aftercare all are closely interrelated so that changes in one organization have definite consequences elsewhere within the system.

The juvenile justice system is made up of three basic subsystems. These subsystems, the police, the juvenile court, and corrections, consist of between 10,000 and 20,000 public and private agencies, with annual budgets totaling hundreds of millions of dollars. Many of the 40,000 police departments across the nation have juvenile divisions, and over 3000 juvenile courts and about 1000 juvenile correctional facilities exist in the United States.[2] Of the 50,000 employees in the juvenile justice system, more than 30,000 are employed in juvenile correctional facilities, 6500 are juvenile probation officers, and the remainder are aftercare officers and staff who work in residential programs. In addition, several thousand more employees work in diversionary programs and private juvenile correctional systems.[3]

The functions of the three subsystems differ somewhat. The basic work of the police is law enforcement and maintaining order. The maintenance of order function, which occupies most of police officers' time, involves such responsibilities as settling family disputes, providing emergency ambulance service, directing traffic, furnishing information to citizens, preventing suicides, giving shelter to drunks, and checking the homes of families on vacation. The law enforcement function requires that the police deter crime, make arrests, obtain confessions, collect evidence for strong cases that can result in convictions, and increase crime clearance rates.[4] The police must also deal with juvenile lawbreaking and provide services needed by juveniles.

The juvenile courts are responsible for disposing of cases referred to them by intake divisions of probation departments, supervising juvenile probation, making detention decisions, dealing with child neglect and dependency cases, and monitoring the performance of youths who have been adjudicated delinquent or status offenders. The *parens patriae* philosophy of the juvenile court charges the court with treating rather than punishing youngsters appearing before juvenile judges. But the treatment arm of the juvenile court goes only so far, and those youths who commit serious crimes or persist in juvenile lawbreaking may be sent to training schools or transferred to the adult court.

Corrections is charged with the care of those youthful offenders sentenced by the courts. Juvenile probation, the most widely used judicial disposition, supervises offenders released to probation by the courts, ensuring that they comply with the conditions of probation imposed by the courts and desist from delinquent behavior in the community. Day treatment and residential programs are charged with preparing youths for their return to the community, with preventing unlawful behavior in the program or in the community, and with providing humane care for youths directed to the programs. Long-term juvenile correctional institutions have similar responsibilities, but the officials of these programs also are charged with deciding when each youth is ready to be released to the community. In addition, officials of long-term institutions must ensure that residents receive their constitutional and due process rights. Aftercare officers, the final group in the juvenile justice system, are delegated the responsibility of supervising youths released from long-term juvenile correctional institutions. Like probation officers, aftercare officers are expected to make certain that youthful offenders fulfill the terms of their aftercare agreements and avoid delinquent behavior.

Comparison of the Juvenile and Adult Justice Systems

The juvenile and adult justice systems have much in common. Both systems are made up of three basic subsystems, and the agencies are interrelated so that the flow of justice ideally follows the same sequence: from law violation to police apprehension, judicial process, judicial disposition, and rehabilitation in correctional agencies. Both justice systems use the same basic vocabulary, and even when the vocabulary differs, no change of intent is involved.

An *adjudicatory hearing* is a trial.
Aftercare is parole.

Commitment is a sentence to imprisonment.

Detention is no different from holding in jail.

A *dispositional hearing* is no different from a sentencing hearing.

Petition is an indictment.

Shelter is often a jail-like environment.

Taking into custody is no different from being arrested.

Group homes usually have the characteristics of halfway houses.

Furthermore, both systems are under pressure from society to "get tough on crime," especially when dealing with offenders who commit violent crimes. Both systems must deal with overload, must operate on a fiscal shoestring, and must deal with the ongoing problems of staff recruitment, training, and burnout. Finally, both juvenile and adult justice systems are faced with problems of violent and inhumane institutions and of the unlawful activities that take place in these facilities.

But juvenile and adult justice systems also differ significantly. The juvenile justice system, with its emphasis on individualized treatment, still gives more attention to offender rehabilitation than does the adult system. In other words, the age-old supposition that juveniles are more malleable than adults still pervades the juvenile justice process and encourages a greater emphasis on correctional treatment. The due process movement, which has gained a great deal of support in juvenile justice in the past fifty years, still does not provide juveniles with as many rights as adults have. The U.S. Supreme Court is reluctant to make a juvenile court hearing into an adult trial. In addition, the juvenile court must deal with status offenders who would not be criminals if they were adults, and this situation has encouraged the development of "soft" and "hard" policies toward juvenile justice. Status offenders and other minor juvenile offenders receive the soft-line approach, while repetitive juvenile criminals receive the hard-line approach. But even here, the punishment of the juvenile criminal, especially one who has committed violent crimes, is much less than what would be dealt an adult criminal. Thus, the death penalty and the life sentence are reserved for adult offenders and for those juveniles who are transferred to the adult court for trial.

The Path of Justice

The means by which juveniles are processed by the agencies of the juvenile justice system are examined in the next four chapters of this unit. The process actually begins when the juvenile is referred to the intake division of the juvenile court; in some jurisdictions a variety of agents can refer the juvenile, while in others only the police are charged with this responsibility. More commonly, the juvenile is taken into custody by the police who have investigated a crime and have made the decision to refer the youth to the juvenile court. Figure 14-1 is a flowchart of the juvenile justice system.

The intake division of the juvenile court, usually operated by a probation officer, has to make the decision on what to do with the referral. A decision is made on whether the youth should remain in the community or be placed in a shelter or detention facility. As indicated in Figure 14-1, the intake officer has a variety of

Figure 14-1 Flowchart for Juvenile System

Source: William B. Parsonage, Hugh B. Urban and Fred W. Vondracek, "Implementing Recent Innovations in Juvenile Justice," *Juvenile Justice* 26 (August 1975), p. 35. Reprinted by permission.

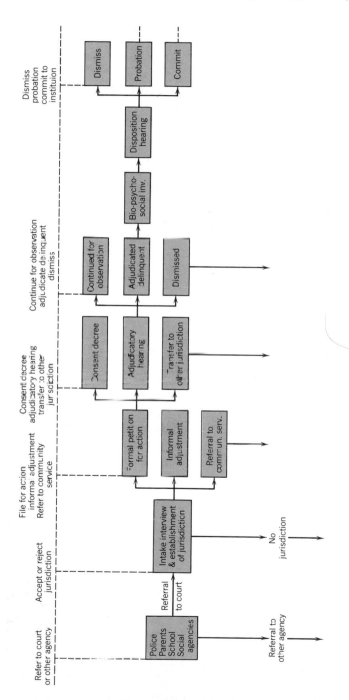

choices in determining what to do with the juvenile lawbreaker, but in more serious cases, the youth usually receives a petition to appear before the juvenile court.

The juvenile court judge, or the referee in many jurisdictions, hears the cases of those youths who receive a petition to the juvenile court. The first stage of the juvenile court proceeding is an adjudicatory hearing. The primary purpose of this hearing is to determine whether the youth is guilty of the delinquent acts alleged in the petition, and the court hears evidence on these allegations. The rights guaranteed to juveniles in the *In re Gault* case include the right to representation by counsel, freedom from self-incrimination, the right to confrontation and cross-examination of witnesses, and, in some states, the right to a jury trial.

A disposition hearing is held when a youth has been found delinquent in the adjudicatory stage or has waived his or her right to an adjudicatory hearing. Most juvenile court codes now require that the adjudicatory and disposition hearings be held at different times. The wide discretion of the juvenile judge permits him or her to warn and release juveniles, place them in a day treatment or residential program, or adjudicate them to the care of the department of corrections, the youth authority, or the youth commission. In some jurisdictions, the judge has the authority to send a youth to a particular correctional facility, but in most jurisdictions, delinquents are adjudicated to the care of the state department of youth corrections.

In small states that have only one institution for males and one for females, the youth committed to a long-term juvenile correctional institution is sent directly to a training school. But in larger states that have several male facilities and perhaps more than one female facility, delinquents must undergo a classification process in which the decision is made about the most appropriate placement for them. Juveniles currently do not spend as long in training school as they have in the past and usually are recommended for release within a year. The institutional staff normally recommend a youth for release, and their recommendation must be approved by the youth commission or youth authority. If the state has an established program of aftercare, the youth released from the training school is placed on aftercare status. He or she must fulfill the rules of aftercare and must avoid unlawful behavior to be released from this supervision.

THE CHALLENGES TO THE JUVENILE JUSTICE PROCESS

The juvenile justice process must deal with three major challenges today: the hard-line mood of society, conflicting philosophies and strategies applied to correcting juveniles, and the limitations of the juvenile justice system.

The Hard-Line Mood of Society

The public has become increasingly intolerant of serious youth crime and advocates in most jurisdictions a "get-tough-with-hard-core-juvenile-criminals" approach. In the mid-1970s, James Q. Wilson, Ernest van den Haag, and politicians across the nation backed a "get-tough-with-criminals" policy. Former Attorney-General William Saxbe was one of the spokespersons for this position. He claimed that "the solution to the crime problem is not rehabilitation programs, but more punishment."[5] Former Governor Dan Walker of Illinois said at this time:

> That message is a simple one. Our criminal justice system is not working—inside jails or out. . . .
>
> It is the people who are afraid; not the muggers, not the robbers, not the rapists, not the murderers, not the lawless.
>
> The people should not fear; the lawless should. That means we have to come up with a system that will make the lawless afraid. We need swift and sure punishment. And tougher punishment.[6]

It did not take long for the get tough mood to be applied to youth crime. First, juvenile judges and probation officers were accused of being soft and permissive. Second, the establishment of community residential programs for delinquents began to meet with marked resistance. Third, officials of juvenile correctional systems found themselves subjected to heavy criticism for the briefness of the stays of youthful offenders in training school. Fourth, the number of youths referred to the adult court began increasing noticeably. Fifth, in more and more jurisdictions nationwide, legislatures lowered the age over which the juvenile court had jurisdiction. Sixth, led by the Juvenile Justice Reform Act in New York State, mandatory sentences for serious juvenile offenses became more common across the nation.[7] Seventh, the state of Washington adopted a determinate sentencing law for juveniles in 1978, and determinate sentencing laws for juveniles have been discussed in a number of other legislatures.

Although practitioners in the juvenile justice system have heard the message, they generally have difficulties knowing what to do about juvenile crime, especially serious and violent youth crime. The most effective approach for dealing with delinquency is currently a subject of debate.

Conflicting Philosophies and Strategies on Correcting Juveniles

To deal with the problem of juvenile delinquency, there are four basic correctional models: the rehabilitation model, which has three variations; the justice model; the crime control model; and the logical consequences model. The existence of these conflicting strategies handicaps juvenile justice and is a major reason no single policy or set of policies currently guide the handling of juveniles. Nearly everyone has an opinion on what can be done to correct the behavior of law-violating juveniles.

The Rehabilitation Model

The goal of rehabilitative philosophy is to change an offender's character, attitudes, or behavior patterns so as to diminish his or her propensities for youth crime.[8] The medical model, the adjustment model, and the reintegration model are all expressions of rehabilitative philosophy.

The concept of the medical model has been accepted in juvenile justice from the time of the founding of the first juvenile court in Cook County (Chicago) in 1899. Juvenile judges turned to professional social workers and psychologists to identify a child's social and psychological needs and to resolve the problems that drove him or her to crime through individual counseling.

Juvenile probation embraced the medical model at the turn of the twentieth century. Graduates of professional social work programs were attracted to jobs as juvenile probation officers, and their training in social diagnosis and social casework made them naturally receptive to the rehabilitative philosophy. The medical model was accepted by the developing field of aftercare in the third and fourth decades of the twentieth century, but the principles of the medical model were most fully developed in training schools. Psychiatrists, soon to be joined by psychologists and psychiatric social workers, looked upon confined delinquents with whom they worked as sick with the disease of criminality and, therefore, in need of treatment.

The medical model, the first treatment model to be developed from the rehabilitative philosophy, contends that delinquency is caused by factors that can be identified, isolated, treated, and cured. Its proponents believe that delinquents should be treated as though they had a disease. Punishment should be avoided because it does nothing to solve delinquents' problems and only reinforces the negative self-image these youths in trouble have. Also, advocates believe that if the causes of delinquents' inappropriate behavior are diagnosed, specialists in such problems have the scientific know-how to provide the cure. The medical model also assumes that the delinquent lacks the ability to exercise freedom of choice or to use reason.[9]

Advocates of the medical model further contend that the legal definition of delinquency should be broad and that victimless crimes and status offenses should remain on the books. Those competent in diagnosis and knowledge of human behavior, according to the medical model, should have wide decision-making authority in the juvenile justice system. In addition, they encourage a much wider use of mental health services.

The adjustment model was developed in the late 1960s and 1970s when some proponents of rehabilitation became dissatisfied with the medical model. Although they agreed with champions of the medical model that offenders differ from non-offenders, need treatment, and can be "cured" by scientific experts (persons trained in a particular counseling technique), they claimed that delinquents are able to be responsible and make law-abiding decisions.

According to the adjustment model, delinquents need treatment to help them deal with the problems that lead them to crime. The emphasis is placed upon delinquents' responsibility at the present time; that is, youthful offenders cannot change the facts of their emotional and social deprivations of the past, but they can demonstrate responsible behavior in the present and can avoid using past problems as an excuse for delinquent behavior. Reality therapy, transactional analysis (TA), guided group interaction (GGI), positive peer culture (PPC), milieu therapy, and behavior modification all are used to help youthful offenders cope more effectively with their personal problems, their peers, and their environment. Offenders are shown that their maladapted behavior got them into difficulty and they are given alternatives that will allow them to live a crime-free life. Most of these therapies are based on insight, but behavior modification is primarily concerned with changing the unacceptable behavior of offenders. These therapies are not based on punishment, since punishment is seen as only increasing delinquents' alienation and behavior problems.

The adjustment approach to rehabilitation also accepts a broad legal definition of delinquency and concurs with the view that scientific experts should have the authority to make decisions in the juvenile justice system. But instead of emphasizing the pathology of offenders as the medical model does, this approach is primarily concerned with helping delinquents reintegrate themselves into society by becoming more responsible in making decisions. This approach discourages the wide use of institutionalization for delinquents.

A basic assumption of the *reintegration model* is that delinquents' problems must be solved in the community where they began. This model also assumes that society has a responsibility for helping law violators reintegrate themselves back into community life. The reintegration model recommends community-based corrections for all but hard-core offenders, offers those hard-core offenders who must be institutionalized a wide variety of reentry programs, and provides the necessary services so that delinquents can restore family ties and obtain employment and education.[10] Supporters of the reintegration model established a wide variety of community-based programs in the 1970s, including diversion programs, residential and day treatment programs, and programs to treat drug abusers.

Rehabilitative philosophy may be less obvious in the reintegration model than in the medical and adjustment models, but the concept of reintegrating the delinquent back into the community clearly contains the mandate that the delinquent must be changed by community-based corrections in order to become a law-abiding citizen. Reintegration advocates strongly support the notion that this change process is more likely to take place in community-based programs than in inhumane training schools. The community is charged with becoming involved in the change process.

The Justice Model

Two philosophical antecedents in juvenile justice can be found for the justice model: due process philosophy and least restrictive philosophy. The *parens patriae* philosophy has been challenged by due process philosophy from the time of the founding of the juvenile court. Although due process philosophy did not have a significant impact until after the U.S. Supreme Court decisions of the 1960s and 1970s, its basic emphasis is to give children better protection through the application of a greater number of due process provisions and procedural safeguards. Due process philosophy holds that the state must justify interfering with a child's life, that current diagnostic and treatment techniques are not sufficiently developed to warrant intervention by the juvenile court, and that children in need of help are different from children accused of crime and must be dealt with differently. It also advocates the establishment of accuracy and fairness in the juvenile justice process.[11]

In the 1970s, proponents of greater fairness in the juvenile justice system were troubled by the contradictions of the juvenile justice philosophy and by the inequities and inadequacies of juvenile justice law, policy, and practice.[12] These reformers turned to Fogel's justice model, which proposes the end of the indeterminate sentence and parole, the initiation of uniform sentencing, and the establishment of correctional programming based solely on the compliance of inmates.[13] Fogel reasons, "If we cannot coercively treat with reliability, we can at least be fair, reasonable, humane, and constitutional in practice."[14]

The development of the justice model also was influenced by least-restrictive philosophy. Edwin Schur and others developed a theoretical framework for the least-restrictive philosophy.[15] They proposed that bad luck and chance are the only reasons many juveniles are caught, labeled, and processed. Once caught, these offenders begin to live up to the labels, which become self-fulfilling prophecies. These offenders become committed to delinquent behavior, especially after being placed in juvenile institutions or detention facilities with youths who have committed more serious crimes. The answer, according to supporters of the least-restrictive philosophy, is for juvenile officials to do no more than absolutely necessary with youthful offenders; if possible, in fact, the best course is to leave them alone.[16] If their offenses are too serious to permit this course of action, juvenile officials should use every available resource before placing them in detention or in institutions. In addition, proponents of this philosophy urge that status offenders be kept out of the juvenile justice system.

The justice model expresses these basic assumptions of the least-restrictive philosophy through its emphasis on decriminalizing status offenders and on diverting minor juvenile offenders from the justice system and to voluntary services. However, this soft-line policy toward status offenders and minor offenders is coupled with a hard-line policy toward juveniles who commit serious crimes. David Fogel believes, as previously discussed, that the punishment should be proportionate to the crime.[17] For those juveniles who have committed serious crimes, "just deserts" demands that they be sent to training school or to long-term placement in residential programs.

Proponents of the justice model advocate a number of changes to bring justice-as-fairness to juvenile justice, urging

- That the enormous discretion granted to juvenile justice practitioners be limited;
- That increasing numbers of youthful offenders be diverted from the justice system to voluntary services.
- That common deficiencies in due process be remedied so as to ensure greater fairness in the transaction between the justice system, the family, and the juvenile offender.
- That curbs be placed upon the indeterminate sentencing practices of juvenile courts and that juveniles be given a fixed sentence by the court at the time of sentencing.
- That status offenders be decriminalized.
- That the governing principle of sentencing be one of "proportionality," which means that there must be a relationship between the seriousness of the offense committed and the severity of the sanction imposed.

- That training schools be made safer and more humane.

- That programs offered in training schools be of a voluntary nature and have no effect on when a youth is released.

- That restitution and community service sanctions be required of more juvenile lawbreakers; these sanctions have the potential for fairness because they give youthful offenders opportunities to atone or make amends for the damage or harm they have inflicted upon others.[18]

Many of these proposed changes are found in the standards developed by the joint effort of the Institute of Judicial Administration and the American Bar Association Joint Commission on Juvenile Justice Standards and are outlined in the report of the Task Force on Sentencing Policy toward Young Offenders formed by the Twentieth Century Fund.[19] The mandatory sentencing law for violent juvenile offenders in New York State, the determinate sentencing law for juveniles in the state of Washington, and the institutional release policy adopted for juveniles in the state of Minnesota are indications of the growing acceptance of the justice model among policymakers.[20]

The Crime Control Model

The third correctional model, the crime control model, emphasizes punishment as the remedy for juvenile misbehavior. Based upon utilitarian punishment philosophy (which was examined in Chapter 4), the crime control model gained popularity in the 1970s because of the apparent rise of youth crime. Supporters maintain that punishment is the preferred correctional model because it both protects society and deters crime. Youthful offenders are taught not to commit further crimes, while noncriminal youths receive a demonstration of what happens to a person who breaks the law.

The supporters of the crime control model claim that the juvenile court has abandoned punishment in favor of individual rehabilitation. They argue for severity and certainty of punishment and advocate greater use of incarceration, especially in training schools. Other basic assumptions behind this approach are that young people who engage in delinquent behavior are abnormal and few in number; that antisocial behavior reflects a character defect that can be corrected through punishment; that punishment can be helpful in teaching responsibility, diligence, and honesty; and that the effectiveness of the juvenile justice system depends upon apprehending and punishing offenders with greater speed, efficiency, and certainty.

The crime control model is grounded on the conviction that the first priority of justice should be the protection of the life and property of the innocent. Consequently, advocates of this model challenge the wisdom of keeping troublesome youths in the community and are quick to support the isolation of juvenile delinquents in detention homes, jails, and training schools. The increased use of transfers to adult courts and the use of mandatory-sentencing laws that specify an extended length of punishment for serious youth crimes are representative of recent hard-line, or crime control, actions. The supporters of this model also believe in a broad definition of delinquency. A great deal of confidence is placed in the police as highly respected participants in the process of administering juvenile justice. That a "get-tough-with-drug-abusers" position is necessary to deal with juvenile crime is another premise of this model.[21]

Many states are now using a combination of the crime-control and the justice model to deal with violent and hard-core juvenile delinquents.

The Logical Consequences Model

The logical consequences model, an emerging model in juvenile corrections, is having increasing impact on how juvenile delinquents are treated. Supporters of this model hold that offenders must be made aware of the cost and the consequences of their socially unacceptable behavior. This model is being widely used in juvenile probation throughout the nation and is also gaining popularity in aftercare and training schools. Two probation officers explain why they are now using the logical consequence model:

> I basically believe in the logical consequence model. If they do such and such which is unacceptable, then they have to pay the consequences.

> It is important for kids to feel something is happening to them. For a lot of kids, to come in and see a probation officer or for a probation officer to stop by the home aren't significant events to them. Restitution is the most important program we can use to help them; it lets them know that there is some kind of consequence for the action they have taken.[22]

The logical consequences model makes at least five major assumptions. One is that juvenile offenders have free will and, therefore, should be held responsible for what they do. Another is that juvenile delinquents know the justice system so well that they are able to take advantage of its permissiveness; that is, delinquents often are aware that another burglary charge will bring only a lecture from the juvenile judge and a continuation of probation. A third assumption is that delinquents will modify their behavior only when the cost of their behavior becomes too high. A fourth is that required community service is necessary because juveniles do not take seriously the regular supervision of probation (i.e., reporting on a regular basis to the probation officer). A final assumption is that it is possible to develop effective relationships with probationers once they have decided to take probation seriously.

The design of the logical consequences model was derived from a logical consequences approach to disciplining children that became popular in American society in the late 1970s and early 1980s. According to this theory the parent, or primary caretaker, should give the child a choice and tell him or her the specific consequences of negative behavior. Its advocates believe this approach puts the responsibility for the behavior on the child rather than on the parent and that the consequences of bad behavior are, therefore, what the child has chosen rather than punishment administered by the parent.

Finally, proponents of the logical consequences model hold that delinquents become more receptive to treatment once they realize that there is a cost to negative behavior. Supporters also claim that putting a cost on behavior when juveniles first come into the justice system reduces the number of delinquents who must later be sent to training school.

Comparison of the Four Models

The rehabilitation model is more concerned that juvenile delinquents receive therapy than that they be institutionalized. The crime control model, on the other hand, is a punishment model that contends juveniles must pay for their crimes. Those who back the crime control model also claim that punishment has social value for both offenders (deterrence) and society (protection). The justice model strongly advocates that procedural safeguards and fairness be granted to juveniles who have broken the law. Yet, proponents of this model also firmly hold that juveniles should be punished according to the severity of their crimes. In other words, the "just deserts" idea demands that juveniles receive punishment proportionate to the harm they have inflicted upon society. Advocates of the justice model also want to keep minor offenders and status offenders out of the juvenile justice system, for they are committed to doing everything possible to keep all but hard-core offenders out of training school. The logical consequences model includes elements of the other three models. It has adapted the concept of utility of punishment from the crime control model, without the repressiveness of the punishment model. The emphasis on rationality in the logical consequences model is similar to that in both the justice and the crime control models; delinquents are seen as having free will and, therefore, are held accountable for their behavior. Those who support the logical consequences model believe that once juveniles realize the cost of their negative behavior, they will become receptive to rehabilitation.

Each of these models has widespread support, but none acts as the guiding force in dealing with juvenile delinquents today. On a larger level, society is using a hard-line, or get tough, approach with hard-core delinquents and a soft-line, or least-restrictive, approach with minor juvenile offenders and status offenders. However, on a day-to-day basis, juvenile justice practitioners are continuing to pick and choose from each of the four models in designing their own approaches. These practitioners' use of different approaches to correcting the behavior of delinquents and the lack of respect they show for those who follow other courses of action results in inefficiency and confusion in juvenile justice.

Fragmentation of the Juvenile Justice System

Ideally, cooperation and communication should exist among the various subsystems of the juvenile justice system to promote efficiency and a smooth flow of justice. Unfortunately, so little cooperation and communication is found among participants in the system that it has become disjointed and fragmented. Indeed, the fragmentation is so evident that the juvenile justice system is sometimes referred to as a nonsystem.[23]

This fragmentation originates in the lack of a common goal among subsystems of the juvenile justice system. The goals of a specific subsystem may change with each new police chief, juvenile judge, chief probation officer, or training school superintendent. The rehabilitation model, which is coming under more and more attack, once had the advantage of being accepted as the stated purpose of the juvenile justice system. But today the goal of the system varies from one jurisdiction to the next and often from one juvenile justice actor to the next. A second cause of fragmentation is that too many governmental agencies control the design of the juvenile justice system within the various states of the nation. Local governmental units usually finance the juvenile court, probation services, residential and day treatment programs for probationers, juvenile detention facilities, and, sometimes, city or county training schools. The states, however, finance training schools, aftercare services, and residential programs for youths on aftercare. A third cause of fragmentation is the proliferation of agencies responsible for juvenile justice in America. These agencies range from diversionary programs with three or four staff members to large state bureaucracies.

Duplication of services represents one of the consequences of fragmentation. For example, families with multiple problems are seen by several different agencies in the same time period. More importantly, fragmentation may have a negative impact on delinquents. Delinquents are sometimes the only ones who know what is taking place in the various subsystems of juvenile justice, and sophisticated delinquents are able to play agencies against one another to avoid having to change their behavior. Another consequence is that local governments are able to set their own standards, which are often reflections of local biases rather than displays of professional competence. Furthermore, fragmentation often creates conflict among professionals working with juvenile delinquents. For example, prosecutors and the police are extremely unhappy with juvenile judges who fail to waive youths who have commited violent offenses to the adult court. The police may be unhappy with the judge who keeps a youth on probation whom they feel should be sent to training school, and the social worker in a training school and the aftercare specialist may be in disagreement over when a youth should be released and to whom.

Obviously, the efficiency, accountability, and fairness of the juvenile justice system depend on the coordination and communication among the subsystems. One of the great challenges facing juvenile justice practitioners today is to overcome the disjointedness and fragmentation of the present system.

THE RESPONSE OF THE JUVENILE JUSTICE PROCESS TO ITS CHALLENGES

The deinstitutionalization movement, the commitment to entry-level and preservice training, and the national trend to improve juvenile justice standards represent three major responses from the juvenile justice system to the challenges it is facing at present.

The Deinstitutionalization Movement

Community-based juvenile corrections is one result of the movement to keep juveniles in trouble out of training school. This deinstitutionalization, or decarceration, movement gained momentum in the late 1960s and early 1970s through the increased public awareness of the brutal and degrading nature of training schools. The idea that community-based corrections is vastly more humane, much more economical, and no less effective than confinement in a training school became widely accepted. It was easy to conclude that few, if any, youths benefitted from institutionalization; many theorists, in fact, began to believe that all training schools should be closed and alternatives developed.

The most important advance toward deinstitutionalization took place when the Massachusetts Department of Youth Services closed all of its training schools in the early 1970s. Deinstitutionalization also became popular in a number of other states during the 1970s.[24] Another important aspect of the deinstitutionalization movement was the attempt to keep status offenders out of training schools. In the early 1970s, 70 to 80 percent of the girls confined in training school were status offenders and up to 30 percent of the boys confined were status offenders, but these figures had been dramatically reduced by the late 1970s.[25]

The public is no longer as receptive to residential community-based programs as it was during the late 1960s and early 1970s, but the commitment to deinstitutionalization in juvenile justice is still apparent in the fact that for the past decade, the population of training schools has not increased and may even have decreased.[26]

Commitment to Entry Level and Preservice Training

Training is one of the most important areas to receive attention from those concerned with the juvenile justice system. A supervisor of custodial staff in a training school notes what used to be a typical problem in juvenile justice:

> We used to be so desperate for staff that we would go out and comb the streets. If a guy was big enough, we would offer him a job and, without any training, would throw him in with the kids. Too many of these staff didn't know what the hell was going on, and they had all kinds of problems with these hard-core offenders.[27]

Fortunately, the time has passed when juvenile justice practitioners received only on-the-job training and "flew by the seat of their pants." All levels of staff in the juvenile justice system now receive far more training than was given before, and this has made a difference in the way juvenile delinquents are handled. Juvenile police officers are receiving specialized training in such matters as juvenile law, interviewing, delinquency prevention, and community resources. Also, the popular ongoing seminars for juvenile court judges at the University of Nevada, as well as the conferences of the National Association of Juvenile and Family Court Judges, have done much to rescue juvenile justice from the hands of judges whose rulings were arbitrary and capricious. Training for probation officers also has been intensified in recent years. Custody and treatment staff members in state training schools are also benefitting from mandatory entry level and inservice training at state correctional training academies.

The National Trend to Improve
Juvenile Justice Standards

Responding to the challenge to improve the juvenile justice system, a number of professional organizations, national and state commissions, and other groups have prepared standards, models, and guidelines to improve the fairness and effectiveness of the system. Among the widely conflicting standards that have been drawn up there are two points of consensus: there is a need to upgrade the procedures and practices of the juvenile justice system, and standards are effective ways to achieve this goal. Several reasons explain the lack of consensus among standards: they have been prepared for different groups; writers of these standards usually do not attempt to conform with any existing standards; and most importantly, the standards are the reflection of the varying ideologies of juvenile justice.[28]

In the late 1960s and early 1970s, several groups recommended special juvenile justice standards, including the President's Commission on Law Enforcement and the Administration of Justice, the National Advisory Commission on Criminal Justice Standards and Goals, many state commissions, the National Council on Crime and Delinquency, the National Conference of Commissioners on Uniform State Laws, the International Association of Chiefs of Police, and the American Correctional Association.

In the mid- and late-1970s, the standards movement accelerated as six important groups added their conclusions to the growing stockpile. The Institute of Judicial Administration and the American Bar Association Joint Commission on Juvenile Justice Standards (IJA/ABA) completed a five-year project in 1977 that carefully reviewed the premises on which the juvenile justice system is based. The Juvenile Task Force, part of the second phase of the 1973 National Advisory Commission on Criminal Justice Standards and Goals (NACCJSG), was charged with formulating a set of objectives and advisory standards that would serve as a model for state and local agencies attempting to improve the juvenile justice system. The Standards Committee was established by the Juvenile Justice and Delinquency Prevention Act of 1974 (JJDPA) to recommend to the president and Congress a set of standards for the administration of juvenile justice. The Twentieth Century Fund Task Force on Sentencing Policy Toward Young Offenders evaluated the indeterminate sentencing policy of the juvenile court. The standards adopted by the National Council of Juvenile Court Judges were intended to standardize juvenile court procedures and to elevate the quality of juvenile justice. Finally, the standards on juvenile corrections of the Accreditation Committee of the American Correctional Association specified the minimal requirements for an agency to receive accreditation.

However, the diversity of the standards proposed by these groups have reduced their potential impact. The IJA/ABA standards propose determinate sentencing, drastic reduction of the powers of the juvenile court, and mandatory sentences for serious crimes. Other standards propose indeterminate sentencing. The National Council on Crime and Delinquency, the Standards Committee of JJDPA, and the IJA/ABA advocate the removal of status offenders from the jurisdiction of the juvenile court, but other proposed standards permit the court to maintain jurisdiction over status offenders. The IJA/ABA and the Twentieth Century Fund Task Force believe punishment should be proportionate to the seriousness of the offense, but other standards makers profess rehabilitative philosophies. The President's Task Force emphasizes community-based corrections, and the National Council on Crime and Delinquency even advocated phasing out training schools. But the IJA/ABA and the Twentieth Century Fund Task Force recommend institutionalization to reduce serious and violent juvenile crime.

The combined efforts of these commissions and organizations to update the philosophy and standards of juvenile justice are impressive. Although conflict among the standards has reduced their impact, the proposals have sparked a lively debate among juvenile justice practitioners, from which nearly every juvenile justice agency across the country has benefited in some way.

POLICY IMPLICATIONS

The problems facing the juvenile justice process are indeed formidable. The serious problem of juvenile delinquency in American society challenges the juvenile justice process to mobilize a coordinated and unified approach. However, conflicting philosophies and strategies for dealing with youth crime and a fragmented system that varies from one jurisdiction to another make it nearly impossible for the juvenile justice process to handle delinquency effectively.

The positive contributions of deinstitutionalization, of in- and preservice training, and of proposed standards have resulted in some improvements in the juvenile justice process. Public training schools are less widely used than before. Overall, fewer status offenders are sent to public training schools; in some states no status offenders are committed to these training schools. The training given to all levels of correctional staff has improved the performance of corrections personnel in the juvenile justice system. The social justice received in the justice process may still leave much to be desired, but the role behavior of practitioners is now probably closer to ideal than ever before. Finally, the development of standards is causing extensive reevaluation of the policies and procedures of the juvenile justice system, and although the conflict among these standards reduces their impact, nearly every juvenile justice agency is benefiting in some way from the resultant debate.

Yet, the actual improvements hardly seem to have scratched the surface of the problem of designing a justice system that will effectively deal with youth crime in American society. The following reforms are necessary for such a system: First, the jurisdiction for the juvenile justice system should belong to one governmental agency. This would better ensure a coordinated flow of youthful offenders and good communication among the subsystems. The best possible solution to this problem would be the establishment of community corrections acts throughout the nation. Such acts, which do exist in a few states, transfer overall jurisdiction and financing to local units of government that elect to be under the community corrections act and to comply with the standards of the act.

Second, as the overall effectiveness of the juvenile justice process is impeded by the conflicting philosophies and strategies for dealing with juvenile delinquents, a possible solution would be for an entire state to decide on one of the correctional models. Some states appear to be moving in this direction, as they implement more and more of the components of the justice model in both adult and juvenile justice. However, the justice model has been accepted more in rhetoric than in reality in the adult justice system and this is even true of the juvenile justice system. A better solution would be for a state or, at least, all the agencies of local juvenile justice systems, to use the best characteristics of the four models in determining the basic goal, or mission, of the juvenile justice process. Perhaps the results would include:

- Decriminalization of status offenders and diversion of both status offenders and minor offenders from the juvenile justice system.
- The granting of due process rights and procedures to all delinquents dealt with by the juvenile justice system.
- Acceptance by probation departments of the philosophy of the logical consequences model in dealing with delinquents.
- Wider use of restitution and community service programs.
- Voluntary participation in correctional treatment programs not connected to the length of correctional stay.
- Wider use of residential and day treatment programs, again relying on the logical consequences model.
- More drug and alcohol abuse counseling and services throughout the juvenile justice process.
- Sentencing of delinquents who have committed serious crimes to training schools that would be smaller, safer, and offer a wider variety of voluntary programs than those in existence today.
- Mandatory sentencing of delinquents sent to training school, with the length of these sentences designed by the National Council of Juvenile Court Judges rather than by state legislatures.
- Requirement of delinquents sent to training school to work or attend school during the day.
- Correctional treatment designed around job preparation of residents and survival skills for use after their release from correctional confinement.
- Enlargement of the network of community support services, especially for those youths who are returning to the community from training school.

Third, the resources of the juvenile justice system must be expanded. The decline of federal dollars has affected the quality of juvenile justice because many worthwhile programs have been forced to close. Local fiscal austerity has also affected the quality of juvenile justice. Few communities offer the variety of programs and services needed for law-violating juveniles. In other words, the resources of the juvenile justice process are vastly inadequate in dealing with the complex problems of youth crime in American society. Interest groups must make a sustained effort to gain better support from federal, state, and local sources.

SUMMARY

Historically, the juvenile justice process developed into a system that was under-girded by the rehabilitation ideal. But today the *parens patriae*, or rehabilitative philosophy, is challenged by other correctional models. The sociocultural context of juvenile corrections has also changed. Only a few years ago the public supported community-based corrections and there was discussion of abandoning institutions. Today, the hard-line mood is gathering momentum in juvenile corrections. The public is concerned that too many streets are unsafe, too many citizens are victimized, and too much property is stolen and destroyed by predatory youths. In terms of the legal context, the juvenile justice system is being given the mandate to control and correct these unlawful youths. This challenge has resulted in a furor of activity to bring about a more effective juvenile justice process. The deinstitutionalization movement, the increased training of practitioners, and the development of standards are strategies that were developed in the late 1960s and 1970s to create a more effective, just, and humane juvenile justice system. However, the conflicting philosophies and methods involved in handling juvenile delinquents and the fragmentation of the juvenile justice system make it very difficult for the system to succeed in its mission of controlling and correcting juveniles in trouble. In the political context, proposed policy changes are that the jurisdiction of the juvenile justice system belong to one governmental agency, that states accept one of the correctional models or adopt the best characteristics of the four models, and that the limited resources of the juvenile justice system be enlarged.

Discussion Questions

1. How severe is the problem of youth crime?
2. The juvenile justice system has devised four ways to deal with delinquency: the rehabilitative model, the justice model, the utilitarian punishment model, and the logical consequences model. Which do you think works best? Why?
3. Why is fragmentation so extensive in the juvenile justice system? What can be done to overcome it?
4. Why is deinstitutionalization a more humane way of dealing with juvenile delinquency?
5. Why are standards of juvenile justice and training of personnel important strategies for juvenile justice?
6. After reading this chapter, do you feel encouraged or discouraged about the ability of the juvenile justice process to deal effectively with juvenile delinquency?

References

Fogel, David. ". . . *We Are the Living Proof*": *The Justice Model for Corrections*. Cincinnati: W. H. Anderson & Company, 1975.

Johnson, Robert; Hoelter, Herbert J.; and Miller, Jerome G. "Juvenile Decarceration: An Exploratory Study of Correctional Reform." In *Crossroads in Corrections: Designing Policy for the '80s.* Beverly Hills, Calif.: Sage Publications, 1981.

Matza, David. *Delinquency and Drift.* New York: John Wiley & Sons, 1964.

Nuernberger, Wilfred W., and Van Duizlend, Richard. "Development of Standards for Juvenile Justice: An Overview." *Juvenile Justice* 28 (February 1977): 3–6.

Schur, Edwin M. *Radical Non-Intervention: Rethinking and Delinquency Problem.* Englewood Cliffs, N.J.: Prentice-Hall, 1973.

Shireman, Charles. "The Juvenile Justice System: Structure, Problems and Prospects." In *Justice-as-Fairness,* edited by David Fogel and Joe Hudson. Cincinnati: W. H. Anderson & Company, 1981.

Van den Haag, Ernest. *Punishing Criminals: Concerning a Very Old and Painful Question.* New York: Basic Books, 1975.

Vinter, Robert D.; Downs, George; and Hall, John. *Juvenile Corrections in the States: Residential Programs and Deinstitutionalization: A Preliminary Report.* Ann Arbor, Mich.: National Assessment of Juvenile Corrections, University of Michigan, 1975.

FOOTNOTES

1. Interviewed in April 1981.

2. N. Paris et al., eds., *Sourcebook of Criminal Justice Statistics—1978* (Washington, D.C.: U.S. Government Printing Office, 1979), pp. 187, 522–526.

3. See National Council of Juvenile and Family Court Judges, *Directory of Juvenile and Family Court Judges* (Reno: University of Nevada Press, 1979), and National Council on Crime and Delinquency, *Probation and Parole Directory,* 17th ed. (Hackensack, N.J.: National Council on Crime and Delinquency, 1976).

4. Gerald D. Robin, *Introduction to the Criminal Justice System* (New York: Harper & Row, 1980), pp. 56–57.

5. Quoted in Michael S. Serrill, "Is Rehabilitation Dead?" *Corrections Magazine* 1 (May/June 1975), p. 3.

6. Ibid., p. 31.

7. The Juvenile Justice Reform Act of 1976 that went into effect February 1, 1977.

8. Andrew von Hirsh, *Doing Justice: The Choice of Punishments* (New York: Hill & Wang, 1976), p. 12.

9. Clemens Bartollas and Stuart J. Miller, *The Juvenile Offender: Control, Correction, and Treatment* (Boston: Holbrook Press, 1978), pp. 13–14.

10. President's Commission on Law Enforcement and Administration of Justice, *Task Force Report: Corrections* (Washington, D.C.: U.S. Government Printing Office, 1967).

11. Frederic L. Faust and Paul J. Brantingham, eds., *Juvenile Justice Philosophy* (St. Paul, Minn.: West Publishing Company, 1974), pp. 574–575.

12. Charles Shireman, "The Juvenile Justice System: Structure, Problems and Prospects," in *Justice-as-Fairness,* edited by David Fogel and Joe Hudson (Cincinnati: W. H. Anderson & Company, 1981), pp. 136–141.

13. David Fogel, *". . . We Are the Living Proof": The Justice Model for Corrections* (Cincinnati: W. H. Anderson & Company, 1975).

14. David Fogel, "Preface" to *Justice-as-Fairness,* p. viii.

15. Edwin M. Schur, *Radical Non-Intervention: Rethinking the Delinquency Problem* (Englewood Cliffs, N.J.: Prentice-Hall, 1973).

16. Ibid.

17. Fogel, *". . . We Are the Living Proof."*

18. Shireman, "Juvenile Justice System."

19. Several standards developed by the Institute of Judicial Administration and the American Bar Association Joint Commission on Juvenile Justice Standards are listed in Chapter 16 published in 1977 by Ballinger Press.

20. New York's Juvenile Justice Reform Act of 1976 went into effect on February 1, 1977; see Michael Serrill, "Police Write a New Law on Juvenile Crime," *Police Magazine* (September 1979), p. 47, for a description of the 1978 determinate sentencing law for juveniles in the state of Washington; see David B. Chein and Joe Hudson, "Discretion in Juvenile Justice," in *Justice-as-Fairness,* pp. 174–188, for a description of the Minnesota program.

21. Daniel Katkin, Drew Hyman, and John Kramer, *Juvenile Delinquency and the Juvenile Justice System* (North Scituate, Mass.: Duxbury Press, 1976), pp. 97–98.

22. Interviewed in 1981.

23. Bartollas and Miller, *Juvenile Offender,* pp. 21–22.

24. Robert D. Vinter, George Downs, and John Hall, *Juvenile Corrections in the States: Residential Programs and Deinstitutionalization: A Preliminary Report* (Ann Arbor, Mich.: National Assessment of Juvenile Corrections, University of Michigan, 1975), p. 35.

25. The National Assessment of Juvenile Corrections study found that 23 percent of the boys and 50 percent of the girls in institutions were status offenders. The Children in Custody census of 1970 revealed that 23 percent of the boys and 70 percent of the girls in public correctional settings were status offenders. The Bartollas and Sieverdes study found that 30 percent of the boys and 80 percent of the girls in the coeducational training schools in North Carolina were status offenders.

26. Rob Wilson, "Corrections Magazine Survey of Juvenile Inmates," *Corrections Magazine* 4 (September 1978), p. 9.

27. Interviewed in April 1973.

28. Bartollas and Miller, *Juvenile Offender,* p. 9.

INTERVIEW WITH JOHN P. CONRAD

I don't think the juvenile justice system "breeds" crime. It just doesn't make enough difference. The trouble is that we have never known what to do with juvenile offenders.

In this interview, John P. Conrad, who is one of the most widely respected authorities on juvenile and adult corrections, discusses some of the most pressing issues facing the juvenile justice system today, such as the handling of status offenders and violent offenders, the role of juvenile correctional institutions, the effectiveness of treatment, the transfer of juveniles to the adult court, and the impact of the juvenile justice system on youthful offenders.

Question: How have society's attitudes and treatment of delinquents changed in the last twenty years?

Conrad: I can look back farther than that, and I will. In 1946, I was employed as a "placement officer" by the California Youth Authority. My title was significant. My duties were indistinguishable from those of an adult parole officer except that my case load consisted of boys and young men under the age of twenty-five—the youngest was eleven or twelve. The reason for the euphemism was that the administrators of the Youth Authority had the notion that juvenile justice was really social work. To use the term "parole officer" would give the boys, their families, their schools or employers, and the community at large the impression that the Youth Authority parolees were criminals.

Some of them weren't. One boy, aged thirteen or fourteen, was the son of a prominent district attorney and his bohemian mistress. He was an inconvenience to both of them and by stratagems that I never understood, it was arranged that he

Interview conducted in January 1984. John P. Conrad is presently a Fellow at the National Institute of Justice, Washington, D.C. He was codirector of the Dangerous Offender Project of the Academy for Contemporary Problems. Conrad has written many books and numerous papers, and, as a career criminologist, he spent twenty years in administration in the California Department of Corrections.

would be committed to the Youth Authority as an "incorrigible." After a spell at one of California's training schools (in those days much worse than they are now), he was to be released to my case load and my unenviable task was to find a foster home that would take him in. I found it, and shortly thereafter went on to a more sensible line of work. A few years later I encountered the boy at San Quentin. Neither the Youth Authority nor the foster home had done him much good, although the plain intent of all concerned was benevolent. Neither of his parents could provide a home for him. He was truant from school, and I suppose it was only a question of time before he would have gotten into serious trouble if the court had not intervened.

He was not the only such boy in my case load. Nowadays we would refer to him as a "status offender" and his commitment to the Youth Authority would be cited as a horrible example of the excesses possible under the standard juvenile court laws. In most states, including California, no court would consider commitment to the Youth Authority or to a state training school. That is a change for the better, and I think it reflects a major shift in the attitudes of the administrators of the system and the general public as well. In the early days of the juvenile court there was a prevailing belief that the mere removal of a boy from a bad environment, even if that called for an institutional commitment, would produce a good result. I don't think any informed person in these times will entertain this notion. We now are inclined to think that state training schools are futile at best, if not much worse. Our perplexity is that we have not thought of a better restraint for a few extremely violent youths who can't be allowed to run loose in the community.

At the other end of the wide spectrum of delinquency to be found in my casebook were a number of young thugs for whom the Youth Authority had accepted jurisdiction even though they were considered too tough for any of its own facilities and had to be housed at San Quentin. They were persistent recidivists—rapists, robbers, and burglars. When they were paroled to my district they became my responsibility. I think they were on to me and my problems. I had a caseload of well over 100. I had no time for the detective work that would have to be done to find these fellows—to say nothing of maintaining effective surveillance over them.

They found me quickly enough when they got into trouble and were arrested. Most of them were well over eighteen—the Youth Authority could and often did maintain jurisdiction to the age of twenty-five. They were interesting young men, and I must confess that I enjoyed the bull sessions I had with them when we finally made connections. I cannot claim that I did them much good, and I am certain that neither the Youth Authority nor San Quentin accomplished anything more than to keep them off the streets of San Francisco for a while. Unfortunately, at that time nobody had any better ideas for their reclamation. I doubt that good ideas for such youths are in any better supply now—more than thirty-five years later.

The consensus is developing that youths over sixteen with long records of recidivism don't belong in the juvenile justice system. In short, we are chopping off both ends of the juvenile court caseload, the status offenders and the chronic thugs. Whether this curtailment of eligibility is a good thing remains to be seen. I doubt that recidivism will be appreciably reduced, but I suspect that the harm done will not be great.

Question: What led to the "get-tough-with-juvenile-criminals" position in the mid-1970s? What is your appraisal of this position?

Conrad: If the Uniform Crime Reports is to be believed, there isn't much to be found in the data of delinquency to justify the drastic changes that have been proposed and, in some states, enacted into law. Between 1972 and 1982 the number of persons under the age of eighteen who were arrested for violent crimes (as reported in the FBI's Uniform Crime Reports) increased from 45,773 to 49,824.[1] That's a leap of 8.9 percent, allowing for modest decreases in the number of homicides and robberies committed by this age group during the course of that decade. Even allowing for some underreporting, this is not a sensational increase.

What has happened, I think, is that the public has been persuaded to accept the contention that the juvenile courts are pretty soft and that kids have to be taught a severe lesson in harsh circumstances. This notion gains credence from horror stories in the news and from word of mouth. Most people know someone who has been mugged or raped or burglarized, or whose car has been stolen, and it is a short jump to the conclusion that some damn punk did it.

I wish I could exclude the inference that the general public has decided that it's mostly black kids who do all these terrible things. Unfortunately, the overrepresentation of black children in the data of delinquency gives some support to this conclusion. What's bad about this conclusion is the racist taint that gets into policymaking. White legislators and judges will be prone to ascribe inferiority to black children in trouble, and to decide that the only way to pound obedience to the law into their heads is to lock them up. The truth is that once a boy or girl has become delinquent, that fact is more critical to the future he or she faces than race. Delinquency is a misfortune that befalls too many black children. There should be more and better resources to help them. Getting tough will get them off the streets for a while, but if toughness is all they get then tougher adult criminals are what we will get a few years later.

Question: What social policy implications does *The Violent Few* have for the practices and procedures of the juvenile justice system?

Conrad: There are three implications that should be taken seriously by all concerned with delinquency as a major social problem. First, interventions should never be nominal, and they should come early in a youth's career. It may be appropriate to let a child off with a warning from the juvenile police bureau when he first gets into trouble. On the second occasion something should happen—at least appearance before the juvenile court and placement on probation with regular and frequent contacts with a probation officer.

Second, the consequences of an offense should be predictable. We found in a statistical study of juvenile court decisions that no variable or combination of variables could predict the action of the court in any case or category of cases in our cohort. That turns delinquency into a gamble, and a gamble that a daring youth will win more often than he loses—provided he takes care not to commit too gruesome an offense. We did not advocate an increased use of the training schools of the Ohio Youth Commission, but we did insist that the system should be predictable. No system of prediction can infallibly forecast the future behavior of a delinquent boy, but the boy should be able to predict the action of the system if he repeats his offense.

Third, it was clear in our data that the time intervening between offenses after the second adjudication became shorter and shorter when the youth was placed in extended custody. There are two contrasting but compatible explanations for that finding. One was that training schools or detention merely produced a more hostile delinquent, indifferent to future consequences to his offenses. The other was that the courts were correctly selecting the worst boys and girls for incarceration. But the implication of this finding is sharp and clear: there may be nothing else to be done with a rough and tough hoodlum, but locking him up in a training school won't accomplish anything positive.

That finding is based on placement in one of the Ohio training schools. So far as I know, Ohio's facilities compare favorably with those in other states. They are modern in construction, adequately staffed—at least in number—and supported by the best of intentions. Unfortunately, they are ineffective in the redirection of the delinquents who are most alarming to the community—the small number of violent recidivists.

Question: What needs to be done to make juvenile institutions safer and more humane? Who should be confined in these long-term institutions?

Conrad: After reading *Juvenile Victimization*, the study of juvenile institutions on which you were

the senior collaborator, I am convinced that nothing at all can be done without people in charge who are able and willing to do whatever is necessary to maintain continuous control. That's a sweeping prescription and I have to hedge it with qualifications. We can't have beatings, a silent system, the lock-step, or "cadet captains" authorized to discipline "cadet" inmates. When I worked for the California Youth Authority all these measures and more were permitted in our "training schools." Those who objected would be loftily told that the Youth Authority wasn't running a chain of Sunday Schools.

Not many kids in these institutions will take on a physically vigorous instructor who has confidence in his skill at controlling others. If these kids are kept busy in realistic training, work, and active sports, they're not likely to try. But if they sense that the staff is scared of them, all will soon be lost. I hear of staff people in youth facilities who come to work in fear and leave at the end of the day relieved that they have survived. Such people should not be employed in the first place, and should be put out of their misery as soon as that misery becomes apparent to others.

Who should be confined? It's easy and trite to say that only violent offenders should be incarcerated. That's the direction in which we are headed, and I hope it's right. But for a long time to come we will need closed facilities for kids with serious chemical dependency problems, for chronic property offenders who consistently fail in community programs, and for some kinds of nonviolent sex offenders who can't be tolerated by their neighbors. As I have already said several times in this interview, I don't think that incarceration in even the best institutions accomplishes good things for those who are incarcerated. It is punishment, and the most severe punishment that can be imposed on a juvenile. I hold that delinquency must have unfavorable consequences, and that the consequences must be graduated in severity. At a point in a delinquent career when all possible lesser consequences have been meted out, the kid should be packed off to a clean and well-managed facility for the detention of youthful offenders.

There is a second purpose for the detention of

such young people. Any failure in the community creates new difficulties for the next plan. Sometimes a closed institution is the only place to keep a kid while figuring out what to do with him or her. This is a good reason for holding a youth so long as it doesn't become a rationalization for not doing anything positive for him.

In a more orderly society we would have less need for locking kids up. I am one of those who distrust incarceration as a solution to human problems. Every step in the direction of effective community programs for delinquents is a step toward civilization and away from the barbarism that is too often under the surface in juvenile corrections.

Question: Are too many juveniles transferred to adult courts? What is your evaluation of transfer procedures as they presently exist?

Conrad: According to the only authoritative source on this question, a survey conducted by Donna Hamparian and associates, there were about 12,300 youths under eighteen who were prosecuted for felonies throughout the country in 1978. In addition there were over 250,000 juveniles age sixteen and seventeen who were referred to adult courts in twelve states that limit juvenile court jurisdiction to persons under the age of sixteen. Of the 12,300 felony prosecutions less than a fourth were for violent offenses.[2]

How many is too many? I am suspicious of the removal from the juvenile court of the nine thousand or so nonviolent juvenile offenders who were sent to the adult court, but Hamparian was unable to make a fine enough analysis to determine the reasons for these waivers.

For me the important question is not the court in which a juvenile is tried but his subsequent fate. Indeed, for some older juveniles the availability of a jury trial in an adult court is an advantage worth the waiver. If trial in an adult court resulted in commitment to an adult prison, no informed person could condone the waiver process. But most youths tried in adult courts are programmed as youths. They don't go to prison or to other adult programs. That doesn't mean that they are placed in programs that are especially beneficial—as I've already said, there aren't many programs for any offenders of any age that make much difference across the board.

Question: Why is it that juvenile justice system tends to breed rather than to reduce crime?

Conrad: I don't think the juvenile justice system "breeds" crime. It just doesn't make enough difference. The trouble is that we have never known what to do with juvenile offenders. Readers of the early works of Sheldon and Eleanor Glueck know that about 80 percent of their sample of 500 juvenile delinquents got into trouble again.[3] I don't think that we have significantly improved the situation in the sixty years that have elapsed since the study was done. We still don't know what to do with the serious juvenile recidivists, but we may be doing better with some who are caught early, before they have acquired an identity as a delinquent. The fact that about 30 percent of our sample in *The Violent Few* were first offenders who didn't get into further trouble is significant evidence that discriminating services are worth trying.[4]

Question: What changes are needed in the juvenile justice system?

Conrad: What changes are needed? I think that as I went along I gave my views in passing, but let me summarize:

1. There must be early intervention. Something must happen to the juvenile if the first offense is a major felony. The second appearance in court for any offense should result in consequences, but not necessarily confinement.
2. The policies of the juvenile court should be sufficiently coherent and widely enough understood so that they are readily predictable.
3. Consequences should be graduated in severity as the individual's offense record lengthens.
4. Probation must become far more intensive. It is a waste of money and a mockery of juvenile justice to maintain case loads in excess of thirty-five. A probation officer should be expected to maintain daily contacts for as long as necessary to assure that the plan for the juvenile is working as expected.

5. Institutions for juvenile offenders must be staffed by men and women who are confident of their ability to keep control of group and individual situations. Programs in the institutions should be as active as possible. Individuals who will be confined for prolonged periods should be programmed with special attention to their needs for evidence of progress and some variety.

6. Postinstitutional supervision should be at least as intensive as probation. There must be an emphasis on surveillance, especially in the case of violent offenders.

7. To the greatest extent possible the concept of case management should be applied throughout the periods of the state's control. The case manager should be the same person throughout.

I won't claim that adoption of this seven-point platform will solve the problem of juvenile delinquency. Faithfully applied by men and women who are properly trained and hired in sufficient numbers, it will eventually make a difference. But the big difference will be made by the community as a whole. Where unemployment is kept to a minimum, where the schools enjoy the confidence of parents and pupils, where mental health services are available to those who need them, the correctional caseload will dwindle. We have hardly started on the road to that utopia.

FOOTNOTES

1. Federal Bureau of Investigation, *Uniform Crime Reports, 1982* (Washington. U.S. Government Printing Office, 1983), p. 170, Table 25.

2. Donna Martin Hamparian et al., *Youth in Adult Courts: Between Two Worlds* (Columbus, Ohio: Academy for Contemporary Problems, 1982), pp. 204–205.

3. Sheldon Glueck and Eleanor T. Glueck, *500 Criminal Careers* (New York: Alfred A. Knopf, 1930).

4. Donna Martin Hamparian, Richard Schuster, Simon Dinitz, and John P. Conrad, *The Violent Few* (Lexington, Mass. D.C Heath & Company, 1978), p. 52.

CHAPTER 15

THE POLICE AND THE JUVENILE

CHAPTER OUTLINE

The process of rehabilitation begins from the first moment the offender comes into contact with the policeman. The youngster who gets himself into trouble generally wants to get himself out of it, too. If the first contact he has with the law is both friendly and understanding, he will probably be more amenable to the treatment he is going to get. . . . If the officer is really in charge of the situation and of himself, the child's attitude will cool gradually, and the job at hand will be easier as a result. This, then, is probably the most important part in rehabilitation an officer can play: to remember that he is the first step in a continuous process which has as its goal the making of a delinquent into a good citizen.

J. D. Lohman[1]

The police are the first line of defense against crime. Having the power to arrest and use deadly force, the police are charged both with preventing and deterring crime and with maintaining peace within the community. Television programs usually portray the police as having glamorous, exciting, and dangerous jobs, but much of the police role is boring, frustrating, and dangerous.

Juvenile crime represents one of the most demanding and frustrating areas of police work. To begin with, youthful lawbreaking and misbehavior place considerable strain upon law enforcement agencies. It has been estimated, for example, that 50 to 75 percent of police agency work directly or indirectly affects adolescents.[2] The leniency of juvenile court codes also makes it difficult for police to deal effectively with youth crime. One of the common complaints of police officers is that arrested juvenile offenders are back on the streets before the officers have had a chance to do the necessary paperwork on them. Furthermore, little status is given in police departments to those dealing with youth crime; indeed, most patrol officers prefer to avoid law-violating juveniles because they are regarded as a poor "bust." Juvenile police officers, in this regard, often have problems in gaining acceptance from fellow police officers who question whether or not the juvenile officer is actually doing *real* police work.

Yet the importance of police-juvenile relations cannot be minimized. The police are usually the first contact a juvenile offender has with the juvenile justice system. As the doorway into the system, the police officer can use his or her broad discretion to either detour youths or involve them in the system. In a real sense, the police officer becomes an on-the-spot prosecutor, judge, and correctional system when dealing with a juvenile offender.

This chapter describes the history of police-juvenile relations, the attitudes that police and juveniles have toward each other, the factors that influence police processing of juveniles, the informal and formal dispositions of juvenile offenders, the rights of the juvenile in custody, the efforts by the police to improve police-juvenile relations, and policy recommendation for police-juvenile relations.

HISTORY OF POLICE-JUVENILE RELATIONS

In the seventeenth and eighteenth centuries, the American colonists and immigrants installed the informal methods of control such as the "mutual pledge," the "watch and ward," and the constable system that they had brought with them in the small colonial towns. These informal methods of control by the family, the church, and the community were sufficient until the expansion of towns in the late eighteenth and nineteenth centuries resulted in increasing disorder.

To deal with the increasing crime problem, New York, Boston, and Philadelphia created police forces in the 1830s and 1840s, and by the 1870s, all major cities had full-time police forces. However, at this time the police were drawn from the least educated segments of society, were ill-treated, and were poorly paid. Furthermore, they often became instruments of political corruption, used for personal gain and political advantage.

In the late nineteenth century, law-violating juveniles received various kinds of treatment from officers walking the beat. Juveniles might receive the same treatment as adult offenders, or they might be treated as erring children and receive slaps on the wrists. Juvenile offenders were sometimes taken to the parish priest for admonition and spiritual instruction.

Some large police departments attempted to improve police-juvenile relations early in the twentieth century. The New York City Police Department began a program in 1914 that helped juveniles develop relationships with local police. In the 1930s, August Vollmer introduced the concept of a youth bureau in the Berkeley, California police department, emphasizing the importance of crime prevention by the police. Youth bureaus were soon established in other urban departments as the need arose for police specialists in juvenile law enforcement. These specialized units were variously called crime prevention bureaus, juvenile bureaus, youth aid bureaus, juvenile control bureaus, and juvenile divisions.

The role of the juvenile officer developed further after World War II, and it was formalized when a group of juvenile officers organized the Central States Juvenile Officers Association in 1955 and the International Juvenile Officers Association in 1957. Through their participation in these regional, national, and international associations, juvenile officers expended considerable effort in developing the duties, standards, procedures, and training necessary for dealing with juvenile lawbreakers. As defined by the officers themselves, the basic responsibility of the juvenile officer was to be helpful, rather than punitive, in handling youthful offenders.

In the 1960s, a number of police programs designed to improve relations with juveniles and to reduce delinquency were developed throughout the United States. Police officers came into the public schools to interact with grade school and high school students and to discuss some aspects of the law with them. The Police Athletic League programs, which had been in operation since the second decade of the twentieth century, also were expanded during the 1960s to cover leadership training, full- and part-time employment opportunities, and moral training, as well as extensive recreational programs. To prevent and control delinquency, the police also became involved in truancy prevention programs, drug abuse rehabilitation, and the actual supervision of youthful offenders.

The degree of involvement in juvenile work varied among different police departments during the 1970s. Although some departments became even more actively involved in juvenile work, the trend in the late 1970s and early 1980s was for police departments to move away from deep involvement in juvenile work. In many departments, juvenile divisions were dropped or their jurisdiction was limited to involving dependent, neglected, abused children, while detective bureaus assumed responsibility for juvenile and adult investigations.

POLICE ATTITUDES TOWARD YOUTH CRIME

The police overall have more positive attitudes today toward youthful offenders than in the past, but three occupational determinants of police work work against even more positive attitudes toward youth crime. First, the police see themselves as skilled in their ability to apprehend criminals, but the leniency of juvenile court codes makes them believe nothing will happen to apprehended youths unless the offense is serious.[3] The police in large cities, especially, think youth crime is out of control because of the permissiveness of the juvenile justice system. In 1977, Edward M. Davis, who was then chief of police for Los Angeles, predicted some grim consequences of this permissiveness:

> As the juvenile justice system continues to operate under present constraints, we know that it is building an army of criminals who will prey on our communities. The benign neglect that we have shown has made children with special problems into adult monsters that will be with us forever. If improvements to this system don't come, it will ensure a generation of criminals who will make the current batch look like kids on a Sunday school picnic.[4]

Second, the dangers inherent in their jobs require the police to be alert to assailants who point to trouble or danger, and, therefore, experienced police officers know they must be especially guarded in a police-juvenile encounter because juveniles' unpredictability and resistance make these difficult arrests.[5] The hard-core offender represents the greatest danger to the police officer. Violent gang members, for example, have few qualms about killing police officers.

Third, the police must always defend the authority of their position, which requires them to quash any verbal or physical abuse from either teenagers or adults.[6] Juvenile offenders, especially those who have had contact with the system before, are likely to challenge the authority of the police officer. They usually know how far they can push the officer, and they are quite cognizant of their rights. Juveniles are even more likely to challenge the authority of the police officer when they are with peers, and, therefore, new officers are advised to avoid talking with a youthful offender in front of his or her peers.

Patrol officers are particularly reluctant to deal with a police-juvenile encounter; their first reaction is to call out juvenile police officers (sometimes called the "diaper squad") to get this "mess" off their hands. But juvenile officers and detectives who work with juveniles on a day-to-day basis are more service-oriented than patrol officers. The positive attitudes that some juvenile officers and detectives have toward youthful offenders enable them to develop remarkable rapport with these offenders.

JUVENILE ATTITUDES TOWARD THE POLICE

The subject of juveniles' attitudes toward the police received considerable empirical examination in the late 1960s and 1970s. Robert Portune's study of almost 1000 junior high students in Cincinnati found that whites had more favorable attitudes toward the police than blacks, that girls had more favorable attitudes than boys, and that students from middle- and upper-class families had better attitudes than those from lower-class families. He also found that hostility toward the law and police increased progressively during grades seven through nine.[7] Donald H. Bouma and his associates administered 10,000 questionnaires to Michigan schoolchildren in ten cities and, while their conclusions agreed with the major findings of Portune's study, they added that the majority of the students felt the police were "pretty nice" and that they would cooperate with the police if they saw someone other than a friend committing a crime.[8] However, R. L. Hoobler's study in San Diego found that a large portion of secondary school students had negative attitudes toward officers in uniform.[9]

Several studies have reported that juveniles with police contacts have more negative attitudes toward police than those without such contacts. L. Thomas Winfree, Jr., and Curt T. Griffiths found in their study of students in seventeen high schools that to a considerable degree juveniles' attitudes toward the police are shaped by contacts with police officers. Negative contacts appear to be twice as important as positive ones in determining juvenile attitudes toward police officers. Negative contacts, according to Winfree and Griffiths, influence juvenile attitudes more than do the factors of sex, race, residence, or socioeconomic status.[10] Chapman, who compared 133 delinquent and 133 nondelinquent boys in Dayton, found that the delinquents felt more negative toward the police.[11] Peggy Giordano, who matched 119 boys who had contacts with the juvenile justice system with 199 who had not, found that juvenile attitudes toward the police seem to be affected more by high levels of delinquent activity and by peers than by the degree of contact a youth has with the system.[12] Delinquent gangs, according to two studies, are particularly hostile toward the police.[13]

William T. Rusinko et al., in examining about 1200 ninth grade students in three junior high schools in Lansing, Michigan, explored the importance of police contact in formulating juveniles' attitudes toward the police. They found that positive police contacts by the white youths in their study clearly neutralized their encounters with police that had negative connotations. But these researchers found that positive police contact did not reduce the tendency for black youths to be less positive in their opinions of police. Significantly, the attitudes of blacks who reported high positive contact were less favorable toward police than the mean attitudes for all black junior high students.[14] The finding agrees with several other studies that shows the development of a culturally accepted view of police among blacks independent of their arrest experience.[15]

Interviewed juvenile delinquents most frequently accuse the police of harassment and of brutality. One juvenile girl complaining about police harassment said, "I can't stand the police because they won't leave me alone. I think it's stupid they pick me up when I run because I've a place to stay. I'm not in trouble."[16] Another juvenile girl added, "I've hated cops all my life. I've had a lot of bum raps from them. If I see a cop, I think they're going to bust me."[17]

A sixteen-year-old female prostitute, in a fairly representative statement, accused the police of brutality:

> Cops don't care. I saw what they did when they arrested my brother. One grabbed him by his hair and threw him around. They loud talk you and harass you. If you're in their custody, they can say and do anything they want to you. Even off-duty, they are still like that. They think they can do anything because they're the law. They can't get into trouble for what they do. The court will always take their word unless there is proven fact that they have done something wrong. And even then, nine out of ten times they get off easy.[18]

Several conclusions can be drawn from these studies. Most youths appear to have positive attitudes toward the police. Younger juveniles have more positive attitudes than older ones. Whites are usually more positive toward the police than blacks, and girls are more positive than boys. Middle- and upper-class youngsters tend to be more positive than lower-class ones. The more deeply committed a juvenile is to crime, the more hostile he or she is toward the police. But the findings about the influence of contacts with the police are mixed. Some researchers have found that the more contacts a juvenile has with the police, the more negative he or she feels about the police, yet others have concluded that for white youths positive contacts tend to neutralize the effect of negative contacts.

PROCESSING THE JUVENILE OFFENDER

Three major aspects of the police response to the juvenile lawbreaker are the various factors that influence police processing of juveniles, the ways that police officers handle juvenile offenders, and the rights of juveniles who have been arrested or taken into custody.

Factors That Influence Police Discretion

Police discretion can be defined as "the choice between two or more possible means of handling a situation confronting the police officer."[19] Discretion is important, for the police actually act as a court of first instance in initially categorizing a juvenile. The police officer thus becomes a legal and social traffic director who can use his or her wide discretion to detour juveniles from or to involve them in the juvenile justice system.

Police discretion has come under attack because many believe the police abuse their broad discretion. However, most police contact with juveniles is impersonal and nonofficial and consists simply of orders to "Get off the corner," "Break it up," or "Go home." Most studies estimate that only 10 to 20 percent of police-juvenile encounters become official contacts.[20] For example, Bordua's 1964 study of the Detroit police found only 5282 official contacts out of 106,000 encounters.[21]

The point can also be made that the juvenile justice system could not function without police discretion. Urban courts, especially, are overloaded at present. Probation officers' caseloads are entirely too high. Many juvenile correctional institutions are jammed to capacity. If police were to increase by two to three times the number of youths they referred to the system, the resulting backlog of cases would be unmanageable.

The police officer's disposition of the juvenile offender is mainly determined by nine factors: the nature of the offense; citizen complainants; sex, race, socioeconomic status, and other individual characteristics of the juvenile; the nature of the interaction between the police officer and the juvenile; departmental policy; and external pressures in the community.

The Nature of the Offense

The most important factor determining the disposition of the misbehaving juvenile is the nature of the offense, in terms of its seriousness. Donald J. Black and Albert J. Reiss, Jr., point out that the great bulk of police encounters with juveniles pertain to matters of minor legal significance, but the probability of arrest increases with the legal seriousness of the alleged offense.[22]

Citizen Complainants

A number of studies have found that the presence of a citizen or the complaint of a citizen is an important determining factor in the disposition of an incident involving a juvenile.[23] If a citizen initiates a complaint, remains present, and wishes the arrest of a juvenile, the chances are that the juvenile will be arrested and processed.[24] If the potential arrest situation results from police patrol, the chances are much greater that the youth will be warned and released.

Sex of the Offender

Girls are less likely than boys to be arrested and referred to the juvenile court for criminal offenses.[25] Yet girls are far more likely to be referred to the court if they violate traditional role expectations for girls, such as running away from home, failing to obey parents, or being sexually promiscuous.[26] In short, the police tend to reflect the views of complaining parents; e.g., that girls should be chaste and should be protected from immoral behavior.

Race

The studies differ on the importance of race in determining juvenile disposition. On one hand, several studies—after results were corrected to account for offense seriousness and prior record—have found that the police are more inclined to arrest minority juveniles.[27] The strongest evidence showing race as a determining factor is found in the Philadelphia cohort study. Wolfgang et al. concluded "that the most significant factor related to a boy not being remediated by the police, but being processed to the full extent of the juvenile justice system, is his being nonwhite."[28] On the other hand, several other studies failed to find much evidence of racial bias. Although it is difficult to appraise the importance of race in the disposition of cases involving juveniles because blacks and members of other minority groups appear to be involved in more serious crimes more often than whites, it does seem that racial bias makes minority juveniles the special targets of the police.

Socioeconomic Status

Substantiating the effect of class on the disposition of cases involving juveniles is difficult because most studies examine race and socioeconomic status together. But lower-class youngsters, according to many critics of the juvenile justice system, receive different "justice" than middle- or upper-class ones; that is, lower-class youths are dragged into the net of the system, while middle- and upper-class juveniles are often sent home. Patrol and juvenile police officers generally agree that there is more concern about "saving" middle and upper-class juveniles than lower-class ones, but they justify this use of discretion by saying that the problematic behavior of upper-class children is more likely to be corrected because their parents can afford psychotherapy and other such resources.

Individual Factors of the Offender

Such individual factors as prior arrest record, previous offenses, age, peer relationships, family situation, and conduct of parents also have a bearing on how the police officer handles each juvenile.[29] If a juvenile is older and has committed several previous offenses, he or she is likely to be referred to the juvenile court. The family of the juvenile is also an important variable. An assistant police chief who has spent several years working as a juvenile officer put it this way:

> Most juvenile problems derive from the parents. You've got to get the parents involved to be successful. You've some parents who are concerned, and you can tell they'll take things by the handle when they're dealing with the problem. Other parents simply don't care. If you want to make any headway in this work, it is necessary to stay on top of the family.[30]

Nature of the Interaction between the Police Officer and the Juvenile

Three studies found that a juvenile's deference to a police officer is influential in determining disposition. Piliavin and Briar discovered that if a youth is polite and respectful, the chances for informal disposition are greatly increased. But if the juvenile is hostile, police will probably judge him or her in need of the juvenile court.[31] Werthman and Piliavin found that the hostility and scorn black gang members displayed toward the police resulted in a high rate of court referral.[32] Richard J. Lundman, Richard E. Sykes, and John P. Clark, in a replication of Black and Reiss' study, concluded that in encounters in which no evidence links a juvenile to an offense, the demeanor of the juvenile is the most important determinant of whether or not formal action is taken.[33]

The personality of the police officer also shapes the nature of the interaction with the juvenile offender. An officer who "just plain doesn't like kids" is more prone to hassle juveniles than one who is concerned, and when a juvenile reacts with profanity or aggressive behavior to this harassment, the officer may decide an official contact is necessary. An officer who loses his or her "cool" may likewise become involved in a confrontation requiring an official contact.

Departmental Policy

Departments vary in their policies on handling misbehaving juveniles. In his study of forty six police departments in southern California, Malcolm Klein found that some departments referred four out of five to the juvenile court while others warned and released virtually all juvenile contacts.[34] Nathan Goldman found in his study of four Pennsylvania communities that the proportion of juvenile arrests varied from 9 percent in one community to a high of 71 percent in another.[35] J. Q. Wilson also concluded that the more professional police departments had higher numbers of juveniles referred to the juvenile court because they used discretion less than the departments that were not as professional.[36]

External Pressures in the Community

Finally, the attitudes of the press and the public, the status of the complainant or victim, and the philosophy and available resources of referral agencies usually influence the disposition of juvenile lawbreakers. The press can do much to encourage a get-tough policy with youthful offenders. In addition, the higher the status of the complainant or victim, the more likely that a juvenile will be arrested and processed for a crime. But a negative reaction to the "wrist slapping" they see in the juvenile court may discourage police officers from arresting and processing juvenile offenders.[37] Finally, the police officer who has community resources available, such as a youth services bureau, responds to juvenile encounters differently from the officer who has no community resources available.

In sum, sufficient studies have been done to provide an outline of an empirical portrait of the policing of juveniles. Of the nine factors determining police officers' dispositions of juveniles, the seriousness of the offense and complaints by citizens appear to be more important than the other seven factors. Yet individual characteristics of the juvenile, as well as departmental policy and external pressures in the community, also affect how police-juvenile encounters are handled.

Informal and Formal Dispositions of Juvenile Offenders

A patrol officer or juvenile officer has at least five options when investigating a complaint against a juvenile or arriving at the scene of law-violating behavior: warning and releasing the juvenile to the community; making a station adjustment; referring the juvenile to a diversionary agency; issuing a citation and referring him or her to the juvenile court; and taking him or her to a detention facility.

Warning and Releasing to the Community

The least severe sanction is applied when the patrol officer decides merely to question and release the youth. Commonly, this occurs when a juvenile is caught committing a minor offense. The patrol officer usually gives an informal reprimand to the youth on the street or takes the juvenile in for a longer interview at the police station.

Up until the 1970s, a patrol officer often might warn the juvenile, "This better not happen again, or I'll beat your ass the next time I catch you." It was not unheard of for a patrol officer to bring out a paddle and to give the erring juvenile two or three whacks. Now, a patrol officer would be reluctant to strike a juvenile under any circumstances because of the potential liability that he or she might face if the juvenile's parents decided to sue.

Making a Station Adjustment

The juvenile can be taken to the station, have the contact recorded, be given an official reprimand, and then be released to the parents. In this situation, the first thing that is done upon bringing the juvenile to the station is to contact the parents. In some police departments, juveniles can be placed under police supervision, to remain under supervision until released from his probationary period.

Referring to a Diversionary Agency

The juvenile can be released and referred to a youth service bureau (YSB), Big Brothers, Big Sisters, runaway center, or mental health agency. With this option, the police officer chooses to divert the youth from the juvenile justice system. When the referral is made to a YSB, the common procedure is to have the patrol officer or juvenile officer contact the YSB, and a staff member of the YSB follows up the contact. In Illinois, several police departments have service units that provide counseling and social services for troubled juveniles and adults, and in these communities, police officers often choose to send misbehaving juveniles to those units.

Issuing a Citation and Referring to the Juvenile Court

The police officer can issue a citation and refer the youth to the juvenile court. The intake counselor of the juvenile court, who is usually a probation officer, then decides whether or not a formal petition should be filed and the youth should appear before the juvenile judge. The juvenile is returned to the family with this disposition.

Taking to the Detention Center

Finally, the police officer can issue a citation, refer the youth to the juvenile court, and take him or her to a detention center. An intake worker at the detention center then decides whether the child should be returned to the parents or left at a short-term juvenile institution. A juvenile is left in detention when he or she is thought to be dangerous to self or others in the community or has no care in the home. A few communities have shelter care facilities that are available for status offenders. In communities that lack detention facilities, juveniles must be taken to the county jail or the police lockup, both of which are inappropriate places for juveniles. Taking youths out of their own homes and placing them in detention facilities clearly must be a last resort.

Rights of the Juvenile in Custody

The rights of juveniles in custody have changed dramatically since the days when the third degree was given at the station. Although some departments have lagged behind others in granting due process rights to juveniles under arrest, the majority of police departments apparently now comply with court decisions concerning the rights of juveniles. However, because few juvenile cases are appealed, police practices by which juveniles are denied their due process rights are usually known only at the local level.[38]

Search and Seizure

The due process rights given to adults in the 1961 U.S. Supreme Court decision, Mapp v. Ohio (367 U.S. 643 1961), concerning search and seizure, have been applied to juveniles in several important cases. A 1966 District of Columbia ruling suppressed evidence seized when the police entered a juvenile's apartment without a warrant at 5:00 A.M. to arrest him. A court held that "the Fourth Amendment to the United States Constitution is a protection designed to secure the homes and persons of young and old alike against unauthorized police searches and seizures."[39]

A Houston police officer stopped a car being driven without lights and issued the driver a traffic ticket for driving without lights as well as without a driver's license. The youth was taken to a police station, for the officer had some question about the automobile's ownership. Another police officer searched the youth five hours after the initial contact, without his consent and without a search warrant, and discovered fifty milligrams of marijuana. For this possession of marijuana, the youth was committed to the Texas Youth Council. However, an appellate court released the youth from training school, finding that a search some five hours after the original arrest for driving without lights "can hardly be justified as incidental to the arrest for a traffic offense."[40]

Interrogation Practice

The U.S. Supreme Court decision Haley v. Ohio (332 U.S. 596, 1948) is an early example of police interrogation excesses. In the *Haley* case, a fifteen-year-old youth was arrested at his home five days after a store robbery in which the owner was shot. Five or six police officers questioned the boy for about five hours; he then confessed after being shown what were alleged to be the confessions of two other youths. No parent or attorney was present during the questioning. The Supreme Court invalidated the confession, stating:

> The age of the petitioner, the hours when he was grilled, the duration of his quizzing, the fact that he had no friend or counsel to advise him, the callous attitude of the police toward his rights combine to convince us that this was a confession wrung from a child by means which the law should not sanction. Neither man nor child can be allowed to stand condemned by methods which flout constitutional requirements of due process of law."[41]

Juveniles taken into custody are entitled to the rights stated in the 1966 *Miranda* v. *Arizona* decision. This Supreme Court decision prohibits the use of a confession in court unless the individual was advised of his or her rights before interrogation, especially of the right to remain silent, the right to have an attorney present during questioning, and the right to be assigned an attorney by the state if he or she could not afford one.[42] The *In re Gault* case made the right against self-incrimination and the right to counsel applicable to juveniles.[43]

But the *Gault* decision failed to clarify whether or not a juvenile could waive the protection of the *Miranda* rules; it also failed to specify what is necessary for a juvenile to waive his *Miranda* rights intelligently and knowingly. For example, is a juvenile's ability to waive his rights impaired if he or she is under the influence of drugs or alcohol or in a state of shock?

Several court cases have held that the minority status of a juvenile is not an absolute bar to a valid confession. A California case upheld the confession of two juveniles from Spanish-speaking families. Although both had been arrested before, one had an I.Q of 65 to 71, with a mental age of ten years and two months.[44] Similarly, a North Carolina court of appeals approved the confession of a twelve-year-old youth who was charged with shooting out a window in a camper truck.[45] Moreover, a Maryland appellate court approved the confession of a sixteen-year-old youth who was a school dropout and had an eighth grade education. He was charged with firebombing and burning a store and a school during a racial confrontation.[46]

To protect juveniles against police interrogation excesses, many jurisdictions have a statutory requirement that a parent or counsel must be present at police interrogation in order for a confession to be admissible. Other states attempt to protect the juvenile by requiring that the youth be taken to the juvenile detention center or to the juvenile court if not returned immediately to the parents' custody. They obviously prefer that police interrogation take place within juvenile facilities rather than at a police station.

Fingerprinting

Fingerprinting, along with pretrial identification practices, is a highly controversial procedure in juvenile corrections. Some juvenile court statutes require that a judge approve the taking of fingerprints of juveniles, that the judge control access to fingerprint records, and that the judge provide for fingerprint destruction under certain circumstances.[47] In many other jurisdictions, the police department determines policy; some police departments routinely fingerprint all juveniles taken into custody and suspected of serious wrongdoing. The Juvenile Justice and Delinquency Prevention Act of 1974 recommended that fingerprints be taken only with the consent of the judge, that juvenile fingerprints should not be recorded in the criminal section of the fingerprint registry, and that they should be destroyed after their purpose has been served.

A 1969 U.S. Supreme Court decision that reversed a Mississippi ruling is the most important case dealing with juvenile fingerprints. In this case, a rape victim had described her assailant only as a black youth. The only leads at the outset of the police investigation were finger and palm prints found on the sill and borders of the window of the victim's home. Without warrants, the police took at least twenty-four black youths to police headquarters, where they were questioned, fingerprinted, and then released without charge. A fourteen-year-old youth who had performed yard work for the victim was brought to headquarters the day after the offense, questioned, fingerprinted, and released. He was interrogated on several additional occasions over the next four days; several times he was shown to the victim in her hospital room but she did not identify the youth as her assailant. The police then drove the youth ninety miles to another city where he was confined overnight in jail. The next day the youth signed a confession statement and was returned to the jail in his community. He was fingerprinted a second time and his fingerprints, along with those of twenty three other black youths, were sent to the FBI for comparison with the latent prints taken from the window. The FBI reported that the youth's prints matched those taken from the window. The U.S. Supreme Court found that the fingerprint evidence used at the trial was the second set, and rejected this evidence because the police had not complied with procedures required in the Fourth Amendment: "The detention at police headquarters of petitioner and the other young Negroes was not authorized by a judicial officer; petitioner was unnecessarily required to undergo two fingerprinting sessions; and petitioner was not merely fingerprinted during the [first] detention but also subjected to interrogation."[48]

Pretrial Identification Practices

The photographing and placing of juveniles in lineups also are highly controversial. The Juvenile Justice and Delinquency Prevention Act recommended that a photograph should not be taken without the written consent of the juvenile judge and that the name or picture of any juvenile offender should not be made public by the media.

The most important case in terms of these pretrial identification practices took place in California. A rape victim was shown pictures of a young male taken by the police in another matter. She could not make positive identification, but a few days later she was asked to come to the probation office at a time when this young male was present. This time she did identify him as her assailant. She was also certain of his identification as her assailant at the detention hearing some six weeks later. But the California appellate court held the one-on-one identification attempts to be constitutionally defective: "The practice of showing suspects singly to persons for the purpose of identification has been widely condemned." However, the judgment was upheld on the basis that the victim's identification of the young male at trial was based on her observation of him during the rape, rather than the three identification attempts.[49]

EFFORTS TO IMPROVE POLICE-JUVENILE RELATIONS

Better training in juvenile matters for line police officers, organization of a police juvenile unit headed by juvenile officers, and prevention and diversionary police-juvenile programs are the three ways police departments are attempting to improve relations with juveniles and do a more effective job of dealing with juvenile offenders. The first two are discussed in this section and the third is examined in Chapter 19.

Better Training for Line Police Officers

Police officers are now receiving more extensive training in juvenile matters, both in training academies for police recruits and in postacademy training, which more and more police departments are conducting on a regular basis for line police officers. Universities are beginning to supplement in-house training on juvenile matters by offering short-term institutes dealing with the problems of delinquency. The Delinquency Control Institute, in the School of Public Administration at the University of Southern California, was the pioneer in offering short-term institutes. Developed by Robert Carter and Dan Pursuit, the USC program offers two intensive eight-week programs each year. Furthermore, the institute has begun to fly its faculty to other communities that are interested in mini-institutes. The National Council of Juvenile Court Judges, located on the campus of the University of Nevada in Reno, also has been offering in-service training to police officers since 1973.[50]

The Juvenile Unit

The juvenile unit (or crime prevention bureau, juvenile bureau, youth aid bureau, juvenile control division, and juvenile division) is charged with the detection, investigation, and disposition of juvenile cases. The San Diego Police Department, for example, has the following responsibilities:

1. Investigating all crimes in which juveniles are listed as the actual or suspected violators.
2. Investigating school, recreation-department, and child-care-center burglaries.
3. Investigating battered-child complaints and taking the appropriate criminal action when indicated.
4. Investigating the cases of missing and runaway juveniles and maintaining appropriate files on them.

5. Investigating stolen and recovered bicycles.
6. Maintaining bicycle-registration files and providing a limited bicycle-license service in conjunction with the Fire Department.
7. Dealing with neglected or abandoned children.
8. Making referrals or other suitable disposition of juvenile offenders.
9. Supervising and regulating teenage dances, in conjunction with other community agencies.
10. Counseling with parents and children.
11. Providing a program of delinquency prevention and control.
12. Checking of crime-prone areas and hangouts.
13. Processing of adult persons charged with or suspected of contributing to the delinquency of a minor.
14. Checking of crime-prone areas and hangouts.[51]

Community relations is a major focus of the juvenile unit. Juvenile officers must cultivate good relations with school administrators and teachers, with the staffs of community agencies, with the staffs of youth service bureaus and youth shelters, with the juvenile court, and with merchants and employees at popular juvenile hangouts. Of course, the juvenile police officer also must develop good relations with parents of youthful offenders as well as with the offenders themselves. The officer who has earned the respect of the youths of the community will be aware of what is happening in the community and will be called upon for assistance by youths in trouble. A director of a youth service bureau, in describing an effective officer, said:

> *Darrell Dirks, a juvenile officer, is beautiful. He talks like a kid. He walks down the halls of school. Kids will punch him in the shoulder. He'll smile and punch them in the shoulder. He solves many crimes simply because he talks with the kids and hangs out with them. They'll tell him who is doing what. The kids have more respect for him than I've ever seen in a juvenile police officer. When I was down there a couple days ago, two kids came in his office just to talk with him. One was a runaway and didn't know what to do, but she went to the police to talk with Darrell because she knew he would help.*[52]

POLICY IMPLICATIONS

The administrative decision on how deeply to become involved in juvenile work, the broad discretionary authority of the police in police-juvenile encounters, and police brutality toward juveniles are three important issues facing policymakers.

The Degree of Involvement in Juvenile Work

A debate currently exists among police administrators over how involved their departments should become in juvenile work. Several questions guide this debate: How much need is there to involve police in delinquency prevention activities? What is the desirability of having police officers establish good relations with youth? How much specialized training is necessary to present cases in juvenile court? How much "downtime" is involved with patrol division officers absent from patrol areas while they process juvenile cases? How appropriate is it to require detectives or other investigators to follow up juvenile cases to the point of final disposition?[53]

Some chiefs maintain a deep involvement in juvenile work. They see it as desirable to have police officers with specialized training deal with youthful offenders. They encourage the juvenile division to sponsor activities such as the Police Athletic League and to develop a variety of prevention and diversionary programs. They may even design policy that elevates the juvenile officer and the juvenile division to the level of other units of the department. But more typically, departmental juvenile units have been phased out, or they handle only cases involving "missing" juveniles and cases of dependent, neglected or abused children. In such departments, detective bureaus have assumed responsibility for juvenile investigations. The most frequently given explanation for the reduced emphasis on police-juvenile relations is that presently scarce resources no longer permit specialized juvenile units and officers.

It would appear a serious mistake to deemphasize specialization in police-juvenile relations. A detective cannot give the time or commitment to juvenile work that a juvenile officer can give. Nor can one detective in charge of investigations with juveniles give the services to juveniles that a separate unit with several juvenile officers can give. Furthermore, the good will fostered among youth by prevention and diversionary interventions is lost with the termination of these programs. If the present trend continues, much of the improvement in juvenile attitudes toward the police may be destroyed, and the hostility that juveniles felt toward the police in the late 1960s and early 1970s may reappear. The ideal would be to develop more, rather than fewer, specialized services with juveniles.

Police Discretion and Police-Juvenile Encounters

It is often thought that decision making concerning youths is limited to the formal justice system. But nothing is further from the truth. As noted in this chapter, the majority of juvenile offenders are informally warned and released, put under surveillance, scolded, or threatened by the police, all without a written record. Informal decision making also occurs when a police officer takes a youth home rather than to the station because he or she knows the youngster's parents or when an officer permits a juvenile offender "to slide by" because he or she knows that the juvenile judge will refuse to take any punitive action.

However, because extra-legal factors intrude into police-juvenile decision making, lower-class and minority youths are likely to receive different "justice" from middle-class juveniles. The explanation usually given for referring more lower-class than middle-class youths to the juvenile court is that lower-class and minority children are involved in serious crimes more often than affluent children. But of equal importance in the discriminatory treatment of lower-class children is the fact that society expects the police to keep poor children in line and to be less tolerant of the behavior of the "dangerous" classes.

However, a disturbing consequence of a policy that reduces police discretion is the greater numbers of youths likely to be referred to the juvenile court. The resolution of this issue probably rests in the development of standards among police departments according to which the decision to refer a youth rests simply upon legal factors, but, at the same time, the least-restrictive model—in which no more is done to a youth than is absolutely necessary—is used throughout the juvenile court proceedings.

Police Brutality toward Juveniles

The police are being accused of using increasing amounts of brutality toward both juveniles and adults. For example, in a case in San Antonio, Texas, a police officer shot a twelve-year-old Mexican-American youth who was under custody in a police car; the officer had been holding the barrel of his gun to the youth's head and playing Russian roulette.[54]

Although no empirical evidence shows that the police are actually becoming involved in more instances of inappropriate physical force, the recent crime control policy of a more conservative U.S. Supreme Court is returning power to the police that was taken away in the late 1960s. This "law-and-order" approach, along with the reduction in numbers of specialized juvenile officers working with juveniles, may result in more instances of police brutality with youthful offenders.

The inappropriate use of physical force in police-juvenile relations is a particularly important issue because taking a juvenile into custody frequently is not an easy matter. Status offenders usually are resistant to or defiant toward authority. Emotionally disturbed youths, as well as those under the influence of alcohol and drugs, are also difficult or occasionally even dangerous. Furthermore, chronic offenders and gang youths may have few qualms about injuring or killing a police officer.

Children's rights groups must become involved in instances of apparent use of inappropriate physical force in police-juvenile encounters. Civil suits, in which police officers who are involved in inappropriate physical force, are assessed punitive damages, are probably the most effective means of deterring police brutality.

SUMMARY

The police, as the first line of defense against crime, must deal with the serious problem of youth crime. The importance of police-juvenile relations cannot be minimized because the police are usually the first contact a juvenile has with the justice system. In the historical context, police-juvenile relations have come a long way in the past two centuries—or for that matter, in the past two decades. In terms of the sociocultural context, juveniles overall now have better attitudes toward the police than in the past. Even juvenile offenders often look upon the police as having a job to do; the police's job is to catch juvenile lawbreakers, and their job is to avoid being caught. In the legal context, the police have wide discretion toward juvenile lawbreaking, but, as several studies have found, about 80 or 90 percent of the police-juvenile encounters result in diversion from the juvenile justice system. The most important factor influencing the police disposition of the juvenile is the crime committed. Juveniles, like adults, have been granted increased due process rights at the time of arrest.

However, factors in the political and economic contexts are impinging upon the progress recently made in police-juvenile relations. Economic constraints, as well as the law-and-order mood of policymakers, are resulting in an increased tendency to do away with specialized juvenile units and juvenile officers. Police departments across the nation do not have the same commitment to prevention and diversionary programs they had a few years ago. Nor do detectives or police officers have the same commitment to providing services to youthful offenders that juvenile officers had in the past. This tendency to withdraw from specialized juvenile work may cause much of the progress achieved in recent years to be lost.

Discussion Questions

1. What occupational determinants of police work affect the police's attitudes toward youth crime?
2. Summarize the attitudes that juveniles have toward the police.
3. What factors influence the police officer's disposition of the juvenile offender?
4. Summarize the rights of a juvenile taken into custody.
5. Why is it a mistake to deemphasize specialization in juvenile-police relations?

References

Kenney, John P., and Pursuit, Dan G. *Police Work with Juveniles,* Springfield, Ill.: Charles C Thomas Company, 1965.

Kobetz, Richard W. *The Police Role and Juvenile Delinquency.* Gaithersberg, Md.: International Association of Chiefs of Police, 1971.

Lundman, Richard J.; Sykes, Richard E.; and Clark, John P. "Police Control of Juveniles: A Replication." In *Police Behavior: A Sociological Perspective,* edited by Richard J. Lundman. New York: Oxford Press, 1980.

Portune, Robert. *Changing Adolescent Attitudes toward Police.* Cincinnati: W. H. Anderson Company, 1971.

Pursuit, Dan G.; Gerletti, John D.; Brown, Robert M., Jr.; and Ward, Steven M. *Police Programs for Preventing Crime and Delinquency.* Springfield, Ill.: Charles C Thomas Company, 1972.

Rubin, H. Ted. *Juvenile Justice: Police, Practice and Law.* Santa Monica, Calif.: Goodyear Publishing Company, 1979.

Winfree, L. Thomas, Jr., and Griffiths, Curt T. "Adolescents' Attitudes toward the Police: A Survey of High School Students." In *Juvenile Delinquency: Little Brother Grows Up,* edited by Theodore N. Ferdinand. Beverly Hills, Calif.: Sage Publications, 1977.

FOOTNOTES

1. J. D. Lohman, "The Handling of Juveniles from Offense to Disposition" (Washington, D.C.: U.S. Government Printing Office, 1963).

2. John P. Kennedy and Dan G. Pursuit, *Police Work with Juveniles* (Springfield, Ill.: Charles C Thomas Company, 1965), p. 5.

3. Jerome Skolnick, *Justice without Trial* (New York: John Wiley & Sons, 1966).

4. Edward M. Davis, "Juvenile Justice since the *Gault* Decision," *Police Chief* 44 (1977), p. 8.

5. Skolnick, *Justice without Trial.*

6. Ibid.

7. Robert Portune, *Changing Adolescent Attitudes toward Police* (Cincinnati: W. H. Anderson Company, 1971).

8. Donald H. Bouma, *Kids and Cops* (Grand Rapids, Mich.: William E. Eerdman Publishing Company, 1969), pp. 69–79.

9. R. L. Hoobler, "San Diego: Secondary Schools' Task Force," *Police Chief* 40 (1973), pp. 28–30.

10. L. Thomas Winfree, Jr., and Curt T. Griffiths, "Adolescents' Attitudes toward the Police: A Survey of High School Students," in *Juvenile Delinquency: Little Brother Grows Up* (Beverly Hills, Calif.: Sage Publications, 1977), pp. 79–99.

11. Bouma, *Kids and Cops.*

12. Peggy C. Giordano, "The Sense of Injustice: An Analysis of Juveniles' Reactions to the Justice System," *Criminology* 14 (May 1976), pp. 105–106.

13. Carl Werthman and Irving Piliavin, "Gang Members and the Police," in *The Police,* edited by David J. Bordua (New York: John Wiley & Sons, 1967), p. 70.

14. William T. Rusinko, Knowlton W. Johnson, and Carlton A. Hornung, "The Importance of Police Contact in the Formulation of Youths' Attitudes toward Police," *Journal of Criminal Justice* 6 (Spring 1978), p. 65.

15. J. P. Clark and E. P. Wenninger, "The Attitudes of Juveniles toward the Legal Instituition," *Journal of Criminal Law, Criminology and Police Science* 55 (1964), pp. 482–489; D. C. Gibbons, *Delinquent Behavior* (Englewood Cliffs, N.J.: Prentice-Hall, 1976); V. I. Cizanckas and C. W. Purviance, "Changing Attitudes of Black Youths," *Police Chief* 40 (1973), p. 42; P. E. Smith and R. O. Hawkins, "Victimization, Types of Citizen-Police Contacts and Attitudes toward the Police," *Law and Society Review* 8 (1973), pp. 135–152.

16. Interviewed in April 1981.

17. Interviewed in May 1981.

18. Interviewed in April 1983.

19. Richard W. Kobetz and Betty B. Bosarge, *Juvenile Justice Administration* (Gaithersburg, Md.: International Association of Chiefs of Police, 1973).

20. James Q. Wilson, "Dilemmas of Police Administration," *Public Administration Review* 28 (September-October 1968).

21. David J. Bordua, "Recent Trends: Deviant Behavior and Social Control," *Annals* 359 (January 1967), pp. 149–163.

22. Donald J. Black and Albert J. Reiss, Jr., "Police Control of Juveniles," *American Sociological Review* 35 (February 1979), pp. 63–77.

23. Robert M. Terry, "Discrimination in the Handling of Juvenile Offenders by Social Control Agencies," *Journal of Research in Crime and Delinquency* 4 (July 1967), pp. 218–230; Nathan Goldman, *The Differential Selection of Juvenile Offenders for Court Appearance* (New York: National Council on Crime and Delinquency 1963), pp. 35–47; Black and Reiss, "Police Control of Juveniles," pp. 63–77; Irving Piliavin and Scott Briar, "Police Encounters with Juveniles," *American Journal of Sociology* 70 (September 1964), pp. 206–214.

24. Terry, "Handling of Juvenile Offenders;" Black and Weiss, "Police Control of Juveniles"; and Robert M. Emerson, *Judging Delinquents: Context and Process in Juvenile Court* (Chicago: Aldine Publishing Company, 1969), p. 42.

25. Gail Armstrong, "Females under the Law—Protected But Unequal," *Crime and Delinquency* 23 (April 1977), pp. 109–120; and Media Chesney-Lind, "Judicial Paternalism and the Female Status Offender," *Crime and Delinquency* 23 (April 1977), pp. 121–130.

26. Media Chesney-Line, "Juvenile Delinquency: The Sexualization of Female Crime," *Psychology Today* 8 (July 1974), pp. 43–46; and I. Richard Perlman, "Antisocial Behavior of the Minor in the United States," in *Society, Delinquency, and Delinquent Behavior,* edited by Harwin L. Voss (Boston: Little, Brown & Company, 1970).

27. Theodore N. Ferdinand and Elmer C. Luchterhand, "Inner-City Youths, the Police, the Juvenile Court, and Justice," *Social Problems* 17 (Spring 1970), pp. 510–527; Goldman, *Differential Selection for Juvenile Offenders;* Piliavin and Briar, "Police Encounters with Juveniles."

28. Marvin E. Wolfgang, Robert M. Figlio, and Thorstein Sellin, *Delinquency in a Birth Cohort* (Chicago: University of Chicago Press, 1972), p. 252.

29. James T. Carey et al., *The Handling of Juveniles from Offense to Disposition* (Washington, D.C.: U.S. Government Printing Office, 1976), p. 419; A. W. McEachern and Riva Bauzer, "Factors Related to Disposition in Juvenile-Police Contacts," in *Juvenile Gangs in Context,* edited by Malcolm W. Klein (Englewood Cliffs, N.J.: Prentice-Hall, 1967), pp. 148–160; Thorstein Sellin and Marvin E. Wolfgang, *The Measurement of Delinquency* (New York: John Wiley & Sons, 1964), pp. 95–105; Ferdinand and Luchterhand, "Inner-City Youths," pp. 510–527.

30. Interviewed in August 1980.

31. Piliavin and Briar, "Police Encounters with Juveniles," pp. 206–214.

32. Werthman and Piliavin, "Gang Members and Police," pp. 56–98.

33. Richard J. Lundman, Richard E. Sykes, and John P. Clark, "Police Control of Juveniles: A Replication," in *Police Behavior: A Sociological Perspective,* edited by Richard J. Lundman (New York: Oxford Press, 1980), pp. 147–148.

34. Malcolm W. Klein, "Police Processing of Juvenile Offenders: Toward the Development of Juvenile System Rates," in Los Angeles County Sub-Regional Board, California Council on Juvenile Justice, Part III.

35. Nathan Goldman, "The Differential Selection of Juvenile Offenders for Court Appear-

ance," in *Crime and the Legal Process,* edited by William Chambliss (New York: McGraw-Hill Book Company, 1969).

36. Wilson, "Dilemmas of Police Administration," p. 19.

37. Donald J. Black, "Production of Crime Rates," *American Sociological Review* 35 (August 1970), pp. 733–748; Joseph W. Eaton and Kenneth Polk, *Measuring Delinquency* (Pittsburgh: University of Pittsburgh Press, 1961); Lyle W. Shannon, "Types and Patterns of Delinquency Referral in a Middle-Sized City," *British Journal of Criminology* 10 (July 1963), pp. 206–214; and Norman L. Weiner and Charles V. Willie "Decisions by Juvenile Officers," *American Journal of Sociology* 76 (September 1971), pp. 199–210.

38. The following section is adapted from H. Ted Rubin, *Juvenile Justice: Police Practice and Law* (Santa Monica, Calif.: Goodyear Publishing Company, 1979), pp. 75–82.

39. *In re Two Brothers and a Case of Liquor,* Juvenile Court of the District of Columbia, 1966, reported in *Washington Law Reporter* 95 (1967), p. 113.

40. Ciulla v. State, 434 S.W. 2d 948 (Tex. Civ. App. 1968).

41. Haley v. Ohio, 332 U.S. 596 (1948).

42. Miranda v. Arizona, 384 U.S. 436 (1966).

43. *In re Gault,* 387 U.S. (1967).

44. People v. Lara, 62 Cal. Reporter, 586 (1967), cert. denied 392 U.S. 945 (1968).

45. *In re Mellott,* 217 S.E. 2d 745 (C.A.N. Ca. 1975).

46. *In re Dennis P. Fletcher,* 248 A 2d. 364 (Md. 1968), cert. denied 396 U.S. 852 (1969).

47. Elyce Z. Ferster and Thomas F. Courtless, "The Beginning of Juvenile Justice, Police Practices, and the Juvenile Offender," *Vanderbilt Law Review* 22 (April 1969), pp. 598–601.

48. Davis v. Mississippi, 394 U.S. 721 (1969).

49. *In re Carl I.,* 81 Cal. Reporter 655 (2nd. C.A. 1969).

50. Thomas R. Phelps, *Juvenile Delinquency: A Contemporary View* (Santa Monica, Calif.: Goodyear Publishing Company, 1976), pp. 141–142.

51. Robert W. Winslow, *Juvenile Delinquency in a Free Society* (Monterey, Calif.: Brooks/ Cole Publishing Company, 1977).

52. Interviewed in October 1982.

53. Rubin, *Juvenile Justice,* p. 60.

54. Paul Takagi, "A Garrison State in a Democratic Society," *Crime and Social Justice* 1 (1974), p. 31.

INTERVIEW WITH ALBERT J. REISS, JR.

"Somehow we must collect some hard, clear-cut evidence that the ends of due process procedures are some positive consequences on kids. . . . Everything we know about bureaucratized models suggest that they don't really work in the best interests of persons, whether juveniles or adults."

In this interview, Albert J. Reiss, professor of sociology at Yale and a widely respected authority on police-juvenile relations, discusses such issues as the effect of due process rights on police-juvenile relations, changes in police discretion in the past twenty years, and the rationale for deemphasizing specialized police work with juveniles.

Question: I sense the attitudes of juveniles are more positive toward the police than they have been in the past. Do you agree?

Reiss: Well, the police think so. But the police have believed for some time that juveniles' attitudes were better than they had been in the past. I think the turning point came with the Civil Rights movement. With this movement, juveniles began to have rights, and the police began to be held accountable for their behavior towards juveniles. This means that the police can't treat juveniles the way they did previously. In the past, they could tell juveniles to get off the corner and to go home: Now, juveniles tell police to shove it, and they do this because they know they have "a right" to be on the corner. They may tell the police officer, "I've a right to be here; you can't do anything about that." The police are also sensitive to the

Professor Albert J. Reiss, Jr. has made a significant contribution to understanding delinquency in America. In the past two decades, his theoretical and empirical contributions have ranged from police-juvenile relations, to control theory, to differential association theory, and to measuring delinquency. The research that Donald Black and he did on processing juveniles has been particularly important in developing an empirical portrait of the police handling of juvenile offenders.

fact that their relationships with parents have changed. They used to be able to take children home and the parents were interested in working cooperatively with the police. Now, the police feel that the parents are more aggressive and hostile towards them and that often they may have an adversary relationship with the parents rather than a cooperative one.

Question: Let's turn the coin over and discuss some of the positive consequences of due process rights for juveniles. Is there less brutality in the system? Is there less misuse of discretion?

Reiss: I wish I knew the answer to that question. My sense is that because of the due process rights emerging from the Supreme Court decisions, there are more formal due process procedures in the system. But I have not seen a study that I thought had convincing evidence that the procedure was somehow in the best interests of the juvenile or in the best interests of the system, whatever the latter might mean. Somehow we must collect some hard, clear-cut evidence that the ends of due process procedures are some positive consequences on kids. Namely, that the increase in lawyers hired to defend kids means that kids are getting more and better counseling. I suspect that the state is represented in the formal sense of due process, but I'm not certain whether that works in the best interest of children. Everything we now about bureaucratized models suggests that they don't really work well in the interest of persons, whether adults or juveniles.

Question: The article you coauthored on discretion has become a classic in police-juvenile relations. Has discretion with juveniles changed since you wrote your article?

Reiss: I think people have forgotten what I said about the nature of discretion itself, although I didn't say it specifically in that article and said it more succinctly later: That is, most sociologists use the term discretion in a way that means nothing more than choice. They say everyone has the right to choose and call that discretionary. Sometimes, it drives me a bit out of my mind because they talk about discretionary choice, but they don't define what they mean by discretionary choice. Now I use discretion in a sense that is consistent with the legal doctine of discretion; a law is discretionary when it is a decision or choice that is not subject to review. What is interesting about the police is that when they arrest somebody, it is subject to review. Therefore, it is not discretionary. So what is discretionary with the police is when the decision is made not to arrest.

So what we were talking about in the article on police control of juveniles is that most of the time the choices of the police were non-reviewable. The minute they made a choice not to arrest a person nobody could review it. This is a very important matter, and it has certain consequences which I tried to pursue in subsequent writings. The interesting thing in the use of police cautioning practices today is that an attempt is made to formalize the procedures and keep track of the person cautioned. What happens then is that police are widening the net. We are beginning to talk about net-widening, particularly at the juvenile level. What we are doing is bringing them officially into the system but at the time I was writing, you see,

they were left outside the system. Now we've invented all these ways to widen the net, such as recording our cautionings or sending them to alternative programs. These youths now have a record and so the next time we can accelerate or escalate the kind of penalties. Thus, the unfettered discretion, in the older system was not reviewable, but in some ways it was a system that labeled less and probably escalated less. In that sense, discretion is used differently now than in the past.

Question: There seems to be a movement in police work today to deemphasize police-juvenile relations. That is, juvenile units and the specialized juvenile officer do not seem to be used as much as they have been in the past. What is your reaction to this movement?

Reiss: Sure, there is now the feeling that the system has moved to the point where you have to justify everything in formal processing procedures. The police are perfectly willing to go along with this. We may be in a transition to a civil justice system. I'm not certain I'm opposed to that but I think it's something we need to look at very closely.

One thing is clear from Zimring's work and that of others is that it's very hard to say that there is an age at which you can feel comfortable about saying a person is still a juvenile or has become an adult. If you look at the behavioral level, it is clear that persons called juveniles commit adult acts. Only if you have some notion of responsibility, can you sense the age at which a juvenile should be treated as an adult.

CHAPTER 16

THE JUVENILE COURT

CHAPTER OUTLINE

Neither umpire nor arbiter; [the juvenile judge] is the one person who represents his community as *parens patriae*, who may act *with* the parents, or
when necessary even in *place* of them to bring about behavior more desirable. As a judge in a juvenile court he does not administer criminal law.
The child before him is not a defendant. There is no conviction, no sentence. There is no life-long stigma of a criminal record. In a juvenile court
the judge administers equity; and the child, still immature and unable to
take his place as an adult before the law, is the recipient of consideration,
of guidance and of correction. The stake is no less than the saving of a human being at a time more favorable than any in an uncertain future.

Gustav L. Schramm[1]

Gustav L. Schramm, a long-term juvenile judge in Pittsburgh, thus describes the
monumental responsibility of a juvenile judge. He, as well as other advocates of the
juvenile court, claims that the informal setting of this court and the parental demeanor of the judge enable wayward youth to be "saved" or "rescued" from their
lives of crime. However, critics challenge these idealistic views of the juvenile court.
They claim that the juvenile court has not succeeded in rehabilitating youthful
offenders, in bringing justice and compassion to them, or even in providing them
their due process rights.[2] Some investigators even accuse the juvenile court of doing
great harm to those appearing before it.[3]

This chapter begins with the historical development of the juvenile court and then
discusses the procedures involved in its administration. It then describes the court's
personnel, including the judge, the prosecutor, and the defense attorney, and examines polices needed for improving it.

CREATION OF THE
JUVENILE COURT

The contextual perspective is helpful in understanding the creation of the juvenile
court, for the court emerged from the interrelationships among the legal, sociocultural, economic, and political contexts.

Legal Context

The juvenile court was founded in Cook County (Chicago) in 1899, when the Illinois
legislature passed the Juvenile Court Act. The *parens patriae* doctrine provided a
legal catalyst for the creation of the juvenile court, as it furnished a rationale for the
use of informal procedures for dealing with juveniles and for expanding state power
over children. The *parens patriae* doctrine also was used to justify the juvenile
court's activities to determine possible causes and to make decisions on the disposition of cases. The kindly parent, the state, could thus justify relying on psychological
and medical examinations rather than on trial by evidence. Consequently, once the

parens patriae rationale was applied to juvenile proceedings, the institution of the juvenile court followed.

Political Context

In *The Child Savers,* Anthony Platt discusses the political context of the origin of the juvenile court. He claims that the juvenile court was established in Chicago and later elsewhere because it satisfied several middle-class interest groups. He sees the juvenile court as an expression of middle-class values and of the philosophy of conservative political groups. In denying that the juvenile court was revolutionary, Platt charges:

> *The child-saving movement was not so much a break with the past as an affirmation of faith in traditional institutions. Parental authority, education at home, and the virtues of rural life were emphasized because they were in decline at this time. The child-saving movement was, in part, a crusade which, through emphasizing the dependence of the social order on the proper socialization of children, implicitly elevated the nuclear family and, more especially, the role of women as stalwarts of the family. The child savers were prohibitionists, in a general sense, who believed that social progress depended on efficient law enforcement, strict supervision of children's leisure and recreation, and the regulation of illicit pleasures. What seemingly began as a movement to humanize the lives of adolescents soon developed into a program of moral absolutism through which youths were to be saved from movies, pornography, cigarettes, alcohol, and anything else which might possibly rob them of their innocence.[4]*

Economic Context

Platt contends that the behaviors the child savers selected to be penalized, such as engaging in sex, roaming the streets, drinking, fighting, attending dance halls, and staying out late at night, were found primarily in lower-class children. Thus, juvenile justice from its inception, he argues, reflected class favoritism that resulted in the frequent processing of poor children through the system, while middle- and upper-class children were more likely to be excused.[5]

The children of the poor were a particular problem to the child savers because the juvenile court emerged during the wake of an unprecedented industrial and urban development in the United States. This process was closely connected with large-scale immigration of people to urban centers who had different backgrounds than the indigenous population. These immigrants brought new social problems to Chicago and other urban centers, and the child savers were determined to rescue the immigrant children and to protect them from their families.[6]

Sociocultural Context

Three social conditions, which characterized the last thirty years of the nineteenth century, led to the founding of the juvenile court. First, many citizens were incensed by the treatment of children during this period, especially the procedure of jailing them with adults. The jails were considered highly injurious to youthful offenders because the deleterious effects of association with adult criminals. Second, urban disenchantment became widespread. The population of Chicago tripled between 1880 and 1890, mostly by immigration, creating such problems as filth and corruption, poverty, the rise of crime, and corruption in city government. Third, the higher status given middle-class women made them interested in exerting their newfound influence to improve the lives of children. Indeed, childsaving became an avocation for some middle-class women who wanted to do something outside the home.[7]

These pressures for social change in Chicago took place in the midst of a wave of optimism that swept through American society during the Progressive Era, the period from 1890–1920. The emerging social sciences assured reformers that through positivism their problems with delinquents could be solved. According to positivism, youths were not responsible for their behavior and needed treatment rather than punishment. The judge and scientific expert could work together in a separate court to discover a child's problem and to provide the cure.

Middle-class religious humanitarianism was another societal level pressure for change in American society. Such writers as Charles Dickens and Mary Carpenter challenged Christians to rescue children from degrading slums. The importance of religious humanitarianism is evident in the fact that many of the well-known child-savers were ministers, and most of the childsaving institutions were private charities, supported, at least in part, by mainline religious denominations.

Thus, the interrelationships of the legal, political, economic, and sociocultural contexts on the societal, community, and individual levels during the final decades of the eighteenth century resulted in the creation of the juvenile court.

THE DEVELOPMENT OF THE JUVENILE COURT

The concept of the juvenile court was rapidly accepted across the nation because the same cultural, political, and economic conditions existed elsewhere. Thirty-one states had instituted juvenile courts by 1905, and by 1928, only two states did not have a juvenile court statute. The amendments that followed the original act brought the neglected, the dependent, and the delinquent together under one roof. The delinquent category was made up of both status offenders and actual violators of criminal law.

Juvenile courts throughout the nation were patterned upon the Chicago court. Children in trouble were offered informal and noncriminal hearings. Their records generally were kept confidential, and the hearings were nonpublic. Also, children were detained separately from adults. Reformers then proposed that the noncriminal aspects of the proceedings be echoed in the physical surroundings of the court:

The courtroom should be not a courtroom at all; just a room, with a table and two chairs, where the judge and the child, the probation officer and the parents, as occasion arises, come into close contact, and where in a more or less informal way the whole may be talked over.[8]

Reformers further advocated that the juvenile judge sit at a desk rather than on a bench and that he occasionally "put his arm around his shoulder and draw the lad to him."[9] But the sympathetic judge was instructed not to lose any of his judicial dignity. The goals of the court were defined as investigation, diagnosis, and the prescription of treatment. Lawyers were deemed unnecessary because these civil proceedings were not adversary trials but informal hearings in which the best interests of the children were the chief concern.

In short, the juvenile court was founded upon several admirable directives: that the court should function as a social clinic designed to serve the best interests of children in trouble; that children brought before the court should be given the same care, supervision, and discipline provided by a good parent; that the aim of the court is to help, to restore, to guide, and to forget; that children should not be treated as criminals; and that the rights to shelter, protection, and proper guardianship are the only rights of children.[10]

Changes in the Legal Norms of the Juvenile Court

The juvenile court has faced various critics during its development, but the constitutionalists have had the greatest impact. The constitutionalists contended that the juvenile court was unconstitutional because the principles of a fair trial and individual rights were denied. They were particularly concerned that the children appearing before the court have procedural rights as well as the rights of shelter, protection, and guardianship. The fundamental assumptions of the constitutionalists were that dependent and neglected children are different from children who break the law and, therefore, must be dealt with through separate judicial proceedings; that diagnostic and treatment technologies are not sufficiently developed to ensure that the delinquent can be treated and cured of his or her misbehavior; and that the state must justify interference with a youth's life when his or her freedom is at stake.[11]

The constitutionalists recommended that these assumptions be incorporated into the structure of the juvenile court by the adoption of separate procedures for dealing with dependent and neglected children and with those accused of criminal behavior; by the use of informal adjustments to avoid official court actions as frequently as possible; and by the provision of rigorous procedural safeguards and rights for children appearing before the court at the adjudicatory stage.[12]

A series of decisions by the U.S. Supreme Court in the 1960s and 1970s demonstrated the influence of the constitutionalists upon juvenile justice. The five most important cases were: Kent v. *United States* (1966), *In re Gault* (1967), *In the Matter of Samuel Winship* (1970), *McKeiver* v. *Pennsylvania* (1971), and *Breed* v. *Jones* (1975).

Kent v. United States (1966)

The Kent decision, the first in which the U.S. Supreme Court dealt with a juvenile court case, concerns the matter of transfer. See Box 16-1 for the facts of this case.

BOX 16-1 *Kent v. United States*

Morris A. Kent, Jr., a sixteen-year-old youth on juvenile probation, was charged with three counts each of housebreaking and robbery and two counts of rape. His mother retained an attorney who had Kent examined by two psychiatrists and a psychologist. The attorney then filed a motion for a hearing on the question of waiver, together with a psychiatrist's affidavit that certified that Kent was "a victim of severe psychopathology" and recommended hospitalization for psychiatric observation. Counsel contended that psychiatric treatment would make Kent a suitable subject for juvenile court rehabilitation. His counsel also moved for access to juvenile court probation records.

Source: *Kent* v. *United States*, 383 U.S. 541, 86 S. Ct. 1045, 16 L. Ed. 2d 84 (1966).

The juvenile judge did not rule on the motions of Kent's counsel. He held no hearings, nor did he confer with Kent, Kent's mother, or Kent's counsel. Rather, the judge entered an order saying that after full investigation, he was transferring jurisdiction to the criminal court. Thus, he made no findings and entered no reasons for the waiver.

On appeal, the U.S. Supreme Court held the juvenile court proceedings defective. The Court held that during a transfer hearing Kent should have been afforded an evidential hearing; that Kent should have been present when the court decided to waive jurisdiction; that the attorney should have been permitted to examine the social worker's investigation of the youth that the court used in deciding to waive jurisdiction; and that the judge should have recorded a statement of reasons for the transfer. Justice Fortas, in the decision, stated:

> There is evidence, in fact, that there may be grounds for concern that the child receives the worst of both worlds; that he gets neither the protection accorded to adults nor the solicitous care and regenerative treatment postulated for children.[13]

The Court decided that withholding Kent's record essentially meant a denial of counsel. The Court also held that a juvenile has a right to be represented by counsel; that a youth charged with a felony has a right to a hearing; and that this hearing must "measure up to the essentials of due process and fair treatment." Finally, a juvenile's attorney must have access to his or her social or probation records.[14]

In re Gault

In May 1967, the U.S. Supreme Court reversed the conviction of a minor in the case of *In re Gault*. This influential and far-reaching decision represented a new dawn in juvenile court history because it, in effect, brought the light of constitutional procedure into juvenile courts. No longer could due process and procedural safeguards be kept out of the adjudication proceedings. See Box 16-2 for the facts of this case.

BOX 16-2 *In re Gault*

Gerald Gault, a fifteen-year-old Arizona boy, and a friend, Ronald Lewis, were taken into custody on June 8, 1964, on a verbal complaint made by a neighbor. The neighbor had accused the boys of making lewd and indecent remarks to her over the phone. Gault's parents were not notified that he was taken into custody; he was not advised of his right to counsel; he was not advised that he could remain silent; and no notice of changes was made either to Gerald or his parents. Additionally, the complainant was not present at either of the hearings. In spite of considerable confusion about whether or not Gerald had made the alleged phone call, what he had said over the phone, and what he had said to the judge during the course of the two hearings, Judge McGhee committed him to the State Industrial School "for the period of his minority (that is, until twenty-one) unless sooner discharged by due process of law."

Source: *In re Gault*, 387 U.S.1, 18 L. Ed. 2d 527, 87 S. Ct. 1428 (1967).

The U.S. Supreme Court in this case overruled the Arizona Supreme Court for its dismissal of a writ of habeas corpus. This writ had sought the release of Gault from training school.[15] Justice Fortas, for the court majority, ruled on four of the six issues raised in the appeal:

1. Notice, to comply with due process requirements, must be given sufficiently in advance of scheduled court proceedings so that reasonable opportunity to prepare will be afforded, and it must "set forth the alleged misconduct with particularity."

2. We conclude that the due process clause of the Fourteenth Amendment requires that in respect of proceedings to determine delinquency which may result in commitment to an institution in which the juvenile's freedom is curtailed, the child and his parent must be notified of the child's right to be represented by counsel retained by them, or if they are unable to afford counsel, that counsel will be appointed to represent the child.

3. We conclude that the constitutional privilege against self-incrimination is applicable in the case of juveniles as it is with respect to adults.

4. No reason is suggested or appears for a different role in respect of sworn testimony in juvenile courts than in adult tribunals. Absent a valid confession adequate to support the determination of the Juvenile Court, confrontation and

sworn testimony by witnesses available for cross-examination are essential for a finding of "delinquency" and an order committing Gerald to a state institution for a maximum of six years.[16]

Justice Fortas, in delivering the Court's opinion, recalled other cases that had provided juveniles with due process of law. In both *Haley* v. *Ohio* (1948) and *Gallegos* v. *Colorado* (1962), the U.S. Supreme Court had prohibited the use of confessions coerced from juveniles, and in *Kent*, the Court had given the juvenile the right to be represented by counsel.[17] Justice Fortas concluded his review of legal precedent with the sweeping statement that juveniles have those fundamental rights incorporated in the due process clause of the Fourteenth Amendment of the Constitution.

The *In re Gault* decision affirmed that a juvenile has the right to due process safeguards in proceedings where a finding of delinquency can lead to institutional confinement. The decision also established that a juvenile has the right of notice of the charges, right to counsel, right to confrontation and cross-examination, and privilege against self-incrimination. But the Court did not decide that juveniles have the right to a transcript of the proceedings or the right to appellate review.

In choosing not to rule on these two latter rights, the Court clearly did not want to make the informal juvenile hearing into an adversary trial. The cautiousness of this decision was underlined by footnote that said the decision did not apply to preadjudication or postadjudication treatment of juveniles.

In re Winship (1970)

In *Winship,* the Supreme Court decided that juveniles are entitled to proof "beyond a reasonable doubt" during the adjudication proceedings.[18] See Box 16-3 for the facts of this case.

BOX 16-3 *In re* Winship

The Winship case involved a New York boy who was sent to a state training school at the age of twelve for taking $112 from a woman's purse. The commitment was based on a New York statute that permitted juvenile court decisions on the basis of a "preponderance of evidence"—a standard much less strict than "beyond a reasonable doubt."

Source: *In re Winship*, 397 U.S. 358, 90 S. Ct. 1968, 25 L. Ed. 2d 368 (1970).

In ruling that the "preponderance of evidence" is not a sufficient basis for a decision when youths are charged with acts that would be criminal if committed by adults, the *Winship* decision not only expanded the *In re Gault* ruling, but also reflected other concerns of the U.S. Supreme Court. The Court desired both to protect juveniles at adjudicatory hearings and to maintain the confidentiality, informality, flexibility, and speed of the juvenile process in the prejudicial and postadjudicative states. The court obviously did not want to bring too much rigidity and impersonality to the juvenile hearing.

McKeiver v. Pennsylvania (1971)

The Supreme Court heard three cases together (*McKeiver v. Pennsylvania, In re Terry,* and *In re Barbara Burrus*) concerning whether the due process clause of the Fourteenth Amendment guaranteeing the right to a jury trial applied to the adjudication of a juvenile court delinquency case.[19] The decision, which was issued in *McKeiver v. Pennsylvania,* denied the right of juveniles to have jury trials. See Box 16-4 for the facts of these three cases.

BOX 16-4 The Right of a Jury Trial for Juveniles

McKeiver v. Pennsylvania

Joseph McKeiver, age sixteen, was charged with robbery, larceny, and receiving stolen goods, all of which were felonies under Pennsylvania law. This youth was found delinquent at an adjudication hearing and was placed on probation after his request for a jury trial was denied.

In re Terry

Edward Terry, age fifteen, was charged with assault and battery on a police officer, misdemeanors under Pennsylvania law. His counsel request for a jury trial was denied, and he was adjudicated a delinquent on the charges.

In re Barbara Burrus

Barbara Burrus and approximately forty-five youths, ranging in ages from eleven to fifteen years, were the subjects of juvenile court summonses in Hyde County, North Carolina. The charges arose out of a series of demonstrations in the county in late 1968 by black adults and children protesting school assignments and a school consolidation plan. These youths were charged with willfully impeding traffic. The several cases were consolidated into groups for hearing before the district judge, sitting as a juvenile court. A request for a jury trial in each case was denied. Each juvenile was found delinquent and placed on probation.

Source: *McKeiver v. Pennsylvania,* 403 U.S. 528, 535 (1971); and *In re Barbara Burrus,* 275 N.C. 517, 169 S.E. 2d 879 (1969).

The Supreme Court, in ruling that juveniles do not have the right to a jury trial, gave the following reasons:

1. Not all rights constitutionally assured for the adult are to be given the juvenile.
2. The jury trial, if required for juveniles, may make the juvenile proceedings into a fully adversary process and will put an end to what has been the idealistic prospect of an intimate, informal protecting proceeding.
3. A jury trial is not a necessary part even of every criminal process that is fair and equitable.

4. The jury trial, if injected into the juvenile court system, could bring with it the traditional delay, the formality, and the clamor of the adversary system.

5. There is nothing to prevent an individual juvenile judge when he or she feels the need from using an advisory jury. For that matter, there is nothing to prevent individual states from adopting jury trials.[20]

A number of states do permit jury trials for juveniles, but most adhere to the constitutional standard set by the Supreme Court. The significance of the *McKeiver* decision is that the Court indicated an unwillingness to apply further procedural safeguards to juvenile proceedings, especially during the preadjudicatory and post-adjudicatory treatment of juveniles.

Breed v. Jones (1975)

The question of transfer to an adult court, first considered in the *Kent* case, was taken up again in the *Breed* v. *Jones* decision.[21] This case questioned whether a juvenile could be prosecuted as an dult after an adjudicatory hearing in the juvenile court. The increased use of transfers, or the binding over of juveniles to the adult court, makes this decision particularly significant. See Box 16-5 for the facts of this case.

BOX 16-5 *Breed v. Jones*

In 1971, the juvenile court in California filed a petition against Jones, who was then seventeen, alleging that he had committed an offense that, if committed by an adult, would have constituted robbery. Jones was detained pending a hearing. At the hearing, the juvenile judge took testimony, found that the allegations were true, and sustained the petition. At the disposi-tional hearing, Jones was found unfit for treatment in the juvenile court, and it was ordered that he be prosecuted as an adult offender. At a subsequent preliminary hearing, Jones was held for criminal trial; an information was held against him for robbery, and he was tried and found guilty. Counsel objected that Jones was being subjected to double jeopardy, but the defendant was committed to the California Youth Authority.

Source: Breed v. *Jones*, 421 U.S. 519, 95 S. Ct. 1779 (1975).

The U.S. Supreme Court ruled that Breed's case did constitute double jeopardy; a juvenile court cannot adjudicate a case and then transfer the case over to the crimi-nal court for adult processing on the same offense. The significance of *Breed* is that prosecutors must determine which youthful offenders they want to transfer to the adult court prior to juvenile court adjudication; otherwise, the opportunity to trans-fer, or certify, those youths is lost.[22]

Today, as will be indicated in more detail in the next section, nearly every state has defined the specific requirements for transfer proceedings in its juvenile code. At present, when a transfer hearing is conducted in the juvenile court, due process law usually requires: (1) a legitimate transfer hearing; (2) a sufficient notice to the juvenile's family and defense attorney; (3) the right to counsel; and (4) a statement of the court order regarding transfer.[23]

Summary

The *In re Gault* and *Winship* decisions have unquestionably effected profound changes in the legal status of juveniles appearing before the juvenile court during the adjudicatory stage. However, the *McKeiver* decision and the more conservative stance of the Supreme Court since 1971 raise some question about whether further decisions will make juvenile proceedings any more like the legal proceedings of the adult court. These decisions have been widely litigated by state courts, and, of course, have received varying endorsements from juvenile courts across the nation. Some juvenile courts gave procedural rights to juveniles even before the U.S. Supreme Court decisions, but other have resisted implementing these decisions.

NATURE OF JUVENILE COURT SERVICES

The types of cases under the jurisdiction of the juvenile court vary widely among and even within states, but they generally include those involving delinquency, neglect, and dependency. Juvenile courts also may deal with cases concerning adoption, termination of parental rights, appointment of guardians for minors, custody, contributing to delinquency or neglect, and nonsupport. The three basic stages of the juvenile court process are intake, adjudication, and dispositional hearings. The juvenile court also holds detention, transfer, and modification hearings.

The Detention Hearing

Legislative acts that govern the juvenile court normally require that the police either take a child to an intake officer of the court or a detention facility or release him or her to the parents. The criteria for detention are based on the need to protect the child and to insure public safety. The decision to detain must be made within a short period of time, usually forty-eight to seventy-two hours, excluding weekends and holidays. Urban courts, which have intake units on duty twenty-four hours a day for detention hearings, frequently act within a few hours.

Intake officers of the juvenile court, rather than juvenile judges, conduct most detention hearings today. Such a procedure represents a progressive move, because having the same judge to hear both the detention and the adjudication hearing is a poor practice. However, most states still require that the juvenile judge be responsible for the policies and operations of the detention facility. Juvenile judges also are usually required to decide whether a child admitted a few days earlier to detention must remain locked up, in order to preclude inappropriate detention or overly long detention.

Juveniles held in detention may be assigned one of four different types of placements. The detention hall or detention home physically restricts the youth for a short period. Shelter care is physically nonrestrictive and is available for those who have no homes or who require juvenile court intervention. The third type of placement is the jail or police lockup. The fourth is the attention home or in-home detention. In attention homes, juveniles receive more services than they would in a typical detention facility, while in-home placement means a juvenile is restricted to his or her home and is supervised normally by a paraprofessional staff member. Each of these detention placements will be described more extensively in Chapter 18.

Case Law Concerning Detention Practices

The U.S. Supreme Court has not ruled on any case relating to detention, but other federal courts and state appellate courts have issued a substantial number of decisions concerning the detention process.[24]

Bail for a juvenile has been a matter of some concern to the courts. Court decisions have differed, finding: that juveniles have a constitutional right to bail; that juvenile act procedures, when applied in a manner consistent with due process, provide an adequate substitute for bail; or that juveniles do not have a constitutional right to bail. Twenty states permit the posting of bail by or on behalf of a minor, but in reality the posting of bail is not widely used in many of these jurisdictions. On the other hand, Utah and Florida deny the constitutionality of bail for juveniles.

Five states have legislated a hearing on probable cause for detained youths, and appellate cases in other states have moved in the direction of mandating a probable cause hearing to justify further detention. Courts in Georgia and Alaska have ruled that a child is entitled to counsel at a detention hearing and to free counsel if indigent. The supreme courts of California and Alaska, as well as an appellate court in Pennsylvania, all have overturned cases in which no reason or inadequate reason was stated for continuing detention. Finally, courts in the District of Columbia, Baltimore, and Nevada have ruled that a juvenile in detention is entitled to humane care. The appeals court in the District of Columbia stated that there is a statutory obligation to provide a juvenile with care "as nearly as possible equivalent to that which should have been given him by his parents."[25]

Intake

Intake essentially means a preliminary screening process "to determine whether the court should take action and if so what action, or whether the matter should be referred elsewhere."[26] By December 31, 1971, thirty-five states and the District of Columbia had provided for some form of screening process, requiring that a judge, juvenile court representative, or a prosecutor approve the filing of a petition.[27] Larger courts usually handle the intake function through a specialized intake unit; probation officers or other officers of the court screen incoming cases in smaller courts.

Intake procedures follow complaints to authorities against children. Juvenile law varies from state to state on who is permitted to sign such a complaint. Typically, most complaints are filed by the police, although they may be initiated and signed by a victim or by the parents of the youth. In some states, parents, victims, probation staff, social service staff, neighbors, or anyone else may go directly to the court to file a complaint. Complaints also may be brought by school officials and truant officers.

After the complaint is received by the intake officer, he or she must first decide whether the court has statutory jurisdiction. If the statutory guides are unclear, the intake officer should seek the advice of the prosecuting attorney. Once legal jurisdiction is established, the second step is to conduct a preliminary interview and investigation to determine whether the case should be adjudicated nonjudicially or petitioned to the court. This evaluation procedure varies from jurisdiction to jurisdiction, principally because so many juvenile courts have failed to provide written guidelines. Thus, the intake officer usually has broad and largely unregulated discretion in making the intake decision.

Options for the Disposal of Cases

The intake unit, especially in larger urban courts, may have up to five options for the disposal of cases: (1) outright dismissal of the complaint; (2) informal adjustment (chiefly, diversion to a nonjudicial agency); (3) informal probation; (4) consent decree; and (5) filing of a petition.

Outright dismissal of the complaint takes place when legal jurisdiction does not exist or the case is so weak that the intake officer questions the feasibility of petitioning the youth to the juvenile court. Informal adjustment means that the intake officer requires restitution from the youth, warns him or her, and then dismisses the case or diverts the youth to a social agency, youth service bureau, or some other such agency. The diversionary agency supervises such referrals and generally reports to the intake unit on their progress; status offenders and juveniles with minor offenses typically are dealt with under this option.

Informal probation, which has been under increased criticism since the 1970s, involves the casual supervision of a youth by a volunteer or a probation officer, who reserves judgment on the need for filing a petition until the intake officer (or other designated persons) sees how the youth fares during the informal probation period. The National Advisory Committee on Criminal Justice Standards and Goals supports the continued use of informal probation, but the President's Task Force on Juvenile Delinquency and Youth Crime and the U.S. Children's Bureau have advocated abolishing informal probation becuase it violates the legal rights of juveniles.

A consent decree, defined "as a formal agreement between the child and the court in which the child is placed under the court's supervision without a formal finding of delinquency," provides an intermediate step between informal handling and probation.[28] The National Advisory Commission on Criminal Justice Standards and Goals recommended that this decree be enforced for a period of no longer than six months; that its use not result in the removal of the child from his or her family; and that its use be based upon sufficient evidence.[29] The consent decree is used less frequently than the other options open to the intake officer at the present time. The consent decree, it should be noted, comes after the petition but before the adjudication hearing.

If none of these options is satisfactory, the intake unit can choose to file a petition. The National Assessment of Juvenile Corrections, in an examination of seven juvenile courts in Maryland, Ohio, Wisconsin, and Massachusetts, found the only relationship existing between type of offense and intake decision was that offenses against persons were more likely to be referred to the court than other offenses (see Table 16-1).

TABLE 16-1 Intake Decisions by Type of Offense Charged

Offense Charged	Dismissal (%)	Informal Handling (%)	Formal Handling (%)	(N)
Status	26	36	38	(77)
Misdemeanor	33	34	33	(123)
Property	29	34	35	(132)
Person	16	32	51	(37)

Source: Mark Creekmore, "Case Processing: Intake, Adjudication, and Disposition," in *Brought to Justice? Juveniles, the Courts, and the Law,* edited by Rosemary C. Sarri and Yeheskel Hasenfeld (Ann Arbor: National Assessment of Juvenile Corrections, University of Michigan, 1976), p. 127. Reprinted by permission.

Unfortunately, the broad discretionary power given intake workers often has been abused. Charles W. Thomas and Christopher M. Sieverdes, studying 346 cases that appeared in juvenile court intake in a small court in the southeastern United States between 1966 and 1969, found that "the seriousness of the most recent offense was clearly shown to be the best predictor of case disposition."[30] But they then made a telling statement: "These findings lead us to conclude that both legal and extralegal factors are being taken into consideration in the determination of whether to refer a given case for a formal hearing in the juvenile court."[31] These extralegal factors, of course, may be a youth's race, sex, social class, or demeanor. In this regard, Terence Thornberry found in his examination of 3475 boys apprehended by Philadelphia police during the period 1965 to 1973 that black youths and those from impoverished census tracts—even when the seriousness of the offense and of prior offenses were held constant—were dealt with more severely by intake workers than others.[32]

Research is needed to determine which approach to intake will mean the greatest services to youth and the least misuse of discretion. But until a systematic examination of the intake process is done, the principles of doing the least harm to the youth as possible and of fairness should guide the intake screening process.

The Transfer Procedure

Judicial waiver and legislative waiver are the two basic mechanisms for transferring (also called binding over or certifying) juvenile offenders to the adult criminal justice system. Judicial waiver, the most common, takes place after a judicial hearing on a juvenile's amenability to treatment or his or her threat to public safety. Legislative waiver narrows juvenile court jurisdiction by excluding from juvenile courts those youths charged with certain offenses.[33]

Judicial waiver, as previously discussed in the *Kent* v. *United States* and *Breed* v. *Jones* decisions, contains certain procedural safeguards for youthful offenders. Most juvenile court judges appear to be influenced primarily by prior record and the seriousness of the present offense in deciding to transfer. However, statutes mandating that the decision to prosecute a juvenile as an adult be made on the basis of the seriousness of the offense charged are inconsistent with the rehabilitative philosophy of the juvenile court. Legislative waiver also is problematic in that it usually has a rationale of incapacitation of chronic offenders through longer sentences than those provided by the juvenile process.[34]

Project MIJJIT, studies undertaken by the Academy for Contemporary Problems of Columbus, Ohio, under the sponsorship of the Office of Juvenile Justice and Delinquency Prevention, found that in 1978, 9352 juveniles were waived by the juvenile court to the adult court. Of the youths who were waived, over 70 percent were seventeen or older, over 92 percent were male, and over 60 percent were white. Surprisingly, only 29 percent of these youths were charged with personal crimes. In adult court, 90 percent were convicted, but 54 percent were placed on probation or fined, 31 percent were committed to prison, 12 percent were sent to jail, and 2 percent were transferred to juvenile facilities.[35]

Because of current pressures on the court to crack down on juvenile hoodlums, the number of juveniles waived to adult court is likely to increase in the future. Thus, this is one of the most critical areas for ongoing research in juvenile justice, because of the potential effect of the political context on judicial decision making.

The Adjudicatory Stage

The adjudicatory, or fact-finding, stage of the court's proceedings usually includes the following steps: the plea of the child, the presentation of evidence by the prosecution and by the defense, cross-examinations of witnesses, and the finding by the judge. These steps serve as protections to ensure that youths are entitled to proof "beyond a reasonable doubt" when charged with an act that would constitute a crime if committed by an adult, and that the judge follows the rules of evidence and dismisses hearsay from the proceedings. Hearsay is dismissed because it can be unreliable or unfair, inasmuch as it cannot be held up for cross-examination. The evidence must be relevant and must contribute to the belief or disbelief of the act in question.

Prosecutors in most juvenile courts today begin these proceedings by presenting the case of the state. The arresting officer and witnesses at the scene of the crime testify, and any other evidence that has been legally obtained is introduced. The defense attorney, who is present in most juvenile courts today, then cross-examines the witnesses. Defense counsel, who may be a public defender, a court-appointed counsel, or a privately retained attorney, also has the opportunity at this time to introduce evidence favorable to his or her client, and the youth may testify in his or her own behalf. The prosecutor then cross-examines the defense witnesses. The prosecution and the defense present summaries of the case to the judge, who reaches a finding or a verdict.[36]

Ten states provide for a jury trial for juveniles, but jury trials are seldom demanded.[37] Statutory provisions often close juvenile hearings to the general public, but this decision varies from one jurisdiction to the next.[38] The right to a speedy trial has been provided by state court decisions and by those statutes that limit the amount of time that can elapse between the filing of a complaint and the actual hearing.[39]

Unfortunately, the typical hearing sometimes falls short of achieving the desired objectives. Hearings are frequently too brief. Cases in large urban courts are sometimes heard so rapidly that they constitute what Lemert refers to as "the three-minute children's hour."[40] In California, the Governor's Commission on Juvenile Justice found that the average time spent on a juvenile hearing is approximately ten to fifteen minutes.[41]

Representation by counsel can also be little more than a legal charade. Judges, by the way they phrase their question about legal representation or even by tone of voice, can persuade parents to waive the right of counsel. Defense attorneys can perform their roles without really affecting the "justice" going on in the courtroom. Although some public defenders do an excellent job of representing their clients, others appear more concerned with maintaining good relations with the judge and the prosecutor. Further, public defenders are sometimes amenable to plea bargaining, an unhappy fact of life in many urban juvenile courts.

In sum, the typical adjudicatory hearing has come a long way since the *In re Gault* decision, but some progressive urban courts appear to provide these constitutional safeguards to a greater extent than smaller, rural courts. While some judges and defense attorneys are exemplary in terms of the support they give to the due process protections of juveniles during this stage of the court's proceedings, other judges and defense attorneys fall short in living up either to the spirit or the letter of post-*Gault* juvenile law. Significantly, as will be examined more extensively later, the prosecutor is becoming a prominent figure at these proceedings.

The Disposition Stage

Once a child has been found delinquent at the adjudicatory stage, some juvenile court codes still permit judges to proceed immediately into the disposition hearing. But the present trend is to hold bifurcated, or split, adjudicatory and disposition hearings because a split hearing gives the probation officer appointed to the case an opportunity to prepare a social study investigation of the youth.

The disposition stage of the court's proceedings normally is quite different from the fact-finding stage, especially when it is held at a different time. Because the dominant purpose is to administer individualized justice or to set in motion the rehabilitation of the delinquent, the judge is not limited as much by constitutional safeguards. Rules of evidence are relaxed, parties and witnesses are not always sworn in, and hearsay testimony may be considered.[42] The starting point of the disposition hearing usually is the written social study of the child prepared by the probation officer. This report examines such factors as school attendance and grades, family structure and support, degree of maturity and sense of responsibility, relationships with peers, participation in community activities, and attitudes toward authority figures. Juveniles are permitted to have legal counsel in this final stage of the proceedings, and the *Kent* decision assured the right of counsel to challenge the facts of the social study.

The factors influencing judicial decision making at the dispositional stage can be separated into formal and informal factors. The three most important formal factors are the recommendation of the probation officer and the information contained in the social study investigation, the seriousness of the delinquent behavior and previous contacts with the court, and the options available. The recommendation of the probation officer in the social study report is followed most of the time by the juvenile judge.[43] The seriousness of the delinquent behavior and the previous contacts with the court probably have the greatest impact on judicial decision making at this stage. Thornberry confirmed that seriousness of the offense and previous offenses have the greatest impact.[44] Studies of the juvenile courts in Colorado, Pennsylvania, and Tennessee revealed that prior decisions by juvenile court personnel are related more strongly to disposition than any other factor.[45] Finally, the juvenile judge is influenced by the options available. The most desirable placement may not be available in that jurisdiction, or the particular placement may have no space for the youth.

The informal factors that sometimes influence judicial decision-making at the disposition stage are: the values and philosophy of the judge; the social and racial background of the youth, as well as his or her demeanor; the representation of a defense counsel; and the political repercussions of the delinquent acts. In terms of the values and philosophy of the judge, some judges work from a legal model, some from an educational model, and some from a medical model, and the model a particular judge emphasizes of course will affect his or her handling of juvenile delinquents.[46]

Thomas and Fitch examined the extent to which social and racial backgrounds of delinquents affect judicial decision making. These researchers reviewed cases processed between 1966 and 1973 in a metropolitan area of Virginia and found that even when the type of offense was controlled, males were treated more harshly than females, blacks more harshly than whites, school dropouts more harshly than those in school, and children from broken homes more harshly than those from intact homes. Furthermore, their study revealed that youths from lower socioeconomic backgrounds tended to be treated more harshly when they were charged with either felonies or status offenses, but that the social classes were dealt with equitably when the offenses were misdemeanors. Still, youths from the upper social classes were much more likely to be put on probation for misdemeanors than were those from lower social classes.[47]

Although studies of the effects of legal counsel on the outcome of cases have yielded conflicting findings, they generally have questioned whether the assistance of counsel in juvenile court is always beneficial[48] For example, some evidence exists that juveniles with counsel are more likely to be institutionalized than those without counsel.[49] Finally, judges occasionally are influenced by the political repercussions of a case, especially when violent crimes are involved.

In sum, the process of judicial decision making at the disposition stage is influenced by a variety of formal and informal factors. The more that informal factors intrude upon the decision-making process, the more problematic the decisions are likely to be.

Judicial Alternatives

The alternatives available to different juvenile courts vary significantly in number. Large urban courts have all or most of the following alternatives, but rural courts may have only a few available.

1. *Dismissal* is certainly the most desired disposition; the fact-finding stage may have shown the youth to be guilty, but the judge can decide, for a variety of reasons, to dismiss the case.

2. *Fine or restitution* also is usually very desirable. Youths may be required to work off their debt with a few hours each week, but their lives are not seriously interrupted.

3. *Psychiatric therapy* as an outpatient, whether in the court clinic, the community mental health clinic, or with a private therapist, is a treatment-oriented decision and is often reserved for middle-class youths to keep them from being sent to unfitting placements.

4. *Probation,* the most widely used disposition, seems to be a popular decision with delinquents as well as a good treatment alternative for the court. Probation is sometimes set for a specific length of time, usually a maximum of two years. The probation officer can be directed by the judge to involve the youth in special programs, such as alternative schools, speech therapy, or learning disability programs.

5. *Foster home placements* are more restrictive inasmuch as youths are removed from their natural homes. These placements are used most frequently for status offenders and dependent, neglected children.

6. *Day treatment programs* are a popular alternative with juveniles because the youths assigned to these programs return home in the evening. However, these programs are few in number and are available primarily in a few states.

7. *Community-based residential programs,* such as group homes and halfway houses, are available to many judges. These residential facilities may be located in the community or in a nearby community, but they are not as desirable as community-based day programs because youths are taken from their homes to live in these facilities.

8. *Institutionalization in a mental hospital* may be seen as appropriate for the child's needs. This placement requires a psychiatric evaluation, after which a recommendation may be made to initiate proceedings for commitment to a mental hospital.

9. *County or city institutions* are available to a few judges across the nation. Placements in these facilities may be deemed appropriate for the youth who needs a placement with more security than probation, but does not require long-term placement in the state training school.

10. *State or private training schools* are usually reserved for those youths who have committed serious crimes or for whom everything else has failed. In some states, state training schools include minimum- (forestry camps, farms and ranches), medium-, and maximum-security institutions.

11. *Adult facilities* are used as an alternative in a few states, if the youth has committed a serious offense and is seen as too hard-core for juvenile correctional institutions.

Other Juvenile Hearings

Juvenile court judges also conducts a variety of other hearings. These vary, depending upon the jurisdiction of the juvenile court, but include modification or review hearings; dependence and neglect hearings; child abuse hearings; children or minors in need of assistance hearings; adoption hearings, and custody hearings.

ROLE EXPECTATIONS OF JUVENILE COURT ACTORS

Judges, referees, prosecutors, and defense attorneys are the main actors in the juvenile court process.

Judges

Juvenile court judges have an enormously important and difficult job. In urban areas they usually are administrators of the court, and unless there is a director of court services, overwhelming administrative tasks are thrust upon them. Their area of supervision encompasses the personnel of the court, which may include other judges, referees, prosecuting attorneys, public defenders, social investigators, probation officers (if probation services are administered by the court, rather than by executive order), clerical workers, and support personnel—psychologists, psychiatrists, and physicians. Judges may be responsible as well for the supervision of foster homes, detention facilities, the court clinic, and aftercare facilities. Judges also must be concerned with financial services, especially because many face shortages of funds.

However, significant changes are taking place in the funding process and in the administration of the juvenile court. In some jurisdictions, separately organized juvenile courts are being recast as juvenile divisions of a multijurisdictional trial court. The central responsibility for budget preparation and presentation then is shared by the trial court administrator and the presiding judge of the trial court. Also, state legislatures are assuming more responsibility for funding trial courts, and this trend probably will continue because it is seen as leading to a more uniform system of justice. Furthermore, some state legislatures are transferring the responsibility for administering juvenile probation and detention services from the judiciary to the state executive branch. Finally, more judges are taking the bench through appointment rather than through a victory in a public election, which means that they will have much different relationships with local funding authorities.

Sophia Robinson sees five role stances among juvenile judges: the parent, the counselor, the chancellor, the lawyer, and the antagonist. The parent judge identifies with the parent more than with the child, and he or she emphasizes obedience to the parents. This judge feels that, like a parent, he or she knows what is best for the child. The counselor judge, in contrast, focuses almost totally on the individuality of each child. He or she is interested in the social history of the child and regards other court personnel as members of a professional team. The chancellor judge balances the child's rights with those of the parent and the community. He or she acts as the arbitrator when difficulties arise. Acting in *loco parentis*, this judge believes that he or she symbolizes the benevolent parent. The lawyer judge perceives his or her role primarily as that of a legal actor and regards the court as the appropriate setting for administering the law. He or she looks upon the court hearing as more or less an adversary trial. Finally, the antagonist judge reacts differently to each situation but generally appears to be hostile to the child; this judge often resents his or her tour of duty on the juvenile bench.[50]

Juvenile judges not only have difficult jobs, but also wield considerable power. Power, of course, sometimes corrupts, and occasionally a judge becomes a despot or dictator in the court. David Matza, addressing the abuse of power in the juvenile court, refers to the justice of some judges as *kadi justice*. The *kadi* is a Moslem judge who sits in the marketplace and makes decisions without any apparent reference to rules or norms; he seems to make a completely free evaluation of the merits of each case.[51] Applied to the juvenile court, the kadi judge might be seen as a special kind of wise person who is able to see and know the whole; but the assumption that juvenile judges are able to discern the problem and quickly arrive at the most desirable solution is both unrealistic and laden with potential problems.

Yet many juvenile judges rise to the challenge and do remarkable jobs. Procedural safeguards and due process rights for juveniles are scrupulously observed in their courts. These judges always are seeking better means of detention and reserve the use of correctional institutions as a last resort. They are very committed, work long hours, and sometimes pass up promotions to more highly paid judgeships with greater prestige. The result is that these judges usually change the quality of juvenile justice in their communities.

Referees

Many juvenile courts employ the services of a referee, who has been called the "arm of the court." In the state of Washington, a referee is called a commissioner and in Maryland, a master. California has both referees and commissioners. A number of states, such as Florida, use only judges in the juvenile court, but referees, masters, and commissioners are the primary hearing officers in other states.[52]

Referees may or may not be members of the bar, but their basic responsibility is to assist judges in processing youths through the courts. They hear cases at the fact-finding stage and sometimes in detention hearings, but if a judicial disposition is necessary, it is usually left to a juvenile judge. Referees generally have a good background in juvenile law, a fundamental grasp of psychology and sociology, and some experience or training in social work.

However, there are some serious problems in the use of referees in the juvenile court. First, the status of the court suffers in the eyes of other members of the judiciary, attorneys, the probation staff, and the community. Second, judicial review of referee findings and recommendations usually does not take place; consequently, referees' decisions are not adequately monitored. Third, referees sometimes fail to clarify or reveal their status; that is, they may wear robes and in other ways take on the role of the judge. Fourth, referee authority confuses legal procedures in the juvenile court and encourages litigation.[53]

Prosecutors

In the juvenile court, the prosecutor represents the state or county and has dual roles that are somewhat contradictory. The prosecutor is expected to protect society but at the same time ensure that those children who would harm society are provided with their basic constitutional rights. The President's Crime Commission in 1967 found that in most juvenile courts there is no prosecutor.[54] Although the prosecutor is still a stranger to small juvenile courts today, one of the consequences of the *Gault* decision is that the participation of prosecutors in larger juvenile courts has expanded greatly.

In larger courts, prosecutors are typically involved at every stage of the proceedings, from intake and detention through disposition. The prosecutor is particularly involved before the adjudication stage because witnesses must be interviewed, police investigations must be checked out, and court rules and case decisions must be researched. In some urban courts, the prosecutor may frequently be involved in plea bargaining with the defense counsel. Prosecutors in some states are even permitted to initiate appeals for the limited purpose of clarifying a given law or procedure.[55] Ted Rubin, in assessing the role of the prosecutor in the juvenile court, predicts that "the prosecutor will come to dominate juvenile court proceedings during the next decade."[56]

Defense Attorneys

The number of juveniles represented by counsel has been gradually increasing since the early 1960s. But, even though more juveniles now are being represented by counsel, considerable confusion exists among defense attorneys concerning their proper role in the courtroom, and even more questions have been raised concerning their effectiveness in court. Defense counsels have at least three roles to choose from: to assist the court with its responsibilities to children; to serve as an adversarial advocate for the child; or to be a guardian or parent surrogate to the child.[57]

Public defenders may do a more adequate job of representing youth than private and court-appointed attorneys, especially when the same public defender must appear in juvenile court day after day. Court-appointed private counsels, especially those who need the work to supplement slim private practices, typically can be easily converted to the court's wishes. Private attorneys, however, may not be comfortable in juvenile court:

> A private attorney in juvenile court . . . noted that there was little an attorney could contribute in this setting. "What can a lawyer say? The probation officers know better about the kids. . . . They aren't out to get them." He usually tried to get the best deal possible for a client, but this procedure has

*no value in a juvenile court. . . . And the lawyer's presence might even de-
stroy the informal atmosphere, if he felt compelled to appear to earn his fee.
"You have to put on a show, a presentation for the client."*[58]

Several 1960s and early 1970s studies, as indicated earlier in this chapter,
showed that children who have counsel may get more severe dispositions than those
without counsel. However, because juvenile courts typically have all the legal trappings of an adversary hearing today, including the presence of a prosecutor, the
defense counsel is necessary.

POLICY IMPLICATIONS

Conflict over the future role of the juvenile court is now focused on two issues: the
jurisdiction of the court over status offenders and the proposed changes advocated
by the Juvenile Justice Standards Project.

The Problem of Status Offenders

Status offenders present an increasing problem to juvenile courts. The jurisdiction of
the juvenile court over status offenders now faces four distinct challenges. First,
legally, the lack of clarity of the status offender statutes often makes them blatantly
discriminatory, especially in regards to sex, and, further, government bodies may
have no legitimate interest in many of these prescribed behaviors. Second, although
status offenders have not committed a criminal act, they frequently are confined with
chronic or hard-core offenders. Third, in the perspective of the *parens patriae* philosophy of the juvenile court, the procedure of processing and confining the status
offender is not in his or her best interest. Some theorists, as mentioned earlier, argue
that the formal intervention of the juvenile court promotes rather than inhibits unlawful behavior. Fourth, many charge that status offenders represent a special class that
must be treated differently from the hard-core or more serious offenders.[59]

Juvenile court judges, however, challenge the movement to strip the court of
jurisdiction over status offenders. One of their most cogent arguments is that status
offenders will have no one to provide for them or look out for them if they are
removed from the court's jurisdiction. This argument makes a valid point—that other
agencies will have to take over if the court relinquishes jurisdiction of these offenders. Given the fragmentation of the juvenile justice system, the result could be
neglect and chaos. Judge David Bazelon responds to this line of thinking by saying:

*The situation is truly ironic. The argument for retaining beyond-control and
truancy jurisdiction is that juvenile courts have to act in such cases because
"If we don't act, no one else will." I submit that precisely the opposite is
the case: Because you act, no one else does. Schools and public agencies
refer their problem cases to you because you have jurisdiction, because you*

exercise it, and because you hold it, and because you hold out promises that you can provide solutions.[60]

Status offenders will probably remain a crucial concern of the juvenile justice system, for there is no evidence that they are decreasing in number. Neither is there any evidence that providing adequate care for "beyond-control" youth will be easy. But if they are removed from the jurisdiction of the juvenile court, nonjudicial agencies will have to assume the work of the court. As more and more jurisdictions keep status offenders out of the court, the idea that other agencies will take over the care and guidance of these youths will be severely tested.

Individualized Justice versus the Juvenile Justice Standards Project

The Juvenile Justice Standards Project, jointly sponsored by the Institute of Judicial Administration and the American Bar Association, recommends the adoption of several guidelines that would alter the juvenile court significantly. The proposed guidelines, which would base sentences on the seriousness of crime rather than on the "needs" of the child, represent a radical departure from the *parens patriae* doctrine.

1. Juvenile offenses would be divided into five classes, three for felonies, two for misdemeanors. A required sentence of two years would be imposed on juveniles who committed crimes for which adults normally would be sentenced to death.

2. The criminal code for juvenile offenders would cover the ages from ten until a youngster's eighteenth birthday.

3. The severity of sanctions for juvenile offenders would be based on the seriousness of the offense rather than on a court's view of the "needs" of the juvenile. Maximum terms for various classes of offenses would be prescribed by the legislature. The court's choice of a sentence within this maximum would be guided by the seriousness of the offense, the degree of culpability indicated by the circumstances of a particular case, and the age and prior record of the juvenile.

4. Sentences should be determinate. The practice of indeterminate sentencing, now prevalent in most states, should be abolished.

5. The least drastic alternative should be utilized as a guide to intervention in the lives of juveniles and their families.

6. Noncriminal misbehavior ("status offenses") and private offenses ("victimless crimes") should be removed from juvenile court jurisdiction.

7. Visibility and accountability of decision making should replace closed proceedings and unrestrained official discretion.

8. Strict criteria should be established for waiver of juvenile court jurisdiction to regulate transfer or juveniles to adult criminal court.[61]

Juvenile court judges are quite concerned about these proposed standards. They feel that the standards attack the underlying philosophy and structure of the juvenile court. Judges also are concerned about how these standards would limit their authority. They see the influence of the hard-liners behind the movement toward standardization and feel that the needs of children would be neglected in the long run. In addition, they view the standards as more a reaction against the original theory of juvenile justice than an affirmative basis for establishing new policy. Too, they challenge the idea that it is possible to treat all children alike.

The extent to which these standards will be adopted in juvenile justice will be determined over the next few years. New York State was the first to act on them, through the Juvenile Justice Reform Act of 1976, which went into effect on February 1, 1977. The act orders a determinate sentence of five years for a Class A felony, such as murder; kidnapping, first degree, and arson, first degree. In 1977, the state of Washington also created a determinate sentencing system for juveniles in line with the recommendations of the Juvenile Justice Standards.

SUMMARY

Three conclusions can be drawn from the examination of the juvenile court and its procedures in this chapter. First, the juvenile court has fallen far short of its idealistic goal of serving the best interests of the child. Obviously, too much has been expected from the court, which lacks sufficient resources and community support to fulfill its mission. Until recently, the court has not had sufficient supervision, which has resulted in abuse on the one hand and in sometimes-moralistic attempts to force improvement on the other.

Second, U.S. Supreme Court and other court decisions from the 1960s and early 1970s have given juveniles more due process rights during court proceedings. Indeed, the typical juvenile court hearing today has many of the trappings of an adult trial. The actors of justice are present, cross-examination of witnesses take place, and proof beyond a reasonable doubt must be established. However, certain U.S. Supreme Court decisions in the 1970s show that the Court appears to be unwilling to transform the activities of the juvenile court completely into the adversary proceedings of the adult court.

Third, critical evaluation of the juvenile court during the past ten years has forced policymakers to rethink the proper role and responsibility of the court. The juvenile court continues its jurisdiction over status offenders, but most juvenile judges no longer have the option of sending status offenders to state institutions as they once did. Indeterminate sentencing, except in the state of Washington, is still accepted for minor offenders, but mandatory punishments are being prescribed for serious offenders in more and more states. In addition, some evidence exists that the age of those under the jurisdiction of the juvenile court is being lowered across the nation and that more youthful offenders are being transferred to the adult court. In short, the future of the juvenile court is currently being debated; the resolution of this debate will have long-term repercussions on juvenile justice in this nation.

Discussion Questions

1. Do you think the structure of the juvenile court should be changed? Why?

2. What can be done to handle the variation in juvenile court procedures from jurisdiction to jurisdiction?

3. How should the status offender be handled by the juvenile justice system?

4. How should juveniles who commit serious crimes be handled?

References

Emerson, Robert M. *Judging Delinquents: Context and Process in Juvenile Court.* Chicago: Aldine Publishing Company, 1969.

Faust, Frederic, and Brantingham, Paul J., eds. *Juvenile Justice Philosophy.* St. Paul, Minn.: West Publishing Company, 1974.

Institute of Judicial Administration and the American Bar Association. *Juvenile Justice Standards.* 24 vols. Cambridge, Mass.: Ballinger Publishing Company, 1977.

Law Enforcement Assistance Administration. *Report of the Advisory Committee to the Administrator on Standards for the Administration of Juvenile Justice.* Washington, D.C.: U.S. Government Printing Office, 1976.

Platt, Anthony. *The Child Savers.* Chicago: University of Chicago Press, 1981.

Rubin, H. Ted. *Juvenile Justice: Policy, Practice, and Law.* Santa Monica, Calif.: Goodyear Publishing Company, 1979.

Schlossman, Steven L. *Love and the American Delinquent.* Chicago: University of Chicago Press, 1977.

Shichor, David. "Historical and Current Trends in American Juvenile Justice." *Juvenile and Family Court Journal* 34 (August 1983. 61–75.

FOOTNOTES

1. Gustav L. Schramm, "The Judge Meets the Boy and His Family," *National Probation Association 1945 Yearbook,* pp. 182–194.

2. President's Commission on Law Enforcement and Administration of Justice, *The Challenge of Crime in a Free Society* (Washington, D.C.: U.S. Government Printing Office, 1967), pp. 79–80.

3. Lisa Aversa Richette, *The Throwaway Children* (New York: J.B. Lippincott Company, 1969); Patrick Murphy, *Our Kindly Parent—The State* (New York: Viking Press, 1974); and Howard James, *Children in Trouble: A National Scandal* (New York: Pocket Books, 1971).

4. Anthony M. Platt, *The Child Savers* (Chicago: University of Chicago Press, 1969).

5. Ibid. See also Sanford J. Fox, "Juvenile Justice Reform: An Historic Perspective," *Stanford Law Review* 22 (1970), p. 1187; and Douglas Rendleman, "Parens Patriae: From Chancery to the Juvenile Court," *South Carolina Law Review* 28 (1971), p. 205, for interpretations similar to Platt's.

6. David Shichor, "Historical and Current Trends in American Juvenile Justice," *Juvenile and Family Court Journal* 34 (August 1983), p. 61.

7. Frederic L. Faust and Paul J. Brantingham, eds., *Juvenile Justice Philosophy* (St. Paul, Minn.: West Publishing Company, 1974), pp. 569–575.

8. Platt, *The Child Savers*, p. 144.

9. Ibid.

10. Faust and Brantingham, eds., *Juvenile Justice Philosophy*, pp. 568–569.

11. Ibid., pp. 574–575.

12. Ibid.

13. *Kent* v. *United States*, 383 U.S. 541, 86 S. Ct. 1045, 16 L. Ed. 2d 84 (1966).

14. Ibid.

15. *In re Gault*, 387 U.S. 1, 18 L. Ed. 2d 527, 87 S. Ct. 1428 (1967).

16. Ibid.

17. *Haley* v. *Ohio*, 332 U.S. 596 (1948); and *Gallegos* v. *Colorado*, 370 U.S. 49, 82 S. Ct. 1209 (1962).

18. *In re Winship*, 397 U.S. 358, 90 S. Ct. 1968, 25 L. Ed. 2d 368 (1970).

19. *McKeiver* v. *Pennsylvania*, 403 U.S. 528, 535 (1971); *In re Barbara Burrus*, 275 N.C. 517, 169 S.E. 2d 879 (1969).

20. Ibid.

21. *Breed* v. *Jones*, 421 U.S. 519, 95 S. Ct. 1779 (1975).

22. H. Ted Rubin, *Juvenile Justice: Policy, Practice, and Law* (Santa Monica, Calif.: Goodyear Publishing Company, 1979), p. 177.

23. Larry J. Siegel and Joseph J. Senna, *Juvenile Delinquency: Theory, Practice, and Law* (St. Paul, Minn.: West Publishing Company, 1981), p. 386.

24. This section on case law concerning detention practices is derived from Rubin, *Juvenile Justice*, pp. 102–104.

25. *Creek* v. *Stone*, 379 F. 2d 106 (D.C. Cir. 1967).

26. H. William Sheridon, *Standards for Juvenile and Family Courts* (Washington, D.C.: U.S. Government Printing Office, 1966), p. 46.

27. Mark M. Levin and Rosemary C. Sarri, *Juvenile Delinquency: A Comparative Analysis of Legal Codes in the United States* (Ann Arbor: National Assessment of Juvenile Corrections, University of Michigan, 1974), p. 26.

28. Richard W. Kobetz and Betty B. Bosarge, *Juvenile Justice Administration* (Gaithersburg, Md.: International Association of Chiefs of Police, 1973), p. 259.

29. National Advisory Commission on Criminal Justice Standards and Goals, *Corrections* (Washington, D.C.: U.S. Government Printing Office, p. 267.

30. Charles W. Thomas and Christopher M. Sieverdes, "Juvenile Court Intake: An Analysis of Discretionary Decision-Making," mimeographed (Williamsburg, Va.: Metropolitan Criminal Justice Center, College of William and Mary, n.d.), p. 19.

31. Ibid., p. 19.

32. Terence P. Thornberry, "Sentencing Disparities in the Juvenile Justice System," *The Journal of Criminal Law and Criminology* 70 (Summer 1979).

33. Barry C. Feld, "Legislative Policies toward the Serious Juvenile Offender," *Crime and Delinquency* 27 (October 1981), p. 500.

34. Ibid., pp. 501–502.

35. John P. Conrad, "Can Juvenile Justice Survive," *Crime and Delinquency* 27 (October 1981), p. 552.

36. Mary E. Murrell and David Lester, *Introduction to Juvenile Delinquency* (New York: Macmillan Publishing Company, 1981), p. 191.

37. Sanford Fox, *The Law of Juvenile Courts in a Nutshell* (St. Paul, Minn.: West Publishing Company, 1971), p. 170.

38. Levin and Sarri, *Juvenile Delinquency,* p. 49.

39. For example, the Laws of Pennsylvania, Act No. 333 (Section 18a) require a hearing date within ten days after the filing of a petition.

40. Edwin M. Lemert, "The Juvenile Court—Quest and Realities," in *Juvenile Delinquency and Youth Crime,* President's Task Force Report (Washington, D.C.: U.S. Government Printing Office, 1967), p. 94.

41. Governor's Commission on Juvenile Justice, State of California, 1959.

42. Rubin, *Juvenile Justice,* p. 137.

43. Jackwell, Susman, "Juvenile Justice: Even-Handed or Many-Handed?" *Crime and Delinquency* 19 (October 1973), pp. 497, 500.

44. Thornberry, "Sentencing Disparities," pp. 164–171.

45. Lawrence Cohen, "Delinquency Dispositions: An Empirical Analysis of Processing Decisions in Three Juvenile Courts," *Analytic Report 9* (Washington, D.C.: U.S. Government Printing Office, 1975), p. 51.

46. Rubin, *Juvenile Justice,* pp. 139–140.

47. Charles W. Thomas and Anthony W. Fitch, "An Inquiry into the Association between Respondents' Personal Characteristics and Juvenile Court Dispositions," mimeographed (Williamsburg, Va.: Metropolitan Criminal Justice Center, College of William and Mary, 1975), p. 17.

48. See Anthony Platt, Howard Schecter, and Phyllis Tiffany, "In Defense of Youth: A Case Study of the Public Defender in Juvenile Court," *Indiana Law Journal* 43 (1968), pp. 619–640; and Anthony Platt and Ruth Friedman, "The Limits of Advocacy: Occupational Hazards in the Juvenile Court," *Pennsylvania Law Review* 116 (1968), pp. 1156–1184.

49. David Duffee and Larry Siegel, "The Organizational Man: Legal Counsel in the Juvenile Court," *Criminal Law Bulletin* 7 (July-August 1971).

50. Sophia M. Robinson, *Juvenile Delinquency: Its Nature and Consequences* (New York: Henry Holt & Company, 1960), pp. 253–262.

51. David Matza, *Delinquency and Drift* (New York: John Wiley & Sons, 1964), p. 118.

52. H. Ted Rubin, "The Eye of the Juvenile Court Judge: A One-Step View of the Juvenile Justice System," in *The Juvenile Justice System,* edited by Malcolm W. Klein (Beverly Hills, Calif.: Sage Publications, 1976), p. 263.

53. Ibid.

54. President's Commission on Law Enforcement and Administration of Justice, "The Administration of Juvenile Justice—The Juvenile Court and Related Methods of Delinquency Control," *Task Force Report: Juvenile Delinquency and Youth Crime* (Washington, D.C.: U.S. Government Printing Office, 1967) p. 5.

55. Rubin, *Juvenile Justice,* p. 177.

56. Ibid., p. 171.

57. Ibid., p. 194.

58. Robert M. Emerson, *Judging Delinquents: Context and Process in Juvenile Court* (Chicago: Aldine Publishing Company, 1970).

59. Charles W. Thomas, "Are Status Offenders Really So Different: A Comparative and Longitudinal Assessment," *Crime and Delinquency* 21 (April 1975), p. 99.

60. David L. Bazelon, "Beyond Control of the Juvenile Court," *Juvenile Court Journal* 21 (Summer 1970).

61. Press release of New York University Press and Broadcast Services, November 30, 1975.

INTERVIEW WITH LOUIS W. MCHARDY

. . . juvenile courts in our society continue to be concerned about female promiscuity and vulnerability. For example, a thirteen-year-old female runaway would be more likely than a male runaway to be confined for less serious offenses because the court wants to protect her. This is the way society has always felt. The courts, as much as other institutions, reflect the values of our society.

In this interview, Louis W. McHardy, Executive Director of the National Council of Juvenile and Family Court Judges and Dean of the National College of Juvenile Justice, discusses several of the most significant issues relating to the work of the juvenile court.

Question: The juvenile court has been subjected to extensive criticism in the past decade. Has this criticism been justified?

McHardy: Extensive criticism of the juvenile court as an institution has occurred throughout the years, and some of that criticism, especially in the past, has been justified. Criticisms have ranged broadly across many spectra. By that I mean that some feel the juvenile court has too much due process, some feel it has too little. Some feel it has been too lenient, and some feel it has been too harsh. Some feel we should be locking up more juveniles

Louis W. McHardy has been Dean of the National College of Juvenile Justice and Executive Director of the National Council of Juvenile and Family Court Judges for the past 12 years. The Council, a professional association of judges having juvenile and/or family court jurisdiction is headquartered on the Campus of the University of Nevada in Reno. It also conducts a research activity, the National Center for Juvenile Justice in Pittsburgh, Pennsylvania. The Council publishes a quarterly journal, Juvenile and Family Journal; *a monthly digest,* Juvenile and Family Law Digest; *and an eight issue yearly newsletter,* Juvenile and Family Court Newsletter. *In addition, the Council publishes numerous texts, monographs, books, and articles on juvenile justice issues. The National College of Juvenile Justice conducts from 35 to 50 continuing education programs each year for judges, court-related personnel, and others.*

Interviewed in April 1984, and used with permission.

to protect the public, and some feel we should never incarcerate a youthful offender for any crime.

I recommend you look at an enlightening article published by John Huxler of our National Center for Juvenile Justice entitled, "Cannon to the Left, Cannon to the Right." This article reviews some of the broad range of attacks which are being made. The author reminds us that we don't have a single juvenile justice system nor do we have one for each of the fifty states. There are literally hundreds of systems and judges. We often have great disparities between two adjacent counties, between urban and rural courts, and even between judges and their staffs.

Specific criticisms have obviously sometimes been justified. But what cannot be justified is the continual lumping together of juvenile court as if the horror story that might take place with a judge in a rural county is representative of what takes place in juvenile courts throughout the nation. The courts are also operating under specific statutes and upholding community standards. Thus, a criticism of the juvenile court cannot be justified until we analyze who is making the allegation and what it is. Considering the crucial and important work the juvenile courts do in our nation, a great deal of the criticism is based on a misunderstanding or unwillingness to accept the basic philosophy of the juvenile court and its role in our society.

Question: Are juvenile courts more uniform in decision-making than they have been in the past? If so, what has contributed to this?

McHardy: I would say so for a number of reasons. The *Gault* decision imposed various decision-making and due process standards on the courts. Some states have recently imposed guidelines or other mandatory schemes to attempt to narrow judicial decision-making. Public scrutiny, including legislative analysis, has imposed increasing awareness of the limits, even the pitfalls, of individualized juvenile justice as we know it.

Judges now also know and talk to each other. They meet and get a chance to exchange ideas. That's what the National Council is all about. Our National College of Juvenile Justice has spent hundreds of hours presenting this topic of decision-making to hundreds of judges throughout the nation. I think juvenile courts, within the limits imposed by the statutes and the resources provided, have increased their professionalism in uniformity of decision-making manyfold the past decade. We have seen some tremendous changes in the role and responsibility of the judge, the specialized training required, the increase and the decrease in the juvenile crime rate, and the demand for public protection from serious juvenile crimes. Yet because of their own awareness and dedication to improve the court, judges themselves deserve credit for having contributed the most to this increased uniformity.

Question: What is your position on jurisdiction of the juvenile court over status offenders?

McHardy: That has been a controversial subject for the past ten years. On the issue of status offenders, I think we need to distinguish between the jurisdiction of the juvenile court and the actual role it chooses or must play. Some states tie the court's hands. However, our council consistently speaks for the least-restrictive alternative for the vast majority of such cases. Nonetheless, after a valid court order has been imposed under a valid state statute and procedure, a judge sometimes has to face the fact that a runaway must be detained in a secure facility for juveniles, until that youth's problem can be treated under the court's jurisdiction. I believe there is a swing in the pendulum concerning the issue of status offenders as the public is starting to realize what happens to runaways and

so forth. Our position is not to remove the jurisdiction of status offenders from the court.

Question: Are adolescent females receiving much different "justice" in court than they have in the past?

McHardy: I would give a qualified yes, because juvenile courts in our society continue to be concerned about female promiscuity and vulnerability. For example, a thirteen-year-old female runaway would be more likely than a male runaway to be confined for less serious offenses because the court wants to protect her. This is the way society has always felt. The courts, as much as other institutions, reflect the values of our society. With regards to more serious criminal offenses, female adolescents probably receive more lenient treatment than males of the same age. Proportionally, we know that females receive fewer incarcerations and more probation sentences. We suspect the male to be more likely to use violence and force, and this might account for a higher rate of males who are incarcerated. In general, I would say that we are seeing about the same proportion of adolescent female and male dispositions as we have in the past.

Question: Are too many juveniles being transferred or bonded over to the adult court? What types of youth offenders should be dealt with by the adult court?

McHardy: Again, this is a question pertaining to values. The public would probably agree that not enough juveniles are being waived or transferred, but they are unmindful that transfer to adult court in no way assumes more severe punishment or even more effective treatment. It is a fact that more juveniles than ever are being tried in adult courts, and I feel this is unfortunate. It is because of increasingly more statutory changes which exclude certain serious offenses or which give the prosecutor the discretion to file a charge directly in the adult court. There has been a significant increase with regard to the number of cases that juvenile courts have waived to adult court.

Most juvenile court judges will make every effort to retain jurisdiction and to rehabilitate youths within the parameter of juvenile justice as we know it today. A recent policy statement adopted by our board states, "The juvenile court and the juvenile justice system are in the best position to respond effectively to the problem of serious juvenile crime. However, there are juveniles for whom the resources and processes available to the juvenile court will serve neither to rehabilitate the juvenile nor to protect adequately the public." Our board feels that such juveniles should be tried and, if convicted, sentenced in adult court.

Remember that only 5 percent of all juvenile offenders commit serious crimes nationally. Of this 5 percent, very few proportionately are ever transferred. In some states, such as Vermont, fewer juveniles are being tried in adult court for the simple reason that the juvenile court jurisdiction has been raised from sixteen to eighteen years of age. Six states have raised the age jurisdiction in the past decade, which balances out the increased adult jurisdiction in other states. In general, those who are waived tend to be serious, chronic, and violent juvenile offenders for whom the individual judge feels must be dealt with in the adult system. The just-deserts philosophy is believed to be more suitable for them than the best interest and treatment philosophy of the juvenile court. The issues of public protection and the unavailability of secure care also influence the court to waive the youth in some jurisdictions.

Question: Are prosecutors starting to play too large a role in juvenile court's proceedings?

McHardy: That's a good question. Some judges would say yes. Several judges in Florida believe that prosecutors have too much discretion. When judicial discretion is limited by the increase of prosecutorial discretion, most judges would agree that they are playing too large a role. Yet in most states, this is not the case. We need effective prosecution, just as we need effective due process rights for the defendant. We also need specially trained juvenile court prosecutors who are aware of and dedicated to the philosophy of the court to treat and rehabilitate the vast majority of young offenders. We need prosecutors who will play a more positive role in assisting the court with an effective and workable disposition. For example, we need prosecutors who understand the effectiveness of restitution as a valid dispositional alternative.

Question: What needs to be done to improve further the services of the juvenile court?

McHardy: This is a difficult question to answer, and I suppose we could write a book on it. Here are some ideas. First, we probably need more legislative and executive advocates for the role and value of the juvenile court in our society. Second, we need more status for the court, higher rank, longer tenure, and assignment of judges based on their professed interest in and dedication to youth, families, and the crucial role of the juvenile court. Third, we need more and better training of the professional staff associated with juvenile courts and, of course, we need more and better judges and referees. The caseloads of some of these courts are astounding. Fourth, we need more resources, including better financial support, and more cooperation with the community, businesses, schools, and volunteer groups. Fifth, we need better allocation of existing resources. Sixth, we need technical assistance, so that good courts and effective programs could be replicated in other places. Seventh, we need better probation services, more innovative programs, and more qualified and better paid staff for the courts. Eighth, we need practitioner-oriented research, which tells us what works, what doesn't, and why. Finally, the courts also need better public relations.

CHAPTER 17

COMMUNITY-BASED CORRECTIONS

CHAPTER OUTLINE

This program has helped me take a look at how serious my crime is. It has helped me take a look at what will happen if I keep stealing cars or doing dope.

Seventeen-year-old male offender in a group home[1]

I had a girl come in who was abused at home and whose mother wanted her to come in. I sat down and talked to her, and she was like living death. She wouldn't communicate or talk with me. That night, her best friend did acid and then stood in front of a train. She opened herself up, stayed here ten days, and straightened herself up.

Female counselor in a runaway house[2]

Probation, residential and day treatment programs, and parole are the basic forms of community-based corrections. These services are alternatives to institutionalization and keep juvenile delinquents out of training schools, jails, and adult prisons. Community-based programs captured the support of the public in the late 1960s and early 1970s because they were regarded as more humane, more economical, and more effective in rehabilitating offenders than training schools. Proponents of community-based corrections argued that they should be used for all but hard-core offenders. A few supporters even advocated closing all the state training schools.

This chapter examines the history and the forms of community-based corrections, as well as the policy needed to make community programs more effective.

ORIGINS OF COMMUNITY-BASED CORRECTIONS

The first community-based corrections for juveniles grew out of juvenile aftercare, or parole, used after institutionalization. Such programs are nearly as old as juvenile correctional institutions. Superintendents of houses of refuge by the 1820s had the authority to release juveniles when they saw fit. Some juveniles were returned directly to their families, and others were placed in the community as indentured servants and apprentices, who could reenter the community as free citizens once they finished these terms of service. This system became formalized only in the 1840s, when states set up inspection procedures to monitor the supervision of those with whom youths were placed.

Juvenile aftercare was then influenced by the development of adult parole in the late 1870s. Zebulon Brockway, the first superintendent of Elmira Reformatory in New York State, permitted parole for carefully selected prisoners. Upon leaving the institution, parolees were instructed to report to a guardian on arrival, to write immediately to the superintendent, and to report to the guardian the first of each month.

Juvenile aftercare programs spread throughout the United States in the early decades of the twentieth century and took on many of the features of adult parole.

Juveniles were supervised in the community by aftercare officers, whose jobs were similar to those of parole officers in the adult system. The parole board did not become a part of juvenile corrections, for in over two-thirds of the states, institutional staffs continued to decide when youths would return to the community.

Probation as an alternative to institutionalization for juveniles arose from the effort of John Augustus, a Boston cobbler, in the 1840s and 1850s. Augustus, who is called the father of probation, spent considerable time in the courtroom and in 1841 persuaded a judge to permit him to supervise an offender in the community rather than to sentence the offender to an institution. Over the next two decades, Augustus worked with nearly two thousand individuals, including both adult and juvenile offenders. As the first probation officer, Augustus initiated several services still used in probation today: investigation and screening, supervision, educational and employment services, and the provision of aid and assistance.[3]

The state of Massachusetts built on Augustus's work with its establishment of a visiting probation agent system in 1869. This system released on probation contrite youthful offenders, who were permitted to return to their parents and to stay with them as long as they obeyed the law.[4] Probation had become statewide in Massachusetts by 1890, although the authority then rested with the courts rather than with municipal authorities. Vermont, Missouri, Illinois, Minnesota, Rhode Island, and New Jersey later adopted probation statutes.

In the twentieth century, probation services changed as they also became more widespread. Probation services spread to every state, and were administered by both state and local authorities. The use of volunteer probation workers had disappeared by the turn of the century, only to return in the 1950s. Probation became more treatment-oriented: early in the century the medical treatment model was used and later, in the 1960s and 1970s probation officers became brokers who delivered services to clients. The upgrading of standards and training also was emphasized in the 1960s and 1970s.

Residential programs, the third type of community-based juvenile corrections to appear, had their origins in the Highfields Project, a short-term guided-group interaction program. Known officially as the New Jersey Experimental Project for the Treatment of Youthful Offenders and established in 1950 on the former estate of Colonel and Mrs. Charles Lindbergh, the Highfields Project housed adjudicated youths who worked during the day at the nearby New Jersey Neuro-Psychiatric Institute and met in two guided-group-interaction units five evenings a week at the Highfields facility. Similar programs were initiated in the 1960s at Southfields, in Louisville, Kentucky; Essexfields, in Newark, New Jersey; Pinehills, in Provo, Utah; the New Jersey centers at Oxford and Farmingdale for boys and at Turrell for girls; and the START centers established by the New York City Division for Youth.

The most dramatic advance in the rise of community-based corrections took place when the state of Massachusetts closed all its training schools in the early 1970s. Jerome Miller, commissioner of the department of youth services, was able to accomplish this correctional reform because he had the support of Governor Francis Sargent and the media. Except for a few girls remaining at Shirley Training School and a few youths sent to private training schools in other states, Massachusetts placed all its adjudicated juvenile delinquents in community-based corrections.

This correctional reform in Massachusetts, along with the reform spirit of the times and the availability of federal funding, caused community-based corrections to be widely discussed in juvenile justice. The idea of deinstitutionalization, or using alternatives to juvenile institutions, became popular in numerous states, and commitments to training schools declined in nearly every state. Soon, South Dakota, Minnesota, Utah, Oregon, North Dakota, and Kansas were placing nearly as many juveniles in residential and day treatment programs as they were assigning to institutions.

In the late 1970s and early 1980s, retrenchment became apparent in community-based corrections. The decline in federal funding, along with the get-tough mood of society, has meant some residential and day treatment programs have been closed. Although probation remains the most widely judicial disposition, both probation and aftercare services have been charged to enforce a more hard-line policy with juvenile offenders.[5]

PROBATION

Probation permits juvenile offenders to remain in the community under the supervision of a probation officer, subject to certain conditions imposed by the court. Probation, which is considered by many to be the brighest hope of corrections, has four different connotations in the juvenile justice system. First, probation is a legal system in which an adjudicated delinquent can be placed. Second, probation refers to an alternative disposition to institutionalization. Third, probation refers to a subsystem of the juvenile justice system. Finally, probation includes the activities, functions, and services that characterize this subsystem's transactions with the juvenile court, the delinquent, and the community.[6]

The Administration of Probation

In thirty-four states, probation is under the control of the juvenile court and is funded by city or county government. In five states, the department of corrections administers probation, and in eleven states other agencies oversee the program.[7] Placing juvenile probation under the control of the juvenile court and funding it through local governmental agencies are probably the best strategies, particularly in those states that provide revenue support or staff to local systems meeting state standards. Providing probation subsidies to local systems complying with state standards can benefit both state and local government agencies. The state thereby ensures uniformity of probation services and practices throughout the state, and the costs of probation services are reduced for local units of government, which are usually operating on a fiscal shoestring.

Procedures vary from state to state. Michigan assigns state-paid probation officers to work with local probation officers. In New York State, local communities that are willing to meet state staffing patterns for probation services are reimbursed for up to 50 percent of their operating costs. California, Washington, Oregon, and Nevada have developed probation subsidy programs that encourage decreased commitments of juvenile delinquents to state training schools by counties. The California Probation Subsidy Program, until it was phased out in 1978, authorized the state to pay each county up to $4000 for every juvenile delinquent not committed to a state correctional institution. Counties were required to raise the number of probation officers, to reduce case loads, and to demonstrate innovative approaches to probation.[8] Washington's juvenile probation subsidy is modeled after the one in California; because 90 percent of Washington's thirty-nine counties participate in the program, the state has been able to reduce commitment rates to juvenile institutions and to improve the quality of probation services.[9]

The Operation of Probation Services

Intake, investigation, and supervision are the basic functions of probation services.

Intake

The intake officer is usually a probation officer, although larger probation departments may have separate intake units in which intake officers are not probation officers. Regardless of the organizational structure of the intake unit, the intake officer is the chief decision maker for juveniles prior to the juvenile court proceedings. He or she has two important decisions to make: what to do with the case and whether to detain the youth until a detention hearing can be scheduled.

The intake officer commonly is faced with one of the following situations: parents bring a child in on their own; parents bring a child in because of a letter requesting their presence; or a police officer brings in a child who has been apprehended committing an unlawful act. Parents who walk in with their child typically complain, "My kid won't obey," "My kid won't do the chores," or "My kid won't come home at night." They want someone in authority to say, "you're going to get punished unless you clean up your act." After interviewing both youth and parents, sometimes each separately, the intake officer may make a contract with the child and parents, by which each agrees to an acceptable compromise solution. Or the intake officer may decide to refer the youth to Big Brothers, Big Sisters, or the youth service bureau.[10]

Parents whose child has been apprehended by the police for a criminal act are commonly instructed by letter to bring their child to the intake unit at a particular time. The intake officer must conduct a preliminary investigation at this time and, based upon his or her findings, make a decision on what to do about the petition. The child ordinarily is released to the parents, not retained in a detention facility.

Police officers also frequently bring juveniles who have been apprehended committing an unlawful act to the intake unit. As part of the preliminary investigation, the intake officer must contact the parents and make an immediate decision about the need for detention. The child is detained, as previously indicated, if he or she is judged dangerous to self or others or if he or she lacks supervision in the home.

Investigation

Investigation requires that probation officers (or youth services counselors as they are called in some jurisdictions) prepare a social history report on a youth ruled delinquent to aid the judge in making the correct disposition. If a juvenile court uses a bifurcated hearing (separating adjudicatory and disposition stages), a social history is ordered by the judge when a juvenile is found delinquent at the adjudicatory or fact-finding stage. But if the court combines the adjudicatory and disposition stages, the social history must be completed before a juvenile appears in front of the judge, who waits until the youth has been found delinquent to read the social history.

The probation officer usually has thirty to sixty days to write the social history. In writing this report, he or she reviews the youth's arrest record, reports of the current offense, any available psychiatric or psychological evaluations, and any pertinent information from social agencies. Furthermore, the probation officer interviews the youth up to eight times and the parents two or three times, usually at least once in the home. It may also be necessary to interview the arresting officer, school administrators or teachers, neighborhood clergy, and peers who know of or were involved in the alleged offense. Peers often volunteer information, saying to the probation officer, "I hear you're Fred's PO. I want you to know that he's a real crazy and did the crime," or "John is a real loser. Let me tell you some of the other shit he has done."

Supervision

When a juvenile judge sentences a youth to probation, the probation officer generally takes the youth aside and explains the meaning of probation. Eloise C. Synder found that juveniles were more receptive to help during these initial interviews with their probation officers than at any subsequent time.[11] The probationer is informed of how frequently he or she will report to the probation officer and of the importance of complying with the conditions of probation. The most widely used conditions of probation include restitution to victims; community service; school attendance; participation in drug abuse programs; avoidance of delinquent peers; refraining from the possession of firearms, dangerous weapons, or an automobile; avoidance of drinking or drug use; living at home and obeying parents; and placement in a foster or group home.

Restitution recently has been widely used in probation. Probation officers like restitution because it both counters the criticism that probation is too soft and provides justice to victims in society. Community service programs are more widely used than are financial restitution programs because many juveniles lack the means to pay financial restitution. Some probation offices have a full-time restitution officer who administers such programs.

The length of time a youth must spend on probation varies from state to state. In some states, the maximum length is up until the juvenile reaches the age of majority, normally sixteen or eighteeen but sometimes twenty-one. Other states limit the length of time a juvenile or adult can spend on probation: in Illinois it is limited to five years, in New York, to two years, in Washington, D.C., to one year, and in California, to six months.[12]

The supervision function is divided into casework management, treatment, and surveillance. Effective casework management requires that a probation officer keep an up-to-date casework file, carry out periodic reviews, decide how each client is to be handled, and divide probationers into several categories—depending upon their needs and the risk they present to the community. The more serious their needs are and the greater risk they present to the community, the more frequent are the visits required of them.

In the 1970s juvenile probation officers often saw themselves as resource managers, or brokers, rather than counselors. The role of community resource manager is based on the premise that "the probation officer will have primary responsibility for meshing a probationer's identified needs with a range of available services and for supervising the delivery of these services."[13] Although E. Eugene Miller noted the reluctance of some probation officers to assume this role because they equated job satisfaction with client involvement, he claimed that "brokerage can effectively eliminate that terrible feeling for the officer of being conscious of helping a few but losing many because of too little time and too large a caseload."[14]

In the 1980s, the logical consequences model has become extremely popular with probation officers, who like the fact that this model places consequences on antisocial behavior. These officers have found that the logical consequences model forces juveniles to take probation more seriously and, accordingly, that the probation officer can more easily form a working relationship with offenders.

But probation officers who regard themselves either as community resource managers or as advocates of the logical consequences model become involved with counseling on an ongoing basis. This counseling may involve crisis intervention with a probationer or with the entire family unit. The probation officer also receives daily calls from irate parents who are ready to give up on their children, and he or she must help them deal more effectively with the youth's unacceptable behavior. Furthermore, the probation officer usually has probationers in his or her caseload who have alcohol or drug problems, and the probation officer often counsels youths about these problems, as well as referring them to such organizations as Al-Anon. Finally, some probation officers conduct group counseling with probationers. One highly respected juvenile probation officer in Ohio tells of his work with groups:

> I just get the boys together and give them a chance to rap about what's on their minds. I say a few things too. I think it has been helpful.[15]

Surveillance requires that the probation officer make certain that probationers comply with the conditions of probation and that they do not break the law. The probation officer has a number of opportunities to observe the behavior of probationers, as he or she sees them in the office, at home, and perhaps visits them at school. The probation officer also visits their parents. If a probationer's behavior is unacceptable, the probation officer is likely to receive reports from school or from law enforcement agencies.

The importance of surveillance was underscored in the mid-1970s when, with the emphasis on law and order, probation services were accused of failing to protect society. If a youth does not comply with the conditions of probation or commits another delinquent act, the probation officer must inform the judge by filing a notice of violation. If the violation is serious enough, the probation officer must recommend that probation be revoked. Thus, the probation officer has a law enforcement role as well as a treatment role.

The Probation Officer

Many juvenile probation officers feel overburdened, underpaid, inadequately trained, and unsupported by community resources. The large caseloads, never-ending paperwork, court time, and the necessary community contacts make the job seem overwhelming. Although the 1967 President's Commission on Law Enforcement and Administration of Justice recommended that probation and parole caseloads should average about thirty-five offenders per officer, the average case load usually ranges from fifty to one hundred. Juvenile probation officers, particularly those in unsubsidized county systems, are often underpaid. Some jurisdictions do a good job of providing training for probation officers, but the average county probation officer does not receive adequate training. Finally, probation officers are frustrated by the lack of community resources. For example, probationers may need mental health or drug counseling services, but these resources are not always available.

Role conflict also places pressure on juvenile probation officers, for the officer is faced with three basic role expectations: treatment, law enforcement, and bureaucratic. The treatment role requires that the probation officer try to introduce probationers to a better way of life and to give them support and guidance as they attempt to solve their own problems. Probation officers who have been trained in human services are especially interested in providing treatment services.

The law enforcement role, however, brings different expectations. The police and citizens of the community are constantly accusing probation officers of allowing dangerous and hard-core delinquents to remain in the community. The law enforcement role encourages probation officers to "trail 'em, nail 'em, and jail 'em" so that the community will be sufficiently protected and justice will be done.

The probation officer must also be a good bureaucrat to be successful. That the system comes first is a reality that probation officers face early in their careers. On Friday afternoon, a probationer may face a crisis situation, but the probation officer who is preparing a social history due to the judge Monday morning knows that the social history must be done before he can deal with the probationer's needs. Richard McCleary's study of parole in Washington, D.C.—which holds true for probation services—demonstrates the pervasiveness of the bureaucratic role in parole officers' jobs.[16]

The Community Volunteer

As previously stated, probation began with volunteers, with professional staff appearing by the turn of the twentieth century. But in the 1950s, Judge Keith J. Leenhouts initiated a court-sponsored volunteer program in Royal Oak, Michigan, which sparked the rebirth of the volunteer movement. Today, over two thousand court-sponsored volunteer programs are in operation, using volunteers to assist probation officers in a variety of ways. In 1975, the Community Crime Prevention Task Force reported that about ten thousand volunteers were working in court-sponsored programs.

These citizens serve as counselors, advisory council members, employment counselors, office workers, public relations workers, record keepers, tutors, and home skills teachers. Once a volunteer has been accepted by the probation officer in charge of the volunteer program, he or she usually undergoes several training sessions. The volunteer is assigned a client when the probation officer is able to make a suitable match. The officer then meets with the volunteer to set goals and expectations for the client, and the volunteer accepts the case. Although critics of volunteer programs charge that they tend to attract persons who are easily manipulated by offenders and that volunteers sometimes create more work than they return in service, proper screening, training, and supervision of volunteers can do much to ensure a high level of volunteer service.[17]

A volunteer usually is encouraged to see the client at least once a week and to do activities with the client that do not cost any money or at inexpensive. A volunteer thus may phone a client once or twice a week and may meet with him or her weekly to give tutoring. They also can take walks, meet after school for a Coke, and occasionally go bowling, skating, to ballgames or movies, and swimming. But more than entertaining the youth, the volunteer is encouraged to develop a positive relationship, in which the youth can find a supportive adult role model.

JUVENILE AFTERCARE

Parole, or juvenile aftercare as it is usually called, is concerned with the release of a youth from an institution when he or she can best benefit from release and can make an optimal adjustment to community living.[18] Because mandatory sentencing is infrequently used and determinate sentencing for juveniles is used only by the state of Washington, the vast majority of juveniles are released from training school to aftercare status.

Once a youth is adjudicated to a state training school, the state normally retains jurisdiction until his or her release. However, in Illinois and in several other states, juvenile judges have the authority to remove youths from training school. The authority to make the decision about when to release a youth from training school is usually given to institutional staff, although in seventeen states other agencies and boards are given the authority to parole juveniles.[19] Often the cottage staff will review the progress of each youth at designated intervals, and, when the staff recommends release, the recommendation is reviewed by a board made up of staff from throughout the institution. If this board concurs, the recommendation must be approved by an institutional coordinator at the youth authority or youth commission.

Cottage staffs usually consider several factors in recommending a youth for release. His or her overall institutional adjustment is reviewed, including performance in school, participation in recreation, and relationships with peers in the cottage. The attitude of the youth also is evaluated; personality conflicts with staff, especially those in the cottage, will usually be interpreted as the result of a poor attitude. The probability of community success is considered: a youth's willingness and ability to set realistic goals is frequently seen as evidence that he or she is ready to return to the community. Finally, reports on the juvenile's performance on the cottage work detail and on his or her personal hygiene generally must be positive before staff will recommend release.

The Administration and Operation of Aftercare Services

State departments of public welfare are the agencies most frequently charged with overseeing released juveniles (in thirteen states), followed by state youth corrections agencies (twelve states), state departments of corrections (ten states), institutional boards (six states), state training school boards (four states), and state departments of health (one state).[20]

An interstate compact is sometimes initiated when a youth has no acceptable home placement within his or her own state. The institutional social worker usually contacts the appropriate agency in another state where the youth has a possible placement and submits an interstate compact for the transfer of the youth to that state after release from training school. The state of original jurisdiction retains authority over the youth and is kept advised of his or her status.

The parole, or aftercare, officer who is responsible for the case sometimes corresponds with the institutionalized youth or may even visit him or her in training school. In many states, a youth cannot be released until the aftercare officer approves the home placement plan submitted by the institutional home worker. This usually involves a visit to the home by the officer to make certain that the home is a good placement. At other times, the aftercare officer must locate an alternate placement, such as a foster or group home.

Part of the problem in juvenile aftercare is that youthful offenders usually are sent back to the same communities (and same families) and exposed again to the same problems they could not handle earlier. Most of their friends are still around, and it is not long before a friend suggests that they commit another crime. If the returnee is determined, he or she might be able to say, "Hey, get out of my face; I don't want to hear that business." But if he or she cannot find a job—and jobs are scarce for delinquent youths who frequently are school dropouts—or feels under financial pressure, it becomes harder and harder not to return to crime.

Most youths on aftercare status are placed on supervision in the community for a year or more after release. As the aftercare officer is expected to monitor the behavior of youths under supervision, he or she provides each youth with a list of rules. These rules usually resemble those given to adult parolees and pertain to such matters as obeying parents, maintaining a satisfactory adjustment at school or at work, being at home a certain time every night, avoiding contact with other delinquents, avoiding the use or possession of any narcotic, and reporting to the parole officer as requested.

If the rules are violated or a law is broken, a youth may be returned to a training school. Although guidelines for the revocation of parole for juveniles have not been formulated by court decisions, revocation of a youth's aftercare status is no longer based solely on the testimony of the aftercare officer, who could be influenced by personality clashes or prejudice toward the client. Today, most jurisdictions have formal procedures for the revocation of aftercare. The aftercare officer may initially investigate the charge but, if he or she finds that the youth did commit the offense, reports the violation to his or her supervisor. The supervisor may review the case and make the decision, or a revocation committee may examine the violation. The aftercare officer may be required to submit a written recommendation or revocation, but he or she is not allowed to testify, and the youth is permitted to speak in his or her defense.[21]

The Aftercare Officer

Parole and probation officers have much in common. Both must handle excessively large caseloads, so that neither is able to spend sufficient time with clients to guide them. Both lack community resources and usually are inadequately trained for their jobs. They also face similar role conflicts and frustrations, although parole or aftercare officers, who work for the state, are better paid than probation officers, who are employed by the county. The aftercare officer, like the probation officer, has certain treatment, or social service, responsibilities. This may involve helping a client enroll in school, finding him or her a job, resolving a conflict with parents, or dealing with a problem that has developed in school. The aftercare officer occasionally must do emergency or crisis-oriented counseling with a youth. Both officers have regulatory responsibilities, but because aftercare officers are dealing with youthful offenders who have already been institutionalized, more emphasis is placed on strict observance of the rules than is true with probationers.

RESIDENTIAL AND DAY TREATMENT PROGRAMS

Residential and day treatment programs are usually reserved for juvenile probationers who are having difficulty dealing with the looseness of probation supervision. In day treatment programs, juveniles attend the program in the morning and afternoon and return home in the evening. In residential programs, which are usually group homes or foster care placements, delinquents are taken away from the supervision of parents and are assigned twenty-four hours a day to their new placement. Some group homes are like the halfway houses used in adult corrections and serve as a placement for juveniles on aftercare status who have nowhere else to go.

The extent, administration, types, and effectiveness of community-based residential programs will be considered next.

Extent of Community-Based Residential Programs

The 1975 study of the National Assessment of Juvenile Corrections (NAJC) found that the average daily population in state-related community-based residential programs during 1974 in the forty-nine reporting states was 110, ranging from zero in six states to a high of 800 in one state. Thirty-four states had an average daily population of 100 or more in state-related community-based residential programs, and three states had over 400 in these community-based facilities.[22]

Administration of Community-Based Residential and Day Treatment Programs

Community-based residential and day treatment programs are either state-sponsored, locally operated, or privately operated. In Minnesota, Oregon, Kansas, California, and Indiana, the state sponsors residential and day treatment programs under community corrections acts.

The Minnesota Community Corrections Act, which has become a model for other community corrections acts, provides a state subsidy to any county or group of counties that chooses to develop its own community corrections system. Juvenile delinquents who are adjudicated to a training school are "charged back" to the county and the costs are subtracted from the county's subsidy. Counties in Minnesota have been understandably reluctant to commit youths to training school because of the prohibitive cost (more than $35,000 a year for each youth) and, therefore, have both established and encouraged a wide variety of residential and day treatment programs.

The deinstitutionalization movement in Massachusetts resulted in the development of a wide network of residential and day treatment programs for youths. The Department of Youth Services administers some of these programs, but more often, the department contracts beds for these youths from private vendors in the community. The department also monitors the services provided by these programs.

California's Probation Subsidy Act, which was replaced by the County Subvention Program in 1978, also led to the development of a network of residential and day treatment programs for youth. At one point, the forty-seven participating California counties were receiving $22 million a year for community based programs. This major state commitment permitted the establishment of the largest number of residential and day treatment programs in the nation. However, the 1978 County Subvention Program, along with the passage of Proposition 13, severely curtailed the funding of such community programs.

Privately run programs usually are administered by a board of directors, who appoint the staff to operate their programs. In addition to the contract funds these programs receive from state and local governments, they also depend on such sources as federal, state, and local bodies and foundations. These programs provide either "halfway-in" facilities for probationers sentenced by the juvenile court or placements for juveniles on aftercare status. Private agencies usually must maintain minimum statewide or court standards.

The Types of Residential and Day Treatment Programs

Foster care, group homes, day treatment programs, wilderness programs, local institutions, and psychiatric services are the main types of community-based programs.

Foster Care

The foster home provides a setting for juveniles who must be removed from their natural homes. Ideally, the foster home simulates a family environment as it provides individualized care, attention, and affection. Foster care allows the placement of a child outside his or her own home without the destructive potential of institutionalization.[23]

Foster parents are subsidized by state or local governments to shelter neglected, abused, or delinquent children. Foster parents are expected to provide food, shelter, clothing, and expenses for their foster children. The management of a foster home is not an easy task, since the neglect and rejection experienced by the majority of foster children generate either overdependency or acting-out behavior. As these children are passed from one home to the next, they generally develop greater feelings of rejection, making it difficult for them to function in a foster home setting. Running away, the use of alcohol and drugs, and property offenses are common with these youths. One experienced foster parent noted:

> I've been a foster parent in three states but, at times, the problems can be overwhelming. Mothers will show up in the middle of the night and demand to see their children. Police will call and say they have your foster child and ask what you want done with him or her. The children are brought to you without any clothes, and you need to buy entire wardrobes for them. On another occasion I came home after shopping for a couple of hours and a new foster [child] had used his own feces to write over the walls of his room.[24]

Yitzhak Bakal and Howard W. Polsky describe a pattern that appears in many foster home placements. The first stage represents a period of negotiation and testing and the beginning of a contract between the youngster and foster parents. This stage can be described as the "honeymoon period," because both the juvenile and foster parents try to please each other and avoid conflict. The second stage is the "feeling comfortable" period. As the foster child begins to feel at home, he or she acts out more often and shows his or her "real self." The foster parents become more frustrated with the youngster, and the relationship deteriorates as both foster parents and child become more critical of each other. Foster children frequently run away at this stage, and foster parents generally need support at this time if the relationship is to survive. The third stage is the change and growth period, during which both parties make progress. The relationship grows, and the child begins doing things to receive approval. The child also starts to identify and develop goals for himself or herself. The fourth stage is again stressful for the foster parent, for the child usually wants to be independent. Parents and child must develop a different contract that alters the relationship and permits the termination of the placement with a minimum of depression, anxiety, and guilt.[25]

Foster placements have been receiving increased public attention. The foster group homes started by Thomas Butterworth in rural Missouri were featured in a television documentary in November 1981. The Villages, supported by the Menninger Foundation, which are located in Topeka, Kansas, are frequently regarded as a model of foster care.

For youths who must be taken from their natural homes, foster care is clearly a better placement than a group home or institutional placement. But, not surprisingly, many youths have negative feelings about foster care placements because few foster homes can replace a real home.

Group Homes

Such terms as group residence, halfway house, group home, and attention home are used in various parts of the United States to identify a small facility serving about thirteen to twenty-five youths. Group homes fulfill several purposes: they provide an alternative to institutionalization; they serve as a short-term community placement, wherein probation and aftercare officers can deal with youths' community problems; and they serve as a "halfway-in" setting for youths having difficulty adjusting to probation or as a "halfway-out" placement for delinquents who are returning to the community but lack an adequate home placement.

Intake criteria, treatment goals, length of stay, target population services, services offered, physical facilities, location in reference to the rest of the city, and house rules of group homes throughout the United States are extremely diverse. Some homes are very treatment-oriented, using a treatment modality like guided group interaction (GGI) to generate a supportive environment among residents and staff. In guided group interaction, residents are expected to support, confront, and be honest with one another so that they may help each other deal with their problems. However, other group homes deliberately avoid establishing a comfortable climate, and staff members may even try to arouse anxiety.[26]

The Silverlake Experiment, which was patterned on the Highfields Project, was set up in Los Angeles County in the mid-1960s. This program, which was in a large family residence in a middle-class neighborhood, provided group living for male youths between the ages of fifteen and eighteen. As was the case at Highfields, only twenty residents at a time lived in the group home, and all participated in daily group meetings.[27]

A well-developed group home model is the teaching-family group home concept, which was developed in 1967 with the establishment of the Achievement Place group home in Lawrence, Kansas. The teaching-family model is currently used in over forty homes in twelve states or more.[28] The Criswell House in Florida, established in 1958, houses twenty-five youths on probation and parole and uses GGI. In the 1970s, Florida developed a network of nine group homes modeled on Criswell House.[29] The Dare Program in Massachusetts is another widely used model. Established in 1964, this program currently has ten specialized programs and thirteen community residences: there are nine group homes, four foster home programs, two residential schools, shelter care programs, and an intensive care high-security facility.[30]

The Philadelphia Youth Development Center (YDC) enrolls 161 juveniles in day treatment programs and 131 in residential programs. The House of Umoja is a YDC group home that serves fifteen youths in a program that creates intensive family feelings within a framework of African-inspired black consciousness. Headed by Sister Falaska Fattah, the House of Umoja deals almost entirely with gang delinquents. It had its beginnings when Sister Falaska's husband, Daoud, who had been a gang member himself, returned to the streets to study the gangs. Sister Falaska saw possible solutions to the violence of gangs in "the strength of the family, tribal concepts, and African value systems." She and her husband then recreated an African-style extended family in which members of the gangs could find alternative values to those of their street life culture. Since the House of Umoja was established in the early 1970s, it has sheltered more than 300 boys, who have belonged to 73 different street gangs.[31]

Day Treatment Programs

Nonresidential day treatment programs multiplied nationwide during the early 1970s. Their popularity can be traced to the advantages they offer community-based corrections: they are more economical because they do not provide living and sleeping quarters; they make parental participation easier; they require fewer staff members; and they are less coercive and punishment-oriented than residential placements.

Nonresidential programs usually serve male juveniles, although California operates two such programs for girls and several coeducational programs. These nonresidential programs have been used widely by the California Community Treatment Project. The New York Division for Youth has also established several nonresidential programs, called STAY. The STAY programs also expose youths to a guided-groups interaction experience.

Another nonresidential program is conducted by the Associated Marine Institutes (AMI) in Florida. Funded by state, federal, and private donations, this privately operated corrections program uses the sea to stimulate productive behavior in juvenile delinquents. Most of the 130 trainees, males between fifteen and eighteen, live at home or in foster homes and attend one of the five centers of AMI (Deerfield Beach—Florida Ocean Sciences Institute, Jacksonville, Tampa, Miami, and St. Petersburg) eight hours a day for up to nine months. They receive training in seamanship, diving, and other nautical skills, as well as attending basic education classes. Youths are referred to this program either by the courts or by the Division of Youth Services.[32]

The United Delinquency Intervention Service (UDIS), based in Chicago, Illinois, began receiving referrals in October 1974. This program primarily serves repeat offenders who are on formal probation. The major goals of UDIS are:

1. To establish an adequate network of community-based services.

2. To reduce commitments to the larger institutional facilities of the Department of Corrections, Juvenile Division, by 35 percent of the commitment rate of Cook County and by 50 percent of the commitment throughout the rest of the state.

3. To provide services at a cost much less than institutional placement with the Juvenile Division.[33]

The UDIS staff uses purchase-of-service contracts, with the range of services including individual and family counseling, vocational testing and job placement, educational and tutoring services, specialized foster care, group home placements, temporary living arrangements, advocacy services, wilderness programs, and residence facilities in the intensive care units. Although some youths receive services for up to twelve months, the average length of involvement ranges from three to six months.[34]

Project New Pride is a day treatment program that offers services to juveniles in Denver, Colarado who have committed serious offenses. Youths involved in this program, which has been designated as an exemplary project by LEAA, receive intensive services for the first three months and then continue with treatment geared to their needs and interests for a nine-month follow-up period. Academic education, counseling, employment, and cultural education are the four main areas of service. For academic education, youths are assigned to either the New Pride Alternative School or the Learning Disabilities Center. The purpose of the counseling is to enhance the youth's self-image and to help him or her cope with the environment. Job preparation is emphasized in this program, as participants attend a job skills workshop and then receive on-the-job training. The purpose of cultural education is to expose participants, most of whom are blacks and Chicanos, to a range of experiences and activities in the Denver area. Project New Pride has been replicated in Chicago; Los Angeles; Boston; San Francisco; Washington, D.C.; Kansas City, Missouri; Fresno, California; Providence, Rhode Island; Haddonfield, New Jersey; and Pensacola, Florida.[35]

Survival Programs

Outward Bound is the most widely used wilderness survival program. The main goals of Outward Bound are to use the "overcoming of a seemingly impossible task" to gain self-reliance, to prove one's worth, and to define one's personhood. An Outward Bound program usually includes rock climbing, rappelling, mountain walking, backpacking, high altitude camping, and survival alone. The wilderness experience generally lasts three or four weeks and has four phases: training in basic skills, a long expedition, a solo, and a final testing period. The locations of these programs include forests, high mountains, canoe country, the sea, and the desert. The first Outward Bound program in the United States was established at the Colorado Outward Bound School in 1962. Other Outward Bound Schools are Minnesota, Hurricane Island, Northwest, North Carolina, Southwest, and Dartmouth College. Variations of the standard Outward Bound course were established throughout the United States during the 1970s; today over one thousand Outward Bound programs or their variations are found, in nearly every state.[36]

VisionQuest, another survival program, was started by Robert Ledger Burton in 1973 in Tucson, Arizona. This program currently has 250 staff members and 250 youngsters enrolled from ten states. Its wide variety of programs includes wilderness training, a mule and horse wagon train, alternative school, nine group homes, and a home-based counseling program. This rigorous twelve- to eighteen-month program requires that youths complete two "high-impact" experiences, such as wilderness training, a sea survival experience, or the mule and horse wagon train. The wagon train, which travels from one coast to the other, has been the subject of a CBS television documentary, a *Life* magazine pictorial article, and innumerable newspaper articles.[37]

Local Juvenile Institutions

Probation departments, especially those in California, operate a number of camps, ranches, and training schools. The Hennepin County Home School (Minneapolis,

Minnesota), described in the next chapter, is the most impressive locally administered juvenile institution.

Mental Health Services

In the late 1970s, many youths referred to the juvenile court were also referred to mental health agencies for evaluations and diagnosis. Some of these evaluations took place in inpatient psychiatric facilities, and others were done on an outpatient basis. Juvenile judges also commonly adjudicated youthful offenders to state diagnostic centers for thirty- or sixty-day evaluation periods.

EFFECTIVENESS OF COMMUNITY-BASED CORRECTIONS

In the minds of many students of juvenile corrections, the effectiveness of community-based corrections is beyond debate. Some proponents of community-based corrections go so far as to look upon the juvenile institution as irredeemably evil and the community programs as unequivocally good.[38] They appear to regard the juvenile delinquent as an underdog who is a nearly helpless victim of society's labeling process and to see flexible and adaptive community care as protecting delinquents from nasty and destructive institutional care.[39]

A more widely held view is that whatever the weaknesses of community-based programs, they do keep delinquents out of inhumane and costly long-term training schools. These more moderate advocates of community-based programs also argue that the further a youth is allowed to penetrate the juvenile justice system, the more difficult it becomes for him or her to be reintegrated successfully into community life. Community-based services also improve the probability of successful client reintegration because staff and clients are closer to community resources.

However, critics question the efficacy of community-based corrections. They claim that community programs tend to supplement rather than replace institutions, thereby leading to a widening of the net of the juvenile correctional system. That is, youths who formerly would have been diverted from the system now are placed in community programs. Critics also challenge the ability of community-based corrections to ensure community safety because of the laxity of probational supervision and because of the excessive number of runaways from residential programs. Critics point to the permissive tendency of many juvenile judges to keep youths on probation regardless of the number or types of crimes they commit. Finally, critics question the ability of community-based programs to correct or rehabilitate delinquents.

Empirical studies on probation tend to demonstrate its effectiveness. Frank S. Scarpitti and Richard M. Stephenson studied 1210 male delinquents in New Jersey for up to four years after their release from one of four programs: probation, a nonresidential program, a residential program, or the state reformatory. They found that only 15 percent of the probationers had to be returned to the juvenile court and sentenced to a punitive disposition, compared to 48 percent of the boys who had been in the residential program, 41 percent of those who had been in the nonresidential center, and 55 percent of the boys from the reformatory.[40] But, of course, the argument can be made that the offenders sentenced to probation were not as deeply involved in delinquency as were those sentenced to residential and institutional settings. Lipton, Martinson, and Wilks, in reviewing the studies done between 1945 and 1963, also found that probation meant a lower rate of recidivism than any other method of rehabilitating delinquents.[41]

Considerable research has been done on residential programs, but the findings are more mixed than those about probation. The California Youth Authority's Community Treatment Project (CTP) found that the overall success rate of project participants was higher than that of offenders in the regular youth authority program.[42] But Paul Lerman, in reexamining this study, questioned its positive evaluation, because youths who were more likely to succeed had been selected for the experimental group and those in the experimental group had committed more offenses than controls and been given more chances than the controls before being sent to training school.[43]

The Unified Delinquency Intervention Service (UDIS), which uses 75 different placement sites in the Chicago area to keep hard-core juvenile offenders out of institutions, has also received mixed evaluations. One study declared this program a success because at the end of the first year of operation, only 15, or 7 percent, of the 221 male and female participants who had completed the program had been rearrested.[44] A 1979 evaluation, however, questioned the success rate of this program.[45]

A study of the impact of the Silverlake Project in Los Angeles revealed very little difference between the Silverlake Project youths and those in the control group after one year, although the cost for the Silverlake program was one-third less than the cost of institutionalizing these youth.[46] In the Pinehills Project in Provo, Utah only 16 percent of the youths who completed the program had been arrested within six months, in comparison with 23 percent of the probation controls and 58 percent of the institutional controls.[47] Research that followed the subjects released from the Provo Experiment for up to six years found that the experimental subjects had lower rates of recidivism than institutional subjects, but that there was little difference between experimental subjects and those who had been probationers.[48]

The Harvard Center for Criminal Justice discovered no significant differences in recidivism rates in most regions between youthful offenders paroled by the Massachusetts Department of Youth Services from its training schools during the fiscal years 1967 and 1968 and a comparable sample of youths released from the department's regional programs in 1973 and 1974.[49] But in regions of the state where integrated networks of community-based programs had replaced institutions, there was a reduction in recidivism; where community programs lacked this integrated network, crime rates remained at previous levels or rose slightly.[50]

The conflicting evidence (as well as the flaws in the research) certainly makes it difficult to conclude that residential programs in the community result in lower rates of recidivism than institutional programs. Nevertheless, a convincing case can be made that residential and day treatment programs are at least as successful as training schools, with far less trauma to youths and less cost to the state.

POLICY IMPLICATIONS

The nature of the linkages between community programs and their social environment is the most distinguishing feature of community-based corrections. As frequency, duration, and quality of community relationships increase, the programs become more community-based. But the quality of community relationships is even more important than the frequency and duration.[51] In terms of quality relationships, the ideal form of community-based treatment should be characterized by a number of basic features. First, the treatment setting should be as similar as possible to the youth's natural environment and, if possible, an integral part of it. Second, as much as possible, youths should be able to remain in their own homes. Third, youths should receive maximum exposure to prosocial peers and minimum exposure to antisocial peers. Fourth, intervention strategies should be designed to enable youths to perform conventional social roles and to assume maximum responsibility for their own successes or failures. Finally, such programs should be situated in agencies that have stable financial support, that have little strain between custodial and treatment goals, and that have high commitment among staff.[52]

However, evidence shows that the decarceration or deinstitutionalization movement is stalled at the present time. The growing popularity of the "get-tough-with-kids" policy, as well as the decline of federal funding, makes it difficult for community-based programs to hold their own, much less expand. For example, Johnson et al., examining the status of decarceration at present in Massachusetts, Ohio, Florida, and Pennsylvania, found a positive trend toward decarceration in Massachusetts, marginal results in Pennsylvania and Florida, and a negative experience in Ohio.[53] But even in Massachusetts, decarceration has come under increased attack in recent years, and more youths now are placed in secure care than in the past.[54] Ronald E. Vogel and Edward A. Thibault, in this regard, claim that the Worcester Secure Treatment Facility in Massachusetts is no more than a juvenile prison.[55]

The implementation of a broad national policy of decarceration, which promises quality relationships for youths, requires three different approaches by policymakers. First, policymakers committed to decarceration must develop a strategy for change. Johnson et al., in the study cited above, provide guidelines for this change strategy. They found that the leadership by executives of correctional systems, as well as the active involvement of private agencies, is crucial to achieving decarceration. Gradual, planned change strategies frequently fail to result in decarceration because gradual change allows interest groups directly affected by decarceration to mobilize and oppose reform efforts. Institutional crises, such as riots or disturbances in a training school, can serve as valuable tools in mobilizing public opinion in favor of decarceration.[56] Second, community-based programs should be seen by policymakers more as a school of citizenship for youthful offenders. This school of citizenship is one in which youths are exposed to "situations of genuine reciprocity, in which the response to services rendered is the willingness to serve others in turn."[57] Third, policymakers must make certain that correctional agencies monitor the quality of programming for residents. Such monitoring is vital both for the delivery of services and for community protection. Too frequently abuses occur in community programs that are not adequately monitored by correctional agencies.

SUMMARY

Community-based corrections is made up of probation, residential and day treatment programs, and aftercare. The development of community-based corrections profited from the spirit of reform that existed at the turn of the twentieth century and later during the 1960s. Within the sociocultural context, support of community programs declined in the 1970s because the hardliners persuaded the public of great extent and danger of youth crime. Instead of being able to consider closing all state training schools, as Massachusetts had done in the early 1970s, proponents of community-based corrections found themselves in a position of defense or withdrawal. The end of Law Enforcement Assistance Administration (LEAA) funding in the late 1970s and early 1980s also resulted in the closing of many community-based programs. Nevertheless, far more delinquents still are treated in the community than are adjudicated to training schools because juvenile judges continue to support the least-restrictive, or soft-line, approach to minor offenders.

The evidence concerning the effectiveness of community-based programs is mixed, but community-based corrections appears to be at least as effective as training schools in reducing recidivism, with far less trauma to youths and less cost to the state. The 1980s should be a good decade for community-based corrections. The prohibitive expense of long-term institutions should mean increased use of alternatives to institutionalization. Perhaps the amount of decarceration of juveniles desired by reformers in the 1970s will never be attained, but the economics of placing juveniles in long-term institutions will probably mean that these end-of-the-line facilities will come to be reserved for hard-core and violent offenders.

Discussion Questions

1. What are the job responsibilities of a probation officer?
2. What are the differences between probation and aftercare services?
3. What are the main types of residential and nonresidential programs for juvenile delinquents?
4. How effective are community-based corrections?
5. What policy changes are needed to expand community-based corrections?

References

Astrachan, Anthony. "Philadelphia's Refuse from Juvenile Gang Wars." *Corrections Magazine* 1 (May/June 1975): 41–48.

Bailey, Ronald H. "Can Delinquents Be Saved by the Sea?" *Corrections Magazine* 1 (September 1974): 77–84.

Coates, Robert B. "Community-Based Corrections: Concept, Impact, Dangers." In Lloyd E. Ohlin, Alden D. Miller, and Robert B. Coates, *Correctional Reform in Massachusetts*. Washington, D.C.: U.S. Government Printing Office, 1977.

Lemert, Edwin M., and Dill, Forrest. *Offenders in the Community*. Lexington, Mass.: D. C. Heath & Company, 1978.

Miller, E. Eugene. "The Probation Officer as Broker." In *Corrections in the Community,* edited by E. Eugene Miller and M. Robert Montilla. Reston, Va.: Reston Publishing Company, 1977.

McCleary, Richard. *Dangerous Men: The Sociology of Parole*. Beverly Hills, Calif.: Sage Publications, 1978.

Scarpitti, Frank F., and Stephenson, Richard M. "A Study of Probation Effectiveness." *Journal of Criminal Law, Criminology and Police Science* 59 (1978): 361–369.

Vinter, Robert D.; Downs, George; and Hall, John. *Juvenile Corrections in the States: Residential Programs and Deinstitutionalization: A Preliminary Report*. Ann Arbor, Mich.: National Assessment of Juvenile Corrections, University of Michigan, 1975.

FOOTNOTES

1. Interviewed in August 1982.

2. Interviewed in May 1981.

3. John Augustus, *First Probation Officer* (Montclair, N.J.: Patterson-Smith Company, 1972), pp. 4–5.

4. Board of State Charities of Massachusetts, *Sixth Annual Report* (1869), p. 269.

5. The most recent statistics indicate that in 1976, 328,854 juveniles were on probation: Law Enforcement Assistance Administration, *State and Local Probation and Parole Systems* (Washington, D.C.: U.S. Government Printing Office, 1978), p. 1.

6. National Advisory Commission on Criminal Justice Standards and Goals, *Corrections* (Washington, D.C.: U.S. Government Printing Office, 1973), p. 312.

7. President's Commission on Law Enforcement and Administration of Justice, *Task Force Report: Corrections* (Washington, D.C.: U.S. Government Printing Office, 1967), p. 35.

8. See Edwin M. Lemert and Forrest Dill, *Offenders in the Community* (Lexington, Mass.: D.C. Heath & Company, 1978), for more information on and evaluation of the probation act in California.

9. *Juvenile Probation Subsidy Program: An Evaluation* (Olympia, Wash.: Community Services Division, Department of Social & Health Services, 1975), p. 3.

10. Larry Grubb, a juvenile probation officer in Sangamon County, Illinois, was extremely helpful in shaping this section on the functions of probation.

11. Eloise C. Snyder, "The Impact of the Juvenile Court Hearing on the Child," Crime and *Delinquency* 17 (April 1971), p. 190.

12. Clifford Simonsen and Marshall S. Gordon III, *Juvenile Justice in America* (Encino, Calif.: Glencoe Publishing Co., 1979), p. 203.

13. National Advisory Commission, *Corrections*, p. 322.

14. E. Eugene Miller, "The Probation Officer as Broker," in *Corrections in the Community,* edited by E. Eugene Miller and M. Robert Montilla (Reston, Va.: Reston Publishing Company, 1977), p. 82.

15. Interviewed in February 1970.

16. Richard McCleary, *Dangerous Men: The Sociology of Parole* (Beverly Hills, Calif.: Sage Publications, 1978).

17. Clemens Bartollas, *Introduction to Corrections* (New York: Harper & Row, Publishers, 1981), pp. 120–121.

18. The statistics are dated, but the most recent ones available indicate that in 1976, 53,347 youths were on parole: LEAA, *State and Local Probation and Parole Systems*, p. 1.

19. President's Commission, *Task Force Report: Corrections*, p. 67.

20. Ibid., p. 151.

21. Peter C. Kratcoski and Lucille Dunn Kratcoski, *Juvenile Delinquency* (Englewood Cliffs, N.J.: Prentice-Hall, 1979), pp. 328–331.

22. Robert D. Vinter, George Downs, and John Hall, *Juvenile Corrections in the States: Residential Programs and Deinstitutionalization: A Preliminary Report* (Ann Arbor, Mich.: National Assessment of Juvenile Corrections, University of Michigan, 1975), p. 35.

23. Yitzhak Bakal and Howard W. Polsky, *Reforming Corrections for Juvenile Offenders: Alternatives and Strategies* (Lexington, Mass.: Lexington Books, 1979), p. 99.

24. Interviewed in February 1978.

25. Bakal and Polsky, *Reforming Corrections for Juvenile Offenders*, pp. 112–113.

26. Oliver J. Keller, Jr., and Benedict S. Alper, *Halfway Houses: Community-Centered Correction and Treatment* (Lexington, Mass.: D.C. Heath and Company, 1970).

27. LaMar T. Empey and Stephen Lubeck, *The Silverlake Experiment: Testing Delinquency Theory and Community Intervention* (Chicago: Aldine Publishing Company, 1971).

28. D. L. Fixsen, E. L. Phillips, and M. M. Wolf, "The Teaching Family Model of Group Home Treatment, in *Closing Correctional Institutions*, edited by Yitzhak Bakal (Lexington, Mass.: D. C. Heath & Company, 1973).

29. Ronald H. Bailey, "Florida," *Corrections Magazine* 1 (September 1974), p. 66.

30. Information from Dynamic Action Residence Enterprise (DARE), Jamaica Plain, Mass.

31. Refer to Robert L. Woodson, *A Summons to Life: Mediating Structure and the Prevention of Youth Crime* (Cambridge: Ballinger Publishing Company, 1981), for the most up-to-date statement on the House of Umoja.

32. Ronald H. Bailey, "Can Delinquents Be Saved by the Sea?" *Corrections Magazine* 1 (September 1974), pp. 77–84.

33. The following materials on UDIS are adapted from John Ortiz Smykla, *Community-Based Corrections: Principles and Practices* (New York: Macmillan Publishing Company, 1981), pp. 209–211.

34. Ibid.

35. The following materials on Project New Pride are taken from U.S. Department of Justice, National Institute of Law Enforcement and Criminal Justice, *Project New Pride* (Washington, D.C.: U.S. Government Printing Office, 1977).

36. Refer to Joshua L. Miner and Joe Boldt, *Outward Bound USA: Learning through Experience* (William Morrow and Company, 1981).

37. Paul Sweeney, "VisionQuest's Rite of Passage," *Corrections Magazine* 8 (February 1982), pp. 22–32.

38. Andrew T. Scull, *Decarceration: Community Treatment and the Deviant—A Radical View* (Englewood Cliffs, N.J.: Prentice-Hall, 1977), p. 43.

39. Ibid.

40. Frank F. Scarpitti and Richard M. Stephenson, "A Study of Probation Effectiveness," *Journal of Criminal Law, Criminology and Police Science* 59 (1968), p. 361–369.

41. Douglas Lipton, Robert Martinson, and Judith Wilks, *The Effectiveness of Correctional Treatment: A Survey of Evaluation Studies* (New York: Praeger Publishers, 1975), pp. 59–61.

42. Nora Klapmuts, "Community Alternatives to Prison," *A Nation without Prisons,* edited by Calvert R. Dodge (Lexington, Mass. D. C. Heath and Company, 1975) pp. 1–2.

43. Paul Lerman, *Community Treatment and Social Control* (Chicago: University of Chicago Press, 1975).

44. Ronald Huff, "Programs Based on Sociology and Social Work," in *Intervening with Convicted Serious Juvenile Offenders,* edited by Dale Mann (Washington, D.C.: U.S. Government Printing Office; National Institute for Juvenile Justice and Delinquency Prevention, 1976), p. 40.

45. This evaluation by the American Institutes for Research in Washington, D.C. is discussed in Kevin Krajick's "A Blow for the Tough Side," *Corrections Magazine* 4 (September 1978), pp. 19–22.

46. William T. Pink and Mervin F. White, "Delinquency Prevention: The State of the Art," in *The Juvenile Justice System,* edited by Malcolm Kline (Beverly Hills, Calif.: Sage Publications, 1976), p. 21.

47. LaMar T. Empey, Maynard Erickson, and Max Scott, "The Provo Experiment: Evaluation of a Community Program," in *Correction in the Community: Alternatives to Incarceration* (Sacramento: California Department of Corrections, 1964), pp. 29–38.

48. LaMar T. Empey, "The Provo and Silverlake Experiments," in *Corrections in the Community,* p. 109.

49. Robert B. Coates et al., "Exploratory Analysis of Recidivism and Cohort Data on the Massachusetts Youth Correctional System" (Cambridge: Center for Criminal Justice, Harvard Law School, July 1975), pp. 1–2.

50. Lloyd E. Ohlin, Alden D. Miller, and Robert B. Coates, *Juvenile Correctional Reform in Massachusetts* (Washington, D.C.: U.S. Government Printing Office, 1977).

51. A. Rutherford and O. Bengur, *Community-Based Alternatives to Juvenile Incarceration* (Washington, D.C.: U.S. Government Printing Office, 1976).

52. Ronald A. Feldman, Timothy E. Caplinger, and John S. Wodarski, *The St. Louis Conundrum: The Effective Treatment of Antisocial Youths* (Englewood Cliffs, N.J.: Prentice-Hall, 1983), pp. 34–35.

53. Robert Johnson, Herbert J. Hoelter, and Jerome G. Miller, "Juvenile Decarceration: An Exploratory Study of Correctional Reform," in *Crossroads in Corrections: Designing Policy for the '80s,"* edited by S. Zimmerman and H. Miller (Beverly Hills, Calif.: Sage Publications, 1981).

54. See John A. Calhoun and Susan Wayne, "Can the Massachusetts Juvenile System Survive the Eighties?" *Crime and Delinquency* 27 (October 1981), pp. 522–533.

55. See Ronald E. Vogel and Edward Thibault, "Deinstitutionalization's Throwaways: The Development of a Juvenile Prison in Massachusetts," *Crime and Delinquency* 27 (October 1981), pp. 468–476.

56. Robert Johnson et al., *The Politics of Decarceration* (Washington, D.C.: U.S. Government Printing Office, 1980).

57. Johnson, Hoelter, and Miller, "Juvenile Decarceration."

INTERVIEW WITH ROSEMARY C. SARRI

> "I understand right now that the Administration is trying to persuade Congress to withdraw all funds for the Juvenile Justice Delinquency Prevention Act. There's also a sizable effort in states to fold the juvenile justice system into the adult system. If that happens, I think we will get even more primitive in social control, despite the fact that we've got fewer and fewer youth in this society."

In this interview, Professor Rosemary Sarri, who is Professor of Social Work at the University of Michigan and co-director of the National Assessment of Juvenile Corrections Project, discusses several of the most important issues related to community-based corrections

Question: The National Assessment of Juvenile Corrections study is acknowledged as one of the most significant studies ever done in community-based corrections. What do you consider to be the most important finding of this study?

Sarri: I think the single most important finding that we learned was about the tremendous variation in juvenile justice system operations among and within the states. There has been no attempt to achieve any kind of standardization. I see this as problematic because we have a society that is extremely mobile, particularly in the youth years. As a result, in the administration of justice there inevitably are problems with regard to fairness and justice.

Second, we learned it is possible to close all of the total institutions for children and youth and operate a viable juvenile justice program. That was achieved to the highest degree in Massachusetts, but it was also achieved to some extent in several states that developed extensive community-based programs with a comprehensive continuum of community-based care.

Third, another very important finding was the very broad and unsupervised discretion of juvenile court judges and staff. The juvenile court judge really operates, to some considerable extent, in isolation from other elements of the justice system in the majority of states. There are very few appeals, and the whole situation of waiver is one in which there is very little accountability or concern about that problem. There is a need to incorporate the juvenile court more effectively under the supervision of the larger judicial structure.

Fourth, we learned that such variables as race, class, and gender are more important in the administration of justice, than variables such as offense. These former variables were more predictive of the kinds of programs that states would develop and how they would proceed, particularly with respect to deinstitutionalization, than were crime rates or specific offense patterns of juvenile delinquents.

Fifth, we learned about the extent to which the social control perspective was dominant in almost all states. This is in contrast to a perspective that would be represented by child and youth well-being, characteristic of the majority of western European countries.

Sixth, a finding that has close parallel is the little concern of juvenile justice personnel (almost

Rosemary C. Sarri is acknowledged as one of the top authorities on juvenile corrections in the United States. She has published widely in the areas of the detention of juveniles in jails and detention facilities, of the impacts of community-based corrections and long-term institutionalization, and of the relationship of gender to the handling of juveniles by the juvenile justice system. She also has been interested in policy formulation in juvenile justice.

throughout the system) about the lack of opportunity structures for youth in our society. There was no real support by the majority of personnel in the juvenile justice system for things such as the National Young Americans Act, a National Service Corps, Job Corps, Youth Employment Opportunities, etc. They decry the kind of situation they have, but there seems to be no advocacy for programs that might be effective prevention and control programs. Finally, staff in the juvenile justice system indicated little willingness to relate on an egalitarian basis to the other youth institutions, such as the school, the labor market, recreational and cultural institutions, in order to develop an effective program for youth.

Question: Why are community-based settings more desirable for youths than placement in long-term training schools?

Sarri: I think that the results from the Massachusetts experiment, as well as the one from our study, demonstrate that community-based programs are as effective and more humane than closed institutions. They are more humane because they have fewer negative, secondary characteristics for youth. They allow youths to remain in contact with their family and community groups. The whole effort at normalization is certainly far more possible in community-based programs than it ever is with long-term training school programs. I think the negative effects of institutionalization are really overwhelming, although evaluators seldom look at this. They look at criteria such as recidivism, but they don't look at some of the other kinds of negative consequences that come from training schools but are not associated with placement in community settings. Another important factor is that staff in community settings focus on the attainment of positive goals for youth and they are far less concerned about coercive control and custody than are institutional staff. Also, overall community-based settings are less costly. Custodial training schools have become extremely costly in our society. Finally, community programs are more desirable because the overwhelming majority of the youth that are processed through the justice system are there for minor offenses and do not need secure custody. There are only a small percentage of

all youthful offenders processed for serious or violent crimes. And even these youths can be much more easily, effectively, and less expensively handled in community-based settings.

Question: Is deinstitutionalization stalled at the present time? If so, why has this taken place?

Sarri: Yes, it's really stalled and, in fact, there's some evidence that institutionalization is increasing, especially for males. The work that Barry Krisberg and Ira Schwartz have done, as well as the work I've done with them, clearly indicates that we have not reduced institutionalization in this country, comparable to the reduction of the available youth population. In other words, we've had approximately 18 percent reduction in the available youth population between the ages of twelve and eighteen since 1968 and, therefore, we should expect to find a similar kind of reduction in the institutionalization patterns in the justice system. This, of course, assumes that the crime rate remains constant. Well, first of all, the crime rate has, if anything, declined; almost all of the indicators of the crime rate show that juvenile crime has declined, especially serious crimes. As a result, one is left with the possibility that we really have a case of a bed-push hypothesis. We have spent a lot of money on correctional facilities and staff. I just noted that the total amount of dollars expended on institutional programs has doubled since 1971; that is, it has gone from 456 million to 839 million. There has been a decline in youth, but there has been a tremendous growth in staff from 43 thousand to over 60 thousand in residential programs. What has happened is that we have created a lot of new facilities. We have more than doubled the number of detention facilities. In other words, we hired new personnel and we have spent more money; therefore, we seem to have to fill the beds.

Deinstitutionalization is stuck because there are a lot of facilities available, and they need to be utilized! The highest risk for institutionalization are male adolescents. What is happening is that we are getting a dramatic increase in length of stay in all types of facilities, including detention facilities. For example, in my own county, the average length of stay in detention has gone to 46 days.

Question: What are the political, economical, and sociocultural factors in American society that have led to the deemphasis on community-based corrections?

Sarri: I think there are a number of reasons why it has happened. First of all, there has been an almost total withdrawal of federal support for deinstitutionalization. Something like deinstitutionalization requires a very heavy social and political commitment by the funding source and that commitment existed when Senator Birch Bayh developed and initiated the Juvenile Justice and Delinquency Prevention Act. When it was amended in 1977, there was also a lot of support for effective deinstitutionalization and a parallel development of community-based programs. All of that federal support is gone for both deinstitutionalization and for prevention and diversionary programs.

Second, the administrative hierarchy at the federal level has been quite willing to support the states in relatively punitive kinds of actions and to provide additional support for reinstitutionalization. Third, the role that the Child Welfare System has played is that we allowed the foster-care dollars to be used to maintain youth in private sector institutions. This has resulted in a tremendous growth in these institutions. In one year, either 1978 or 1979, there was a 7 percent reduction in the incarceration of youngsters in public institutions, and a 7 percent corresponding rise in private institutions. The numbers were not parallel, but it was a very interesting coincidence that you had this take place at the same time, and it continues to happen.

In terms of economic factors, it doesn't really make sense because institutional programs are more costly. What I think has happened is that there's been a withdrawal of federal dollars for diversionary, prevention, and residential community-based care, and, as a result, many communities are left only with institutional placements available. Another economic factor is the increase in single parenthood so that you have youngsters at somewhat greater risks because we don't have other kinds of community support that could exist to help single parents.

Question: Is jailing juveniles as much a problem as when you wrote *Under Lock and Key?* What policy changes need to be made to eliminate the jailing of juveniles?

Sarri: Well, the jailing of juveniles is still very bad. I think we are beginning to get in place some efforts, particularly by church groups and certain other community groups, that will probably move us gradually away from the jailing of juveniles. But to this date, I think the figures that we found in 1974 still hold now. I am unable to make any estimates which do not indicate that at least 500,000 are still held in adult jails each year in the United States. It's very disproportionate among states. There are some states that have very large numbers, and there are few states that have none.

We now have a lot of research on in-house detention of youngsters and alternatives to detention that could be used, but juvenile judges apparently do not wish to use them. In Michigan there has been an effort in the Upper Peninsula, a very large area with very few people, to develop effective alternatives to placing youth in jail, and they have been able to reduce that to nothing.

Detention certainly has changed very little. There still are about 400,000 youth per year being detained, far more boys than girls. What is equally disturbing is that the length of stay is really going up in detention in many states. We're back to holding youth for status offenses in both jails and detention facilities. I think some of the reasons for the very heavy social control of youngsters is that we have withdrawn so much money from education and we have a terrible problem of youth unemployment. So we're left with the situation in which many youth are doing things that adults in this society find offensive for a variety of reasons. We then subject them to a lot of social control, without any consideration of the long-term consequences for doing this.

Question: You've done a lot of research on gender. What have been your recent findings?

Sarri: I think there are many problems with respect to gender issues. There has still not been a movement away from the processing of females for promiscuity and other sex-related status offenses. We still continue to do this and do not address the seriousness of this problem. What's happening is that we don't find these female sexual offenders as much in public training schools as we did when we did the NAJC study; what we are finding today is that many of the girls are being cycled into mental health facilities, where they may remain for very long periods of time for their status offenses. Females are a particular risk in the justice system because their families, more than the police in many instances, are the persons who bring them to the attention of the official system. If a family cannot advocate and support its youth, that youngster is in greatest risk in the justice system. A runaway girl without family support is in a worse predicament than a male who commits armed robbery but has the support of his family. This male will move more quickly through the justice system than the girl.

Another problem that is becoming more recognized now is that females are at a far greater risk for sexual abuse. Many of the adolescent females who come to the attention of the justice system come because they are reacting against the sexual abuse that they experienced in their families. When they became adolescents, they began to recognize this sexual abuse for what it is.

Males are at much greater risk for institutionalization than they were ten years ago. We are moving males into the closed training schools and long-term group facilities, while we are moving females into the child welfare private sector and mental health kinds of programs. In a study that we did, we found that the person that is at greatest risk in the juvenile justice system for long-term, punitive incarceration is the black male, even when you control for offense. The person who is most likely to get probation or diversion is the white male. The white female is more likely to get a group home placement or a mental health place, and a black female is more or less a 50/50 between institutionalization and probation placement.

Question: What are your predictions for community-based corrections in the next decade?

Sarri: I understand right now that a bill is before Congress to withdraw all funds for the Juvenile Jus-

tice Delinquency Prevention Act. There's also a sizable effort in states to fold the juvenile justice system into the adult system. If that happens, I think we will become even more primitive in social control, despite the fact that we have fewer and fewer youngsters in society. I hear people talking about the declining crime rate, and give the explanation that the police and justice system are more effective. Such statements cannot be made unless one controls for the decline in the available population.

I think we will continue to be punitive with youth, until we get a really invigorated interest in the development of community-based corrections along with some very strong federal guidelines and incentives for the states to move in that direction. The current involvement of many of the church groups in the justice system is perhaps one of the more positive things today because they have been advocates for progressism in juvenile justice in the past five or ten years. The church groups are organizing themselves and working with various private coalition groups that are interested in progressive programs in juvenile justice. They are catalysts for getting things going at the community level and sometimes at the state level. I've seen a number of them take a very active role in trying to get statutory change in the juvenile code. I think this positive force is probably going to grow.

Overall I'm not very optimistic about the remainder of the 1980s. If there is a change in administration, that could begin to get a reversal of the kinds of things that have gone on since 1980s. But I don't think it will be a complete turn-around because the juvenile justice system is a low priority on the federal agenda. I think by about 1990 or certainly by about 1995 that changes toward more humane treatment of youth will take place simply because of demographic factors. I think another thing that will happen is that we will gradually see a movement away from so much emphasis on blacks, and there will be more attention to the problems with Hispanics. All the things we have attributed to blacks, we seem now to attribute to Hispanics, because of their lowered status in our society.

CHAPTER 18

JUVENILE INSTITUTIONS

CHAPTER OUTLINE

> However good an institution may be, however kindly in spirit, however ge-
> nial its atmosphere, however homelike its cottages, however fatherly and
> motherly its officers, however admirable its training, it is now generally . . .
> agreed that institution life is at the best artificial and unnatural, and that the
> child ought to be returned at the earliest practicable moment to the more
> natural environment of the family.
>
> *Hastings Hart*[1]

Juvenile institutions, as this seventy-year-old statement declares, are no substitute for the home. Some feel that juvenile institutions do irreparable harm to juveniles and should be closed; others look upon them as a measure of last resort that should be used only when everything else has failed; and still others encourage their increased use because of their supposed deterrent effect upon youth crime. This chapter describes and evaluates these short- and long-term facilities. Detention homes, shelters, county jails, and police lockups are the short-term facilities used by society to confine juveniles for a few days.[2] Long-term institutions include reception or diagnostic centers, ranches, forestry camps, farms, and training schools; they provide placement of adjudicated delinquents for periods ranging from a few weeks to a year or more. A brief history of juvenile institutions is helpful before proceeding to such topics as the extent and types of juvenile facilities, the nature of inmate life, and the effectiveness of juvenile institutions at the present time.

HISTORY OF JUVENILE INSTITUTIONS

Before the end of the eighteenth century, the family was commonly believed to be the source or cause of deviancy, and, therefore, the idea emerged that perhaps the well-adjusted family could provide the model for a correctional institution for children. The house of refuge, the first juvenile institution, reflected the family model wholeheartedly, for it was designed to bring the order, discipline, and care of the family into institutional life. The central concern was to separate youths from the degradation and temptation of the vice-ridden cities; thus, the idea was for the institution to become the home, the peers the family, and the staff the parents.[3]

The first house of refuge was chartered for females in New York in 1824. New York also started the first school for males in 1825, and over the next decade or so, Boston, Philadelphia, Bangor, Richmond, Mobile, Cincinnati, and Chicago followed suit in establishing houses of refuge for males. Twenty-three schools were chartered in the 1830s and another thirty in the 1840s. The vast majority of the houses of refuge were for males. The average capacity of these was 210; the capacity ranged from 90 at Lancaster, Massachusetts, to 1000 at the New York House of Refuge for Boys.[4]

Although founded under different correctional philosophies, these houses of refuge resembled existing state prisons and county jails. Some were surrounded by walls to maintain security. The buildings were usually four stories high; the five- by eight-foot rooms were windowless and had iron-lattice slabs for doors. Upon entering the institution, youths were dressed in identical clothing and given identical haircuts. Troublemakers were punished by a diet of bread and water, by solitary confinement, or by whipping with a cat-o'-nine-tails or manacling with a ball and chain.[5]

The development of the cottage system and the construction of these juvenile institutions outside cities were two reforms of the mid-nineteenth century. The cottage system was introduced in 1854 and quickly spread throughout the nation. The new system housed smaller groups of youths in separate buildings, usually no more than twenty to forty youths per cottage. Early cottages were log cabins, and later cottages were built from brick or stone. Now called training schools or industrial schools, these juvenile facilities were usually constructed outside cities, so that youths would be reformed through exposure to the rural and simpler way of life. It was presumed residents also would learn responsibility and new skills as they worked the fields and took care of the livestock. Their work would enable the institution, in turn, to provide its own food and perhaps even realize a profit.

Several significant changes occurred in juvenile institutionalization during the first several decades of the twentieth century. First, because it had become clear that custody was the primary effect of these industrial or training schools, reformers advocated treatment on several fronts. Case studies were used to prescribe treatment plans for residents; reception units were developed to diagnose and classify new admissions; individual therapies, such as psychotherapy and behavior modification, were used; and group therapies, such as guided group interaction, became popular means of transforming the inmate subculture. Second, institutional programs became more diverse. Confined juveniles could graduate from state-accredited high school programs; home furloughs and work release programs were permitted in many training schools; and vocational programs were expanded in well equipped training schools to include printing, barbering, welding, and automobile repair. Finally, the types of juvenile correctional facilities were increased to include ranches, forestry camps, and farms, as well as the traditional prison-like training schools.

In the 1960s and 1970s, reformers began to accuse training schools of being violent, inhumane, and criminogenic. Jerome Miller, who closed all the training schools in Massachusetts in the early 1970s, aptly expressed this viewpoint when he said:

> Reform schools neither reform nor rehabilitate. The longer you lock up a kid in them, the less don't protect society. They're useless, they're futile, they're rotten.[6]

The widespread criticisms of training schools, along with court decisions and pressure groups in the legislature, led to a number of changes in the mid- and late-1970s. These humane reforms included the withdrawal of status offenders from training schools, a dramatic reduction in staff brutality, more extensive staff training programs, the growing acceptance of grievance procedures for residents, and the tendency to convert single-sex institutions into coeducational facilities.

THE TYPES OF JUVENILE CORRECTIONAL INSTITUTIONS

In 1979, the most recent statistics available, there were nearly 2600 short-term and long-term juvenile institutions in the United States. Although the public facilities were nearly equally divided between state and locally operated and between short-term and long-term institutions, most of the private institutions were long-term facilities.[7] (See Tables 18-1 and 18-2.) An examination of these tables shows that detention centers, training schools, and ranches, camps, and farms outnumber other facilities and hold the bulk of institutionalized youth. The population of jails is not included in these figures, but they house more juveniles each year than any other type of correctional facility.

Jails

Jails—which have been called "sick,"[8] "the ultimate ghetto,"[9] "the most glaringly inadequate institution on the American correctional scene,"[10] and "brutal, filthy cesspools of crime"[11]—hold 500,000 or more juveniles each year.[12] The reason why so many youths are confined in county jails and police lockups is that 93 percent of the juvenile court jurisdictions (totaling 2800 counties and cities in the United States) must use these institutions when detaining juvenile lawbreakers.[13]

Many problems confront the juvenile incarcerated in a jail. First, health problems are created by the shortage of items such as soap, towels, toothbrushes, clean bedding, and toilet paper. Second, most small jails and many large ones offer little treatment or recreational programming, because they lack space, staff, and fiscal resources. Third, the lack of professionally trained staff reduces the quality of jail life. The county sheriff, who is usually responsible for the jail, sees himself as a law enforcement officer and tends to regard the supervision of the jail as a millstone; new deputies often are assigned to jail duty, and they typically cannot wait until they get back to "real" law enforcement on the streets. Fourth, jails, like other adult institutions, are overcrowded, and this condition creates idle and restless prisoners. Overcrowded conditions and idleness also foster a lawless jail society, in which the strong take advantage of the weak. Jail victims are most frequently women, children, and first-offender males.[14]

The physical and sexual victimization of children in jails by adult prisoners is especially offensive. Pat Barker, an official of the Oklahoma Crime Commission, recalls his own jail experience:

> [It's] frightening. You're in a detention room with sleeping accommodations for 32 and there are 40 people. Some people have to sleep on the floor. I've seen people raped, especially young kids. You can get a kid as young as 14

TABLE 18-1 Number of U.S. Public Juvenile Detention and Correctional Facilities and Number of Juveniles Held, by Type of Facility, 1971, 1973, 1974, 1975, 1977, and 1979[a]

Type of Facility	Number of Facilities						Number of Juveniles[b]					
	1971	1972	1974	1975	1977	1979	1971	1972	1974	1975	1977	1979
All facilities	722	794	829	874	892	933	58,429	47,385	46,753	46,794	48,032	47,642
Short-term facilities	338	355	371	387	448	458	14,280	12,706	12,566	12,725	11,929	NA[b]
Detention center	305	319	331	347	NA	NA	11,767	10,782	11,010	11,089	NA	NA
Shelter	17	19	21	23	NA	NA	360	190	180	200	NA	NA
Reception or diagnostic center	16	17	19	17	NA	NA	2,153	1,734	1,376	1,436	NA	NA
Long-term facilities	384	439	458	487	544	535	40,449	32,988	32,356	34,255	32,167	NA
Training school	191	187	185	189	NA	NA	34,055	26,427	25,397	26,748	NA	NA
Ranch, forestry camp, and farm	115	103	107	103	NA	NA	5,471	4,959	5,232	5,385	NA	NA
Halfway house and group home	78	149	166	195	NA	NA	973	1,602	1,727	2,122	NA	NA

[a]NA means statistics not available.
[b]Based on average daily number of residents.

Source: Adapted from U.S. Department of Justice, *National Criminal Justice Information and Statistics Source* (Washington, D.C.: U.S. Government Printing Office, 1977, p. 17; 1979, p. 2; and 1981, p. 129.

TABLE 18-2 Number of U.S. Private Juvenile Detention and Correctional Facilities and Number of Juveniles Held, by Type of Facility, 1974, 1975, 1977, and 1979[a]

Type of Facility	Number of Facilities				Number of Juveniles[b]			
	1974	1975	1977	1979	1974	1975	1977	1979
All facilities	1,337	1,277	1,600	1,558	31,384	26,740	29,611	28,556
Short-term facilities	76	66	126	74	797	830	843	NA
Long-term facilities	1,261	1,211	1,474	1,484	30,952	26,460	28,227	NA
Training schools	61	65	NA	NA	4,078	3,660	NA	NA
Ranches, forestry camps, and farms	395	295	NA	NA	16,955	13,094	NA	NA
Halfway houses and group homes	805	851	NA	NA	9,919	9,706	NA	NA

[a]Based on average daily number of residents.

[b]NA means statistics not available.

Source: Adapted from U.S. Department of Justice, *National Criminal Justice Information and Statistics Source* (Washington, D.C.: U.S. Government Printing Office, 1977, p. 18; 1979, p. 3; and 1981, p. 131.

years old, and several 16. These young people would come in, and if they were fresh and young, the guys [inmates] who run the tank and lived in the first call, they would take these young guys if they wanted to. They would take the kid, forcibly hold him, and someone would rape him right in the rear. I just flat saw it happen. The guards in jail make rounds periodically, but they don't have enough manpower. Some of [the kids] go to pieces, just right there and then, kids who can't hack it and are torn apart. They cry all the time, just nervous, scared of their shadows. Others just get embittered and next time some young kid comes in they turn around and become the raper instead of the rapee. So it depends on the individual. If the kid tells the guards [about a rape], they better yank him out of there or his life isn't worth a nickel.[15]

The sexual victimization of juveniles in the Philadelphia jail system has been well documented. Victimization began in the sheriff's vans that transported prisoners from the police stations to the jails, courthouses, and prisons. These vehicles, without windows and totally lacking in staff supervision, provided the opportunity for sexual assaults of children in huge numbers.[16] In a hearing before a Senate committee, the district attorney of Philadelphia noted that half of the sexual victims in this correctional system were juveniles who could not protect themselves against adult predators.[17]

What is so unfortunate about the failing of juveniles is that so many are confined for acts that would not be considered violations if committed by an adult. John

Downey's study of juveniles detained in jails within eighteen states found that 41.6 percent were apprehended for such acts. The lack of seriousness of their acts is underlined by the brevity of their stays: 70 percent were confined in the jail for two days or less, and 80 percent were sent home or otherwise remained in the community following release.[18] The Children's Defense Fund study of children in jail found that less than 20 percent had been jailed for a violent act.[19]

The practice of jailing juveniles is considered so offensive that it has been objected to by the International Association of Chiefs of Police, the National Sheriffs' Association, the U.S. Children's Bureau, and the National Council on Crime and Delinquency. But some evidence exists that the jailing of juveniles is declining because of the Juvenile Justice and Delinquency Prevention Act (JJDPA). In 1980, Congress strengthened the JJDPA with a tough new amendment. States would have to cease sending youths to adult jails within five years if they wanted to receive federal funding for juvenile justice; a two-year extension would be permitted beyond that to states that reduced the number of juveniles in adult jails by the end of 1985. The Office of Juvenile Justice Delinquency Prevention later reported that twenty-nine states had achieved "substantial compliance" by the end of 1982.

Detention Centers

Detention homes, also called juvenile halls and detention centers, were established at the end of the nineteenth century as an alternative to jail for juveniles. Their purpose is to serve as temporary holding centers for juvenile offenders who need detention either for their own safety or to ensure public safety. According to the 1975 National Criminal Justice Information and Statistics, 347 detention facilities held 11,089 children that year.[20] California's 45 detention centers held over 30 percent of the total number of children detained in 1975.[21]

Detention centers are administered by state agencies, city or county governments, welfare departments, or juvenile courts. The states of Connecticut, Vermont, and Delaware and Puerto Rico have complete responsibility for administering juvenile detention centers. Georgia, Massachusetts, New Hampshire, Rhode Island, and Maryland operate regional detention facilities; Utah and Virginia also encourage the establishment of regional detention centers by reimbursing counties for their construction. The majority of detention facilities are administered by the county. Juveniles are usually detained in these centers from three to twenty-one days, but the juvenile codes of most states now require that detention not continue over forty-eight hours without a detention hearing.

The traditional model of detention for youths was woefully inadequate. A grim-looking detention facility usually was attached to the building that housed the administrative offices and hearing rooms of the juvenile court. Locked outer doors and high fences or walls prevented escapes. The lack of programming made it clear that these facilities were intended merely to be holding centers. A former resident described her experience in a traditional detention home:

It [the facility] sucks. It was the worst place I've ever been in. They're [staff] cruel. They used to give work details for punishment. For an entire hour, I scrubbed the kitchen floor with a toothbrush. They can get away with this, and it is not against the law. The place is falling apart. They are just not very caring people. They didn't do much for me except scare me.[22]

Fortunately, the nationwide movement to develop standards for detention and innovative detention programs resulted in marked improvement in the overall quality of detention facilities and programs during the 1970s. The bureau of detention standards in those states that have such overseeing units usually inspects detention centers once a year; this inspection also insures a better quality of detention practices.

Attention Homes, initiated in Boulder, Colorado, by the juvenile court to improve the detention process for children, have spread to other jurisdictions. The stated purpose of the Attention Homes program is to give youths *attention* rather than *detention*. Problem resolution is the focus of the program, and professional services are provided to residents on a contractual basis. These nonsecured facilities have no fences, locked doors, or other physical restraints. They also are characterized by more extensive programming and by more intensive involvement between residents and staff than is typical.

Home detention, a nonresidential approach to detention, was first used in St. Louis, Newport News, Norfolk, and Washington, D.C., and now is being used throughout the United States. The in-home detention program is commonly within the organizational structure of the juvenile court and is administered by the community services unit of the probation department. An in-home detention coordinator typically will meet with the intake officer, with a field probation officer, and sometimes with a juvenile officer prior to the detention hearing to decide whether a youth is an appropriate candidate for in-home detention. Some jurisdictions use a release risk evaluation to decide whether in-home detention for a particular youth should be recommended to the juvenile judge. Youths placed on in-home detention are required to remain at home twenty-four hours a day; the in-home detention worker visits the youth and family seven days a week and also makes random phone calls throughout the day to make certain that the juvenile is at home. A recent study of the first two years of the San Diego County Home Supervision Program showed that the program provided effective supervision, while it cost less than one-third the amount required to place a youth in secure detention.[23]

The Camden County Children's Center in Lakeland, New Jersey, is one of the most impressive detention facilities in the United States. Residents publish a newspaper, make use of such treatment programs as psychodrama, are permitted to care for a St. Bernard, go on sledding and skiing trips, play basketball games with teams from other detention facilities, attend movies and plays and visit museums in the community, and go every Tuesday night to radio and television studios to learn about the use of radio and television equipment.[24]

Shelter Care Facilities

Shelters are primarily used to provide short-term care for status offenders and for dependent or neglected children. Although only twenty-three public shelters existed in 1975, an increase in the number of shelters has resulted from the funding mandate of the Juvenile Justice and Delinquency Prevention Act requiring that noncriminal youths be placed in such facilities.

The length of stay usually varies from overnight to a few days, but occasionally a youth must stay several weeks because of hearing delays in the juvenile court or because of difficulty in scheduling court-required family therapy sessions. Delinquent youths may also be placed in shelter care if a county has no detention center and the juvenile judge does not want to detain the youth in the county jail or if a judge decides to reward the positive behavior of a youth in the detention facility by transferring him or her to the more open shelter care.

With the development of shelter care standards across the United States, these facilities are becoming more responsive to the needs of children. These units are more open than most detention facilities and permit residents to enjoy home visits on weekends and field trips into the community during the week. However, shelter care facilities have problems similar to those of detention facilities. One staff member noted:

> The real frustration of working here is that we're just a holding place for kids. We don't get to see any changes or to do any treatment. We see so many, and nothing seems to change. We don't deal with the families. We also don't have any controls here; no backup system like a control room.[25]

The constant problem with runaways is a headache to all administrators of these nonsecure facilities. The openness of these settings also leads to minor disciplinary problems among residents.

Reception and Diagnostic Centers

In 1975, seventeen reception and diagnostic centers were in operation in the United States, and they held an average of 1734 juveniles per day. The purpose of these reception and evaluation centers, which are under the sponsorship of the youth authority, the youth commission, the department of youth services, or the department of corrections, is to determine which treatment plan suits each adjudicated youth and which training school is the best placement.

The evaluation of each resident usually takes between four and six weeks. Evaluations are done by a psychiatrist, a clinical psychologist, a social worker, academic staff, and a chaplain. The psychiatrist does a psychiatric evaluation, and a psychologist administers a battery of psychological tests measuring intelligence, attitude, maturity, and emotional problems. The social worker, meanwhile, develops a social case study of each youth. The academic staff during this orientation period determines the proper school placement and attempts to identify any debilitating learning problems. Physical and dental examinations also are typically given the youth at this time. Finally, child-care workers in the living units evaluate institutional adjustment and peer relationships. Once all the reports have been prepared, a case conference is held on each resident, to summarize the needs and attitudes of the youth and recommend the best institutional placement.[26]

In large youth commissions, or departments of youth services, the recommendation must be approved further by an institutional coordinator, but once it is approved, the youth is transferred to the approved institutional placement, and the diagnostic report is sent with him or her. But because many training schools have their own orientation programs, it is not unusual for the report to receive little attention and for the youth to undergo something of the same process over again in the reception cottage.

Ranches, Forestry Camps, and Farms

Minimum-security institutions, such as ranches, forestry camps, and farms, are typically reserved for youths who have committed minor crimes and for those who are committed to the youth authority for the first time. In 1975, there are 103 state and county and 295 privately administered ranches, forestry camps, and farms. In that year, private facilities held 13,094 residents and private programs held 5385 delinquents.

Forestry camps are popular in a number of states. Residents usually do conservation work in a state park, cleaning up, cutting grass and weeds, and doing general maintenance. Treatment programs usually consist of group therapy, individual contacts with social workers and the child-care staff, and one or two home visits a month. Residents also may be taken to a nearby town on a regular basis to make purchases and to attend community events. Escapes are a constant problem because of the nonsecure nature of these facilities.

County and privately administered ranches are especially widely used in California and several other states. Horseback riding is the most popular recreational activity, but work detail usually consists of taking care of the livestock, working in the garden, and performing general maintenance duties. Guided group interaction is the most widely used treatment program and one or two home visits a month give residents an opportunity to reintegrate themselves to community living.

Farms now receive infrequent use in juvenile corrections, chiefly because the acceptability of juveniles doing farm work waned during the 1960s and early 1970s. That is, the value of such outdoor activities as taking care of the livestock and cultivating the garden no longer receives the support they once had in juvenile corrections.

Residents are generally much more positive about a placement at a forestry camp or ranch than about placement at a training school. They like both the more relaxed approach to security and the more frequent community contact. Residents also respond to the shorter stays of these minimum-security institutions, and, given the looser atmosphere of these settings, it is not surprising that they have better relations with staff here than in training schools. However, some youths who are homesick or are victimized by peers cannot handle these settings and repeatedly run away until they are transferred to more secure institutions.

The Hennepin County Home School, one of the most interesting juvenile institutions in the nation, combines features of both camps and ranches. It is an open facility, located in a beautiful 160-acre wooded site approximately seventeen miles from downtown Minneapolis. It serves a coeducational population, ranging in age from eleven to eighteen, with the average age sixteen. The school receives no status offenders; the largest group of offenders is made up of those charged with burglary and car theft. The typical resident has had at least five prior court involvements, and well over half of the residents have been involved in some type of out-of-home placement prior to their commitment to the County Home School. The institution is divided into five Alpha cottages and one Beta cottage. The average stay in the Alpha cottage is five months; residents stay about three weeks in the Beta program, which is a short-term restitution program for Hennepin County youth. Each resident of the Alpha program has received an indeterminate sentence and is required to move through the four stages of the treatment program to be released. The sophisticated treatment program of this institution uses such modalities as MacGregor family therapy, transactional analysis, token reinforcement, reality therapy, and life space theory. Horseback riding and canoeing are favorite activities, and residents leave the institution to attend football games, to watch movies, or to go shopping.[27]

Public and Private Training Schools

Training schools, the end-of-the-line placement for the juvenile delinquent, are being used less today than in the past. For example, a 1978 survey by *Corrections Magazine* found 26,000 youths in secure and semisecure state facilities, a 28 percent drop from the 36,507 confined on January 1, 1970.[28] statistics for private training schools are less complete, but a 1977 *Children in Custody* report documented that 4078 youths were confined in private training schools.[29] This trend away from training schools in the 1970s is chiefly explained by the diversion of status offenders from these institutions and by the popularity of the deinstitutionalization philosophy in juvenile corrections.

Public Training Schools

The larger states, such as California, New York, Michigan, and Illinois, each have several training schools; smaller states commonly have one training school for boys and another for girls. Massachusetts and Vermont have no training schools. The traditional policy of separating males and females in training schools now is being abandoned in several states that are opening up one or more coeducational facilities. All the training schools in North Carolina are presently coeducational.

Physical Design

The physical structure of public training schools ranges from the homelike atmosphere of small cottages to open dormitories, which provide little privacy for residents, to fortress-like facilities with individual cells. Maximum-security training schools generally have high fences and sometimes even walls around them. Their interiors are characterized by bleak hallways, locked doors, and individual cells covered by heavy screens or bars. Medium-security training schools usually have cottages or dormitories and also maintain perimeter security by high fences. But their atmosphere is more relaxed, in that residents are trusted to move around more freely on the campus and are permitted more off-campus visits than are allowed in maximum-security training schools. Few training schools are minimum-security, because it is assumed that many residents are there because they could not handle less restrictive placement facilities.

Organizational Goals

David Street, Robert D. Vinter, and Charles Perrow, in a 1966 study of several public and private training schools in Michigan, identified three basic organizational goals: obedience/conformity, reeducation/development, and treatment. They found that staff in obedience/conformity institutions kept inmates under surveillance, emphasized rules, reacted punitively to residents, and did not become involved with residents. Staff members in reeducation/development institutions, in contrast, demanded conformity, hard work, and intellectual growth, but they were more willing to reward positive behavior and to develop relationships with residents. Staff members in treatment institutions were the most involved with residents since they interacted more with them and also put more energy into working with their problems.[30]

However, regardless of their official goal, the fact that training schools experience such large number of runaways from training schools means that most actually emphasize custody. This custodial emphasis gives most training schools a punishment-oriented atmosphere. Custodial staff members are reprimanded, and sometimes even suspended, for violations of security that lead to escapes. Treatment staff members often have their treatment recommendations about offenders refused because particular residens are poor security risks. Superintendents are frequently fired when the number of runaways brings unfavorable publicity to the youth authority or youth commission.

Programs

The programs offered by training schools are superior to those of other juvenile institutions. The medical and dental services that residents receive tend to be very good. Most larger training schools have a full-time nurse on duty during the day and a physician who visits one or more days a week. Institutionalized delinquents typically are unhappy with the medical and dental care they receive, but, on balance, it is true that most youths are receiving far better medical and dental care than they have in the past.

The educational program is usually accredited by the state and is able to grant a high school diploma. It probably also offers classes to prepare residents for the general education examination. Furthermore, basic education classes usually are available, consisting of a review of the necessary skills in reading, writing, and mathematics. Reading laboratories and programmed instruction are sometimes used to help residents develop skills in these areas. Classes tend to be small, and students are permitted to progress at the rate most satisfactory to them. However, a visit to a typical classroom in a training school does not result in a favorable impression as many students are bored and a few even may be asleep.

Vocational training provided by training schools for boys consists of such courses as automotive design, welding, carpentry, printing, barbering, machine shop, and drafting. Vocational courses in training schools for girls are more limited but usually include beauty culture, sewing, food service, and secretarial skills. However, because residents have difficulty being admitted to the necessary labor unions following release, this vocational training is generally not helpful in finding future employment. But a few residents do leave the institution and find excellent jobs with the skills they have learned.

Recreation has always been emphasized in training schools. Male residents are usually offered such competitive sports as softball, volleyball, flag football, basketball, and sometimes even boxing or wrestling. Cottages may compete against each other, and the institution may have a team that competes against other institutional teams. Other popular recreational activities include attending weekly movies; building model cars; participating in talent shows, dramatics, and choir; decorating the cottage at Christmas; and playing Ping-Pong, pool, and chess. Some training schools offer sailing or canoeing for residents; some have swimming pools; and still others sponsor dances with residents of nearby training schools.

Religious instruction and services are always provided in state training schools. A full-time Protestant chaplain and a part-time Roman Catholic chaplain are available in most schools. Religious services offered include Sunday mass and morning worship, confession, baptism, instruction for church membership, choir, and religious counseling. However, few residents usually respond to these religious services, unless attendance is compulsory, and then there is frequently considerable resistance to them.

The punishment administered to misbehaving residents varies from training school to training school. Fortunately, blatant staff brutality has disappeared from most schools. Adult correctional systems have had enough problems with the federal courts that they do not want confinement conditions in their juvenile institutions declared unconstitutional as cruel and unusual punishment. The amount of time spent in solitary confinement is also much less than it was a decade ago. The use of tranquilizers, such as Thorazine, for disruptive residents has also declined over the past few years. The most widely used means of discipline today are withholding institutional privileges, postponing community activities or visits, placing the youth in isolation for short periods of time, and delaying institutional release.

Prerelease programs are also an important component of institutional life. Some training schools conduct a formal prerelease program, in which residents are transferred to a prerelease program. In most training schools, home visits, off-campus visits, and work release are made available to responsible residents before release.

Private Training Schools

Privately administered training schools are usually better known to the public than are state institutions because private institutions' soliciting of funds has kept them in the public eye. Proponents of private institutions claim that they are more effective than public training schools because they have a limited intake policy, which means they choose whom they want to admit; because they have more professional staff; because they have a better staff-client ratio; because they are smaller; and because they are more flexible and innovative.

Some of these claims are more true than others. While private training schools have the right to limit their intake, the increased interstate commerce of children has resulted in some private schools taking as many children as they can get. In short, some private institutions exploit the inadequate licensing procedures of states to warehouse children as cheaply as possible and thereby to reap higher profits.

It is also true that private training schools are smaller than public ones; yet, one-half still house one hundred or more residents, numbers too large for effective work with institutionalized juveniles. The recent tendency to send status offenders to private institutions may result in private facilities as large as state institutions.

The claim that private training schools are more flexible and innovative than state facilities also appears to be accurate. They do have the advantage over state institutions of being free from political process and bureaucratic inertia. Also, they seem to have more professional and treatment staff: 70 percent of the private institutions employ full-time professionals, as compared to 60 percent of public training schools.

But, the studies of private institutions, such as Howard Polsky's *Cottage Six*, fail to show that private training schools have a higher quality of institutional life than private ones.[31] Overall, it would appear that the best private training schools are better than state facilities, and that the average private training school is possibly a little better than the average state facility, but that the most inhumane training schools in the United States are also private ones.

THE QUALITY OF INMATE LIFE IN A TRAINING SCHOOL

The nature of the inmate social system, the pains of imprisonment, and the ways used to cope with institutional life are important factors in appraising the quality of inmate life in a training school.

The Inmate Social System

The many empirical studies on the inmate social system have consistently challenged the efficacy of juvenile institutionalization. These studies also have found that there are more similarities than differences in inmate life in single-sex and coeducational institutions.

Training Schools for Boys

Studies of training schools for boys, with few exceptions, show an inmate society in which the strong take advantage of the weak. In their study of the State Industrial School for Boys in Golden, Colorado, Gordon H. Barker and W. Thomas Adams found two types of inmate leaders: one held power through brute force, and the other ruled through charisma. According to these researchers, residents were involved in an unending battle for dominance and control.[32]

Howard W. Polsky studied a cottage in a residential treatment center in New York. Supported by the Jewish Board of Guardians and devoted to individual psychoanalytic treatment of emotionally disturbed children, the staff in Cottage Six were unable to keep inmate leaders from exploiting peers. The social hierarchy that developed in this cottage had the following pecking order: leaders, their associates, "conartists," "quiet types," "bushboys," and "scapegoats." The tougher the youth the higher he ranked in the social order. Polsky also found that boys in higher classes in the hierarchy used ranking, scapegoating, aggression, "threat-gestures," and deviant skills and activities to keep lower-class boys in place. Those at the bottom of the status hierarchy found life so debilitating that most of them ended up in mental hospitals.[33]

In an examination of the social structure among residents at the California Youth Authority's training schools, Allen F. Breed identified five levels: (1) "el Presidente"—"duke"; (2) lieutenants, vice presidents—"tough boys"; (3) "straight"—"conformists"; (4) "messups"; and (5) "scapegoats"—"Punks"—"stoneouts." While the names and titles varied among training schools, the creation of a status hierarchy in which the strong dominated the weak was found in every institution.[34] Seymour Rubenfeld and John W. Stafford, in a study of a boy's training school in Washington, D.C., characterized the relationship among residents as a sadomasochistic struggle for privilege, power, and material goods. They discovered three passive homosexual roles—"punk," "sweet boy," and "girl"—each more passive and correspondingly more stigmatized than the one before it.[35]

Sethard Fisher, who studied a small training school in California, identified victimization and patronage as two of the major behaviors taking place. He defined victimization as "a predatory practice whereby inmates of superior strength and knowledge of inmate lore prey on weaker and less knowledgeable inmates."[36] Patronage referred to youths building "protective and ingratiating relationships with other more advantageously situated on the prestige ladder." Fisher also saw victimization as made up of physical attack, agitation, and exploitation, with agitation a form of verbal harassment, and exploitation "a process whereby an inmate will attempt to coerce another by means of threat and duress."[37]

Clemens Bartollas, Stuart J. Miller, and Simon Dinitz's *Juvenile Victimization: The Institutional Paradox* examined the culture that end-of-the-line delinquents established in a maximum-security institution in Columbus, Ohio. In this "jungle"—as residents frequently called the training school—dominant youths exploited submissive ones in every way possible. Ninety percent of the 150 residents were involved in this exploitation matrix: 19 percent were exploiters who were never themselves exploited, 34 percent were exploiters and victims at different times, 21 percent were occasionally victims and never exploiters, 17 percent were chronic victims, and 10 percent were neither victims nor exploiters.[38]

Bartollas et al. draw this conclusion about the lawless environment of this training school:

> *The training school receives the worst of the labelled—the losers, the unwanted, the outsiders. These young men consider themselves to be among the toughest, most masculine and virile of their counterparts and they have the societal credentials to prove it. Yet in much the same way that they themselves are processed, they create, import, and maintain a system which is as brutalizing as the one through which they passed. If anything, the internal environment and the organization and the interaction at TICO are less fair, less just, less humane, and less decent than the worst aspects of the criminal justice system on the outside. Brute force, manipulation, institu-*

tional sophistication carry the day, and set the standards which ultimately prevail. Remove the staff, and a feudal structure will emerge which will make the dark ages seem very enlightened.[39]

Training Schools for Girls and Coeducational Training Schools

Until 1960, studies about the confined juvenile girl were as numerous as those about the incarcerated adult female. The early studies found that girls in training school became involved in varying degrees of lesbian alliances and pseudo-family relationships. In the past twenty years, only two major studies have been done on the female's adjustment to training school: Giallombardo's *The Social World of Imprisoned Girls* and Propper's *Prison Homosexuality: Myth and Reality.*[40]

Rose Giallombardo examined three training schools for girls in various parts of the United States and found that a kinship system existed, with some variation, in each of the training schools. Pseudo-family membership organization was pervasive in all three institutions, whether called the "racket," the "sillies," or "chick business": it embraced 84 percent of the girls at the eastern institution, 83 percent at the central, and 94 percent at the western. Some of the social roles identified were "true butches," "true fems," "trust-to-be butches," "trust-to-be fems," "jive time butches," "jive time fems," "straights," "squealers," "pimps," "foxes," "popcorns," and "cops."[41]

The "parents," the leaders of these families, had considerable authority vested in their role. One resident explained they deferred to the "parents":

> *The mother and the father—they're the ones that have the say. If they say, "Don't go to school," you say you have cramps, a backache, a stomachache, anything, but you don't go.*[42]

Alice Propper's *Prison Homosexuality* examined three coeducational and four girls' training schools scattered through the East, Midwest, and South, of which five were public and two were private Catholic training schools. Residents reported homosexual behavior involving from 6 to 29 percent of the inmates in the various institutions. Propper found that the best indicator of homosexual participation during the present term of institutionalization was previous homosexuality: only 12 percent of those who had been homosexual virgins upon entering the institution admitted engaging in homosexuality, as compared with 71 percent of those with previous homosexual experience. In contrast to previously held assumptions, she found very little overlap between pseudo-family roles and homosexual behavior; participation in homosexuality and make-believe families was just as prevalent in coeducational as in single-sex institutions, and homosexuality was as prevalent in treatment-oriented as in custody-oriented facilities. She also reported that residents sometimes continued homosexual experiences when they were released, even when their first experience was as the unhappy victim of a homosexual rape.[43]

Bartollas and Sierverdes's study of six coeducational institutions in a southeastern state drew the following conclusions: Females adhered more strongly to inmate groups and peer relationships than did males. They felt more victimized by peers than did males, but they did not harass or manipulate staff as much as males did.

They also were more satisfied with institutional life than were males.[44] Pseudo-families existed among girls, but they were based much less on homosexual alliances than were those in all-girls training schools.[45] Status offenders, who made up 70 percent of the girls and 30 percent of the boys, were the worst victims in these training schools and had the most difficulty adjusting to institutional life.[46] White males and females experienced high rates of personal intimidation and victimization by black and American Indian youths.[47] Social roles were anchored by three general coping orientations: (1) dominance and aggressive; (2) manipulative; and (3) passive or submissive. Each of the seven roles had a male and a female counterpart. The male social roles were "bruiser" and "bad dude" (aggressive roles), "cool" and "daddy" (manipulative roles), and "weakling," "punk," and "asskisser" (passive roles). The complementary female roles were "bruiser" and "bitch" (aggressive roles), "lady" and "bulldagger" (manipulative roles), and "child," "girlfriend," and "asskisser" (passive roles).[48]

The Pains of Confinement

Undoubtedly, the greatest pain of confinement for a juvenile is the loss of freedom. As an institutionalized girl in one of the training schools studied by Giallombardo expressed it:

> You miss being free more than anything. . . . What you hate is the doors
> being locked at night. When you hear that key turning, it really does some-
> thing to you. . . . You hate being locked in your room. Everybody hates be-
> ing locked in. You miss your freedom most of all. Being able to take a
> walk—even just a little walk—whenever you feel like it. Some days, I feel
> like I'm going to jump right out of my skin if I can't go off by myself from
> everyone in the cottage, and just think by myself. You miss your freedom.[49]

Confined juveniles generally find the institutional atmosphere oppressive. Residents used to be given standard haircuts, were required to wear state uniforms, had their mail censored, and had to surrender most of their personal possessions; that is, they were stripped of anything providing a sense of security, identity, or independence. Although such procedures are usually things of the past, residents are still subjected to rigid rules and regimented programs. They also must deal with the restriction of physical movements, with a strip search each time they return to the institution, with an occasional search line to determine whether contraband is being moved from one part of the facility to another, and with placement in solitary confinement for unacceptable behavior. Furthermore, a politics of scarcity generally becomes a way of life, and every prized item, such as cigarettes, desired foods, and toilet articles, has a value far out of proportion to its value in the free community.

Most juveniles find institutionalization stressful from the day they arrive to the day they leave. Gaining the acceptance of peers is one of the early stresses of confinement. All newcomers are tested, and it is necessary for them to walk a fine line: to appear strong enough that predatory peers will not exploit them but yet not so strong that inmate leaders will look upon them as a threat to their social positions. Adjusting to a social role represents another stress of confinement. If residents permit themselves to be sexually victimized, they must then deal with the nearly over-whelming degradation of a victim status. But even if youths have the necessary credentials and the desire to earn a highly esteemed role, they must literally claw their way to the top. Dealing with staff presents a further stress. Delinquents soon discover that making a "good presentation of self" to the staff earns the desired institutional privileges, but because they typically have problems with authority figures, it is difficult for them to overcome their resentment of staff control.

Adaptations to Confinement

The most popular mode of adaptation to confinement is making the most of institutional life. Residents try to meet their needs the best way they can and, at the same time, seek to avoid all unpleasant tasks. Another mode of adaptation is to "play it cool," simply "doing time" and giving allegiance to neither staff nor peers. These residents learn to keep their emotions under control and to do whatever is necessary to shorten their institutional stay. A third mode of adaptation is rebellion: these inmates confront staff in every possible way, instigating others to riot against staff, stage a mass protest, or set institutional fires. Withdrawal is a fourth adaptation. Running away is the favored means of withdrawal, but other possibilities include the use of drugs, mental breakdown, and suicide. Adopting prosocial attitudes and using the training school experience to prepare for the future is the least common way to cope with institutional life. Inmates who adopt this mode typically develop close relationships with staff and become deeply involved in a treatment modality, such as transactional analysis.[50]

In summary, there is little good that can be said about the quality of life in most training schools. The "strong shall survive" inmate culture that is found in most training schools for boys creates a lawless society, characterized by intimidation, force, and victimization. Male residents do not feel safe and, indeed, are not safe in these settings. Training schools for girls typically have a pseudo-family, or kinship system, which is controlled by girls who play male roles. Coeducational training schools were looked upon in the 1970s as a much more humane approach to juvenile institutionalization. Although they do appear to have less victimization than single-sex training schools, they still have their kinship systems or pseudo-families in girls' cottages and exploitation matrixes in both boys and girls' living units. Finally, all confined juveniles must deal with the loss of freedom, the oppressiveness of institutional life, and a highly stressful environment. Of the various ways to cope with confinement, it is disturbing that adopting prosocial attitudes and using the present experience to prepare for the future is the least popular adaptation. Equally disturbing is the number of youths who choose to withdraw through running away, drugs, mental breakdown, and suicide.

RIGHTS OF CONFINED JUVENILES

The rights of institutionalized juveniles have received much less attention from federal courts than have the rights of adult prisoners. On one hand, the courts have paid less attention to juvenile institutions because they are assumed to be more humane and to infringe less upon the constitutional rights of offenders than adult prisons. On the other hand, juveniles must depend upon advocacy groups to file writs to federal courts. However, as part of the broader children's rights movement, increased attention has been given to the rights of confined juveniles. The courts have to date mandated two major rights: the right to treatment and the right to be free from cruel and unusual punishment. Institutionalized juveniles also must be granted the rights to refuse treatment, to be free from arbitrary punishment, and to be safe.

Right to Treatment

Several court decisions have held that a juvenile has a right to treatment when he or she is committed to a juvenile institution. The *White* v. *Reid* (1954) decision held that juveniles could not be kept in facilities that did not provide for their rehabilitation.[51] The *Inmates of the Boy's Training School* v. *Affect* (1972) decision also held that juveniles have a right to treatment because rehabilitation is the true purpose of the juvenile court.[52] The Indiana Seventh Circuit's decision in *Nelson* v. *Heyne* agreed with the district court that residents of the Indiana Boys' School have a right to rehabilitative treatment.[53]

In the *Morales* v. *Thurman* decision (1973), the U.S. District Court for the Eastern District of Texas issued the most extensive order ever justified by a child's right to treatment.[54] The court held that a number of criteria had to be followed by the state of Texas in order to assure that proper treatment would be provided to confined juveniles. Included in these criteria were minimum standards for assessing and testing children committed to the state; minimum standards for assessing educational skills and handicaps and for providing programs aimed at advancing a child's education; minimum standards for delivering vocational education and medical and psychiatric care; and minimum standards for providing a humane institutional environment. But the order was vacated on procedural grounds by the Fifth Circuit Appeals Court on the grounds that a three-judge court should have been convened to hear the case. On certiorari to the U.S. Supreme Court, that Court reversed the Court of Appeals and remanded the case. Whether the order of the District Court can withstand the assault against it may affect future considerations of the right to treatment of confined juveniles.[55]

Right to Be Free from Cruel and Unusual Punishment

Considerable case law has also been established assuring confined juveniles of the right to be free from cruel and unusual punishment. The *Pena* v. *New York State Division for Youth* decision held that the use of isolation, hand restraints, and tranquilizing drugs at Goshen Annex Center was punitive and antitherapeutic and, therefore, violated the Fourteenth Amendment right to treatment and the Eighth Amendment right to protection against cruel and unusual punishment.[56] The court in the case of *Inmates of the Boy's Training School* v. *Affect* condemned such practices as solitary confinement and strip-cells, as well as the lack of educational opportunities, and established the following minimum standards for youths confined at the training school:

1. A room equipped with lighting sufficient for an inmate until 10:00 P.M.
2. Sufficient clothing to meet seasonal needs.
3. Bedding, including blankets, sheets, pillows, pillow cases, and mattresses. Such bedding must be changed once a week.
4. Personal hygiene supplies, including soap, toothpaste, towels, toilet paper, and a toothbrush.
5. A change of undergarments and socks every day.
6. Minimum writing materials: pen, pencil, paper, and envelopes.
7. Prescription eyeglasses, if needed.
8. Equal access to all books, periodicals, and other reading materials located in the training school.
9. Daily showers.
10. Daily access to medical facilities, including the provision of a twenty-four-hour nursing service.
11. General correspondence privileges.[57]

Federal courts have also held that extended periods of solitary confinement and the use of Thorazine and other medications for the purpose of control represent cruel and unusual punishment.[58]

Rights That Confined Juveniles Must be Granted

Institutionalized juveniles also should have the right to refuse treatment; that is, treatment programs should be voluntary and have nothing to do with the length of confinement. The state of Washington at present is the only state in which juveniles have the right to refuse counseling and treatment. Residents further should have the right to be free from arbitrary punishment. The California grievance process, which gives wards of the state the right to protest the disciplinary decisions made against them, is the type of formalized procedure that should be made available to juveniles throughout the nation. Federal support has helped New Jersey, Michigan, and Illinois to establish advocates for youths in residential institutions. Delaware, Indiana, and New York are currently in the process of establishing such programs. Furthermore, juveniles must have the right to be safe while they are confined in a correctional institution.

POLICY IMPLICATIONS

There are a number of reasons why short- and long-term juvenile institutions are better today than they were in the past. First, the federal legislation in the Juvenile

Justice and Delinquency Prevention Act caused most states to withdraw status offenders from long-term juvenile facilities, with some states no longer placing status offenders with delinquents in short-term facilities. It was not only unwise correctional policy to confine the runaway and the murderer together, but it was also unjust, because status offenders often ended up staying longer than delinquents. Second, the deinstitutionalization movement in juvenile justice has reduced the number of youths confined to training school and has put pressure on correctional officials to improve juvenile institutions. Third, many institutional officials have contributed to improving short- and long-term juvenile facilities through their in-house reforms; e.g., curtailing the use of physical force and drugs on troublesome inmates, converting single-sex facilities to coeducational ones, and making solitary confinement more humane. Finally, and perhaps most importantly, the intervention of the courts has persuaded policymakers that juvenile facilities within their jurisdictions must live up to minimum standards.

Yet, while it can be argued that long-term juvenile facilities have improved in the past decade, some critics still charge that they should be closed because they are prohibitively expensive, are inhumane, and are schools of crime. The charge that juvenile institutions are prohibitively expensive cannot be denied. Some states spend as much as $35,000 to $50,000 a year to confine a youth in a training school; few states spend less than $1000 a month. Juvenile institutionalization clearly is a luxury that can be afforded only for violent and hard core delinquents.

The accusation that juvenile institutions are still inhumane also has considerable merit. Too many long-term institutions are violent and lawless, and only the strong survive in these predatory jungles. The high levels of stress in most training schools also make them inhumane. From the day they arrive until the day they leave, juveniles are faced with continuous stress. Some are able to cope with this ordeal better than others, but few seem to profit from their institutional stay, and some suffer irreparable harm. Furthermore, the rigidity of institutional rules, the monotony of everyday programming, the unfairness of release procedures, and the negative effects of organizational labeling create an inhumane environment. Finally, too frequently juvenile institutions become garbage dumps for the children of minority groups and the have-nots.[59]

However, the charge that juvenile institutions are schools of crime is open to debate. One position argues that training schools actually deter juveniles from future antisocial behavior. In a study of juveniles arrested in Newark, New Jersey, A. Horwitz and M. Wasserman found that those who had received the least severe dispositions had a higher recidivism rate than those who had been institutionalized.[60] Also, Charles A. Murray and Louis A. Cox, Jr., in evaluating the United Delinquency Intervention Services in Chicago, concluded that the more intense the intervention with chronic offenders, the greater the likelihood that the intervention would suppress postprogram delinquent behavior.[61]

But critics of training schools generally charge that they are schools of crime. This position is undergirded by three assumptions: (1) that the recidivism rates are extremely high; (2) that residents of short- and long-term juvenile facilities expand their repertoires of potential crimes while they are confined; and (3) that residents' experiences in the institution increase their chances of continuing a delinquent career. The first assumption can be supported more easily than the other two. I. J. Goldman found that 51 percent of the youths released from juvenile correctional institutions in New York State were reapprehended by the police within a year of achieving their freedom.[62] Stuart J. Miller also found in a study of 443 consecutive training school releases that the recidivism rate increased with the number of years after discharge; four years after release, the recidivism rate was 54 percent.[63]

A moderate position that training schools vary in terms of their criminogenic impact upon residents appears to be more reasonable than the other two. That is, training schools may do little good, and sometimes greater harm, but both individual factors and organizational variables must be examined before it can be determined whether youths are any more likely to commit crime when they leave than they were when they arrived. Theodore Newcomb's survey of juvenile institutions found that, on the average, residents in smaller institutions, regardless of their precommitment offense levels, tended to have lower postcommitment levels; youths committed to large institutions, no matter what their precommitment offense level, tended to have higher postcommitment levels.[64]

In summary, a more progressive correctional policy requires various strategies: If at all possible delinquents should be kept in their home communities. If detention is necessary, confinement in jails should be avoided at all costs. Instead, juveniles should be placed in detention homes or shelter care facilities, with the population not to exceed thirty and with an adequate number of programs and staff to provide for their needs. If a juvenile has committed a crime so serious that placement in a long-term institution is necessary, the facility should be a small, coeducational institution with well-trained staff, good programming, and a safe environment. Either a determinate sentencing structure should be used or a time management structure should be implemented, so that inmates know early in their stay when they will be released. Participation in treatment programs should be voluntary and have nothing to do with the length of institutional stay. Inmates should be allowed increasing amounts of decision-making responsibility. Following a logical consequences model, rather than using drugging or punitive isolation of troublesome inmates, appears to be a more effective way of handling disciplinary problems in training school. Community resources, both public and private, should be extensively used; as soon as residents can handle it, they should be reintegrated into community programs. Finally, correctional officials of both public and private short- and long-term juvenile correctional institutions should be required to maintain minimum standards for all phases of institutional life.

SUMMARY

This chapter summarizes the history and present status of juvenile institutionalization. Such short-term institutions as jails, detention homes, and shelter care are primarily used to detain juveniles until a disposition is made by the juvenile court. Long-term institutions consist of camps, ranches, farms, reception centers, and training schools. Although the proportion of juveniles who are sent to these long-term facilities is small, these institutions of last resort are an integral part of society's control of law-violating juveniles.

Jails are no place for juveniles, and there is little in the jail that can be beneficial to them. Detention homes and shelters also provide few positive experiences for juveniles. Reception and diagnostic centers usually do a good job of evaluating the problems of residents, but their recommended treatment plans frequently are not implemented when youths are transferred to a camp or training school. Some camps, ranches, and farms provide an open setting and good staff support for offenders, but opponents of these institutions argue that most of these youths could function as well in community programs. Training schools—whether private or public, single-sex or coeducational, old or new, large or small—have more critics than they do supporters. There has been marked improvement in long-term institutions in the past two decades; yet, they still do irreparable damage to some youths, and few youths profit from institutional confinement. Long-term institutionalization is an expensive process, and too many of these facilities are still violent and inhumane.

Today, as has been true since the first houses of refuge were established in the 1820s, both long- and short-term juvenile institutions are among the best examples in juvenile justice of the interrelationships among the historical, legal, sociocultural, economic, and political contexts. The legal context determines who will be sent to training schools and other juvenile institutions, but the juvenile court is influenced in its decision making by what society wants, by the local political pressure placed on juvenile judges, and by the increased cost of training schools. Unquestionably, the hard-core delinquent poses a problem for the juvenile justice system, and, given the present mood of the public, these youths will continue to be confined in long-term institutions. The task now is to design facilities, provide programs, and train staff that will ensure these offenders a humane and, if they choose, a beneficial stay, while they are confined for their socially unacceptable behavior.

Discussion Questions

1. What experiences is a juvenile likely to have in each of the types of correctional institutions?
2. Compare private and state training schools.
3. Evaluate the quality of life in training schools.
4. Evaluate the effectiveness of training schools. What can be done to make training schools more effective?

References

Bartollas, Clemens; Miller, Stuart J.; and Dinitz, Simon. *Juvenile Victimization: The Institutional Paradox.* New York: Halsted Press, 1976.

Bowker, Lee H. *Prisoner Subcultures.* Lexington, Mass.: D.C. Heath & Company, 1977.

Feld, Barry C. *Neutralizing Inmate Violence: The Juvenile Offender in Institutions.* Cambridge: Ballinger Publishing Company, 1977.

Giallombardo, Rose. *The Social World of Imprisoned Girls: A Comparative Study of Institutions for Juvenile Delinquents*. New York: John Wiley & Sons, 1974.

Polsky, Howard W. *Cottage Six: The Social System of Delinquent Boys in Residential Treatment*. New York: Russell Sage Foundation, 1963.

Propper, Alice. *Prison Homosexuality: Myth and Reality*. Lexington, Mass.: D.C. Heath & Company, 1981.

Richette, Lisa Aversa. *The Throwaway Children*. New York: J. B. Lippincott Company, 1969.

Street, David; Vinter, Robert D.; and Perrow, Charles. *Organizations for Treatment: A Comparative Study of Institutions for Delinquents*. New York: Free Press, 1966.

Wooden, Kenneth. *Weeping in the Playtime of Others*. New York: McGraw-Hill Book Company, 1976.

FOOTNOTES

1. Hasting Hart, *Preventive Treatment of Neglected Children* (New York: Charities Publication Committee, 1910), p. 12.

2. Juveniles, especially those charged with violent crimes, may be detained in these "temporary" facilities for several months.

3. David J. Rothman, *The Discovery of the Asylum* (Boston: Little, Brown & Company, 1971), pp. 53–54.

4. Ibid., p. 65.

5. Ibid., pp. 225–227.

6. Sid Ross and Herbert Kupferberg, "Shut Down Reform School?" *Parade* (September 1972), p. 4.

7. U.S. Department of Justice, Law Enforcement Assistance Administration, *National Criminal Justice Information and Statistics Service* (Washington, D.C.: U.S. Government Printing Office, 1982), pp. 129–131.

8. Richard A. McGee, "Our Sick Jails," *Federal Probation* 35 (March 1971), pp. 3–8.

9. Jack Newfield, *Bread and Roses Too: Reporting about America* (New York: Dutton, 1972), p. 333.

10. President's Commission on Law Enforcement and Administration of Justice, *Task Force on Prisoner Rehabilitation* (Washington, D.C.: U.S. Government Printing Office, 1967).

11. *Correctional Trainer* (Newsletter for Illinois Correctional Staff Training, Fall 1970), p. 109.

12. The estimated number of youth confined in jails during a year ranges from 900,000 (Children's Defense Fund) to 100,000 (National Council on Crime and Delinquency). Rosemary Sarri estimates that there are at least 500,000 juveniles jailed each year. See the interview following chapter 17.

13. President's Commission on Law Enforcement and Administration of Justice, *Task Force Report: corrections* (Washington, D.C.: U.S. Government Printing Office, 1967), pp. 124–128.

14. Clemens Bartollas, *Introduction to Corrections* (New York: Harper & Row, 1981), p. 219.

15. Ben Bagdikian, "A Human Wasteland in the Name of Justice," *Washington Post* 30 January 1972, p. A-16.

16. William G. Nagle, "Prison Architecture and Prison Violence," in *Prison Violence,* edited by Albert K. Cohen, George F. Cole, and Robert G. Bailey (Lexington, Mass.: D.C. Heath & Company, 1976), p. 105.

17. Testimony of Arlen Specter, district attorney of Philadelphia, Pennsylvania in hearings before the Subcommittee to Investigate Juvenile Delinquency of the Committee on the Judiciary, U.S. Senate, 91st Cong., 1st Sess., 4695 (1970).

18. John J. Downey, "Why Children Are in Jail and How to Keep Them Out," *Children* 17 (January-February 1970), pp. 3–4.

19. Thomas J. Cottle, *Children in Jail: Seven Lessons in American Justice* (Boston: Beacon Press, 1977), pp. viii–ix.

20. U.S. Department of Justice, *National Criminal Justice Information and Statistics Service* (Washington, D.C.: U.S. Government Printing Office, 1977), p. 17.

21. U.S. Department of Justice, *National Criminal Justice Information and Statistics Service,* (Washington, D.C.: U.S. Government Printing Office, 1977), pp. 18, 20–21.

22. Interviewed in May 1981.

23. Thomas M. Young and Donnell M. Pappenfort, *NEP Phase 1 Summary Report: Secure Detention of Juveniles and Alternatives to Its Use* (Washington, D.C.: U.S. Government Printing Office, 1977), p. 15.

24. Information primarily compiled from residents' newspaper, "What's Happening," n.d.

25. Interviewed in June 1981.

26. Thomas R. Phelps, *Juvenile Delinquency: A Contemporary View* (Pacific Palisades, Calif.: Goodyear Publishing Company, 1976), pp. 221–222.

27. Information contained in the brochure developed by Hennepin County Home School (n.d).

28. Louisa Fraza, "*Corrections Magazine* Survey of Juvenile Inmates," *Corrections Magazine* 4 (September 1978), p. 4.

29. U.S. Department of Justice, *Children in Custody* (Washington, D.C.: U.S. Government Printing Office, 1977), p. 63.

30. David Street, Robert D. Vinter, and Charles Perrow, *Organization for Treatment: A Comparative Study of Institutions* (New York: Free Press, 1966).

31. Howard W. Polsky, *Cottage Six: The Social System of Delinquent Boys in Residential Treatment* (New York: Russell Sage Foundation, 1963).

32. Gordon E. Barker and W. Thomas Adams, "The Social Structure of a Correctional Institution," *Journal of Criminal Law, Criminology and Police Science* 49 (1959), pp. 417–499.

33. Polsky, *Cottage Six,* pp. 69–88.

34. Allen F. Breed, "Inmate Subcultures," *California Youth Authority Quarterly* 16 (Spring 1963), pp. 6–7.

35. Seymour Rubenfeld and John W. Stafford, "An Adolescent Inmate Social System—A Psychological Account," *Psychiatry* 26 (1963), pp. 241–256.

36. Sethard Fisher, "Social Organization in a Correctional Residence," *Pacific Sociological Review* 5 (Fall 1961), p. 89.

37. Ibid., pp. 89–90.

38. Clemens Bartollas, Stuart J. Miller, and Simon Dinitz, *Juvenile Victimization: The Institutional Paradox* (New York: Halsted Press, A Sage Publication, 1976), pp. 131–150.

39. Ibid., p. 271.

40. Rose Giallombardo, *The Social World of Imprisoned Girls: A Comparative Study of Institutions for Juvenile Delinquents* (New York: John Wiley & Sons, 1974); Alice Propper, *Prison Homosexuality: Myth and Reality* (Lexington, Mass.: D.C. Heath & Company, 1981).

41. Giallombardo, *Social World of Imprisoned Girls,* pp. 145–211.

42. Ibid., p. 210.

43. Propper, *Prison Homosexuality.*

44. Christopher M. Sieverdes and Clemens Bartollas, "Institutional Adjustment among Female Delinquents," in *Administrative Issues in Criminal Justice,* edited by Alvin W. Cohn and Ben Ward (Beverly Hills, Calif.: Sage Publications, 1981), pp. 91–103.

45. Ibid.

46. Clemens Bartollas and Christopher M. Sieverdes, "The Victimized White in a Juvenile Correctional System," *Crime and Delinquency* 34 (October 1981), pp. 534–543.

47. Ibid., p. 540.

48. Christopher M. Sieverdes and Clemens Bartollas, "Social Roles, Sex, and Racial Differences," *Deviant Behavior* 3 (1982), pp. 203–218.

49. Giallombardo, *Social World of Imprisoned Girls,* p. 241.

50. Bartollas, Miller, and Dinitz, *Juvenile Victimization,* pp. 173–179.

51. 125 F. Supp. 647 (D.D.C.) 1954.

52. 346 F. Supp. 1354 (D.R.I. 1972).

53. 355 F. Supp. 451 (N.D. Ind. 1973).

54. 364 F. Supp. 166 (E.D. Tex. 1973).

55. Adrienne Volenik, "Right to Treatment: Case Developments in Juvenile Law," *Justice System Journal* 3 (Spring 1978), pp. 303–304.

56. 419 F. Supp. 203 (S.D.N.Y. 1976).

57. 346 F. Supp. 1354 (D.R.I. 1972), p. 1343.

58. See *Lollis* v. *N.Y. State Dept. of Social Services,* 322 F. Supp. 473 (S.D.N.Y. 1970); and *U.S. ex rel. Stewart* v. *Coughlin,* No. C. 1793 (N.D. Ill., November 22, 1971).

59. Lois G. Forer, *No One Will Listen: How Our Legal System Brutalizes the Youthful Poor* (New York: John Day, 1970).

60. A. Horwitz and M. Wasserman, "A Cross-Sectional and Longitudinal Study of the Labeling Perspective" (Paper presented at American Society of Criminology Annual Meeting, Atlanta, Georgia, 1977).

61. Charles A. Murray and Louis A. Cox, Jr., *Beyond Probation: Juvenile Corrections and the Chronic Delinquent* (Beverly Hills, Calif.: Sage Publications, 1979), pp. 51–52.

62. I. J. Goldman, *Arrest and Reinstitutionalization after Release from State Schools and Other Facilities of the New York State Division for Youth: Three Studies of Youths Released January 1971 through March 1973* (Albany: New York State Youth Division, 1974).

63. Stuart J. Miller, "Post-Institutional Adjustment of 443 Consecutive TICO Releases" (Ph.D. diss., Ohio State University, 1971).

64. Theodore Newcomb, "Characteristics of Youths in a Sample of Correctional Programs: Differences Associated with Programs and the Time Spent in Them," *Journal of Research in Crime and Delinquency* 15 (1978), pp. 3–24.

INTERVIEW WITH PEARL WEST

Innovation now in dealing with young people is happening at the local level. It has been spurred by small and generally private persons. . . . To me the heartening thing about it is that some people not in the system are taking responsibility.

In this interview, Pearl West, former director of the California Youth Authority, discusses long-term juvenile institutions, California and its present approach to youthful offenders, and the social policy needed to deal more effectively with youth crime in the United States.

Question: In the early and mid-1970s, juvenile institutions were criticized for being inhumane, violent, and criminogenic, but in the late 1970s and early 1980s, advocates of institutionalization began to urge that institutions were improving. What is your general reaction to where long-term juvenile facilities have been in the past decade and are today?

West: A very broad question! Look inside of the juvenile institutions. The commitments have changed in the course of the last decade. The young people no longer include the very young. They have, therefore, changed patterns of commitment offense. They have also changed in numbers. These factors have all impacted institutions in a variety of ways.

First, it has meant that institutions of juveniles have gotten larger. By definition, that is almost a guarantee that they are going to be less helpful to most young people. Second, the commitment numbers and the lengths of time served both rose

During 1975–1976, Pearl West was a member of the California Youth Paroling Board. From 1976–1981, she was the director of the California Youth Authority. Beginning in 1976, she also has been an adjunct professor of political science at the University of Pacific. She is presently the president of Associates West, a consulting firm on criminal justice issues and public policy and a consultant to the California Senate Judiciary Subcommittee on Corrections and Law Enforcement Agencies.

during this decade you ask about. Now, happily, from my point of view, both are falling again. A decade or so ago, most young people who were locked up were status offenders. But today's populations can be characterized as harder and more volatile. They have committed crimes that are more offensive and more frightening to society. But locking them up for long periods proved counter-productive, apparently raising the old question of whether or not juvenile institutions aren't really just "schools for crime"—with longer sentences producing "better students."

Throughout this decade, it has also been observed that there is an enlarging percentage of ethnic minorities being admitted to institutions. This is particularly true on the coastal areas and in the southern areas of the United States. These populations bring special cultural and language problems with them. One of the things that seems to be constant all the way through, but is gradually increasing today, is that the influence of the peer group is rising. That seems to be true irrespective of whether the young person comes from a poor neighborhood and a family that has had other criminals in it, or whether the young person comes from the middle class or upper class and has not had prior contact with the system. Another of the conundrums that I don't even pretend to understand is that there doesn't seem to be any real differences in the characteristics of those who come from single parent homes as opposed to two parent homes.

In terms of institutionalization in the future, I see three trends that will likely continue. I see the rise and fall of violent acts that the young people are committing with some soft evidence that alcohol and drugs play a critical role. Whatever the causes, society will increasingly institutionalize those who have committed serious offenses. I see the increase in ethnic composition of juvenile institutions. Finally, although I am very much distressed that the original intent of the Juvenile Justice and Delinquent Prevention Act to provide other services for status offenders has somehow been overlooked, I note with a greater sense of relief that status offenders have been released from institutions in large numbers.

Question: When I was working in juvenile institutions in the late 1960s and early 1970s, we always looked to California as the pacesetter of juvenile corrections. Where is California today in terms of juvenile corrections?

West: I agree that California did lead the country for many years and, until recently, was at the forefront of almost every area of juvenile and adult corrections. However, California also leads the country with its infamous proposition 13 and its reduction of property taxes, that has made a real difference in the number of governmental services available to young people. The support dollars simply are not available.

There are some other basic differences that have affected juvenile corrections in California. One is that California's adult system has legislatively abandoned the principle of rehabilitation for adults in the prisons, and that philosophy is pushing against the doors to juvenile institutions. Additional limiting pressures have come with determinate sentencing for adults. Proposals for the full array of civil rights, including jury, and bail for young people are being toyed with elsewhere. While none of these seem to have happened yet in California, nevertheless, there were bills that are attempting to establish these things in California in the current legislature (1984). This would have been unheard of a few years ago. Furthermore, as the population of institutions has increased at both the county and the state levels, there has been ever less money, less flexibility, and more bodies to contend with. This has meant that there has been virtually no experimentation in terms of new programs. What we now call research in California basically is counting the heads—where do they come from, what do they do, and where are they going? This, as you know, is a far cry from

the research California has done in the past. It is simply trying to keep track of the population traffic. I regret that very much because we need to do a great deal more of research before we can begin to do the kind of creative planning programming young people need. Nobody can be locked up, abandoned, and then be expected to return to normal society and to perform in constructive ways. I wish I could say that California is still leading the country, but, as far as I can tell now, I think we are leaning toward the very repressive, and several midwest states are currently in the lead.

Question: You have been very much involved in the policy arena for young people for a number of years. What is the state of the art today in terms of juvenile justice policy?

West: I wish I could say I absolutely knew. Let me ruminate a bit and share with you what I am aware of. Innovation now in dealing with young people is happening at the local level. It has been spurred by small and generally private individuals or groups. But where it occurs, there has unfortunately been even poorer record keeping than in the publicly supported efforts, which has required at least a track record, if not a research design. For lack of that information, it is hard to evaluate whether we are seeing anything more than desperate attempts at filling the breach. The one heartening thing about it is that some people not in the system are taking responsibility. An effective aspect seems to stem from the fact that they are small programs. The one thing that happens in public institutions in California is that there is a tendency to put a bed in every corner before anything new is tried. This is a redundant and non-creative approach that is not helpful to young people. This inhibits and prohibits the normal life experiences. I consider this approach antithetical to progress.

There is a push at the national level, as well as at the state level, for smaller programs. But policymakers are not receptive because they are still running on tight budgets. Indeed, there is still much breast-beating about who's going to have the lowest budget. The translation of that into human services always means that those people who have no representation—the nonconspicuous, the non-visible, non-constituent groups—will get hit the hardest. I am greatly disturbed about our tendency to make decisions exclusively on the basis of cost. The cheapest is often not the best when you are buying our future.

To be entirely candid, at least in California, there is enough concern about young people still that there is more money per capita going into the Youth Authority than there is to the Dept. of Corrections for adults. It's not adequate, but at least it is a recognition that, regardless of immediate political necessity, the future must be invested in, and one must believe that young people can change and are worthy of the investment.

But overall it is not a pretty picture. I wish it were very, very different. The private attempts are hopeful, but some of the private networks are falling apart. Standards and oversight are often lacking. We particularly need services to runaway populations. We now know, with some certainty, that these young people are characterized by high levels of physical abuse and frequently come from incestuous families. Services to this group are virtually nonexistent except for spotty small-type efforts. Young people are not running away from the world; they are running away from their families. They run to and live with their peer culture because the peer group will help to show them that they are worthy human beings. These small efforts that now take place are grossly inadequate for providing for their nurturing needs. That they succeed at all is a testimonial to the possibility of overcoming impossible odds.

PRIMARY AND SECONDARY PREVENTION, TREATMENT, AND THE SUMMARY

CHAPTER 19

PREVENTION OF DELINQUENCY

CHAPTER OUTLINE

In the last analysis, the most promising and so the most important method of dealing with crime is by preventing it—by ameliorating the conditions of life that drive people to commit crime and that undermine the restraining rules and institutions erected by society against antisocial conduct.[1]

This statement, which is taken from the 1967 *Task Force Report on Juvenile Delinquency and Youth Crime,* emphasizes the importance of prevention as a policy direction for the justice system. Subsequently, this emphasis on prevention was written into federal law in the Juvenile Delinquency Prevention Act of 1972, the Juvenile Justice and Delinquency Prevention Act of 1974, and the Juvenile Justice Amendments of 1977.[2]

Three different levels of delinquency prevention have been identified. *Primary prevention* is focused on modifying conditions in the physical and social environment that lead to delinquency. *Secondary prevention* refers to intervention in the lives of juveniles or groups identified as in circumstances disposing toward delinquency. *Tertiary prevention* is directed at the prevention of recidivism.[3]

Primary prevention and secondary prevention, or diversion, are seen as much more likely to have positive results than tertiary prevention, or control of delinquency, because interventions by the justice system often result in the behavior of juveniles getting worse rather than better. Or to express it another way, the juvenile justice system is often accused of creating more crime than it cures.

The first part of this chapter discusses primary prevention, while the second part examines secondary prevention. The chapter concludes with the policies that are necessary to improve interventions aimed at preventing delinquency in the United States.

PRIMARY PREVENTION

Following a historical review of delinquency prevention, a typology of prevention interventions and the models of delinquency prevention are discussed in this section.

History of Delinquency Prevention

The highway of delinquency prevention is paved with punctured panaceas.[4] A member of the Subcommittee on Human Resources of the Committee on Education and Labor put it this way:

> *The public is looking for an inexpensive panacea. . . . These periodic panaceas for delinquents come along every 2 to 3 years in my experience. The harm they do is they divert the attention of the public from any long-term comprehensive program of helping youth, working to strengthen school*

systems, communities, job opportunities, housing and recreational pro-grams.[5]

One reason for society's seeking of panaceas stems from the tendency to seek easy answers to complex problems.[6] Another reason is the frustration and sense of futility in a continuous, losing battle with juvenile crime that makes policymakers eager to discover a solution. Another reason for the receptivity toward panaceas is found in the belief society has in prevention (i.e., "An ounce of prevention is worth a pound of cure").

The panaceas, which will be described in the next section, have ranged from biological and psychological interventions to group therapy, gang intervention, recreational activities, job training and employment, community organization, and even to structured reorganization of the entire society. A model of delinquency prevention popular in the late 1970s was based on scaring delinquents or suspected delinquents straight. "Scared straight," a label derived from the title of an award-winning documentary film about the Juvenile Awareness Project as the New Jersey's Rahway State Prison, refers to programs whereby inmates used the realities of prison life to frighten the wits and, consequently, crime out of teenagers. This panacea, as had many others before it, met with initial enthusiasm and then was submerged under criticism from all sides.[7]

In the 1970s, several studies examined the effectiveness of delinquency prevention programs. Michael C. Dixon and William W. Wright concluded from their examination of these programs that "there is a relative paucity of research of evaluative information available in the field of juvenile delinquency prevention."[8] Even when adequate evaluation is performed, these researchers added, "few studies show significant results."[9] Dixon and Wright also emphasized that several types of programs, such as individual and group counseling, social casework, detached street gang workers, and recreational programs, have not consistently been shown to reduce or prevent delinquency.[10]

Richard J. Lundman, Paul T. McFarlane, and Frank Scarpitti drew the same pessimistic conclusion: "it appears unlikely that any of these [delinquency prevention] projects prevented delinquent behavior."[11] In concluding that little or nothing of what they had looked at seemed to work, they noted that one of the possible explanations for the failures they found was the poorly conceptualized or incomplete theories supportng the prevention efforts. In short, the projects typically failed to establish any clear link between what was causing the delinquency and how they were trying to prevent it.[12]

Lundman and Scarpitti collaborated on a later study of delinquency prevention and, adding fifteen projects to the twenty-five previously studied, concluded: "A review of forty past or continuing attempts at the prevention of juvenile delinquency leads to the nearly inescapable conclusion that none of these projects has successfully prevented delinquency."[13] These researchers even went on to say that "researchers should expect future projects to be unsuccessful," because, given the poor history of past attempts at delinquency prevention, there is little reason to expect any greater success with any efforts.[14]

A Typology of Cause-Focused Strategies of Delinquency Prevention

The National Juvenile Justice Assessment Centers have developed a typology for conceptualizing and organizing approaches to delinquency prevention according to the causes of delinquency they address. They also include within this typology a framework for systematically planning and evaluating delinquency prevention efforts.[15] This typology promises to provide a solid basis for developing an effective technology of delinquency prevention. The twelve strategies of this typology are listed in Box 19-1 and are based upon a presumed cause of delinquent behavior.

BOX 19-1 Strategies of Delinquency Prevention

A. Biological/psychological strategies assume that delinquent behavior derives from underlying physiological, biological, or biopsychiatric conditions. These strategies seek to remove, diminish, or control these conditions.

B. Psychological/mental health strategies assume that delinquency originates in internal psychological states viewed as inherently maladaptive or pathological. They seek to directly alter such states and/or environmental conditions thought to generate them.

C. Social network development strategies assume that delinquency results from weak attachments between youth and conforming members of society. They seek to increase interaction, attachments, and/or involvement between youth and nondeviant others (peers, parents, other adults) as well as the influence which nondeviant others have on potentially delinquent youth.

D. Criminal influence reduction strategies assume that delinquency stems from the influence of others who directly or indirectly encourage youth to commit delinquent acts. They seek to reduce the influence of norms toward delinquency and those who hold such norms.

E. Power enhancement strategies assume that delinquency stems from a lack of power or control over impinging environmental factors. They seek to increase the ability or power of youth to influence or control their environments either directly or indirectly (by increasing the power or influence over communities and institutions in which youth participate). (Efforts to increase community or institutional influence or power over youth are *not* power enhancement.)

F. Role development/role enhancement strategies assume that delinquency stems from a lack of opportunity to be involved in legitimate roles or activities which youth perceive as personally gratifying. They attempt to create such opportunities. To meet the conditions of role development, roles developed or provided must be perceived by youth as worthwhile (i.e., sufficiently valuable or important to justify expenditure of time and effort).

G. Activities/recreation strategies assume that delinquency results when youths' time is not filled by nondelinquent activities. They seek to provide nondelinquent activities as alternatives to delinquent activities.

H. Education/skill development strategies assume that delinquency stems from a lack of knowledge or skills necessary to live in society without violating its laws. Education strategies provide youth with personal skills which prepare them to find patterns of behavior free from delinquent activities, or provide skills or assistance to others to enable them to help youth develop requisite skills.

I. Clear and consistent social expectations strategies assume that delinquency results from competing or conflicting demands and expectations placed on youth by legitimate organizations and institutions such as media, families, schools, and communities which impinge on the lives of youth. Inconsistent expectations or norms place youth in situations where conformity to a given set of norms or expectations results in an infraction of another set of norms or expectations.

J. Economic resource strategies assume that delinquency results when people do not have adequate economic resources. They seek to provide basic resources to preclude the need for delinquency.

K. Deterrence strategies assume that delinquency results because there is a low degree of risk or difficulty associated with committing delinquent acts. They seek to change the cost-benefit ratio of participation in crime. They seek to increase the cost and decrease the benefit of criminal acts through restructuring opportunities and minimizing incentives to engage in crime.

L. Abandonment of legal control/social tolerance strategies assume that delinquency results from social responses which create youths' behaviors as delinquent. . . . such responses—whether in the general form of rules or in the more specific form of an instance of legal processing—may cause youths whose behaviors are so treated to perceive themselves as "outsiders" and, consequently, to engage in delinquent acts.

Source: J. David Hawkins et al., *Reports of the National Juvenile Justice Assessment Centers: A Typology of Cause-Focused Strategies of Delinquency Prevention* (Washington, D.C.: U.S. Government Printing Office, 1980), pp. vii–ix. Reprinted by permission.

Each of these twelve strategies is based on an assumption regarding the cause of delinquency and aims at modifying or eliminating that cause.[16] Because the strategies are ideal types, prevention programs may utilize combinations of several of these strategies, or in some cases may not address any presumed causes of delinquency.[17] See Figure 19-1 for the development scheme of the presumed cause of delinquency, the strategy for dealing with the cause, and the goal of this strategy.

Models of Delinquency Prevention

The Cambridge-Somerville Youth Study in Massachusetts; the New York City Youth Board; Mobilization for Youth in New York City; detached gang workers; Walter C. Reckless and Simon Dinitz's self-concept studies in Columbus, Ohio; the Chicago Area Projects; La Playa de Ponce in Puerto, Rico; mediation with youth gangs; Jobs

FIGURE 19-1 Causes of Delinquency and Associated Strategies of Delinquency Prevention

Presumed Cause	Strategy	Goal of Strategy
Physical abnormality/illness	Biological-physiological -Health Promotion -Nutrition -Neurological -Genetic	Remove, diminish, control underlying physiological, biological or bio-psychiatric conditions
Psychological disturbance disorder	Psychological/Mental Health -Epidemiological/early intervention -Psychotherapeutic -Behavioral	Alter internal psychological states or conditions generating them
Weak attachments to others	Social Network Development -Linkage -Influence	Increase interaction/involvement between youth and nondeviant others; increase influence of nondeviant others on potentially delinquent youth
Criminal influence	Criminal influence reduction -Disengagement from criminal influence -Redirection away from criminal norms	Reduce the influence of delinquent norms and persons who directly or indirectly encourage youth to commit delinquent acts
Powerlesness	Power-enhancement -Informal influence -Formal power	Increase ability or power of youth to influence or control their environments, directly or indirectly
Lack of useful worthwhile roles	Role development/role enhancement -Service roles -Production roles -Student roles	Create opportunities for youth to be involved in legitimate roles or activities which youth perceive as useful, successful, competent
Unoccupied time	Activities/recreation	Involve youth in nondelinquent activities
Inadequate skills	Education/skill development -Cognitive -Affective -Moral -Informational	Provide individuals with personal skills which prepare them to find patterns of behavior free from delinquent activities
Conflicting environmental demands	Clear and consistent social expectations	Increase consistency of expectations/messages from institutions, organizations, groups which affect youth
Economic necessity	Economic resources Resource maintenance -Resource attainment	Provide basic resources to preclude the need for delinquency
Low degree of risk/difficulty	Deterrence Target hardening/removal -Anticipatory intervention	Increase cost, decrease benefits of criminal acts

FIGURE 19-1 (*continued*)

Presumed Cause	Strategy	Goal of Strategy
Exclusionary social responses	Abandonment of legal control/ social tolerance -Explicit jurisdictional abandonment Implicit jurisdictional abandonment -Covert jurisdictional abandonment -Environmental tolerance	Remove certain behaviors from control of the juvenile justice system; decrease the degree to which youths' behaviors are perceived, labeled, treated as delinquent

Source: J. David Hawkins et al., *Reports of the National Juvenile Justice Assessment Centers: A Typology of Cause-Focused Strategies of Delinquency Prevention* (Washington, D.C.: U.S. Government Printing Office, 1960), p. 13. Reprinted by permission.

for Youth in Boston and Cambridge; and alternative schools are the most widely hailed models of delinquency prevention. In this section each model will be described and then will be evaluated according to the typology presented above.

Cambridge-Somerville Youth Study

This individual approach to delinquency prevention presumed that psychological disturbances lead to delinquent behavior and, therefore, it focused on efforts made through a counseling relationship to alter the psychological states of respondents, as well as their ability to function in school and at home.

The project began in 1935 when 325 eleven-year-old boys were nominated by their teachers, police, welfare agencies, or churches as either "difficult" or "average" children, and each was assigned a counselor who acted as academic tutor, social worker, or counselor as the situation required. Another group of 325 boys was matched as to personality and family situation but given no treatment other than that usually provided by the community as part of the growing-up process. The examination after the conclusion of the project in five years indicated that the counseling had had little positive effect on the treatment group. For example, about equal numbers of treatment and control boys were committed to juvenile institutions.[18]

However, when the boys reached young adulthood, almost twice as many control boys were sentenced to correctional institutions. The follow-up examination further revealed that those who had been seen weekly by their counselors had fewer convictions than those seen less frequently and that female counselors had been more effective than male counselors.[19] In summary, although the model had mainly discouraging results, the claim can still be made that it may have had some long-range positive effects upon participants.

New York City Youth Board

This study also presumed that psychological disturbances lead to delinquent behavior and provided psychiatric and social worker services to identified predelinquents.

The study was conducted in 1952 to 1953, when researchers used the Glueck Prediction Table to examine 223 boys in the New York City school system. Twenty-one were identified as predelinquents, but initial examination at the conclusion of the study revealed that the services had had little positive effect. But because the tretment group of predelinquents was less criminal than the control group after ten years, it was concluded that the psychiatric and social work services may have had some long-term positive effects upon participants.[20] Still, the results of this study also were acknowledged as disappointing.

Mobilization for Youth Project

This project built upon Cloward and Ohlin's "delinquency and opportunity" theory sought to reduce the gap between the social and economic aspirations of youth and their opportunities to achieve these goals through legitimate means. The program took place in the 1960s in a 67-block area of New York City and included many blacks and Puerto Ricans in its population. The goals of the project were to improve the opportunities of area youth in work and education, to make services available to individuals and families, and to provide assistance in community organization.[21]

Employment services included a subsidized work, vocational guidance, and job-training program for all unemployed, out-of-school youth between sixteen and twenty-one in the target area. The educational aspects of the program included increasing parent-school contacts, developing curriculum and methods consistent with the needs of these youth, and providing high school tutors for students who needed them. Neighborhood service centers were designed to provide assistance with paperwork in applying for Social Security or welfare benefits and to furnish babysitting, family counseling, and classes in homemaking skills. The Mobilization for Youth Project also provided recreational activities for youth in the area, a detached worker program in which workers were sent into the street to work with alienated youth, and various programs to help residents of the target area fight for improved living and housing conditions.[22]

Unfortunately, this project encountered continuous resistance from one of the city's largest newspapers, as well as from governmental units and public officials. Although millions of dollars were spent on this multidimensional delinquency prevention effort, it was judged only a partial success.

Detached Gang Workers Projects

These projects were based on the strategies that assume that delinquency stems from the influence of peers and from weak attachments between youths and conforming members of society. Such projects were widely used in Boston, New York, Chicago, and Los Angeles during the 1950s and early 1960s, and trained workers (usually social workers) were thought capable of providing positive role models to delinquent-prone youths and persuading members of youth gangs to pursue prosocial behavior.

Irving Spergel listed the following goals of street work with gangs:

1. Control (principally of gang fighting).
2. Treatment of individual problems.

3. Providing access to opportunities.

4. Value change.

5. Prevention of delinquency.[23]

However, intervention by the community in terms of detached gang workers often served only to magnify the delinquency problem, increase its seriousness, and reinforce the symptoms.[24] That is, detached gang workers sometimes went into an area in which a group of boys were loosely associated with what has been called a "near group" and succeeded only in developing this group into a cohesive gang.[25] Not surprisingly, participants in the gang then became involved in higher rates of delinquency than before the arrival of the detached worker.

Self-Concept and the Prevention of Delinquency

Walter C. Reckless and Simon Dinitz, as discussed in Chapter 7, used role development and educational strategies in an attempt to improve the self-concept of students who were veering toward delinquency. These investigators concluded that the major difference between the so-called "good" boys and the so-called "bad" boys is that the good boys have a better self-concept than the bad boys.

In the late 1950s and early 1960s, the Columbus school system permitted Reckless and Dinitz to set up pilot projects in elementary schools in high-delinquency areas. The basic purpose of these pilot projects was to improve the self-concept of male students who had been identified as delinquency-prone. At first involving only sixth-graders for the last hour of the school day, the project eventually expanded to include seventh-graders of eight junior high schools for one school year. The guiding principles of the program were to provide boys more appropriate role models and to present participants with appropriate insights into life situations, so that they would be able to improve their self-concepts.[26]

In all, 1726 boys were examined at four consecutive yearly periods—at the end of the seventh, eighth, ninth, and tenth grades. But the researchers found that in none of the outcome variables were the experimental subjects significantly different from the controls. This was especially evident in the school-performance and police-contact data.[27] Reckless and Dinitz concluded that perhaps the most important reason for failure of the program was that the exposure to role-model internalization was not intensive enough; that is, it did not reach the boys' inner selves.[28]

Chicago Area Projects

In 1934, Clifford Shaw and Henry McKay founded the Chicago Area Projects in order to help communities deal with social problems on the local level.[29] This delinquency prevention project was based theoretically on such strategies as social network, criminal influence reduction, power enhancement, role development, and activities/recreation.

The first projects were set up in three areas: South Chicago, the Near West Side, and the Near North Side. Shaw and his colleagues had lost confidence in official agencies' ability to deal adequately with the needs of youth and, therefore, they recruited local leaders to intervene with neighborhood youth.[30] The organizers of the Area Projects believed that instead of throwing youths so quickly to the justice system, the community should intervene on the behalf of youth. In the fifty-year existence of the Area Projects, community citizens have intervened by showing up in juvenile court to speak on behalf of youth in trouble and by organizing social and recreational programs so that youths have constructive activities in which to participate. They also have given special attention to local youths who are having difficulties at home or school or with the law.

The Area Projects have served as an exemplary model of what grass-roots organizations in the community can achieve in preventing juvenile delinquency. However, there is some evidence that the Area Projects have been ineffective in coping with delinquency in its most serious forms in the areas of the city with the highest rates.[31]

La Playa de Ponce

Delinquency prevention, based on similar strategies as the Chicago Area Projects, has been one of the major goals of this community redevelopment project in the port section of Ponce, Puerto Rico. Since 1968, Isolina Ferre, a Sister of the Order of Missionary Servants of the Blessed Trinity, has worked to unite citizens in self-directed efforts against La Playa's social problems, including juvenile delinquency.[32] Sister Isolina noted, "Our aim is to prevent juvenile delinquency by helping the community provide self-help opportunities for their neighborhood youths."[33] She added:

> We have thirty-five ongoing programs. We began little; we began going to the courts, taking care of the youth affected by the courts. In 1969, for example, there were seventy juvenile delinquents found guilty by the courts. This year we only had eight cases in juvenile court. What has happened to the rest? We divert them.
>
> We go to the police station and pick them up there. The community brings them to us. We have all kinds of programs to involve them so they're not arrested and brought before the juvenile courts. These eight juvenile cases were given back to us, not sent to institutions. It is very seldom we cannot take care of a kid.[34]

Programs include vocational workshops to prepare youths for jobs in industry, formal tutoring in academic subjects, and many social and recreational activities.[35] But in addition to providing programs for youths and the advocacy provided by adults, this organization has been successful in involving youths in the affairs of the community. Youths are accepted as valued members of the community and are expected to play important functions in the development of community life and activities.[36]

The Playa de Ponce delinquency prevention project has not received outside evaluation, but it appears to be an exemplary model of grass-roots community groups dealing effectively with youth crime.

Mediation with Youth Gangs

The previously mentioned House of Umoja (Philadelphia), the Youth-in-Action (Chester, Pennsylvania), El Control del Pueblo (New York City), the Inner City

Roundtable of Youth (New York City), the Youth Identity Program, Inc. (New York City), the South Arsenal Neighborhood Development Corporation (Hartford, Connecticut), and SEY Yes, Inc. (Los Angeles) are community projects that mediate with youth gangs. These programs have defused to a certain extent the violence of youth gangs within these urban communities and have involved gang members in more constructive activities.[37]

The success of these grass-roots community groups in involving youth gangs in constructive activities owes much to the charismatic leadership of these programs. Although these programs show the potential of grass-roots groups in dealing with the prevention and control of serious youth crime, the future of such groups depends upon their gaining the support of city and state political leaders and of local bureaucratic structures.

Jobs for Youth

This program, using the strategies of role development, education, and economic resources, serves economically disadvantaged high school dropouts (ages sixteen to twenty-one) in the cities of Boston and Cambridge. Nine hundred and fifty youths (60 percent male) are involved annually. The program assists youths with little or no work experience to prepare for employment, find jobs, and succeed in work situations.[38]

Evaluations of this program indicate that only half of those who gain employment stay at the job for more than a month. This may be the consequence of inadequate job readiness, but it also may result from the fact that the jobs provided are menial and offer low starting salaries. Although the program's effectiveness in preventing delinquency is unknown, evaluations of other such youth employment programs have not shown positive delinquency prevention results.[39]

Alternative Schools and Other School Delinquency Prevention Programs

Programs that bring students into the decision making process, programs that link the school more effectively with the community, drug education programs, therapeutic intervention with difficult students, and alternative schools for disruptive students are the main types of delinquency prevention programs used in the public school system.[40]

Alternative schools are the most widely used and the most promising of these programs. They incorporate such strategies as role development/role enhancement, education/skill development, and activities/recreation in their work with disruptive students. Alternative schools often are able to handle pupils who have been disruptive in the public school setting because they have smaller classes and individualized instruction, a low student-adult ratio, competent teachers, and a goal-oriented classroom environment focused on work and learning. Alternative schools also usually deal more appropriately with both positive and negative behavior in the classroom.

More empirical examination is necessary to demine the actual effects of alternative schools on delinquency prevention, but there is some evidence that they tend to reduce absenteeism and dropout rates, that they provide a more positive educational experience for students, and of course that they relieve the public schools of the disruptive behavior these youths display in regular classrooms. Yet, the overall impact of these programs has been reduced because of the increasingly difficult students referred to them and because of declining federal funding.

Evaluation of Delinquency Prevention Programs

Grass-roots groups in the community, such as the Chicago Area Projects, La Playa de Ponce, and mediation groups with youth gangs, represent the most effective means of preventing and controlling juvenile delinquency. But it must be remembered that these few successes are still greatly outnumbered by those delinquency prevention programs that have had little impact in curbing delinquency in their areas. (See Figure 19-2 for a comparison of the programs discussed in this section.) Recommendations for improving the effectiveness of delinquency prevention programs will be offered in the policy section of this chapter.

SECONDARY PREVENTION, OR DIVERSION

The emphasis on diversionary programs began only in 1967 when the President's Commission on Law Enforcement and Administration of Justice recommended the establishment of alternatives to the juvenile justice system:

> The formal sanctioning system and pronouncement of delinquency should be used only as a last resort.
>
> In place of the formal system, dispositional alternatives to adjudication must be developed for dealing with juveniles, including agencies to provide and coordinate services and procedures to achieve necessary control without unnecessary stigma. Alternatives already available, such as those related to court intake, should be more fully explored.
>
> The range of conduct for which court intervention is authorized should be narrowed, with greater emphasis upon consensual and informal means of meeting the problem of difficult children.[41]

Theoretical Rationales for Diversion

Theoretically, this recommendation was based on the labeling perspective and Sutherland's differential association theory. First, as discussed earlier, labeling theorists argue that adolescents tagged as delinquents by social control agencies are likely to live up to their labels. Society's reaction is critical, as Edwin Lemert contended, in determining whether juvenile lawbreaking remains situational or develops into a consistent pattern of delinquent behavior.[42] The National Strategy for Youth Development and Delinquency Prevention tied labeling theory to diversion in identifying three processes that block juveniles from satisfactory maturation and weaken their ties to societal norms: the entrapment of negative labeling; the limited access of acceptable social norms; and the resulting process of rejection, alienation, and estrangement.[43] (See Figure 19-3 for a diagram of this theoretical scheme.)

Second, Sutherland's differential association theory provided another justification for diversion as it holds that individuals learn delinquent behavior from "significant others." Policymakers began to be concerned about placing status offenders and minor offenders in with hard-core delinquents because they feared that status offenders and minor offenders would learn delinquent motives, techniques, and rationalizations from such offenders.[44]

Early proponents of diversionary programs also claimed that these interventions offered a number of other advantages that would lead to a more effective and humane justice process; these included the reduction of case loads, the more efficient administration of the juvenile justice system, the freeing of the juvenile court to handle the more difficult cases, the development of an advocate role apart from the formal justice system, and the provision of therapeutic environments in which children and parents could resolve family conflicts.[45]

Undergirded by these rationales and advocated by the President's Crime Commission, diversionary programs required only a funding base in order to be put into operation as a viable alternative to formal processing in the juvenile justice system. The first stages of funding were passed by Congress in the Omnibus Crime Control and Safe Streets Act of 1968 and the Juvenile Delinquency Prevention and Control Act of 1968. In 1970, Congress amended the Safe Streets Act, requiring that a portion of the funds received under the LEAA block grant program be allocated to juvenile and adult community-based corrections program. The Juvenile Delinquency Act of 1972 focused on creating new and maintaining old diversionary programs in the community, and the Juvenile Justice and Delinquency Prevention Act of 1974 continued funding diversionary programs.

Diversionary Programs

Diversion can come either from the police and the courts or from agencies outside the juvenile justice system. With diversion initiated by the courts or police, the justice subsystems retain control over youthful offenders. But even with diversion outside the formal jurisdiction of the justice system, youthful offenders are usually referred back to the juvenile court if they do not participate in these programs.

The Police

The police officer frequently warns and releases juveniles without formal processing, and police discretion may account for as much as 90 percent of all diversion. Formal police diversionary programs multiplied rapidly in the 1970s; California alone has more than 150 police diversionary programs. Police programs include predelinquent intervention as well as diversion of actual offenders.

Community predelinquent programs include courses in high school, junior high, and elementary school settings about school safety, community relations, drug and alcohol abuse, city government, court procedures, bicycle safety, and juvenile delinquency. The Officer Friendly Program, which as been established throughout the nation, is used to develop better relations with younger children. The Police Depart-

FIGURE 19-2 Prevention Program Matrix

Prevention Program	System of Intervention	Prevention Level	Prevention Strategies	Level of Intervention	Program Effectiveness	Program Location	Catchment
Cambridge-Somerville	Community, school	Primary	Psychological, education	Individual	No short-term effects	Urban	Whole area
New York City Police Board	School	Primary	Psychological	Individual	No effect	Urban	Whole city
Mobilization for Youth Program	Community	Primary	Social network, criminal influence reduction, power enhancement, role development, activities/recreation, education, economic resource	Individual, community, gangs	Incomplete information	Urban	Local, neighborhood
Detached gang workers	Community	Primary, secondary	Social network, criminal influence reduction, role development, activities/recreation	Individual	No effect	Urban	Local, neighborhood
Self-concept and delinquency prevention	School	Primary	Education Role Development	Individual	No effect	Urban	Residential

Chicago Area Projects	Community	Primary, secondary	Social network, criminal influence reduction, power enhancement, role development, activities/recreation	Individual	Incomplete	Urban	Community
Jobs for Youth	Work	Primary	Role development, education, economic resources	Individual	Not evaluated	Urban	Greater metropolitan area
Mediation with gangs	Community	Primary, secondary	Social network, criminal influence reduction, role development, power enhancement	Individual group	Incomplete information	Urban	Whole city
La Playa de Ponce	Community	Primary, secondary	Social network, criminal influence reduction, power enhancement, role development, activities/recreation	Individual	Incomplete information	Urban	Community
Alternative schools	School, classroom	Primary	Role development, role enhancement, education/skill development	Individual	Incomplete information	Urban	School

Source: John S. Wall et al., *Reports of the National Juvenile Justice Assessment Centers Juvenile Delinquency Prevention: A Compendium of 36 Program Models* (Washington, D.C.: U.S. Government Printing Office, 1981), pp. 7–16.

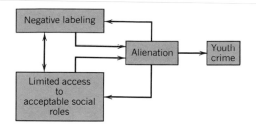

Figure 19-3

Source: Adapted by permission from *Phase I Assessment of Youth Service Bureaus, Summary Report of Youth Service Bureau Research Group for LEAA* (Boston: Boston University, 1975), p. 17–18.

ment of St. Petersburg, Florida, hired a ventriloquist with a dummy in the 1970s to represent the police department. The Kentucky State Police set up an island camp for the purpose of working with predelinquent and underprivileged boys aged ten to fourteen years. Other predelinquent programs existing across the nation include the ride-along program and the Law Enforcement Explorer Posts, jointly sponsored by the Boy Scouts of America and police departments.[46]

The police refer many juveniles to such social agencies as youth service bureaus, mental health clinics, child welfare departments, the Big Brother and Big Sister associations, YMCA and YWCA, boys' clubs, religious groups, and recreational groups. A number of police departments have established police youth service bureaus, which offer youthful offenders counseling on drug and alcohol abuse and on family problems, tutoring, and job assistance.[47]

The Juvenile Court and Probation

Informal probation appears to be the means of diversion most widely used by the juvenile court. Although juveniles may be kept out of formal proceedings of the juvenile court by informal probation, there is still reason to believe that the rights of youths are frequently violated through this informal procedure.

The juvenile judge may choose to divert a juvenile to a crisis intervention program or to a long-term counseling and treatment program. For example, the 601 Project of the Sacramento Probation Department provides short-term family crisis counseling instead of court processing for status offenders and for those charged with offenses involving petty theft, possession of drugs, drunk and disorderly conduct, and receiving stolen property.[48]

The court also may divert juveniles to shoplifters' programs, drug and alcohol abuse clinics, and alternative school programs. The Santa Clara County Juvenile Probation Department has a program for drug abusers. Among the different treatment technologies used are educational and counseling programs, transactional analysis (TA), and psychodrama. Parents frequently must attend these clinics with their children, and the failure of a youth to participate in the program usually means his or her return to the juvenile court.

Diversion outside the Juvenile Justice System

Youthful offenders also may be diverted to drop-in centers, alternative schools, social and mental health agencies, and youth service bureaus. Assistance was given to states, localities, and nonprofit private agencies by the Runaway and Homeless Youth Act, Title III of the 1974 Juvenile Justice and Delinquency Prevention Act, in order to create temporary shelters for runaway youths. Now such centers exist throughout the United States. One New York City center includes three temporary care shelters, where thirty homeless youths can stay from three to eight months; two "crash pads," where nineteen youths can stay up to three weeks; and a reentry program, called Last Stop, where fourteen youngsters can prepare for as long as a year for independent living.[49]

In some of the larger programs for runaways, youths may be involved in such activities as drug abuse counseling, job preparation, prenatal counseling, and even dance or theater workshops. Runaway programs provide youths with temporary food and shelter, as well as support and crisis counseling. These programs represent the best example of diversion, because youths who fail to respond are not sent back to the juvenile justice system.

Social agencies and mental health agencies have always been widely used by the juvenile court. Indeed, reliance on mental health agencies appeared to increase during the 1970s because of the belief among juvenile judges and probation officers that youth in trouble had a great number of mental health problems.[50]

In 1967 the President's Commission on Law Enforcement and Administration of Justice gave the major impetus to the establishment of youth service bureaus by recommending that such agencies be used to work with juveniles outside the juvenile justice system. Youth Service Bureau is the most frequent name, but the agency may also be called Youth Resource Bureau, Youth Assistance Program, Listening Post, or Focus on Youth.

Sherwood Norman, one of the pioneers of YSBs, identified the basic objectives of this diversionary agency:

> The Youth Service Bureau is a noncoercive, independent, public [or sometimes private] agency established to divert children and youth from the justice system by (1) mobilizing community resources to solve youth problems, (2) strengthening existing youth resources and developing new ones, and (3) promoting positive programs to remedy delinquency-breeding conditions.[51]

One hundred and fifty YSBs were established throughout the nation during the late 1960s and early 1970s. A 1971–1972 survey of one hundred and forty YSBs conducted by the Youth Development and Delinquency Prevention Administration found that during the two-year period approximately 50,000 of the 150,000 youths participating in YSB programs were diverted from juvenile court proceedings.[52] However, the decline of federal funding in the late 1970s and early 1980s left many YSBs unable to keep their doors open.

Youth service bureaus typically provide a variety of services. Drop-in centers, crisis intervention hotlines run by volunteers, truancy and school outreach programs, and twenty-four-hour crisis intervention programs are common. But some larger YSBs also make arrangements for temporary care for runaways, conduct programs for pregnant teenagers, and provide school dropouts with employment.

YSBs have been criticized recently for a number of reasons. They have been seen as coercive because they may return a youth to the juvenile court if he or she fails to cooperate with staff or refuses to participate in the program. Critics contend that YSBs enlarge the net of the juvenile justice system because before these bureaus existed youths now referred to them would have had their cases dismissed by the court. YSBs also are criticized for providing more services to middle-class than to lower-class youths. Finally, YSBs are seen as so dependent on the approval of the juvenile justice system and the community that they often cannot serve as an effective change agent.[53]

Evaluation of Diversionary Programs

The most positive characteristic of diversionary programs is that they minimize the penetration of youthful offenders into the juvenile justice system. However, empirical studies of diversion have not generally demonstrated that doing something (treatment or services) is necessarily better than doing nothing. Although several studies have indicated that diversionary programs do tend to reduce recidivism, other researchers warn that the overlooked consequences of diversion challenge the viability of this concept.[54] Some of these negative effects include widening the net of juvenile justice by increasing the number of youths who are contacted by the system, increasing the size of the system (budget and staff), creating new legal entities, altering traditional programs, and ignoring clients' due process rights.[55]

POLICY IMPLICATIONS

Research seems to show that: (1) the younger a child is when first involved with the juvenile justice system, the more likely that the child will persist in delinquent behavior; (2) the more contact a juvenile has with the juvenile justice system, the more likely that he or she will persist in delinquent behavior; and (3) the farther a youngster is processed into the juvenile justice system, the less chance there is that he or she will be diverted successfully from the system.[56] These findings readily lead to the conclusion that primary and secondary prevention are much more desirable than later control of delinquency. That is, if at all possible, the child should be prevented from becoming delinquent, but if it is impossible for some reason, the child should be diverted from the system before his or her delinquent behavior gets any worse. However, a different strategy clearly is needed, because delinquency prevention programs have generally been unsuccessful and diversionary programs have sometimes done more damage than good.

In terms of developing a new strategy, a first step is to identify and evaluate the three levels on which delinquency prevention takes place: (1) ecological alterations, (2) individual intervention, and (3) systematic social change.[57]

Ecological alterations, which refer to environmental manipulation by increasing street lighting, improving supermarket and department store security, or developing secure architectural designs, are the least promising of the three levels. Improved lighting or security may discourage youngsters from committing delinquent behavior at one location, but the youths are likely to move to another location.

Individual intervention takes place at two key points. First, the family, the school, and the community are expected to provide adequately for the needs of children. As the primary source of socialization, the parents have the responsibility of caring for, loving, and promoting the independence of the child. Neglect or abuse can be extremely detrimental to the growth and well-being of the child. The school also is critically important in helping children have positive experiences and develop constructive goals. Research evidence strongly supports the conclusion that the more success a student experiences in school, the less likely he or she is to become involved in delinquent behavior. Further, the community is important in the socialization of a child. A grass-roots community organization can be particularly successful in building bridges between the adults and youths in the local community and between the local residents and the institutions of the larger community.[58] The Chicago Area Projects, La Playa de Ponce, and the House of Umoja are examples of grass-roots community groups that provide a network of youth services and serve as youth advocates in the social and justice institutions of the wider community.

The identification of potentially delinquent youths represents the second key point where individual intervention can take place. The evaluation of delinquency prevention programs in this chapter shows that individual intervention at this point has generally been unsuccessful. Intervention can be made more effective by improving the quality of delinquency prevention programs. These programs must be based upon sound theory, which deals realistically with one or more of the presumed causes of delinquency. Program designs also must do what they purport to do; that is, each program must have the integrity that the theoretical development of the intervention demands. Finally, effective prevention programs must be subject to rigorous evaluation. The importance of appropriate theory, sign, and evaluation for effective programs is developed more extensively in Chapter 20.

Finally, significant reductions in delinquent behavior will not take place without massive changes in American society. Widespread poverty, unemployment, violence, social isolation, urban ghettos, racism, and sexism encourage high rates of delinquent behavior. Gregory P. Falkin, in evaluating delinquency prevention strategies, concluded that redistributing income is the most feasible method of reducing delinquency:

> *Redistributing income is essentially a "costless" method of preventing crime. Compared to the other policy options, income redistribution was found to be the most cost-effective method of reducing delinquency. Furthermore, income redistribution directly enhances distributive justice. In conclusion, of all the programs studied, income redistribution was found to be the most cost-effective and the most just method of reducing delinquency.*[59]

In sum, societal change and intervention at the family, school, and community level are far more likely to succeed than ecological alterations or programs designed for potentially delinquent youths. But the more that delinquency prevention strategies are focused on helping all children realize their potential, the more likely that these interventions will be effective.

SUMMARY

The examination of delinquency through the contextual perspective suggests that the definition of delinquency results from the inter-relationships among the historical, legal, sociocultural, economic, and political contexts. If the definition of delinquency is restricted to the legal context, then the focus of delinquency prevention strategies will be to intercede in the lives of potential delinquents in order to prevent delinquency before it can occur. If that fails to happen, turning juveniles away from further processing by the juvenile justice system becomes an important social goal. But if a delinquent is defined as a youth who commits socially unacceptable behavior, then most American adolescents are delinquents because at one time or another most commit unlawful behavior. To prevent delinquency among the majority of American youth is quite different from preventing delinquency among those youths who come to the attention of the juvenile justice system.

Diversion, in its broad sense, comes from programs sponsored by the police, the juvenile court and probation officers, and agencies outside the justice system. The youth service bureau is the most widely used diversionary agency outside the juvenile justice system. Although in the late 1960s and early 1970s diversionary programs often were looked upon as a panacea for youth crime, mounting evidence now challenges the efficacy of diversionary programs; the most serious criticism is that they result in more youths getting caught in the net of the juvenile justice system.

The most desirable strategy is to prevent delinquency before it can occur, but delinquency prevention programs have generally fallen far short of controlling youth crime. Of the various delinquency prevention programs reviewed in this chapter, the grass-roots community groups appear to offer the most promising approach. But for delinquency prevention programs to have a real impact on youth crime in America, it will be necessary to modify the social, economic, and political conditions of American society that lead to crime. Until that happens, primary and secondary delinquency prevention programs are chipping at the tip of the iceberg rather than dealing with the base of the problem.

Discussion Questions

1. What are the three types of prevention? Explain and illustrate each type.
2. Why have delinquency prevention programs been so popular in the United States?
3. Why is designing a program around a presumed cause of delinquency a promising strategy?
4. Which delinquency prevention program described in this chapter do you find the most interesting? Why?
5. Why are diversionary programs seen as being coercive?
6. Discuss the youth service bureau. What are some shortcomings of this diversionary agency?

7. What are the three broad levels on which delinquency prevention can take place? Evaluate the possibilities at each level.

8. Do you believe that income redistribution is a real possibility in American society?

References

Carter, Robert M., and Klein, Malcolm W. *Back on the Streets*. Englewood Cliffs, N.J.: Prentice-Hall, 1976.

Dixon, Michael C., and Wright, William E. *Juvenile Delinquency Prevention Programs: Report of the Findings of an Evaluation of the Literature*. Washington, D.C.: National Science Foundation, 1974.

Finckenauer, James O. *Scared Straight! and the Panacea Phenomenon*. Englewood Cliffs, N.J.: Prentice-Hall, 1982.

Gibbons, Don C., and Blake, Gerald F. "Evaluating the Impact of Juvenile Diversion Programs." *Crime and Delinquency* 22 (October 1976): 411–420.

Hawkins, J. David; Pastor, Paul A., Jr.; Bell, Michelle; and Morrison, Sheila. *Reports of the National Juvenile Justice Assessment Centers: A Typology of Cause-Focused Strategies of Delinquency Prevention*. Washington, D.C.: U.S. Government Printing Office, 1980.

Lundman, Richard J.; McFarlane, Paul T.; and Scarpitti, Frank R. "Delinquency Prevention: A Description and Assessment of Projects Reported in the Professional Literature." *Crime and Delinquency* 22 (July 1976): 297–308.

Phase I Assessment of Youth Service Bureaus, Summary Report of Youth Service Bureau Research Group for LEAA. Boston: Boston University, 1975.

Rutherford, Andrew, and McDermott, Robert. *National Education Program Phase I Summary Report: Juvenile Diversion*. Washington, D.C.: U.S. Government Printing Office, 1976.

Walker, Jerry P.; Cardarelli, Albert P.; and Billingsley, Dennis. *The Theory and Practice of Delinquency Prevention in the United States: Review, Synthesis, and Assessment*. Columbus, Ohio: Ohio State University Press, 1974.

Wall, John S.; Hawkins, J. David; Lishner, Denise; and Fraser, Mark. *Reports of the National Juvenile Justice Assessment Center's Juvenile Delinquency Prevention: A Compendium of 36 Programs' Models*. Washington, D.C.: U.S. Government Printing Office, 1981.

Woodson, Robert L. *A Summons to Life: Mediating Structures and the Prevention of Youth Crime*. Cambridge: Ballinger Publishing Company, 1981.

Woodson, Robert L. *Youth Crime and Urban Policy: A View from the Inner City*. Washington, D.C.: American Enterprise Institute for Public Policy Research, 1981.

FOOTNOTES

1. President's Commission on Law Enforcement and Administration of Justice, *Task Force Report on Juvenile Delinquency and Youth Crime* (Washington, D.C.: U.S. Government Printing Office, 1967), p. 41.

2. J. David Hawkins et al., *Reports of the National Juvenile Justice Assessment Centers: A Typology of Cause-Focused Strategies of Delinquency Prevention* (Washington, D.C.: U.S. Government Printing Office, 1980), p. 1.

3. See U.S. Consultative Group, *Prevention of Crime and the Treatment of Offenders* (Geneva: United Nations Publication, 1968), for development of these levels of prevention.

4. James O. Finckenauer, *Scared Straight! and the Panacea Phenomenon* (Englewood Cliffs, N.J.: Prentice-Hall, 1982), p. 4.

5. U.S. Congress, House, Subcommittee on Human Resources of the Committee on Education and Labor, *Hearings, Oversight on Scared Straight!,* 96th Cong., 1st Sess., 4 June 1979, p. 305.

6. David Rothenberg is quoted in Finckenauer, *Scared Straight!, p. 4.*

7. See Finckenauer, *Scared Straight!,* for a criticism of the scared straight phenomenon.

8. The review of these studies on delinquency prevention is derived from Finckenauer, *Scared Straight!,* pp. 8–9; and Michael C. Dixon and William E. Wright, *Juvenile Delinquency Prevention Programs: Report of the Findings of an Evaluation of the Literature* (National Science Foundation, October 1974), p. 2.

9. Finckenauer, p. 35.

10. Ibid., p. 36.

11. Richard J. Lundman, Paul T. McFarlane, and Frank R. Scarpitti, "Delinquency Prevention: A Description and Assessment of Projects Reported in the Professional Literature," *Crime and Delinquency* 22 (July 1976), p. 307.

12. Finckenauer, *Scared Straight!,* p. 9.

13. Richard J. Lundman and Frank R. Scarpitti, "Delinquency Prevention: Recommendations for Future Projects," *Crime and Delinquency* 24 (April 1978), p. 207.

14. Ibid.

15. Hawkins et al., *Typology of Cause-Focused Strategies.*

16. See Hawkins et al. for the development of this typology and the goals of each strategy, pp. 11–25.

17. See Jerry P. Walker, Albert P. Cardarelli, and Dennis Billingsley, *The Theory and Practice of Delinquency Prevention in the United States: Review, Synthesis, and Assessment* (Columbus, Ohio: National Institute of Law Enforcement and Criminal Justice, Ohio State University, 1976), p. 147.

18. Edwin Powers and Helen Witmer, *An Experiment in the Prevention of Delinquency* (New York: Columbia University Press, 1950).

19. Joan and William McCord, "A Follow-Up Report on the Cambridge-Somerville Youth Study," *Annals of the American Academy of Political and Social Sciences* 322 (March 1959), pp. 89–99.

20. Reported in Jackson Toby, "An Evaluation of Early Identification and Intensive Treatment Programs for Predelinquents." *Social Problems* 13 (Fall 1965), p. 168.

21. Marylyn Bibb, "Gang-Related Services of Mobilization for Youth," in *Juvenile Gangs in Context; Theory, Research and Action,* edited by Malcolm W. Klein (Englewood Cliffs, N.J.: Prentice-Hall, 1967), p. 177.

22. Ibid., pp. 175–182.

23. Irving Spergel, *Street Gang Work* (Reading, Mass.: Addison-Wesley, 1967), pp. 28–32.

24. Malcolm W. Klein, ed., *Juvenile Gangs in Context* (Englewood Cliffs, N.J.: Prentice-Hall, 1967), p. 6.

25. Lewis Yablonsky, "The Delinquent Gang as a Near Group," *Social Problems* 7 (Fall 1959), pp. 108–117.

26. Walter C. Reckless and Simon Dinitz, *The Prevention of Juvenile Delinquency: An Experiment* (Columbus, Ohio: Ohio State University Press, 1972), pp. 47–52.

27. Ibid., p. 153.

28. Ibid., p. 158.

29. The description of the Area Projects found in this section is largely derived from Harold Finestone, *Victims of Change: Juvenile Delinquents in American Society* (Westport, Conn.: Greenwood Press, 1976), pp. 125–130.

30. A book by one of these local leaders describing the Area Projects on the Near West Side is Anthony Sorrentino's *Organizing against Crime* (New York: Human Sciences Press, 1977).

31. See Solomon Kobrin, "The Chicago Area Project—a 25-Year Assessment," *Annals of the American Academy of Political and Social Science* 322 (March 1959), pp. 20–29, for another evaluation of the Area Projects.

32. Robert L. Woodson, *A Summons to Life: Mediating Structures and the Prevention of Youth Crime* (Cambridge: Ballinger Publishing Company, 1981), p. 91.

33. Robert L. Woodson, *Youth Crime and Urban Policy: A View from the Inner City* (Washington: American Enterprise Institute for Public Policy Research, 1981), p. 17.

34. Ibid., p. 18.

35. Woodson, *Summons to Life*, pp. 91–92.

36. Ibid., pp. 92–93.

37. See Woodson, *Youth Crime and Urban Policy*, for a description of the gang intervention programs and strategies of these groups.

38. John S. Wall et al., *Reports of the National Juvenile Justice Assessment Centers Juvenile Delinquency Prevention: A Compendium of 36 Program Models* (Washington, D.C.: U.S. Government Printing Office, 1981), pp. 60–61.

39. Board of Directors, Manpower Demonstration Research Corporation, *Summary and Findings of the National Supported Work Demonstration* (Cambridge: Ballinger Publishing Company, 1980), pp. 111–115.

40. See Wall et al., *Compendium of 36 Program Models*, for a description of these programs.

41. President's Commission, *Task Force Report on Juvenile Delinquency and Youth Crime*, p. 2.

42. Edwin M. Lemert, *Social Pathology* (New York: McGraw-Hill Book Company, 1951).

43. Youth Development and Delinquency Prevention Administration, *The Challenge of Youth Service Bureaus* (Washington, D.C.: U.S. Government Printing Office, 1973).

44. Edwin H. Sutherland and Donald R. Cressey, *Criminology* (Philadelphia: J.B. Lippincott & Company, 1974).

45. Andrew Rutherford and Robert McDermott, *National Evaluation Program Phase I Report: Juvenile Diversion* (Washington, D.C.: U.S. Government Printing Office, 1976), pp. 2–3.

46. See Dan Pursuit et al., *Police Programs for Preventing Crime and Delinquency* (Springfiled, Ill.: Charles C Thomas Publishers, 1972), for a description of these and other police diversionary programs.

47. Ibid.

48. Roger Baron and Floyd Feeney, *Juvenile Diversion through Family Counseling: A Program for the Diversion of Status Offenders in Sacramento County, California* (Washington, D.C.: U.S. Government Printing Office, 1976).

49. Subcommittee of the Committee on the Judiciary, U.S. Senate, 96th Cong., *Homeless Youth: The Saga of "Pushouts" and "Throwaways" in America* (Washington, D.C.: U.S. Government Printing Office, 1980), pp. 35–44.

50. Conclusion based on interviews conducted with juvenile judges and probation officers in several departments in three states during 1981 and 192.

51. Sherwood Norman, *Youth Service Bureau: A Key to Prevention* (Paramus, N.J.: National Council on Crime and Delinquency, 1972), pp. 12–13.

52. Youth Development and Delinquency Prevention Administration, *"The Challenge of Youth Service Bureaus,"* in *Back on the Streets,* edited by Robert M. Carter and Malcolm W. Klein (Englewood Cliffs, N.J.: Prentice-Hall, 1976), p. 284.

53. See *Phase I Assessment of Youth Service Bureaus, Summary Report of Youth Service Bureau Research Group for LEAA* (Boston: Boston University, 1975), pp. 45–46, for an expansion of these criticisms.

54. Rutherford and McDermott, *Juvenile Diversion,* p. 5.

55. Ibid.

56. Donald R. Cressey and Robert A. McDermott, *Diversion from the Juvenile Justice System* (Washington, D.C.: National Criminal Justice Reference Service, Law Enforcement Assistance Administration, 1974).

57. Sarnoff A. Mednick, "Primary Prevention of Juvenile Delinquency," in *Critical Issues in Juvenile Delinquency,* edited by David Shichor and Delos H. Kelly (Lexington, Mass.: Lexington Books, 1980), p. 264.

58. Harold Finestone, *Victims of Change: Juvenile Delinquents in American Society* (Westport, Conn.: Greenwood Press, 1976), p. 126.

59. Gregory P. Falkin, *Reducing Delinquency: A Strategic Planning Approach* (Lexington, Mass.: Lexington Books, 1979), p. 134.

INTERVIEW WITH ROBERT L. WOODSON

Those who are experienced with the problems of juvenile crime in the community at the local level and those who have demonstrated the capacity to solve the problems should play the principal role in designing policies and programs to prevent juvenile delinquency.

In this interview, Robert L. Woodson, who is currently the president of the National Center for Neighborhood Enterprise and adjunct fellow at the American Enterprise Institute for Public Policy Research in Washington, D.C., talks about the revitalization of urban communities through grass-roots groups in neighborhoods. He also explains how these groups offer the best programs for the prevention of delinquency in urban areas.

Question: You have been critical of traditional approaches to youth crime. Would you say more about this?

Woodson: I think that many of the liberal advocates for poor and minority kids have misled the American public in describing the problems and plight of these young people. These so-called experts have used many strategies to secure money from the federal government to mount delinquency prevention programs that do not work. However, if you examine how the $600 million earmarked for prevention was spent from 1975–1981, you would

---

Woodson has been investigating the problem of youth crime for the last fifteen years. He is now in the midst of a three-year research project on urban revitalization, which is aimed at determining what mix of public policies and neighborhood strategies is likely to produce successful community development. He has been on several presidential committees and is currently a member of the President's Council on Private Sector Initiatives. Woodson has written numerous articles and three books, including A Summons to Life: Mediating Structures and the Prevention of Youth Crime *and* Youth Crime and Urban Policy: A View from the Inner City. *Interviewed in June 1983, and used with permission.*

---

find that the bulk was spent not on delinquency prevention but on the deinstitutionalization of status offenders.

Question: A number of studies have found that the lower-class minority male commits a disproportionately high number of serious juvenile crimes. Why is this so?

Woodson: I challenge those who say that it is possible to avoid talking about socioeconomic conditions in explaining youth crime. Many official efforts to intervene with disadvantaged minority youngsters actually led them into crime. The foster care system is probably the most problematic of these official interventions. In fact, minority youngsters are the most defenseless segment of American society. They have no advocates and are regularly placed in foster care by the system. And once in the system, they are trapped—not only because they are there but also because they are moved more frequently. Consequently, many experience severe psychological and sociological trauma. If we scrutinize our foster care system with the same vigor that we condemn minority youngsters—especially males—to it, I think we would find that it actually incubates tomorrow's criminals.

Question: Would you describe your approach of using the neighborhood as the basis for dealing more effectively with youth crime?

Woodson: The neighborhood is one of the primary ways we can deal with youth crime, and it is the most effective approach. The neighborhood approach builds on a natural kind of environment analogous to the human body. In the human body, for example, if there is an injury or deficiency, antibodies are drawn to the point of injury. I believe this strategy—a natural one—applies generally. The same phenomenon occurs with neighborhoods. If one applies local antibodies to social problems within the neighborhood, then the neighborhood can cure its own illnesses at the source. Thus, the most effective means of treatment then is to strengthen a system's own capacity to ward off disease. Of course, effective cures are also influenced by and may be dependent on factors or information external to the neighborhood. Cures are inherently costly and limited in availability. Therefore, if neighborhoods are too economically and socially depressed, they will require boosters to restore and enhance their capacity. However, we must take care to maintain the proper balances because the parachuting of assistance programs into neighborhoods in a vacuum is not only ineffective but criminal.

Question: Grass-roots community organization is an exciting concept, but will it work in the depersonalized, fragmented, and economically depressed urban societies today?

Woodson: It is already working. The more economically depressed, the more stressful the environment, the more people turn to their indigenous resources. This is the beauty of this approach. It effectively transforms economic conditions. What it offers a troubled youngster, in effect, is an extended or surrogate family. And families don't dissolve if income is cut off—in contrast to those programs where funding is cut off. The staying power of grass-roots community groups and their long-term commitment to young people distinguish them from other bureaucratic programs.

Question: How can these grass-roots community groups mediate with youth gangs?

Woodson: They mediate with youth gangs in several ways. First, they accept gang membership as being essential for inner city kids. In other words, they don't try to break up gangs, they redirect their energies to positive activities and away from criminal activities. Neighborhood groups start from a position of respect for their young people; they set up programs that allow these young people to gain respect via nonviolent tactics. For example, one strategy in one urban neighborhood was to engage the support of people they call "oldheads," older gang members who have gotten married and outgrown gang membership. Because these oldheads are still respected on the street, they play a parental role for younger gang members.

Question: You have written widely about the House of Umoja. Why does this Philadelphia project excite you?

Woodson: This project has accomplished more in eliminating gang violence than any other. Sister Falaka Fattah and her husband extended the influence they had over the youngsters in a residential facility to the entire city. One of the big questions that is raised time after time is: How do you replicate a successful program? Umoja demonstrates how that is done. You need not have the exact program, rather you adapt the program from one setting by applying the concepts that work to a broader audience or different setting. Umoja demonstrated that by extending its influence over the youth who had passed through its program during five years of operation to as many as 85 youth gangs and 5000 young people in Philadelphia.

Question: How about La Playa de Ponce in Puerto Rico? Why do you see this as a promising experiment in delinquency prevention?

Woodson: Ponce is a rural place. You don't hear much about what happens to kids in rural settings. Yet drug addiction was high among its youth, and it exhibited all the problems of its urban counterparts. Even in the face of extreme deprivation and isolation, Sister Ferre, director of this program, was able to create a sense of community among La Playa's 18,000 residents.

Question: What policy recommendations do you consider most important in preventing juvenile delinquency?

Woodson: Those who are experienced with the problems at the local level and those who have demonstrated the capacity to solve these problems should take the lead in designing policies and programs to prevent juvenile delinquency. We seldom ask people with a direct stake in the outcome of a problem to take a significant role in the design of the solutions. Sister Falaka and Sister Ferre have a stake in their communities. We need to give more of the allocated money to those who have a chance to be victimized by the problem and not to large bureaucracies from the outside or to those *not* directly involved in the problem. This is such an obvious strategy.

CHAPTER 20

TREATING THE JUVENILE DELINQUENT

CHAPTER OUTLINE

Does treatment work? It worked for me.

Seventeen-year-old male delinquent

He [foster parent] taught me how to love. He wouldn't give up on me, and his love turned me around.

Thirty-year-old former male delinquent

I don't want to let Betty [staff member in a Youth Service Bureau] down. She has really done a lot for me.

Fifteen-year-old female delinquent[1]

The rehabilitation of juvenile delinquents remains the established purpose of the juvenile justice system. In the twentieth century, every conceivable method has been used in the effort to acomplish the task of rehabilitating delinquents so that they refrain from further unlawful behavior. The variety of treatment technologies still in use includes classification systems, treatment modalities, skill development and self-help techniques, restitution interventions, and service programs. Since the early 1970s, however, the rehabilitative ideal has been so sharply attacked that some have even recommended its burial.

This chapter examines correctional treatment by discussing the treatment debate, evaluating the various classification systems and treatment modalities, defining the ingredients of effective rehabilitation programs, and developing a policy statement to improve correctional treatment.

THE TREATMENT DEBATE

Correctional treatment came under increased criticism in the late 1960s and early 1970s. In 1966, reporting on the results of one hundred empirical evaluations of treatment, Walter C. Bailey concluded that there seemed to be little evidence that correctional treatment is effective.[2] In 1971, Robison and Smith added that "there is no evidence to support any program's claim to superior rehabilitative strategy."[3] Then in 1974, the late Robert Martinson startled both correctional personnel and the public with the pronouncement "With few and isolated exceptions, the rehabilitative efforts that have been reported so far have had no appreciable effect on recidivism."[4] The media quickly simplified Martinson's statement into the idea that "nothing works" in correctional treatment. In 1975, Douglas Lipton, Martinson, and Judith Wilks published the *Effectiveness of Correctional Treatment,* which critically evaluated the effectiveness of correctional treatment programs.[5] In that same year, Martinson announced on "Sixty Minutes" that "there is no evidence that correctional rehabilitation reduces recidivism."[6] A spirited debate on the "nothing works" thesis has continued to rage since the late 1970s.

Ted Palmer, a correctional researcher in California, challenged Lipton, Martinson, and Wilks's research, by tabulating eighty-two studies mentioned in the book and showing that thirty-nine of them, or 48 percent, had had positive or partly positive results on recidivism.[7] Palmer used Martinson's own words to reject the "nothing works" thesis:

> *These programs seem to work best when they are new, when their subjects are amenable to treatment in the first place, and when the counselors are not only trained people, but "good people" as well.*[8]

In the late 1970s, Martinson conceded that "contrary to [his] previous position, some treatment programs *do* have an appreciable effect on recidivism. Some programs are indeed beneficial."[9]

Paul Gendreau and Robert R. Ross reviewed the literature published between 1973 and 1978 and found that 86 percent of the 95 intervention programs studied reported success.[10] According to Gendreau and Ross, this success rate was "convincing evidence that some treatment programs, when they are applied with integrity by competent practitioners in appropriate target populations, can be effective in preventing crime or reducing recidivism."[11] But, despite Martinson's recantation of his "nothing works" thesis and Palmer's and Gendreau and Ross's defense of correctional treatment, the general mood regarding offender rehabilitation in the late 1970s and early 1980s was one of pessimism and discouragement.

Today, three positions or camps exist concerning treatment in juvenile corrections in America. One group has given up on rehabilitation, claiming that correctional treatment is defective in both theory and practice. Proponents of the utilitarian philosophy and conflict theory fall into this first camp. Those who hold the utilitarian punishment position discredit correctional treatment because they assert that it does not reduce recidivism among delinquents. They also are critical of the leniency and permissiveness of juvenile justice based on the rehabilitation model. Advocates of utilitarian philosophy propose that punishment is a more desirable goal for the juvenile justice system because it is more likely to deter delinquents than rehabilitation and, at the same time, provides greater protection for society.[12] Conflict theorists also question whether the rehabilitative ideal can result in reduced recidivism, but they further charge that rehabilitative philosophy actually encourages the continuation of the abuses of an exploitative correctional system.[13]

A second group holds that a humane justice system requires that treatment services be available for those youthful offenders who want them and can benefit from them. Treatment should be voluntary, however, and unrelated to the length of an offender's confinement. David Fogel, Andrew von Hirsch, Norval Morris, and John Conrad are proponents of this position.[14] Thus, while treatment may not work for every offender or even for the majority of offenders, it should be available for those who want it. This group also generally recommends the replacement of interminate sentencing and the parole board with indeterminate sentencing structures. Punishment is again seen as the basic purpose of the correctional process, but delinquents should be punished because they deserve to be punished, rather than to deter crime or protect society.[15]

A third group continues to support rehabilitation as the primary purpose of the correctional process. Proponents of this position, which is much more widespread in juvenile corrections than in adult corrections, claim either that correctional treatment has been unfairly evaluated and in reality is effective in reducing recidivism or that correctional treatment made a number of impressive gains in the 1970s and is much better than it was in the past.[16] Francis T. Cullen and Karen E. Gilbert claim that rehabilitation should be supported because it "is the only justification of criminal sanctioning that obligates the state to care for an offender's needs or welfare."[17] Although most holding the third position are content to retain indeterminate sentencing and the parole board, increasing numbers of this group agree that participation in programs should become less a condition of release than it has been in the past. Finally, there is a growing acceptance among those in this third camp that the utilization of theory and research will lead the way to discovering such information as what measures work with what offenders in what contexts.[18]

CLASSIFICATION SYSTEMS

Throughout the twentieth century, classification has been considered the first step in treatment in juvenile corrections. Psychiatric evaluations and psychological workups of juvenile delinquents were done in child guidance clinics by the second decade of this century. A number of reception and diagnostic centers were built in the 1930s and 1940s so that delinquents could be assigned to programs compatible with their psychological, educational, and vocational needs. Classifying youths in terms of their personality dynamics, world view, and behavior were the three most popular schemes in the 1960s and 1970s. But in the last few years, classification systems in juvenile corrections have lost much of their former popularity.

Psychological Evaluations

Most juvenile delinquents are involved in psychiatric interviews and psychological workups on one or more occasions. Psychiatric interviews may be used to determine the psychological problems of a youth, and the therapist may use such terms as psychoneurotic, antisocial, passive-aggressive, passive-dependent, adjustment reaction to adolescence, group delinquent, and unsocialized in describing the problems of a youth. Psychiatric interviews also are frequently conducted before a delinquent who has committed violent offenses is released from training school to provide corrections officials with assurance that a youth is no longer dangerous before they release him or her. Various psychological tests, such as the Jesness Personality Inventory, categorize youthful offenders according to concepts such as: social maladjustment, value orientation, immaturity, autism, alienation, manifest aggression, withdrawal-depression, social anxiety, repression, denial, and asocial index.

I-Level Classification System

The Interpersonal Maturity Level (I-Level) Classification System, developed by J. Grant and M. Grant in the late 1950s in California, assumes that personality development follows a normal sequence and attempts to identify the developmental stage of offenders by focusing on their perception of themselves, others, and the world.[19] A seven-point classification scheme ranges from I_1 (infantile in interpersonal maturity) to I_7 (ideal social maturity). Researchers have found that most delinquents can be classified at the I_2, I_3, and I_4 levels; these levels are further divided into nine delinquent subtypes.[20] That is, the delinquent is fixated at one of the lower levels of social maturity. Because the I-Level system contends that the impact of treatment varies from one youth to another according to his or her developmental stage, this scheme represents the theory of differential treatment: i.e., what works with one may have no effect on another or even a negative impact.[21] The I-Level system was rigorously evaluated at the California's Community Treatment Project (CTP) and at the Preston Boys School in California during the 1960s and has been widely used in juvenile corrections throughout the nation.[22]

The Quay Classification System

Herbert C. Quay developed a classification system that evaluates delinquents in terms of their behavior rather than their world view. The Quay classification system is based on five types of personality: inadequate-immature, neurotic-conflicted, unsocialized aggressive or psychopathic, socialized or subcultural delinquent, or subcultural-immature delinquents. Inadequate-immature offenders behave childishly or irresponsibly. Neurotic-conflicted delinquents are anxious, insecure youths whose internal conflicts create problems for themselves and others. Unsocialized delinquents adhere to the values of their delinquent peer group. Offenders in the subcultural classification are usually involved in gang delinquency. Subcultural-immature delinquents are youths who violate the law but feel alienated from delinquent peer groups.[23] The Quay classification and treatment model was used at the Robert F. Kennedy Youth Center in the early 1970s, and the center's director was able to determine the types of counselors who would work best with youths in each classification.[24]

Evaluation of Classification Systems

The broad psychiatric and psychological categories have rarely been translated easily into concrete treatment plans. Critics rightfully contend that clinical staff are long on diagnosis and short on treatment prescriptions. The Robert F. Kennedy Youth Center eventually rejected the Quay system because staff members questioned whether the behavior of offenders in each particular category is indeed distinctive. In addition, staff members charged that the Quay system created serious behavior problems among residents, especially incorrigibility and attempted escapes, and that it led to racially homogeneous groups or cottages. Administrators were forced to withdraw the Quay system because of lack of commitment by the line staff.[25] The I-Level system, which has been widely used in juvenile corrections, has been subjected to extensive criticism since the 1970s. Critics frequently charge that the I-Level system also leads to racially homogeneous groups or cottages and that institutional problems are caused by the lack of commitment by security staff to this scheme of differential treatment; they also point out that union agreements prevent line staff from being shifted from cottage to cottage to match residents' needs with available staff services. Thus, classification systems are less accepted in juvenile corrections today than they were previously, a condition that is not likely to change in the near future.

TREATMENT MODALITIES

Treatment modalities are widely used in community-based corrections and have been instituted in nearly every training school in the United States. Psychotherapy, psychodrama, transactional analysis, reality therapy, behavior modification, family therapy, guided group interaction, positive peer culture, and the therapeutic community are the treatment modalities most frequently used in juvenile corrections. Self-help modalities, such as teaching motivation, Emotional Maturity Instruction, and skill development are also commonly used.

Psychotherapy

Various adaptations of Freudian psychotherapy have been used by psychiatrists, clinical psychologists, and psychiatric social workers since the early twentieth century. In either an one-to-one relationship with a therapist or in a group context, delinquents are encouraged to talk about past conflicts causing them to express emotional problems through aggressive or antisocial behavior. The insight that delinquents gain from this individual or group psychotherapy supposedly helps them resolve the conflicts and unconscious needs that drive them to crime. As a final step of psychotherapy delinquents become responsible for their own behavior.

Acceptance of the therapist is a key to successful psychotherapy, for youths must discover all adults are not like their rejecting parents. A trusting therapeutic relationship, coupled with firmness and justice on the part of the therapist, is intended to help offenders acquire a new sense of dignity and worth.

However, psychotherapy has been ineffective as a rehabilitative technique with delinquents. Of ten studies of psychotherapy with delinquents reported in the literature, eight had completely negative findings.[26] In one of the remaining two, the results were negative except for those youngsters defined as "amenable."[27] In a study that had positive findings on eight of nine criteria, Thomas examined the use of psychotherapy in a public school setting with delinquency-prone adolescents and found that psychotherapy in this setting involved more steps than simply talking with the youth.[28]

On balance, it appears that psychotherapy, as it is now practiced, will be unsuccessful in rehabilitating the majority of juvenile delinquents.

Psychodrama

Jacob Moreno introduced psychodrama into the United States in 1925 , as a model for allowing the psychiatrist to treat social situations. The promise of psychodrama is that in dealing with conflicts openly delinquents learn. In psychodrama individuals are involved in role-playing situations that demand they act out their real feelings or behaviors. Ideally, delinquents in a psychodrama group can spontaneously create new behaviors and improve their behavioral repertoire, obtain feedback, see themselves as others do, and improve their communication with others. Within the society of the group delinquents can experience various feelings and observe the effects these feelings have upon others.[29]

The Santa Clara County Juvenile Probation Department used psychodrama as a technique for dealing with first-time drug offenders. Youths were challenged to stage and act out human situations, as a vehicle for understanding the motivations for their behavior, including drug abuse.[30] Psychodrama was also used at the National Training School in Washington, D.C.[31] Herman evaluated the effectiveness of psychodrama with institutionalized delinquent boys in New York.[32] However, in none of these three settings was psychodrama statistically significant in reducing recidivism.[33]

Although psychodrama in its pure form is rarely found in community-based programs or training schools, such related techniques as role playing, improvisational theater, and other theater games are common. For example, role play has been used with Ohio youths on probation to teach them the consequences of their behavior. Theatre Without Bars uses arts-in-education techniques in the New Jersey training schools, and in the mid-1970s Ma Goose, Inc. established a twice-weekly improvisational theather workshop at the San Francisco Juvenile Court's Hidden Valley Ranch for youthful offenders.

In summary, psychodrama and such related techniques as role playing, improvisational theater, and theater games in themselves probably have little impact on reducing delinquency, but when combined with other interventions, they help youths focus on their relationships, take on new roles or switch roles, and develop desired relationships.

Transactional Analysis

Transactional analysis, a therapy based on interpreting and evaluating personal relationships, has proved of immediate value to many delinquents and, thus, has generated considerable interest. Using catchy language, TA promises delinquents who feel "not OK" that several easy steps can make them "OK."

A TA leader first performs a "script analysis" with each delinquent under his or her care. The purpose of the script analysis is to estimate the effect that past "tapes" have on an individual's present behavior. TA theorizes that delinquents become "losers" or "nonwinners" because they continue to play self-defeating tapes. The TA leader then teaches the delinquent that it is possible to become a winner and to achieve life's goals. Treatment begins at this point if the delinquent decides that he or she is willing to negotiate a treatment contract with both short- and long-range goals.

Delinquents willing to commit themselves to treatment are taught the basic premises of this modality in a TA group. They are shown that they act according to three roles in dealing with others: the "child," the "parent," and the "adult." One purpose of TA therapy is to help each offender use the adult ego state more frequently and to turn off the "not OK" feelings buried in the child tape.[34] Offenders further learn that four "life positions" describe the judgements they make about themselves and others: "I'm OK—You're OK"; "I'm not OK—You're OK"; "I'm not OK—You're not OK"; and "I'm Ok—You're not OK." A major purpose of TA therapy is to help participants accept "I'm OK—You're OK," meaning that they see value in people and feel that both the self and others are well adjusted to life.[35] Offenders also learn that people play games to protect themselves from knowing themselves and growing up. TA claims that these games serve negative purposes, such as keeping an individual from intimacy with others and causing him or her to act in the impulsive, immature child role too much of the time.[36]

TA has been used in training schools throughout California, Ohio, and various other states because it offers several advantages: (1) it is relatively easy to teach to interested staff; (2) it appeals to offenders because it offers hope; (3) it reduces disciplinary problems in units where it is used; and (4) it provides a future job possibility for offenders who become highly skilled in its use.

However, not all youthful offenders respond to this modality. One offender noted:

> [T]hey are just trying to brainwash you into being a middle American dude. The staff and all are liberal, but they are just trying to get you to conform, not smoke marijuana and stuff.[37]

Another youth was even more critical:

> I think [TA] is a bunch of bullshit. It makes no sense at all.[38]

TA appears to have little success with offenders who are not motivated to examine their own problems, who are evading personal change, and who have serious behavior problems. Offenders with borderline intelligence, with sociopathic tendencies, and with immature personalities also rarely profit from this insight therapy. But overall, TA remains a promising modality for certain juvenile delinquents.

Reality Therapy

Reality therapy, developed by William Glasser and G. L. Harrington, is based on the principle that individuals must accept responsibility for their behavior. The goal of the reality therapist is to lead the person being treated to act "responsibly." But in order for an offender to act in a responsible way, two basic needs must be fulfilled—the need to love and be loved and the need to feel that one is worthwhile to oneself and to others. Reality therapy contends that these basic human needs are achieved through actions that are realistic, responsible, and right—the three R's of this modality.[39]

Richard L. Rauchin outlined the fourteen steps an effective reality therapist takes to become involved with and influence the behavior of clients:

1. **Personalizes** The reality therapist becomes emotionally involved. He or she carefully models responsible behavior and does not practice something other than what he preaches.

2. **Reveals self**   He or she does not need to project an image of being all-knowing or all-powerful.

3. **Concentrates on the "here and now"**   He or she does not allow the person to use the unfavorable past as a justification of irresponsible action in the present.

4. **Emphasizes behavior**   The reality therapist is not interested in uncovering underlying motivation or drives; rather, he or she concentrates on helping the person act in a manner that will help him meet his needs responsibly.

5. **Rarely asks why**   The reality therapist takes the posture that irresponsible behavior is just that, regardless of the reasons.

6. **Helps the person evaluate his behavior.**   He or she repeatedly asks the person what his current behavior is accomplishing and whether it is meeting his needs.

7. **Helps him develop a better plan for future behavior**   If the person cannot develop his own plan, the reality therapist will help him develop one. A contract is drawn up and signed by the person and the reality therapist.

8. **Rejects excuses.**

9. **Offers no tears or sympathy.**

10. **Praises and approves responsible behavior.**

11. **Believes people are capable of changing their behavior.**

12. **Tries to work in groups.**   People are also more responsive to the influence and pressure of their peers. People are also more likely to be open and honest with a peer group.

13. **Does not give up.**

14. **Does not label people**   Behavior is simply described as responsible or irresponsible. The therapist does not classify people as sick, disturbed, or emotionally disabled.[40]

Glasser worked as a psychiatrist with the girls at the Ventura Training School in California, where he came to believe that while offenders need both consistent discipline and warm acceptance, neither warmth nor discipline should supersede the other. Delinquents should be given increased responsibilities at the same time they are receiving consistent discipline and warm acceptance.[41]

More empirical evidence on reality therapy is necessary before any conclusions can be drawn about its effectiveness. Glasser reported that reality therapy had close to an 80 percent success rate with the girls at the Ventura School because only 43 of 370 program graduates returned while he was a therapist there.[42] An in-house study of the reality therapy program for adult and juvenile sex offenders at the Western State Hospital in the state of Washington showed that from 1958 to 1968 only 8.9 percent of the exoffenders involved were rearrested.[43]

Reality therapy is frequently well received by youthful offenders because its emphasis on present behavior makes sense to many who are "turned off" by modalities oriented to insight therapy. Staff members in the juvenile justice system also are attracted to reality therapy. They usually feel that the basic concepts of this modality are easily learned. They also like its present focus and the authority and power it gives them. In addition, they like the emphasis reality therapy places on responsibility and discipline. However, critics charge that reality therapy oversimplifies human behavior and that it can lead to an authoritarian attitude on the part of the therapist. They also question whether it is wise to ignore the past.

Reality therapy is used throughout community-based corrections and juvenile correctional institutions despite these criticisms. Because many of its assumptions are agreeable to line staff members, the popularity of reality therapy will probably endure long after many of other technologies have been forgotten.

Behavior Modification

Behavior modification, which has been used widely in juvenile corrections in the past ten years, rewards appropriate behavior positively, immediately, and systematically, and it assumes that rewards increase the occurrences of desired behavior. Similarly, behavior that is not reinforced decreases in frequency.

Behavior modification, also called behavior therapy or contingency management, uses many techniques to reinforce positive and extinguish negative behavior. The basic tools are systematic desensitization, extinction of undesirable responses, assertiveness training, conditioning against avoidances response, counter-conditioning, and tokens. Positive reinforcers consist of attention, praise, money, food, and privileges; negative reinforcers include threats, confinement, punishment, and ridicule.[44]

Behavior modification therapy depends on consistency, which means that each staff member in the environment must consistently provide positive and negative reinforcers. Behavior therapists also usually recommend brief time-out periods during which offenders receive no reinforcements of any kind. Behavior modification further assumes that the negative attitudes prompting undesirable behavior will ultimately disappear if the undesired behavior is eradicated.

Schwitzgebel and Kolb's study of behavior modification is one of the most frequently cited. They involved twenty delinquent boys in Boston in a nine-month project, in which the youths were paid for talking into a tape recorder about their life experiences. The boys came to their appointments on an individual basis, two to three times a week. The measured result of the program was that attendance became more prompt. After three years, follow-up data showed significantly fewer arrests and less months incarcerated for those in the program than a matched control group. But there was no significant difference in recidivism, as measured by those youths who went on to the reformatory or prison. The authors attributed the success that was achieved to the fact that individualized rewards were used and that the experimenters were empathetic, direct, and unorthodox in their relationships with the youths.[45]

However, Dennis A. Romig, in reviewing fourteen studies of behavior modification involving almost two thousand delinquent youths in programs across the United States, concluded that behavior modification is no panacea for juvenile delinquency. Although behavior modification has been effective in changing certain behaviors, such as those related to school attendance, test scores, promptness, and classroom behavior, it has had less impact on such global factors as delinquency or arrest rates. Romig concludes that the more delinquents are involved in the process of behavior modification and the more the behaviors to be changed are specific and behaviorally simple, the more likely the results will be positive.[46]

Overall, behavior modification is helpful in improving institutional behavior and in conveying certain skills, but it is questionable whether this modality will have any long-range impact on reducing juvenile delinquency in American society.

Family Therapy

Treating the entire family has become a widely used method of dealing with a delinquent's socially unacceptable behavior. The Sacramento 601 Diversion Project is one of the most successful examples of family therapy. This project was designed to determine whether youths in need of supervision (status offenders) could be more effectively diverted from delinquency through short-term family crisis counseling involving the entire family than through involvement in traditional juvenile court intake procedures. The evaluation of the 601 Project indicated that it had successfully achieved its four major goals: (1) to reduce the number of cases ending in juvenile court; (2) to reduce the number of repeat offenders; (3) to decrease overnight detentions; and (4) to accomplish these goals without increasing the cost required for regular processing of cases.[47] Romig postulates that the positive results of the 601 Project "can be attributed to the involvement of the youths' families at the crisis points and the subsequent attempts by the project staff to improve the communication patterns of the family."[48]

Alexander and Parsons evaluated three different approaches to family treatment: a short-term behavior program intended to improve the communication patterns of delinquent youths and members of their families; a didactic group discussion of adolescent problems; and a psychodynamic, insight-oriented family therapy program. These researchers found no significant difference between any of the three treatment groups and their control groups in recidivism.[49]

Romig, in evaluating the above two studies and ten others involving 2180 youths, concluded that family treatment did not reduce delinquent behavior. However, when such therapy focused upon the positive goal of improving communication among family members, significant decreases of delinquency occurred. Further, crisis intervention counseling, especially when used to teach systematic problem solving, was successful.[50]

Overall, family therapy appears likely to be more effective when it is focused on teaching parents communication, problem-solving, and disciplining skills. Status offenders and their families, particularly, should be able to benefit from effective family therapy.

Guided Group Interaction (GGI)

Guided group interaction, a popular modality in juvenile corrections, is used in state institutions of eleven states: New Jersey, South Dakota, Minnesota, West Virginia, Illinois, Georgia, Florida, New Hampshire, Maryland, Michigan, and Kentucky. In addition, GGI has been one of the most widely used modalities in community-based programs and was first used with youthful offenders in the Highsfield Project in New Jersey in the early 1950s.

GGI, whether it takes place in the community or in an institution, places youthful offenders in an intensive environment under the direction of adult leaders. Although the GGI group meets several times a week and the interaction is intense, the atmosphere is typically neither hostile nor authoritarian. Indeed, in institutional contexts, members of GGI groups are usually given considerable say and often make decisions ranging from when a group member will be released or granted a home furlough to how a group member will be punished to whether the front door will be locked at night.[51]

The guided group interaction process usually consists of several stages. In the first stage, new participants are encouraged by group members and the leader to relax their defenses. During the second stage residents share their life stories and problems as they begin to trust the group. In the third stage, participants frequently discuss how they got into crime as well as the problems of living outside and in the correctional environment. Youths may feel secure enough to be open to change by the fourth stage, and in the fifth stage, they make their own plans for change. Participants make conscious decisions about their futures during the guided group interaction process.[52]

Several studies, mentioned in Chapter 17, found that noninstitutional GGI programs are at least as effective as and much less costly than correctional confinement. But little research has been done on the efficacy of GGI in institutional settings.

GGI has several strengths, which partly explain its wide use in juvenile corrections. GGI is a comprehensive treatment strategy that substitutes a whole new structure of beliefs, values, and behaviors for the values of delinquent peer subcultures. More staff members can be involved in this treatment process than others without significantly increasing costs because GGI can be led by trained custodial staff members. Further, GGI teaches offenders to take responsibility for their own lives and to reduce their dependency on the delinquent peer group. Finally, GGI has been somewhat successful in avoiding the development of delinquent subcultures in treatment groups.

GGI also has several shortcomings. Most importantly, the wide variations among GGI programs prevents the development of clear, consistent, and repeatable treatment designs. The shortage of trained leaders is also a major problem. In addition, the emphasis on peer group norms may leave too little room for individualism, and the achievements made are not always easily transferable to life in the community.

GGI continues to be widely used in juvenile corrections, but the popularity of this modality has waned dramatically in the past decade.

Positive Peer Culture (PPC)

Positive peer culture, like its parent model GGI, is a group approach for building positive youth subcultures, and it encompasses a total strategy extending to all aspects of daily life. Developed by Harry Vorrath and his associates, PPC has been used in all the state juvenile institutions in Michigan, Missouri, and West Virginia.[53]

The main philosophy of PPC is to "turn around" the negative peer culture and to mobilize the power of the peer group in a positive way. PPC does this by teaching group members to care for one another; caring is defined as wanting what is best for a person. Vorrath believes that once caring becomes "fashionable" and is accepted by the group, "hurting goes out of style."[54]

PPC involves the same stages as GGI, but it places considerably greater emphasis on positive behavior. Group members learn to speak of positive behaviors as "great," "intelligent," "independent," "improving," and "winning." In contrast, negative behavior is described as "childish," "unintelligent," "helpless," "destructive," "copping out," and "losing."

Positive peer culture is especially concerned about the destructive power of "negative indigenous leaders" (NIL) and has developed strategies to neutralize the power of these negative peer leaders. The basic strategy is to undercut the foundations of negative peer leaders' support by winning the leaders' lieutenants away from them.

Jerry D. Mitchell and David L. Cochrum, in one of the few studies conducted on the effectiveness of positive peer culture, found that the use of PPC means fewer incidents and a smoother, less traumatic program in an adolescent treatment facility.[55] However, Jerry O'Rourke, superintendent of Red Wing Training School in Minnesota, questioned the efficacy of PPC:

> PPC came in and rode the crest of newism. PPC worked well for three years [here]. But by 1975/1976, this institution began to have trouble in several areas: runaways were high, assaultive incidents were high, and the community was up in arms. When I evaluated PPC, I saw that people had forgotten about the concepts behind the group program. They were only following the routine of the book. It had become a routine or ritual, and so it was necessary to get rid of PPC.[56]

PPC has the same strengths as guided group interaction, in that both programs undermine the negative values of the delinquent peer culture, depend on comprehensive strategies for treating delinquents, and place responsibility for change on the shoulders of offenders. However, three limitations on the efficacy of PPC have been cited. Critics claim that PPC underestimates the ingenuity and resourcefulness of peer subcultures; that the success of this model appears to depend on staff members' abilities to remain unpredictable to their groups—and such inscrutability is an uncommon trait; and that it is questionable whether or not it is possible to teach caring relationships to youthful offenders who have experienced exploitation and deprivation all their lives.

Nevertheless, PPC—which requires more extensive evaluation—appears to be one of the most promising ways to treat juvenile delinquents.

The Therapeutic Community

The purpose of the therapeutic community is to create environments supportive of socially acceptable behavior. The concept of the therapeutic community evolved from the contributions of Maxwell Jones, who felt that it was possible to overcome passivity toward therapy by giving clients responsibility for the operation of the units in which they live. The theory is based on reducing role differences between the keepers and the kept and giving patients every opportunity to analyze their own behaviors.

Therapeutic communities are used infrequently in juvenile corrections because such communities are self-enclosed and tend to shut youthful offenders away from the network of community services they need. The Monzanita Lodge, which houses the California Youth Authority's Drug Abuse Program, is the best example of a therapeutic community in a juvenile correctional institution.[57] Elan, which is located in Poland Springs, Maine has incorporated many of the concepts of the Daytop therapeutic community in a diversion program that supporters cite as exemplary and foes regard as brutal to participants.[58] Juvenile drug abusers also are sometimes sent to adult therapeutic communities. A former resident of a Minnesota progam tells of his first day:

> It was a real mellow sort of place, but it made you suspicious. I didn't think this place could be for real. I was there for four hours when I had my family interview. There were fifteen or sixteen residents and four staff members there. I tried to be cool about the whole thing, but it scared me to death. They were evaluating how honest I was with myself, whether I had enough motivation to change, or whether I was going to play a bunch of games. They kept saying I was lying to them. Then they told me, "If you really want to stay here, stand up on a chair and let a guy know four blocks away that you want to be here. He is waiting to catch a bus and if he catches that bus without your getting his attention, you're on your way to training school." So I stood on that chair and I felt like a fool, but I yelled as loud as I could. They let me stay in the house; it was the best thing that ever happened to me.[59]

The usefulness of therapeutic communities in juvenile corrections is limited by the reluctance of community-based and training school administrators to allow the degree of resident self-government that is necessary to make this concept functional. In addition, therapeutic communities do tend to shut residents off from the network of supportive services juveniles need, and they establish such rigid environments that many juveniles are unable to tolerate them.

Emotional Maturity Instruction (EMI)

A treatment program that is beginning to appear throughout the South is Emotional Maturity Instruction (EMI). The basic assumptions of EMI, as developed by Dan MacDougald in the late 1960s, are that subconscious goals and attitudes are influenced by the comprehension of key words. In a fifteen-week course, EMI teaches students the proper meaning of such words and concepts as "judgmental love," "truth," "patience," and "reacting to criticism." Three tools are used in this course: an ancient Aramaic manuscript of the social teachings of Jesus, the Socratic method of dialogue, and the belief that people can change attitudes and behaviors by controlling their own minds.[60]

An in-house evaluation indicated that this program had positive results at the East Texas training school for girls, but more empirical evaluation is necessary before any conclusive statement can be made about EMI.

Teaching Motivation to Juvenile Delinquents

Among the popular motivation courses taught in training schools throughout the nation are Zoom, Winners, Insight Incorporated, Guides for Better Living, and Feminine Development Programs. Fifteen thousand juvenile and adult offenders at 175 institutional sites have completed the Guides for Better Living course. This course is based on the philosophy of businessman and millionaire W. Clement Stone, as described in *I Dare You,* by William Danforth, *Think and Grow Rich,* by Napoleon Hill, and Stone's *The Success System That Never Fails.* These self-motivational materials teach offenders principles of success so that they can become winners rather than losers in life.[61]

Although motivation courses do teach positive attitudes and assure residents that they have the power to change their lives, it is not clear how helpful such middle-class success-oriented programs are for lower-class delinquents when they are released in the community.

Skill Development Programs

Skill development programs are currently experiencing considerable popularity in juvenile corrections. These progams teach communication, decision-making, daily living, educational advancement, vocational, and career skills. Dennis A. Romig, in evaluating the efficacy of institutional treatment for delinquents, concluded that skill development has been more successful than any other rehabilitative technique.[62] He used skill development as his focus to design the following model for rehabilitating delinquents:

1. Get the youths' attention.
2. Obtain staff who have empathy.
3. Objective diagnosis.
4. Set behavioral goal.
5. Teach youths new behaviors using effective teaching methods:
   a. Individualized diagnosis.
   b. Specific learning goal
   c. Individualized program based upon personally relevant material.
   d. Teach basic academic skills.
   e. Multisensory techniques.
   f. Sequential presentation, breaking complex skills into simple steps.

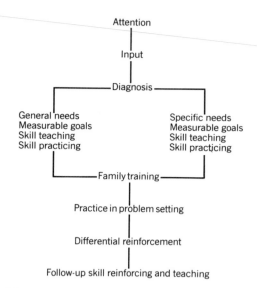

Figure 20-1 Model of Delinquency Rehabilitation

Source: Dennis A. Romig, *Justice for Our Children: An Examination of Juvenile Delinquent Rehabilitation Programs* (Lexington, Mass.: Lexington Books; D.C. Heath: Company, 1978), p. 111. Reprinted by permission.

    g. Initially rewarding youths' attention and persistence.

    h. Differential reinforcement of learning performance.

6. Teach skills in the following areas:

    a. Communication skills

    b. Daily living and survival skills

    c. Career skills, such as career decision making and career advancement.

7. Practice skills in problem solving.

8. Differentially reinforce.

9. Family training in communication, problem-solving, and disciplining skills.

10. Follow-up skills training and reinforcement.[63]

    Romig believes that the use of this model of delinquency rehabilitation, which is built around skill teaching and skill practicing, would result in a dramatic reduction of juvenile delinquency in American society. See Figure 20-1 for a diagram of this model of delinquency rehabilitation.

    Although the teaching of social survival skills, such as interpersonal, problem-solving, and learning skills, has not been given the attention that other treatment technologies have, it may well be one of the most promising modalities in juvenile corrections.

POLICY IMPLICATIONS

The overall quality of treatment in juvenile corrections is not impressive. Enforced offender rehabilitation has sometimes resulted in making delinquents worse rather than better through treatment. The frequent criticism that offender rehabilitation is defective in theory and a disaster in practice has been true on too many occasions. Program designs have often given little consideration to what a particular program can realistically accomplish with a particular group of offenders and have frequently relied on a single cure for a variety of complex problems. In addition, programs have generally lacked integrity, because they have not delivered the services they claimed with sufficient strength to accomplish the goals of treatment. Furthermore, the research on offender rehabilitation has generally been inadequate, with many projects and reports on rehabilitation almost totally lacking research design.[64]

To improve the quality of correctional treatment, three basic steps appear to be necessary: (1) more programs must include the ingredients of effective interventions; (2) programs must be based upon better program design, assure higher program integrity, and be evaluated by more rigorous research methods; and (3) research must provide more information on what works for whom and in what context.

Ingredients of Effective Programs

Effective programs usually have a number of ingredients in common. They usually are set up by an inspired individual or group of individuals, have developed a unified-team approach among staff, have a transmittable philosophy of life, trust offenders with decision-making responsibilities, help delinquents develop needed skills, are regarded as unique and different by delinquents, avoid isolation from social institutions, and provide a support network for offenders following release or graduation.[65]

The Inspired Leader Who Means Business

The inspired individual or group of individuals who means business in setting up a program has been found time after time to be one of the chief ingredients of effective programs. In Outward Bound, Kurt Hahn was able to generate enthusiasm and support among those who contacted him.[66] An inspired woman and her husband also set up the House of Umoja in Philadelphia, seeking to deal with the gang problem in that urban community.[67] The inspiration of Clifford Shaw continues to influence the Chicago Area Projects long after his death.

Unified Treatment Team

A program is more likely to have an impact upon offenders if the treatment team is unified. In a unified treatment team, all staff members become treatment agents as they design the program, develop short- and long-range goals for the program, and involve themselves with offenders.

Philosophy of Life That Is Transmittable

Effective programs also generate a sense of mission or purpose among delinquents by transmitting a philosophy of life. Martin Groder has noted that "It's not that the guy has to adopt the philosophy of the program, but he's got to learn it well enough to integrate it with his own life experience and come out with his own version."[68] Bartollas, Miller, and Dinitz reported that having a mission or purpose in life is one characteristic of hard-core offenders who are later successful in the community.[69]

Involvement of Offenders in the Decision-Making Process

Effective programs also frequently provide decision-making responsibilities for juvenile delinquents. Although many correctional interventions treat delinquents as helpless children incapable of making decisions for themselves, the more noteworthy programs encourage decision making and then make participants responsible for the decisions they make. The more delinquents are permitted to make choices concerning what happens to them, the more likely they are to be involved in a treatment program and to seek to profit from it.

Skill Develoment

Effective programs, as previously noted, help delinquents develop skills that prepare them for adjustment in the community. These range from educational and vocational to interpersonal and problem-solving skills. Such skills make delinquents feel that they can accomplish something or they have acquired important insights about themselves or about life.

Uniqueness

The most disinguishing characteristic of effective interventions is sometimes their very uniqueness. That is, the components of these programs that make them different from other correctional interventions are sometimes the most important factors in "grabbing" the attention of youthful offenders and in getting them involved in these interventions.

Participation in Social Institutions

Effective correctional interventions for juvenile delinquents and status offenders rely on good communications and effective working relationships with those institutions that juveniles come into contact with each day, such as the family and the school. Grass-roots interventions, which arise because of a recognition of need at the community level, have sometimes been very effective in providing advocacy services with parents, school authorities, and officials of the justice system.

Adequate Community Support Networks

Community-based and institutional programs also require adequate community follow-up in order for delinquents to sustain positive changes in their lives. Outward Bound is a prime example of a program with great initial impact that diminishes over time because of the lack of community follow-up.

Strategy for Improving the Effectiveness of Correctional Programs

To improve program effectiveness requires that program designs be based upon theoretical premises, that programs be implemented with integrity, and that programs be evaluated with rigorous research methods.

Program Design

The theoretical premises, or constructs, of programs must be examined in order to determine whether the theoretical constructs are appropriate for any particular group of offenders. The processes by which any set of interventions will change delinquent behavior must also be examined in order to determine whether the treatment has sufficient strength to produce the desired behavior or attitudinal change. Finally, the theoretical constructs must be meshed with the setting in which treatment takes place to ensure that programs are implemented in appropriate settings.[70]

Program Integrity

Delinquents must be placed in the right program at the optimal time for them to benefit from treatment. Effective interventions must actually deliver the services they claim to deliver, with sufficient strength to accomplish the goals of treatment. In addition, program integrity requires that personnel be equipped to deliver the specified services—thus, treatment personnel must have some degree of expertise in what they are doing, must have sufficient training to do it, and must receive adequate supervision. Finally, it must be possible to modify interventions according to the changing interests and needs of offenders.[71]

Program Evaluation

The Panel on Research on Rehabilitative Techniques concluded after nearly two years of examining offender rehabilitation that "the research methodology that has been brought to bear on the problem of finding ways to rehabilitate criminal offenders has been generally so inadequate that only a relatively few studies warrant any unequivocal interpretations.[72] Sample sizes must be large enough to measure subtle effects, such as changes in interactions. True randomized experiments must be conducted whenever feasible because they permit some certainty about causal relationships. Researchers need to identify the common elements of effective programs and to determine how these elements affect success with particular groups of offenders. In addition, researchers need to determine how effective programs can be replicated in other settings. Finally, more empirical work must be done on measuring the outcomes of correctional treatment.[73]

Who Gets What Treatment

Correctional treatment also needs to discover what works for which offenders in what context. In other words, correctional treatment could work if amenable offenders were offered appropriate treatments by matched workers in environments conducive to producing positive effects.[74]

To match up individual offenders with the treatments most likely to benefit them will be no easy task. Only through well-planned and soundly executed research will the information necessary be gained. The Panel of Rehabilitative Techniques recommends the use of the "template-matching technique".[75] This technique creates a set of descriptors, or a "template," of the kinds of people who are most likely to benefit from a particular treatment according to the theory or basic assumptions underlying it.[76] Because of the scarcity of treatment resources, matching programs to those offenders most likely to profit from them is only sensible.

SUMMARY

As indicated in this chapter, we may have expected too much from correctional treatment. Violent and inhumane training schools are among the least promising places for treatment to take place. But even in community-based programs, the lack of resources for overworked staff, clients' histories of failure, and drug and alcohol addictions result in far more failures than successes. The danger, however, is to expect too little from correctional treatment. Some delinquents do profit from treatment in community-based and institutional settings. The programs may simply make their present confinement more bearable, or they may provide a sense of mission or purpose for offenders so that they can go on to live crime-free lives. In sum, some programs are effective, and some treatment agents do have positive impacts on delinquents.

The future effectiveness of correctional treatment in juvenile corrections ultimately depends on three conditions: (1) funding research so more effective technologies can be developed; (2) identifying what works for which group of offenders so that delinquents interested in treatment can be given the interventions most compatible with their needs and interests; and (3) creating more humane environments so that environmental conditions will not interfere with the treatment process.

Treatment was buried in the mid-1970s with considerable fanfare, although programs continue to exist in communities and institutions. The same amount of energy should be put into reemphasizing treatment, not as a panacea for youth crime or as a condition of release, but as a viable option for those offenders who are interested in change, growth, and positive movement in their lives. Any less will be cruel and unusual punishment.

Discussion Questions

1. What are the three basic positions on the usefulness of correctional treatment?
2. Why are classification systems on the decline in juvenile corrections?
3. Why is TA popular with many delinquents?
4. Why do line staff frequently favor reality therapy over other treatment techniques discussed in this chapter?
5. What attitudes and changes do GGI and PPC hope to bring forth in the peer culture?

6. Define the basic ingredients of effective programs. Why is each important?

7. In terms of policy for improving correctional treatment, what are the three recommendations given in this chapter? Why would each recommendation improve the quality of offender rehabilitation?

8. Which modality do you believe is the most promising for use in correctional institutions? Why?

References

Berne, Eric. *Games People Play.* New York: Grove Press, 1964.

Cullen, Francis T., and Gilbert, Karen E. *Reaffirming Rehabilitation.* Cincinnati: W. H. Anderson Company, 1982.

Harris, Thomas. *I'm OK—You're OK.* New York: Harper & Row, 1967.

Lipton, Douglas; Martinson, Robert; and Wilks, Judith. *The Effectiveness of Correctional Treatment.* New York: Praeger, 1975.

Martin, Susan; Sechrest, Lee; and Redner, Robin; eds. *Rehabilitation of Criminal Offenders: Directions for Research.* Washington, D.C.: National Academy of Sciences, 1981.

Sechrest, Lee; White, Susan O.; and Brown, Elizabeth, D.; eds. *The Rehabilitation of Criminal Offenders: Problems and Prospects.* Washington, D.C.: National Academy of Sciences, 1979.

Vorrath, Harry H., and Brendtro, Larry K. *Positive Peer Culture.* Chicago: Aldine Publishing Company, 1974.

Wicks, Robert J. *Correctional Psychology.* San Francisco: Canfield Press, 1974.

FOOTNOTES

1. Interviewed in early 1981.

2. Walter C. Bailey, "Correctional Outcome: An Evaluation of 100 Reports," *Journal of Criminal Law, Criminology, and Police Science* 57 (June 1957), pp. 153–160.

3. J. Robison and G. Smith, "The Effectiveness of Correctional Programs," *Crime and Delinquency* 17 (1971), pp. 67–70.

4. Robert Martinson, "What Works?—Questions and Answers about Prison Reform," *Public Interest* 35 (Spring 1974), pp. 22–54.

5. Douglas Lipton, Robert Martinson, and Judith Wilks, *The Effectiveness of Correctional Treatment* (New York: Praeger, 1975).

6. CBS Television Network. Excerpted from "60 Minutes" Segment, "It Doesn't Work" (24 August 1975).

7. Ted Palmer, "Martinson Revisited," *Journal of Research in Crime and Delinquency* 12 (July 1975), pp. 133–152.

8. Ibid., p. 137.

9. Robert Martinson, "New Findings, New Views: A Note of Caution Regarding Sentencing Reform," *Hofstra Law Review* 7 (Winter 1979), p. 244.

10. Paul Gendreau and Robert Ross, "Effective Correctional Treatment: Bibliotherapy for Cynics," *Crime and Delinquency* 27 (October 1979), pp. 463–489.

11. Robert R. Ross and Paul Gendreau, eds. *Effective Correctional Treatment* (Toronto: Butterworth, 1980), p. viii.

12. See James Q. Wilson, *Thinking about Crime* (New York: Basic Books, 1975), and Ernest van den Haag, *Punishing Criminals: Concerning a Very Old and Painful Question* (New York: Basic Books, 1975).

13. See Anthony Platt, *The Child-Savers: The Invention of Delinquency* (Chicago: University of Chicago Press, 1968).

14. See David Fogel, *". . . We Are the Living Proof": The Justice Model for Corrections* (Cincinnati: W. H. Anderson Company, 1975); Andrew von Hirsh, *Doing Justice: The Choice of Punishments* (New York: Hill & Wang, 1976); Norval Morris, *The Future of Imprisonment* (Chicago: University of Chicago Press, 1974); and John P. Conrad, *Justice and Consequences* (Lexington, Mass.: D. C. Heath & Company, 1981).

15. Fogel, *". . . We Are the Living Proof"*; and von Hirsch, *Doing Justice*.

16. See Robert R. Ross and Paul Gendreau, "Offender Rehabilitation: The Appeal of Success," *Federal Probation* 45 (December 1981), p. 46.

17. Francis T. Cullen and Karen E. Gilbert, *Reaffirming Rehabilitation* (Cincinnati: W. H. Anderson Company, 1982), pp. 247, 253, 257, 261.

18. See Lee Sechrest, Susan O. White, and Elizabeth D. Brown, eds., *The Rehabilitation of Criminal Offenders: Problems and Prospects* (Washington, D.C.: National Academy of Sciences, 1979); and Susan Martin, Lee Sechrest, and Robin Redner, eds., *Rehabilitation of Criminal Offenders: Directions for Research* (Washington, D.C.: National Academy of Sciences, 1981).

19. See Roy L. Austin, "I-Level and Rehabilitation of Delinquents," in *Justice and Corrections*, edited by Norman Johnston and Leonard D. Savitz (New York: John Wiley & Sons, 1978), for an account of the history and development of I-Level.

20. Marguerite Q. Warren, "The Community Treatment Project: History and Prospects," in *Law Enforcement Science and Technology*, edited by S. A. Yefsky (Washington, D.C.: Thompson Book Company, 1972), pp. 193–195.

21. See Ted Palmer, "The Youth Authority's Community Treatment Project," *Federal Probation* (March 1974), pp. 3–14.

22. See Austin, "I-Level and Rehabilitation," for a discussion of the evaluation of these two projects.

23. Roy Gerard, "Institutional Innovations in Juvenile Corrections," *Federal Probation* 34 (December 1970), pp. 38–40.

24. Peter C. Kratcoski and Lucille Dunn Kratcoski, *Juvenile Delinquency* (Englewood Cliffs, N.J.: Prentice-Hall, 1979), pp. 294–295.

25. Gerard, "Institutional Innovations," pp. 38–40.

26. See Dennis A. Romig, *Justice for Our Children: An Examination of Juvenile Delinquent Rehabilitation Programs* (Lexington, Mass.: D.C. Heath & Company, 1978), pp. 82–83, for a description of these studies.

27. Stuart Adams, "Effectiveness of Interview Therapy with Older Youth Authority Wards: An Interim Evaluation of the PICO Project," Research Report No. 20 (Sacramento, Calif.: California Youth Authority, 1961).

28. E. S. Thomas, "Effects of Experimental School Counseling of Delinquency-Prone Adolescents," *Dissertation Abstracts* 28 (1968): 2572.

29. Clemens Bartollas, *Correctional Treatment: Theory and Practice* (Englewood Cliffs, N.J.: Prentice-Hall, 1984).

30. F. Berkowitz, *Evaluation of Crime Control Programs in California: A Review* (Sacramento, Calif.: California Council on Criminal Justice, April 1973).

31. G. L. Ingram, et al., "An Experimental Program for the Psychopathic Delinquents: Looking in the 'Correctional Wastebasket' *Journal of Research in Crime and Delinquency* 7 (1970), pp. 24–30.

32. L. A. Herman, "An Exploration of Psychodrama," *Group Psychotherapy* 21 (1968), pp. 211–213.

33. T. M. Ostrom, et al., "Modification of Delinquent Behavior," *Journal of Applied Social Psychology* 1 (1971), pp. 118–136.

34. Eric Berne, *What Do You Say after You Say Hello?* (New York: Grove Press, 1972).

35. Thomas A. Harris, *I'm OK—You're OK* (New York: Harper & Row, 1965).

36. Eric Berne, *Games People Play* (New York: Grove Press, 1964).

37. Peter Scharf, Lawrence Kohlberg, and Joseph Hickey, "Ideology and Correctional Intervention: The Creation of a Just Prison Community," in *Correctional Counseling and Treatment*, edited by Peter C. Kratcoski (Monterey, Calif.: Duxbury Press, 1981), p. 412.

38. Interviewed in July 1972.

39. William Glasser, *Reality Therapy* (New York: Harper & Row, 1965), pp. xii, 7.

40. Richard L. Rachin, "Reality Therapy: Helping People Help Themselves," *Crime and Delinquency* 20 (January 1974), pp. 51–53.

41. Glasser, *Reality Therapy*, p. 70.

42. Ibid., p. 68.

43. George J. MacDonald et al., "Treatment of the Sex Offender," mimeographed (Fort Steilacoom, Wash.: Western State Hospital, 1968).

44. Carl F. Jesness et al., *The Youth Center Research Project* (Sacramento, Calif.: American Justice Institute, 1972), p. 7.

45. R. Schwitzgebel and D. A. Kolb, "Inducing Behavior Change to Adolescent Delinquents," *Behavior Research Therapy* 1 (1964), pp. 297–304, analyzed in Romig, *Justice for Our Children*, p. 11.

46. Ibid., pp. 20–21.

47. Berkowitz, *Evaluation of Crime Control Programs*.

48. Romig, *Justice for Our Children*, p. 87.

49. B. V. Parsons and J. F. Alexander, "Short-Term Family Intervention: A Therapy Outcome Study," *Journal of Consulting and Clinical Psychology* 41 (1973), pp. 195–201.

50. Romig, *Justice for Our Children*, pp. 92–93.

51. See Clemens Bartollas and Stuart J. Miller, *The Juvenile Offender: Control, Correction, and Treatment* (Boston: Holbrook Press, 1978), pp. 298–306, for a more extensive presentation of guided group interaction and positive peer culture.

52. Robert J. Wicks, *Correctional Psychology* (San Francisco: Canfield Press, 1974), pp. 50–51.

53. See Harry H. Vorrath and Larry K. Brendtro, *Positive Peer Culture* (Chicago: Aldine Publishing Company, 1974), for the philosophy and principles of PPC.

54. Ibid.

55. Harry D. Mitchell and David L. Cochrum, "Positive Peer Culture and a Legal System: A Comparison in an Adolescent Treatment Facility," *Criminal Justice and Behavior* 7 (December 1980), pp. 399–406.

56. Interviewed in September 1981.

57. See Michael S. Serrill, "California," *Corrections Magazine* 1 (September 1974), pp. 44–45, for a description of this program at Monzanita Lodge.

58. See Phillip B. Taft, Jr., "Elan: Does Its Bizarre Regimen Transform Troubled Youth or Abuse Them?" *Corrections Magazine* 5 (March 1979), pp. 18–28, for a more extensive description of the program.

59. Interviewed in March 1980.

60. Carl H. Schmidt, "A Research Proposal for Evaluating the Effectiveness of Emotional Maturity Instruction," mimeographed (August 1978).

61. Harry H. Woodward, Jr., and Frederick M. Chivers, "Teaching Motivation to Inmates," *Federal Probation* 20 (March 1976), pp. 41–48.

62. Romig, *Justice for Our Children*, p. 109.

63. Ibid., p. 110.

64. Sechrest, White, and Brown, eds., *The Rehabilitation of Criminal Offenders*; and Martin, Sechrest, and Redner, eds., *Rehabilitation of Criminal Offenders*.

65. These elements of effective programs are suggested by the work of Martin Groder and of Alden D. Miller, Lloyd E. Ohlin, and Robert B. Coates. See "Dr. Martin Groder: An Angry Resignation," *Corrections Magazine* 1 (July-August 1975), p. 3; and Alden D. Miller, Lloyd E. Ohlin, and Robert B. Coates, *A Theory of Social Reform: Correctional Change Processes in Two States* (Cambridge: Ballinger Publishing Company, 1977).

66. Joshua L. Miner and Joe Boldt, *Outward Bound USA: Learning through Experience in Adventure-Based Education* (New York: William Morrow & Company, 1981).

67. See Robert L. Woodson, *A Summons to Life: Mediating Structures and the Prevention of Youth Crime* (Cambridge: Ballinger Publishing Company, 1981), for a biographical sketch of Sister Fattah and her husband.

68. "Dr. Martin Groder," p. 33.

69. Clemens Bartollas, Stuart J. Miller, and Simon Dinitz, "Boys Who Profit: The Limits of Institutional Success," in *Reform in Corrections: Problems and Issues,* edited by Harry E. Allen and Nancy J. Beran (New York: Praeger Publishers, 1977), pp. 18–19.

70. Sechrest, White, and Brown, eds., *The Rehabilitation of Criminal Offenders*, pp. 35–37.

71. Herbert C. Quay, "The Three Faces of Evaluation: What Can Be Expected to Work?" *Criminal Justice and Behavior* 4 (December 1977), pp. 341–353.

72. Sechrest, Brown, and White, eds., *The Rehabilitation of Criminal Offenders*, pp. 3–4.

73. Martin, Sechrest, and Redner, eds., *Rehabilitation of Criminal Offenders*, p. 6.

74. Sechrest, Brown, and White, eds., *The Rehabilitation of Criminal Offenders*, p. 45.

75. The template-matching technique was originally proposed in D. Bem and D. Funder, "Predicting More of the People More of the Time: Assessing the Personality of Situations," *Psychological Review* 85 (1978), pp. 485–501.

76. Martin, Sechrest, and Redner, eds., *Rehabilitation of Criminal Offenders*, p. 82.

INTERVIEW WITH DONALD R. CRESSEY

"If you say 'nothing works,' you're implying that nobody changes or can be changed. That's nonsense. We all change, all the time. . . . Here's the principle, the simple principle taught to me when I was a young student of psychology: Anything that is learned can be unlearned."

In this interview, Donald R. Cressey, who is professor of sociology at the University of California, Santa Barbara, answers a number of pressing questions about correctional treatment, such as—what it is, whether it works, whether it should be compulsory, whether the state can be trusted to administer rehabilitative programs, and whether it has improved. Professor Cressey has been interested in the subject of correctional intervention for many years and recommends in this interview that the focus of correctional intervention be changed from a psychological to a social learning model.

Question: What is your reaction to the "nothing works" statement by Robert Martinson?

Cressey: It's baloney. There's no evidence that nothing works. For a number of years, corrections was in the hands of people who used psychiatric theory rather than theory like social learning or differential association. They thought they could "treat" and "cure" criminality, but they were wrong. Their programs didn't work, but that doesn't mean that nothing will work.

Think about the theory behind most of the programs Martinson reviewed. The assumption, based on a medical model, was that through his or her social experiences, the person gets infected with a

Donald R. Cressey in acknowledged as one of the top criminologists in the United States. He is the author of books such as Other People's Money *and* Theft of the Nation *as well as coauthor of the classic text,* Criminology *(with Edwin H. Sutherland) and of such books as* Diversion from the Juvenile Justice System, Social Problems, *and* Justice by Consent.

bad personality—call it X—and that persons with an X kind of personal or emotional makeup almost automatically become Y, which is delinquent or criminal. To illustrate, if a person gets infected with tuberculosis, the bacillus is X, and it follows that X leads to Y—poor breathing ability, poor lung capacity, gasping, hacking, and coughing. Now if you want to get rid of Y, you put infected people in hospitals or clinics and treat them for X. You need pay no attention at all to the process by which a person contracted tuberculosis. On this analogy, the juvenile institution and the adult prison was going to be a clinic that would treat the disease of X that causes crime and send the offender out the back door cured.

I've been analyzing prison programs for thirty years, and during all those years—long before Martinson—I've been saying that rehabilitation programs based on this understanding of treatment won't work. The reason they won't work has little to do with prisons or institutions for delinquents. It has to do with the faulty view of the nature of crime and of personality. The idea of "curing" someone of delinquency or criminality is ridiculous if you think of the change process in terms of differential association or some other form of learning theory.

I wrote an article about changing criminals way back in 1955.[1] It said, boiled down, that if you want to change people, you must change their so-

[1] Donald R. Cressey, "Changing Criminals: The Application of the Theory of Differential Association," *American Journal of Sociology,* 61:116–170, September, 1955.

cial relationships. You can't take a man or boy out of an environment where there is a wild excess of criminal behavior patterns, casually expose him to a treatment program in prison or a juvenile institution for a couple of years, send him back to the same old environment, and then expect him to not violate the law. You may say that he violates the law because he has not been cured, but you will be wrong. He picks up where he left off because you never dealt with his social relationships. You don't "cure" social relationships. You can't "treat" them either, but you can change them. It works.

Here's a boy whose fun and excitement during high school was stealing hubcaps and siphoning gas. When he gets into a university he finds such behavior to be "kid stuff" that's not done by university students, so he doesn't do it anymore. There is nothing magical about this. Nothing about his personality or his biology has changed. Nevertheless, his delinquency disappears because his social relationships have changed.

If you say "nothing works," you're implying that nobody changes or can be changed. That's nonsense. We all change, all the time. Some people change from being noncriminal to being criminal at the age of 25, 52, or even 64. By the same token, these and other, younger, criminals can be changed back to noncriminals. Here's the principle, the simple principle taught to me when I was a young student of psychology: Anything that can be learned can be unlearned.

I don't think it's possible to find a psychologist who will disagree with that principle. Now, I maintain that criminality and delinquency are learned. That's what the differential association theory is all about. It follows then that delinquency can be unlearned. Therefore, "something works." But giving the delinquent vocational training or counseling or group therapy or individual therapy or drugs isn't going to change him because those "treatments" aren't directed at getting him to unlearn his delinquent behavior. But if your concern is with changing the social relationships in which he learned the delinquency in the first place, then you will find that he unlearns that behavior.

Question: How about applying differential association to the use of guided group interaction or posi-

tive peer culture, both of which are based on social learning theory? Would you agree that this would make correctional interventions more effective?

Cressey: Yes. I would agree because such programs ideally deal with social interaction. But I would add another twist: If I want to change you, the best thing I can do is to get you in a "peer culture" program and encourage you to try to change other people. If you're a delinquent and you try to help another person unlearn his or her delinquency, you are probably going to have very little effect on that person, but your efforts will have a lot of effect on you. There is nothing new or mysterious about this principle, but it is rarely used in correctional programs. It was used by the early Christians who sent every person out as a missionary. They might not have made many converts, but they certainly reinforced their own faith. The Mormons use the same principle, as do Jehovah witnesses and members of AA [Alcoholics Anonymous]. If you ask me why so few probation officers are criminals, my answer will be two-fold. First, throughout the formative years of their lives, they have not experienced an excess of associations with criminal behavior patterns. Second, continually telling people not to be delinquents reinforces the lawabiding values they have learned.

So something works, particularly with youngsters. The "nothing works" ideology that is now so popular usually refers to prisons for adults, but most criminals are juveniles. The idea is to incapacitate criminals and, at best, to achieve deterrence through punishment. Because nothing works, the idea goes, we should forget about providing positive, interventionist programs in prison. Just lock them behind walls of concrete and steel, and then ensure that they don't climb over them. This "do nothing" ideology hasn't permeated as deeply into institutions for juveniles. One reason for this is that even the "punishment is the answer" nuts—especially those who are parents—recognize that young people learn and unlearn. They are malleable and easily changed if attention is directed to their social relationships. The "do nothing" folk ought to know that old criminals are easily changed too, if you go about it properly.

Question: In *Reaffirming Rehabilitation,* one of Cullen and Gilbert's concerns is that the state would dismantle rehabilitation programs if inmates were no longer required to participate in them. Is the state to be distrusted as much as they appear to distrust the state?

Cressey: The important point here is that we are the setters of public policy. So, we, the people, once said there should be so-called rehabilitative programs in prisons as well as in juvenile correctional institutions. The state ran them. Now the "nothing works" supporters say that state has done such a terrible job that we should no longer mandate prison officials to try to change inmates by positive means. The argument is attractive because the state is much better able to punish than it is to do anything else. After all, the purpose of the criminal law is punishment. Each criminal law says that whoever behaves in a certain way ought to be punished. Nothing is said about rehabilitation or, for that matter, about doing something for victims. Now ever since the *Gault* decision this same criminal law has increasingly been used to undermine the "correctional" philosophy of the juvenile court. This means that the juvenile justice system is also becoming a system that is concerned solely with the administration of punishment.

Being a libertarian, I have my own distrust of government. But saying that the state should engage in radical deregulation and therefore should not run rehabilitation programs is absurd. If the state stops helping people, as we sometimes hear it proposed in national politics, we are doomed.

Question: What about compulsory treatment?

Cressey: The basic objection to compulsory treatment is that the actual aim of the so-called treatment or rehabilitation programs has been to control inmates rather than to change them. I long ago voiced this objection myself. In California twenty years ago, any inmate who wanted to get out of prison had to participate in group therapy. Hundreds of people went through the motions of participating in the programs. Ostensibly, as I said earlier, the idea was to let a man out of prison when he was "cured" of his criminality. To decide whether he had in fact been rehabilitated, the parole board was supposed to examine his participation in the group counselling program, talk with the leader and other group members, and look for signs of change. Instead, the board looked at his criminal record, his current offense, his social background, his prison disciplinary record, and other conditions that had nothing to do with so-called "treatment." Requiring participation in group counselling turned out to be a requirement that the inmates be quiet and docile. Any program that requires inmates to "work their way out of prison" by showing signs of being rehabilitated is bound to fail because such programs are always restricted by custodial and punitive concerns.

Question: Has correctional intervention improved? Has the technology been refined? Is it better today than it has been in the past?

Cressey: No, I think not. Here's an eight-year-old kid marching toward San Quentin. Should the state intervene? Of course it should intervene. But how to intervene is a different matter. Intervention techniques are no better today than they were twenty years ago or even thirty years ago. They still interfere with civil liberties too. The reason, primarily, is the one I mentioned earlier—most intervention techniques are still based on the mistaken notion that delinquency stems from a deformed or otherwise inadequate personality. Techniques for changing people's social relationships without abridging constitutional rights are still to be tried.

CHAPTER 21

JUVENILE DELINQUENCY IN THE 1980S

CHAPTER OUTLINE

Juvenile delinquency in American society is a serious matter but a common phenomenon today. The public is "fed up" with juvenile crime, especially violent crime, and exerts considerable pressure on officials of the juvenile justice system and on policymakers to do something about youth crime. The vast majority of juveniles commit some form of law violations at sometime during adolescence, but most go on to become law-abiding citizens. Some youths commit serious offenses, including violent crimes, and a few become chronic juvenile criminals.

This final chapter will summarize briefly the contents of this book and present policy recommendations that should better prevent and control juvenile delinquency in American society.

CONTEXTUAL PERSPECTIVE

A major theme of this book is that delinquent behavior in America takes place in and is shaped by five contexts: the historical, the legal, the sociocultural, the economic, and the political. These five contexts do not exist in and by themselves, for all are interrelated with each other. Furthermore, each of the five contexts operates on three levels: (1) the societal or state level, (2) the neighborhood or community level, and (3) the individual level. Thus, this contextual perspective is multidimensional and avoids the tendency to become entrapped in one context and subordinating all the others to that particular frame of reference.

Historical Context

A sociological interpretation of delinquency needs to account for the origins and emergence of typical patterns of delinquency by locating such origins in time and place. Much of recorded history has revealed abuse and indifference to be the fate of many children. However, during the seventeenth and eighteenth centuries in America, children began to be viewed as less threatening, and parents became more concerned with training and socializing them than with conquering their spirits. Since the mid-twentieth century, parents have attempted to meet the expanding needs of their children in a democratic and supportive environment. In the late nineteenth century, the concept of adolescence evolved out of changing conceptions of childhood. Adolescence, a term defining the life interval between childhood and adulthood, was acknowledged as a new stage in human growth and development.

The history of juvenile justice in the United States has been one of taking authority away from the family and giving it to the state. This process actually began in the early eighteenth century when reformers became disillusioned with the family and looked for a public substitute that would provide an orderly, disciplined environment similar to that of the "ideal" Puritan family. Houses of refuge, which were intended to protect wayward children from corrupting home environments, were established beginning in the 1820s. In 1899, the first juvenile court was created in Cook County (Chicago), and while the juvenile court movement established a justice system for juveniles separate from that of adults, the court was legally empowered to act as a substitute parent for youths in trouble. In the 1960s and 1970s, the expansion of community-based and diversionary programs continued the trend to deemphasize the role of the family and to bring more juveniles into the net of the juvenile justice system.

The prevention and control of delinquency has been a major part of the history of juvenile justice in the United States. Primary prevention, long the basic goal of those concerned about juvenile delinquency, has received more criticism than praise over the past century. Minor successes have occurred here and there, but the overall pattern has not been impressive. The prevailing attitude toward diversion, or secondary prevention, has gone in the past decade from widespread acceptance to wholesale criticism. Diversion has been accused of enlarging the net of the juvenile justice system, of saving those who need saving the least, and of denying the due process rights of juveniles. The treatment of delinquents has also been characterized as a history of good intentions. Nearly every conceivable method has been tried to remodel, remake, reshape, and rehabilitate delinquents. But these strategies have fallen far short of accomplishing the goals of curing delinquency or of deterring youths from returning to the justice system.

On the community level, each community has developed its own history of dealing with juvenile crime. Some communities provide a network of services for youths in trouble, while others have only limited services. For example, police departments in some communities offer a number of specialized services for juveniles; others have very few. Similarly, the number of day treatment and residential programs available for youthful offenders varies. But more importantly, the quality of services communities provide juveniles varies. Typically, those interventions that do have a positive impact upon juveniles are led by charismatic and caring persons.

Education is a vital part of community life that especially affects adolescents. The U.S. Constitution says nothing about public education, but by 1918, education was both free and compulsory in nearly every state of the Union. The baby boom of the 1950s resulted in larger enrollments and more formalized student-teacher contacts in public schools in the 1960s. In the 1970s, public education came under increased criticism, as several studies documented the harm done to children by repressive educational systems.[1] However, the quality of public education sometimes varies significantly between the suburban and the urban school.

On the individual level, crime is an act that is a product of the time and experience of the actor. Each juvenile develops his or her own history in the larger community. Youths who are looked upon as good boys and girls generally want to maintain the positive image that others hold of them. But youths who are looked upon as troublemakers because of histories of law-violating behavior also have reputations to uphold.

Legal Context

Delinquency is a legal term that was initially used in 1899 when Illinois passed the first law on juvenile delinquent behavior. The juvenile court, from its establishment, has based its philosophy of handling juveniles on the legal concept of *parens patriae*. This concept means that the state is to step in and provide the care to a child that a good parent would provide. Children are to be treated not as criminals, but as young persons not totally responsible for their behavior.[2] The purpose of the court ultimately is to rescue or save juveniles from lives of crime. However, critics have challenged these idealistic goals. They claim that the juvenile court has not succeeded in rehabilitating juvenile delinquents, in bringing justice and compassion to them, or in providing them due process rights.[3]

The capricious and arbitrary justice handed out by the juvenile court, resulting in the lack of due process rights for juveniles, led to a series of decisions by the U.S. Supreme Court in the 1960s and 1970s (*Kent* v. *United States,* 1966; *In re Gault,* 1967; *In the Matter of Samual Winship,* 1970; *McKeiver* v. *Pennsylvania,* 1971; and *Breed* v. *Jones,* 1975). The *In re Gault* decision, in the most far-reaching of these cases, stated that a juvenile has a right to due process safeguards in proceedings where a finding of delinquency could lead to confinement and that juveniles have rights to notice of charges, to counsel, to confrontation and cross-examination, and to privilege against self-incrimination.

The childrens' rights movement also sprang up during the 1960s to ensure greater rights for young people in all areas of their lives. While unable to form a coalition, interest groups have made significant progress on special issues of due process rights in school, questions of custody in divorce cases, guardianship for foster children, protection of the rights of privacy, independent access to medical care, and child abuse legislation. Supporters of the childrens' rights movement have gone so far as to urge that a bill of rights be enacted, in which children are provided the rights to a relevant education, to a supportive home, to personal property, to sexual relationships of their choice, to all available information without censorship and to expression of political opinions.[4]

Juvenile court codes, which are found in every state, specify the conditions under which the state may legitimately interfere in a juvenile's life. Since the passage of the 1974 Juvenile Justice and Delinquency Prevention Act, the definition of delinquency has been restricted more and more to acts committed by a juvenile that are violations of criminal law. In many states, juvenile court codes have recently been modified to lower the age of jurisdiction of the juvenile court and also to make it possible to transfer more youthful offenders to the adult court.

On the community level, the juvenile court has three legal approaches to youthful offenders. On one end of the spectrum, the *parens patriae,* or rehabilitation, model is used to deal with status offenders and minor offenders. At the other end of the spectrum, juveniles who commit a serious crime or continue to break the law are presumed to deserve punishment rather than treatment because they possess free will and know what they are doing. In between these two groups are those juveniles who see crime as a form of play and commit delinquent acts because they enjoy the thrill of getting away with illegal behavior or because they are bored. Their acts typically are looked upon more as mischievous than as delinquent and, therefore, they usually are excused or diverted from the system.

To express this another way, the philosophical viewpoint of positivism is used with the majority of juvenile offenders. It is presumed that they cannot help committing socially unacceptable behavior; that is, biological, psychological, and sociological antecedent conditions cause such behavior. But juveniles who commit serious crimes or continue to commit delinquent acts are presumed to be acting of their own free will and, therefore, are responsible for their behavior. The delinquent acts of these serious or repeat offenders are viewed as purposeful activity resulting from rational decisions.

On the community level, the juvenile court is charged with controlling the behavior of law-violating juveniles. But the juvenile court finds it difficult to fulfill its mission of controlling juvenile crime for several reasons. Lack of a unifying philosophy makes it difficult to deal effectively with youth crime. The fragmentation of the juvenile system continues to pose major problems in presenting an effective and orderly response to youth crime. In addition, the juvenile justice system continues to receive meager funding and to be a marginal area of governmental concern. Finally, the juvenile justice system tends to breed, rather than reduce or cure, delinquency; that is, the more that delinquents are processed through the juvenile justice system, the more likely they will continue their law-violating behavior.

Improved police-juvenile relations in the past decade are attributed largely to the proactive interventions of the police in dealing with juveniles. Probation is criticized as being too soft, but supporters claim that the emerging logical consequences model will result in improving the effectiveness of probation services. Community-based corrections appear to be at least as effective as training schools in reducing recidivism, with far less trauma to delinquents and less cost to the state. The decisions made by juvenile courts still reflect a policy of saving middle-class youngsters and of dumping lower-class ones into long-term juvenile correctional institutions. While training schools may be more humane than they have been in the past, they are still acknowledged as ineffective means of dealing with delinquency.

On the individual level is the youthful offender who breaks the law. First, why does this youth commit delinquent acts? Second, what do the official and unofficial means of measuring delinquent behavior tell us about such a youth?

In response to the first question, the neoclassical approach argues that juvenile lawbreakers have free will and make rational decisions to commit delinquent acts. In contrast, biological and psychological positivism theories contend that delinquents cannot help committing crimes because they are controlled by socio-biological or psychological antecedent factors. Sociological explanations also fit within a positivistic framework because they conclude that social factors cause youths to be predisposed to delinquent behavior. Social structure explanations of delinquency claim that delinquents commit crime because they are poor, because they live in disorganized communities, and because they cannot achieve middle-class success patterns. Social process theories, also within the general framework of sociological positivism, state that youths commit delinquent acts because they learn such behaviors from other delinquents, because the group encourages them to take a moral vacation from the law, because they lack commitment to the social bond, because they have poor self-concepts, and because they are labeled by society. Finally, radical criminologists argue that it is the economic exploitation of the lower classes that causes delinquent behavior.

However, no one causal scheme appears sufficient in itself to explain delinquent behavior, or, for that matter, no one causal scheme is able to explain why youths do not become involved in delinquent behavior.[5] Some theories, of course, explain the behavior of some youths more than others, but generally the reasons a youth becomes involved in delinquency includes social process, social structural, psychological, and sometimes even sociobiological levels of explanation. Integrated theory, which generally includes linking social control and other social process theories, is increasingly being used to develop more multidimensional explanations of delinquent behavior.

Official and unofficial measurements of delinquency lead to the following observations about delinquent behavior:

- Delinquency in a serious problem in American society in terms of the prevalence and frequency of law-violating behavior.
- Delinquency is spread throughout all social classes.
- A few delinquent youths, who have been called chronic offenders, commit a disproportionate number of antisocial acts.
- Minority youths appear to commit more frequent and more serious delinquent acts than do white youths.
- Boys still commit more delinquent acts and more serious delinquent acts than do girls.
- Girls appear to commit delinquent acts for many of the same reasons that boys do.
- Female delinquents, especially those who commit moral offenses, are treated unfairly by the juvenile justice system.
- Youth gangs are a serious problem in urban areas and the public schools, and their expanding organizational structures are making it more difficult for agencies of the justice system to handle them.

Sociocultural Context

A knowledge of the particular social structure and the social processes within and through which delinquency occurs are important in understanding youth crime. In terms of the societal level, the public today is very concerned about the seriousness of youth crime. The perceptions of the public, which are determined largely by the media, are that youth crime is out of control, and, consequently, the public is putting pressure on policymakers to curb the serious problem of juvenile delinquency. The public also is concerned about the amount of violence and vandalism in the public schools. But a child-centered culture still provides the broader social context for handling youth crime. This child-centered culture dictates a generally permissive approach to children and, accordingly, the least restrictive model has been widely used with status offenders and minor offenders. While this soft-line policy is being used with status offenders and minor offenders, the public wants a hard-line policy taken with delinquents who commit serious personal and property crimes.

On the community level, the family and the school are two critical institutions for understanding delinquency in American society. Family conflict and poor marital adjustment appear to be more closely related to delinquent behavior by children than is the structural breakup of the family. But the likelihood of delinquency also increases when parents are indifferent or rejecting, when siblings are delinquent, or parents criminal, when parents unable to provide for the emotional and financial needs of children, and when discipline is inadequate.

Child abuse and neglect also have a profound effect on the behavior and attitudes of adolescents and children. Neglected and abused adolescents are more likely to run away from home and, if placed in foster care, to have difficulty in adjusting. Neglected and abused adolescents frequently have school problems, which can lead to truancy or being labeled disruptive students. Neglected and abused adolescents may also become involved in drug and alcohol abuse in order to blot out the emotional pain experienced at home. Sexually abused adolescents are often self-destructive, which can be expressed in drug or alcohol abuse, involvement in prostitution, or suicidal behavior. Adolescents, especially males, sometimes express their anger over being abused in ways that hurt others. In short, victimization within the home sometimes has a profound effect on adolescents and may influence them to become involved in status offenses or in delinquent behavior.

The repressiveness of public education has created bored, frustrated, dissatisfied, and alienated students. Urie Bronfenbrenner has noted that "the schools have become one of the most potent breeding grounds of alienation in American society."[6] Not surprisingly, vandalism and violence are serious problems in this nation's schools.

A number of studies have established a direct relationship between delinquent behavior and poor academic achievement.[7] The 1967 report by the Task Force on Juvenile Delinquency pointed out that boys who failed in school were seven times more likely to become delinquent than those who did not fail.[8] However, the explanations for poor academic achievement are more complex than lack of general aptitude or intelligence. The link between learning disabilities and juvenile delinquency is at present a popular subject for research. Although the link between LD/JD is questionable, considerable evidence supports the contention that youngsters with learning disabilities frequently fail in school and that officials of the justice system are influenced by their school failure to process them through the juvenile justice system. The relationship of delinquency to absenteeism from school is also a complex one. Delbert Elliot and Harwin Voss found that dropouts' delinquent behavior declined dramatically in the period immediately after they left school and continued to decline thereafter. In contrast, the official delinquency and self-report delinquency of those youths who remained in school gradually increased during the studied years.[9]

On the individual level, adolescents, like adults, are influenced by the values and norms of the larger society. The violence of youth gangs is not surprising in view of the infatuation with violence in American society. Property offenses can be seen as merely an extension of the behavior found among adults. "Beating the system" is another norm that juveniles learn from adult society. Further, youths' dependency on things outside themselves for pleasure has been learned from adults dependent on alcohol and drugs.

The adolescent period, during which the individual passes from childhood to adulthood, is one strongly affected by environmental influences. Some youngsters find this period to be a time of calm, easily adjusting to the various pressures facing them. But other youngsters find this period one of crisis, and are influenced by the crises they face to become involved in delinquent behavior. The peer group, or teenage society, appears to exert a strong influence on those adolescents who are alienated from families and other social institutions. Chronic running away and the abuse of alcohol and drugs also may cause adolescents to become further involved in socially unacceptable behavior.

Economic Context

The relationship between economics and delinquency has a long history. The studies by Clifford R. Shaw and Henry McKay, by Albert K. Cohen, and by Richard A. Cloward and Lloyd E. Ohlin, all of which are considered classics, found a direct relationship between economics and delinquency.[10] But because of the consistent finding in self-report studies that delinquency is spread throughout the social classes, the relationship between economics and delinquency was deemphasized by mainline sociologists in the 1970s. However, in the 1980s, a number of studies have again found higher offense rates among lower-class juveniles.

Robert Gillespie's survey of fifty-seven studies provides considerable support for a positive relationship between unemployment and the committing of property crimes.[11] Allen Calvin also documents an extremely strong association between the unemployment of black youths and street crime.[12] Furthermore, Berk, Lenihan, and Rossi found that unemployment increases recidivism among exoffenders.[13] Finally, Phillips, Votey, and Maxwell found a strong relationship between unemployment and crime.[14] These studies, which substantiate a strong relationship between unemployment, social class, and delinquency, generally contend that those studies not reporting higher rates of delinquency for lower-class youths are susceptible to theoretical and methodological criticisms.

Meanwhile, radical criminologists have argued over the past decade that the economic exploitation of lower-class youths by the capitalist class is the chief reason for youth crime. These radical conflict theorists, with a Marxist orientation, believe that crime and delinquency in capitalist society emerge because of the efforts of the powerful to maintain their power at all costs, with the result that the working class is exploited. Radical theorists contend that true economic, social, and political equality for all cannot be achieved under the present capitalist system.[15]

The danger is either to over- or under-emphasize the role of economics in understanding delinquency. Although growing up poor may increase one's likelihood of becoming delinquent, economics is only one of the contexts that affects an adolescent on a daily basis.

On the community level, the economic context is especially important in impoverished neighborhoods. Unemployment rates are typically extremely high in these neighborhoods. Families live on the edge of economic survival. The necessities of life, such as nutritious food, warm clothing, adequate heat in the home, and proper medical care are not available. The futility of this type of existence may breed resignation or rage. Parents may neglect or strike out against their children. Or they simply may be so preoccupied with economic survival for the family that they have little time or energy left for supervision of their children.

On the individual level, juveniles are affected by the economic conditions of society in at least two ways. First, children from an impoverished home background must accept on a daily basis the consequences of economic deprivations in their lives. Not surprisingly, the children of the poor frequently turn to crime to acquire what their families cannot provide. Second, youngsters today must deal with economic hard times that makes unemployment rates extremely high. Adolescents who drop out of school find making it in the marketplace particularly difficult. Among minority youths in urban areas, for example, unemployment rates are sometimes 50 to 60 percent.

Political Context

The political aspects of delinquency theory and practice are receiving more attention today than they have in the past. The policy used to deal with youth crime is made in the political arena, and it is in this arena that the policy for the prevention and control of delinquency is developed, implemented, and evaluated. But social policy is determined in environments in which diverse groups compete for scarce resources. Many conflicting groups are present, and the power bases of these interest groups are critical factors in terms of achieving desired policy changes.

Achieving constructive policy changes for dealing with delinquents in American society is difficult because juvenile justice is at present a relatively marginal area of governmental concern. Juvenile justice has little general support within the states, few interest groups regularly support it, coalitions of interest groups and political governmental leaders seldom push for change, and reports on important events relating to juvenile justice are frequently relegated to the back pages of the newspapers.[16]

But even more difficult to ensure are the policy changes needed to deal with such social problems as unemployment, poverty, substandard housing, urban slums, child abuse, and repressive public education. These larger societal problems relate directly to the ability of young people in American society to realize their potential. As has been suggested throughout this book, delinquency constitutes only a small part of the social problems plaguing American society.

Another thesis of this text is that the more policy changes are interlocked among social systems, the more likely they will have a deterrent effect upon delinquency. That is, the more that overlapping relationships can be created among such social systems as the school, family, and community, the more likely these integrated socialization processes operating at different levels within the social system are to have a positive impact upon delinquency prevention and control.

On the community level, citizens who want a more effective approach to preventing and controlling delinquency must become involved in interest groups working for a more humane and just society. The task of such groups will be to influence policymakers on all levels. Although many battles will be lost, partly because of conflicting interests, persistence and intelligence should eventually pay off in positive policy changes. Paul Lerman emphasizes the importance of formulating interest groups to fight for youth in trouble:

> *What is required is search and experimentation to evolve a variety of social-planning models that can be used adaptively to deal with the existing realities of interest groups, conflicts, and scarce resources. In pursuit of this strategy, planners may have to trade off a value they cherish—rationality—in order to realize other values they prize—humanitarianism, fairness, and effective treatment. . . . [O]ther participants in the criminal justice system have been engaged in trade-offs for a long time. If planners want to have a voice in guiding the system, they may have to become participants and act like an interest group too. This might compromise their adherence to rationality—but they may have no other choice if they are to exercise influence.*[17]

Interrelationships of the Contexts

The history of juvenile justice is sometimes presented as a steady march of ideas toward more humane and enlightened conceptions of childhood and democracy.[18] But in every period since the colonial one, political and economic forces have intertwined with sociocultural and legal forces at the societal, community, and individual levels to shape society's methods of handling troublesome youths. That is, the contextual perspective proposes that the definitions of delinquency, the social forces conducive to delinquency, and the prevention and control of delinquency emerge from the interrelationships of the five contexts, each of which has societal, community, and individual levels. This perspective helps the person studying the problem of delinquency in several ways.

First, the contextual perspective helps the person studying delinquency from getting entrapped in one context and subordinating all the others to that frame of reference. Second, the contextual perspective reminds the person studying delinquency that youth crime is affected by a variety of forces on several levels. As one examines delinquency at the three levels, from the broad societal to the perspective of the individual delinquent, he or she will understand why easy answers do not exist. Third, the contextual perspective provides a direction for developing more effective strategies for dealing with delinquency in American society. This method of analysis proposes that delinquency prevention and control interventions should be restructured according to interlocking perspectives. Indeed, the more the interventions are interlocked on societal, community, and individual levels, the more likely that delinquency prevention and treatment programs will be more than Band-aid therapy. Fourth, the contextual perspective reminds one studying delinquency that theories about delinquent behavior must be placed in the economic, social, political, and cultural conditions of their time. That is, this approach emphasizes the importance of why people thought as they did, how their creations reflect the time in which the theories were brought to light, and what role they played in their particular historical setting in which they lived. Finally, the contextual perspective helps provide a more authentic expression of the delinquent in action. It does this by giving a multidimensional view rather than a unidimensional one, by reporting accurately how delinquents interpret the events that happen to them, and by interpreting the effects of interactions with others.

ISSUES FACING JUVENILE DELINQUENCY

In the early 1970s, four trends became apparent in handling youthful offenders: due process, diversion, deinstitutionalization, and decriminalization.

The movement toward due process rights of juvenile offenders took place during the 1960s when several U.S. Supreme Court cases defined the due process safeguards juveniles have when they are taken into custody and when they appear before the juvenile court. In the late 1960s, support from federal fundings was used to establish diversionary programs across the nation. Supporters of such programs urged that diversion spared youths the stigmatization and the negative impact of the juvenile justice system. Deinstitutionalization, or keeping youths in the community rather than using long-term institutions, also developed in the 1960s because of the belief of the negative impact of institutionalization on juveniles. Finally, decriminalization, which has to do with no longer regarding status offenses as criminal offenses, took place throughout the nation in the 1970s. Most jurisdictions decided that they would be handled in different facilities than delinquents, but they would continue to be under the jurisdiction of the juvenile court.

In the late 1970s and early 1980s, the due process and decriminalization trends still received strong public support, but diversion and deinstitutionalization received weaker support than they had earlier in the decade. Diversion has come under increased criticism in recent years for enlarging the net of the juvenile justice system, for ignoring the due process rights of juveniles, and for stigmatizing participants in these programs. Deinstitutionalization meanwhile was affected primarily by the increased popularity of a "get-tough" attitude with youthful offenders. Some states, as Rosemary Sarri indicated in her interview following Chapter 17, are even beginning a process of reinstitutionalization.

A number of controversial issues, some of them new and others merely more pronounced than they had been before, are facing juvenile delinquency today.

- There is a growing acceptance of the lack of effectiveness of traditional rehabilitation models.
- There is a renewed interest in the biosocial factors of juvenile misconduct.
- There is a growing concern about the ineffectiveness of the juvenile justice system and the desire to merge the juvenile into the adult justice system.
- There is a growing concern about the seriousness of youth crime, especially among lower-class and minority youth.
- There is a growing concern on how to deter the behavior of gang delinquents because of the greater sophistication of gang structure and organization.
- There is a growing intolerance concerning the ineffectiveness of the public schools with American adolescents.

- There is a continued interest in the lack of rights and responsibilities given to adolescents.
- There is an emerging interest in international aspects of delinquency.[19]

Liberals, radicals, and conservatives differ in how these issues today should be handled. Liberals generally want to continue the trends of the early 1970s and support the least-restrictive approach to juveniles; that is, do not do any more than absolutely necessary with law-violating juveniles. They frequently support providing programs for those youthful offenders who want them and urge that the rights of adolescents be increased in American society.

Radicals claim that the real causes of delinquency are rooted in the existing social system. They are extremely critical of liberal criminologists because they claim that they have been co-opted by the establishment. Thus, radicals charge that the liberal stance is a conservative one because it supports the status quo. Radicals concentrate on policies that would bring a total change of the capitalist socio-economic system. The actual course of action proposed by radical criminologists is the involvement in political activism.[20]

The conservative approach suggests a "get-tough" policy for juvenile crime. The basic purpose of the juvenile justice process, according to conservatives, is punishment. Incapacitation, rather than rehabilitation, should be used to show juveniles the cost of delinquent behavior. Determinate sentencing, lowered ages of jurisdiction for the juvenile court, and transfer to the adult court are also means recommended by conservatives to deter youth crime.

The author of this text supports the least-restrictive model for youthful offenders. In the context of the least-restrictive model, he recommends an expansion of due process safeguards, deinstitutionalization, and decriminalization. He also upholds the position that adolescents must be given more rights and responsibilities in American society. Furthermore, he believes that macro social changes are needed in order to impact the extent and nature of delinquent behavior. Finally, increasing the cost or consequences of youth crime is needed, such as requiring restitution or community service programs, but the danger is to place too much confidence in punishment. The juvenile justice system, as well as the means of handling adolescents in American society, is far too punitive already. Specific policy recommendations are contained in the next section.

POLICY RECOMMENDATIONS

Important factors in the creation of public policy are theoretical and research advances, grass-roots community delinquency prevention, urban policy and the prevention and control of delinquency, the family and the prevention and control of delinquency, the school and juvenile delinquency, and the control of delinquents in the justice system.

Theoretical and Research Advances

Theoretical and research advances are critically needed to enable society to improve its ability to prevent and control juvenile delinquency. For example, prevention, diversionary, and treatment programs must be based upon more adequate theoretical underpinnings or foundations. Research is also necessary to identify which programs work for whom and in what setting. In addition, research must identify at what point it is desirable to take a child out of an abusive home and to ascertain the best placements for those youths taken from their natural homes. Furthermore, interventions used by the public school for disruptive students must be based upon sound theory and good research methods. Finally, policymakers would find it beneficial to examine other cultures to understand better the problem of delinquency in American society. In a real sense, the crosscultural context belong with the other five described in this book. Crosscultural comparisons of delinquency, especially in Western societies, are now receiving attention, and these comparisons offer fruitful insights and directions for policymakers in our society.

Grass-Roots Community Delinquency Prevention

Efforts to prevent delinquency must avail themselves more of community resources. The more that community members are involved in the social problems of the community, including youth crime, the more likely that these problems will be resolved. Robert Woodson recommends the following guidelines for establishing grass-roots community groups for dealing with youth crime:

- Those close to or experiencing the problem to be addressed should play a primary role in its solution.
- The needs of the child should be satisfied first within the context of the family, either nuclear or extended, and within the culture in which that child resides.
- If existing neighborhood facilities are unable to provide the services needed, every effort should be made to develop such a resource by educating and training indigenous people and institutional representatives, with professional providers of services supplying technical assistance in a spirit of voluntarism.
- When the nature of the problem is such that outside professional assistance can respond effectively, service should be provided in such a way that those being helped will participate fully in the decision making.[21]

Urban Policy and the Prevention and Control of Delinquency

The serious nature of urban youth crime mandates that extensive attention be given to improving the quality of life in urban neighborhoods. Woodson recommends the following guidelines for improving the quality of urban neighborhoods:

- The principal aim of public policy should be to strengthen the capacity of economic institutions within neighborhoods, and to identify and support activities that will create wealth within the communities as well as increase the resilience and diversity of the economics. Programs should be designed to produce the fullest employment of the resources of the neighborhood, including its people, its indigenous capital, and its land. . . .

- In accordance with the minimalist proposition of the mediating structures paradigm, under no circumstances should public policy directly involve larger bureaucratic institutions in the establishment of a local mediating structure. Nor should public policy intervene directly in the operation of a local structure or otherwise exercise control over its decision-making process. Any program of economic aid should not depend on subsidy for its long-term continuation.

- It is necessary to identify and assess the needs of a neighborhood as perceived and interpreted by residents directly experiencing the problems associated with urban decline, as opposed to the current reliance upon census data or other special macrostudies.

- Programs to motivate and train young people for work should use local mediating structures as the principal vehicle for offering such services. . . .

- Every effort should be extended to institute programs that better redistribute existing resources and avoid increasing public expenditures that contribute to inflation.[22]

The Family and the Prevention and Control of Delinquency

The goal of family life is for children to maximize their potential and to feel love and acceptance within the family unit. However, many families fail to meet the psychological, social, and even physical needs of their children. Indeed, the physical and emotional abuse children receive at home sometime affect their adjustment and happiness the rest of their lives.

In terms of primary prevention, income redistribution or some means whereby family units are assured adequate financial resources would be a first step in dealing with abuse and neglect. Increasing the number of services that help parents deal with their children and with their other responsibilities would be another important step in preventing or at least minimizing neglect and abuse in the home. Tertiary prevention, or treating the abused or neglected child, must be provided a greater number of programs throughout the nation. The Santa Clara program shows that it is possible to develop more effective programs for dealing with child abuse.

The School and Juvenile Delinquency

The school's inability to meet the educational and social needs of lower-class minority children, as well as its difficulty in dealing with the educational and social needs of students with learning problems, has contributed to the fact that school has a negative impact upon many students. It is not surprising that they withdraw from school or become disruptive in the classroom. To make the public school a positive experience for more of its students, the following recommendations are appropriate:

- Students who have difficulty functioning (i.e., working up to their abilities) in traditional classrooms must be provided opportunities to learn in educational settings more compatible with their academic and social skills.

- Students must be given more opportunities to participate in decision making in the public school, so that they will take more responsibility for the problems experienced in the public school setting.
- The school environment must be safe for school officials and for students.
- The educational inequality that presently exists in public schools in lower-class, or urban, areas must end. A neighborhood's or a community's wealth or property tax base should not mean that middle-class youngsters have better schools than lower-class juveniles.

The Control of Juvenile Delinquency

To deal more effectively with the problem of youth crime in American society, the following recommendations are useful:

- Total-system planning must be a top priority. Citizens in the community should be involved in any decision planning, as should law enforcement officers, intake officers, juvenile judges, probation and aftercare officers, residential staff in community programs, and institutional staff in short- and long-term correctional facilities. Statewide and national juvenile justice seminars should be available, for they provide personnel with an understanding of the broader goals of the system.
- A humane and fair system of juvenile corrections must always be the priority of all those concerned with juvenile justice. Every effort must be made to insure that youthful offenders are dealt with fairly and are guaranteed full rights under the Constitution. All Juveniles, regardless of age, sex, race, creed, or national origin, should be dealt with uniformly and without discrimination.
- The treatment of juvenile delinquents must be conducted under the least-restrictive model and, as often as possible, troublesome youths should be handled outside the juvenile justice system. From the point of first contact, juvenile correctional officials should make every effort to minimize the contact of juvenile offenders with the justice system.

  Detention homes or training schools must be used only as a last resort. Juveniles should never be placed in jails, and transfer to the adult court should be instigated only if everything else within the juvenile justice system has failed.
- The recruitment, training and support of all staff throughout the juvenile justice system must be of the highest possible quality. Personnel employed by the agencies to oversee programs concerned with the correction and rehabilitation of delinquents should be well trained, sensitive to youth, and committed to their jobs. The brutal or insensitive staff member can do considerable damage in a residential or institutional-based program.[23]

In conclusion, the challenge in juvenile delinquency is great. For several decades the imposing challenges have meant that the various areas of delinquency—causation, prevention, social institutions, and correction and treatment—have made little progress. Dealing more effectively with delinquency in America requires major changes in society, as well as changes within social institutions and within the various agencies of the justice system. There are no easy answers. If we care for children, we will see to it that our ideas are presented forcefully and clearly to policymakers. And if we care for children, we will not wait until the system finally works, but instead, we will reach out and help those youngsters seeking to find themselves.

Discussion Questions

1. What is social policy? How does it affect juvenile delinquency?

2. What are the main policy recommendations offered here for juvenile delinquency? What is involved in each policy recommendation?

3. How do the recommendations contained in this chapter reflect the aims of a democratic society rather thana totalitarian one?

References

Kassebaum, Gene. *Delinquency and Social Policy*. Englewood Cliffs, N.J.: Prentice-Hall, 1974.

Lerman, Paul. *Delinquency and Social Policy*. New York: Praeger Publishers, 1970.

Shichor, David, and Kelly, Delos H. *Critical Issues in Juvenile Delinquency*. Lexington, Mass.: Lexington Books, 1980.

Woodson, Robert L. *A Summons to Life: Mediating Structures and the Prevention of Youth Crime*. Cambridge: Ballinger Publishing Company, 1981. ˊ

FOOTNOTES

1. See Jonathan Kozol, *Death at an Early Age* (Boston: Little, Brown & Company, 1968); and John Holt, *Why Children Fail* (New York: Pitman, 1967).

2. Roscoe Pound, "The Juvenile Court and the Law," *National Probation and Parole Association Yearbook* 1 (1944), p. 4.

3. President's Commission on Law Enforcement and Administration of Justice, *The Challenge of Crime in a Free Society* (Washington, D.C.: U.S. Government Printing Office, 1967), pp. 79–80.

4. Richard Farson, *Birthrights* (New York: Macmillan Publishing Company, 1974).

5. Travis Hirschi, *The Causes of Delinquency* (Berkeley: University of California Press, 1969).

6. Urie Bronfenbrenner, "The Origins of Alienation," *Scientific American* 231 (1973), pp. 41–53.

7. Hirschi, *Causes of Delinquency*; LaMar Empey and S. G. Lubeck, *Explaining Delinquency* (Lexington, Mass.: Lexington Books, 1971); Martin Gold, *Status Forces in Delinquent Boys* (Ann Arbor, Mich.: Institute for Social Research, 1973).

8. Task Force on Juvenile Delinquency, *Juvenile Delinquency and Youth Crime* (Washington, D.C.: U.S. Government Printing Office, 1967), p. 51.

9. Delbert S. Elliott and Harwin L. Voss, *Delinquency and Dropout* (Lexington, Mass.: Lexington Books, 1974), pp. 127–128.

10. See Chapter 6 for a discussion of these studies.

11. Robert Gillespie, "Economic Factors in Crime and Delinquency: A Critical Review of the Empirical Evidence," U.S. Congress, House, Subcommittee on Crime of the Committee of the Judiciary, Serial 47, 95th Cong., pp. 601–625.

12. Allen D. Calvin, "Unemployment among Black Youths, Demographics and Crime," *Crime and Delinquency* 27 (April 1980), pp. 234–244.

13. Richard A. Berk, Kenneth J. Lenihan, and Peter H. Rossi, "Crime and Poverty: Some Experimental Evidence from Ex-Offenders," *American Sociological Review* 45 (October 1980), pp. 766–786.

14. L. Phillips, H. L. Votey, Jr., and D. Maxwell, "Crime, Youth and the Labor Market," *Journal of Political Economy* 80 (May-June 1972).

15. Richard Quinney, *Class, State, and Crime,* 2d ed. (New York: Longman, 1980), pp. 57–66.

16. Rosemary C. Sarri and Robert D. Vinter, "Justice for Whom? Varieties of Juvenile Correctional Approaches," in *The Juvenile Justice System,* edited by Malcolm W. Klein (Beverly Hills, Calif.: Sage Publications, 1976), p. 169.

17. Paul Lerman, *Delinquency and Social Policy* (New York: Praeger Publishers, 1970), p. 417.

18. Barry Krisberg and James Austin, *The Children of Ishmael: Critical Perspectives on Juvenile Justice* (Palo Alto, Calif.: Mayfield Publishing Company, 1979), p. 569.

19. David Shichor and Delos H. Kelly, *Critical Issues in Juvenile Delinquency* (Lexington, Mass.: Lexington Books, 1980), p. 1.

20. Shichor, "Some Issues of Social Policy in the Field of Juvenile Delinquency," in *Critical Issues in Juvenile Delinquency,* pp. 321–322.

21. Robert L. Woodson, *A Summons to Life: Mediating Structures and the Prevention of Youth Crime* (Cambridge: Ballinger Publishing Company, 1981), pp. 129–130.

22. Ibid., pp. 137–138.

23. These statements are derived from National Commission on Criminal Justice Standards and Goals, *Corrections* (Washington, D.C.: U.S. Government Printing Office, 1973)

JUVENILE GLOSSARY

adjudication Juvenile court judge decides, during the adjudicatory hearing, whether the juvenile is a delinquent, a status offender, or a dependent, or whether the allegations in the petition can be sustained.

adjudicatory hearing This stage of the juvenile court's proceedings usually includes the plea of the child, the presentation of evidence by the prosecution and by the defense, cross-examination of witnesses, and the finding by the judge whether the allegations in the petition can be sustained.

adolescence Term defining the life interval between childhood and adulthood, usually the years between 12 to 18.

adult court Juveniles who have committed serious crimes can be waived to the adult court or in some states the adult court has jurisdiction over juveniles who commit certain offenses.

adult justice system The adult justice system must deal with those juveniles who are waived to this system.

adversary system The juvenile justice system, like the adult justice system, is characterized by an adversarial relationship between the defense and prosecution, with the judge acting as arbiter of the legal rules. For the judge to determine guilt, the prosecution must prove the charges beyond a reasonable doubt.

aftercare Supervision given juveniles who are released from correctional institutions so that they can make an optimal adjustment to community living.

aftercare officer This juvenile justice actor supervises juveniles following their release from institutional care.

anomie Robert K. Merton states that a state of anomie or normlessness occurs when the integration between cultural goals and institutional means are lacking in a society.

appeal Review of juvenile court proceedings by a higher court. Although no constitutional right of appeal exists for juveniles, this right has been established by statute in some states.

appellate review A higher court reviews the decision of a juvenile court proceedings. Decisions by apellate courts, including the U. S. Supreme Court, have greatly affected the development of juvenile court law.

arrest The process of taking a juvenile into custody for an alleged violation of the law. Juveniles under arrest have nearly all the due process safeguards accorded to adults.

bail The payment of an amount of money to be released from pretrial detention, but juveniles do not have a constitutional right to bail as do adults.

behavior modification This treatment technology rewards appropriate behavior positively, immediately, and systematically, and it assumes that rewards increase the occurrences of desired behavior.

beyond a reasonable doubt   Degree of proof needed for a juvenile to be adjudicated a delinquent by the juvenile court during the adjudicatory stage of the court's proceedings.

binding over   The process of transferring (also called certifying) juveniles to the adult court. This takes place after a judicial hearing on a juvenile's amenability to treatment or his or her threat to public safety.

biological positivism   Belief that the biological limitations of juveniles drive them to delinquent behavior.

biopsychosociological factors   Differs from other theories of biological positivism because this theory links genetic, environmental, and psychological factors in explaining delinquent behavior.

blocked opportunity theory   The role of blocked or limited opportunity in explaining delinquent behavior has received considerable attention in the sociological analysis of both male and female delinquency.

body type theory   William Sheldon and Sheldon and Eleanor Glueck found that the mesomorphic (bony, muscular, and athletic) body type is more likely to be delinquent than endormorphic (soft, round, and fat) or ectomorphic (tall, thin, and fragile) body types.

booking   Record of an arrest made in police stations. In some jurisdictions, photographing and fingerprinting of the juvenile are also part of booking.

chancery court   The philosophy of *parens patriae* was developed from the chancery court in England.

child abuse   Physical abuse refers to intentional behavior directed toward a child by the parents or caretaker to cause pain, injury, or death. Emotional abuse involves a disregard of the psychological needs of a child. Sexual abuse, or incest, refers to any sexual activity that involves physical contact or sexual arousal between nonmarried members of a family.

child neglect   Refers to disregarding the physical, emotional, or moral needs of children. It involves the failure of the parent or caretaker to provide nutritious food, adequate clothing and sleeping arrangements, essential medical care, sufficient supervision, and normal experiences that produce feelings of being loved, wanted, secure, and worthy.

children's rights movement   Efforts of interest groups during the 1960s and 1970s to extend the rights of children.

chronic offender   The Philadelphia cohort study identified chronic offenders as youths who committed five or more delinquent offenses. This term is used by other studies to refer to a serious and repetitive youthful offender.

citation   A summons to appear in juvenile court.

classical school of criminology   The basic theoretical constructs of this school are developed from the writings of Beccaria and Bentham and look on human beings as rational creatures who, being free to choose their actions, could be held responsible for their behavior.

cohort studies   These studies usually include all persons born in a particular year in a city or county and follow them throughout part or all of their lives. The most important cohort studies were conducted in Philadelphia, Columbus (Ohio), and Racine (Wisconsin).

commitment   Action of a juvenile judge at the disposition stage of the juvenile court proceedings that a juvenile be sent to a juvenile correctional institution.

commitment to delinquency   David Matza uses this phrase to refer to the attachment that a juvenile may have to delinquent identity and values.

commitment to the social bond   Travis Hirschi uses this phrase to refer to the attachment that a juvenile has to conventional institutions and activities.

community-based corrections   Probation, residential and day treatment programs, and parole are the basic forms of community-based corrections. The nature of the linkages between community programs and their social environments is the most distinguishing feature of community-based corrections. As frequency, duration, and quality of community relationships increase, the programs become more community based.

community service project Court-required restitution in which a juvenile spends a certain number of many hours working in a community project.

community volunteer Individual who donates his or her time to working with delinquents in the community.

complaint The charge made to an intake officer of the juvenile court that an offense has been committed.

concentric zone theory Robert Burgess' theory that urban areas grow in concentric circles was used by Clifford Shaw and Henry McKay to measure delinquency rates in Chicago and elsewhere. Shaw and McKay found that the delinquency rates were progressively higher as zones moved away from the central city at three different points of time.

conflict theory Theory that conflict is explained by socioeconomic class, by power and authority relationships, and by group and cultural differences.

consensual model A model of society viewing the social order as a persistent stable structure that is well integrated and that is based on a consensus of values.

consent degree Formal agreement between the juvenile and the child in which the juvenile is placed under the court's supervision without a formal finding of delinquency.

containment theory Walter C. Reckless' containment theory postulates that strong inner and reinforcing external containment provide insulation against delinquent and criminal behavior.

contextual perspective A method of analysis found in this book that uses the interrelationships of five contexts (historical, legal, sociocultural, economic, and political) on three levels (societal, community, and individual) to understand delinquent behavior as well as the means to prevent and control delinquent behavior.

control theory Containment and social control theories, the most widely discussed control theories, agree on the fundamental point that human beings must be held in check, or somehow controlled, if delinquent tendencies are to be repressed.

crime control model Supporters of this model, such as James Q. Wilson, Ernest van den Haag, and others, believe that discipline and punishment are the most effective means of deterring youth crime.

criminogenic influences Characteristics of a society or an institution that lead to youth or adult crime.

cruel and unusual punishment The Eighth Amendment to the U. S. Constitution guarantees freedom from cruel and unusual punishment while juveniles and adults are under correctional custody.

cultural conflict theory Thorsten Sellin, the best-known proponent of this perspective, holds that delinquency or crime arises because individuals are members of a subculture that has its own particular conduct norms.

cultural deviance theory Clifford R. Shaw and Henry D. McKay, as well as Walter B. Miller, view delinquent behavior as an expression of conformity to cultural values and norms that are in opposition to those of the larger American society.

culture The customs, beliefs, values, knowledge, and skills that guide an individual's behavior along shared paths.

day treatment programs Juveniles attend these court-mandated, community-based corrections programs in the morning and afternoon and return home in the evening.

decriminalization This term is used in juvenile corrections to refer to the process of no longer regarding status offenses as delinquent offenses.

deinstitutionalization The process of closing long-term institutions and moving residents to community-based corrections. Deincarceration is another term used to describe this same process.

delinquent act An act committed by a minor that violates the penal code of the government with authority over the area in which the act occurred. If committed by an adult, this act could be prosecuted in a criminal court.

delinquent career Delinquents who commit one offense after the other and who appear to be committed to deviant values are sometimes said to be involved in a career.

delinquent subcultures Albert Cohen and others have defined delinquent subcultures as made up of lower-class juveniles who are experiencing strain or alienation from the larger culture.

dependency Legal status over which the juvenile court has assumed jurisdiction because of inadequate care of parents or caretakers.

detention Temporary restraint of a juvenile in a secure facility because he or she is acknowledged as either dangerous to himself or to others.

detention facility This facility, also known as detention center or home, provides custodial care of juveniles during juvenile court proceedings.

detention hearing The hearing, usually conducted by an intake officer of the juvenile court, makes the decision whether or not a juvenile will be released to his or her parents or be detained in a detention facility.

determine sentencing This form of sentencing, which is used only by the State of Washington for juveniles at the present time, provides fixed forms of sentences for offenses. The terms of these sentences are generally set by the legislature rather than determined by judicial discretion.

deterrence The assumption that delinquency can be prevented by the threat of legal sanctions. Utilitarian punishment philosophy or proponents of the crime control model particularly advocate this belief.

differential association theory Delinquent behavior is expected of those individuals who have internalized a preponderance of definitions favorable to law violations.

disposition Stage of the juvenile court proceedings in which the juvenile judge decides the most appropriate placement for a juvenile who has been adjudicated a delinquent, a status offender, or a dependent.

diversion Juveniles are referred to dispositional alternatives outside the formal juvenile justice system.

diversionary programs Diversion can come either from the police and the court or from agencies outside the juvenile justice system.

double jeopardy *Breed* v. *Jones* decision (1975) ruled that juveniles cannot be tried in juvenile court and then be referred to the adult court. This would constitute double jeopardy and, according to the Fifth Amendment to the U. S. Constitution, no person may be subject to twice being put in jeopardy of life or limb for the same offense.

drift theory Juveniles, according to David Matza, neutralize themselves from the moral bounds of the law and drift into delinquent behavior.

drug abuse Excessive use of a drug, which is frequently accompanied by physical and/or psychological dependence.

due process rights Constitutional rights guaranteed to juveniles during their contacts with the police, their proceedings in court, and their interactions with the public school.

ego The ego, according to Sigmund Freud, mediates between the id and the superego and is important in the socialization of the child.

emotionally disturbed offenders Youths whose emotional problems interfere with their everyday functioning and whose behaviors bring them into the juvenile justice system are included in the broad category of emotionally disturbed offenders.

false negative A prediction is made that crime will not occur and it does.

false positive A prediction is made that crime will occur and it does not.

family court In some jurisdictions, such as New York, the family court hears all matters pertaining to juveniles, including delinquency and status offenses.

family therapy Treating the entire family has become a widely used method of dealing with a delinquent's socially unacceptable behavior.

felony Criminal offense punishable by death or by incarceration in a state or federal correctional institution usually for one year or more.

financial restitution Court-ordered condition of probation in which a juvenile is required to make financial restitution to a victim of his or her crime.

focal concerns   Walter B. Miller contends that lower-class youths have different values or focal concerns (toughness, smartness, excitement, fate, and autonomy) than middle-class youths.

foster care   The foster home provides a setting for juveniles who must be removed from their natural homes.

free will   Proponents of the classical school of criminology, as well as advocates of the punishment approach today, believe that juveniles are rational creatures who, being free to choose their actions, could be held responsible for their behavior.

gang   A youth gang is bound together by mutual interests and with identifiable leadership who act in concert to achieve a specific purpose that generally includes the conduct of illegal activity.

gender roles   Societal expectation of what is masculine and what is feminine behavior.

generation gap   The widely accepted belief in the 1960s that there was a difference in values, or generation gap, between juveniles and adults.

gentlemen reformers   The reformers who advocated the development of houses of refuge, or juvenile institutions, in the early part of the nineteenth century as a means to deal with problem youths.

group delinquency   Research findings have generally found that most delinquent behavior takes place with peers and is group related.

group homes   A placement for adjudicated youth by the court, which is also called a group residence, halfway house, and attention home, that serves about 13 to 25 youths as an alternative to institutionalization.

guided group interaction   Interaction which, whether it takes place in the community or in an institution, places youthful offenders in an intensive group environment under the direction of an adult leader. The guided group interaction process substitutes a whole new structure of beliefs, values, and behaviors for the values of delinquent peer subcultures.

halfway house   A residential setting for adjudicated delinquents, usually for youths in need for a period of readjustment to the community after an institutional confinement.

hard line approach   A get-tough-with-juvenile-criminals mood that is presently found among some policymakers and the public.

hidden delinquency   Unobserved or unreported delinquency makes up what is known as hidden delinquency.

home detention   A form of detention used by some jurisdictions in which the juvenile remains at home but receives intensive supervision by staff of the probation department.

houses of refuge   These institutions were designed by eighteenth-century reformers to provide an orderly disciplined environment similar to that of the "ideal" Puritan family.

id   Freud's theory of the personality refers to the id as the raw instincts and primitive drives of the person. The Id wants immediate gratification of its needs and, therefore, tends to be primitive and savage.

index offenses   The most serious offenses reported by the FBI on the *Uniform Crime Reports,* including murder and nonnegligent manslaughter, forcible rape, robbery, aggravated assault, burglary, larceny-theft, motor vehicle theft, and arson.

indeterminate sentencing   This type of sentencing is used in most jurisdictions other than those that have mandatory or determinate sentencing. In indeterminate sentencing, the juvenile judge has wide discretion and can commit a juvenile to the department of corrections or youth authority until correctional staff make the decision to release the juvenile.

infanticide   The murder of a child. This practice was widely practiced by parents in the past.

in loco parentis   A guardian or an agency is given the rights, duties, and responsibilities of a parent.

inmate subculture   The organization of inmates in a training school into a culture that has its own norms, social roles, and leadership.

institutional abandonment   Parental practice of assigning caretakers, such as wet nurses, the responsibility of raising children.

intake   The first stage of the juvenile court proceedings in which the decision is made whether to divert the referral or to file a petition in juvenile court.

Interpersonal Maturity Level Classification Scheme I-Level, as this classification scheme is commonly referred to, assumes that personality development follows a normal sequence and attempts to identify the developmental stage of offenders by focusing on their perception of themselves, others, and the world.

jail Juveniles are sometimes confined in county jails or police lockups. These adult facilities have few services to offer juveniles.

jury trial Juveniles do not have a constitutional right to a jury trial but several jurisdictions permit juveniles to choose a jury trial.

just deserts This pivotal philosophical basis of the justice model holds that juveniles deserve to be punished if they violate the law. But the punishment given the offender must be proportionate to the seriousness of the offense or the social harm inflicted on society.

justice-as-fairness This justice-as-fairness perspective, as David Fogel calls his justice model, advocates that it is necessary to be fair, reasonable, humane, and constitutional in practice.

Juvenile Justice and Delinquency Prevention Act of 1974 A federal law established a juvenile justice office within the LEAA to provide funds for the prevention and control of youth crime.

juvenile justice standards Jointly sponsored by the Institute of Judicial Administration and the American Bar Association, this project proposes that sentences of juveniles be based on the seriousness of crime rather than on the "needs" of the child.

labeling theory The labeling perspective claims that society creates the delinquent by labeling those who are apprehended as "different" from other youth when in reality they are different only because they have been "tagged" with a deviant label.

law-and-order perspective This "get-tough-with-criminals" approach became popular in juvenile corrections in the mid and late 1970s.

Law Enforcement Assistance Administration (LEAA) This Omnibus Crime Control and Safe Streets Act of 1968 established this unit in the U. S. Department of Justice to administer grants and provide guidance for crime prevention projects. Until funding ended for LEAA in the late 1970s, LEAA's grants permitted the expansion of community-based programs throughout the nation.

learning disabilities (LD) Children with special learning problems exhibit a disorder in one or more of the basic psychological processes involved in understanding or using spoken or written language. Some support exits for a link between juvenile delinquency and learning disabilities.

least restrictive model This model is based on the assumption that a juvenile's penetration into the system should be minimized as much as possible because the system tends to breed rather than to reduce youth crime.

logical consequences model Advocates of this model believe that delinquent behavior should exact a cost and that youthful offenders should be made aware of the consequences of their socially unacceptable behavior.

mandatory sentences Some states require that juveniles who commit certain offenses should receive a specified length of confinement.

masculinity hypothesis Several studies of female delinquents propose that as girls become more boy-like and acquire more "masculine" traits, they become more delinquent.

medical model Proponents of the medical model believe that delinquency is caused by factors that can be identified, isolated, treated, and cured.

minor Person who is under the age of legal consent.

Miranda warning A 1966 U. S. Supreme Court ruling has given arrested subjects three rights before interrogation: the right to remain silent, the right to consult with an attorney, and the right to court-appointed counsel if the suspect cannot afford private counsel. Juveniles also have these rights at the time they are taken into custody.

misdemeanor An offense that is punishable by incarceration for not more than one year in jail.

modification hearing Review, or modification, hearings are held in many juvenile courts in which the judge reviews the progress of an adjudicated youth every six months or so.

National Council of Crime and Delinquency This council, which publishes *Crime and Delinquency*, has been a long supporter of deinstitutionalization and of the due process model in juvenile corrections.

nonjudicial agencies Diversionary programs that are outside the formal juvenile justice system.

norms The guidelines individuals follow in their relations with one another; they are shared standards of desirable behavior.

"nothing works" Robert Martinson and colleagues claimed in the mid 1970s that correctional treatment is ineffective in reducing recidivism of correctional clients.

Office of Juvenile Justice Delinquency Prevention (OJJDP) This office was established with the passage of the 1974 Juvenile Justice and Delinquency Prevention Act.

official juvenile delinquency The main sources of official juvenile delinquency are the *Uniform Crime Reports, Juvenile Court Statistics,* institutional and aftercare records, and cohort studies.

Omnibus Crime Bill of 1978 in New York State This bill, commonly known as the "juvenile offender law" stripped the Family Court of jurisdiction of thirteen year olds accused of murder and fourteen year olds accused of murder, attempted murder, and other violent offenses.

orthomolecular imbalances Chemical imbalances in the body, resulting from poor nutrition, allergies, and exposure to lead and certain colors, that are said to lead to delinquency.

parens patriae This medieval English doctrine sanctioned the right of the Crown to intervene into natural family relations whenever a child's welfare was threatened. The philosophy of the juvenile court is based on this legal concept.

petition The intake unit files a document in juvenile court asking that the court assumes jurisdiction over the juvenile.

plea bargaining In urban courts, the defense counsel and the prosecution frequently agree that the juvenile will plead guilty for a reduction of the charges or dropped charges.

police discretion The choice between two or more possible means of handling a situation confronting a police officer.

positive peer culture This group modality, like its parent model GGI, is a group approach for building positive youth subcultures and encompasses a total strategy extending to all aspects of daily life.

positivism This view has been the dominant philosophical perspective of juvenile justice since the time the juvenile court was established at the beginning of the twentieth century. It holds that, just as laws operate in the medical, biological, and physical sciences, laws govern human behavior, and these can be understood and used. The causes of human behavior, once discovered, can be modified to eliminate many of society's problems, such as delinquency.

private training schools Juveniles are frequently committed by the juvenile court to training schools that are under private auspices; the county then pays a per diem rate for the care of these youths.

probation A court sentence by which the juvenile's freedom in the community is continued or only briefly interrupted, but under which the person is subject to supervision by a probation officer and the conditions imposed by the court.

probation officer This officer of the court is expected to provide social study investigations, to supervise persons placed on probation, to maintain case files, to advise probationers on the conditions of their sentences, to perform any other probationary services that a judge may request, and to inform the court when persons on probation have violated the terms of that probation.

program integrity Effective interventions must actually deliver the services they claim to deliver, with sufficient strength to accomplish the goals of treatment.

Progressive Era During this era (the period from around 1890 to 1920), the wave of optimism that swept through American society led to the acceptance of positivism. The doctrines of the emerging social sciences assured reformers that through positivism their problems could be solved.

proletariat Karl Marx contended that, with capitalism, society is splitting up into two great classes facing each other—bourgeoisie (capitalist class) and proletariat (working class).

prosecutor   The representative of the state. Also called county's attorney, district attorney, or state attorney.

psychoanalytic theory   Sigmund Freud contributed three insights that have shaped the handling of juvenile delinquents: (1) personality is made up of three components—id, ego, and the superego; (2) all normal children pass through three psychosexual stages of development—oral, anal, and phallic; and (3) personality traits of a person are developed in early childhood.

psychopath or sociopath   This personality disorder is frequently acknowledged as the personality type of hard-core juvenile criminals. The claim is made that the psychopath or sociopath is chiefly the unwanted, rejected child who grows up but remains as an undomesticated child and never develops trust or loyalty to an adult.

psychotherapy   Various adaptations of Freudian therapy have been used by psychiatrists, clinical psychologists, and psychiatric social workers to encourage delinquents to talk about past conflicts causing them to express emotional problems through aggressive or antisocial behavior.

Quay Classification Scheme   A scheme developed by Herbert C. Quay that evaluates delinquents in terms of their behavior. It is based on five types of personality: inadequate-immature, neurotic-conflicted, unsocialized aggressive or psychopathic, socialized or subcultural delinquent, or subcultural-immature delinquents.

radical theory   Criminologists who apply Marxist theory to the study of delinquency contend that the dominant classes create definitions of crime to oppress the subordinate classes, that the economic system exploits lower-class youths, and that social justice is lacking for lower-class youths.

ranches, forestry camps, and farms   Public and private juvenile correctional institutions that are usually less secure and keep residents for a shorter stay than do training schools.

rationality   The quality or condition of being reasonable, rational, or the possession or use of rea-

son. Juveniles, according to hardliners, have free will and rationally calculate the cost of lawbreaking.

reality therapy   William Glasser and G. L. Harrington base this treatment modality on the principle that individuals must accept responsibility for their behavior.

reception and diagnostic centers   Juveniles committed to juvenile institutions frequently are sent first to these centers that then diagnose their problems and develop a treatment plan.

recidivism   The repetition of delinquent behavior when a youth has been released from probation status or from training school.

referees   Many juvenile courts employ the services of these juvenile justice personnel. They may or may not be members of the bar, but their basic responsibility is to assist judges in processing youths through the courts.

reference group   The group with which a juvenile identifies or to which he or she aspires to belong.

rehabilitation model   The medical model, the adjustment model, and the reintegration model are all part of the more inclusive rehabilitative philosophy because they are all committed to changing the offender.

rehabilitative philosophy   The goal of this philosophy is to change an offender's character, attitudes, or behavior patterns so as to diminish his or her delinquent propensities.

reliability   Related to the consistency of a questionnaire or interview; that is, whether repeated administration of a questionnaire or an interview will elicit the same answers from the same juveniles when they are questioned two or more times.

right to treatment   Several court decisions have held that a juvenile has a right to treatment when he or she is committed to a training school.

runaway behavior   Usually defined as being away from home for 24 or more hours without permission of parents or caretakers.

search and seizure   Juveniles, as adults, have constitutional safeguards to protect them against unauthorized police searches and seizures. To search a person or location, the Constitution requires that a lawfully obtained search warrant be obtained.

self-reflexive human beings Delinquent behavior is not merely the product or consequence of societal and community forces but is also the creation of symbol-using, self-reflexive human beings.

shelter care facilities Shelters are primarily used to provide short-term care for status offenders and for dependent or neglected children.

skill development programs These programs teach communication, decision making, daily living, educational advancement, vocational, and career skills.

social class A term used to describe those who have similar incomes, educational achievements, and occupational prestige.

social control theory Delinquent acts, according to Travis Hirschi and others, result when a juvenile's bond to society is weak or broken.

social development model This model, based on the integration of social control and cultural learning theories, proposes that the development of attachments to parents will lead to attachments to school and a commitment to education as well as a belief in and commitment to conventional behavior and the law.

social disorganization theory Juvenile delinquency, according to Shaw and McKay and others, results from the breakdown of social control among the traditional primary groups, such as the family and the neighborhood, because of the social disorganization of the community.

socialization The process by which individuals internalize their culture, for from this process, an individual learns the norms, sanctions, and expectations of being a member of a particular society.

social justice Radical criminologists claim that social injustice is present in the juvenile justice system because poor youth tend to be disproportionately represented, because female status offenders are subjected to sexist treatment, and because racism is present and blacks are dealt with more harshly than whites.

social process theories These theories examine the interactions between individuals and their environments that influence them to become involved in delinquent behavior.

social structure theories The setting for delinquency, as suggested by social structure theories, is the social and cultural environment in which adolescents grow up or the subcultural groups in which they choose to become involved.

sociobiology A recent expression of biological positivism stresses the interaction between the biological factors within an individual and the influence of the particular environment.

soft determinism David Matza claims the concept of soft determinism contains the best resolution of the free will and positivism debate; that is, delinquents are neither wholly free nor wholly constrained but fall somewhere in between.

soft line approach The desire to treat leniently those youths who pose little threat to the social order.

state training school Long-term juvenile correctional facility that is operated by the department of corrections or youth commission of state government.

station adjustment A juvenile can be taken to the police station, have the contact recorded, be given an official reprimand, and then be released to the parents.

status offender A juvenile who commits a minor act that is considered illegal only because he or she is underage. Various titles given to status offenders include MINS (minors in need of supervision), CHINS (children in need of supervision), CHINA (children in need of assistance), PINS (persons in need of supervision), and FINS (family in need of supervision).

strain theory Social structure exerts pressure on those youths who cannot attain the cultural goal of success to engage in nonconforming behavior.

superego The superego, or the conscience, according to Freud, internalizes the rules of society.

supremacy of parental rights A presumption for parental autonomy in child rearing and the philosophy that coercive intervention is appropriate only in the face of serious harm to the child.

symbolic interactionist theory This theory in social psychology that stresses the process of interaction among human beings at the symbolic level has been influential in shaping the development of several social process theories of delinquent behavior.

take into custody The process of arresting a juvenile for socially unacceptable behavior.

template matching technique This technique creates a set of descriptors, or a "template," of the kinds of people who are most likely to benefit from a particular treatment intervention.

therapeutic community The purpose of this treatment modality is to create a total environment supportive of socially acceptable behavior. The modality is based on reducing role differences between the keepers and the kept and giving offenders every opportunity to analyze and take responsibility for their own behaviors.

tracking systems Classifying students according to their abilities in public and private schools.

transactional analysis (TA) A therapy, based on interpreting and evaluating personal relationships, that has proved of immediate value to many delinquents. Using catchy language, TA promises delinquents who feel "not OK" that several easy steps can make them "OK."

true negative A prediction is called a true negative if the prediction is made that delinquency will not occur and it does not.

true positive A prediction is called a true positive if the prediction is made that delinquency will occur and it does.

utilitarian punishment philosophy James Q. Wilson and Ernest van den Haag, leading spokespersons for this position, contend that punishment is necessary to deter youthful offenders and to protect society from crime.

validity A serious question concerning self-report studies rest with their validity. For example, how can researchers be certain that juveniles are telling the truth when they fill out self-report questionnaires.

values the general ideas individuals share about what is good or bad, right or wrong, desirable and undesirable.

youth service bureau (YSB) An agency that is outside the juvenile justice system designed to divert children and youth from the justice system by (1) mobilizing community resources to solve youth problems, (2) strengthening existing youth resources and developing new ones, and (3) promoting positive programs to remedy delinquency-prone conditions in the environment.

CREDITS

Chapter 1   Sepp Seitz/Woodfin Camp
Chapter 2   Richard Hutchings/Photo Researchers
Chapter 3   Michael Rothstein/Jeroboam
Chapter 4   Leonard Speier
Chapter 5   Joel Gordon
Chapter 6   Joel Gordon
Chapter 7   Charles Gatewood/The Image Works
Chapter 8   Barbara Alper/Stock Boston
Chapter 9   David White/Black Star
Chapter 10   Franklin Wing/Stock Boston
Chapter 11   Charles Gatewood/The Image Works
Chapter 12   Stephen Shames/Black Star
Chapter 13   Ira Berger/Woodfin Camp
Chapter 14   South Carolina Department of Correction
Chapter 15   Susan Kuklin/Photo Researchers
Chapter 16   John Maher/EKM-Nepenthe
Chapter 17   Maureen Fennelli/Photo Researchers
Chapter 18   Stephen Shames/Black Star
Chapter 19   Martin A. Levick/Black Star
Chapter 20   Eric A. Roth/The Picture Cube
Chapter 21   Marion Bernstein

AUTHOR INDEX

SUBJECT INDEX